THE GHOST DANCE

THE GHOST DANCE

For what are the comprehensible terrors of man compared with the interlinked terrors and wonders of God!

Herman Melville, *Moby Dick, or the Whale*

THE
GHOST DANCE

Origins of Religion

WESTON LA BARRE

A DELTA BOOK

To my Fathers
of the flesh and of the spirit
who posed me these problems
and to Jean-François Lefebvre
Chevalier de La Barre
burned at the stake in Abbeville
1 July 1766 at the age of eighteen

Contents

Preface

THIS book is a psychological and anthropological study of religion. Naturalistically approached, human religion turns out to be an *entirely* human phenomenon, and entirely derived from the nature of human nature. Religion has never been explainable in the terms provided by religion, and the long search for knowledge of the gods or of God has given us no knowledge whatever that is acceptable to all men. Why not then look carefully at man himself for an understanding of this human phenomenon?

It may startle those who would find God to be asked first to look at Australopithecine ape-men, at the nature and vicissitudes of individual childhood, at the historically recoverable childhood of our species, and at the peculiar "neoteny" or biological infantilization of *Homo sapiens*. But if religion is in fact something that people think and feel and believe, then in order to understand religion we obviously need to know more about people, and their unique biological environment, human society. We must likewise look seriously at the way the human mind works both waking and dreaming, in serenity and under duress.

Since the awesome *mana* or compelling power of god-men and of gods is at the very least a psychological phenomenon, we must look psychologically at these apprehensions of the *mysterium tremendum et fascinosum* universal to all religions. Similarly, since a strange "charisma" seems to accompany the vatic spokesmen of the supernatural powers—their prophets and priests, culture heroes and shamans—then we must also try to understand the psychological and cultural nature of charisma. And finally, since we would not wish projectively to reconstruct a pseudo-historical Just-So past, we must also discover and understand the actual ethnological and archeological past of man, insofar as we can, from the available "ethnographic present" (a somewhat movable date, the time before massive acculturation and change when specific peoples were first sufficiently well known to modern scientists), and from the fixed and time-stratified data of prehistory, documented for us by archeology.

This ambition would seem to demand both anthropological and psychological competence so that, modestly or otherwise, I should state that by training and predilection I am in any case a psychiatrically oriented anthropologist. I do not pretend to have chosen the American Indians for a study of religion on any impressive a priori methodological grounds. It is simply that by field experience I am primarily an Americanist. Theoretically it would not matter where one found the data, insofar as the interest lies in meanings and functions and relationships; for my purpose it suffices that the Indian be human. But in years of preoccupation with the American Indian, hindsights have gradually emerged concerning further advantages of method.

For one matter, American Indian cultures are largely obsolescent, now politically impotent, and constitute no epistemological threat to us. For another, the Americas affiliate culture-historically with ancient Asiatic arctic cultures, and through these with archaic Mesolithic cultures of Europe; and behind these, when studied comparatively, we can still discern the outlines of the Paleolithic. And, somewhat surprisingly, the Paleolithic ur-culture in this light also lies discernibly behind the Hebrews and the Greeks, the great formative peoples and the psychic ancestors of modern man. It is in the areas of Greek and Hebrew studies that I feel consciously most amateur and prone to error. But I would argue strongly in any case that, on certain technical grounds of uniqueness, these must necessarily be the two favorite folk of the world ethnologist, as well as of the modern humanist.

A specialist's frankly admitted admiration for two striking human societies and cultures should not blind us, however, to the fact that man is a higher primate, with a unique body I am obliged to take seriously for its being, I think, the base of man's unique biological adaptation, culture. The approach to this specifically human ecology is, further, I believe, necessarily psychoanalytic, since psychoanalysis was the first and still is the only psychology to take seriously the whole growing human body as a place to live in and to experience—for, as we will show, the emotional predicaments of this body-experiencing profoundly shape adaptive personality, the historic character of groups, and human institutions alike. Psychoanalysis is the first psychology to preoccupy itself with the symbolic *content* and *purpose,* as opposed to the mere modalities and processes, of thinking. It is the first authentically human as opposed to animal psychology. It is naturalistic, rather than experimental. We can not expect to find the human essentials—the family, the oedipal predicament, incest taboos, history, culture and language—lurking in rats and other experimental animals and birds. The human body, meanwhile, is a dependably cross-cultural phenomenon. And, finally, psychoanalysis is the first truly naturalistic psychology that consistently attends to live and functioning human beings, not statistically dismembered into safe, quiddity-denuded categories that control out of controlled experiments the very threatening data that would best edify us about ourselves.

The structural logic of this book is largely that of order of presentation of data. But there are also didactic considerations. The Introduction presents, in a moment, possibly upsetting or even irritating flat statements of what are, properly speaking, summarized conclusions, which the rest of the book must subsequently justify. But the author must play fair, if only to warn the reader to stop reading. Immediate scrutiny of our own society would be too strong medicine to take. There are practical problems about developing insights elsewhere before applying them to our society and culture too. Every culture, though a living room, is also a great trashy museum. Each old cobbler's bench is refurbished into a cocktail table. An empty old whiskey jug becomes a familiar decoration to please the eye as once its contents did the palate; an old coffee grinder becomes a new lamp; and a *churinga* opens the daily mail. Our vested interests in cocktail tables and paper knives must dissuade such conceptual housecleaning.

Another metaphor, that of a certain view from a plane, discloses another methodological advantage in beginning with the American Indian. As one flies over the *sunderbands* of India—the huge marshy home of the royal Bengal tiger in the endless Ganges-Brahmaputra delta—the eye is struck by the visibly different time-depths of the various river courses. The contemporary channel is marked by a tangled marginal growth; newly abandoned tracks still show some of this; and fainter and fainter in the earth we can see all the old and still older courses of the rivers, as a half-erased parchment palimpsest is written on and over-written again. The *sunderbands* represent an ethnological paradigm of Old World literate cultures—much documented, but enormously complex in the flow and counterflow of human life and cultural deposits.

In most of Asia, for example, the specialist may spend a lifetime in sorting out the various strata and influences even in a single limited area. Africa too, after its first human origins at least somewhat a cul-de-sac like the New World, has "culture areas" only by courtesy of our tacit understanding that the modern Stone Age Bushman-Hottentot kind of art once anciently spread northward to an "Aurignacian" or "Capsian" period of the Mediterranean paleolithic, and that these present-day South African relict peoples share culture traits remotely with the Abyssinian eastern Horn; that a Neolithic "Hamitic" cattle complex is newer in some parts than Negro agriculture, and perhaps older in other parts; and that the many-layered Guinea Coast of West Africa may even have distant influences from prehistoric Egypt. In short, we have not so much discrete culture "areas" here as we have varyingly overlapped and merging ecological adaptations, of different historic time and geographic provenience.

America is flatter, simpler in its time depth. It is true that Pueblos, Mexico-inspired, rest on Basketmaker territories; Mexico itself had many imperialist ebbs and flows from its different geographic areas; and Mexico perhaps ultimately inspired some culture traits in the southern Mississippi basin and even in the early Eastern Woodlands. Again, culture may have spread in an eastward arc along the Guiana coasts, curled back and spread up the Amazon to its farthest tributaries, and southward down the Brazilian coast and inland over early Marginal folk. Tropical Forest traits took Antillean steppingstones to Florida, to account perhaps for some "Amazonian" traits of some eastern agriculturalists of the United States, such as the Iroquoian blowgun. Northwest Coast tribes and Eskimos seem to have had later inspirations from northeast Asia. And the exposed western coasts of the New World from Canada to Peru offer a suspiciously large target for late influences from the Vikings of the Pacific, the Polynesian island-hoppers.

Nevertheless, it is still possible to think of the Americas in terms of authentic culture areas, without any great archeological confusion. In their relatively naïve religious conceptions, both aboriginal Americas contain only variations on the single theme of shamanism, except for those religions of a few high cultures, but these, however, are still quite demonstrably local derivations from shamanism. But it is the Americas' magnificent archeological and cultural integration with ancient Eurasia that is the most exhilarating—such that one can be sure a trait like a conical hut in the Eastern Woodlands of the United States sweeps across the Plains and Canada and reaches around the Pole westward clear across Asia and Europe to Lapland; and that in religion "bear ceremonialism" for example is continuous in circumpolar orbit around the earth, and even continues in time a bear cult of the late Old Stone Age in the eastern Alps. These are breath-taking cultural perspectives indeed!

Best of all, the Americas constitute a kind of Mesolithic fossil, through the comparative study of whose cultures one can creep up on Eurasiatic history and protohistory so to speak from the flank, and along an immense time depth, secure in the knowledge that each step of diffusion can be proven with overwhelming data. But this book is not primarily on the American Indian and, it is hoped, not solely for my specialist colleagues who demand the specific evidence. However, I would ask the general reader to allow me some minimal presentation of the evidence for ancient psychotropic drugs that I think I can show are behind the rationale both of Eurasiatic (even Indoeuropean) and Amerindian Mesolithic religion.

By understanding the Sibero-American ur-culture I believe we can have some authentic culture-historical clues for understanding both the archaic Indoeuropean Greeks and the most ancient Hebrews. Even the carefully condensed and summarized evidence for this claim may not be enough for each specialist, whom I must ask to assess with his own special knowledge my wide-ranging hypotheses; the present volume has been laboriously condensed from a manuscript three times as long, in an attempt to reach the general reader as well. At any rate, this patient paleo-ethnology is about the only "method" of which I can boast. I will therefore ask the reader generously to accept for the moment that, just as chapters on human biology and human psychology summarize data indispensable for my exposition, so also minimal chapters on the American Indian and ancient Asiatic shamanism are required before I may summarize crisis cults all over the primitive world, and finally our own Graeco-Hebraic religion.

Man is the culture-bearing animal, who never is and never can be alone and still remain human. A peculiar organism, a man is the precipitated experiences of many minds, reified knowledge, the word made flesh. The individual man therefore potentially lives as many millennia as his knowledge of the past can span. But it must be conscious and articulate knowledge, for otherwise a living man is partly the passive present-day residue of the pathology of past history, since tradition is in part as neurotic as any patient. The past imprisons the present only because we have not mastered our own history; a first step is to attempt a prehistory of modern man and to sketch, so to speak, his intellectual autobiography.

It is repeatedly astonishing how short the range of conscious knowledge is, in space and time, of men imprisoned in the ethnographic here and now; and, as T. E. Lawrence noted, astonishing what a poor conductor of knowledge the ordinary man is. Nevertheless, as has been observed, history is what you cannot resign from. Every culture is a bar to the exercise of free rationality—and yet each nation gratuitously offers, even forcibly, the sorry detritus of its own past, a treasure to share in acculturating other old lands. Still, one should discuss European religion with respect and circumspection, knowing that the subject matter is, profoundly, oneself.

THE GHOST DANCE

THE GHOST DANCE

Introduction

THERE is no mystery about religion. The genuine mysteries lie in what religion *purports to be about:* the mystery of life and the mystery of the universe. But religion itself is the beliefs, behaviors, and feelings of people. As such, when societies are concerned, religion is a proper subject for anthropology and history; and when the individual is concerned, for psychology and psychiatry. That is to say, any religion is completely open to naturalistic study, so long as religious acts and attitudes are viewed as descriptive *fact* and no one bothers about final metaphysical truth. Any religion, including our own, can be studied thus detachedly as folklore, if we put aside the question of ultimate validity. Of course this approach will give us no answers to the "questions" asked by religions; but in the process we may learn something about the nature of religion itself. Religion then as a legitimate subject matter, not as a technique of knowledge, concerns us here.

Wittgenstein[1] has observed that most propositions are not false but merely senseless, hence we cannot answer questions of this kind but can only expose their senselessness. Many metaphysical problems arise because we do not understand the logic of language (as Socrates did not) or what language itself is (Plato did not), and consequently such philosophical "problems" are no problems at all. They are only quibbles over what we do not know or understand: our linguistic behavior. For example, if (behavioristically) "God" be our term for the Unknown, then we cannot assert anything whatever about it—not even to predicate its "unknowability" for this is to claim knowledge that it is unknowable. But theologians insist on smuggling in their own private connotations and denotations for the term (or, just as dangerously, they rely on ours), thus giving rise to all manner of theological "problems" when the only problems are the theologians themselves (or ourselves), none of whom we know.

Here are some senseless non-problems: Is the galactic universe *really* like my father or like the creative male progenitor in the species *Homo sapiens?* How do you know that it is not? Do I matter to Matter; does Mother Nature *care* about me? Does the constituency of the man who was God, who died and did not die, the son who was his own father, by a virgin mother, the uncreated created One, legitimately extend to the planets Mars and Venus? To Betelgeuse? Do I, who am a mortal metazoan, *really* have immortality? Can I get godhood by eating a god? How many angels, who do not occupy space, can dance on the point of a pin, which does not occupy space?—et cetera, et cetera. If God is unknown, then theology is a science without subject matter, and the theologian is one who does not know what he is talking about. If he has only forgotten what he was talking about—the premises lurking hidden in his unconscious connotations and denotations—then these must be made explicit if we are to discuss them meaningfully. We can proceed only if we have more verifiable meanings attached to our terms. Meanwhile we may reasonably raise questions about him such as: Why was it he did not know what he meant? Why does he have these meanings? How many people mean what he meant and why? But these are questions about psychology, human biology and culture, not about God, who remains elusively Unknown.

Of course, if, meanwhile, we are still interested in the truth or falsity of stated beliefs, then we must make a quite different and separate search and take one of several choices of means. We may ransack experience to discover if there is an entity that corresponds exactly to what we have defined, study the observable behavior of the entity and set up hypotheses in search of verification, as scientists do. Or we may suppose that because the mind has been able to think of it clearly and to verbalize it logically and grammatically, the entity then necessarily exists in fact—which is the technique of dialectic Greek rationalism, a philosophic tradition reaching as far down toward our time as Kant who insisted, somewhat surprisingly, that subjective idealism is subjective. Subjectivity that omnipotently confers "ontological" status upon ideas is also the technique of magic and of schizophrenia, for both of which the stated wish or fantasy is equivalent to its accomplishment or reality.

Alternatively, we may suppose that a belief is true simply because we have been told it by prestigious other persons, and we have never thought to question what traditional sources have taught us. But this is to burden *people* with the validation of what only reality can validate. Besides, the theologian and the metaphysician do not really know, or recognize as such, but merely *rely* on the contents of their minds and their unexamined personalities for the stuff of their propositions. The fundamentalist likewise does not know the origins of or the ancient reasons for the beliefs, but relies on his fellows and their culture to supply the authority for the beliefs, which reference to appropriate aspects of reality alone would provide; as such, the beliefs remain folklore. Neither the man of god who originated the beliefs nor the faithful communicant seems to realize that neither personality nor culture are adequate grounds for belief. Personality is the precipitate of what a man has learned, and for this rock-bottom reason he *trusts* his personality, because he has experienced it; but personal experience is limited, often atypical and sometimes even distorted. Culture is the precipitate of what men have learned, and therefore they trust it too; but culture may be personal error compounded.

Inevitably, each man often must discriminate between what he has been taught and what he has learned. He must make his peace with the past, his own and that of the race, and choose at times between the wisdom of the fathers and his own direct experience. This is the method of daily common sense and of science. The person using this touchstone of knowledge may then look upon the magic world-view as interesting material for the scientific folklorist, the ethnologist and the psychiatrist, but he would never choose personally to use the magic knowledge-technique of mere reference to self-wish (the magician being all the while contemptuous that the scientist does not have the omnipotence or the omniscience of the sorcerer). Similarly, the scientist may look on past world-views as interesting data for a history of science or a sociology of religion, but not accept mere antecedence as establishing the validity of beliefs (the religionist all the while pitying or mocking the scientist for not having the certitude of the true believer).

Thus those who depend on the largest possible current experience of the world to shape their world-view may (infuriatingly) eschew religious tribalism entirely, impiously discard the opinions both of Plato and St. Paul—and trust instead to a scrutiny by biochemists of deoxyribonucleic acid in double spirals in genes and chromosomes for their knowledge of the facts of life, or to a scrutiny by astrophysicists of the red shift of distant nebulae and the bending of light by matter for their views of the cosmos. The magician knows everything simply because it is he who thinks it. The religionist knows because the wisdom of the ages, the authority of the past, has told him so. The scientist candidly admits the tentative nature of his "knowledge" of the unknown that stretches out from him on all sides, and invites us to look at and talk about the evidence for his current hypotheses. The theologian insists on our sharing his fixed opinions about the Unknown, when all we may feel entitled to is an open mind. There are doubtless differing opinions about the epistemological predicaments of these respective thinkers. But these opinions are probably beyond rational argument, since they are ultimately based on different emotional stances toward the cosmos. Meanwhile, that opinions in these matters differ so widely is itself an interesting datum; and indeed it may be possible to examine these differing emotional stances.

As a scientist, the anthropologist has an especially difficult epistemological problem. He is a culture-bearer studying the culture of other culture-bearers. But the anthropologist is also a kind of official drop-out, ostensibly using alien tribes as his mouthpiece, and allowed to conduct his private rebellion in the arcane language of academic books—strong medicine for those who would understand him, for he casts up relativities fully as threatening as those of Freud, Einstein, and Marx. Ideally, perhaps, he should no longer be in flight from the natal culture he found uncomfortable and that impelled him to become an anthropologist, and no longer use native cultures as mere polemic substitutes for it, though he may and must use his humanity in order to perceive the human. He should have made a separate peace with his culture, because ideally also he should now recognize what culture operationally is and does for (as well as does to) human beings. And ideally too—to pile up impossibilities —he is a person psychiatrically learned in the origins of his own personality, and whose fieldwork is therefore not a species of unwitting autobiography, as theology so often is bad lyric poetry. Perhaps acute and constant awareness of the many ways in which a man may lie is a first rough defense against lying. The problem is, how much method is needed to keep one from lying? Some people, it is true, can lie without any method at all; but with all the method in the world other people can still tell lies. The only way we can tell a truth-teller is to be able to see what he sees when he points to it. Since human nature is what the anthropologist points to, we may take it that little preoccupation with method is needed, since no formal method beyond articulateness and agility in pointing may serve quite well, and much more method serve not at all. The subject matter is the reader. And the reader must be critic-scientist about the subject matter too.

Without vouching for their utility we may sample some definitions of God. Of course Herodotus[2] held sturdily that no man knows more about the gods than any other. Logically this might mean that no man knows anything about the gods; but doubtless, in his own shrewd sense, he was right, since any man is willing and able to produce the definitive statement about God at the drop of a hat. But it was a rash statement for a world traveler like Herodotus to make. What of all the priests and oracles he met, self-admitted specialists in the supernatural—priests ministrant of sacred revelation (come to some man sometime but now safely embalmed in tradition) as well as the living shaman-oracles he encountered still getting fresh messages from the spirit world? How does anyone know anything about the gods anyhow, if not these vatic specialists on whom knowledge of the gods depends! And what do they deal with? *Primus in orbe,* said the Romans,[3] *deos fecit timor*—but fear seems an odd commodity to batten on, and exploiting it gives vatics scant moral dignity.

The late Greeks thought God the Supreme Good, but many men since them have quibbled over the ontological status of this Idea, perhaps understandably given the state of the world. Besides, embarrassingly, any fantasy, nightmarish and evil as well, can be dragged into existence by the same logodaedaly and supposed omnipotence of thought. But in their view, since omniscience, omnipotence and omnibenevolence that exist would all constitute a greater Good than their merely conceptual non-existing equivalents, God defined as the Supreme Good is therefore now in business, omniscient, omnipotent and omnibenevolent. Unfortunately, these three Absolutes immediately collide and have grave logical trouble coexisting. *Si Deus bonum, unde malum?* Whence the existence of evil?—for an omnipotent benevolence could not let evil exist. And since evil does exist, God must be either not all-powerful or poorly informed. Or is evil not real? Or is evil really good? One of these absolutes must yield right-of-way, whatever the rules!—unless of course it is a question of *Credo quia absurdum.* Why not believe *any* nonsense then; why just *this* nonsense?

Again, Omnipotence that grants his sons free will runs into similar difficulties, since the one makes impossible the other. Further, an Absolute defined as unknowable and ineffable cannot be talked about in any case, given either predication. We observe apparent causality; but some ask, who *caused* causality? The uncaused Cause. But what value is this additional postulate? "Impertinent," says Bacon: we simply *observe* causality happening. Who made me, asks the child. God. But who made God, asks the child; and we are no better off than if we admitted, simply, that existence appears to exist. Perhaps Being was not created— just because the individual was! If God is Eros, the synthetic ordering principle, there is also Thanatos, death and dissolution, just as surely. If God is Love, then evidently he is not found everywhere; perhaps he is immanent somewhere and modestly limited, but evolving. But if God is Love, then how can evil be Desire, as Buddhists claim? Only frustrated and unfulfilled desire is evil, a Greek would say! And if God is redeeming Love, how can he be inviolable Justice at the same time? As Unmoved Mover, God seems merely a logically impossible trick like the Uncreated Creator to get creation moving; and a Love that moves the sun and stars must surely be something else than what mortals mean by Love, especially since human love (the only kind we know) turns out to be categorically sinful.

Besides, with the same rationale, the Gnostics took one look at the world and decided that Existence must be evil, and the reigning God really the Devil. Surely Goodness can not be the essence of the universe as early hellenized Christians maintained, and at the same time evil be the nature of the world we live in as medieval Christians felt. Furthermore, when examined closely, neither good nor evil inhere in the physical world at all. Good and bad are subjectively judged qualities attending selective relationships that human (and other) organisms enter into, with respect to quite identifiable portions or states of the physical environment. Therefore even relative good and evil cannot exist apart from organisms; life *creates* good and evil out of organic wishes and needs that did not exist before life. A man and a cow might differ fundamentally on the "good" of beefsteaks, and yet each be relatively right. Since there are many kinds of organisms, with different needs, good can scarcely be Absolute; while an objective Good that is not *good for* some organism is good for nothing. If, operationally, "good" is, after all, only a relativistic adjective, what has happened to our Noun-entity, Absolute Good? It is an Idea that, by its own definition as Absolute and by the relative nature of the good, logically can not exist. "Absolute" is an absurd word.

Evidently this term God is more protean than Zeus, being now one thing and now another: absolute good, and evil incarnate; creative love, and the creature of fear; Love and Desire opposed; Omnipotence and particulated free wills; an Entity experienced, but unknowable and indescribable; inflexible Justice and pliant Grace combined; immanent and transcendent; who acts from his own necessity but in complete freedom, etc. Theology, like obsessional neurosis, deals with problems cleverly (if unconsciously) contrived to be insoluble! For example, Calvin upheld without compromise the Augustinian view of God as predestinator; but this makes God both the helpless benefactor of the unworthy (who sin) and the capricious foe of the good (who nevertheless suffer). An immoral God? But why strive for morality if this is either unnecessary (given God's grace) or impossible to choose (given predestination)?

Theology is fabricated of such contradictions. (Is there perhaps something wrong about the postulates or the definition?) If the earnest man asks, "Why must I accept your predicates of God for their exact opposite?" the vatic personage replies, "Who are you to know the inscrutable nature of God?" But bad logic may lose out to good, and the vatic lose clients: "Well then, if I can not know your God, I will not," and leave theologians talking to themselves. The transcendentalist Margaret Fuller solemnly, if somewhat comprehensively, asseverated, "I accept the Universe," which was magnanimous of her, assuming that she knew entirely what she was talking about—but hardly what every organism including herself is actually doing that busily edits the environment *selectively* accepted and appropriated into itself. Obviously she could *not* accept the universe in its entirety and stay in business as Margaret Fuller.

Witness to many definitions of God, the subtle Nicholas of Cusa[4] finally decided that God was the totality of possible subjective visions. Every face that looks into God's sees nothing but its own truth. He who beholds with loving look feels a loving gaze directed toward him; who beholds with anger sees an angry face; with joy, joyfulness. God is the mirror of oneself. Indeed, Sartre's Zeus[5] complained of confusion on this score, for he was the dread and the love and everything else that men fantasied of him. His slow ritual dance must hold their eyes so intent on him that they forget to look into themselves. If once he forgot himself for a moment and let their eyes turn, then men once created would be no longer his—which is to forget they were not his creation but he theirs.

But, cried Jane Harrison,[6] accustomed to Greek clarity, to say Alpha is Omega, life and force the same as moral good, and to call all of them and much else God is to darken counsel! None of these postulates about the Absolute, observes the scientist, serves proposition-making or allows operational testing. Since That Which Is must include everything from the valency of carbon to the Second Law of Thermodynamics, this is too big a mouthful for everyday use, and Cosmos or Universe are easier locutions when needed. Your absolute god as Stimulus surely evokes diverse Response!, observes the psychologist. Agreed, answers the anthropologist, there are more gods than tribes. Yes, says the poet Wallace Stevens,[7] with a poet's licensed ambiguity, "God and the human imagination are one."

The definitions of God become more psychological as we reach modern times. "God is collective desire personified," wrote E. Doutté[8]; that is, God is what everyone wants. But he is also what no one really seems to want; he is "something not ourselves which makes for righteousness," said Matthew Arnold.[9] But is this second contradictory God not identical with the first, if we may substitute the term "enculturational conditioning"? Further, "this something not ourselves," as some have impolitely observed, could be characterized somewhat more exactly by specifying anything from father to tribesman and policeman to tax collector. Besides, why exclude conscience, *within oneself,* from righteousness? And in the last analysis, where does this god, this cultural compulsion reside if not *in* "ourselves," myself and my fellow tribesmen? However, in actual practice, we make God accomplice to our *crimes* if we busy him with absolution, a kind of bail-bondsman for our misdemeanors. Is it then crime that we desire? And use God to secure? What on earth can we be talking about when we use this chimerical little Word!

"God is my desire," wrote Tolstoy with magnificent ambiguity. The psychiatrist might read interminable volumes of Tolstoy to fathom what this uncomfortable man could have meant by it; otherwise, each one will choose among alternative interpretations according to his own temperament. "God is my desire. God is the One that I love. God is the Other of my infinite longing. God is desire, the voice of my Id. God is the organic compounds of carbon and nitrogen and whatever else it is in me that desires: God is my literal life and my future life forever that I desire. God is my yearning narcissism and I am God. God is my moral father as I desire righteousness. God is Everything I wish to incorporate. My desire is earnestly to adapt myself to That Which Is. God is the Second Law of Thermodynamics, Thanatos, my essential Death Instinct, since this is the process and the end of which I am desirous, or to which I am inexorably compelled to go: God is the death of me; my merging of self with the infinite Self means non-entity, inescapably, passionately, Universe, surcease. I can only desire or "will" what must be: God is the deterministic definition of my creatureliness. God is my hunger for what I am not and have not; he is the negative template of what I am; he is the Supplement in total reality of what I limitedly am; he is the All outside my own skin. God is my infantile envy of omnipotence —and there we have paraded before us a whole menagerie of psychiatric dispositions. All these, and doubtless more, are possible meanings of the definition of Tolstoy. It is poetry, to which each brings his own meaning. But this poetic ambiguity makes the definition somewhat useless for prosaic discourse!

Still, this book purports to be one on religion. Cannot we do somewhat better in defining religion than we have in defining God? First of all, the etymological definition: *religare* means "to bind fast" as it were in ob*liga*tion, a word built on the same root. "Religion" is not derived from *relegere,* "to go over again" in reading or speech or ritual, as the lawyer Cicero[10] thought in his treatise *De Natura Deorum* on the "nature of the gods"; or from *relegere,* "to gather together" in the sense of collating religious formulae or collecting legal precedents. So long, therefore, as we use the correctly derived term "religion" we must not lose this sense of the binding, compulsive, obligatory, in some sense moral and customary aspect of religion. Religion demands behaviors, loyalties, commitment.

Already several pagan authors, including Polybius,[11] had made familiar a concept of the *utility* of religion as a kind of *panem et circenses* to divert and amuse the impoverished masses, to take their minds off their troubles and their condition of life. This notion was taken over much later by Marx, the view that religion served a useful narcotizing of the people for the purposes of economic exploitation by the elite; indeed, to the rationalist unbelievers of the eighteenth century, the elitist function had been a favorite explanation of religion, though the Philosophes tended to emphasize rather the intellectual and political exploitation by priests and kings. But all these formulations suffer from a number of inadequacies. First of all, use is not essence. Nor do these conceptions do justice to the subjective *psychological* nature of religion for its practitioners. Further, this view wrongly supposes that sacred culture is witting, planned, consciously created, and always or often or even ever reaches foreseeable conclusions. It also does violence to the fact of sincere beliefs, mistaken or not; and to the fact that the officiants of cults are characteristically as "deluded" as their communicants—if indeed not more so, to the degree that the more needful vatic personality originated the belief, whereas his communicants merely gratefully accepted it at secondhand. Given its nature, religion doubtless can be *used* for a number of purposes. But to suppose that everywhere the purpose of religion is exploitative is to propound a paranoid-persecutory theory of history and culture-by-plot.

Psychologically more convincing is the humanistic functional view of Gilbert Murray. He believes that "religion essentially deals with the uncharted region of human experience. A large part of human life has been thoroughly surveyed and explored; we understand the causes at work; and we are not bewildered by the problems. That is the domain of positive knowledge. But all around us on every side there is an uncharted region, just fragments of the fringe of it explored, and these imperfectly; it is with this that religion deals."[12] Religion, therefore, is the human way that *sapiens* the "knower" has of dealing with the unknown. As Santayana says, religion is the poetry in which we believe.

An objectivist view, with understandably much currency among religionists, is that of Rudolf Otto.[13] A response, he implies, must obviously have a stimulus. Religion then is the human responses to the *Mysterium tremendum et fascinosum* which God is. The formulation has much psychological reality. But the Mystery (Wach[14] thought, and I think him mistaken) would ultimately defy any attempt to describe, analyze and comprehend it scientifically. Certainly it will if we persistently look for it in the wrong direction! Indeed, until we know the nature of the Mystery, any response remains subjective and the whole problem *psychological.* Thus we know a great deal about responses, religions, which moreover are accessible to study, but we seem condemned never to know about the Stimulus, which apparently is not. Very well, if our only data are psychological, why not approach them psychologically?

What could the Stimulus be? Frazer[15] believed that the fear of the dead is, on the whole, the most powerful source of primitive religion; Malinowski[16] would have it that the source is fear of individual death itself. Descriptively, there is much ethnographic evidence to support both these related views. However, both taken together do not appear to exhaust the content of religion. And neither explains in any way just why the spirits of the dead, or death itself, should be feared.

To be more precisely objectivist and concretely ethnographic, we should scrutinize the specific religion of one group, and for this none serves better than that of the well-documented Greeks. But as Jane Harrison points out,[17] our imaginations are so filled with the vivid personalities and clear-cut human images of the Olympian gods, it takes a severe mental effort to realize that at the origins of Greek religion *there were no gods at all,* only clay-daubed ritualists, earth-serpents, and other animal familiars of human shamans. Gilbert Murray, her predecessor, and E. R. Dodds, her successor, would agree with her: behind the manlike gods was only man, and at the root of Greek humanistic religion was only the human shaman, the dancing sorcerer, masked like an animal. Is the *Mysterium* man, perhaps, and not the Universe?

The Chinese sage Mencius said that "He who brings all his intellect to bear on the subject will come to understand his own nature; he who understands his own nature will understand God."[18] The Chinese were humanists too; perhaps they can give us a clue, for Chinese Taoism began in shamanism also. Just who is the shaman, psychologically and functionally? Some person or persons we all know? And just what are the tremendous and fascinating mysteries? The mystery of life, and the mystery of the universe, perhaps indeed the two confounded? But since belief

and attitude and response are properly subjective and psychological matters, let us first explore further what religionists have to say about them.

"Religion," says Schleiermacher,[19] "consists of an absolute sense of
our dependency." Murray[20] regards it worth remarking that Schleiermacher placed the essence of religion in this feeling without attempting to
define the object toward which it was felt. Bonnard[21] considered that
"The religious feeling of primitive man can be almost wholly defined as
a feeling of the presence of the Other." But who is this Other? Jean-
Marie Guyau thought that "Religion is universal sociomorphism; the
religious sense is the sense of dependence in relation to wills which primitive man places in the universe"—and of all the definitions he knew,
Salomon Reinach[22] thought this one indisputably the best. Is it Society
that we are dependent on? The most elementary form of the religious
life, Durkheim believed,[23] was the totemic celebration of the group's
own sacred ingroupness. God and Society are one: ancestors are the
guardians of morality; initiation means being formally taken into group
membership, a ritual of socialization; religious rites are the dramatized
expression of social solidarity; and group belief makes all collective representations "true." But behind Society is there not some more fundamental entity? What is this awesome Other?

Claude Bernard viewed disease as the body's attempt at homeostasis,
appropriate in kind but faulty in amount. Is religion the mind's attempt
at homeostasis, appropriate in amount but faulty in kind? Is religion an
autotherapy of the body politic when other cultural means fail? Are not
magic, religion, medicine and art—visual, sung, ritualized or danced—
all forms of primitive psychotherapy, techniques for the liquidation of
anxiety in primitive societies? Thus, religion seems to be a kind of phatic
social hormone, to spread and share and contain common fears. But what
fears? And is religion only spiritual gregariousness, a group's cognitive
patriotism, Society celebrating itself? If so, why all the mystery about it?
And if so, why do not gregarious monkeys and apes—and in fact other
gregarious species like cows and antelopes and bees—why do they not
have what we can identify as religion, this response to an objective social
Mysterium tremendum et fascinosum?

But in the last analysis, is religion essentially public, or is it not really
private? However social in its form, is religion not really somehow acutely
individual in its origin and intensity? Indeed, in defining religion as the
"art and theory of the internal life of man," Whitehead regarded his
definition as "the direct negation of the [Durkheimian] theory that religion
is primarily a social fact."[24] Had not William James called religion the
"experiences of individual men in their solitude"?[25] In fact, Whitehead

concluded, religion is "what the individual does with his solitariness," and collective acts are only the "trappings of religion." Allport pointed out that not only does this personal religion differ widely among individuals but it "resists all attempts at its communication to others."[26] What is it in the individual that makes for the shaping of group religion? What private-public *Mysterium* is it that all individuals have in common but do not share?

A secular scrutiny of religion makes the Referent quite clear; and further study also explains the fearsome hiddenness, ambivalent projection, psychological ambiguity, and the strikingly individual and ethnic variety in the *Mysterium tremendum et fascinosum*. The Mysterium *is* in a sense objective, and, in fact, *has* been experienced; but each individual has forgotten its erstwhile nature and original location. Religion is what a man thinks and feels concerning this unique unknown, and what he does with his ignorance. An understanding of the phenomenon embraces also the explanation of why religious response is uniquely human. *The context is the universally human nuclear family, the condition is individual human neoteny.* In religion the projected parent still stands, as of yore, between us and physical reality, and is still sometimes confused with it, the divine attributes being those of creator, ancestor, lawgiver, protector, feared ally, lover and friend. At the base of every religion is the familial experience, and all religions consequently contain some basic oedipal story in their myths. Who is the magic shaman? And when do we first feel awe?

At times God has traits of the mother; but her psychic presence is more often discernible, as we shall see, in the para-system magic. As the dominating power-figure in the family and ultimate sanctioner of behavior, toward whom intensely ambivalent feelings are typically directed, in religion (here, properly so called) God most often is the psychic ghost of the father—eternal as his imago is in the unconscious mind, but in ritual often imitated, sometimes symbolically killed, and not infrequently even eaten. The origin of the imago in a real father is the reason for his intensely personal and individual quality; and the human universality of social fatherhood is the reason individual persons in society can join together in passionate confrontation of the culturally similar paradigm in the group. In the words of Ernest Jones, "religious life represents a dramatization on the cosmic plane of the emotions, fears, and longings which arose in the child's relation to his parents."[27]

In a sense religion is the group dream, or perhaps nightmare, that teaches men the proper stance *vis-à-vis* the parental divine, as characteristically shaped in that society, but in either case now "unreal" except psychically. More precisely, every religion historically begins in some dramatic individual revelation or dream, culturally diffused to others, and gradually edited into the necessarily vague and contradictory entity appropriate to a whole group. The intensity of feeling about God and his intrinsic contradictoriness together explain the violence of the *odium theologicum* and the historic fact that men earnestly murder one another over religion. But to the degree that any temporary consensus can be achieved, "God" will change with the needs of the group and with the experience each successive generation has of changing styles in parents.

Religion also entails mutual forgiveness for a vaguely felt disloyalty to current common sense, a kind of conspiratorial fellowship; and with a consequent group fervor, individuals mutually support their necessary myth. From this guilt derives, in part, both the quality of positive agglutination and the usual invidious ingroupness of communicants in any religion. In order for this kind of defense mechanism adequately to defend the psychologically suspect individual, an exaltation of the group as such is required (which in this context it the less deserves). *Mon patrie quand même!* That the function of religious belief is equilibrium-seeking is shown not merely by the characteristic content of such belief, and not only by the intense mutual phatic support which members of the group give one another in holding to the group-dream, and their rage at any defection from orthodoxy, but most especially in the successively renewed and re-rationalized *defenses* of the same old beliefs. Often all that is new in religious history are the new ways of defending old beliefs—defenses often borrowed from changes in *secular* cognitive styles, which would otherwise tend to corrode archaic belief—imitation being the homage eternal holy belief pays to changing common sense. Again, in their cults men earnestly and in good faith copy—through ritual mimicry, magic identifications, masks—the strengths of the fathers, not daring to recognize that, on occasion, those ritual strengths were dreamed up by other mere men in the despair of living, and were not there before human need created them. If mere manhood shows through the frayed garments of godhood, then new ritual and new myth must be dreamed.

Fervent mutual support of "right thinking" easily results in a complacent conviction of invidious righteousness. However, no religion has anything whatever to do with goodness as such. Membership in the group may signalize assent to or coerce the individual toward the group's definition of good and evil; and in the practice of whatever outlandish orthodoxy, those who are in fact intrinsically kind and loving persons will doubtless inevitably express their uncomplicated goodness and social integration. But no belief in any myth has any final relation whatever to individual kindliness and goodness. On the contrary, religious groups can be and frequently are quite as wicked as any political or military or other mobs. For kindliness and goodness, and their opposites, are the qualities of individuals; and they are shaped far earlier in life and by other means than by group-shaping cult myths. In fact, since any cultural "rightness" is ultimately sanctioned by the society, *it is especially in intense group situations* that the disciplines of the individual conscience are loosed, and each repressed wickedness finds an acting out in the permissive mob context, with the new contagious mystique and authority of the mob substituting *pro tem* for the individual conscience. The psychopathy of the mob leader that propels him to antinomian leadership in crisis, now releases and mobilizes the hidden psychopathy in each mob member. To understand the dynamics of mobs is to forbid oneself the sleazy indulgence of such acting-out. And if anything, group membership blunts ethical perception and fetters moral imagination, because we then uncritically and passively let others think for us.

The function of the group ethic, of course, is simply to maintain the group. Thus, in meeting real tests of contemporary goodness (for example toward Jews in Germany and toward Negroes in America), established religious institutions, as compared with secular ones, have been by no means notable for superior or even equivalent goodness, or for priority in perceptiveness. It is unreasonable to expect any human group, despite its protest of supernatural rationale, to be superhuman; and there are intrinsic reasons to anticipate in group emotion the "less than human." Groups at best merely compound the mixed goodness and badness of constituent men; but as mobs they elicit the repressed evil in individuals. Goodness is far oftener the possession of clear-headed individuals in cool secular and commonsense non-mob contexts, than of those whose judgment is chronically warped by habits of assiduously believing self-deceptive nonsense about themselves, and who are unduly complacent in their conviction of automatic godliness through membership in the group. Group membership as such, therefore, may actually militate against effective goodness. The function of the group is to make us *feel* that we are good, not necessarily to make us good. Operating with such human mixtures, how could it be otherwise? A cult is not Maxwell's demon.

Far more fundamentally, the function of the cult is to assuage individual suffering from common human vicissitudes. Limited in power as each one discovers himself to be, group-adherence promises omnipotence; religion is an attempt to overcome any lack of equipment to deal with a threatening situation alone. And faced as each one is by inevitable personal extinction, in the religious group he seeks the image of the omnipotent father of childhood who created him, or the ancestors who created men or the cultural group. Did not once these creators also preserve and protect us? So will they now!

The *psychic presence* of these fathers as vague feelings in our minds is one base of the belief in spirits. Submission to them and instinctual renunciation secure the promise of triumph over difficulties and over the final insult to narcissism, death. One bargains portions of life to retain life. This is the commodity, the price, and the binding bargain or covenant. It is easier in these matters for the average man to buy the ready-made group neurosis than to make up his tailor-made own. In supposing that the physical environment cares about the well-being and survival of the individual animal—a proposition for which there exists no positive and much negative biological evidence—religion is the "delusion of reference" of human beings. In place of the "persecution" by death (at the hands of the angry environment-father), narcissism substitutes the "benign paranoia"[28] of religion (and omnipotent protection by him). Fear has been transformed into love, though in each case environment has been confounded with father.

There is a certain irony in the fact that the society which makes, or accepts, the paranoid claim that a given shaman is the father-god, is, so to speak, punished by his becoming, thereby, charisma-laden, immortal, a very god; and that, commonly enough, the communicants then murder this symbolic father to reclaim and re-incorporate the surrendered potency. In this whole process men are not so much being good as they are being human. What they are all compelled to do, group membership tells them is somehow appropriate and hence "good." It is nevertheless difficult to concede that ritual father-murder and symbolic cannibalism in such totemic communions make together for any special righteousness. The dramatization of persistent ambivalence toward the father is not so much necessarily moral "good" as it is merely catharsis, and that *feels* good.

Religion is meaningless unless there is in some manner a *persistence* of the mana and awe of the father, *mysterium tremendum et fascinosum,* and his continued psychic presence. In this sense, Tylor long ago made the most accurate definition of religion as a "belief in spiritual beings"[29] —and useful both for its psychological appositeness and its ethnographic comprehensiveness. To define religion in any other way than Tylor's is to lose descriptive reality and essence (with the reservation that magic, properly so called, is a discernibly different if related phenomenon). As Spiro points out,[30] anthropologists would have to invent some other term to define the obsessive human concern with supernaturals that help or harm men, if as scientists they would wish to continue discussing what we understand by religion—to which we might add that at the same time the erstwhile term "religion" would be gutted of all psychological and ethnographic content, a proper wraith. Durkheim properly noted that religion cannot be defined except by the traits found everywhere religion is found. But of the several human *loci* suggested for religion, Freud has the claim over Durkheim for precision: it is the *society of the family* in which it begins, and religion is only subsequently institutionalized in Society. In biological terms, only human animals have religion, since only they have the human family. Mere sociability creates no cult in other animals.

To see the ghost-father God thus safely distant from us in time turns out to be surprisingly easy. Who, indeed, is now afraid of his father! What is really difficult however, but not to be shirked, is to discern the residual eternal infant *present now* in each one of us. For this is precisely the painful recognition which our sacred behavior is in fact carefully contrived to hide from us—as well as to hide recognition that a monstrous unsurrendered infantile omnipotence is the ultimate paradigm of God and the first of his many psychosexual metamorphoses.

Death. No one can really contrive to believe in his own total extinction. So long as one lives vividly aware of his experience-shaped and hence inevitable thoughts, a conviction of the manifest inevitability and eternity of his personality accompanies his consciousness of it; psychological insight into his personal past only reconfirms the almost frightening persistence in him of past personality. And what is more real than consciousness? *Cogito ergo sum!* The time is the eternal present, and one has experienced an infinity of presents before. Experience an ending? Absurdity! Without retrospection how could one even properly *experience* it, since being can only be compared in perspective with being? Even logic argues pitiably here for personal immortality! But there is a quite logical alternative to this impasse: the admission that no man can have any experienced conception of his own mortality. In the abstract, having observed it, one knows that death is something that happens to other people. But in metaphysical perspective this insight expands infinitely to the alarmed generalization that death is what happens to every man, every animal, every plant—and, in other ways, perhaps to every solar system, every galactic universe!

Still, it manifestly cannot happen here. Since every jot and tittle of his personality is based on solid experience, one *trusts* his personality and its infallible judgments. What fact is so obdurate as not to fit easily somewhere in the infinitely expandable filing cabinet of one's understanding? Otherwise, thinking would have encountered an unassimilable fact—and then where would thinking be! Indeed, we enter consciousness with one of the prime attributes of God, omniscience, and from child to dotard this delicious conviction never really leaves us. We *know* everything that we know, so that obviously we know *everything* we know, which in the absence of any further knowledge is tantamount to admitting we know everything; just listen to any child, any adolescent, any adult, any old man! It is only some dim memory of a time when we did not know what we now know that chastens us to know that sometime we may know more than we now know—but of course at each "then" we did not know any better! Am I not now writing the final word on this matter?

We begin existence possessing another prime attribute of God, omnipotence. To the child in the womb, every subliminal wish, every organic need in that perfected environment is in that fact accomplished instantly. We scarcely dare ascribe to him even consciousness of his blissful oneness with his universe. It is a magic time. Then wish equals fact, and fact wish. This omnipotence begins to erode at birth, that first unwilling bum's rush, humiliating to a god, of being cast out of Eden—just as he will one day learn to fear the unceremonious and undignified bum's rush out of life, quite without any justice or reason or proper deference to his wishes.

Omnibenevolence, perhaps, one experienced—if experience it can be called—only of that uterine utopia, unless the pale "oceanic state" of mystic oneness with nature is a ghostly recall of that lost bliss. Certainly the first cry after birth is an entirely reasonable one of godly and total rage. Possibly parents provide in their asseverations the henceforth unlikely supposition that they, or any other environment, could be omnibenevolent. One can yearn in vain for omnibenevolence in the environment and for total "understanding" (of one's organic wants and psychic hungers), but this does not seem to be what environments are in business for; being a fetus turns out to have been a misleading experience, and the nearest thing in this line, to be sure of the best available quality, is merely a fallible mother's ministrations, at any rate when she is around. The world is a deceiver, if we thought it modeled on that first one, and the progress thenceforth of every god is fated to be inexorably downhill.

Sometime in babyhood we encounter a vast remote and awesome Presence, prepotent even over mother. And since experienced power was total when thought was omnipotent, then clearly this obdurate and irascible Will gradually filches omnipotence as he filched mother from us, and now outrageously possesses both omnipotence and mother himself. Suddenly one is little, unworthy and weak. These gigantic Others countenance our existence only at the cost of difficult renunciations and unasked-for disciplines. It is a furious time of outraged feeling, of first-realized abject dependency, of towering tides of ambivalence which range between total hatred and seeking the assurance of love, of wickedness and earnest moral faith and hope. Since in his consciousness the child was lately the whole universe, and is still the center of it, death is the talion punishment for an untamed wish in the child to annihilate his father. But to avoid his own death and to accomplish his father's, he must now repress his murderous feelings and wait until he is grown up to kill god. As a child one wondered, how can I record this knowledge of what it is to be a child? For obviously when I am an adult I will no longer understand, since adults do not. Being an adult seems mostly to consist in having forgotten childhood, and in compensation to indulge now in sheer joyously arbitrary power over the child. Perhaps it is possible, for an adult who has to, to recover these feelings in all their murderous gut reality and overwhelming total love. But it is very difficult, and in both emotional tone and content not wholly alien to religious experience.

Gradually, with speech and walking and the discovery of its sex, the child achieves awareness of the exhilarating miracle, a conscious organism's power to live. Each time we enter some new psychic environment, not walled about with protections and comforters, we struggle anew for mastery; and every adaptation tells us we have not really lost all the old secret power. But the child's supposed "omnipotence" gradually dwindles into the adolescent's equally illusory "omnipotentiality" seemingly with only the problem of choice of what to become. Each real becoming, however, narrows down infinite potential—often with a delayed recognition that things just happened in sequence, without much conscious choice at all. When finally he comes to achieve the major trait of godliness, the power to create life, omnipotentiality sadly evaporates into mere potency: the adolescent has shrunk into a man. As a father he learns the rueful secret that his awesome responsibility for creating the psychic universe, which in fact does create and shape the personality of the child, is not accompanied by the omniscience and omnipotence the job requires. He can only shakily and dubiously pretend to omnibenevolence—which the little terror all the time uses all his effort to try, to undermine, and to prove false. And sometime, in sheer self-defense, the father is provoked into the use of *force majeur,* like an unjust god. The process has come full cycle: adults just do not understand a child's legitimate claim to omnipotence!

At each severer test of adequacy as one grows, there remain all these earlier experiences of power; and each discovery of weakness or limitation makes it easy to retreat into the sacred family of childhood securely bounded by omnipotent love, or to some earlier phase of the encounter with omnipotence. Discovering less and less omnipotence in the self, the individual seeks the same vain commodity in the Not-Self (which he still secretly hopes to control or to persuade). It is not there: only the endless task of accommodating, through triple book-keeping, Soma, Self, and Society to one another.

In subsequent life, the individual may encounter many other fathers, whose charisma matches the degree of his unassuaged childlike need. But in demanding submission as a child, does not such a shaman rob the individual of his power as a man, in order to collect and assert vatic omnipotence and make of himself a god? Behind each God is only a paranoid messiah, the shaman and false wonderworker; he has somehow retained everyman's infantile omnipotence. But can one truly become a man by conforming to his myth, by serving him, by imitating the god, or by ritually aping his god-impersonating ancestors? It is too late really; we know the fallibilities of fathers. As Rilke[31] knew, God, the-no-longer-sayable, is stripped of his attributes: eternity, omnipotence, infallibility return to the dead universe without a father. A god is only a shaman's dream about his father.

When I discern that the bargaining is only for a child-lost omnipotence, and that the cult is only that of the urgency of my needs, I can no longer worship. The omnipotence of anyone exists only in the child's imagining. The only omniscience and omnipotence now lie in the *claims* of the shaman; and these I am ready to believe only because I thought I saw them in my father. The only proper attitude toward myself and my needs is simply respect, not worship. And I know that in the end, each one of us, alone, meets death. But since no man can kill his father and the secret will is omnipotent, I know he did not, could not die! The immortality of God—again to confound mortal father with immortal universe—is His very essence! I swam into mind out of nowhere, and now must I learn we all swim back into nothingness? Surely I am like my Father? Surely now He will lend me his eternity this once and leave me immortal! Have I not, in my conscience, loyally kept Him alive?

Here we may discern how an absolute fundamentalist ethic is related to an eternal God: He is needed to take responsibility for Good, He must remain saddled with the sanctioning of good behavior, He is the Caretaker—not the fallible conscience. But God as Absolute Goodness, we have seen, is immediately self-contradictory with the other absolutes we require of him, and lives nowhere. By operational definition of the nature of the good, every "good" must be relevant to an organism. Then only what is *good for* man is any good for man. Hence the system "man" is sufficient to define goodness—whether he be ignorant of what it is, misguided, perverse, or whatever. If culture, if personality are further speciations of man, then perhaps good must be still further refined down to what is good for a single individual (like an improbable, and probably mistaken, taste for the music of Alban Berg or Edgar D. Varèse).

Is God to be (as he logically should be) the sum total of all the contradictory goods of all living organisms? Why not call it "environment" and let it go at that! Other animals may have their species-adapted ethology, but for men the only possible ethics are human ethics. Ethics may seem to be of God; but "God" is only a biopsychological relationship peculiar to human biology. Likewise, ethics only seem to be external to man, or anti-individual, because their compulsions were once outside the self. Any ethic would be in desperate straits if it had to depend on non-natural "supernatural" miracle, on the authority of absolute fiat and not on real biological relationships, on a "transcendent" Absolute, on any encountered irrationality, and on gaps in our scientific experience-explanations. In these gaps, ethics could lead at best only a temerarious existence, likely at any moment to be squeezed out of reality by some new understanding of ours.

Obviously, ethics *belong to* man and *belong to* the individual. One must therefore be careful to demand only the best-quality goods, for anything else is not good enough! This requires constant comparative shopping and consumer choice—certainly this is what *de facto* every individual is burdened with! Man came into being out of blind and accidental processes in the purposeless environment that did not have him in mind. The universe is useless until organisms use it. Man is only the heir of antecedent organisms' purposes, or more precisely the only purpose of man is himself. His only faith, his only possible loyalty is toward man, and the purposes he makes. If it be argued that he exists for God's sake or for God's purposes, this is only a confused and somewhat pretentious way of saying that man exists for his own sake. Only in man can "ought" become "is" —and in a wholly operational, rationally understandable, wholly secular way.

It is therefore necessary to keep constantly in mind the *function* of religion. Curiously, however, in calling human motivations and psychological meanings outside the domain of anthropology, classical British Functionalists outdo their ancestor Durkheim, who was certainly not antipsychological. At one time (though he later changed his mind), Firth[32] stated that in studying ritual the anthropologist had no concern with the inner state of the subjects, but only with the objective kinds of social structures that are maintained by ritual. This is to sweep out all human motivation that sets the system going, and all meaning to communicants as well! The study of religion cannot by exclusion of psychological reality be made Behaviorist or objectivist, since its essence is subjective. To ignore the subjective means not to study religion as a subject matter. The subjective is here the reality; and in a psychiatrically sophisticated study of Tallensi religion, Fortes noted that "All the concepts and beliefs we have examined are religious extrapolations of the experiences generated in the relationships between parents and children"[33]—thus comprehensively including both psychological and social realities and giving them meaning in terms of one another.

Basic problems in our day are less objective-scientific than subjective moral ones. In the scientific method we already have an effective way of solving problems, of understanding and making things. Politico-economic and social ills derive from moral failures in the using and sharing of things. Indeed, murderously competing dogmas on how to do this actually constitute the most real danger to mankind, in a new round of religious wars, the politico-economic ones of our day. In science we are willing to make experiments to uncover facts; in morals we are not. In order to be moral at all we think we have to be absolutists, so hiddenly insecure are we as moral beings. And yet all ethnic history is in fact a series of unwitting, blind, and undirected moral experiments—the human evolutionary equivalent of random mutation in animal genes. Absurdly, we try to suppose that on all moral questions the eternal and unchanging truths have been handed down once and for all, as though morality had no adaptive ecological context at all, and as though the solutions—forged in other social, economic and ethnic climates—must nevertheless be applicable to the new problems of the day.

To insist we already have the solutions is often to remain possessed of the problems. We need the phyloanalysis of ideologies much as we need the psychoanalysis of neuroses and the scientific critique of past hypotheses. Neuroses operate in terms of obsolete and misdrawn emotional maps, they interfere with the effective processing of new interpersonal information, and hence they impugn current realistic response; the same is often true of moral culture. Religious behavior is not so much genuinely adaptive behavior as it is symptom formation; to understand this, let the reader reflect, not on his own "true religion," but on some exotic alien or primitive religion he knows about. Are we not permitted to doubt that the sacrifice of children to Moloch was good for Phoenician society? That the ten thousands of human sacrificial skulls in aboriginal Mexico City actually secured the Aztec state? Do earnestness or energy prove moral truth? Or does zealousness? Did the Inquisition benefit Europe?

As Freud maintained, "religious phenomena are to be understood only on the model of the neurotic symptoms of the individual, which are so familiar to us, as a return of long-forgotten important happenings in the primæval history of the human family [and] owe their obsessive character to that very origin and therefore derive their effect on mankind from the historical truth they contain."[34] Cultural man is the only animal with a psychic past—and consequently the only animal with a moral future.

Neurosis, in individuals or groups, is a frightened clinging to the past, and remaining a slave to the forgotten. History and life-history are both in part *events to be recovered from,* through unearthing and re-viewing forgotten premises behind the bitterly defended false answers. History that cannot be understood and neutralized is the neurosis of the society. Time-binding man is also time-bound. We already know the *Prometheus Bound* of Aeschylus; the truly most sought-for of all classic documents is *Prometheus Unbound.* Each man must be his own Prometheus or "future-wise" man—but this is possible only in being also his twin Epimetheus or past-remembering man. To be sure, our power over the past within us is limited. But fortunately the power of the past over us is limited too— unless of course we espouse the binding faith of the Culturologists, for whom Culture is the omnipotent god who allows us no freedom but determines our every act—as though rebellious organisms were not part of the act and one of the determinants, and as though each individual were the perfectly enculturated zombie of omnipotent Society—no oedipus, no adolescence, no culture change, no people here! Nor is man entirely freedom, as the Existentialists preach, though multiplication of possibilities in complex systems is certainly in the direction of freedom. He is also responsibility—unless we perform "ritual value-washing" like the positivist Wienerkreiser[35]—for we cannot escape responsibility for the judgments we cannot escape making.

The mood of science is to discard or accept theories with articulate and conscious premises. And this should be the aim of the healthy individual ego. But the mood of sacred culture is to preserve at all costs preferred obsessive hypotheses, such as God and immortality, and for this purpose oedipal "mystery" is to be preferred. Epistemologically, the flaw in religion is to rely for judgment on external human sources of the special sort we call divine, because they have been purveyed to us by vatic characters considered charismatic. These occupy the psychic space and authority of a child's father, and if accepted their spurious paternity will falsely infantilize us. We must, therefore, in studying these spokesmen of the gods, explore the psychic history of human infancy, and of man's cultural childhood. Freud pointed out that every internal barrier of repression is the historical result of some external obstruction.[36]

Any culture is in part made up of a corpus of taboos that may need re-examination—but in part culture is also made up of valuable adaptive clues. To discriminate the one from the other is the mature psyche's task.

The humanist (and this I take it must by definition include the anthropologist) necessarily looks to the past, in order to understand the present. But such use of the past can not be a slavish and uncritical worship. Those who uncritically admire and unselectively worship the past are in the dangerous position of supposing the past will carry them in its arms—whereas it is more properly we who carry the past on our backs: all the old neuroses of forgotten time, the premature or over-easy or wish-contaminated conclusions, the comforting fantasies of men more burdened with anxieties than information. Until we shall have some godly and "absolute" knowledge of good and evil, we must content ourselves with Schweitzer's existentialist *Interimsethik,* and do the best we can.

Culture (or more properly the *power* of individuals in a society committed to the culture) frustrates raw animal wish, and yet it promises secure gratifications. The question is, how effectively and efficiently does it do this, at what price, and can we make a better bargain? Can we buy greater authentic gratifications at a lower price of repression; and can we be sure that every repression, well invested, yields the highest possible gratification income? If we do not possess the democratic process of thus modifying our lives, then culture truly is arbitrary tyranny, since as individual wills we did not enter into the earlier social contracts that made the culture. Libidinal contracts must be renewed in each generation, and they must avoid the binding covenant of mortmain. But we are not free not to make any social contracts whatever.

We are all Epicureans; but we must all be Stoics too. We cannot make Society a womb into which we can crawl back and become immortal because unborn. To anthropomorphize God is to limit the Other to one's own limited fantasies. Reality is richer than thought, and no man is clever enough to program a computer to factorize reality into thought terms. He would be programming it! Belief in deity is basically immoral if it means we need not face the world without cringing, accept our problems without whining, and avoid the illusion of escape from inexorable predicaments like death. Perhaps, indeed, if we avoided absurd fantasy about death, we might consequently live more significant lives. And would soldiers who knew they were mortal rush so gloriously to death in battle for their fantasies? Or the dubious motives of other men?

The peculiar nature of religious "knowledge" is shown by the fanaticism with which men defend the sacred. Religious dogmas do not discover new knowledge for us, whereas scientific hypotheses do. The reason for this is that dogma must be believed unquestioned, since it insists it is ultimate knowledge itself; on the contrary, if dogma generates no new knowledge, it is not even a good hypothesis! But scientific hypotheses must be reality-tested; and they are valued both for their "fit" to experience and for their vexatious ability to show up new facts, often by no means immediately welcome. Again, the difference lies partly in the nature of religious versus scientific language, since wrongly or irrelevantly phrased questions (absolutes, angelic spirits or unbodied life in spaceless space, non-dying metazoans) get no answer at all from nature.

Religion too is ultimately based on hypotheses—hypotheses that do not admit themselves to be such, hypotheses that call themselves "revelations" irrefutable and unchanging, historically discarded hypotheses, hypotheses whose meaning is not known or has been forgotten, and hypotheses which time has hidden and which we must rediscover to make examinable, if indeed either recovery or examination is possible. Above all, the difference between secular and sacred lies also in the willingness to lay aside the postulates underlying a propositional statement (Riemannian versus Euclidean geometry, the wave or particle theory of light), in contrast to men's notorious unwillingness to discard the postulates (God and immortality) behind their religious beliefs.

The difference between the sacred dogma and the secular hypothesis suggests that the religion of an individual is an autobiographical statement, defended in the same way and with the same means that he defends his personality. A man's religion is what he *feels* about the Unknown; and what he feels is based on what he has experienced in his emotional growth and individual life history, his own positive and inescapable "truth." A man's religion is his moral Rorschach. What he sees in the cards is not so much a function of the unknown (the inkblots) as it is of his personality, unwittingly projected. What he thinks he sees is ultimately a statement about his unknown self. A man's religion is thus literally his character.

Since history has left them unproved, the sacred statements made by any society are of the same nature and human locus. A religion is the Rorschach of a society, hotly defended as is everything else tribal and hence sacred. And for the same reasons. As in much of personality, so in much of culture, dogmatic constructs are erected on old, painful and unresolved problems in the individual's forgotten life history, and in the society's forgotten past. Both neurosis and sacred culture are the frantic nonce-solutions of people under stress which are frozen into permanence by fear. Religions therefore constitute not so much objective statements about the universe as subjective statements about people, projective crisis-cult statements about people, collectively or individually. Theology, then, is not so much a science without subject matter, as it is the misplaced locus of a subject matter for the sciences of psychology and anthropology. Beliefs, of course, do not have to be true in order to be psychologically real and socially functional; the falsity of a belief can do nothing to impugn the fact that it is a belief. Such special facts, therefore, can be studied scientifically through a sociology of knowledge.

Consequently, an understanding of the religion of a half-mad Siberian *olonist* or a drunken Shawnee Indian may provide us with the human self-knowledge needed to prevent the destruction of mankind. As always, insight is best nourished on humble details; and one can learn much about God likewise from Eskimo culture and from Eskimo grammar. For this understanding we need to examine belief in its ecological context. From Alaska to Greenland, the Eskimo are a littoral people living on Arctic seashores. They have a curiously dual economy. In summer they hunt land animals, gather berries, and get such plant foods as are seasonably available. In winter they fish and hunt sea mammals through the sea ice. To the Eskimo, summer is an easy and jolly time. It is winter that is hard, when great storms come up, sometimes stopping hunters for weeks from getting food, and then the people starve.

Knowing their chief life problem and their major ecological predicament, we can almost predict, projectively, how the religion of the Eskimo will be structured. Is the aleatic element of anxiety and uncontrol involved with land animals? Not at all; for land-hunting is comparatively easy and within relatively sure technological control of the remarkable Eskimo material culture, and a man can accept direct ego-responsibility for this. It is the winter sea that is his concern. Are there then gods in the sea who will succor him? Not quite. For when the male hunter, the father, is helpless to give food, who then regressively is the earlier source of security? It is Sedna, a goddess, who lives in the sea. Who is she? And what, indeed, does she do? In a legendary stress-situation, the girl Sedna became the supernatural Owner [progenitor] of the Animals, and she sends seals to the hunters as food for the people. But why are there storms that prevent hunting; and why are there sometimes no seals; and who sends the storms? It is Sedna, who is angry at them. And why? They have broken one of her taboos. Taboos about what? Taboos about the most contingent and uncontrolled and anxiety-laden area in life: taboos about food. Someone has secretly cooked the flesh of land animals and sea animals together, and for this reason Sedna is enraged. What is the remedy? That the culprit publicly confess his breach of taboo, and then Sedna will send seals and the storms will subside.

A study of Eskimo grammar would clarify conclusions already reached on ethnographic grounds. When we approach the ostensible Object of our search, "God," the term turns out to be curiously changeable indeed. When we try to define God there is very little consensus on the proper connotations and denotations of the word. We may try to communicate with one another through the use of this term, and yet we will constantly find ourselves in fundamental disagreement concerning what we are talking about. This is not surprising, since what we are talking about is our projected selves, which differ somewhat. The chief difficulty with "God" is his grammatical behavior. The term parades as a noun, behaving with complete propriety as subject and object in sentences properly shaped in any Indoeuropean language. He formally possessivises in case forms ("God's"), having an interesting if arbitrary grammatical gender (masculine), and pluralizes with syntactic if not theological correctness ("Gods").

And yet, functionally speaking, "God" is really a pronoun, a pronoun whose referents, connotations and denotations differ with every person and every society using it! "God"—we learn from the Eskimo, which has a rich set of locative pronouns like "this," "that," "that-one-in-sight," "that-one-not-in-sight," "that-one-up-north," "that-one-down-south," etc., including "that-one-down-there-in-the-sea" *used only to refer to Sedna* —"God" for us is a special pronoun "It" that we use when we vocalize concerning something we know absolutely nothing about, the Unknown. English is not nearly so tidy and clear locatively about this Pronoun as is Eskimo! For us, "God" seems to be a special kind of third-person pronoun: what you and I and they feel phatically about the universe and man. Theology is therefore phatic vocalization in the human primate, not referential speech. God is the Pronoun whose antecedents differ with each individual and society. The locus of the subject matter, obviously, is somehow in societies and in men's minds, not in the outside physical universe.

We are therefore gravely mistaken about the locus of the unknown. We have supposed it is outside us, in the not-self or cosmos, when indeed it is the equally unknown inner self—the personality that we project in our theologies. There are as many special connotations and denotations of this Pronoun, in the last analysis, as there are men. The Unknown is (unknowingly) inside each one of us. Gods are born in the individual's unconscious mind, dreams made of his own psychic substance. The term "God" refers, then, to a specific but varying "It" which in the mouth of any man means "my inner character." Thus alarmingly, this protean Pronoun turns out to be not a third-personal but a first-person-singular pronoun in another guise! This It, in a sense, is each man's own Id—omnipotence trailed again to its lair!

Can we wonder, then, that theologies differ as widely as personalities do? Or that finally each man must be his own priest (wrestle with his own oedipal problems), just as every man must do his own dreaming? Technically, all that we say about "God" as the Unknown is a statement of ignorance concerning our inner selves—an arrogance with grave moral consequence, as many later examples in this book will demonstrate. To paraphrase the mystics, when we seek the Self we encounter the self. When we talk about God, let us be more careful about locatives; when we theologize, let us remember the greater precision of Eskimo grammar in its pronouns!

NOTES

(Introduction)

1. Ludwig Wittgenstein, *Tractatus Logico-Philosophicus* (London: Routledge and Kegan Paul, 1933, p. 63).

2. Herodotus, *Histories* (New York: G. P. Putnam's Sons, 1926, 4 vols., tr. A. D. Godley, II:3).

3. *Deos fecit timor* was a view current among Epicureans: the words are also found in Lucretius and Petronius, but the best claim is that of Statius (W. Robertson Smith, *Lectures on the Religion of the Semites,* New York: Macmillan, 3rd ed., 1927, p. 518 fn.).

4. Nicholas of Cusa cited from E. Cassirer, *Individuum und Kosmos in der Philosophie der Renaissance* (Leipzig & Berlin: Teubner, 1927, p. 34).

5. Jean-Paul Sartre, *No Exit and The Flies* (New York: Knopf, 1947, pp. 134, 136, 157).

6. Jane Ellen Harrison, *Themis, A Study of the Social Origins of Greek Religion* (Cambridge: At the University Press, 1927, p. 535).

7. Denis Donoghue, "Wallace Stevens Imperator," *New York Review of Books,* 7 ⅓⁄9 (1 December 1966) 6ff., p. 8.

8. E. Doutté, *Magie et Religion dans l'Afrique du Nord* (Alger: Jourdan, 1909, p. 601).

9. Matthew Arnold quoted by Theodor Reik, *The Mystery on the Mountain* (New York: Harper and Brothers, 1958, p. 167).

10. Cicero, *De Natura Deorum* (New York: G. P. Putnam's Sons, 1933, ii, 28, 72); cf. Aulus Gellius, *The Attic Nights* (New York: G. P. Putnam's Sons, 1927, 3 vols., I:iv, 9).

11. Polybius cited from H. J. Muller, *The Uses of the Past* (New York: Oxford University Press, 1952, p. 184).

12. Gilbert Murray, *Five Stages of Greek Religion* (originally *Four Stages* [1912], the addition of a chapter [1925] made it *Five Stages;* the 3rd ed. [1951] contained additionally an introduction, the whole being New York: Doubleday Anchor Books, 1955, pp. 4–5).

13. Rudolf Otto, *The Idea of the Holy* (New York: Oxford University Press, 1923; also Galaxy Books, 1958).

14. Joachim Wach, *Sociology of Religion* (Chicago: University of Chicago Press, 1944, p. 14).

15. Sir James George Frazer, *The Golden Bough, A Study in Magic and Religion* (New York: Macmillan, 1930, p. vii).

16. Bronislaw Malinowski, *Magic, Science and Religion* (New York: Doubleday Anchor Books, 1954).

17. Jane Ellen Harrison, *Prolegomena to the Study of Greek Religion* (Cambridge: At the University Press, 2nd ed., 1908, p. 162).

18. Quoted in R. F. Johnson, "Worship (Chinese)" in James Hastings (ed.), *Encyclopedia of Religion and Ethics* (New York: Charles Scribner's Sons, 13 volumes, 1908–26, 12:759–62, p. 760).

19. Friedrich Schleiermacher, in Salomon Reinach, *Orpheus, A General History of Religions* (London: William Heinemann, 1909, p. 2).

20. Murray, *op. cit.,* p. 121 fn.

21. André Bonnard, *Greek Civilization from the Iliad to the Parthenon* (London: George Allen & Unwin, 1957, 3 vols., I:333).

22. Jean-Marie Guyau in Reinach, *loc. cit.*

23. Emile Durkheim, *The Elementary Forms of the Religious Life* (London: George Allen & Unwin, 1915; Free Press Paperback, 1965).

24. Alfred North Whitehead, *Religion in the Making* (New York: Macmillan, 1930, p. 6).

25. William James, *The Varieties of Religious Experience* (London: Longmans, Green and Co., 1902, p. 31; Modern Library, 1936; also New Hyde Park: University Books, 1963).

26. Gordon Allport, *Institutional Behavior* (Chapel Hill: University of North Carolina Press, 1933, pp. 427–28).

27. Ernest Jones, "The Psychology of Religion," in Sandor Lorand (ed.), *Psychoanalysis Today* (New York: International Universities Press, 1944, 315–25, p. 316).

28. T. S. Szasz, "A Contribution to the Psychology of Bodily Feelings," *Psychoanalytic Quarterly*, 26 (1957) 25–49, p. 36.

29. E. B. Tylor, *Primitive Culture* (New York: Henry Holt and Company, 2 vols., 3rd American ed., 1889, I:424).

30. M. E. Spiro, "Religion: Problems of Definition and Explanation," in Michael Banton (ed.), *Anthropological Approaches to the Study of Religion* (London: Tavistock Publications, 1966, 85–126, p. 91); compare with Spiro's position J. Goody, "Religion and Ritual: The Definitional Problem," *British Journal of Sociology*, 12 (1961) 142–64; and R. Horton, "A Definition of Religion and its Uses," *Journal of the Royal Anthropological Institute*, 90 (1960) 201–26.

31. Rainer Maria Rilke, in a letter to Ilse Jahr, 22 February 1923, in Erich Heller, *The Disinherited Mind* (Baltimore: Penguin Books, 1961, p. 140).

32. Raymond Firth, *Elements of Social Organization* (New York: Philosophical Library, 1956, p. 224); cf. "Problem and Assumption in an Anthropological Study of Religion," *Journal of the Royal Anthropological Institute*, 39 (1959) 129–48, p. 133.

33. Meyer Fortes, *Oedipus and Job in West African Religion* (Cambridge: At the University Press, 1959, p. 78). Robin Horton ("Destiny and the Unconscious in West Africa," *Africa*, 3 [1961] 110–16) severely criticizes Fortes, however, since the fate of Oedipus was not part of his personality (in contrast to the Tale notion) and also because classical Fate could not be modified (as it could among the Tale). Horton properly advises that the Freudian concept of the unconscious would much better explain the Tale data.

34. Sigmund Freud, *Moses and Monotheism* (London: Hogarth Press, 1940, p. 91; cf. p. 129).

35. D. N. Morgan, "Ritual Value-Washing among the Wienerkreiser," *American Anthropologist*, 59 (1957) 871–74, p. 874.

36. Freud, in a letter to Ernest Jones, 1 August 1912, in Ernest Jones, *The Life and Work of Sigmund Freud* (New York: Basic Books, 3 vols., 1953–57, II:455).

I

Anthropology and Psychology of Religion

THE historic situation of people profoundly shapes their anthropological view of themselves. In the eighteenth century, when national states still had some economic and military reality, the world seemed made up of many tribes, essentially separate, with quaint and sometimes edifying differences. In turn, the colonial nineteenth century of rival empires was nostalgically romantic and a little sad about the "evolutionary inferiority" of the lesser societies they were busy consuming and dominating. However, in cultural status, European states impinging on one another in the eighteenth century were relatively near-equals; by contrast, in the nineteenth century, mother country and colonies were widely apart in power potential.

In the twentieth-century world, grown crowded, where already obsolescent statehood is still being grasped at in recently tribal and colonial regions, political history seems to be moving ambiguously in two directions at once. The United States earnestly exports its own paradigm of democratic self-determination to an unready or unwilling or indifferent postcolonial world—only to be accused of crypto-imperialism as it multiples new nations to its own discomfort and cost. Simultaneously, a late-comer Russian imperialism seeks to expand an archaic autocracy—all the while protesting that its mission is liberation. In between was the curiously revivalistic, messianic mixture of Charlemagne, the Sun King and Napoleon, the French Quixote—spreading a world evangel at the same time he handed away colonial *outre-mer*.

There is fiction of course in all these political mythologies; and in each of these mystiques a cultural imperialism is implied. In our own cultural evangel, we are often naïvely baffled at the world's incomprehension of our manifest goodwill. But on the intellectual level, we deeply suspect that to be culturally rightist is not necessarily to be right; and we have long since become sophisticated to a kind of ethical relativity, ethnological egalitarianism, and weary existentialism, which at times—and perhaps for similar psychological reasons—strikingly resembles Hellenistic cynicism and despair. For international conflicts are not solely political and economic. More profoundly and basically, conflicts arise from cultural incommensurabilities, of which Americans, in their innocent possession of dominant political and economic power, seem peculiarly unwitting. These conflicts are in essence world crises of acculturation. However, both acculturation and crisis may be open in our time to anthropological analysis and understanding.

As the last fragments of an "untouched primitive" world begin to disappear and the international communication of scholars at the same time very greatly increases, the study of man appears to be moving into a stimulating new phase, though beset, perhaps, with its own problems of epistemological acculturation. Meanwhile, astronomy, biology and psychology in turn have destroyed each cherished narcissistic Eden of man-centered uniqueness. Man is only one kind of accidental animal, asymmetrically placed in a fairly ordinary galactic universe, whose adaptive mind *eo ipso* contaminates his potential knowledge of himself and of his world.

Cultural relativity, with its existentialist view of culture, has now destroyed the final prop of fundamentalist tribal man—that inveterate absolutist whose very animal nature it is to embody experiments in value-paradigms. This latest threat to human narcissism seems shattering, for it means that the culture heroes and charismatic ancestors of the sacred past are no longer gods, but only men like ourselves. Still, the struggle with each successively dethroned vanity has always heretofore been edifying; and from each discovered limitation we can learn. But it means the scrutiny of a most sacred belief—that our culture is the distilled essence of a cumulative and historic evolution toward an ultimate new Eden of knowledge and truth, as embodied especially in that seemingly truest of geometries, our basic religion, be that Science or some traditional faith. It means that we must examine both culture and religion, not in the context of "truth" at all, but rather as animal phenomena that *do something for us adaptively*—leaving aside for the moment the question *which* reality, inside or outside our human skins, they may be in turn adaptive to—but which may often be irrelevant to a serenely indifferent universe. Culture and its most comforting component, religion, may be only adaptive mechanisms peculiar to this kind of animal, whose unique biology we must therefore scrutinize.

The eighteenth century[1] saw religion in the model of its own rational and revolutionary ethos. Religion was essentially an exploitative historic plot, and its tyranny would end when the last king was strangled in the entrails of the last priest. However, it is possible that the religionist, leader or led, is more victimized by his belief than is the skeptic, and the rational may be the least important or essential part of any religion. Marx retained this old-fashioned view of history-by-plot in the next century (as though his new interpretation of history had been known to his predecessors as a truth they quickly exploited), seeing religion as "the opium of the people" in the dialectic of class struggle.

The nineteenth century inherited the rationalism of the eighteenth, but otherwise, except for Marx, somewhat less of its aggressive revolutionary iconoclasm. Indeed, the nineteenth century[2] viewed religion largely in terms of its own ethos and faith in Progress. Religion was a gradually evolved perfection, a progressive unveiling of an ultimate truth, a piecemeal revelation of God from Moses to the Established Church. Anthropological students of religion would therefore interest themselves in the problem of origins, in order to discover and depict the cultural evolution of Revelation, twin sister to Science. (Each century has its own brand of rationalism, the function of which is to rationalize its unexamined cultural assumptions; only the twentieth century has discovered, painfully, the massive irrationality of man—which changes the whole context of discourse.)

The intellectual paradigm of the late nineteenth century, clearly, was Darwinian evolution. But it is not always clear just when biological evolutionism is being extrapolated (illegitimately) in the early British studies of culture, and just when a supposed human *consensus gentium* is being implicitly used not to explain but to justify contemporary faith (as though primitive animism were a partial "feeble first glimpse" of the now manifest "loftier truth," the Englishman's God). But from the beginning, non-evolutionist American Boasians were accustomed to report ethnographic facts, however outlandish, with a straight face—often intentionally to distance themselves from ready sermonizers who easily knew which was a "higher belief" and which "lower" in the evolutionary and hence cognitive scale. Partly it was a habit of cool, non-judgmental scientific sobriety. But partly, at times perhaps, non-editorializing was a protective mask, a still necessary genteelism in studies of religion, a tone that had lasted at least until William James, a gentlemanly wisdom that hesitated to offend. Such ambiguous urbanity, however, was often mistaken for assent by those motivated to do so, and the reported ethnographic fact was somehow felt to confirm theological argument, belief supporting belief.

But a twentieth-century rejection of the legitimacy of the Culture-Evolutionist analogy, certainly as applied to the study of religion, nevertheless does not allow us easily to impugn the motives of early anthropologists who seized on exciting and illuminating new ideas. If animals evolve, do not then also the ideas of men? But ideas and animals are insufficiently alike, we think. The new criterion, by our own explicit standard here, is *what are the facts being used for,* either consciously or unconsciously—used to explore difficult and unwelcome knowledge of ourselves, or for theological ax-grinding? Unfortunately (as will be shown in a moment) some schools of European anthropology did betray theological intent. The present intention is to explore, not to justify faith. Ethnographic data are only ethnographic data. Let us then be careful of what we do with them; systematic and self-examining skepticism is nowhere more necessary than in the study of religion. Not what we can push them to, but where the facts may lead, should be the goal.

In attempting to understand religion, early Evolutionist anthropology made a search for origins and universals. In the view of the founding father of modern anthropology, Edward Tylor, all religion is based on animism, the ancient and widespread belief in a soul separable from the material body, a sort of potentially brain-less mind, unbodied consciousness, extra-organic life, spirit or *anima*. After a tacit assessment of the ethnographic evidence, Tylor proposed his famous definition of religion as the "belief in spiritual beings." Tylor's view was that animism—the projective peopling of the world with self-like psyches—was the pristine and still universal view on which all later religion was built and elaborated, by a kind of further evolutionary speciation. Tylor's contemporary, the sociologist-philosopher Herbert Spencer, was even more organic-evolutionary in his thinking. He attempted to generalize the ethnographic facts into a kind of historical law of growth or paleontological phylogeny of religious development. Using the "age-area hypothesis," Spencer arranged the data into a successively smaller-tiered ziggurat or set-back wedding cake, the oldest and simplest and geographically most widespread beliefs at the bottom, the newer and more defined and refined beliefs being higher in this confection. Spencer thought that religion began in ancestral ghost-worship—for Victorian England a view not astonishing to us perhaps (though, on ethnographic grounds of spread, Spencer might better have begun with a more nearly universal and logically simpler Tylorian animism, since a Spencerian ghost is already specialized, i.e., a *person-originated* spirit, not just simple cosmic soul-stuff). The whole edifice was crowned at the top with the figure of the monotheistic God.

Bishop Codrington, however, on concrete ethnographic grounds, disturbed the thesis of pan-animism. Codrington discovered among supposedly "ethnologically earlier" Pacific primitives a belief in *mana* or impersonal force. Typologically, logically, and on quasi-evolutionary grounds, the Melanesian concept of *mana* would seem to antedate historically the animistic belief in spiritual beings or more individuated personal spirits. On these grounds, Marett argued a thesis of the "preanimistic" origin of religion. Frazer, with his large book-knowledge of primitives, was understandably ambivalent about the conflicting evidence (and indeed to call *mana* earlier because it was believed in by "ethnographically earlier" contemporary primitives would seem to be circular reasoning). In the early versions of *The Golden Bough,* Frazer at first considered that religious belief in spiritual beings preceded magical belief in impersonal forces, for science also deals with impersonal forces. But later Frazer came around to the dissidents' view that magic logically preceded religion. Unfortunately, however, logic is not history, much less a history of religion. *Mana* and *anima* are types of concepts, not stages of belief.

Tylor, Codrington, Marett and Frazer all to some degree had been arguing within the assumptions of an evolution of religion. Consequently, additional field evidence again upset the supposed evolutionary sequence. Andrew Lang discovered that many "ethnographically primitive" peoples (meaning simple in material culture) had the concept of a monotheistic "High God"—which, historically and typologically, ought to be the latest of all! In the evolutionist game of which-came-first, Lang was not an evolutionist but a devolutionist and degradationist: man had fallen from monotheistic grace. Lang saw at the beginning a sempiternal primitive High God, from whose worship (he argued) man, whoring after more venal deities and more manageable gods, as he put it, inevitably backslid into trafficking with these spirits—man being, in his view, what he was—and finally even into arrogant godless magic that usurped the omnipotence of God.

On this discovery of a High God, worshiped even by "ethnographically primitive" peoples, the Catholic *Kulturkreis* anthropologists of Vienna gratefully erected an *Urmonotheismus,* fundamental to revealed theological truth, an Eternal One where Frazer had seen at the roots of European religion only a Dying God. It was as though even primitives had discovered the objective truth; and the ancient and universal *consensus gentium* concerning the truth would be maintained if only an historic authoritative institution could prevent the human Adam from retreating from this monotheistic revelation into polytheistic and other errors. English Protestants, relying on history and evolution, saw the established faith as having been arduously evolved-toward; the Austrian anthropologists relied on a catholic *consensus gentium* of all peoples *semper ubique* ethnographically to discover and establish God.

Implicitly, *all* these views followed a more or less biological metaphor —even the Catholic, so compelling was the hegemony over thought of Darwinian evolution. The British sought a logical paleontology of religion and an historical evolution of belief. The Germans' "culture-cycle" was even explicitly an *organism,* migrating and filiating as a complex or bundle of genetically related traits, like gametes and zygotes. "Cultural fossils" were consciously sought for—by both British and Germans, as though religion were a developing organism undergoing evolutionary adaptation, and as though a paleontological stratigraphy of its successive forms could be ascertained, as it were geologically laid down.

With the classic fieldwork of Spencer and Gillen on Australian Bushmen, all factions seemed to have found the critical culture fossil, totemism, with its curious beliefs in the association of men with animals and plants, an association that regulated food, fertility, marriage, descent, and social organization in various tribal combinations. Since the geographically long-isolated Australians were a very primitive phrasing of man physically, and possessed an exceedingly simple material culture, it seemed reasonable to suppose that their religion must then be the missing fossil that would finally settle all questions of priority.

To the French sociologist Durkheim, this elementary form of religious life was a kind of ritual celebration of the group's own ingroupness; the French have always magically emphasized the group because, an intensely family-centered society, effective larger unity has always been for them a chronic political problem, successively the more difficult with each larger concentric circle of people to be conceptually embraced.[3] But Durkheim gained from his study of totemism certain penetrating insights into the social nature of religion which are still fundamental; he might just as well have discovered them elsewhere, however, than in totemism. Following Durkheim, the great English classicist Jane Ellen Harrison[4] found chthonic snakes and the totemic ritual of Titans at the root of Greek religion; and the renowned Semitist Robertson Smith discerned totemic elements in early Semitic religion. Finally Freud, projecting the oedipal conflict into the archaic past, found totemic murder and the ensuing cannibalistic feast to be the origin of totem and taboo. In this most wrong-headedly Jungian of his books, Freud saw in parricidal totemism the inherited original sin behind all society. However, since the essay on totemism by Lévi-Strauss, it is clear why many different persons see in totemism many different things, since the term "totemism" embraces many diverse social phenomena. Indeed, Australian totemism (which is in no sense "primitive" either in time or in simplicity but a very complexly developed structure) is only one instance of a far more nearly universal phenomenon: the inveterate and deep-seated interest of man in other animals, and his tendency to think about them naïvely in human terms as if they were human. To embrace all the phenomena referred to by totemism, the grandiose term must be eroded down to mean merely man's social anthropomorphizing of animals. For precision, the specific society and the features referred to must in any case be stated. A term as generic as "totemism" in this loose sense can hardly be the origin of anything.

The late-nineteenth- and early-twentieth-century search for a necessary logic of culture-evolution ended, as is so often the case, not in a solution of the problems it laid bare, but in the rise of new ways of looking at the same data—and indeed all these great figures developed new insights into the data of religion through their theories, which is what theories are for. For example, despite his methodological error, as we see it (and it was after all based on a very Athenian Greek view of the psychological unity of mankind), Frazer was a deeply learned classicist, and his descriptive discrimination between magic and religion is a permanent intellectual heritage. Just as each generation owes a debt to its great Semitists, so also it learns constantly from its Hellenists. Gilbert Murray quite properly admired his predecessor, Sir James George Frazer. But Murray moved far from a monolithic "psychological unity of mankind"—which in new guise a new generation of "social anthropologists" again seeks—to show, in his classic *Five Stages of Greek Religion,* how affective-cognitive styles actually change rapidly in time, even among the same people. Another classicist, Marett, successor to Tylor in anthropology at Oxford, rejected a certain residual intellectualist rationalism in his teacher, attended more to Tylor's seminal psychologism, and went forward to emphasize the conspicuously non-rational emotional components in religion—a tradition another great classicist, our contemporary E. R. Dodds, has further enriched in *The Greeks and the Irrational.* Jane Harrison too, especially in the *Epilegomena,* last volume of her great trilogy, had seen that the gods are in large measure projections of societies and their emotional states. And Rohde has deepened immeasurably our understanding of the *anima* bequeathed us by Tylor. There is little question that modern anthropology would be much the poorer without the stimulus of these Greek-nourished minds.

From Le Bon to Durkheim, and from Levy-Bruhl to Mauss and Lévi-Strauss, the French have been consistently psychological-minded (though they sometimes lose sight of the individual in their preoccupation with the group). In a related tradition Van Gennep, while perceiving in the *rite de passage* an important function in maintaining group solidarity, also saw that such rituals typically transcend a psychological crisis in the life-cycle of the individual. Both Durkheim and Levy-Bruhl significantly drew our attention to a kind of group "will to believe"—but this is already the phrase of the greatest American psychologist of religion, William James.[5] James was the intellectual ancestor of a whole generation of American psychologists of religion, Ames, Coe, Leuba, Pratt, Starbuck and Stratton, who had their British counterparts in Flower, Thouless and Uren, as well as in the German Protestant psychologists of religion. But the acknowl-edged leader in religious psychology among German-speaking peoples, and indeed the world, was Freud, intellectual father of Abraham, Reik, Jones, Ferenczi and Róheim.[6] It is now fashionable, among those who have learned least from him, to be condescending about Freud. But it was Freud who accomplished a revolution in our way of thinking about re-ligion. In the words of Auden, "If often he was wrong and at times ab-surd, to us he is no more a person now but a whole climate of opinion."[7]

In nineetenth-century Europe the Establishment vigorously combated the corroding influence of Darwinian evolution on received belief; and yet theologians soon found themselves expounding the *evolution* of "the idea of God" in their very arguments, so pervasive was the biological pattern of thought of that time. In the end, scientific biology triumphed over traditional theology as authority on biology, quite as earlier the Copernican astronomy had triumphed over traditional religious cosmology. And in the process, having been wrong again despite its categorical assurance, re-ligion again lost intellectual caste. Similarly, psychology and anthropology have seemed to dissolve traditional religious belief into mere folklore—small loss, however, since in the study of folklore, belief, and culture at large we may gain the most sustaining insights into our human condition today.

It is a cliché that in the anthropology of the first half of the present century, the study of religion has been a much neglected field as com-pared, say, with social structure. The same general neglect of the human-istic approach to the study of religion is apparent also. As one of the most distinguished humanists of religion, Mircea Eliade,[8] has written,

Let us recognize it frankly, History of Religions, or Comparative Religion, plays a modest role in modern culture. When one recalls the passionate interest with which the informed public in the second half of the nineteenth century followed the speculations of Max Muller on the origin of myths and the evolution of religions and followed his polemic with Andrew Lang; when one recalls the considerable success of *The Golden Bough,* the vogue of *mana* or of the *mentalité prélogique* and *participation mystique;* and when one recalls that *Les Origines du Christianisme,* the *Prolegomena to the Study of Greek Religion,* and *Les Formes élémentaires de la Vie religieuse* were the bedside books of our fathers and grandfathers, one cannot contemplate the present situation without melancholy.

The reason for this neglect of the old "history of religion" approach lies in the changing motives for the study of religion. Lingeringly in the nineteenth century there was still a sometimes unacknowledged interest, even among serious students of religion, to find some intellectually respectable basis for personal belief, presumably to be found in a comparative eclectic study of the "more advanced" world religions. But for the intellectual public of the mid-twentieth century, all the issues seemed permanently resolved by simple nonbelief, the data safely embalmed in the tedious and neglected folklore of past errors and superstitions. No one had had anything new to say on the study of religion for some decades. As a guide to personal belief and behavior, intellectuals were just no longer interested in the subject.

Changed motives and viewpoints have brought us again to the study of religion. The motive now is not to find belief but understanding, the viewpoint not biological but psychological. The present approach, however, remains biological, and deliberately so, though it is less evolutionary than ecological in emphasis: culture is man's major mode of adaptation at the same time that culture alters, and to a degree provides, the ecological situation to which we adapt; and religion, as a part of culture, is *one kind* of cultural adaptation, and a rather special one.

Often in spite of ourselves and of what we think we are about, ours is undoubtedly the psychological century. Psychological insight has tended to destroy at the same time that it explains faith to us. Anthropology has contributed to the same end. In a period of massive culture-contact, field workers, no longer finding "untouched native groups" to study, have become interested in problems of acculturation and the sometimes bizarre cults accompanying it. The whole approach to the study of religion has changed. Gradually we have come to see that whatever is recoverable of an *Urreligion* is useful mainly to help us understand motifs in subsequent religion, quite as knowledge of antecedent culture of any period illuminates the culture that follows. Archeology indeed gives us genuinely datable information about paleoreligion, too, if only we know how to read the data. But we do not need to recover all the lost origins in order to understand the dynamics of religion, for with each new crisis cult we can see an "origin" of religion before our very eyes.

In any inquiry we must learn to seek information from unexpected sources. To the degree that the fossil remains of animals, the accompanying fauna and flora, paleoclimatology and the like all tell us much about the ecology of extinct animals, so also the actual morphology and context of fossil protohominids can give us many clues as to their food ecology—and hence some of their major life concerns. The function and meaning of belief become clear in the ecological context—a point no more abundantly confirmed than in the rich Old Stone Age cave art. The historical origins of religion were what they were. But perhaps they would have been the same in any case? Comparative anatomy tells us unmistakably that the main change from ape to man was one of habitat and food ecology. *Because* earliest man was a gatherer of available savannah plant foods, he must have been intelligently interested in plant growth, the seasons and weather; *because* he was a game hunter, concerned with killing and not being killed himself, and hence preoccupied with life and death, then (given these concerns) in some sense primitive animism was an "inevitable" idea, an explanation of the "life stuff" that was his main commodity.

In order to understand religion, we must study the nature and function of belief itself. In earlier quasi-evolutionary studies, the exotic separate species of religion tended to be exploited for polemic-epistemological or system-building purposes; but now we are more impressed by the significant similarities and continuities in the histories of religions. In the new psychological approach, ethnological history then becomes merely the context of careful study of meanings and dynamics, much as in the case of any new field data. Preoccupied with descriptive facts concerning religion, we may perhaps be freed from any necessity of defending the "in some sense" truth of contemporary religion. Assuming only a simple uniformitarianism regarding crisis cults—similar situations, then as now, have similar results—we may even turn again to a more disinterested scrutiny of our own religious origins. But to be free in the pursuit of ethnographic and psychological fact, we must give up the search for theological truth. The gain may be greater than we anticipate. In fact, in our value-disoriented world, *the understanding of religion may be the key to an understanding of the nature and function of culture at large and hence the survival of our species*—and for this we have some continuing appetite and need.

It is an irony that our initial insights come from a most unpsychological source, a semi-governmental report in a late-nineteenth-century field monograph on American Indians. This is James Mooney's now celebrated work on *The Ghost Dance.*[9] Briefly, the "Ghost Dance" of 1890 was an intertribal movement, mostly among Plains Indians, in response to the loss of hunting territories, the virtual disappearance of the once enormous buffalo herds on which the Indians depended, a succession of crushing military defeats, new and usually fatal diseases, and protracted droughts—all together meaning the breakdown of their whole hunting economy and prowess-warfare, as they were herded onto successively smaller and smaller reservations. The Ghost Dance was a typical crisis cult in being a largely fantasied "autistic" solution for all their problems: a new skin would slide over the old earth, covering up the whites and all their works, and bringing upon it new trees and plants, great buffalo herds, the ghosts of the dead, and the great departed warriors and chiefs. This utopian dispensation would occur if only the tribes danced the Ghost Dance, each person carrying the magic feather that would lift him up onto the new world when it came.

Another great pioneering study, of similar significance for Oceania, was an even obscurer government report in frontier New Guinea, Williams'[10] classic paper of 1923 on the "Vailala Madness" which instituted the cargo cult. The "cargo cult" arose among colonial New Guinean natives who needed to explain to themselves just why they had to work so hard, whereas the idle and powerful white commanded great wealth—somehow mysteriously implicated with the great cargo ships that took away native products like copra, and came back laden with the many mysteries like machines and radios that made white men so powerful. The cargo cultists preached that all these objects were actually forged by their own native ancestors in some far-off volcano, and were intended to be sent to them, only to be intercepted by the whites. If only the New Guineans would throw away their old native cult objects and ceremonies, and imitate the behaviors of the whites, such as sitting solemnly and speechlessly around tables, then the cargoes would come to their proper recipients.

Since the appearance of the government reports by Mooney and by Williams, anthropological field data have multiplied greatly, so that the interested student has a veritable embarrassment of riches before him. It is not proposed to summarize these many acculturational cults, or the theories about them, in the present place; for a précis of this major development both in American and in European anthropology see my article on the "History of Studies of Crisis Cults." The importance of these grotesque acculturational cults for a general theory of culture can hardly be overestimated, since it is so often in the study of pathological functioning (as in medicine and psychiatry) that we can gain insight into normal functioning.

Nowadays hardly a month passes that we do not learn of some new "Alice" cult in Africa or some new "Johnson cult" in remote Oceanic islands. These are not lightly to be dismissed as mere ethnic oddities. That they are pathetically mistaken or ludicrous to us does not matter, since we are not concerned with epistemological dignity or theological truth; that they are human is enough reason to study them here. What should also be noted here is the immense *practicality to Americans* of these studies of acculturational conflicts in the modern post-colonial world—a world largely produced, in fact, by powerful American pressures to export a democratic American ethos, all the way from Korea to Rhodesia, and from Nigeria to Vietnam. We still make today huge human sacrifice to our ignorance.

A quarter-century ago, Ralph Linton[11] proposed to designate accultura-tional phenomena like the Ghost Dance and the Cargo Cult by the term "nativistic movements," implying by this some revamping of old native cultures to meet new needs. However, many acculturational cults are not properly "nativistic" at all in Linton's sense; and many of the other terms used are generically unsuitable because they are descriptive only of geo-graphically specific types ("ghost dance" and "cargo cult"). Since Linton's time a veritable industry of compulsive taxonomies of crisis cults has arisen both here and abroad to express the various millennarian, chiliastic, es-chatological and other features of crisis cults. Unfortunately these minutiae of classification have not always been contributory to insight. I have adopted the simple term "crisis cult" both for its brevity and its inclusive-ness, intending only to imply the insight of Malinowski that there is no cult without crisis. That is to say, there must be an unresolved problem or crisis, chronic or acute, and unresolved by ordinary secular means, be-fore there is cult response. The term "cult" also implies a distinction from ordinary secular actions or social movements such as war, legal or fiscal reform, economic, technological or other social change. "Cult" also im-plies the typically dereistic and in some cases the minority aspects of the response.

Man lives in two worlds, a matter-of-fact one of common public ex-perience, the other of mysteriously "supernatural" and compelling private dream or trance. More precisely (since for reasons to be discussed men sometimes share their sacred life as they do the secular), these two "worlds" of man are really *two modes of psychic experiencing* in the individual. William James and others have long studied the trancelike state in the "mystical experience."[12] In recent years psychologists have been experimenting with the aloneness-state of the mystic, cut off from the sensory world in his search for God. Experimenters have suspended subjects in a tank of body-temperature water, as alike to the womb as one can make it, to isolate the subject as much as possible from all sensory stimulation. In this state of sensory deprivation, the "self" or conscious ego regresses amazingly. After a period, varying from individual to individual but beginning in most after about three-quarters of an hour, quite normal persons, robbed in the tank of all sensory cues, begin to do a strange thing. With the screen of consciousness not filled with sensory images from the environment, the individual himself begins to fill the screen projectively with his own inner uncorrected fantasies. In the language of the psychiatrist, the subject hallucinates; this is what he does with his aloneness.

The same phenomenon is known to anthropologists, for example in the solitary "vision quest" of the American Indians. A young man, usually at the time of puberty, goes out to some isolated place to fast and pray for four days and nights, and, depriving himself of sleep as well, he may be visited by what, he thinks, are supernatural beings. The phenomenon is widely known in other self-induced trance states, as when in many parts of the world the individual is "possessed" by "spirits" (strangely alien psyches or psychic states). Explorers like Admiral Byrd in the South Pole hut described in his book *Alone*,[13] isolated from other people for a long time, especially in featureless landscapes, have also touched upon such uncanny experiences as these. There is also the famous case of Captain Slocum, who sailed around the world alone and was visited during heavy storms by supernatural helpers he hallucinated.

These facts contain a moral: we need our tribal fellows to help criticize our dreams; and we need the outside world lest, like the man in the tank, we begin helplessly to hallucinate. Again, when reality becomes too threatening, as to the man in the boat on stormy seas, then too we begin to hallucinate. There is no comfort for the haughty "normal" mind in these phenomena. Admiral Byrd, Captain Slocum, and the young Indian may be as normal and healthy men as one can find. But how threatening to find a normal man own twin to a psychotic! Not twin, but the same man. Each conscious mind reigns over a raging lunatic within. Is not the dream a temporary psychosis, somehow needed to face daily waking life, and cured only when the world returns to our possession? Certainly the scientist is under no illusion about the objective "reality" of the kind of world presented to him by his senses. The mathematical physicists' reality, like Einstein's universe, is an intellectual construct, a disciplined and stately dream, far removed from "commonsensical" experience indeed! And any anthropologist knows that the world which natives in some societies appear to see is certainly a strange one in terms of his own cultural experience.

Anthropologists have often noted that most societies divide their culture into sacred and secular parts, the "holy" and the "profane," either conceptually or in their behavior or in both. The secular is the realm of mundane workaday technology, of ego control, and of constantly evolving adaptation to the environment. The secular is a realm of relatively low emotional charge. By contrast, the sacred is a realm of adaptation to anxieties, to crises both social and personal, and to common unsolved problems like death. The sacred is a realm of high emotional potential. But if we were to suppose there is only one objective supernatural world, we quickly learn that the sacred realm differs radically from society to society. The subject matters are widely different; only the basic religious mood is the same or similar. Further, religious attitudes change in historic time as well as in ethnographic space. Change is not suprising; secular culture changes too. What is interesting is that religions are always tailor-made, projectively, to fit current individual and group anxieties—as we noted of the Eskimo. Thus, material culture, technology and science are adaptations to the outside world; religion, to the inner world of man, his unsolved problems and unmet needs.

Charismatic leaders, in the social context of their rise, are culture heroes come in response to stress situations in the culture. A society's culture is a set of defense mechanisms, both technological and psychological. If technical means fail to protect the people against anxiety and stress, then psychological means must be fabricated to maintain homeostasis. All religions, perhaps, began as crisis cults, the response of society to problems the contemporary culture failed to resolve. Historically, acculturation itself is a common stressor, in particular of sacred culture. Faith, once lost, can never be regained, for it is the nature of authentic belief never to have been questioned; all that is possible now is ever more frantic asseverations in the face of doubt, protestations of cultural loyalty, and an attempted nativistic journey back into the sacred past. Each religion is the Ghost Dance of a traumatized society.

The Ghost Dance of 1890 was the revelation of a Paviotso messiah, partly a mixture of borrowed Christian notions with earlier Indian cults, and partly the autistic vision of the messiah. The fantasy of a new heaven on earth and the miraculous reappearance of dead ancestors and leaders as helpers was a response to the disintegration of Indian cultures under the pressure of the advancing white frontier. The historic context is quite clear and well known—the great Sioux Uprising, Custer's last stand, Sitting Bull, and the Battle of Wounded Knee.

The insights derived from a study of the Ghost Dance apply equally to the famous Hellenistic "failure of nerve" (in Bury's phrase), the ghost dance of our own historical tradition, when Greek culture collapsed after the long and disastrous Peloponnesian War, and when Hebraic culture suffered destruction of the Temple in the razing of Jerusalem in 70 A.D. and the Diaspora of the Jewish people. The old Roman Republic had been destroyed by a cynical and exploitative Caesarism when Graeco-Judaic Christianity appeared during this multiple crisis of the classic world. Christianity spread still further as the Roman Empire proved unable to solve its social and economic and moral problems through the familiar institutions of slavery, militarism, and the autocratic deified Emperor. Our sacred culture is the ghost hovering over dead Graeco-Judaeo-Roman cultures, the ghost dance of our forgotten psychological past. Small wonder that sacred beliefs must be "religiously" protected against rationality and contemporary common sense, for that would reopen old wounds not to be probed! The intensity of the reaction instituted an autistic response that lasted in force for at least a millennium and a half. Nor is this ghost of the dead classic world quite laid yet.

Religion is the feeling of what is desirable and comforting in crisis situations. "There are no atheists in the foxholes" ran a familiar cliché in a former war. That is, when under severe stress, men must have credence in some larger ultimate reasonableness than their immediate experience would seem to give them. Similarly, in everyday situations, men have to call upon an inherited morality to regulate their raw animal impulses. Religion is thus a kind of moral geometry to help triangulate one's way through social reality; commonly joined to it too is the cognitive map of a new cosmology. Morality is not immediately given biologically. It is the larger social context in which we must try to place our biological impulses meaningfully. Mentally sick people, we would agree, are those who do not know how to handle their emotional life meaningfully in social context. But what an outrage it is to imply that whole societies can be functionally and descriptively insane! And that our most sacred beliefs are the group-neurosis of our traditional society!

Knowledge of the past is doubtless therapeutic, but it is also both subversive and dangerous. It is subversive because through it we escape the confining but protective parochialism of the present, the to some perhaps unfelt tyranny of contemporary tribalism, the necessary Absolute Goodness that some think they need in order to live. It is dangerous because escape from the present seems to be total alienation from the human, at least of the human we know, a psychopathic detour around the historic compulsions that make us human, and that are "good" in at least the only ways we know. Worse, knowledge of the past discovers to us the frightful burden of freedom of choice and responsibility. Where was God when the bomb fell on Hiroshima? Outrageous blasphemy! It was the holy duty of patriotism! Does God then stand behind each flame-thrower today that sears to agony and charred lifelessness a peasant woman and her baby? Belief in God-and-country is sickeningly immoral if it so leads us to shirk moral responsibility; with modern communications we cannot even invoke the German claims that "we did not know." Worship of the sacred contemporary tribal group in the new secular religion of patriotism is no escape from ourselves either or from our moral responsibility; the free distribution of guilt does not lessen the sum. Such worship is anti-intellectual as well, especially hostile to the lone protester, hostile to real moral distinctions, hostile to all moral perceptiveness more sensitive than one's own. In this cult of the contemporary, how can we understand the nightmare of the present if we refuse to look at the dreams of the past?

In unbearable crisis situations, religious prophets are culture innovators who are able to contrive new social forms and new symbolisms to keep all men in the society from going individually insane; but what a monstrous pathology then is the new "normality"! Religiously gifted individuals, often madmen in the eyes of their contemporaries, are poets of culture, able to invent new kinds of moral feelings and institutions. Their myths so much resemble dreams because at one time they *were* dreams, the actual dreams of culture heroes in response to social stresses. Historically, gods and religions are condensations of the culture hero's dream and the dream supernatural, at times even of the culture hero himself, as in Buddhism and Judaism and Christianity. The same is true of "primitive" religion, for this is the identical conclusion we can reach on the basis of Shirokogoroff's great study of Tungusic shamanism[14]: the shaman and his supernatural are strangely the same, like Moses and Yahweh, Jesus and God.

In order to see clearly how a whole society can be as disoriented as any individual, it is necessary to examine the false dichotomy between culture and personality. Spiro[15] has shown brilliantly and convincingly that what we call "culture" is an abstraction from the observed behaviors in common of many individuals in a specified group. But at the same time, what we call "personality" is equally an abstraction from human behavior, that of an individual. Thus culture is the observed consistency in the behavior of a number of individuals in a society; personality is the consistency of pattern in the observed behavior of one individual. *The concrete empiric source of these abstractions is identical,* viz. the mutually patterned and resonant behavior of human beings in society. No human behavior exists apart from definable human beings; and *it depends only on the way we look at it whether we see "personality" or "culture."*

Grave difficulties arise when platonizing minds try to reify cultural behaviors, turning verb-like activities into a noun-like thing, and erecting mere behaviors into a transcendental absolute called Culture—with the astrological outside influence of Culturology's Culture moving helpless men about like mindless chessmen. Culture was once outside each and every individual in the society; everyone must be enculturated. But this does not mean that culture ever was at any one time or is now completely outside all individuals in the society. When we try to find a place to put this transcendental Culture, we run into still more trouble. For of course the only place for this kind of Culture to live in is another reification, Society or the Group Mind or the Collective Unconscious, or some such never-never entity. Culture is not omnipotent God! Society is not a transcendent Absolute! There is nobody here but us people.

Similarly, when we reify personality we get a Soul, together with the mystery of its Free Will—that is, the mystery of an absolutely unconditioned activity, such as we nowhere observe in the whole universe. The free-willed soul is a god-thing. This Soul has a fragment of omnipotence (that is, if total power can be partial), borrowed from Omnipotence (despite what this local omnipotence does to God's). The hallmark of such platonizing is to land us instantly in absurdity; and total incomprehensibility does not make this mystery metaphysically true. When both are defined as absolutes and as disguised omnipotencies, Culture and Personality obviously cannot abide in the same universe. On the other hand, if we see personality as behavior (learned from others) and culture as behavior (learned from others), then we can avoid such nonsense as "culture in personality" and "personality in culture" as though one were enclosed inside the other. The trouble with absolutes is that there is nowhere to put them in this universe, so we have to "transcendentalize" them to metaphysical Limbo. Personality *as behavior* is only the culture of an individual. And culture *as behavior* is only the personalities of individuals. The mystery evaporates when we look at the actual phenomena and try to remember what we are talking about.

Since culture and personality are abstractions—abstractions from observed human behavior but differently delimited and observed from different points of view—and since the concrete human behavior is the same in either case, Spiro has provided us with a naturalistic bridge "between" culture and personality (the two islands are only our conceptual categorizings), hence the possibility for a psychiatric study of cult behaviors. Thus we can see the dynamics of the charismatic individual in a disturbed society as seen by Devereux,[16] and understand with Wallace the ghost dance behaviors of societies.[17] A charismatic leader is an individual responding to stress; a ghost dance is a society of individuals responding to stress. The mystery of "charisma" as a kind of supernal omnipotent compulsion streaming out from an individual like animal magnetism or high-voltage psychokinesis also evaporates. The culture hero's charisma, that uncanny authority and supernatural ascendance he seems to have over his fellows, is in purely naturalistic terms merely the phatic attractiveness of his teaching to others under the same stress, an attractiveness aiding its diffusion from individual to individual. Charisma is only shared unconscious wishes and symbiotic thought-paradigms in leader and communicants. Diffusion of a cult is identical with the diffusion of a culture.

Traditional anthropologists are entirely happy to present quite large generalizations about behavior in a group if only we call it "culture." And yet certain British and American sects in anthropology are sure that personality does not exist (i.e. cannot be talked about, which only means they can not or do not want to talk about it) and can be safely ignored in any anthropological discussion. But where on earth did they get this "culture" if not by questioning individual after individual, in a specified group living on a specified acreage in a specified country? Meanwhile, if Culture is covertly defined by them as omnipotent, then of course there is no use to talk about the individual, human biology, learning, enculturation, acculturation, or anything having to do with the adaptations of real people. Very neatly, definition of any entity as an Absolute always prevents any further discussion about it and other related entities.

Again, these anthropologists are able to see that an individual can be disoriented with respect to a specified cognitive map, that provided by his native culture; he is "crazy." But they throw up all kinds of smokescreens of objection if it is suggested that, through consistency (via diffusion) with the individual's disorientation, a whole society can be disoriented too—say, in a cargo cult ideology, with respect to the realities of European economic behavior, and the European cognitive maps concerning it. They stoutly defend some native shaman or messiah from the gross imputation of being psychotic—"certainly not in terms of the native culture"—ignoring that, in this very fact, the society is joining his cult!

Like other people, many anthropologists find it anxiety-arousing to talk about individual mental illness, and need to distance themselves conceptually from it. The next logical step, discussion of disoriented societies, is too much. Culture and personality must somehow be too disparate for this to happen! how can you talk about a whole society being disoriented? etc., etc.[18] The anxiety we feel on discovering the merely existential nature of culture is deeply psychological, and it is another root of the distaste for discussing sick societies. Many persons are uneasy enough at the psychiatrist's expressed suspicion that the brain is not an organ for grinding out rational truths, but is rather the major homeostatic organ in the body (Cannon, Selye, Freud).[19] To suggest that the function of culture is homeostatic also (Róheim)[20] is to be very disconcerting indeed.

Naïve rationalists talk as if all cultures were always mechanically and rationally adaptive, and adaptive only to features of a real external world; as if cultural differences were only ecological differences of environment rationally adapted to; as if all psychic and social mutations were necessarily adaptive (all genetic mutations are not); as if all cultures were "equally good" adaptively when, historically, they manifestly are not; as if, apart from the manifestly absurd native rationale of native custom, by its very existence the custom must have a good reason in terms of rationalizations comfortable to us (circumcision reduces the incidence of uterine cancer); as if there were a "wisdom of the ages" in every culture since each one is old; as if there were a natural selection among culture traits, and so on.

To argue that there are neurotic (maladaptive) elements in every culture is not to say that all culture is never based on any reality; certainly every neurotic and psychotic still breathes, digests, circulates his blood, and carries on all kinds of adaptive animal activities. To point out disorientation is merely to allege that the mechanism in the forefront of every human society's and individual's adaptation, viz. symbol-using and value-making, is not operating properly (adaptively) both in neurosis and in the crisis cult. Dynamically oriented anthropologists insist that some areas in every culture are *irrational* and can be best studied by clinical techniques already developed in psychology and psychiatry to study the irrational—a position still widely combated in the more naïve quarters in anthropology.

I am not concerned with being ingratiating but only realistic on this point. Any culture-and-personality specialist who does not command modern dynamic psychiatry—and I mean command, not that he has readily producible superstitions based on a fifth-hand acquaintance with Freud contaminated by five sets of personality-configuration between, and has never read a line of Abraham, Jones, Ferenczi, or Róheim, or perhaps has never even heard of them—is in the same position as a modern astronomer ignorant of Einstein, an economist ignorant of Marx, or a biologist ignorant of Darwin. It is a fatuity to suppose that just because we are conscious we automatically know ourselves, or that because we know of many cultures we know what culture *is*. What we think we know is the enemy of our knowledge.

Objections to the psychiatric study of religion are two: the methodological one (which Spiro has disposed of) and the emotional. The second difficulty is, of course, that in making a naturalistic study of religion we are really examining the psychological defenses of a society. We must expect to encounter the same irrational and fanatic defenses against the analytic process as occurs in the analysis of the individual. If the society so studied is our own, we must expect the same defense mechanisms to bristle as in the case of the individual neurotic patient undergoing a psychiatric analysis of his defense mechanisms. We need to recognize that it is extraordinarily *difficult psychologically* to know ourselves. This difficulty, which only a few students have as yet acknowledged or understood, is that the study of man is beset by the presence of these defense mechanisms within man himself, which all of us share, though it is to be hoped in varying degrees.

The dynamic study of religion is no place for the genteel mind to stray into, hoping to garner a nosegay of sublime truths by a kind of philosophical daisy-picking. He is only trying on neuroses for size. For my parallel between sacred culture and neurosis is not an idle one. A society of individuals defends its unexaminable sacred culture because this sacred culture is in fact a complex of defense mechanisms, usually diffused from an identifiable charismatic individual, and usually a paranoid one. These socio-religious defense mechanisms against anxiety come from culturally institutionalized responses to earlier historical stresses and to traumata with which the secular means of that time were unable to cope. Secular science has constantly reopened these questions, indeed has long since solved some of them and is continually solving others. But sacred culture bearers prefer to keep these questions arcane mysteries, precisely as the individual neurotic wishes to ignore the anxiety-arousing traumatic origins of his stress-induced behaviors. Both are frozen stances of ignorance and fear. (God did not die! I shall not die!)

Freud has shown that a compulsion neurosis, with all its peculiar dogmas and rituals, is a private religion. And Reik has further shown us religions that are like a compulsion neurosis diffused among many cultists.[21] The compulsive neurotic half knows his behavior is irrational but "cannot help himself." The cultist likewise, joining with his fellows, defends his faith so fanatically precisely because he half knows it *is* only a faith. The secrets of the *kachina* mask, the Arunta *churinga* or bull-roarer—the Eucharist, the Trinity and the Resurrection—must be kept sacred mysteries, certainly for women and children, even though properly initiated men know all about them anyway. This ambivalent-compulsive attitude is psychologically identical, in one individual, in a *folie à deux,* in a cult, or in a culture. The function of the belief is the same in each case, to protect individuals against anxiety rising from hidden, unresolved, and at least onetime unresolvable problems.

While psychiatrists have been studying cults and cultists, and anthropologists have been assembling descriptions of crisis cults to illustrate "contemporary origins" of religions, psychologists have been pursuing two trends of research that need only to be integrated with the others for a fresh understanding of the human propensity for religion to emerge. These two developments are the studies of sensory deprivation, and of the psychophysiology of sleep and dreams. To these may be added new psychiatric developments in ego psychology and the study of patients suffering from "cultural shock." Since it is the most readily summarizable, I discuss this last, culture shock, first.

In American wars of this century it is not uncommon for returning soldiers to bring home with them brides from exotic lands, since we prefer our wars to be overseas. These culturally uprooted women, perhaps especially in isolated smaller towns where there are no similar others to join with, often understand only a few words of English, and they depend for social communication in a strange country entirely upon the husband. The alien wife of course brings with her the notions of her country concerning the position of women. The husband, away from home most of the day, likewise makes implicit, but culturally American, assumptions about the social adequacy and independent personality of women. Perhaps too, in some cases, he has unconscious ambivalence about the alien race of his wife and hence contributes further to her social isolation.

After a time, often only a few months, the alien wife may suffer a psychotic breakdown, usually with bizarre depressions and hallucinatory experiences of a mild to severe paranoid-persecutory nature. These reactions are not unlike the mild paranoia in some deafened people, and remind us again how much the individual depends on language for the social commerce, emotional reactions, and complex cultural communications that give the person constant ego support and definition. Much of the self is socially mirrored and must be continuously reaffirmed. That is, the ego must be supported not only for "identity" purposes but also for successful ego management of recurrent superego (social) and id (organism) conflicts. When suddenly and massively deprived of customary reactive stimuli to the ego, the personality suffers deflation and severe depressive loss, and the isolated individual begins to make conflictual paranoid projections in order to people this void. "Culture shock" (like the alienation-anomie which it partly resembles) is an increasingly common clinical entity.[22] Even in densely metropolitan areas and in, seemingly, socially privileged diplomatic circles, tragedies of culture shock have been known to occur.

Out of professional pride, anthropologists seldom admit the quite characteristic depression and paranoia of "culture shock" they have all experienced during the first few weeks or months of fieldwork. However, in contrast to alien wives, anthropologists in personal motivation are already themselves alienated from their own culture in typical characterological ways professionally. The conquest and mastery of exotic new "cognitive maps" gratifies the inbuilt personal need and professional appetite. Successful fieldwork therefore constitutes a kind of cumulative triumph of personality—such that, very commonly, the anthropologist comes out of the field experience with a mildly fanatic love for "his" particular primitive people, and even with deeply gratifying personal friendships that over-ride great cultural and age differences. It is possible, however, that the anthropologist's need and effort contributed more to these friendships than did spontaneous native admiration for his uniquely valuable personality. They have merely rescued his humanity, for which, in context, he is perhaps overly grateful; even deeper friendships are possible, in fact, with one's own tribesmen—and at home for that matter. Be that as it may, the anthropologist is professionally in a position peculiarly fitted, if he is self-perceptive and honest, for an understanding of the reality and dynamics of culture shock—specifically, if he naïvely and stubbornly knows what he knows and does not join the available professional cult of those concerned to mask anxieties with sterotyped hairy-chested posturings. Is the anthropologist forbidden to learn about people from himself? The examination of "counter-transference"[23] to cultural phenomena yields insights into culture also: how can the fieldworker pretend there is no fieldworker in the field!

For the self-perceptive person, even pleasure-travel is an illuminating discovery of oneself and one's deeper identity, as well as an obvious enrichment in knowledge and experience of human alternatives. But it is astonishing how much an effective command of foreign languages is necessary for the genuinely pleasurable excitement of travel. It is easy enough to daydream at home of the romance of far places and of the vacation from oneself. It is another matter to shoulder triumphantly the sheer ego-burden of daily adaptation in alien lands, unbuffered by the PX, the local American colony, or the ubiquitous Hilton home-away-from-home. It seems probable that variations in rigidity of personality are related both to language ability and to fundamentalist hostility against or real love for travel. For at the opposite end of the gamut from our ideal self-discerning anthropologist is the angry American of the moneyed middle class, who thinks louder shouting conveys meaning better to a stupid foreigner who *will* not understand good English even when graciously pidgined for the foreigner's benefit; the good citizen, illiterate in the language and history of each land hastily visited, who comes to feel that foreignness is a deliberate plot by conniving, alien, inferior and evil beings to humiliate, harass, victimize and persecute the right-thinking American taxpayer. Will I be glad to get back home!

In any case, foreign wars, foreign travel and war-brides are all common enough nowadays to make us all at least a little aware of the fact of culture shock. Culture shock is perhaps a special case of a larger phenomenon that might be called "social deprivation." We have already briefly alluded to the experience of Captain Joshua Slocum[24] who, at the turn of the century, sailed around the world alone. His case is worth considering in more detail. Once, in a South Atlantic gale, he double-reefed his mainsail and left a whole jib instead of laying-to, then set the vessel on course and went below, because of a severe illness. Looking out, he suddenly saw a tall bearded man, he thought at first a pirate, take over the wheel. This man gently refused Slocum's request to take down the sails and instead reassured the sick man he would pilot the boat safely through the storm. Next day Slocum found his boat ninety-three miles further along on a true course. That night the same red-capped and bearded man, who said he was the pilot of Columbus' *Pinta,* came again in a dream and told Slocum he would reappear whenever needed. Several times later on the voyage, the apparition did indeed return during gales to help him. Despite its vividness and obviously reassuring function, Captain Slocum, a hardy soul, knew it to be a hallucination.

Slocum's experience calls to mind the "imaginary companion"[25] that lonely children sometimes invent for themselves, in the lack even of a doll or dog or blanket comforter. So social an animal is man that even in solitude, as William James knew,[26] we address our thoughts and acts to some ultimate infinite Socius who will understand and approve. The idealized condensation of all our earlier rewarded experiences of others, he is the projected *Doppelgänger* of us all.

Another well-known example of the mysterious stranger is the presence that haunted Sir Ernest Shackleton and his companions in the Antarctic. Vast empty areas like snow-fields and deserts and featureless open sea seem especially evocative of hallucinatory projection. Like Admiral Byrd, Christiana Ritter had similar experiences during her long winter isolation. Stypulkowski, a Russian prisoner in Lubianka Prison, experienced such hallucinations; so also did Jan Baalsrud, a Norwegian resistance-fighter, who spent twenty-seven days alone, injured on a mountain plateau, before rescue. Major General William Dean reported that long solitary confinement was one of the techniques used for "brain-washing" in North Korean Communist prison camps; and Hebb gives evidence that this was also a factor in conditioning to the curious "confessions" common in the earlier Russian "propaganda trials."[27]

An ethnographic parallel is the *kayakangst* often found among the Eskimo of West Greenland, reported as early as 1806. Kayakangst[28] affects the hunter out alone in a kayak in the open sea. At first there is a trance-like lowering of consciousness resulting from a kind of hypnotic "fixing" (perhaps of foveal vision?), accompanied by curious kinesthetic shifts in the body image and body ego. This disoriented and disorganizing experience is deeply frightening and severe panic ensues, together with acute phobias and symptoms of conversion hysteria. Kayakangst seems to have features in common with the "windigo psychosis"[29] affecting lone hunters in winter among high-latitude Algonquian Indians. Siberian "olonism" and Tibetan "chöd" (in a later discussion of the circumpolar shamanic self-induced vision quest) have resemblances to arctic kayakangst and subarctic *windigo*. Arab folktales are also full of encounters with evil *jinn* in lonely places in the featureless desert; Jacob, when alone, seems to have encountered one of these Semitic demons by the ford at Jabbok. One wonders if this is not the same phenomenon described in Hippocrates,[30] of a man traveling in a wild and lonely place where terror seizes him as the result of seeing an apparition—for "panic" we know is literally possession by Pan, the god of lonely places.

In his book *Solitary Confinement,* Christopher Burney enforces upon us the specific inhumanity of punishing human beings by social isolation, from which brutal experience the most hardened and psychopathically isolated individuals at times emerge as "stir crazy" psychotics. In Burney's eloquent words, "We need the constant ebb and flow of wavelets of sensation, thought, perception, action and emotion, lapping on the shore of our consciousness, now here, now there, keeping even our isolation in the ocean of reality, so that we neither encroach nor are encroached upon . . . we have our shape, and we preserve it best in the experience of many things."[31]

In early "sensory deprivation" experiments, the psychiatrist Bressler and his colleagues[32] were disturbed to find young subjects both male and female were emerging from the experiments with symptoms of "artificial traumatic neurosis" for which the experimenters felt morally bound to provide therapy. One wonders, indeed, whether the fantasies of schizophrenics, especially fantasies of depersonalization and body-dismemberment, are not the result of the social and sensory isolation present in some self-absorbed catatonic states; certainly superstitions of dismemberment by demons are found in places as far apart in space and time as Melanesia, Tibet, and ancient Egypt. Self-hypnotic, motionless, self-absorbed meditation in remote places may aid in inducing this quasi-catatonic state. Without containment of consciousness by a constant steady flow of information from the environment, the self itself disappears. Even our prized "identity" depends on constant bounding by the cosmos.

Culture shock, I have suggested, is a sub-variety of social deprivation; and social deprivation is an instance of a still larger category, sensory deprivation. These in turn relate to the universal human phenomena of the vision, the hallucination, and the dream. Concerning these psychic states an especially fascinating knowledge has emerged, only during the last decade, from the scientific study of sleep. Kleitman of Chicago and Dement, now of Stanford, have been the pioneers in this research.[33]

All mammalian (that is, large-brained) animals appear to dream. Strangely, though we know they sleep, despite millennia of human preoccupation with dreams and the meaning of dreams, no one before these investigators seems to have recognized the objective and visible proof that animals dream too. This dramatic discovery was first touched on, simply, by observation of sleeping human beings. Formerly, sleep was supposed to be merely a resting state of sensory withdrawal from the world, during part or all of which (depending on recoverable memory to prove it) a state of dreaming occurred. It was now discovered that only during part of sleep an odd activity was going on: behind the closed eyelids of the sleeper there was a rapid skittering of the eyeballs, which was designated "Rapid Eye Movement" or, for short, "REM sleep." By awakening subjects during both REM and non-REM sleep and inquiring if they remembered anything, it was quickly established that REM sleep coincides exactly with the dream state; and, since REM sleep can be observed in mammals also, it is reasonably inferred that mammals dream too.

One would suppose that brain activity would naturally be greater during the conscious waking state. But as measured by encephalograms, the spontaneous discharge of nerve cells in REM sleep goes on more furiously ever than in the waking state, being tremendously accelerated in every region of the brain studied thus far. On the polygraph, which records many functions simultaneously, speed-up and irregularities of heartbeat and breathing occur at the same time as visible REM and the characteristic REM electro-encephalogram (EEG) brain waves appear. Blood pressure also is increased; as research proceeds, perhaps every body function studied will be found to show some characteristic change related to REM sleep (for example in males, variable degrees of penile erection invariably accompany REM sleep). We once thought that the dream-state was merely light sleep, with consequent recoverable memory of the dream content. Although, quite as Freud thought, there appears to be constant and unremitting unconscious mentation in the living brain, asleep or awake, the specific nature of the intermittent dream-state was a surprise to everyone.

The refinement discerned recently is in the various stages and types of sleep, REM and non-REM. Mentation in non-REM sleep appears to be apocopated and fragmentary, but it is still matter-of-fact, like most ego-oriented conscious thinking. REM sleep, by contrast, is extravagantly dereistic and hallucinatory, arrantly "autistic" or self-constituted, self-willed. In REM sleep the brain clearly appears to be "in business for itself." REM sleep seems in some way to be a special redintegrative action of the nervous sytem. By many objective measures such as the EEG, the brain is *more* active in REM sleep than when the person is wide awake. The REM state is not mere sleep either. Dement believes that "the REM period is more accurately considered a third state of being."

How have we managed to suppose for thousands of years that this period was one of quiet repose? Only by reason of the fact that during REM sleep there is an almost total cut-off of the body-ego, with a special mechanism blocking or inhibiting the discharge of central nervous system (CNS) effects upon the motor neurones, so that the body lies motionless, for all the frantic happenings in the brain. REM sleep is a spree of the CNS. It is a furious activity independent of the body-taught ego; one is reminded of Aristotle's observation that the dream state lacks the element of judgment ($\tau\grave{o}\ \dot{\epsilon}\pi\iota\kappa\rho\hat{\iota}\nu o\nu$). It is suggested that "the dream would truly appear to be born in the brain-stem but clothed in the cortex"— which implies in dreams a self-exploratory character, a kind of housekeeping scrutiny or inventory of organic id needs by the cortical ego.

What happens to sensory input during sleep? Although it was admitted that such input is greatly reduced, an older mechanistic theory of dreaming supposed that it was various external stimuli (including bodily proprioception) that in fact produced the dream. On the contrary, however, the dream appears rather to be internally autonomous, and even proprioceptive stimuli (indigestion, bladder pressure) are distorted and woven into the fabric of the imperiously self-willed dream.

Can drugs affect REM sleep? LSD seems to exert a specifically stimulating effect on the REM mechanism. Dexedrine sulfate, administered at bedtime, considerably reduces the normal amount of REM sleep in humans, hence the constant use of it may be psychologically deleterious. It has been suggested also that alcohol suppresses REM activity, so that *delirium tremens* in chronic alcoholics may be an explosive return to hallucination in REM-deprived states. Interestingly, by using Oswald's technique of taping eyelids, Rechtschaffen has shown that REM dreaming can occur with the eyes wide open: the dreamer (he told Dement) gives the uncanny impression of being wide awake and looking about, though judging from the EEGs he is undoubtedly asleep. Perhaps schizophrenic hallucination is just such "wide-awake" dreaming.[34] The curious affliction of narcolepsy, once thought to be merely overpowering attacks of daytime sleep, is now viewed as being persistent recurrence of specifically REM states.

The REM state does not usually come immediately with the onset of regular sleep, but characteristically a little over an hour later—though a daytime nap will usually bring on a REM state (was that why one wanted a nap?) and in fact much sooner than at night-time—after which several separated REM states will occur during the night, and commonly one just before normal awakening, when the REM dream leaves the male body at least sometimes in a shocking state.[35] What is dreaming for? One rather mechanistic explanation, plainly imaging the brain as a gigantic computer and mindful of the "clear" buttons on an electric calculating machine, has it that the dream is only the adventitious epiphenomenon to the kind of scanning "clearance" that keeps all systems afferent —in other words, dreaming is only the meaningless mental representation of the nightly unscrambling that keeps the computer usable and accessible to new input. This computer analogy makes the brain rather a cold machine—and the dream does seem more interesting and meaningful than that, less passive certainly and its activities somehow more "chosen." Besides, a sensitively discriminatory "clearance" must be actively at work, since dreaming does not destroy memory. On the contrary: dreams often are made up partly of very old memories, and dreams themselves are frequently remembered. Such a calculating-machine concept is not necessarily wholly incorrect, but it does not seem adequate to encompass a perhaps *adaptive* function of a *psychological* nature in a complex *organism;* nor is it, incomplete or not, necessarily inconsistent with a psychoanalytic view that offers a more psychological-organic view of the adaptive function of dreaming. For Freud, dreaming is a discharge, not possible when awake, of potentially noxious tensions, which, if blocked, might accumulate as conscious mental disturbances. That is, dream-sleep is a kind of normal built-in therapy or "regression in the service of the ego." The success of artificially prolonged "sleep therapy" in traumatic neuroses would seem to bear this out.

Since all mammals studied thus far have REM states, any sound explanation will have to account for these animals too. One student reasons that dreaming first emerged with ancestral mammals as a kind of adaptive "sentinel" state, a part-awakening several times a night with manifest physiologic preparation of the earlier deeply sleeping animal for instant alertness and possible action. Though the eyelids are closed, the fact that scanning *eye* movements are invariable components of REM dreams makes this theory attractive. However, it is not established that REM sleep is "lighter" with respect to accessibility to sensory input of a selective danger-warning kind than is non-REM; and REM states "incorporate" and mask problems like bladder fullness and in fact *autistically substitute for* actual need gratification with a "dream"; and one still has to account for the seemingly autonomous and active nature of the dream, so that the sophisticated expert who advances it calls his own theory *simpliste,* which it doubtless is. Nevertheless, it is interesting that spontaneous awakening tends to occur at the beginning of a REM state, and anxious and depressed or otherwise fearful people often awaken in what would seem to be the middle of a REM period; there is also the nightmare to account for. But, again, theoretically semi-scheduled (though internally determined) REM states would not appear necessarily to be adapted to outside exigencies, which randomly come when they come. Furthermore, if REM states regularly *followed* external sensory stimuli that should invite semi-awake scanning, then the "sentinel" theory would be more plausible; but such is not the case. Indeed, as Freud observed, one function of the dream seems to be to "preserve sleep" against the intrusion of even proprioceptive stimuli related to some physiological need. Dreaming may be adaptive —but clearly it is adaptive inwardly, psychologically, not outwardly, environmentally. Surprisingly, dream-deprived animals even seem in Dement's judgment to be "improved" adaptively with respect to their environment; hence he properly notes it is difficult to account for the persistence of a mammalian function, not absolutely necessary for the maintenance of life in the adult animal, as being adaptive in the wild state. Is dreaming, then, a subjective indulgence, a cognitive onanism, a supererogatory ebullience of otiose play? Is autism unnecessary?

Or is the dream somehow homeostatic, like the neurotic symptom? Or is dreaming inversely related to ego growth? It is a fact that the amount of REM sleep declines rapidly from birth to the age of two, and declines again to the age of five, when it levels off at two or three hours of the twenty-four, and thenceforth decreases slowly throughout the rest of life. A newborn baby sleeps three-fourths of the time, spending 30 per cent of his life in non-REM but fully 45 per cent of his life in REM sleep. At two, he sleeps only 58 per cent of the time, with 46 per cent of the twenty-four hours in non-REM and now only 12 per cent in REM sleep. Since these are the years of rapid brain growth, are dreams just brain-building noises in the night? At five, the child sleeps only 50 per cent of the time, 42 per cent in non-REM but only 8 per cent of his life now in REM time. Since the intervening years are those of rapid ego growth, does the inverse relation of REM-time and ego attainment mean that dreaming is the sound and fury of struggles in ego growth? It is not true that adolescents sleep almost not at all; they make it up in school, and they sleep almost as much as five-year-olds.[36] But at fifty a man spends only 22 per cent of his life in non-REM sleep, plus 7 or 8 per cent in REM sleep—as if older people, with achieved identity, did not want or need to dream, or it may be could not, as much as younger people do. We will remain puzzled about all these matters until we know better what REM dreaming is for.

What happens when people are experimentally deprived of REM sleep, by systematic awakening each time the EEG indicates a REM state? Subjects REM-deprived from two to fifteen days (but not of non-REM sleep) were noticeably more impulsive, and one rather schizoid individual indulged in paranoid flights of speech. The recording on one subject was discontinued about 5:30 A.M. on the fifteenth night because it was nearly impossible to let him sleep at all, so rapidly did REM sleep intervene. The experiment on another subject was stopped on the sixteenth REM-deprived night on the appearance of frankly autistic and paranoid waking ideation, in order to avoid the possible danger of a full-blown psychosis; on this subject's subsequent first undisturbed recovery night, although it did not appear immediately, the first REM period lasted 176 minutes, the longest period of continuous REM sleep yet recorded. In general, loss of REM sleep, totally or in part, leads to an increasing tendency for it to occur, and the amount of increase roughly parallels the amount of cumulative deprivation—as if the subject "remembered" the exact amount of loss and was stubbornly determined to make it up when he could. Some persons, on waking up at night, even have a fairly exact notion of the time (or the amount of time they have slept) because of their sense of relative satiations of REM need. Sleep studies are still in their infancy. But Dement nevertheless has repeatedly stated that he considers it unproven that REM sleep is necessary to life in the *adult* animal. REM sleep, however, we may safely say, seems highly desired by many people!

For most men, the dream is the only experience they have of escaping their strange and unwilling imprisonment in obdurate waking space and time. Thus if one of man's two worlds seems remolded nearer to the heart's desire, there is no wonder he is reluctant to attribute reality only to the more vexing waking world. Indeed, the two realms of sacred and secular are at least as "real" as man's two psychic worlds. Jane Harrison, W. H. R. Rivers, and Karl Abraham[37] all knew that revelatory dreams are close to myth, which is the dream-thinking of a society just as the dream is the mythology of the individual. Róheim thought dreams and myths not only similar but that much of mythology actually derives from dreams. Indeed, the Australian Bushmen themselves equate dream-time with the myth-time that is mysteriously brought back in ritual; myth is as timeless as the unconscious mind.[38] It is the delectability of dreams that makes them desirable, and it is their desirability that (along with lowered critical threshold) gives them their intense "reality" and conviction.[39] The fact that he dreams first forces on man the need to epistemologize.

Historically, revelation in the crisis cult is often the literal dream-vision of the charismatic founder of the cult. But the term "crisis cult" can be criticised on two grounds: is not every moment in history in some sense a "crisis" and does not "cult" imply invidious reality judgment? The only answer to the criticism is, yes it is, and yes it does. But that is what life is like, a chronic crisis; and that is what science is, making invidious judgments of the reality value of competing hypotheses or belief systems. Two criteria for truth we commonly use are very dubious. The duration of a belief in time has nothing to do with its reality-value. The durability of a cult in becoming successively a sect, denomination, and ecclesia is really a measure of its seeming ability to serve in new crises, and is otherwise only a measure of cultural mass and respectability.

Epistemologically, then, we are bound to make reality judgments discriminating sacred cult responses from secular measures such as war, law, political, economic, technological and other social change—and this despite a ready concession that every war may have its secondary dereistic cult rationalization, that the effect of law may be in part magical, and that each political and economic myth may embody a subcultural autistic mystique *sub specie aeternitatis*. I do not deny our predicament. I assert it. This is also an admission that we do not really know at any time the boundaries of the technological (externally oriented) and the cult (internally oriented) change. We may not know whether there is primary operation of conscious ego functions or of unconscious id functions. Cultural speciation is blind. That is to say, not only do "natives" not know whether their actions are to be designated sacred or secular, but also *we do not know either about ours,* the ambiguous nature of adaptive culture being what it intrinsically is. Nevertheless, tentative scientific judgment in these matters is at least as astute as our ability to discriminate between waking reality and dream.

In this examination of culture we are reduced to the humility (and the strength) of the scientist: if culture is the specifically human adaptive technique, then we may not know beforehand which cultural mutation or speciation is ultimately adaptive and which not. Or more probably perhaps, as also with genetic traits, it may be potentially both adaptive and non-adaptive in "balanced polymorphism," depending on complex combinations of ecological circumstance, in part of our own creation, and often with minuscule or marginal selectiveness. With an existentialist understanding of the nature of culture, our final protective anthropocentric arrogance will have to be discarded. Cultural man proposes, but (unknown) reality disposes, for man is only another kind of animal. In a universe where the very stars whirl and wheel in places we discern only light-years later, and even the great planets wander exquisitively responsive to bodies we incompletely descry in the night, a necessary wisdom is humility, a knowledge that we do not know but can only say that, blessed and burdened with our current projective fantasies, this is the way it seems, now.

NOTES

(I Anthropology and Psychology of Religion)

1. Peter Gay, *The Enlightenment* (New York: Knopf, 1966) is a good recent summary. For specific works see: David Hume, *Dialogues Concerning Natural Religion* (New York: Social Sciences Publishers, edited by Norman Kemp Smith, 2nd ed., 1948); A. Koch and W. Peden (eds.), *The Life and Selected Writings of Thomas Jefferson* (New York: Modern Library, 1944); Immanuel Kant, *The Critique of Pure Reason*, in Theodore M. Greene (ed.), *Kant Selections* (New York: Charles Scribner's Sons, 1929); and Edward Gibbon, *The Decline and Fall of the Roman Empire* (New York: Modern Library, 2 vols., 1932). In the same eighteenth-century tradition is a work first published in 1895, Andrew D. White, *A History of the Warfare of Science with Theology in Christendom* (New York: Braziller, 1955).

2. For the nineteenth century, formative classics include: Karl Marx and Friedrich Engels, *Marx and Engels on Religion* (New York: Schocken Books); Edward B. Tylor, *Religion in Primitive Culture* (New York: Harper Torchbooks); Herbert Spencer, *Principles of Sociology* (London: Williams and Norgate, 3 vols., 1882–96, Chs. 20–25 in vol. I, pp. 322–440); R. H. Codrington, *The Melanesians* (Oxford: Clarendon Press, 1891); Andrew Lang, *The Making of Religion* (London: Longmans, Green & Co., 1898); and J. H. King, *The Supernatural: Its Origin, Nature and Evolution* (London: Williams and Norgate, and New York: G. P. Putnam's Sons, 2 vols., 1892). Belonging also to the nineteenth-century tradition are: Sir James George Frazer, *The Golden Bough* (London: Macmillan, 12 vols., 1914–19; the Macmillan one-volume paperback is to be preferred to the Anchor one edited by Gaster); R. R. Marett, *The Threshold of Religion* (New York: Macmillan, 1941, pp. 1–32); see also the chapter on "Frazer and his Critic Marett" in Franz Steiner, *Taboo* (New York: Philosophical Library, 1956) and R. R. Marett, "Preanimistic Religion," *Folklore* [London], 11 (1900) 162–82; Wilhelm Schmidt, *Der Ursprung des Gottesidee* (Münster: Aschendorff, 12 vols., 1912–55) or the H. J. Rose-edited translation, *The Origin and Growth of Religion* (New York: L. MacVeagh, 1931); and Emile Durkheim, *The Elementary Forms of the Religious Life* (London: George Allen & Unwin, 1915; Free Press paperback, 1966).

3. For a social understanding of French sociology an indispensable sidelight is Margaret Mead and Rhoda Métraux, *Thèmes de la "Culture" de la France, Introduction à une Etude de la Communauté Française* (Le Havre: Institut havrais de sociologie économique et de psychologie des peuples, 1957); also Lawrence Wylie, *Village in the Vaucluse* (Cambridge: Harvard University Press, 1957).

4. Jane Ellen Harrison, *Prolegomena to the Study of Greek Religion* (Cambridge: At the University Press, 2nd ed., 1908; Meridian paperback), *Themis: A Study of the Social Origins of Greek Religion* (Cambridge: At the University Press, 1927), and *Epilegomena to the Study of Greek Religion* (Cambridge: At the University Press, 1921). *Epilegomena* and *Themis* have been reprinted together (New Hyde Park: University Books paperback). W. Robertson Smith, *The Religion of the Semites* (New York: Macmillan, 1927; Meridian Books). Sigmund Freud, *The Future of an Illusion* (London: Hogarth Press, translated by W. D. Robson-Scott, 1949; in James Strachey [ed.], *The Standard Edition of the Complete Psychological Works of Sigmund Freud*, London: Hogarth Press, 23 vols., vol. 21, 1949; Anchor Books); *Totem and Taboo* (New York: W. W. Norton & Co., 1952; Standard Edition, vol.

13; the Brill translation [New York: Random House, 1960, and Modern Library paperback] is inferior). Claude Lévi-Strauss, *Totemism* (Boston: Beacon Press, 1963; Beacon paperback); of course this conclusion was reached forty-seven years earlier by the dozen-some authorities in W. Schmidt (ed.), "Das Probleme des Totemismus, Eine Diskussion über die Natur des Totemismus und die Methode seiner Erforschung," *Anthropos*, 9 (1914)-11 (1916). Recently, adding to Harrison on Greek and Smith on Semitic origins in totemism, is Wen-shan Huang, "Totemism and the Origin of Chinese Philosophy," *Bulletin of the Institute of Ethnology* [Academica Sinica, Nanking-Taipei-Taiwan, China], 9 (1960); see also "The Origins of Chinese Culture: A Study of Totemism," in Leroi-Gourhan, P. Champion and M. de Fontanés (editors), *VIᵉ Congrès Internationale des Sciences Anthropologiques* (Paris: Musée de l'Homme, 1963, pp. 139-43). Gilbert Murray, *Five Stages;* E. R. Dodds, *The Greeks and the Irrational* (University of California paperbacks); and Erwin Rohde, *Psyche: The Cult of Souls and Belief in Immortality among the Greeks* (New York: Harcourt, Brace & Co., 1925). Arnold van Gennep, *The Rites of Passage* (Paris: E. Nourry, 1909; reprinted, Chicago: University of Chicago Press, 1960).

5. The psychologists of religion include: William James, *Varieties of Religious Experience;* J. B. Pratt, *The Religious Consciousness* (New York: Macmillan, 1920), and *The Psychology of Religious Belief* (New York: Macmillan, 1907); E. S. Ames, *The Psychology of Religious Experience* (Boston: Houghton Mifflin Co., 1910); J. H. Leuba, *The Psychology of Religious Mysticism* (New York: Harcourt, Brace & Co., 1929); G. A. Coe, *The Psychology of Religion* (Chicago: University of Chicago Press, 1916); R. H. Thouless, *An Introduction to the Psychology of Religion* (New York: Cambridge University Press, 1923); G. M. Stratton, *Psychology of the Religious Life* (London: G. Allen & Unwin, 1911); A. R. Uren, *Recent Religious Psychology* (New York: C. Scribner's Sons, 1929); J. C. Flower, *The Psychology of Religion* (London: Kegan Paul, 1927); and E. D. Starbuck, *The Psychology of Religion* (London: Walter Scott, 1899).

6. After Freud, the major psychoanalytic writers on religion are: Karl Abraham, *Dreams and Myths* (New York: Nervous and Mental Disease Monograph Series 18, 1913); Otto Rank, *Das Inzestmotif in Dichtung und Saga* (Vienna: F. Deuticke, 1912); Ernest Jones, *Essays in Applied Psychoanalysis* (London: Hogarth Press, 1923); Franz Riklin, *Wishfulfillment and Symbolism in Fairy Tales* (New York: Nervous and Mental Disease Monograph Series 21, 1925); Theodore Reik, *The Ritual* (New York: International Universities Press, 1959), *Ritual: Psycho-analytic Studies* (New York: Farrar, Straus & Co., 1946), *Myth and Guilt* (New York: George Braziller, 1957), *The Mystery on the Mountain* (New York: Harper and Brothers, 1958), *The Temptation* (New York: George Braziller, 1961); Sandor Ferenczi, "Gulliver Fantasies," *International Journal of Psycho-Analysis*, 9 (1928) 283-300; Géza Róheim, *Australian Totemism* (London: Allen & Unwin, 1925), *Animism, Magic, and the Divine King* (London: Kegan Paul, 1930), *The Riddle of the Sphinx* (London: Hogarth Press, 1934), *Primitive High Gods* (Supplemental Volume to *Psychoanalytic Quarterly*, 1934), *The Eternal Ones of the Dream* (New York: International Universities Press, 1945), and "Transition Rites," *Psychoanalytic Quarterly*, 11 (1942) 336-74—but see also the voluminous bibliography of Róheim's works in G. B. Wilbur and Warner Muensterberger (eds.), *Psychoanalysis and Culture: Essays in Honor of Géza Róheim* (New York: International Universities Press, 1951, pp. 455-62). Good summaries are by Robert F. Casey, "Oedipus Motivation in Religious Thought and Fantasy," *Psychiatry*, 5 (1942) 219-29, and "The Psychoanalytic Study of Religion," *Journal of Abnormal and Social Psychology*, 33 (1938) 437-52. For a bibliography of more recent works, see Weston La Barre, "The Influence of Freud on Anthropology," *American Imago*, 15 (1958) 275-328, especially footnotes 57 to 62, pp. 316-17.

7. W. H. Auden, *The Collected Poetry of W. H. Auden* (New York: Random House, 1945, p. 166).

8. Mircea Eliade, "Crisis and Renewal in History of Religions," *History of Religions*, 5 (1965) 1–17, p. 1. For characteristic statements on recent anthropological neglect of religion, see Claude Lévi-Strauss, in T. A. Sebeok (ed.), *Myth: A Symposium* (Philadelphia: American Folklore Society, 1955, p. 50), S. T. Kimball (Introduction to Van Gennep, *op. cit.*, p. xvii), J. J. Honigmann (*American Anthropologist*, 61 [1959] 121–22, p. 121), and W. A. Lessa (*loc. cit.*, 123–24, p. 123).

9. James Mooney, *The Ghost Dance Religion and the Sioux Outbreak of 1890* (14th Annual Report, Bureau of American Ethnology, part 2 [1896] 641–1136). A. F. C. Wallace has edited an overly shortened paperback version in *The Ghost Dance* (Chicago: University of Chicago Press, 1965).

10. F. E. Williams, *The Vailala Madness* (Port Moresby: Territory of Papua, Anthropology Report ##4, 1923; available also in the Bobbs-Merrill Reprints in Anthropology ##A-241). See also Williams' paper on "The Vailala Madness in Retrospect," in E. E. Evans-Pritchard, Raymond Firth, Bronislaw Malinowski and Isaac Schapera (eds.), *Essays presented to C. G. Seligman* (London: Kegan Paul, Trench, Trubner & Co., 1934, pp. 369–79).

11. Ralph Linton, "Nativistic Movements," *American Anthropologist*, 45 (1943) 230–40.

12. William James, *Varieties of Religious Experience*, esp. Lecture I, "Religion and Neurology," pp. 1–25.

13. Admiral Richard Byrd, *Alone* (New York: G. P. Putnam's Sons, 1938); Captain Joshua Slocum, *Sailing Alone Around the World* (New York: Century, 1900).

14. S. M. Shirokogoroff, *Psychomental Complex of the Tungus* (London: Kegan Paul, Trench, Trubner & Co., 1935).

15. Melford E. Spiro, "Culture and Personality, The Natural History of a False Dichotomy," *Psychiatry*, 14 (1951) 19–46, especially page 43.

16. George Devereux, "Charismatic Leadership and Crisis," in Géza Róheim (ed.), *Psychoanalysis and the Social Sciences* (New York: International Universities Press, 1955, IV, pp. 145–57).

17. A. F. C. Wallace, "Revitalization Movements," *American Anthropologist*, 58 (1956) 264–81, p. 268.

18. But Ruth Benedict, long ago and in a much-read book, pointed out that "Tradition is as neurotic as any patient" (*Patterns of Culture*, Cambridge: Riverside Press, 1934, p. 273; cf. p. 237).

19. W. B. Cannon, *The Wisdom of the Body* (New York: W. W. Norton & Co., 1932); Hans Selye, *The Stress of Life* (Montreal: Acta, Inc., Medical Publishers, 1950, New York: McGraw-Hill, 1956); Sigmund Freud, *The Future of an Illusion* (London: Hogarth Press, 1949).

20. Géza Róheim, *The Origin and Function of Culture* (New York: Nervous and Mental Disease Monographs, 1943; New York: Johnson Reprint Corp., 1969).

21. Theodor Reik, *Dogma and Compulsion* (New York: International Universities Press, 1951).

22. I. A. Kishner and W. Muensterberger, "Hazards of Culture Clash: A Report on the History and Dynamics of a Psychotic Episode in a West-African Exchange Student," in W. Muensterberger and S. Axelrad (eds.), *The Psychoanalytic Study of Society* (New York: International Universities Press, 1966, IV:99–123).

23. The only serious extended examination of counter-transference in the social sciences is by George Devereux, *From Anxiety to Method in the Behavioral Sciences* (The Hague: Mouton, 1967), to which I was honored to write the Preface. But see also J. P. Spiegel, "Some Cultural Aspects of Transference and Countertransference,"

in J. H. Masserman (ed.), *Science and Psychoanalysis*, II, (New York: Grune and Stratton, 1950) for another slant on the problem.

24. Slocum, *op. cit.;* cf. Walter Gibson, *The Boat* (Boston: Houghton Mifflin, 1953), and Hannes Lindemann, *Alone at Sea* (New York: Random House, 1958, pp. 19, 128, 144, 152, 157–59, 161 and 171).

25. Clara Vostrovsky, "A Study of Imaginary Companions," *Education*, 15 (1895) 393–98; N. A. Harvey, *Imaginary Playmates and Other Mental Phenomena* (Ypsilanti: Michigan State Normal College, 1919); E. B. Hurlock and M. Burnstein, "The Imaginary Playmate: A Questionnaire Study," *Journal of Genetic Psychology*, 41 (1932) 380–92; and Margaret Svendsen, "Children's Imaginary Companions," *Archives of Neurology and Psychiatry*, 32 (1934) 985–99.

26. William James, *Principles of Psychology* (New York: Henry Holt & Co., 1890, 2 vols., I, 315–16).

27. Shackleton's "presence" is noted in Dodds, *op. cit.*, p. 117; Christiana E. Ritter, *A Woman in the Polar Night* (E. P. Dutton & Co., 1954); the observations of General Dean, Stypulkowski, and Jan Baalsrud are noted in P. Solomon, P. J. Leiderman, J. Mendelson, and D. Wexler, "Sensory Deprivation, A Review," *American Journal of Psychiatry*, 114 (1957) 357–63. Experimental work on sensory deprivation stems from D. O. Hebb of McGill University, in his attempts to understand "brainwashing" and the "confessions" in Russian propaganda trials. The initial paper appears to be that of Hebb's students, W. H. Bexton, W. Heron, and T. H. Scott, "Effects of Decreased Variation in the Sensory Environment," *Canadian Journal of Psychology*, 8 (1954) 70–76. Other basic studies on sensory deprivation: John C. Lilly, "Illustrative Strategies for Research on Psychopathology in Mental Health," *Group for the Advancement of Psychiatry, Symposium No. 2*, 1956, pp. 13–20, 44; *idem*, "Mental Effects of Reduction of Ordinary Levels of Physical Stimuli on Intact, Healthy Persons," *Psychiatric Research Reports, American Psychiatric Association*, 5 (1956) 1–28; J. A. Vernon, T. E. McGill, and H. Schiffman, "Visual Hallucinations During Perceptual Isolation," *Canadian Journal of Psychology*, 12 (1958) 31–34; L. Goldberger and R. R. Holt, "Experimental Interference with Reality Contact," *Journal of Nervous and Mental Diseases*, 127 (1958) 99–112; S. J. Freedman and M. Greenblatt, "Studies in Human Isolation," *U. S. Armed Forces Medical Journal*, 11 (1960) 1330–1497; S. J. Freedman, H. Gruenbaum, and M. Greenblatt, "Perceptual and Cognitive Changes in Sensory Deprivation," *Journal of Nervous and Mental Diseases*, 132 (1961) 17–21; D. Wexler, J. H. Mendelson, H. Leiderman, and P. Solomon, "Perceptual Isolation, a Technique for Studying Psychiatric Aspects of Stress," *Archives of Neurology and Psychiatry*, 79 (1958) 225–33; P. Solomon and J. Mendelson, "Hallucinations in Sensory Deprivation," in J. L. West (ed.), *Hallucinations* (New York: Grune & Stratton, 1962, pp. 135–45; B. D. Cohen, G. Rosenbaum, S. I. Dobie, and J. S. Gottlieb, "Sensory Isolation: Hallucinogenic Effects of a Brief Exposure," *Journal of Nervous and Mental Diseases*, 129 (1959) 486–91; and A. J. Silverman, S. I. Cohen, B. M. Shmavonian, and George Greenberg, "Psychophysiological Investigations in Sensory Deprivation," *Psychosomatic Medicine*, 23 (1961) 48–61. Books on the subject: P. Solomon, P. E. Kubzansky, P. H. Leiderman, J. H. Mendelson, R. Trumbull, and D. Wexler (editors), *Sensory Deprivation* (Cambridge: Harvard University Press, 1961); and C. A. Brownfield, *Isolation, Clinical and Experimental Approaches* (New York: Random House paperback). See also N. Rosenzweig, "Sensory Deprivation and Schizophrenia: Some Clinical and Theoretical Similarities," *American Journal of Psychiatry*, 116 (1959) 326–29.

28. Zachary Gussow, "A Preliminary Report of 'Kayakangst' among the Eskimo of West Greenland: A Study in Sensory Deprivation," *International Journal of Social Psychiatry*, 9 (1963) 18–26. K. I. Taylor and W. S. Laughlin give a somewhat me-

chanical explanation based on grounds of skill and training in use of the kayak, in their "Sub-Arctic Kayak Commitment and 'Kayak Fear'" (Paper presented at the Annual Meetings of the American Anthropological Association, San Francisco, 1963). Cf. kayakangst with a similar phenomenon in aviation, A. M. H. Bennett, "Sensory Deprivation in Aviation," in Solomon *et al.*, *op. cit.*, pp. 161–73.

29. Ethnographic materials on "windigo" may be found in A. Skinner, "The Plains Ojibway," *Anthropological Papers, American Museum of Natural History*, 11 (1914) part vi, pp. 500–5; J. E. Guinard, "Witiko among the Tête de Boule," *Primitive Man*, 3 (1930) 69–71; J. E. Saindon, "Mental Disorders among the James Bay Cree," *Primitive Man*, 6 (1933) 1–12; F. G. Speck, *Neskapi* (Norman: University of Oklahoma Press, 1935, pp. 71–74); and F. W. Hodge (ed.), *Handbook of the American Indians North of Mexico* (Bulletin 30, Bureau of American Ethnology, 2 vols., 1907, under "Weendigo," II:930). John M. Cooper, "The Cree Witiko Psychosis," in Alan Dundes (ed.), *Every Man His Way* (Englewood Cliffs: Prentice Hall, 1968, pp. 288–92) has a basic bibliography on *windigo*. The best modern understanding of windigo is by V. Barnouw, "A Psychological Interpretation of a Chippewa Origin Legend," *Journal of American Folklore*, 68, nos. 267–69 (1955) 73–85, 211–23, 341–55. See also W. M. Bolman, "Hamburger Hoarding: A Case of Symbolic Cannibalism Resembling Whitico Psychosis," *Journal of Nervous and Mental Disease*, 142 (1966) 424–28; Ruth Landes, "The Abnormal Among the Ojibwa Indians," *Journal of Abnormal and Social Psychology*, 33 (1939) 14–33; and S. Parker, "The Windigo Psychosis in the Context of Ojibwa Culture and Personality," *American Anthropologist*, 62 (1960) 603–24.

30. The reference to the Hippocratic corpus (*Int.* 48, vii, 286L) is cited from Dodds, *op. cit.*, p. 117.

31. Christopher Burney, *Solitary Confinement* (London: Clerke and Cockeran, 1952, p. 16).

32. Bernard Bressler, A. J. Silverman, S. I. Cohen, and B. Shmavonian, "Research in Human Subjects and the Artificial Traumatic Neurosis: Where Does Our Responsibility Lie?" *American Journal of Psychiatry*, 116 (1959) 522–26.

33. The pioneering work on REM was announced by E. Aserinsky and Nathaniel Kleitman in "Regularly Recurring Periods of Eye Motility and Concomitant Phenomena during Sleep," *Science*, 118 (1953) 273. See also N. Kleitman, *Sleep and Wakefulness* (Chicago: University of Chicago Press, 1963), and "The Nature of Dreaming," in G. E. W. Wolstenholm and M. O'Connor (editors), *The Nature of Sleep* (Boston: Little, 1961, pp. 349–63). Important sources: William Dement, "The Effect of Dream Deprivation," *Science*, 131 (1960) 1705–7; "Studies on the Function of Rapid Eye Movement (Paradoxical) Sleep in Human Subjects," in M. Jouvet (ed.), *Aspects Anatomo-Fonctionnels de la Physiologie du Sommeil* (Paris: Centre National de la Recherche Scientifique, 1954), and "Experimental Dream Studies," in J. Masserman (ed.), *Science and Psychoanalysis* (New York: Grune, 1964, 7:129); C. Fisher and W. Dement, "Studies in the Psychopathology of Sleep and Dreams," *American Journal of Psychiatry*, 119 (1963) 1160–68; W. Dement and C. Fisher, "Experimental Interference with the Sleep Cycle," *Canadian Psychiatric Association Journal*, 8 (1963) 400–5; W. C. Dement, "Dreaming: A Biologic State," *Modern Medicine*, 5 July 1965, pp. 184–206; W. Dement and S. Greenberg, "Changes in Total Amount of Stage Four Sleep as a Function of Partial Sleep Deprivation," *Electroencephalography and Clinical Neurophysiology*, 20 (1966) 523–26. See also M. Kramer, R. M. Whitman, B. J. Baldridge, and P. H. Ornstein, "The Pharmacology of Dreaming, A Review," in G. J. Martin and B. Kisch (editors), *Enzymes in Mental Health* (Philadelphia: Lippincott, 1966, pp. 102–16). David Foulkes, *The Psychology of Sleep* (New York: Scribners, 1966), is written for the layman. A very significant paper is by Charles Fisher, "Dreams, Images, and Perception: A Study of Unconscious-Pre-

conscious Relationships," *Journal of the American Psychoanalytic Association*, 4 (1956) 5–48. Dement on dreams as the "third state of being" is quoted from his *Modern Medicine* article, *loc. cit.*, p. 190; Rechtschaffen on "open-eye dreaming" from Dement in Jouvet, p. 605. On narcolepsy as REM sleep, W. Dement, A. Rechtschaffen, and G. Gulevish, "The Nature of the Narcoleptic Sleep Attack," *Neurology*, 16 (1966) 18–33; also Dement in *Modern Medicine, loc. cit.*, p. 205. Frederick Snyder has advanced the evolutionary theory of the "sentinel" function of dreaming; another interesting theory, based on the dual-memory system, that dreams select for long-range memory from recent short-range memory content, is presented by Christopher Evans in "Sleeping and Dreaming—A New 'Functional' Theory," *Trans-Action*, 5, no. 2 (December 1967) 40–45.

For Freud (*The Interpretation of Dreams*, Standard Edition, vols. 4–5; Avon Books) the discharge of noxious tensions in dreaming was a *psychological* phenomenon. But there now seems to be proof of a *chemical* substrate of this, *i.e.*, an actual toxin. Dement theorizes that REM-deprivation accumulates a substance that must be metabolized in comparable quantity in later undisturbed sleep; preliminary experiments in transferring the cerebrospinal fluid from a REM-deprived cat to another which then manifests excessive REM need, would seem to support the theory (William C. Dement, "Recent Studies on the Biological Role of Rapid Eye Movement Sleep," *American Journal of Psychiatry*, 122 [1965] 404–8, p. 406). The notion that the dream serves to preserve sleep appears to be as old as Descartes (see Bertram D. Lewin, "Dreams and the Uses of Regression," in *Freud Anniversary Lecture Series*, New York: International Universities Press, 1958, pp. 50ff). On animals as "improved" by REM-deprivation, see W. C. Dement's "Discussion" in the *International Journal of Psychiatry*, 2 (1966) 41–46, p. 45. The most primitive animals proven polygraphically to have REM sleep are birds (significantly, like mammals warm-blooded), but their REM periods are exceedingly brief, three-tenths of one percent of sleep (see next citation, p. 607).

For age-variations in amount of sleep and REM-proportion, see H. P. Roffwarg, J. N. Muzio, and W. C. Dement, "Ontogenetic Development of the Human Sleep-Dream Cycle," *Science*, 152 (29 April 1966) 604–19. That penile erections are specific to REM periods, with detumescence occurring as non-REM sleep ensues, see the above, pp. 605, 606 (citing C. Fisher, J. Gross, and J. Zuch, "Cycle of Penile Erection Synchronous with Dreaming (REM) Sleep," *Archives of General Psychiatry*, 12 [1965] 29–45—a discovery surprising even to psychoanalysts, who had argued the sexual function of dreams on other grounds—and a paper presented by Fisher and Gross at a symposium of the Association for the Psychophysiological Study of Sleep in March 1965). Interestingly for Freud's and Abraham's observations on the oral libidinal zone, just as, in infants, lessening of muscle tone heralds a REM period, so also do progressive increases in mouth movements resembling sucking; but past a certain threshold of activity, the REM period appears to give way to arousal from sleep (*Science, loc. cit.*, pp. 610, 611). On REM and LSD, *loc. cit.*, p. 614; on dexedrine sulfate, Rechtschaffen and Maron, cited by Dement in Jouvet, *op cit.*, p. 587. On alcoholism and REM-states, see R. Greenberg and C. Pearlman, *Delirium tremens and Dream Privation* (Washington, D.C.: Association for the Psychophysiological Study of Sleep, 1964). On REM sleep as not being necessary to the biological well-being of the *adult* animal, see Dement, *Modern Medicine, loc. cit.*, p. 198, and *American Journal of Psychiatry, loc. cit.*, p. 407.

34. Before Freud, Kant said "the lunatic is a wakeful dreamer" and Schopenhauer wrote "a dream is a short-lasting psychosis, and a psychosis is a long-lasting dream" (quoted in P. Radestock, *Schlaf und Traum, eine physiologish-psychologische Untersuchung*, Leipzig: Breitkopf und Härtel, 1879; see also M. Katan, "Dream and Psychosis: Their Relationship to Hallucinating Processes," *International Journal of*

Psycho-analysis, 41 [1960] 341–51; and other references in Kleitman, *Sleep and Wakefulness,* p. 106.

35. Dement has informed me (in correspondence) that he believes the analogue occurs also in females.

36. Is it possible that the truly fantastic answers college students sometimes write on examinations are evidence that note-taking in class was contaminated by dreams?

37. Karl Abraham, *Dreams and Myths;* Jane Harrison, *Epilegomena,* p. 32; Géza Róheim, "Fairy Tale and Dream," in *The Psychoanalytic Study of the Child* (New York: International Universities Press, 8 [1953] 394–403); W. H. R. Rivers, "Dreams and Primitive Cultures," *Bulletin of John Ryland's Library,* 1918, p. 26; Clyde Kluckhohn, "Myths and Rituals: A General Theory," *Harvard Theological Review,* 35 (1942) 45–79 (also in Bobbs-Merrill Reprint Series); and Alan Dundes, "Earth-Diver: Creation of the Mythopoeic Male," *American Anthropologist,* 64 (1962) 1032–51.

38. For the Bushman's "eternal dream time" (Elkin) see A. E. Jensen, *Myth and Cult among Primitive Peoples* (Chicago: University of Chicago Press, 1962, p. 117). Pater Wilhelm Schmidt, writes Jensen (p. 103), believed "mankind may have penetrated to the concept of the Highest Being in a purely rational way, even prior to any primal revelation." Ethnocentric condescension aside, with such intersubjective indeed crosscultural consensus apparently so widespread and for so long, and rational as well, why is it that ordinary rational proof is so lacking? Is He then, curiously, only to be found somehow inside? And what, epistemologically, is revelation? Given the discrepancy of wishful dreams and rational waking life, is theology then primarily our rationalizing dream-associations?

39. Classical writers have also had their say on dreams. Heraclitus seems to have been the first to note the public nature of waking life versus the private nature of dreaming; Aristotle shrewdly noted the lowered critical threshold in dreaming. For Herodotus on dreams as day-residues, see Godley edition of *History,* III: p. 329, bk. 7, sect. 16). The Greeks thought truly prophetic dreams passed through the "gate of horn" but deceitful dreams through the "gate of ivory" (*Odyssey,* Bk. 19, line 560). Jews traditionally believed that morning dreams just before awakening were "the ones that come true" (Louis Ginsberg, *The Legends of the Jews,* New York: Simon and Schuster paperback, 1961, p. 226). For a psychoanalytic view of another dream-function, see M. M. Willey, "Sleep as an Escape Mechanism," *Psychoanalytic Review,* 11 (1924) 181–83. The best ethnographic work on the subject is Jackson Steward Lincoln, *The Dream in Primitive Cultures* (Baltimore: The Williams and Wilkins Company, ?c1935; reprinted, New York: Johnson Reprint Corporation, 1969); for subsequent anthropological work on dreams see Weston La Barre, *Influence of Freud,* p. 316 fn. 55.

II

The First Men

RELIGIOUS behavior appears to be unique to man among all the animals. Further, religious behavior is present in all known human societies, past and present. It would therefore seem useful to explore the peculiar biology and ecology of the human species as a reasonable, if unexpected, way to help us arrive at an understanding of religious behavior. For this purpose it is logically necessary to extend our study back in time to those primates who may first be called functionally "human," the African Australopithecines, and to contrast them with other primate species.

There is now general agreement among anthropologists that the biologically most significant traits of man are his wholly terrestrial habitat, bipedality, meat-eating, sexual dimorphism, nuclear family and incest taboos, his culture, massive use of symbols and tools, and his peculiar social, economic, and psychological structure. It might be supposed that comparative primatological evidence, fast accumulating in the last two decades, were irrelevant to this project, since man is not descended from any living primate. But such comparative evidence nevertheless is useful, to describe alternative primate dispensations, and to silhouette the fact that the human is specifically one such primate dispensation. For this purpose, large primates, living in much the same region as early human-like primates, would be the most critically contrastive. Morphologically and genetically men are closest to the great apes; but *ecologically* early man was closer to the baboon. We can therefore better understand man by a glance at his contrasts with the baboon.[1]

Baboons (a term covering several cercopithecine *Papio* species) like man are largish terrestrial primates. Moreover, their habitat, south of the Sahara in Africa, includes the territory in which the first human-like primates arose. Baboons have several specializations adaptive to ground-living, notably the formidably long and sharp canines of adult males for the defense of the whole troop against predators. From birth to death, baboons live within the troop, never venturing away from it except in the case of temporarily near-ranging adult males and perhaps rarely a lone post-mature male expelled from the troop. But the lone animal probably cannot long defend itself against predators; has no further biological relevance to the closely knit social group; and females and juveniles always remain with the group. The baboon troop forages as a unit, and it is specifically to group life that sexual dimorphism and adult-juvenile differences are adapted.

That is, the total *biomass* of a baboon troop is distributed among a number of adult males who protect the group, a larger number of considerably smaller females to maintain the troop reproductively, and a number of juveniles demarked by pelage and other traits. Evidently both the larger number and distinctly smaller size of the females are adapted to the necessities of the troop foraging for food as a group, as is also the smaller number of adult males whose larger size requires more food to maintain them. The peculiar biomass of baboons is clearly the most economical one, ecologically, to balance protection and reproduction within total food availability. Too many adult males would bear nonadaptively upon the limited food supply by usurping the food of females and young needed to maintain the group, but only a single male with a harem of females would be insufficient for the protection of the group. Likewise, given the vicissitudes of terrestrial baboon life, reproductive replacement most efficiently employs a larger number of females who are smaller, again in relation to a limited food supply. Speedier motility than baboon troops have would doubtless tend to increase the total amount of food, but troop speed is limited by the biological necessity of protecting defenseless juveniles and gravid females. To this situation, the long fangs of adult baboon males are evidently an evolutionary response.

Baboons are almost entirely vegetarian, though they also eat insects, young birds and eggs that they encounter in their slow foraging, as well as an occasional small animal hiding immobile in the grass. However—perhaps surprisingly in view of the long male fangs—baboon troops never aggressively hunt and kill any of the large quadrupeds that are abundant in many of their areas. In fact, baboons often mingle peacefully with them, and even have a quasi-symbiotic mutual warning of the nearby presence of common predators, with sharp primate eyes supplementing an acute ungulate sense of smell. Again, slow baboon motility and the necessity of guarding the troop both lead us to suppose that baboon fangs are primarily protective in function.

Baboons have distinct food-based territoriality and are organized around a serial dominance-hierarchy of adult males. One should not, however, anthropomorphically imagine a baboon potentate and feudal subservients, for near co-dominance of males occurs; and, indeed, the relatively stable dominance hierarchy itself serves to minimize inter-male aggression by substituting dominance-communication for active fighting among adult males, which would certainly tend to reduce the number of necessary troop-protectors. Some students believe that the differing pelage of juvenile baboons, as well as the bright blue scrota of juvenile males, are "markers" which exclude these juveniles from either sexual or aggressive approach by adult males.

Certainly the oestrous female, with her highly colored and tumescent sexual skin, is a positive stimulus to sexuality, and at such times consort pairs may be temporarily formed, with very little fighting over females in oestrous. The muting of inter-male fighting within the troop is evidently adaptive to the necessity of having enough males in the troop to protect it. As for juvenile males, they are not functionally adult until the late eruption of the long canines—again as markers of their adult status— at which time only do they begin to find a place in the male dominance hierarchy. Less dominant animals tend to groom more dominant animals more often than the reverse, and it is probable that such grooming is part of the communication and fixing of the dominance-hierarchy. Biologically, baboon aggression is best directed outward, toward predators and toward other baboon troops that might compete for the same limited food supply, rather than inward within the troop.

A baboon mother with a newborn infant is the object of much interest on the part of other adult females, and adult males have an interested concern for the safety of all juvenile animals in the troop. After the short suckling period, a baboon mother almost never gives any kind of food to her infant. In fact, mothers have repeatedly been observed to grab food from their young and otherwise to treat them roughly. Similarly, dominance behavior in the larger males is implicated with food, since subservient animals will move away from a dominant male establishing a food claim (can this food "selfishness" have been another factor in the contrastive size of baboon males and females?). *Baboons do not share food*, any more than do arboreal fruit- and vegetation-eating primates or even the quasi-terrestrial anthropoid apes closest to man—unless perhaps it is a question of captured meat, which would be more worth fighting for. But even when one baboon by chance acquires meat food, the dominance hierarchy is still respected, a dominant animal expropriating, and a subdominant one quietly begging but at the dominant animal's choice.

Baboon fathers show no specific recognition of their own young, but only a generalized adult male attitude toward all juveniles. There are no stable "families" within the baboon troop, beyond the temporary breeding consorts, the significance of which is solely genetic. The "social fatherhood" of baboon males is limited to mere concerted troop protectiveness of the young, and the same protection is moreover extended also to the small adult females. Baboons are terrestrial but unlike hominids they are quadrupedal in gait. They are fanged but not carnivores. The contrast of many of these baboon traits with those of humans is marked, and these latter will be the subject of the rest of this chapter.

Since most primates are tree-living, but baboons and men ground-living, some great ecological change must have occurred to effect the differences between baboons and other monkeys, and between semi-terrestrial anthropoids and men. Besides deriving from different immediate primate origins (monkey versus ape), baboons and men have taken divergent terrestrial paths, since the same climatic event in their common territory has affected both species in diverse ways.

Recent finds are forcing a revolution in our views concerning human evolution, although experts are still arguing the finer significance of the new fossil evidence. The Australopithecinae—*Australopithecus africanus, A. robustus* ("Paranthropus"), "Zinjanthropus boisei" and possibly *Meganthropus paleojavanicus*—have been accepted by most authorities as hominids. But, in the view of some, the australopithecines are too recent to have been directly ancestral to man, while "Australopithecus prometheus" has been rejected as a user of fire, the earliest user being, to date, still Peking man.[2] The australopithecines were, in part, coexistent with an apparently still older form, *Homo habilis,* whose indisputable tool-using and larger brain firmly establish him as human and a probable speech user. The australopithecines therefore are now somewhat displaced by *Homo habilis* as the more probably direct ancestor of modern man. But the evidence is not yet all in, and evolution is a continuous process, so that we should not be surprised if more facts will revise views on minor points. The long-known Pithecanthropi—*Pithecanthropus erectus* and "Sinanthropus pekinensis" of Asia, to which some add *Homo heidelbergensis* of Europe—now take a place later in time than *Homo habilis.* "Telanthropus" of Africa is probably interstitial between the australopithecines and the pithecanthropines, while *Homo erectus* or Neanderthal man is probably an early sub-species of *H. sapiens,* specifically *Homo sapiens neanderthalensis,* to which group the African *Homo rhodesiensis* is evidently allied.

At Olduvai Gorge, where both *H. habilis* and australopithecines have been found, there is evidence of a major climatic change between earlier and later beds. Somewhat speculatively—although the differing monkey-ape *versus* human endpoints are well known, and each one of the transitions must be accounted for at some point in time—the following general picture may be described. Somewhere in the *Australopithecus-Homo habilis* area in Africa, man added the hunting of large mammals to the primate gathering of plant foods. The presence in African caves of both australopithecine and baboon bones has led to the question as to which was the hunter and which the hunted species.[3] We think that australopithecines were the hunters of baboons, and for several reasons. Firstly, australopithecines seem to have had a firm knee joint which first enabled hominids to *run* in hunting—versus the slow-moving quadrupedal baboon troops. Secondly, humans in the same area are still hunters, whereas even modern baboons have never become massively neo-carnivorous (in the sense of actively hunting large game as opposed to eating insects and merely passively encountered small or immature animals) despite their long fangs. Thirdly, australopithecine use of weapons in the bipedally-freed hands may have prevailed even over long baboon canines. And fourthly, a matter to be expanded on later, a differing *geographic* social structure made humans more mobile hunters than baboons in troops could be.

Hominid neo-carnivorousness is the major ecological event in the early formative history of mankind. Because meat is a far more concentrated food than vegetable materials, and hence more easily transported and more worth sharing, active animal-hunting meant that *for the first time among primates,* these early humans became habitual food sharers—an event of major biological significance. From physical evidence to be presented shortly it is evident that hominids had all-male hunting groups that left females behind during this activity. That males separated from females of the horde during the hunt was critically important not only for all subsequent human evolution but also for man's peculiar social nature, species-specific psychology and cultural institutions—in particular his religion. Hunting ecology, sexual dimorphism and human psychology are all closely related functionally.

Because animals are reproduced according to templates of complexly arranged amino acids, in the "information"-laden ribonucleic acids of parental chromosomes, each animal species tends to be replicated according to a standard pattern. Organisms never consciously or willingly plan a change in their evolutionary direction. Instead, they cope with change with what they have; and the changed environment selects for survival those random mutations best adapted to the environmental change. However, of necessity animals must be conservative of successful adaptations already achieved. Thus we should not say that our ground-living primate ancestors abandoned the trees, but rather that the trees deserted them.

During the East African Miocene, this indeed seems to have been what happened. The evidence of geology shows that, once or several times, slow climatic changes in the Miocene diminished the extent and density of jungles, and grasslands grew at their expense until in some places there were only scattered groves of trees in open savannas. Those monkeys and apes that retreated with the retreating jungles remained monkeys and apes. Those anthropoids that never quite abandoned their arboreal existence were ancestral to the modern great apes. In retaining successful adaptation to jungles, their modern habitat is consequently still restricted to jungles.

But other anthropoids, in order to preserve the old adaptation intact (Romer's Rule), migrated over increasingly open spaces to another forest territory. Modern African apes, the gorilla and the chimpanzee, are semi-terrestrial feeders, even though they still live in jungles and retreat to trees for protection and at night. It is reasonable to infer that the common anthropoid ancestor of bipedal australopithecines and semi-terrestrial apes, through supplemental ground feeding, was thus pre-adapted enough to cross open territory when necessary. Those successful and strong enough to defend the new groves, once reached, were the ancestors of the apes. Meanwhile other bands of anthropoids led a marginal existence in the competition for diminishing groves, and these were the precursors of the terrestrial Australopithecines and *Homo habilis* (a similar fate happened to some monkeys, and these became the ground-living baboons of Africa). It is not to be imagined that in either case this was a single "Just So" drastic event, but rather that these were the adaptive pressures that led different species of primates to take different directions.

Our ancestors were the ape-failures. They did not leave the trees because they wanted to but because they were thrown out, either by climate or by better apes. This would be a conservative ape's-eye view of things. But those migrant anthropoids which had gained successful enough adaptation to migrate over open country at all went on under these same pressures, selectively as individuals, to adapt still further to open country. These Miocene waifs that did not make the grade became the australopithecine or the *Homo habilis* ancestors of bipedal man.

Only new predicaments force new adaptations and change, and it was to such predicaments that the middling-size African hominids made progressive adaptation. Apes are known to use branches and thrown objects as weapons, and sometimes also to seize small animals and birds immobilized by protective hiding or helplessness in nests. Baboons in the open parks and grasslands also encounter such passive prey in their foraging. It was probably the richness of African grasslands in other mammalian species, baboons included, that enabled our hominid ancestors to survive in their changed environment. Two selective pressures advantaged these hominids to persist in the trend toward a permanently bipedal stance: to peer above the grasses to see predators and game, and to carry in their freed hands the weapons to use against both.

The specific size of australopithecines, relative either to their primate competitors, to their land predators, or to the game they hunted, was significant. They did not match some ape competitors in size or strength, but at the same time they were small and light enough to attain speed in the hunt. Only an initially lightweight anthropoid could remain upright constantly, run, and achieve adaptively a laterally stable knee joint; even today, after two million years of evolution, heavy football players easily abuse this still imperfected joint with lateral strains. Thus, close as they are in the many ways derived from a common anthropoid ancestry, gorillas and men took divergent evolutionary directions: the heavy and slow, though immensely powerful, vegetarian and still partly arboreal gorilla, in contrast to the lighter, smaller, fully bipedal and swifter neo-carnivorous hominids.

Besides being critically important for the evolution of a stable knee joint, the small size of early hominids had further implications. They were small and agile enough, and yet big enough—*at least in bands*—successfully to hunt animals. At the same time they were not clawed or fanged or fast enough to become lone hunters, as were some of the feline carnivores in the same territory. Thus, small hominids retained the same earlier primate gregariousness as did baboons, but for different reasons. Vegetarian terrestrial baboons live in troops primarily for protective reasons, but hominids had additionally to co-operate for the purposes of the hunt. A *group* of hunters was necessitated by the small size, anatomic defenselessness, inadequacy and weakness of the individual hunter in chasing and surrounding swift or dangerous prey—and yet the nature of the hunting group must have selected for the same muting of inter-male aggressiveness that we find in baboons and other multi-male primate groups with dominance hierarchies.

There must also have been some relationship between the small size of early hominids and the size and speed of the animals they hunted. It is possible to envisage an australopithecine group preying upon baboons that, for their own group-ecological reasons, stood their ground. But it is difficult to imagine even *Homo habilis,* with his known crude weapons and despite putative group organization, to have hunted, say, the abundant antelopes of Africa. We need much more archeological evidence of the animals that the most ancient hominids hunted, for such facts would be significant with respect both to their anatomy and to their social structure; *both ecology and social structure are ultimately to be critically important for an understanding of human religion.*

If *Australopithecus* had been overlarge, he would have needed correspondingly large amounts of food to feed him, yet he was not equipped to go it alone as a hunter—and even group hunting, initially with poor weapons, cannot be supposed to have been uniformly successful in providing plentiful meat. At the same time, hunted animals must have been large enough, or often enough successfully hunted, to make group hunting, with a still larger biomass to serve, effective. Similarly, gut length is necessarily greater in plant eaters like the ancestral anthropoids than in meat eaters like the emergent hominids, and some sense of the proportion of foods ancient man ate would allow us a basis for inference about such aspects of his changing anatomy, especially since a more compact digestive system would serve his adaptive need to be light in weight.

Gregariousness had advantaged arboreal primates in the main protectively. In fact, the combined tree-ground adaptations of some gregarious anthropoids like the gorilla in time allowed them a far greater size than that of the earliest paleontologically known anthropoid apes. But fruit can be picked, insects caught, and vegetable food gathered by the individual ape, male or female or juvenile. Hunting, however, as opposed to fruit eating, under ancient conditions must have required multiple-individual co-operation, especially in view of the inefficient weapons of early hominids.[4] The complex equation must therefore include variables for species-specific anatomy and bodily skill, individual hunter size, hunting-group size, biomass distribution, size and available number of the animals hunted, and such directly cultural factors as weapon type and efficiency.[5]

In this differential equation, only greater hunting efficiency (anatomical and social), better weapons (cultural), and larger hunted animals (ecological factors) would selectively allow for progressively larger individual hominids or affect variable group size. Therefore selective pressures on hunters would seem to be both on weapons and on more adaptive social organization, both affecting the development of culture. And cultural accomplishment in turn would be, reflexively, a selective factor on physique (only one among many of such examples of the influence of culture on biology). For example, would an age-long use of spears select for a more linear "asthenic" body type; the use of the bow, for a more broad-shouldered and muscular "athletosome"; and the later conditions of agriculture for a more "pyknic" peasant type of physique?[6] (Such at least would seem to be the case with Sioux bow-men as contrasted with Pueblo agriculturalists, both of the same race.)

In later times, Eskimos and certain east Africans are all primarily meat eaters, so that climate must also enter into the differences in body configuration between chunky compact Eskimos and tall linear East Africans —all members of the same species, but with different environmental problems of metabolic heat conservation versus heat diffusion. If so, then climatic factors must also have affected primitive *Homo habilis* and the australopithecines, since both lived in specific climates. Moreover, within the same African race of Negroids, is it possible that primitive hunting methods even continued to select for the virtually "australopithecine" size of modern African pygmies, versus the taller agricultural Negroes, versus the tallest Nilotic herders of them all? (Indeed, pygmy hunters and agricultural Negroes, and agricultural Negroes and herding Nilotes, are in symbiotic relations with one another in food exchange, so that the later picture is further complicated by inter-tribal socio-economic cultural factors). We would therefore conclude that climatic and cultural influences must also affect human biology, even that of primitive *Homo habilis* and the australopithecines, and hunting with alloplastic weapons developed from matter outside the species' genetic system is already a cultural phenomenon.

The greater complexity of hunting as compared with fruit eating, and the swiftly changing contingencies of the hunt, also evidently favored a change from closed, species-wide "phatic" ape cries—closed in the sense that each monolithic one of these cries can serve to display in the individual ape, and diffuse to the group, only one endocrine phatic state each: fear, anger, amorousness and the like—into the more elaborated communications of merely group-wide articulate speech. Hominid hunters need language. But not only in the hunt. The adaptive necessity of intense group life among aggressive hunters also demands better communication and management of both aggressive and erotic drives in early man. Not the "Cyclopean" nuclear family but hunting bands of co-operating adult males must be postulated for ancient African hunting—no less than for the hunting of huge mammals like mammoths and gigantic wild bulls by Old Stone Age man in the later European Pleistocene, even though *Homo neanderthalis* was by then far larger and stronger than *Homo habilis* had been.

Uncontaminated aggression can in fact serve erotic drives in many wild animals,[7] but not among human animals in whom primate sexuality and gregariousness are both greatly increased. Under primitive conditions, hunting, moreover, demands great physical aggressiveness—and yet, in the predicament of required group life for hunters, some management of raw aggression and arranged sexual claims were both absolute necessities.[8] For these reasons, we would infer that a hunting ecology, in its totality, pressed toward the formation of cohesive nuclear families within the band.[9] Other biological considerations, to be noted later, forced family exogamy, in which every individual must leave his infant family-of-origin for a new adult family-of-procreation—a social situation incidentally which also favored the "opening" of closed phatic ape systems into more flexible and society-diffused language.[10]

The hunting group economy favored, therefore, a progressively larger forebrain, not alone to increase hunting efficiency through better communication in more complex situations, but also to inhibit ingroup aggression and to direct it outward in the hunt. We believe that early man in this situation was already saddled with problems and inhibition-founded guilts concerning both his aggression and his sexuality—if for no other reason than that the earliest cave art, as we shall see, repeatedly mixed up hunting and sexuality symbolically, repeatedly confused men and animals, and invariably confounded fear of conscience (superego anxiety) with fear of reality (ego anxiety). It is also visibly rooted in some of the very anatomical changes that progressed with human evolution: *man's religion is intricately and inextricably tied up with the specific kind of animal that he is.*

It is imperative to see that hunting culture is a *culture.* That is, hunting posed new ecological conditions, *cultural conditions,* to which man's anatomy itself adapted. It is biologically wrong to suppose that men anatomically like ourselves slowly discovered culture, because what we have to begin with are only middling-sized, bipedal, but small-brained *Homo habilis* and australopithecines—whereas at the other end of the process we have big brains and many other traits besides to account for. *Our socioanatomical structure is in part the result of our early weapon-using hunting culture.* Bipedality plainly preceded big brains, for this the new fossil evidence incontrovertibly shows. And bipedal hunting plainly set the predicaments to which larger brains were progressively an adaptation.

Further, it is now clear that the decrease in size of the anterior teeth, related to progressively decreased prognathism, and the tripling of brain size both came *after* man first had tools and perhaps also fire. That is, smaller teeth and larger brains are consequences of the *changed ecologi-*

cal conditions created by the cultural use of hunting weapons, tools, and fire. Even the final perfection of the hand, with its longer and fully opposable thumb, may have been an adaptation responsive to the increased use of tools, since brachiating apes, although prehensile-fingered, are stub-thumbed. In the evolutionary sense, tool culture changed ape paws into human hands.[11] We need no longer seek, thus far in vain, a long-thumbed ape as ancestor of man, because the modern hand is the result of perhaps two thousand millennia of now archeologically established tool use in paleontologically proven bipeds, australopithecines and *Homo habilis*. But human evolution is not only anatomical. We have reason to believe that it is also involved with the invention of, for primates, strikingly new social forms.

No primates other than man are hunters. Any evolutionary explanation, consequently, must deal with the massive adaptive change which added meat eating to a vegetarian diet. Ancestral fruit eating had given early hominids no anatomical preadaptations to become land carnivores. This preadaptation, instead, was a social one. For other good adaptive reasons, their primate tree ancestors had been gregarious—and now the weakness of these small, grounded primates was a further factor pressing for a more intensified gregariousness, co-operation, and the forming of tight protective social groups. A quite parallel case is that of the monkey-derived baboon, which also has an intense gregariousness, such that the individual is never more than a few feet physically from the rest of the troop. The biological meaning of baboon gregariousness is evident in the autoplastic (genetic) evolution of male fangs: tight geographical gregariousness enables adult males to protect the whole "symbiotic" biomass of the troop. But baboon troops cannot be hunting bands—even despite their carnivorelike canines—because all forage slowly *en masse*.

The distinctions between these two grounded primates in Africa, baboons and early man, are critical. With weapons instead of fangs, hominid hunters adapt alloplastically, *culturally*. But these hunters made a further *social* innovation drastically modifying earlier primate gregariousness: *the temporary topological separation of males from females and young*. This part-time geographic discreteness of hunting males from females and young emancipated them from the identical impediments that prevented baboons from being hunters. Once again, we must not imagine a "Just So Story" of the single cataclysmic event. We would envisage, rather, a slow foraging anthropoid band from which, on the appearance from time to time of obtainable game, active males would gradually more and more detach themselves in the chase, and gradually for longer times if such activity were adaptive for the group, viz. in the obtaining of more effi-cient and concentrated and hence sharable meat food.

Such separation, often necessarily by considerable distances, brings with it a problem. Either the slow, remnant band must continue to forage in much the same closeby vicinity, perhaps unrewardingly, so it may be re-found, but is meanwhile more vulnerable to predators, or, now depleted of active males, it may tend to seek a familiar, more protected locality. Females and young can perhaps meanwhile remain gatherers, but at least the male hunters must be able to refind them. Hunting thus implies some understood focus for re-meeting, ideally one meanwhile safer for females and the young. Instead of *ad hoc* nesting where whole gorilla groups hap-pen to find themselves at night, hominid hunter-gatherers need some foyer where they may rejoin and to which gathered plant booty and animal prey can be transported.[12]

A differing sex-ecology eventuates in differing male physiques, since different adaptive pressures play upon males who hunt than upon females who do not. That ancient hominid females in fact did not hunt is further signalized in their own diverse specializations. In all kinds of *social* ani-mals, birds, and even termites, arachnids and insects, male-female and sometimes intersex differences in morphology are commonplace, depend-ing upon diverse functions in the mutually adapted and so to speak "sym-biotic" social group. The small hominid horde must have had at least as much inter-individual influence on sexual dimorphism as baboon troops have, though the specific dimorphisms would be adapted to a specifically human situation. There can be no question whatever that these differ-ences are reflected in contrasting male and female anatomy and physiology.

The human male has relatively larger muscles and bones, especially longer leg bones, larger hands and feet, less subcutaneous fat, a larger thyroid, larger lungs, and more red corpuscles per cubic centimeter than the human female. These dimorphisms obviously serve the massive spurts of energy that are needed for the hunting of animals. The fat-nakedness of males allows a more rapid diffusion of metabolic heat produced by the higher metabolic rate, though not body temperature, of human males. The same factor operates in greater human male body-linearity, relative both to chunkier adult females and to bulky and slower vegetarian goril-las. Again, the human loss of typical mammalian hair[13] over most of the body would also serve this same function of rapid diffusion of body heat. Gorillas can be bulky, and furred like all other primates, because they do not need to move fast in their food quest. That other tropical animals such as the elephant, the hippopotamus and the rhinoceros are also non-furred must be related to the great bulk of these herbivores, rather than to heightened heat-metabolism as in hominid hunters.

Assuming the normal primate and mammalian brown skin for early hominids in Africa, then local "racial" specialization in a still darker black color is further explainable functionally—for the rapid diffusion of body heat built up from the massive rapid movement incident to primitive hunting in a tropical climate. Fat-nudity, linearity, body glabrousness, and skin color therefore all argue the tropical origin of hominid hunters, evidently in Africa. The depigmentation of the skin in other human races, as an opposite specialization, would then be a later response to colder and less sunny climates than that of Africa, since too rapid a diffusion of body heat would not be adaptive in the cold climates of northern Europe and Asia, for Caucasoids and Mongoloids respectively.

Apparent contradictions to the principle of body hairlessness and metabolism in hominid hunters are worth pursuing. That Caucasoid males are hairier than Negroid and Mongoloid males suggests that the ancestral stock of Caucasoids moved into a colder climate before the process of body-hair loss had reached its completion, and that Negroid hunters, under continuing tropical conditions, continued to progress toward human glabrousness, as did also, for other reasons, the Mongoloids. That Caucasoid males are hairier than Caucasoid females would argue that the tropical conditions inducing adaptive glabrousness in African hunters ceased to operate in the colder latitudes of European hunters, and that better fat-clad Caucasoid females could progress farther toward human hairlessness because also they more characteristically enjoyed the advantage of caves and fire than did hunting males—for whom furs, too, in a cold climate would now seem a necessity, given both their greater exposure anatomically and climatically and prior partial loss of body hair. Certainly fire was very early known in the caves of China, if this is a factor in Asian glabrousness. But perhaps the matter is more complex than this, since male body hair in Caucasoids is a gerontomorphic trait; and endocrine factors may be further involved.

Primate comparisons may be useful in understanding human body-hairlessness also. Active, linear, small, furred primates like the gibbon have smaller body-surface ratios than larger, linear, glabrous man. Many primates have partly bare skins, on the face, chest, armpits, and elsewhere, that allow heat diffusion when the body is extended as in characteristic brachiating and feeding attitudes, but these parts are covered up when the animal bundles itself more compactly together to conserve body heat during the colder nights. By contrast, humans have long axial hair, which probably serves to reduce friction between the arm and torso against which it is more characteristically moved in economic activities, arms to the sides rather than raised in brachiation. Similarly, anthropoid hair is not notably longer on the head than that on other parts of the body, and a larger amount is evidently not needed to protect them from the sun in shady jungles. In general, human groups have wide geographic variability in hair form and body distribution, which must be regarded as the result of more widely varying environments among humans than among more uniformly furred tropical and subtropical primates. But the pan-human anomaly (for primates) of near body-hairlessness must still be explained on some ground uniformly affecting the hominids ancestral to man, and this factor we believe to have been early hominid hunting in tropical Africa.

In an earlier study, *The Human Animal,* I suggested that human neoteny[14] and self-domestication—possible within the peculiar protections of hominid society—are very prominent in human evolution. It will be evident now that discrete-sexed hunting provides the ecological context of such domestication and neoteny. Among ancestral African hominids, evidently only males hunted. For otherwise females would show the same adaptations that males do. On the contrary, however, hominid females specialized in the opposite direction toward femaleness, and thus provided the conditions in which human infants could specialize in prolonged infancy as well. For the conditions of domestication to operate, whether in animals or in humans, three criteria must be met: protection from natural wild enemies, a provided food supply, and human sexual selection. All three criteria are precisely met in the human situation.

Lionesses, for example, are as much hunters as male lions are, and some students even argue that lionesses at times do more hunting than lions because they also hunt for their cubs. By contrast, when the first male hunters bring home their kill to be shared by females, juveniles, and the post-mature or otherwise non-hunting individuals, then all these latter are domesticates to this degree removed from the operation of natural selection as in wild animals. The adaptations of the non-hunters then serve the uses of the whole social biomass, as initially did those of the hunting males. That is, they do not need to maintain in their physiques the adaptations to hunting that active males did, in order for the group to survive. Insofar as the human female—within the protection, food supply, and sexual selection provided by the male—is now freed for adaptation to other humanly desirable traits, she is the direct and literal "domesticate" of the human male. And not only for "feminine" traits sexually selected by the male, but also, in the differential survival of her offspring, for *female* traits that advantage her young protectively, in the kinds of human beings that can be born, and the kinds that survive.

Physiologically, the human female is adapted to the expenditure of energy at a lower rate but for a longer period than the human male. Both sexes have different fatigue patterns, and both respond with marked contrast to environmental heat conditions. By contrast with males, human females have more subcutaneous fat, and more fat reserves in general, a smaller stature, smaller bones and lungs and muscles—and, more significantly, permanent breasts (a trait of domestication also present in man's milch animals, long after the fact and paralleling the same model), and a wider pelvis (even though they are shorter-legged) than the males. Female specializations are evidently for the production and long care of the dependent young. The pregnant human female, heavy and short-legged and wide-hipped, is not very effective as a hunter of wild animals, certainly not of swift ones—and, biologically, should not be, of dangerous ones—and certainly not with rude weapons under primitive conditions. Indeed, she could not have specialized in maternity, as she manifestly has, had she had to hunt. But so long as she does not need to, it does not matter at all, adaptively. Instead of going out to hunt and kill wild animals, through her own special adaptations she does something perhaps more important biologically, the nurturing of the longer-dependent, increasingly neotenous, and increasingly big-brained human animal.

In many forms of life, notably among birds, the female is the arbiter in the acceptance or rejection of sexual suitors (hence the wide variety in plumage and color in male birds), whereas the lone human female, being smaller and weaker than the male, is to some degree sexually vulnerable to all adult males. At the same time, males, necessarily larger and stronger owing to the selective pressures of hunting, may prefer and hence sexually select for more docile and feminine females whom they may dominate without further ado—but whom they must protect from the sexual aggression of other males if their own individual traits are to be significant in selective breeding. Reciprocally, to the degree that they could, hominid females may have sexually selected for such protective traits in the males with whom they bred. Thus males selected for docility, females for aggressiveness, in the other sex.

These traits have an endocrine base, and they are also evinced in differential morphology. Phylogenetically, one change, conspicuous in the evolutionary series of hominid fossils, has been the progressive reduction of the supraorbital ridges. This change has certainly been related to the reduction of prognathism (hand feeding, adaptive head globularity, perhaps also tools and the use of fire), with a consequent change in angle of muscle action and a reduced need to buttress against muscle pull the thin-shelled orbits with heavy brow bone. However, the decrease in size of brow ridges can not be accounted for solely by the muscle mechanics of the face. There must also have been an endocrine component of the phenomenon. For brow ridges also decrease in domestic animals such as the unrelated pig, cow, horse and cat, none of which was selectively bred for smaller brow ridges as such.

It seems, rather, that in his domestication of mammals, man selected for more docile and manageable individuals, for altered milk and meat production, etc., all of which traits were in fact related to unknown but concomitant endocrine differences. Interestingly enough, the same is true also for rats, in which the endocrine differences are well known. Wild rats have larger brow ridges and larger faces than tame rats; and wild rats have larger adrenal glands, are more prone to rage, and are much harder to handle than domesticated rats. In selecting for more tame animals, man has also unwittingly selected for smaller adrenals, and smaller adrenals are in turn partly responsible for anatomical differences in the skull.

Thus a number of mechanisms may be operating in the progressive evolution of hominids, as evidenced in the meaning of this one trait only, brow ridges. For example, one might infer from adrenal and brow ridge differences that hominid hunters were closer to natural selection for aggressiveness than were females more domesticated in this trait and functionally less in need of it. At the same time, sexual selection by males for female docility, and by females for male aggressiveness, would be operating toward the observed dimorphously dissimilar ends. Hence the smaller brow ridges of the female may be a concomitant of her greater docility, relative to both traits in the male—for all that he too may have been selected for progressively less endocrine irascibility.

Less ape-browed individuals, then, may have been just as much selected under early human conditions as were bigger-brained ones with greater cortical control. Indeed, brow ridges in the service of large prognathous jaws, versus relatively larger brain cases, are functionally as well as mechanically antagonistic in the skull. That the process of brow reduction is, in males, incomplete, suggests that males still need aggressiveness for socially useful ends, but under progressively greater cortical control, whereas the special socio-biological functions of females culminate in morphologically smaller brow ridges. One might even speculate whether the ancient traditional social organization of the Sinitic branch of man, the greatly extended patrilocal family and its aggression-suppressing requirements, in contrast to nuclear-family oriented virilocal Europeans, may have operated in producing different racial results with respect to brow ridges! If so, in an extreme case, this would be only another cultural factor operating selectively upon physical morphology—but of course we must already suspect that the complex process is probably "over-determined," that is, affected by multiple causes.

In any case, we must be prepared to find human culture a species-specific factor in human selection, inasmuch as culture creates new conditions to which physical traits selectively adapt. Thus, selective ecological pressures on aggressive but co-operative hunters, as well as differential sexual selection, and even "social" selection under changing conditions, may all be implicated in the observed differences between ancient and modern, male and female, Caucasoid and Mongoloid brow ridges—and these be related, too, to the complex jaw versus brain-case evolution of the human skull. It is probable that many other human traits, if persistently enough studied, would give us the same wealth of insight that the apparently insignificant brow ridge is capable of yielding. That we may be mistaken in our initial judgment concerning the relative importance of various factors should not militate against this kind of holistic thinking about man.

Australopithecines, despite a bipedality suitable for hunting, nevertheless had only ape-size brains. Hominid skulls placed in evolutionary time sequence show a striking and progressive increase in brain size. The new "hunting ecology" of hominids, therefore, evidently entailed an intensified social symbiosis placing an adaptive premium on larger forebrains—not only to invent better tools and weapons, and not only to manipulate and store up the developing symbolisms of human speech, but also to filter, qualify and modulate unedited raw hindbrain impulses of erotism and aggression. The continuing adaptiveness of social life, even under changed conditions, evidently continued selective pressure toward the same ends in still later hominids and humans. These are functional considerations. There are also anatomical ones.

Male specialization for successful hunting and the provision of more concentrated sharable meat food was the enabling factor behind the increased dimorphism of the female pelvis, a domesticated trait not suitable for and not relevant to natural selection in hunting. Further, inasmuch as female specializations were in turn the enabling factor behind the increasing infantilization of the infant, hunting ecology is ultimately behind not only human anatomy and sexual dimorphism but also the human neoteny that is the basis of human culture. The widened pelvis has the function of producing not bigger-bodied but bigger-brained infants, and the massive human specialization in forebrain transformed man into a culture-bearing, learning animal.

The human infant is normally born head first not only mechanically but also metaphorically. Fully one seventh of the baby's birth weight is brain. There have been progressive changes favoring maximal brain volume in the neonate, that is, a reduced face and jaw allowing relative increase in brain case in an increasingly globular skull. But there is evidently an upward limit to the absolute size of a skull that can be born even through a dimorphously enlarged female pelvis. Consequently, relative to other animals, human infants are all born so to speak prematurely when this mechanical maximum for the species is reached, and babies must continue their still unfinished brain growth postnatally during a period of helpless dependency. Only much later can the body afford to catch up, because brains are needed *from the beginning* for the business of becoming a new human being; indeed, the face-braincase and body-brain proportions are all plainly directed to this end.

Brain comes first. With so much emphasis on the production, both prenatally and postnatally, of a huge brain, and so little on the unfinished rest of the body, the function of all these changes is manifest. Even the final myelin-sheathing of the nerves is not complete until about thirty-six months. From infant to adult, the skull height doubles, for in the topography of a baby's skull the face and jaws also are almost only an afterthought to the in every way emphasized early preparation of a huge brain. Only postnatally does the tiny body increase greatly to its adult size: torso length triples, arm length quadruples, and even the humanly long leg quintuples in length from baby to man. It is to this strikingly unfinished bodily dependency that the human female's specialization in maternity is the response.

Technically, the human baby is the domesticate of the female, with respect to protection and food supply. In this, the major adaptation to post-uterine life is the sucking reflex, one of the few responses neurologically ready in striated muscle at birth. Among primates in a phylogenetic scale, the infant is suckled for a progressively longer and longer time, in inverse proportion to its non-preparation and infantilization at birth. Among primitive tribes, the baby is suckled ordinarily for at least two years, and notably longer than this among some primarily meat-eating modern tribes such as those in central Siberia.

Physically, the literal domestication of the baby is evidenced in the neoteny of his feeding and self-protective functions. Likewise, his greatly delayed sexual maturity, with the profound significance this has for human culture, is another consequence of his neotenous domestication. Human fathers permit the oral dependency but not the sexual competition of their sons within the nuclear family, hence the selective pressures favoring sexual neoteny have resulted in a still longer dependency and learning period in humans. Thus, ultimately, both specialized mothers and fathers are responsible for the biological neoteny of their young in the human family. For the purposes of the present study, it may be well to emphasize in anticipation the thesis that human neoteny not only provides conditions for learning both of group culture and individual character, *but also forms the experiential matrix for magic and religion, and indeed for the scientific world-view as well.*

Male hunting and sharing of the meat kill changes the survival conditions not only of morphologically feminized females and infantilized infants, but also of other members of the hominid group, the disabled and the post-mature. We must not expect that under archaic conditions this ecological burden could have been very great. Nevertheless, the maintenance, by hunters, at the home focus, of males disabled through hunting or otherwise unfitted for hunting, would greatly change the conditions of survival and genetic fate of home males. And not only that. The activities of home males could at times change the "cultural environment" of the whole society, including that of male hunters.

If all males were hunters, and if hunters had time only to hunt and to breed, not much change in a hunting culture could be expected to occur. But if "biological leisure" from hunting permitted, say, a hunt-crippled male to stay behind and invent a fire-hardened point on a long wooden spear to replace a thrown or hand-wielded club or rock; and then to invent a sharpened stone point for the spear; and then, say, a myopic or short-sighted male to improve the fineness of a stone point necessary for a newly invented arrow and bow (such as occurred in the African Aurignacian or Capsian period)—all usable by the hunter at greater stalking distances limited by his comparative speed in running, or at progressively greater protective distances from dangerous prey—then the hunting success and even the survival of the hunter would be enhanced, and hence the survival potential of the whole group. The fact is that the very myopia of the male that disadvantaged him for the hunt would be precisely the trait that enabled him to make finer weapon points. Genetically, then, there would be a "balanced polymorphism" among myopic males and keen-sighted hunters in the group. Meanwhile, if Hephestus was lame, he nevertheless won Aphrodite. The first division of labor was by sex, probably of male hunters and female gatherers. But variety is the life of evolution, and further specialization would advantage the survival of the *group.*

In the evolution of man away from the other anthropoids, there is also a critical change in the nature of the group. In monkeys and apes, the social group is usually structured into one serial dominance-hierarchy. The adaptive function of the dominance hierarchy appears to be the minimizing of male ingroup aggression over food and sex and the maximizing of the male function of protection against outgroup competition, both of which systems tend to operate through symbolic gesture and threat-displays, not usually actual fighting. By contrast to the single dominance hierarchy, among all human groups there is an emergence of nuclear families. It is suggested that the human father's social paternity is asserted through his increasing functional success as a food-getter; that is as a hunter, the provider of a concentrated food that partly emancipates the female as an individual food-gatherer, through (for primates, anomalous) food sharing, heightens the male-female bond; and simultaneously permits the respective female-infant specialization. Social paternity in a family depends on a stability of male-female relationship which, to judge from all later forms of the family, may be as much *economic* as sexual. The perception of uterine siblinghood and hence the origin of conceptual kinship would likewise depend on this initial stability of the family.

Human group-ecology has changed in other ways too. Baboons eject old males from the foraging group when they can no longer exercize their group-protective sexual function. But if, among hunting humans (since evolution advances by tiny steps), there were even a slightly greater survival of post-mature males and females, then this condition also would advantage the group—again with selective pressure for large, remembering brains to preserve group lore. Contact with past group experience, both in problems and answers, is the essence of culture. And since the variety of answers, to progressively different questions in the varying environments encountered in man's spread, would advantage groups differentially, then fixed instincts adapted to one ecological niche would be gradually replaced, selectively and advantageously in human groups, by more labile adaptively-invented culture. Human neoteny embodies not prepared adult-adaptive instincts but a greater freedom and curse, labile learning from others. And some human *drives* (not "instincts") mature in their operation only after the influence of culture has long been brought to bear upon the individual. Thus man is both the heir and, to a degree, the continuing slave and child of the past, as the influence of the cultural fathers upon the individual progressively increases.

For in the random blind speciation of culture traits, all traits are not necessarily adaptive to the outer environment. And some parts of culture are autistically "adaptive" only to society-posed predicaments and inner anxieties of men. Our abundant witnessing of anti-adaptive traits in cultures,[15] including our own, must force us to this conclusion concerning their blindness—despite the blow to narcissistic rationalism and tribalism that this admission constitutes. Culture possesses authority, but not necessarily truth. With symbols and ideologies we adapt on a level different from that of animal genes. But even the random mutations of animal genes are not all necessarily adaptive for the animal species. Our brains are no more omniscient concerning the total environment than are chromosomes. The seeming eternal truth in culture is only an artifact of our neoteny and needful learning. We think it demonstrated that culture traits and genes equally share random mutation, ultimately subjecting all cultural "species" of men like all species of animals to inexorable natural selection.

NOTES

(II The First Men)

1. Sherwood Washburn and Irvin DeVore, "Social Behavior of Baboons and Early Man," in S. L. Washburn (ed.), *Social Life of Early Man,* Viking Fund Publications in Anthropology, 31 (1961) 62–71; "The Social Life of Baboons," *Scientific American,* 204, #6 (June 1961) 62–71; Irvin DeVore and K. R. L. Hall, "Baboon Ecology," pp. 20–52, and *idem,* "Baboon Social Behavior," pp. 53–110, both in Irvin DeVore (ed.), *Primate Behavior* (New York: Holt, Rinehart and Winston, 1965); and John Buettner-Janusch, *Origins of Man* (New York: Wiley and Sons, 1966, pp. 268–74).

2. Kenneth P. Oakley, "Use of Fire by Neanderthal Man and his Precursors," in G. H. R. von Koenigswald (ed.), *Hundert Jahre Neanderthaler 1856–1956* (Utrecht: Kemink en Zoon, 1958, pp. 267–69); H. S. Harrison, "Fire-Making, Fuel, and Lighting," in C. Singer, E. J. Holmyard, A. R. Hall [and T. I. Williams for II–V] (eds.), *A History of Technology* (New York: Oxford University Press, 1954–58, 5 vols., I:216–37).

3. S. L. Washburn, "Australopithecines: the Hunters or the Hunted?" *American Anthropologist,* 59 (1957) 612–14. If humans hunted baboons, perhaps they succeeded because they were "species-ignorant" of the meaning of baboon phatic territorial cries; or, if they understood these they succeeded because of the useful heresy of not obeying or responding to them. If hominids at that time used referential language, in this situation too it would have been more adaptive than animal cries.

4. A provocative book about paleolithic hunters: Andreas Lommel, *Die Welt der frühen Jäger, Medizinmänner, Schamanen* (München: D. W. Callwey, 1965); a vivid reminder of the conditions of primitive hunting, Elman R. Service, *The Hunters* (Englewood Cliffs: Prentice-Hall, 1966); see also R. B. Lee, I. DeVore and Jill Nash (eds.), *Man the Hunter* (Chicago: Aldine, 1968). But the classic work is Åke Hultkrantz, "Type of Religion in the Arctic Hunting Cultures: A Religio-ecological Approach," in H. Hvarfner (ed.), *Hunting and Fishing,* (Luleå: Norbottens Museum, 1965, 265ff.); also "An Ecological Approach to Religion," Ethnos, 31, 1-4 (1969) 131-50.

5. Important recent works affecting the general viewpoint presented: F. Clark Howell and François Bourlière (eds.), *African Ecology and Human Evolution* (Chicago: Aldine Press, 1963); and S. L. Washburn (ed.), *Social Life of Early Man* (Chicago: Aldine Press, 1961).

6. Alice Brues, "The Spearman and the Archer—An Essay on Selection in Body Build," *American Anthropologist,* 61 (1959) 457–69, reprinted in A. Montagu, (ed.), *Culture and the Evolution of Man* (New York: Oxford University Press, 1962, pp. 202–15). Beyond anthropologists' general agreement that culture sets new ecological conditions for selection, Frederick S. Hulse gives a number of specific examples in *The Human Species* (New York: Random House, 1963).

7. Aggression and sexuality are so closely related in birds indeed that exposure of special markers or special ethological behaviors are necessary to communicate the fact that apparently aggressive behavior is really sexual in intent.

8. On sexual tolerance among primate males, see DeVore, *Primate Behavior,* pp. 196, 203, 207 and 455; see also 183, 471. Note that among baboons (p. 38) and howler monkeys (pp. 287, 617–18) *membership in the group* is a prerequisite to

coitus, and individuals do not change groups in these closed systems. By contrast, humans must leave the nuclear family, and exogamy rules may extend to ever-larger groups with each generation as the remembered ancestor of the common descent group recedes in time. Besides having direct biological significance, such exogamy also favors the *spread* of group-knowledge or culture.

9. Judgments concerning the family are governed by the following considerations. Discernment of uterine siblinghood requires dependency of sufficient duration, and adequate birth rate, for one child to identify with and to rival another. But social paternity depends on a stability of male-female relationships, in part *or even predominantly* economic, though non-seasonal sexuality is an important but not exclusive part of such relationship. Encumbrance by offspring foments a more leisurely foraging by females, but non-encumbrance fosters more active male ranging in the hunt; thus the division of labor by sex and further sexual dimorphism are derived from a division of sexual functions, *viz.* hunting versus reproduction and nursing. The evidence is that neither the single-family male, with only primitive weapons, could be a big-game hunter alone; nor, without control of sexuality could a familyless horde of hunters cohere, given the intensification of both mammalian sexuality and nurture in humans; and, besides, proto-human anthropoids were probably already gregarious primates, as indeed their nearest African relatives, gorillas and chimpanzees, and their fellow-terrestrials, baboons, all still are. Countenance is also lent to the family-cum-society position on hominid hunters by the earliest demographic data we have, that on the Mesolithic deer-hunters of Star Carr, whose at least minimal (winter hunting) group was about four families of some five members each, all encamped together on one crannog or wooden bog-island. Larger aggregations also depend on economic-ecologic factors: Star Carr evidenced c. 13 persons/100 mi.², the early agricultural village of Jarmo, 2737, and Sumer, 5000 (Robert J. Braidwood and Charles A. Reed, "The Achievement and Early Consequences of Food Production: A Consideration of the Archeological and Natural-Historical Evidence," *Cold Spring Harbor Symposia on Quantitative Biology,* 22 [1957] 19–31).

10. On exogamy and language, see Weston La Barre, *The Human Animal* (Chicago: University of Chicago Press, 1954, pp. 167, 305); the "opening" of human speech may be related to the opening of the endogamous primate band.

11. The "precision grip" of baboons is like that of men (Buettner-Janusch, p. 268) so that, if baboons had been bipedal, they presumably could have enjoyed all the advantages of fully bipedal handedness. But the more swiftly perfectible alloplastic weapon versus the slower evolution of the autoplastic canine, and the separability of males in human hunting groups versus baboon troops, together made the difference. The non-human use of "tools" is unquestioned, and yet there are distinctions. The caddis insect *Hydropsyche* builds an underwater seine to catch food, but the net is made from its own metaplasm and is not an alloplastic tool. The *Ammophila* wasp uses a small pebble to tamp down the soil over its nest tunnel, but this is an instinctual not a cultural act; the *Oecophylla* ant's use of its own larva (moved back and forth in the adults' mandibles while the larva secretes silk strands to unite leaf edges pulled together by adult ant chains) does not quite fit our criteria for "tool" either (Ross E. Hutchins, *Insects,* Englewood Cliffs: Prentice-Hall, 1966, pp. 180, 43 and 201–2). A chimpanzee can fit two sticks together to reach a banana, but this is *ad hoc* insight, not traditional culture. Human tool use has all the features these infra-human uses lack; and for the rest, the great quantity and variety of human tool-uses constitutes a real qualitative change of phase.

12. Since tools can be, and usually are used in a sitting position, there is much to be said for Hewes's argument that *carrying food* was a significant impetus to bipedalism (Gordon W. Hewes, "Food Transport and the Origin of Hominid Bipedalism," *American Anthropologist* 63 [1961] 687–710, p. 688; also "Hominid Bipedal-

ism: Independent Evidence for the Food-carrying Theory," *Science* 146 ✕3642 [1964] 416–18). Hewes does not accept Dart's argument that the use of weapons favored a change to bipedalism. However, the weapon-using and food-carrying theories are not necessarily incompatible, since the activities may have reinforced one another in shaping bipedality (note the theory that the first "clothing" was a weapon- and tool-carrying belt—which would leave hands free for carrying food). Shared *carrion* could be consumed on the spot by the undivided group; but if the larger-sized males *actively hunted* (which would take them afield from the foraging band) large and swift animals (which females encumbered by pregnancy and nurselings could not pursue) and then transported the weapon-killed food back to the lair, we have meat food-sharing doubly behind bipedalism and also significant as a further explanation of dimorphism and sexual division of labor. Therefore splitting of the group in hunting seems to me a critical issue.

13. Weston La Barre, "Comments on the Human Revolution," *Current Anthropology,* 5 (1964) 147–50, also *Bobbs-Merrill Reprints in the Social Sciences,* 1965; see also on human hairlessness *Current Anthropology,* 7 (1966) 201–3 where these arguments are expanded. William Montagna points out (personal conversation) that "glabrous" here should mean not "hairless" but, strictly speaking, only the absence of coarse visible hair, since even a "bald" man's scalp is covered with fine barely-visible lanugo-like hair. The suggestion of Desmonde Morris that man is hairless because of a cetacean-like *marine* phase in East Africa I regard as farcical (Weston La Barre, review of M. F. Ashley Montagu [ed.], *Man and Aggression* [New York: Oxford University Press, 1968] in *American Anthropologist,* 7 [1969] 912–15).

14. La Barre, *Human Animal,* pp. 303–6. Neoteny could scarcely develop in a solitary primate; and it is still anti-adaptive insofar as adult members of the group must bear the additional burden of the individual with prolonged human infancy. Therefore neoteny must in some way ultimately benefit the *group, viz.,* pooled experience transcends knowledge independently obtainable by the individual, hence the adaptive function of prolonged youth is to give the animal time enough to learn. Individual neoteny is the group's way of accumulating and preserving its adaptive lore of past experience (cf. S. L. Washburn and D. A. Hamburg, "The Implications of Primate Research," in DeVore, *Primate Behavior,* 607–22, pp. 612–13).

15. See discussion of Burridge, Harris, and Frazer in Ch. VIII.

III

The First World

It IS very doubtful that any wild animal, in need or under duress, ever imperiously commands its environment to change and adapt to the animal's needs. Nor does a wild animal seem ever to beseech the environment to love, take pity on, or care for it—for to do either, in place of adaptive behavior of its own, would swiftly prove anti-adaptive, the environment being what it is. Nevertheless, on occasion, these two attitudes of magic and religion are precisely those that the human animal, in need or under duress, abundantly manifests. Magic and religion, then, may be only species-specific responses, peculiar to this kind of animal, to which it is somehow conditioned, as somehow apposite behavior that somehow *does something for him.*

We can see now the acute relevance of human biology to these psychological responses and adaptations, beyond the merely physical aspects of neoteny and domestication noted earlier. As a neotenous domesticated animal, the human baby does not immediately or very significantly meet the material environment to which in some degree he must later be adapted as an adult. Instead, in his most formative period, the effective environment of the infant is *other people,* in particular his long-nurturant and protective parents. The experiential matrix of his later responses in magic and religion thus lies in these traits so conspicuous in human biology. This is a more relevant use of biology. It is not in the elusive pseudo-evolutionary history of religion as a quasi-organism that we will find understanding, for this is a misleading analogy. More rewarding is a study of the characteristic and ascertainable life history of the human individual, developing as an authentic organism within his peculiarly human "environment." Hence the present inquiry concerns the biological basis of the capacity and the propensity for magic and religion in man, which is a legitimately biological affair since only man manifests these behaviors.

Human pregnancy is long in absolute terms, but less so relative to human longevity; and still less so considering the developmental distance to be covered, and the functional prematurity of the baby's birth in preparation for the business of becoming human. For the brain, maximally big within mechanical limits at birth, continues growth during an appreciable postnatal period. Is there any significance in the very fact of a big brain at birth as a real basis for quite early experiencing? We consider that there is, that the significance can be expressed psychologically, and that the experience is verifiable. Just as the brain grows physically, the mind grows psychologically through its specific situational experiences. Within the womb the baby is orginally totally "omnipotent" with respect to need and the gratification of need. Every metabolic wish is continuously granted. This world is biologically contrived to be his. He is a god, blissfully at one with the world he knows. It is a problemless environment; he owns his universe; there is no Other.

This psychological picture would seem far-fetched were it not for overwhelming evidence that the experience is deeply registered in the organism at least as a feeling tone; and it is precisely the biological exaggeration of brain that is the substrate for registering inchoate and archaic pre-verbal experience. Clinically, it is the experience-time to which in fact some schizophrenics return, if deeply disturbed in their first postnatal learning, the dependent oral adaptation to the first Other, the mother. Some catatonics even take a literally fetal posture. Ideationally, the schizophrenic state as we know it clinically is one of complete narcissism, self-concern and magic omnipotence, with feeble or absent ego boundaries, so that the self and the fantasied world are one. The schizophrenic is a fetus that is yet in the world. And the nightly dream, when we withdraw from the world, is an analogue of this psychosis that we all know.

Concerning the extravagantly heightened mammalian dependency of the unfinished organism, biologically there can be no doubt, for schizophrenia is the psychological artifact of desperately unmet and overwhelming biological needs. But this is not all our evidence. In the mystical state some individuals can at times massively regress to a condition of de-individuation, to the "oceanic feeling" in which Self and Not-self are one in pantheistic harmony and union. The mystical state is an authentic phenomenon psychologically. It is also a cross-cultural phenomenon ethnographically: in Indian religious symbolism, the retreat to a desireless

Nirvana is explicit. "O thou jewel in the flower of the lotus!" in Buddhist symbolism means literally the desireless fetus in the womb.

At birth the baby is mostly blind wish and organic demand. He greets the light with his first platonic cry of rage at this imperfect world; there is no doubt that the newborn baby's face is flushed with a towering and total anger. He learns anguish and anxiety through his first frustration. Gone is the Golden Age in an unforgotten Eden. Soon, again he mostly sleeps. Interestingly, new evidence indicates that a far larger portion of the newborn infant's sleep-time is spent in active dreaming than is the case by the time of adolescence or in adulthood, when dreaming is only episodic. Only the painful problem of hunger awakens the baby, and he is quite willing to announce his state of mind concerning the situation. And again he sleeps, ignoring the world for his dreams.

Birth is the first harsh meeting with reality, the first experience of problem and pain. The infant organism must promptly learn to breathe and to exercise a new anatomically prepared method for oxygenating blood. His body now has independent circulation, independent heat-homeostasis, and many other complex functions to perform besides. It is his first state of being a person, an individual, an independent organism. Normally, the species-elaborated maternity of the human mother, phys-iologically prepared anatomically and hormonally and in other intricate biochemical ways, promptly meets her baby's inescapable requirements. It is necessary to realize that the normal mother enjoys a distinct sensual gratification in suckling her child. It is pleasure that binds her love, organic love as real as the biological process. With a loved child, the mother achieves her deepest femininity. With a loving mother, the baby is placated into the burden of living in this world. Mother and child are psychologically symbiotic, theirs a shared narcissism that is invincible.

Beyond the struggle of birth, then, there are further real functional problems. And problems pose the possibility of their non-solution. But breathing, heartbeat, digestion and heat control are mostly autonomic and anatomical, and physiology soon proceeds automatically without need for thought. Sucking, however, is the first situation in which the baby must *do something* with striated, consciously controlled muscles. Success at this basic biological task shapes the first adaptive layer of the ego, *learned* in coping with the world. Later—and not unreasonably if that is its growth limit—this archaic ego will at times attempt to cope with the world in the same way, though now inappositely to a larger extra-human world of things. Magic is, thus far, an oral-context adaptation: the magic cry summons succorance, coerces reality, and the inchoate infant ego emotionally consumes the world.

But some babies, in a state of marasmus,[1] refuse to suckle. In un-willingness to meet the new task, this stubborn *preference* for an earlier state is a literal death *wish* that ends in death. Similarly, the schizophrenic stubbornly refuses to meet the hateful and frustrating world psychologically, if his needs have not been comfortingly and pleasurably gratified. He will know no Other, ever, unless this first biologically significant fragment of reality, the mother, can organically love him in his first need. Here is the first note of our tragic *vulnerability to people* and to their human imperfections. The condition of being human is also the possibility of being psychotic. For at each growth stage, only the appropriate kind of love assuages the anguish of new need. Every failure of Eros to lead us to a newer and more difficult integration with each more complex Other, means a crippling arrest of growth, a frightened retreat to an earlier known and safer but now less problem-adequate position, and a part-death that is a triumph of Thanatos. For at each stage we must adapt or die—or at least stay alive only at a limited level that is the death of future potential. All people have some psychic scars that inhibit and distort action in new encounters and situations. More extremely, psychotics and neurotics mutilated in their growth, are two forms of psychic living death. They live, but only like the wasp-stung caterpillar[2] that can never metamorphose into a resplendent butterfly.

To live adaptively in this world and to grow psychologically, the child must relinquish his seductively gratifying infancy, and learn to live with frustration.[3] For the rest of the world does not, in fact, behave as the first-known reality, mother, does. Each new kind of reality we encounter invariably frustrates and always disappoints the godlike will we start with. To deal adequately with each emergent new reality we must continually replace *hubris,* or overweening narcissistic arrogance, with a more service-able *aretē,* or real functional power.[4] Interestingly, this new learning is initiated by certain behaviors of mother herself. Sometimes she is there, sometimes she is not. At times the magic cry brings suitable automatic obedience to the baby's wish—yet, even so, this magic act requires of him some action and some sense both of himself and of the otherness of his only known world, his mother. Unease is his first awareness of himself; and frustration, the encounter with the obduracy of the Other.

Through this experience, the infant gradually learns to discern dim ego boundaries. Somehow the painful need is within himself, and some-how the rescue from it comes from outside. Because of its succor, there-fore, he can love this outside part-world—indeed, if he can later love the mater-ial world, it is perhaps literally through transference, with a libidinal residue from this first successful coping with mater as a phenomenon. Sometimes, he feels, he can command its gratifying presence, and indeed he really does, but experience teaches him that sometimes also he really can not. He learns his first lesson in biology, so to speak, concerning what is inside his skin, and what outside. The infant is forced to discriminate out of his undifferentiated self-world a *separate* world beyond his wish and will, but without giving up organic id demands lest the bargain be worthless. Psychologically, a new function and consciousness emerge, a case-hardened tuition of raw need: the problem-taught ego, rewarded, has learned. Ideally this executive ego—increasingly disenchanted, matter-of-fact and acerb—will grow in power as its grows in discipline; and in scope, with knowledge, for the rest of a man's life. Here, the infant begins to discern the difference between subject and object: *ob-ject,* that which literally is "thrown athwart" his will, and *sub-ject,* that which is "cast under" him as the ground of his being.*

* The "ground of being" theologians talk about is, of course, one's own physical body, temporarily on loan from the material universe. As "Creator" only *parents* are the genetic "ground of being"—but parts of parents *are* embryologically oneself, never in this sense "outside" but a living continuum with oneself. Meanwhile, the environment is the source of life energy, truly once-outside but also now truly inside organically; but the physical environment is not the organizer or father of one's being. To name the personified cosmos one's father or "ground of being" in this derived sense is not to know one's own father, and to confound one Other (father) with another Other (cosmos). The universe is only the *location* of one's life, not its "ground" as organic Creator—and, besides, there are two of these Creators, genetically. To become metaphysical is *not to know what we are talking about.* Subjects and objects and *kinds of objects* must be discriminated and kept apart: we begin to philosophize when we no longer know what our words mean. In this context, theology is really, ignorantly and unwittingly, discussing human biology under the pretense of discussing a grandiose cosmology—actually discussing the "facts of life" after having quite illegitimately identified two distinct Others, father and cosmos, as One. The theologian here is a poor biologist, because he has not adequately located his subject matter.

Of course, since the body is the physical locus or psychological focus of pain, frustration, anxiety and guilt, one can mislearn to hate and fear the body, and to lay the emotional ground for world-hating platonism. But thus to hate the body is a twisted metaphysic, based on the assumed legitimate "omnipotence" of arrogant and unchastened infantile will (or the misuse, misapprehension and mislocation of man-created categories, as though these subjective demiurges created the world). *Of course* the body is sometimes frustrating, like all material things, and the mind non-omnipotent even over it. But the body is also the *sine qua non* of all the mind's many pleasures. When he knows who he is and then loves life, a sound man finds his body dear. It is the ground of his being. As were his father and mother, whom he will therefore love too. And, intellectually, to a moderate degree at least, his society and tradition, which verges, dangerously, into a love of mankind. But the platonic ideality of "ideas" is merely the caitiff obedience of words to the thinker's infantile-omnipotent wish; and he ought not be self seduced by his fantasies if he would get on in the world.

The increasing awareness of the mind as subjective and of the body as one portion of the objective world—all here again only partly known— is added to in a second stage of learning. When nerve myelination is completed, the infant begins to have a more active relation to the world, more satisfyingly will-directed, and giving a part command of it. Instead of the passive dependency of the protected oral phase, he can now walk and talk. These are immense accomplishments, and they are undoubtedly great satisfactions—but then the child inevitably encounters new problems in the physical world, and comes into conflict with the social world of people about him. There is real new power over the body and its functioning. With more active body mastery the child now invades the physical world; but at the same time social demands invade his body autonomy.

It is a time of power, but of conflict of wills, the anal phase; the affect we feel over the use of this stubborn term is of course a measure of the emotion once surrounding a baby-mother conflict over it. Who totally owns one's body anyway? The fact is that society has a part-equity in it. Often it takes a long time to acknowledge the obduracy of this new Other, society and its demands as mediated by mother. It means placing disciplines on formerly uncomplicated pleasures at simple satisfaction of organic needs. The control of excretory functions, because of society's strong feelings in the matter, is the focal point of this phase, physically and psychologically. Enforced discipline first asserts society's power. However, sphincter control is only one of the several features of the socialization and enculturation period designated by this fighting term for the self / society conflict. And of course individual mothers and societies may differ in the "tone of voice" in which they teach and enforce these universally human disciplines to their particular taste. But for those capable of honest self-perception it is even useful to retain, without compromise or prettification, the emotion-laden term as intrinsically edifying. If enculturation forces repression of some wishes, then the body becomes evil; for it is the body that has the wishes, hence the body-self is fearful and wicked. Social discipline is the origin of sin.

Sphincter morality, "lowly" and hateful as it may be, is therefore the first germ of the "loftiest" human artifact, the conscience or socially shaped superego. It is the first concession of self-will to the interests of society, and thenceforth the superego, in the normal person, will have a part-hegemony over the ego. Earlier, in the oral phase, the ego served the interests only of the organic id; now the ego is further burdened with social demands. Once again ego boundaries between self and not-self become more sharply defined, with respect both to subject and objects, whether persons or things. The residual tone of anal-phase learning experience colors not only these ego discriminations but also the continuing problems of dominance-submission in larger social contexts later. But, as usual, frustration teaches, if mastered; cripples, if not. The learning about persons as other "subjective" objects, and of things as another kind of object, and of the complex differences between the two, can rewardingly occupy the individual for the rest of his life. Nevertheless, there are still people who attempt to treat people like feces, or like things: Hitler was one of them.

In his classic observations, Sir James Frazer noted two kinds of sympathetic magic, which we can now view in psychological terms. It is no accident that in one kind, "contagious magic," there is an attempt to control or punish a person through magic manipulation of his exuviae (feces, blood, hair, sputum) as onetime material parts of the person. In the other, "homeopathic magic," matter shaped in the form of the person and symbolically representing him is manipulated. Contagious magic assumes a spurious "law of contact" in which the part supposedly influences the whole—but which at best could operate only in an intact organism (such as one had subjectively experienced in his own body) and not with respect to parts removed from it. Homeopathic magic in turn assumes a spurious "law of similarity" in which the symbolic effigy supposedly commands the real body. Exuvial magic misapprehends the nature of organic things; effigy magic, the nature of symbols. The two kinds of magic now misuse precisely the two accomplishments of the second ego phase, body control and symbolic speech. In one we have extrapolation of the self's real body control into an imagined control of another person's body; in the other, an equally illegitimate extrapolation of the power of speech and symbol. Speech can, indeed, but within limits, coerce and control other people; but the magic word can not control inert matter merely symbolizing the other person.

Both kinds of magic are failures to discern the objective limitations of real subjective powers: the learned ability to use muscles and symbols. One does in fact have control of one's own body and body contents, but not those of other people; only muscles, or their alloplastic analogues, can move matter for people, and symbols can "move" only other people, not things. Exuvial magic, however, pretends to be "anal omnipotent" and symbolic magic "oral omnipotent." Magic, then, uses earlier phase adaptations—but these are inadequate and inapposite to later contexts of larger reality that the individual is unwilling to learn emotionally and hence unable intellectually to know. Magic does not reflexively examine the self as a will but takes its necessities for granted, and hence magic narcissistically and complacently indulges the subjective Pleasure Principle.[5] Magic does not discern the object as discrete, and hence misses real coping with the Reality Principle. Magical belief, therefore, is self-delusory fixation at the oral-anal phases of adaptation, with purely fantasied operation of the omnipotent will. It is a narcissistic failure to discern ego boundaries and the limitations of ego control. Emotionally, it is *hubris;* intellectually and in cognitive potential, Thanatos. In the superb metaphor of Frazer, magic pulls strings to which nothing is attached.[6]

As the child begins to learn about things, so also he begins to learn about people. The reality of other persons depends, in part, on the discernment of oneself, both as body and mind, so that other persons are in a sense the projection of awareness of self. (Animism, further, is the illegitimate projection of mind and will into non-person objects—rocks, streams, trees, fire, lightning, wind—that in fact lack both consciousness and volition.) Gradually, as the mother emerges from a fuzzy focus as mere breast and becomes successively a face, a body, and a person— another figure looms significant beyond the mostly gratifying mother, father. He is an unmitigated problem. The child, it seems, is not— strangely and unjustly!—the only loved one in this new family world. For mysterious but manifestly unreasonable reasons, mother even seems to love father at the behest of a more imperious love than that with which she loves the child; brothers and sisters are a nuisance, but at least they are in the same boat libidinally as oneself. Sometimes she even joins the Enemy.

Father somehow dominates the trinity, and Oedipus is not king after all. This is a shocking way to treat infantile omnipotence. Was it father who usurped king baby's right to the kingdom of mother's body? Was it he who separated the weanling from the breast? Worse, he is no substitute. Indeed, father is more remote. He has no anatomical modality for loving the child as the mother did. For good biological reasons, mother loved categorically; father acerbly demands performance to earn his approval and love, lest, strangely, one be a hateful, rejected and debased sinner. Father's love is at best abstract, at worst ambiguous: he protects and rewards the righteous, but he also threatens the wicked with outright chastisement. He is the father of conscience, far more potent than an indulgent mother in mediating society's demands. This new Object is a *mysterium tremendum et fascinosum.* He is hateful, but powerful with *mana*—indeed, he seems to possess the awesome omnipotence the child once thought he had himself. He persecutes, and we cannot understand his ways.

The only escape is to seek to be like him—to become a moral creature and bearer of culture—and for man to be made in God's image, if the irascible moral thunders are to be stilled. What is one's wickedness? The child's oral love for the mother that seems to rival the father? Or the oedipal adulteration of the naïve first kind of love, with fantasies surrounding newly discovered body pleasures, those secret powers that belong only to God? Is this the mysterious bond between the parents? At this juncture the child has encountered the universal human incest taboo, that belongs biologically to this animal and to no other one. As his object-love style changes in phase and in libidinal body-zone, the loss of the mother as love object is the tragedy of Everyman.

This process is necessarily "biological" since the incest taboo is, perhaps, in part, a product of intrinsic biological phase-growth: intense and prolonged conditioning to the child-method of loving precludes the possibility of learning quite opposite conditioning to a different kind of relationship to the same person. That is, human neoteny—long dependency, largely instinctless learning and long delayed puberty alike—may lie at the base of the universal incest taboo as an exclusively human phenomenon, since only humans have this unusual neoteny psychologically. We must not neglect, however, the importance of the father for the taboo, since there is *simultaneous* and *heightened* functioning of both breeding and nurturance behavior in the human female biologically (as opposed to the separate *alternation* in time of these female functions in other animals), such that the body of the mate/mother is inevitably destined to be the battleground for diverse biological concerns of father and child.

As a later phase of body discovery, of one's own and others', and of mother's and father's bodies in particular, comes the puzzling awareness that human beings are, of all things, sexually dimorphous. A new lesson in biology: even people are not necessarily all like the narcissistic self! This discovery can be a shock, even frightening. What does the difference mean? In naïve male terms, it means that females once had, but have now lost, the proud parts of males—hence females are sinful, inferior and to be despised, and terrifying. For the girl, the difference represents a cosmic unfairness, not to have what boys have. For the boy, then, the difference is a threat, the possibility of losing this new source of intense pleasures; for the girl, that she has already (and *why?*) been unjustly punished. Is there to be for both an unending line of losses, of "separation anxiety" from all pleasures, to be experienced only to be taken away? At birth the individual lost a homeostatic heaven, at weaning the breast, at socialization body autonomy—and now the phallus?

For both sexes the father's secret genital is the symbol of paternal *mana,* the manifest source of male dominance over women and children.

Compared to the magnificent and powerful father, the boy is small and inferior. And yet the boy is like him in body pattern. In witness of his father's likeness to him, somehow a promise, and in envious admiration of his father's overwhelming power and potency in the greater world of people and things, the boy now enters into an enthusiastic discovery and valuation of his own sex, and into appropriate sex-typing through emulation, identification and learning of masculine skills and attitudes. Only male things are admirable and worthwhile now. It is the time for competitive games and athletic mastery and measurement against male opponents, activities in which the boy also can exercise his most obvious superiority over females, his greater strength and speed and physical prowess. The boy's normal love of things male is abstract; it is masculinity of spirit, abstract male *mana,* that is to be possessed and internalized, introjected and made one's own. Only when the loved and admired object, the male Other, remains concrete and forever outside, unpossessable as a *logos* or pattern by the dejected child's inferiority, and only when the child uses earlier body zone modalities to incorporate maleness, does this love become perverse and thus miss its biological goal, the becoming of a man.

It is worth returning on a more abstract level to the human family as the laboratory of the subtler dimorphisms of femininity and masculinity, since both of these shape the projective systems of magic and religion. Phallic Prometheus did not, in fact, "steal" fire from Olympus, for fire is infinitely divisible and grows; and he will not be punished by the eagle of Zeus tearing at his vitals, except insofar as he maliciously "deprives" Zeus of it (nor did Zeus in fact need to mutilate his father Ouranos to become king in his own heaven). Masculinity is comfortably shared logos. In conceding this logos to father and to other men, each man has his own. But it is always at the price of relinquishing easy childish omnipotence that the boy can take his place among men.

The psychological indispensability of the father, both in posing the new competitive problem of the phallic period and in the resolution of the father-son conflict, is clearly manifest. Both son and daughter depend partly upon the father for their respective masculinity and femininity. No doubt "tertiary sexuality"—that is, characterological masculinity and femininity, as opposed to primary-genital, and secondary-hormonal traits —is shaped differently in different societies and to different expectancies. And yet panhuman anatomical and physiological considerations force us to conclude that generic and generalizable facts do exist. The very experience of living in a male or a female body must differ as much psychologically as bodies differ morphologically; and as for panhuman sexual dimorphism it is indisputably there biologically. So long as human males are larger and stronger than females, so long as males have external genitals and females do not, and females menstruate while males do not, so long will the male and female body-based "castration complex" of the phallic period be as universal as the family-based oedipus. The abundant ethnography of puberty rites and initiation ceremonies[7] is merely adjunctive evidence for the primary human biological facts.

First, the male. A baby does not need a father psychologically, but a boy does. Mothers can grow babies, but only fathers can make men. Women *do not know how* to teach boys to become men, for a mother's viewpoint toward both child and boy is limited by her femininity: he was a loved child, he is anatomically and automatically an admired male. Mother can believe all her children are equally lovable (were equally pleasure-giving), and quite rightly so if this means all children need nurturance. Nevertheless, in the competitive extra-familial male world, individuals just are not equal, and some are manifestly better than others, whether in prowess, skill, knowledge, courage, or abstract social worth. It would ultimately be dangerous nonsense for a mother-mystique, operating alone, to crush competition for excellence and superiority in males, since males inevitably make comparisons in size and strength, this having been the burning issue between child and father, boy and man (note, in our society, how mostly women teachers in early schooling seem to seek and certainly do succeed in fomenting dull conformity and mediocrity, through the here-misplaced egalitarianism of the feminine mystique; what boy in this situation would not be restive and turn all the more avidly to sports!).

In their very role as mothers and females, then, women do not provide an astringent enough atmosphere for boys realistically to become men in a man's larger world. The father, with his biological remoteness, is a necessary bridge to increasing discernment of the Reality Principle, psychologically. An exclusively woman-raised boy (lacking even father surrogates and sometimes also even womanly appreciation of males in general) would be bound to feel later in his adult situation either somehow swindled in his birthright to automatic love and hence obscurely resentful, spuriously superior reactively, and imperiously love-demanding without earning it—or else somehow hopelessly weak, inferior or a failure in a man's world. Without a father a boy never learns who he is, with respect both to power and the limitation of power. Mothers give love unconditionally, but men, lacking a mother's biology of loving, demand proof of worth and respect. Fathers are the first more massively real surrogates of society, the first really demanding Reality Principle and foil for moral learning, since indulgent mothers represent primarily the Pleasure Principle.

Women love persons, child or man, concretely, anatomically, and are better mothers and monogamists for it. But men, having been once oedipally displaced from a specific object, and more drastically at that, tend to love women generically, and to admire men, if grudgingly, more abstractly. Mothering alone breeds passive narcissism; fathers breed stern standards and the necessity of actively earning approval. The very biological remoteness of the father from his child accounts for the generic and abstract quality of masculinity as a spiritual state. It is not who (child) but what (man) you are that counts. It is not each special case (every mother's child) but ability to toe the same line (abstract standards).

The girl has a different characterological fate.[8] The father, being male, indulges his daughter with a different love, and expresses affection longer in physical contact with a little girl than with a boy. The father, who looks upon the son as an extension of himself, is threatened, angered, and aroused to action by his son's passivity, which is so untypical of his own masculinity; a daughter's passivity, encouraged, can maintain longer a childlike quality. Since father is the strongest and dominant in the family, and the indulged daughter closer to the child, the feminine Electra is not so stressful and categorical as the masculine Oedipus. Thus the daughter characteristically enjoys indulgence as a child-person from both mother and father, and learns a feminine concreteness in object-love as a result. Indeed, since it is the dominant parent himself who must distance his daughter from himself, and at that not from any once-biological tie as close as suckling, and moreover relatively late at her puberty—and with less formidable threat from mother since a girl cannot lose external genitals—an hysteric daughter may find difficulty in giving up the safe child-love of father for the more threatening and damaging love of other men. Males suffer from the *drasticness* of oedipal displacement from a biologically (orally) loved object; females suffer from the nowhere-implemented *ambiguity* of the electra, and a continuing child-love from the father that imprisons but merely supplements the mother's in tenderness. Masculine rules do not quite apply to the girl—anyway she has been "wronged" and the world "owes" her special treatment therefore—and her feminine superego is mostly acquired from her softer mother, under milder feminine pressures and threats, and with less to lose. By contrast, the male superego tends to be more rigid and dependable, more rigorous and inflexible: a good man is more predictable than a good woman. His masculinity is bound to abstract principle, her femininity more free for *ad hoc* situational feeling-response.

Adolescence, for the girl, in acquiring the mature breast, is achieving in herself what she earlier lost in her loss of mother at weaning, and this facilitates a direct identification with her mother; but the feminine experience of menarche reawakens both castration anxiety and cleanliness taboos. In this unaccountable bleeding lies further "proof" of her deprived and mutilated state; the functional uncontrollability of the bleeding is a new "offense" against cleanliness morality: women are "unclean"— and men especially fear them in this state as a reminder of "supernatural" danger to themselves. Femininity is intrinsically inward, passive and secret, for anatomical, physiological and psychological reasons; masculinity for similar reasons intrinsically active and overt. For the girl, maleness and father are foils for growth in femininity. Whomever she "blames" for her femaleness, she still longs to possess maleness. But she can not; she must settle for possessing a male. Since he is the first significant male in the family constellation, it is inevitable and natural that she should love her father as the first male object, his masculine attitudes toward a daughter also being what they are. But again one may love only in rivalry, for mother somehow possesses him. The girl must both initially "lose" maleness, and then lose her father, another of the recurrent tragedies of the human condition. He is forbidden.

For the boy, adolescence is an almost giddy pleasure in experiencing now unforbidden feelings and achieving new physical and intellectual mastery, the only price for this growth and freedom being the poignant one of totally giving up his first love, too, in order psychologically to possess and to exercise his potential for genital love He has discovered —since father encourages and elicits his masculinity—that he does not have to give up his sexuality but only its first tentative object. Thus, in early adolescence, boys are in full flight from mother and, for a while, from everything degradingly feminine. As he matures, however, the late-adolescent is disenchanted of both his father's and his own omnipotence, and the "over-evaluation" of maleness is muted. As the youngster grows to become a man, his father simultaneously diminishes in relative size to become simply a man too. The once seemingly unbounded adolescent now shrinks into a man. And, as once did his father, the young man returns to his first love, a changeling to a changeling, a man to a woman but not his mother. There is a characterological hard-bitten quality about a man in having made a final hard bargain to possess his manhood, and it is the more jealously possessed for this reason. However, since, child or man, male love for women is always directly organic and relatively uncomplex, loss of his mother in death is straightforward reawakened mourning. But since in some ways the father is oneself, complexly and ambivalently imbricated into one's very character, Freud rightly says that the most important event in a man's life is the death of his father. For his manhood, his character, his morality and his final worldview will take their tone from his ultimate feeling toward his father.

There are of course pathologies in the phallic phase of sex-identification as well. If the male child relinquishes neither his own fantasied omnipotence nor the fantasied omnipotence of his father, and if he cannot enter into his male heritage of limited and contingent potency, he can become locked lifelong in the phallic "paranoid" stance. Who has the omnipotence—prophet-mouthpiece of male mana, or God! In the paranoid state, these ego boundaries are quite fluid and precarious, the prophet and his god often indiscernible clinically, and the same individual may at one time insist only on his oracular function, and at another claim godhood for himself. In longing for identity with the father, the paranoid self often merges with the Self, omnipotence regained. For in paranoia neither has the psychological boy grown in potency nor has the father diminished in omnipotence, the attempted identity thus being of child with god, and not man with man.

The paranoid precariously possesses "omnipotence" but only at the price of potency, real and symbolical, as a man. The paranoid *can not* identify with his father as the lover of his mother, except at the cost of madness. Nor, in a non-abstract (sexualized but really narcissistic) love of his father's maleness can he escape other terrors. Feminized, he seeks his father's love and is persecuted by it as well. In winning the fantasy battle for phallic omnipotence, he has lost the whole war. The impotent worshiper of his father's majesty is a tragic Kafka, forever outside the castle, endlessly baffled and abused by petty powers and thrones—pseudo-gods themselves with only society-borrowed bureaucratic omnipotence —forever on trial, an ugly insect.

Institutionally, the paranoid is the *vatic personality,* the priest of his father's godhood, condemned to a child's poverty, chastity and obedience —or he is himself spuriously a paranoid omnipotent god. This is not the proud outcome of a man's struggle for potency! The term "vatic" is derived from the Latin *vates,* a "seer, prophet or poet," ultimately from an old Celtic word, in Old Irish *faīth,* "prophet," appearing also in Greek (Strabo) as οὐάτης, "priest"—one oracular or inspired. The vatic personality is only the seer or humble witness of an external omnipotence, the oracle his "utterance" of the words of the god, his inspiration a being passively inspirited or "breathed into" by the god. The prophet is not one who predicts but literally one who "speaks forth" as the mouthpiece of omniscience, which latter it is that knows all, including the future.

The vatic personality, in sum, is the individual driven by inner need and conviction to speak with the voice of god, as if the voice were not his own. Hence the prophet is psychologically parasitic upon a supposed external omnipotence that is really an equally fictive internal one. Every paranoiac is a god in person, every god a paranoiac projected into space.

Only human fatherhood and sonhood form a sufficient biologic cause for this curious phenomenon—the psychological neoteny of the human child. There is no other empirical basis in experience for these projections of the vatic stance. The vatic personality exists in two closely related forms, shaman and priest, depending upon ego boundaries and the psychological space occupied, the attained stage of psychosexual maturity, and their respective institutional contexts socially and culturally.[9] There clings about the vatic personality an inescapable aura of femininity, because of the frozen passivity before the father, and because of an essentially feminine technique of controlling or cajoling the father, rather than in the direct, unafraid, manly expression of will. Both shaman and priest are psychologically feminized. Ethnographically, and in many separate parts of the world, the shaman characteristically becomes transvestite, a *berdache* socially and psychically. The priest's masculinity is masculine protest only; indeed, in some equivalent guise, in many culture-historically quite independent parts of the ethnographic world, the priest takes off his necktie, so to speak, and dresses in woman's garb. In India, for example, he is the feminized transvestite Vaishnavite worshiper of the Lover.

Psychologically and socially the more primitive of the two, the shaman is preposterously and magniloquently a fatuous child, for he uses mother-learned magic, not the secular ego-techniques of mastery that other men use. For the shaman is at base a magician: external powers invade and leave his body with practiced ease, so feeble are his ego boundaries and so false his fantasies of Total Mana anywhere, inside or out. His "supernatural helpers" are only vaguely conceptualized as persons, certainly less clearly than individuated gods; in fact, his "spirits" are commonly those of animals, the unbearable psychic struggle being displaced from the family arena "totemistically" onto animals. The shaman's "powers" are curiously half-*mana*, half-*anima*. At times he "incorporates" the spirits that enter his body; at times, in metamorphosis, he becomes the animal itself. The shaman is the paranoid "father" of his tribesmen and protects them from supernatural assault and invasion, but even in this imagery he is not wholly a man—indeed, though relatively rarely, hysteroid women are often shamanesses too. The shaman is a culture hero to the frightened and the infantilized, but psychically he is a child too.

By contrast, the priest has arrived, and speaks to a clientele, at the oedipal level. He does not magically command, he implores Omnipotence. Instead of child-mother he uses child-father techniques. Students of magic and religion have almost endlessly argued the differences on institutional grounds, but vainly, because institutionally magic and religion are quite often mixed ethnographically.[10] When he uses holy water and saints' bones and magic formulas, the instituted priest is really a shaman operationally. With more personified powers whom he placates by sacrifice, the shaman functionally, and in attitude, is really a priest. The real difference between magical and religious practice is not in real outside entities but in *the psychic attitude of the practitioner*. Clinically and ethnographically, attitudes can be, and often are, psychosexually mixed, and the same individual manifest both.[11]

Insofar as he "masters" the spirits, and orders them about at will to do his bidding, the practitioner is a shaman. But insofar as he is possessed and managed by them, he is only the prophet-mouthpiece of a god. Shamans are indeed often both, ethnographically; but there is little ambiguity about who the "god" of the magician basically is: himself. In total submission to a personified God beyond his command, the practitioner is just as plainly a priest, presiding in group worship of an Omnipotent Father. Both types of vatic personality alike speak with the voice of a god, self or Self, but each at a terrifying price, his very manhood. In duress or need, both have retreated to an unrelinquished paranoid stance in neotenous coping with omnipotence. The real difference between shaman and priest is who and where the god is, inside or out.

The intense narcissism of the phallic phase, in between the oral-anal and the oedipal, is made very clear in the story of Aladdin (his name means "height of faith" in Arabic). Aladdin rubs his magic lamp of wish-gratification—and a gigantic *jinn* swells forth, omnipotently to do his bidding. But after all Aladdin literally *owns* his jinn. The jinn is of course vaguely male, but he is not really a person. The male jinn is still commanded as irresponsibly as the baby summoned the mother. It never enters Aladdin's head to consult the jinn's convenience as a person, or to question his power over the jinn. He never concerns himself about the jinn's reward or will as a person. The jinn is mere vaguely anthropomorphic smoke; he is almost only an impersonal borrowed mana.[12] Aladdin never worries about jinn hunger or fatigue, jinn wages or working hours; he merely summons the jinn at will. Aladdin is clearly a narcissist with incompletely defined ego boundaries, poised at the height of faith in phallic omnipotence.

The religionist, just as clearly, is psychosexually more mature in

ascribing a Personality to the Other than is the magic maker. The religionist assiduously reminds all around of his own finite "creatureliness"
at the feet of his Other. Mothers make magicians; fathers, gods. The
religionist, quite naturally and characteristically, both fears and contemns
the magic maker, since the latter represents his own regression to an
earlier outgrown and rejected stage. The magician is fixed at the more
archaic psychological state in which other powers have not yet really
become human persons. The magician is the only Person when he
commands only a vaguely impersonal mana or abstract outside Power.
The religionist, by contrast, has progressed to seeking his Father as a
discretely defined moral Person beyond his control. He does not control,
he beseeches this Other. He eagerly follows categorical moral or even
bizarre cultural commands, if only such obedience will placate a Personal
Other and enable him to cope with His aweful unpredictability: not my
will but Thine be done. The religionist has more fully discovered
emotionally the persons of the familial trinity. Consequently he inveterately uses a family imagery: god the father, the loving mother of god,
and the suffering son. The symbolic oedipal lineament of these figures is
complete.

Just as the shaman and his god are indiscriminable in the preoedipal,[13]
prepersonal stage, so later a woman's way of adaptation to a putative projected father becomes a way of containing her residual infantile hysteria.
And since it is the father and the father's love that are now predominantly
significant for him too, in a man's attempt to manage an oedipalized
world, religion is his way of containing his infantile paranoia.[14] Thus, the
human person—an intensely social animal, family-protected throughout
a long apprenticeship to childhood, and ecologically dependent upon a
symbiosis both in family and in society—is easily accustomed in stress
situations to call upon some human Other, and usually with some success. Moreover, under conditions of extreme stress, when no human other
—and indeed the whole society's techniques of coping with problems—
can successfully aid him, it is also not surprising that he would, though
illegitimately, seek succor in his non-human environment, or might
projectively apperceive that non-human environment, animal[15] or physical, in anthropomorphic terms. For other humans have been his experienced source of succorance.

In the same human terms too, because of his clear biological responsibilities, the adult human would be that one who could most successfully
minister to the dependencies of others. That is, the adult person would
be emotionally disposed to do so; and as an adult he would discriminate
intellectually between self, human others, and the non-human environ-

ment, since it is on his successful discrimination that his dependents must rely. Of course such a hypothetically adult human being scarcely ever exists, or if he does, only segmentally and temporarily. In his disposition to protect his tribesmen from supernatural dangers, the shaman is in fact, in this function, a "father" to them. It is only that he now uses infantile modalities in doing so. He and they operate with a child's eye view of what fatherhood is.

If no one has ever witnessed a perfectly adult father, how can one be expected always to be perfectly adult himself? But that does not prevent him from projecting such a perfect model, made up perhaps of the humanity of many segmentally imperfect men, selectively synthesized into a Perfect Man as a "pure type." Such a godlike figure takes up the slack, so to speak, between idealized perfection and an imperfect father. A father's failures provide the need for God. Much of the time most human beings, even children, swing along matter-of-factly, reasonably hard-bitten and ego-dependent. But each adult encapsulates, and has been, a child; and no person is the god this formula demands him to be. Under stress, many adults easily regress to the childhood "paranoid stance." Omnipotence *must* exist, because I now need it! In this, vacillating, one either *is* (magic) the omnipotence each child felt he preserved invincibly in the experience of his mother; or, having thought he saw it in his father, he cries out, often inappropriately, to some omnipotence in the larger non-familial environment (religion). Ultimately both magic and religion reflect the individual narcissism that insists, inalternatively, that somewhere there *must* be an omnipotence to minister to one's here wholly conscious and clear, categorically sanctioned, sacred id need. The environment *must be* what I, unself-questioningly, demand that it be. The absoluteness of the imperious id creates the Absolute.

It is not a matter for cavil, but for acceptance. The human condition does not allow any man a wild animal self-sufficiency, and never in his life does he experience it. Each man carries his own childhood and its paranoid potential within him. He knew dependency and he has experienced power. He *will* see that his organic and other needs are met; he would be the poorer animal for it, were he not thus unrelenting. Under stress, however, and under continued need, he regresses to earlier power-techniques, and tends incorrectly to define both dependency and power as absolutes. Understandably then, every man may be at times the Self of magic shamanism, at times the religious supplicant of the not-self Other's power. For, given his peculiar human biology, these techniques *had* experienced success, in earlier ego growth.

It is therefore a fundamental error in psychological epistemology to suppose that archaic world-views are mere bundles of dead errors, to be dismissed by comfortable rationalism. Religion and magic arise from *quite different emotional stances,* deep in the unconscious minds of individuals. There can be no "rational" argument with the magic-maker, because he does not emotionally *know* a not-self Other; he will merely rationalize his failures and maintain the same stubbornly narcissistic position. Nor can there be "rational" arguing with religionist categories, for the religionist will irresistibly find and inevitably talk about connotatively only the *kind* of Not-Self he apperceives and emotionally needs. There is, consequently, an equally irreconcilable conflict between magic and religion, and between religion and science, for they are all based on different phatic-emotive hypotheses about the world. The individual who maintains there is no conflict between science and "true" religion either means that he thinks his religion is as true as science, thus indicating his misunderstanding of the nature of both, or that he is using the merely contingent authority of contemporary scientific "truths" as though these were like apodictic religious Truths.

"God" is not a semantic term, therefore, but a phatic one. It does not point to an unambiguously objective outer state-of-affairs, such as is accessible to all in scientific language. It refers, rather, to an inner subjective oedipal constitution, which is as varying as individuals are. "God" is how a man *feels* about the universe, and one man's theology is manifestly his oedipal disposition to another. That is, we all feel as our life experience has taught us to feel, inexpugnably.[16] And that's an end to it, for the rest is rationalization. Thus arguments about the nature of "God" are an irrational hurling of individual oedipal convictions at one another; and it is fruitless because each is talking about ontogenetically somewhat different phenomena. If "God" here behaves curiously like the first personal pronoun, it is because the god-concept is somehow inseparable from ego-experience and one's residual infantile narcissism.

We can now understand certain "institutional" differences between magic and religion. Many scholars have noted that magic trends toward the individual, whereas religion trends toward the social. The psychiatric reason for this contrast is plain. Magic trends toward the individual because it corresponds to a more narcissistic stage of ego development. Religion trends toward the social because it corresponds to a more mature stage of other-person awareness. The medicine-man obtains magic power in himself, and his clients are individuals seeking the benefit of his power for themselves. But religion always tends to become a group cult, and for larger social ends. Again, the institutional "mixtures" of the two are not the issue, but rather the epistemological stance of the persons concerned.

The "institutional" contrast is not empirically absolute, since the shaman is sometimes half a medium of and half a mediator to the spirits. Furthermore, his function as a culture hero caring for his tribe is already a shared narcissism, and already social when his vision becomes the property of a wider cult. The epistemological-psychological contrast is, however, deep and abiding. A full-blown ethical religion must always guard itself against backsliding into a more primitive magic as it becomes more assured and institutionalized. Religion must always focus on a god as the repository of power. In magic the power is a man's.

Significantly also, the differences are always reacted to institutionally, and with infallible emotional logic. The desperate quarrel of early Christianity with Gnosticism was legitimate and proper, for the thrice-powerful Hermes was essentially the shaman of a magic cult. But is Christianity so different from Gnosticism ultimately? Logically, if even one god-man obtains the immortality (the messiah) intrinsic only to the other (the universe), the door is opened to Everyman when the shaman shares his gift. Thus in this sense Christianity is a back-slid Judaism when a human messiah obtains and shares the Eternity belonging only to That Which Is; and the Papacy is in turn a back-slid Christianity in which the mystic descendant of Peter again exercises the god's omniscience merely delegated to him as a medium.

The fundamental contrast between religion and science is also evident in a certain psychological difference in feeling tone with respect to epistemology or the problem of knowledge. Religion fervently believes, and ever reasserts its faith[17]; science carefully preserves its independent skepticism.[18] Religion yearns for the settled and the final, and looks backward to the first sacred revelation; science insists upon its own intrinsic non-finality, and looks forward to the new fact and the new hypothesis. Religion confidently asserts its knowledge, once and for all, of the Unknown; but science modestly admits its contingency and partial ignorance. Religion is psychic anthropomorphism; but science scrupulously seeks to rid itself of all subjective human factors in the observer. Religion is wishful, oedipal-narcissistic, and tenderminded; science is acerb, impersonal, and toughminded. Religion knows gods; science only fallible men. Religion is fettered to the sacred past; science looks forward to the secular future. Religion looks backward to a Golden Age and imagines an unworldly future Heaven; science peers into a mundane here and now. Religions all derive ultimately from some individual's mystic state that is ineffable and passes all human understanding; science endlessly devises new languages to point to the bases for everyone's seeing and understanding. Religion depends on faith in revelation; science on evidence in experience. Religion tends to the exclusive and the invidious in the group cult, and as each oedipal disposition differs individually, to belief as a private matter; but science is public, international and panhumanly inclusive. Religion supposes that values come from gods; science knows that man must and does make his values and hypotheses by himself. Religion seeks some inscrutable Person to submit to; science seeks an understandable impersonal reality it would dominate. Religious ritual tends to forget its meanings and to substitute the compulsive masking symbol for the fact, and theology constantly forgets what it was talking about; science knows that its symbols are merely revealing tools, and cheerfully throws away language that no longer expresses its newer understandings. Religion seeks vainly to refind the ontogenetic past; science successfully makes the future of the species. Religion emphasizes man's burning inner needs; science the indifferent outer facts. And in its defense of old beliefs, religion becomes through time ever more sophistic; but in the discarding of inadequate for more adequate views, science becomes ever more sophisticated.

All men are variously infantile ontogenetically. Men meet life not alone or even mainly with individual genetic adaptations, but with his traditional society's cultural accumulation of the pasts of many other persons. Some at least of these persons have been possibly mistaken in their solutions of human problems. Each literate civilization is a vast grab bag of "solutions" each of which may match some epistemologic-oedipal disposition, and a variety of such oedipal constitutions continues to be manufactured. Each civilization, therefore, is an incredible mélange of magic and superstition, of ethical faith and religion, and of ego-oriented rationalism and science. Each maturer world view does not gain a clear-cut and inevitable victory, since not every one, and not each of us always, is completely a man epistemologically. In the emotional market, bad coin may drive out good, in a kind of Gresham's Law of psychological economy. Still, perhaps religion has also tended widely to drive out magic, for it is humanly more beautiful. Perhaps, in continuously striving to provide a psychosexually more advanced social ambience, more and more individuals can come to learn the beauty of a still greater epistemological maturity beyond.

Biologically, these projective systems rest upon species-specific human nature, and upon the experiences of the neotenously *instinctless* child as he enters successively new worlds not walled about with prepared adaptations. At each step he must *learn* his humanity. The first world of the baby is the beloved breast of his mother; then, slowly, he discovers himself; soon, beyond, is his father and a humanity of brothers. But always for the new human animal "the first world" is the people who environ him. The experiences of his mother and his own body underlie the mystique of magic. The first god of the baby is himself, his ultimate god the ghost of his struggle with the Omnipotent Other, his father. The psychic rationale of religion, too, lies in the human family.

But a scientific ego-tonus toward the world is possible too. Fathers are fallible. If we can accept them in their non-omniscience and know why this omniscience cannot be, minds and symbols being what they are; and if we can accept fathers' non-omnipotence, and see why our neoteny only seemed to see omnipotence in them, we can then humanly identify with real fathers. And if we can accept even their non-omnibenevolence, and know why and forgive them, then we may be able to acknowledge the necessity of creating human values and striving for them. Our fathers were only men. The ethos of science, too, lies in the human family —from having fathers whom we must come to distrust for their having been merely human.

All values, moral and intellectual, are constructs of human experience and need. So also are aesthetic values. It is understandable that art[19] should have the overwhelming power that it does over sentient human beings. In art men of all times are kin. For art, always and everywhere, speaks with secret power to the human condition. In the sacredly beautiful cave of Lascaux, the artist magically created the great beasts that men depended on then for sustenance, and we know his awe when we see them. Song, it would seem, began in the language of the bard Orpheus, calling to the rocks, hills and animals of his shaman's world. And who, now, can hear Bach on the great organ at Trondheim, and not know the thrilling majesty of Bach's God? Who, seeing the sun-blazing glory of the Parthenon, soaring white against the sky on the high Acropolis, cannot feel the protecting nurturance of the Athenian Maiden born of the Thunderer, almighty Zeus? And who, standing below the starlit towers of Senlis, does not sense the deep reverence and longing that built this first Gothic cathedral to the glory of God? It is quite simply true that, through all history, the greatest creations of art have been in the service of religion, and even the latest artist and poet put forth worlds born yearningly only in themselves. Religion is a poetry that speaks of those the little child tenderly loved.

We can know and reverence this art, and still know that it is art, for this only deepens its poignancy. In religion and art we but exalt our own humanity. Long before the child meets, in any full sense, the sublimely heartless and beautiful, the inseductible and implacable cosmos, his responses to it will have been shaped inexorably by the child's first adaptations to people, including himself. But we wish never to be seduced back to the prison of childhood! Beyond, for some chastened few, is the psychic manhood of science. Such a person has learned the equal legitimacy in Being of the man within his body and that mysterious, but surely unmanlike, inhuman and impersonal Total Other, the physical universe. He earnestly struggles to discriminate both and to fear neither, and is gradually disciplined to relinquish infant godhood for brief finite power as a man. He will live his clever primate life with as much satisfaction and meaning as he can contrive,[20] for he knows that he can rejoin that longed-for Ultimate Other only in death.

Science is not a new "magic" and it is not in any sense a "religion" but something quite different, since it takes a wholly different ego-stance toward the world. It is true that the scientist uses symbols and hypotheses in his search, but the authentic scientist tries carefully to remember that man-made symbols and hypotheses are only just that, his psychic tools. He may not trust too far the seeming "magic" of symbols. The purpose of words is to point to the world and to convince by the clarity of shared discernment. Words have no other magic—not even poetry, wherein the poet points to himself and to the human truths he labors to share with other men. All art is only that, in some fashion, and all religion.

Science is not religion, because it tries not to see the world in man's image, and not to worship man's image projected into the unknown. The scientist knows that he is a man, and would serve men; but even humanism, become a religion, can slip into worshipful arrogance.[21] Is it necessary to impute one's having been created, and ultimate death, to the whole uncreated and undying universe? Is it possible that the nature of Being is simply to be, without beginning or end? Does my loved father yet live? What anthropomorphic arrogance is it that steals the essence of cosmic eternity and absurdly imputes it to our immortal selves! Must we always confuse the attributes of man and of the universe! To be a man means to suffer vicissitudes, and also to contemplate with equanimity the ultimate horror and humiliation of animal "omnipotence," death—one's own death and the death of all lovers and friends, perhaps the death of our feisty and admirable species, even the death of this planet at the death of its central star. Small matter: for at one place in this cold cosmos there once lived values, and mind.

NOTES

(III The First World)

1. On marasmus and related oral pathologies, see Margaret A. Ribble, "Clinical Studies of Instinctive Reactions in Newborn Babies," *American Journal of Psychiatry*, 95 (1938) 149–58; "The Significance of Infantile Sucking for the Psychic Development of the Individual," *Journal of Nervous and Mental Diseases*, 90 (1939) 455–63; "Disorganizing Factors in Infant Personality," *American Journal of Psychiatry*, 98 (1941) 459–63; and *The Rights of Infants* (New York: Columbia University Press, 1943). The classic paper on orality is that of Karl Abraham, "The First Pregenital Stage of the Libido," *Selected Papers*, pp. 248–79.

2. *Ammophila* wasp paralyzing of caterpillars as food for their own young: Hutchins, *Insects*, p. 125. I have observed this in my own North Carolina woods. The organ-pipe mud-dauber wasps under the eaves use spiders instead.

3. On ego growth, S. Freud, *The Ego and the Id* (London: Hogarth Press, 1950), and *Three Essays on the Theory of Sexuality* (London: Hogarth Press, 1962; New York: Basic Books, 1963) are basic; also Anna Freud, *The Ego and the Mechanisms of Defence* (London: Hogarth Press, 1937). Modern ego analysis stems from Sandor Ferenczi and Franz Alexander, the foremost recent proponent being the late Heinz Hartmann, *Ego Psychology and the Problem of Adaptation* (New York: International Universities Press, 3rd printing, 1964).

4. On *hubris* and *aretē*, see La Barre, *Human Animal*, pp. 311–12, 325–26, 329, 332. Incidentally, Culturology ascribes an "omnipotence" to culture only through persistently ignoring both the organic biological base of culture and the psychological needs culture undoubtedly serves. Culturology is thus an anthropology minus *anthropos*.

5. S. Freud, *Beyond the Pleasure Principle* (London: Hogarth Press, 1922).

6. J. G. Frazer, *The Golden Bough* (Macmillan editions, p. 57).

7. The classic book on puberty rites is that by Arnold van Gennep, *Rites of Passage*. For modern studies, see J. W. M. Whiting and I. L. Child, *Child Training and Personality* (New Haven: Yale University Press, 1953); J. W. M. Whiting, R. Kluckhohn, and A. Anthony, "The Function of Male Initiation Ceremonies at Puberty," in Eleanor E. Maccoby, T. M. Newcomb, and E. L. Hartley (eds.), *Readings in Social Psychology* (New York: Henry Holt and Company, 1958, pp. 329–70); and F. W. Young, *Initiation Ceremonies* (New York: Bobbs-Merrill Company Paperback, 1965).

8. On tertiary sexual characteristics, see W. La Barre, "Anthropological Perspectives on Sexuality," in D. L. Grummon and A. Barclay (eds.), *Sexuality: A Search for Perspectives* (Lansing: Michigan State University Press, 1971); on the maturation of tertiary traits, see *idem*, "Personality from a Psychoanalytic Viewpoint," pp. 65–87, in E. Norbeck, D. Price-Williams, and W. M. McCord (eds.), *The Study of Personality: An Interdisciplinary Approach* (New York: Holt, Rinehart and Winston, 1968). A good recent anthology is by Eleanor Maccoby (ed.), *The Development of Sex Differences* (Stanford: Stanford University Press, 1966). An acute sense of the critical dynamic differences is manifest in Robert J. Stoller, *Sex and Gender, On the Development of Masculinity and Femininity* (New York: Science House, 1968).

9. The contention of the French sociologists Henri Hubert and Marcel Mauss ("Esquisse d'une théorie générale de la magie," *Année Sociologique*, 7 [1902–3] 1–146)

that magic is not part of an organized cult and hence private, secret and illicit, simply does not fit the ethnographic facts. Many magical rites—for hunting, rain-making, fertility, protection—are done on behalf of the whole tribe, and moreover within organized, public cults (*cf.* Jan de Vries, "Magic and Religion," *History of Religions,* 1 [1962] 214–21). Marett's view (*Threshold, passim*) that magic is basically anti-social is likewise untenable; only "black magic" is anti-social. Indeed, E. A. Hoebel, summarizing much cross-cultural evidence, writes that "magic, the use of the supernatural for moral ends, long remains the handmaid of the law, mopping up where the broom of the law fails to sweep clean" (*The Law of Primitive Man,* Cambridge: Harvard University Press, 1954, quoted in E. V. Winans and R. B. Edgerton, "Hehe Magical Justice," *American Anthropologist,* 66 [1964] 725–64, where typical evidence is collected in considerable amount from a specific tribe).

However, still influenced by Hubert and Mauss, Irving King again sought the difference in the social character of religion and the individualism of magic (*The Development of Religion,* New York: Macmillan Co., 1910). Malinowski's distinction between magic as practical and utilitarian, and religion as neither, can hardly be maintained (for a recent view of this, see Michael M. Ames, "Buddha and the Dancing Goblins: A Theory of Magic and Religion," *American Anthropologist,* 66 [1964] 75–82—which also, incidentally, gives a good Sinhalese example of the ethnographic mixture of magic and religion, and despite a clear distinction of the two *in Sinhalese theory* as well). Again, I can accept De Vries' view (p. 221) that the magician's act "constitutes an audacity" only in the context that "he coerces to his service what his community regards as venerable"—for this is a *conflict* of magic and religion and not intrinsic to magic as a world-view. An objection to the magic "my will be done" can arise psychologically only with a Thou to whom one says "Thy will be done."

10. The real difference between magic and religion therefore lies in the ego-level of the practitioner's (and participants') *attitudes* toward the supernatural. The view of magic is more narcissistic and feebler in its object-discrimination, that is, it is *ontogenetically* more archaic. But this is not the same as the historically more ancient or the culture-evolutionist more "primitive." Karl Beth properly notes that from the beginning religion and magic have acted from two completely different attitudes of mind, and such a psychological position alone can explain the characteristic "mixtures" we commonly find ethnographically (*Religion und Magie, Ein religionsgeschichtlicher Beitrag zur psychologischen Grundlegung der religiösen Prinzipienlehre,* Berlin: B. G. Teubner, 2nd ed., 1927, p. 397).

11. None of the prepsychological theories ever offers an explanation of the *psychic origins* of magic and religion, or why (given their irrelevance and untestability in external reality) they are *plausible modes of behavior,* but simply takes them, unexplained, for granted. In its clarification of these points lies the further advantage of the psychoanalytic view: each attitude is *learned* adaptively, but *inappropriately used* regressively. An oral modality is adaptive, certainly, but only with respect to people —adaptive to the mother in sucking, and adaptive to other persons, later, in speech— but not with respect to the universe, in the "magic cry" or the schizophrenic-created world. An anal-mastery modality is adaptive, too, with respect to muscles and, within limits, to things. An oedipal modality is also adaptive—to the father and, to a degree, to society—but not to the physical universe which is unmoved by interpersonal techniques. Magical and religious views come from honest experience—of people, misplaced projectively onto the non-human world. Thus, religious "conviction" derives empirically from familial experience of the protection, concern, etc., of our human environment; it has no empirical base in any experience of the non-human physical environment. We have all experienced arbitrary "grace" also—the child, of his parents, and adults, of one another—but never on the part of non-human reality.

118   THE GHOST DANCE

12. Frazer's notion that magic is a primitive kind of science (since both deal with impersonal forces) is another "objectivist" theory that misses the point, though Frazer is by no means as uncritically naïve as secondhand critics who have not read him allege (*The Golden Bough,* Macmillan editions, pp. 48, 711–12). Magic, psychologically, is sets of uncritical and uncriticized beliefs; science, a consistently skeptical method of validating or invalidating suspect beliefs. A scientific hypothesis is a fantasy that knows and admits it is a fantasy, hence magic and science could hardly be more polar and opposed in the subjective sense. Further, *in order to be forced to* the epistemological sophistication of science, the individual must first be disenchanted of the "omnipotence of thought" in infantile magic or regressive schizophrenia as an adequate or apposite adaptive technique; and next he must suffer the further oedipal trauma of discovering that neither his parents nor the tribe they represent are divinely all-knowing. The matter is so clear, it is astonishing how few individuals manage really to achieve emotionally this epistemological toughness of mind. Most remain "authoritarian personalities" fanatically defending the eternal rightness of their tribal gods and prophets, i.e. remain father-worshipers.

An excellent example of the ethnographic mixture of magic and religion is found in Menangkabau, where the pagan magician is an honored guest at even the most important Moslem ceremonies: "Usually the magician called on Allah at the start of the rite and finally he begged forgiveness for showing himself so powerful. It is claimed that some magicians have familiar spirits at their command" (F.-C. Cole, *Peoples of Malaysia,* New York: D. van Norstrand Co., 1945, p. 269). In this, Allah the god is used as a familiar spirit! An objectivist-institutionalist approach could never decide whether such a ritual was "magic" or "religion"—which is not to annihilate their difference. On the other hand, the psychoanalytic approach can even discriminate among types of parental image and the subsequent "nature of the gods" (J. W. M. Whiting, "Socialization Process and Personality," in F. L. K. Hsu [ed.], *Psychological Anthropology: Approaches to Culture and Personality,* Homewood: Dorsey Press, 1961, pp. 355–80, in which an excellent, though brief, bibliography lists the relevant modern studies).

13. The "fuzziness" between self and object can best be described in terms of the voluminous empirical researches of Jean Piaget (*The Child's Conception of the World,* New York: Harcourt, Brace & Co., 1929, and other studies of Piaget's subsequently translated into English, in particular *The Construction of Reality in the Child,* New York: Basic Books, 1954). As H. Hartmann points out, for the young child, "The object is nothing but a prolongation of the child's activity" ("Contribution to the Metapsychology of Schizophrenia," in *The Psychoanalytic Study of the Child,* 8 [1953] 177–98, p. 181). Indeed, all scientific knowledge is *operational.* A stimulating discussion of the ontogenetic emergence of objects may be found in K. R. Eissler, *Leonardo da Vinci: Psychoanalytic Notes on the Enigma* (New York: International Universities Press, 1961), pp. 213–14, with special reference to the hand (pp. 115–19) and to the eye (p. 216). Hallowell believes that man could not have evolved without a conceptual distinction of the subjective and the objective, of which culture is the integration ("The Role of Dreams in Ojibwa Culture," in von Grunebaum and Caillois, pp. 267–89).

14. Functionally and historically, the system-building philosopher is close to the theologian and the priest. But all suffer the same limitation of attempting to make up the answer from inside. "A philosophical problem has the form: 'I don't know my way about.' For philosophical problems arise when language *goes on holiday*" (L. Wittgenstein, in E. N. Hiebert, "The Uses and Abuses of Thermodynamics in Religion," *Daedalus,* 95 [Fall, 1966] 1046–80, p. 1076). The history of philosophy even seems to recapitulate the ontogenetic sequences. Before Hume, philosophers were "synthetic" system-builders who put forth whole worlds from the magic mouth;

only with Kant did they become "analytic" of their own tools and behavior, examining *what symbols and propositions mean.*

15. In his oedipal encounter with his father, Kafka, more masochistic, felt himself to be the animal; but Freud's "Little Hans" and Ferenczi's "Little Árpád," healthier totemists perhaps, changed the father into an animal. Franz Kafka, *The Castle* (rev. ed., New York: Knopf, 1954), *The Trial* (New York: Modern Library, 1957), "The Metamorphosis," in L. Hamalian and E. L. Volpe (editors), *Seven Short Novel Masterpieces* (New York: Popular Library [paperback]), *Letter to My Father* (New York: Schocken Books, 1966 [paperback]). S. Freud, "Analysis of a Phobia in a Five-Year-Old Boy," in *Collected Papers* (III:149–295 in Hogarth Press ed. of 1925; vol. 10 in *Standard Edition;* Philip Rieff [ed.], New York: Collier paperback, 10 vols., 1963, BS190v, pt. IV, pp. 47–183). Sandor Ferenczi, "A Little Chanticleer," in *Sex in Psychoanalysis* (Boston: Richard G. Badger, Gorham Press, 1916, pp. 240–52).

16. The non-mention of the most potent of his premises for belief—the philosopher *trusts* his temperament–and the matter that "there is no fact so brutish and unmalleable as not to fit into the frame of his philosophy"—is wittily discussed in F. M. Cornford, *The Unwritten Philosophy, and Other Essays* (Cambridge: At the University Press, 1950, pp. 2, 33–36). On the logical conflict of magic and religion, see Ralph Lerner, "Maimonides' Letter on Astrology," *History of Religions*, 8 (1968) 143–58, p. 155.

17. There is no relationship whatever between the Old Irish *fáith* for the vatic and English "faith," although vatic faith is parasitic manhood. The latter is from an Indoeuropean root *$\phi\iota\theta$, "to move by entreaty," which curiously has come to mean empirically non-substantiated belief. In Locke's words, "Faith . . . is the assent to any proposition, not . . . made out by the deductions of reason, but upon the credit of the proposer as coming from God in some extraordinary way of communication" (*Essay on Human Understanding,* New York: Dover Publications, 2 vols., 1959, IV, xviii, 2). Thus faith meaning "to pray" has become faith meaning "to believe." An edifying etymology.

18. "Karl Popper once remarked that genuine science does not primarily seek to prove, but challenges refutation" (Theodor Reik, *Mystery on the Mountain,* p. 159). "The great revolutions in human history do not change the face of the earth. They change the face of man, the image in which he beholds himself and the world around him. The earth merely follows suit. It is the truly pathetic fallacy of empiricism that it offers as safe harbour what is the ocean itself, the storms, the waves, and the shipwrecks, namely man's experience of himself and the 'objective' world. The history of human kind is a repository of scuttled objective truths, and a museum of irrefutable facts—refuted not by empirical discoveries, but by man's mysterious decisions to experience differently from time to time. All relevant objective truths are born and die as absurdities. They come into being as the monstrous claim of an inspired rebel and pass away with the eccentricity of a superstitious crank" (Erich Heller, *The Disinherited Mind,* p. 232).

19. "We have *Art* in order not to *perish of Truth*" (F. Nietzsche, *Werke,* München: Musarion-Ausgabe, 1922, 23 vols., XIX, p. 229). "For with every new gain in poetic creativity the world as it is, the world as created without the poet's intervention, becomes poorer; and every new impoverishment of the world is a new incentive to poetic creativeness. In the end the world as it is is nothing but a slum to the spirit, and an offense to the artist" (Heller, pp. 149–50).

20. The consensus of biologists: man is the result of a long and purposeless material process, in the sense of not being preplanned by any initial Cause. Purposes belong only to organisms, not to physical environments; organisms *make* environments have purpose (for organisms) for the first time, through the organism's own physico-chemical plan. Personified Evolution had no purpose, certainly not man;

man must create purposes for himself. "There are no ethics but human ethics, and a search that ignores the necessity that ethics be human, relative to man, is bound to fail" (G. G. Simpson, *The Meaning of Evolution,* New Haven: Yale University Press, 1952, p. 307; see also pp. 292, 310, 344). That ethics must be naturalistic and cannot maintain themselves in gaps of scientific explanations of nature is also shown by Ernst Cassirer, *Determinism and Indeterminism in Modern Physics* (New Haven: Yale University Press, 1956, p. 50). Further, the more complex man becomes, the more improbable, and statistically the less likely to exist in infinite time.

21. Regarding the longevity of our particular primate species we should note that the roughly 2500 families of animals that have left a fossil record have had an average longevity of less than 75,000,000 years; about a third are still living; and although a few families became extinct by evolving into new ones, the majority dropped out of sight without descendants. At or near the end of the Permian nearly half of the known families of animals throughout the world disappeared, including 75% of the amphibian and 80% of the reptile families; the late Cretaceous extinctions eliminated a quarter of all the known families of animals of that time. Man himself has aided the extinction of more than 450 species of animals (Norman D. Newell, "Crises in the History of Life," *Scientific American,* 208 [February 1963] 76–92).

Concerning the death of our sun, the sequence of stars from blue giants to red dwarfs is of course a commonplace of modern astronomy. "That man is the product of causes which had no prevision of the end they were achieving; that his origin, his growth, his hopes and fears, his loves and his beliefs, are but the outcome of accidental collocations of atoms; that no fire, no heroism, no intensity of thought and feeling can preserve an individual life beyond the grave; that all the labours of all the ages, all the devotion, all the inspiration, all the noonday brightness of human genius are destined to extinction in the vast death of the solar system, and that the whole temple of man's achievement must inevitably be buried beneath the debris of a universe in ruins—all these things, if not quite beyond dispute, are yet so nearly certain that no philosophy which rejects them can hope to stand" (Bertrand Russell, *Mysticism and Logic,* New York: W. W. Norton, 1929, p. 47, quoted in Sir William Dampier, *A History of Science and Its Relations with Philosophy and Religion,* New York; Macmillan, 1932, p. 487).

That the nature of Being seems simply to be, without beginning or end, is indicated by the First Law of Thermodynamics. Accepting Einstein's proviso of the $E=mc^2$ *equivalence* of mass and energy, we observe that no natural process violates the principle of "conservation of energy." It is impossible, by any means—mechanical, chemical, thermal, radioactive or atomic—to build a perpetual-motion machine that creates energy from nothing. Not even the universe is such a perpetual-motion machine. The dysteleology of my last paragraph in this chapter derives, of course, immediately from the Second Law of Thermodynamics, empirically as inexorable as the first. Student engineers, somewhat less solemnly, have long paraphrased the Laws of Thermodynamics as follows: "(1) You can't win, (2) You can't even break even, (3) Things are going to get worse before they get any better, and (4) Who says things are going to get better?" (J. L. Greenstein, "Dying Stars," *Scientific American,* 200 #1 [January 1959] 46–53, p. 46).

IV

The First Americans

FIFTEEN or twenty thousand years ago, at the end of the fourth great Ice Age or before, the first men reached the New World. These were the ancestors of the American Indians. They came in small bands of several families, following the hunters who got them food. Straggling out of Asia in pursuit of game, they had no notion of the two enormous continents that lay ahead of them, empty of men. At the peak of the last glaciation (called Wurm in Europe, and Wisconsin in America) an appreciable portion of the earth's water was frozen into mile-thick land-borne glaciers, and the Alaska-Siberia land bridge was no narrow isthmus but a broad land mass connecting Asia and America. Alaska was to them only an extension of Siberia, richer in unhunted animals, and it was these that drew them on. Over the slow centuries these driblets of Paleoasiatic peoples, even then evidently of several different language families, fanned out slowly southward, spread and bred and wandered until they reached the southernmost tip of South America in Patagonia, around 9000 years ago.[1]

These are conservative dates. But every year the first entry of man into the New World seems to be pushed deeper into antiquity. Fifty years ago, cautious anthropologists would have agreed that men were in the Americas no longer than 10,000 years ago—although some botanists argued a greater time-depth was needed, among other reasons to account for the domestication of corn, which does not occur in the wild state.[2] In recent years archeologists have given us more generous estimates. In the cave of Palli-Aiké near the Straits of Magellan in Patagonia, Carbon$_{14}$ dating indicates that hunters lived there with now extinct animals some 8,700 years ago. Since this site is at the tip of South America, an unknown number of years must be allowed for man's diffusion southward from the region of the present Behring Straits.

The earlier claim for human presence at Tule Springs, Nevada, some 23,800 years ago is failing to find recent consensus. And yet, charred dwarf mammoth bone from a Channel Island find (sample L-290R) seems to indicate the presence of man on the west coast of North America 29,000±3000 years B.P. (before the Present, in Carbon$_{14}$ dating). The difficulty with remote dates of the order of 30,000 years ago, however, is that man of a Neanderthaloid type would seem to be implied, of which we quite lack paleontological or genetic evidence in the New World; if present, he must have lived in few localities, and in very small numbers. At such a date he should also have a Mousterian-like cave-man culture,[3] or the "chopper-chopping" tool industry of East Asia; but neither men nor artifacts of the right type and antiquity have been found in southern and eastern Siberia. As for fire and hunting, "Peking Man" of course had these in East Asia at a far earlier date, hence the possibility that a few hominids could have arrived at so ancient a time must be kept open. At the present, however, the scarcity and the uncertain or controversial nature of such finds must leave us with the Scotch verdict, "not proven." Nor do we anticipate that such early dates will be authenticated, for this would put New World archeology out of phase with the growing volume of Old Stone Age C$_{14}$ dates for the Old World.

Since American Indians are of distinctly modern physical type, it would be more conservative to look for the earliest evidence of their ancestors in *Homo sapiens* types of East Asia.[4] Men of modern type were certainly in China toward the end of the fourth Ice Age. Much of southern Siberia was not glaciated during the Pleistocene, and in the upper Yenesei and Lena river valleys as well as around Lake Baikal there are a number of advanced Paleolithic sites. These do not correspond exactly to the "Upper Paleolithic" of western Europe, though they are culturally connected with the late Paleolithic of the west. These southern Siberians lived in a tundra climate and hunted the mammoth, woolly rhinoceros, cave lion, arctic fox, and bison; there is good evidence that they followed the mammoth northward with the retreating ice until their hunting of it made this furry elephant extinct. They lived in permanent semi-subterranean houses, and made long flint knives struck from a prepared core, a technique diagnostic of the late Paleolithic period in Europe and elsewhere. The finds at Malta near Irkutsk, and at Bureti in the Angara Valley, show artifacts and a way of life roughly similar to the late Solutrean and early Magdalenian of western Europe. On scanty evidence their physical type is said to resemble Upper Paleolithic types to the west. The advanced Paleolithic populations of southern Siberia lived there between 15,000 and 10,000 B.C.

These archeological finds conform better with New World geological and archeological horizons. By 14,000–12,000 B.C. there was a corridor between the Rocky Mountain and continental glaciers in western Canada; that is, there was clear access from northern Alaska, through northwest and western Canada, to the plains area in the south. American Indians were certainly in the United States by 12,000–10,000 B.C., for we have radiocarbon dates of about 11,000 years ago from Rocky Mountain areas, and also implied evidence (in their characteristically fluted flint blades) that these "Paleo-Indians" lived as well in the eastern and southeastern United States south of the retreating Wisconsin glaciation at about the same time—a dating that allows for the fact that the cultures of these fluted-blade Paleo-Indians had begun to show regional diversities.

These earliest definite cultures in the New World have no associated skeletal remains. But crania dated about 8000 B.C. have the same general traits as those associated with the advanced Paleolithic cultures of Siberia. Interestingly, Sapir has related the Athapaskan family of tone-languages, spoken by the Indians still inhabiting the Canadian corridor, to the Sinitic family of tone-languages of Asia; and Sapir's pupil, Mary Haas, has shown lexicostatistically that the Muskhogean languages of the southern United States split from the Algonkian languages on both sides of the Canadian border from west of the Great Lakes eastward around 8000 or more years ago.[5]

The first American Indians flourishing between 9000 and 5000 B.C. on the high plains in eastern New Mexico, Colorado and Texas were hardy men. With lances tipped by their finely flaked blades they hunted, on foot, large and now extinct animals, including the mastodon, and the hairy mammoth as did their contemporary or slightly earlier big-game-hunting Siberian confreres (the shouldered lanceolate blades of the lower layers in the Sandia Cave of New Mexico some think may date back to before 15,000 B.C.). Certain of their flint types, like the Clovis and Folsom points, may even be New World inventions. The Iztapan and Lerma finds of central and northeastern Mexico, the Venezuelan El Jobo points, the Aympitín industry of the Andes and southern South America, and the Magellan I culture of the Straits show the wide geographic range of the early American big-game-hunting societies. After 7000 B.C. and the glacial retreats, the climate became drier, and the intermountain basin and range country of western North America, where the giant herbivores could be hunted, shrank correspondingly, as did also the old grasslands of South America. After 5000 B.C., hunting gradually shifted to the buffalo in North America, and to the large cameloid guanaco in South America.

The date 8000 B.C. is a convenient archeological divide between the Paleo-Indian big game hunters and the early Archaic cultures to the east, for after this date the distinctive fluted projectile style tends to disappear, the climate had changed and most of the Wisconsin ice had moved north, leaving the Great Lakes. The year 4000 B.C. is also an approximate cultural watershed too. Up to 4000 B.C. the eastern cultures were largely of American origin, slowly responding to changing local climates. Between 4000 and 1500 B.C., however, artifacts new both in form and function, and resembling northern Eurasian ones, began to appear.[6] It was formerly thought that pottery was an independent American invention that diffused northward and southward from Mexico. Now archeological evidence seems to indicate that pottery is part of a considerable "Mesolithic" later diffusion from Asia.

The bow and arrow, so characteristic of Indians in both the Americas, is also a significant diagnostic trait.[7] The bow and arrow seems to have originated in the Capsian period of Africa and came, possibly via Spain, to western Europe in the Aurignacian. It may not have diffused over the enormous distance eastward across Eurasia in time to be the weapon of the first American mammoth hunters, but it was certainly the characteristic weapon of the bison hunters. Thus, although migrations from Asia to America occurred over a definable range of several thousand years, through a careful assessment of widespread or universal culture traits in both Americas, we can get a fairly clear picture of the primary culture base of the New World in relation to the Old. This culture horizon again is roughly from the Magdalenian (late Paleolithic of Eurasia) to the Mesolithic. Perhaps because the high latitudes significant for land migration were sparsely populated hunting territories and were already occupied by hunters from the late Paleolithic onward, no important migrations from Asia seem to have occurred since the arrival of the Eskimo-Aleut in Alaska (with the possible exception, farther south and by sea, of some few Polynesians *from* Oceania *to* the Americas, in contravention of the notorious "Kon-tiki" hypothesis). The Neolithic in America—since all the cultivated plants, with one very dubious exception, the sweet potato, and all the domesticated animals, except the dog, are different from those of the Old World—is clearly an independent New World development.

The core culture of the Americas is therefore Asiatic Magdalenian-Mesolithic in base, with later specialized local developments independent of Asia. The earliest New World cultures correlate directly with those of the Old, of appropriate period. Further, in their lack of later outside influence and in their remarkable homogeneity, American Indian cultures preserve for us genuine ethnographic insights into the late Paleolithic-Mesolithic cultures of Eurasia. It is important to realize that the Asiatic-American connection is not based on mere remote inference, but on actual geographic culture-continuities. For example, the semi-subterranean house that goes back to the advanced Paleolithic peoples of southern Siberia, is found also among modern Siberians now farther north, including the Kyzil-Khakasy, Ostyak, Samoyed, Lamut, Goldi, Gilyak, Chukchi, Koryak and Kamchadal, as well as the Siberian Eskimo and Alaskan Eskimo-Aleut; in North America, the semi-subterranean house extends from both Alaskan Indians and Eskimos through western Canada to the American Southwest (the Mandan earth-covered lodge of the Plains and the subterranean ceremonial Pueblo *kiva* must be recognized as related forms).[8]

Again, the conical, skin-covered *tipi*,[9] found in central-western Canada south to the American Plains, is also found among such Siberian tribes as the Buryat, Tuvan, Tofalar, Nentsy, Ngansan, Samoyed, Kets, Tungus, Yakut, Nanay, Orochi, Yukaghir, Chukchi and Koryak. In North America, bark-covered wigwams[10] are found among almost all the eastern Woodlands Algonkians and Iroquoians; in Siberia, tribes using the wigwam include the Yakuts, Altai, Kachin-, Kyzil- and Sagay-Khakasy, Tuvans, Shors, Tofalars, Khant, Nentsy, Ngansan, northern Sel'kup, Kets, Evenk, Tungus, Orochen, Birar, Manegry, Evens of Okhotsk, Negidal, Nanay, Ul'chi, Udegey, Orok, and the Reindeer Yukaghir. The birchbark canoe, widespread among Iroquoians and Algonkians of the United States and Canada, is used in Siberia by the Yakuts, Goldi, Gilyak, Evenk and (formerly) Udegey; Orochi legends also mention birchbark boats.[11] The Koryak have a skin-covered hunter's boat like the Eskimo *kayak,* and so also do the Aleuts. Skis are Scandinavian and eastward to the Altai, Ostyak, Goldi, and the Kamchadal of Kamchatka, though the Kamchadal mostly use snowshoes; snowshoes are of course Alaskan and Canadian eastward to the Indians of Maine. The travois, or inverted V-drag over the dog's back for carrying goods, is Altai and Tuvan, as well as Canadian and Plains. Slit-eyed snow goggles are Yakut and Tungus, as well as Eskimo; the cradleboard is Gilyak, as well as North American. The sweat-lodge, equivalent to the *sauna* of the Swedes and Finns, extends eastward around the world across Siberia to most of Canada, and into much of the northern United States.[12] The distribution of sleds, sledges and toboggans when plotted on a Mercator-projection map would show long, concentric, circumboreal ovals from Finland to Maine centering upon the Behring Straits, with the more specialized new types central and the simpler older types successively more peripheral and widespread.[13] It is the overwhelming mass and consistency of evidence that leads scholars universally to agree on a Siberian-Asiatic origin for the American Indians. Racially, for example, Indians are early unspecialized Mongoloid types (e.g. without "slant eyes") with the appropriate blood-group proportions, etc.—which fits all the other *kinds* of evidence.

Nor are Asiatic-American shared traits merely those of material culture. Bear ceremonialism has a circumboreal distribution even wider than that of the sled-sledge-toboggan complex. The "magic flight" legend, in which the pursued figure in folklore casts behind him objects to deter the pursuer, succeeding only with the last, is Eurasiatic and American alike[14]; the Orpheus legend of the shaman's descent to the underworld is widespread in North America, as well as in Eurasia.[15] Scalping is ancient Scythian in south Russia eastward to New England and south to the Plains and west to the Great Basin; it reappears in a slightly different form in the shrunken whole head-skins of Amazonia.[16] Shamanism of a specifically Eurasiatic type is distributed from ancient Scandinavia to eastern Siberia, and continues from Alaska eastward to Greenland and southward to Patagonia in the New World.[17] There can be no question of the relatedness of these ancient, continuous and far-flung traits in both material and non-material culture.

The "pan-American" base culture inferred for the first Indians is well known since the classic studies of Kroeber. The earliest mammoth hunters may have had only spears; certainly the spear-thrower (Aurignacian at least, in Europe) has a wide, though interrupted, occurrence which suggests that it is very old in the New World; at the same time, the bow and arrow is so nearly universal in both North and South America as to appear very early indeed also. The archaic Americans had dogs for hunting, and fire, which they made with a fire-drill of one stick hand-twirled upon another. They had woven and also twisted two-ply "twined" basketry; distributionally, coiled basketry must have come later. Only late-comers, apparently, had pottery. Their clothes were at best rude and untailored wrap-around furs; and in warmer climates farther south they discarded even these to go nude in parts of California, middle America, and most of Amazonia, though in parts of this huge area woven clothing was later used. But again in bleak and windswept Patagonia, their only coverings in the coldest weather are even in historic times only a rough furred hide held around the body, and a coating of animal fat rubbed on the skin. In material culture these ancient Americans had at best achieved only a late Old Stone Age culture much like that we know archeologically from the caves of France and western Europe.[18]

On the same trait-distributional grounds we can be reasonably certain also about the social culture of these peoples, even though they issued from an obscure and historyless part of the globe. For example, since monogamy was required only in the Pueblos and in a few other places, we may safely infer that our first Americans at least permitted polygyny, even if every man did not actually achieve it economically. Among bison and guanaco hunters, polygyny might depend mainly on a man's power to pre-empt several wives and to provide for them through his hunting; but among mammoth hunters, adult male mortality may have been high and polygyny a natural consequence in that biomass.

Few traits are so conspicuous as the male-centeredness of society among American hunters. The early Americans had no agriculture and no domesticated animal except the dog, and probably few food reserves beyond what they hunted and gathered. Especially in the lean times of winter, everything depended on the strength and ability of the hunter for continued survival of the group. Hunting pitted against hunger was a constant area of anxiety, as is evident in basic Indian religion and folklore. For example, in the "windigo psychosis" of high-latitude Canadian Algonkians, the unsuccessful winter hunter was believed to become possessed by the spirit of a cannibal giant whose bones were made of ice, and the failed hunter came back to camp a raving-mad cannibal attempting to eat his dependents. It is remarkable that even among the wealthy sedentary folk of the warm Northwest Coast, the purpose of the prestigious "Cannibal Society" winter dance was ritually to tame an initiate gone cannibal-mad in the woods—a ceremony with echoes in the "olonism" of the Siberian Tungus, to be described later. Despite the awesome and unquestionable antiquity of these rituals and myths found both in Siberia and America, their details are discernibly related.[19]

Since only males are hunters, aboriginal American society had a distinctly masculine cast. And since hunting rests on the skill of each man's strong right arm, it was also competitive, individualistic and open. No man owed subservience to another. But generosity with the products of the hunt was absolutely basic in American society, and generosity remained the foundation of prestige systems even among later more highly developed tribes.[20] The original basis of this is plain: after the dreadful dangers of the ancient mammoth group hunt, a share in the kill by all survivors is only to be expected; and among lone stalk-hunters, if one man had bad luck in his hunting, it was simple life insurance to share food, as among Eskimo seal hunters. But again it is remarkable how this early hunting

ethos persisted, often quite unnecessarily and irrationally, in later-elabo-
rated forms. For example, in the Northwest Coast *potlach,* conspicuously
wealthy people still fiercely compete in generosity to obtain symbolic social
prestige. To honor an institutionalized "favorite child" in the Plains,[21]
food and property are lavishly given away; and at most Indian feasts
everywhere, guests are supposed to take home the inevitable surplus food.
Plains Indian "vowed" ceremonies, from the Sun Dance to Peyotism, all
imply a feast provided by the vower. It is possible that the Amazonian
"great house" of the chief, where tribesmen gather from their single family
farm huts in the bush for tribal dances and feasts, grew out of this
same basic custom of generosity in giving. Even developed Inca "com-
munalism" had an expected outflow of goods to balance the economic
inflow. Indian giving implied reciprocity. But he who could not return
in full amount or better lost status, while the conspicuously lavish giver
gained permanent social status. The roots of this pattern in hunting, and
the trauma to male character when this prestige system was historically
no longer possible, have been insufficiently emphasized in Americanist
studies.

It is necessary, moreover, to recognize both sides of the situation. The
lavish giver is socially conspicuous and admirable; and yet his success
bred in others a deep and curious dependency of character among American Indians, which also has been insufficiently attended to.[22] It has been
suggested that the ease with which Indian bands attached themselves,
under near-aboriginal conditions, to fur-trading agents rested on this same
habit of dependency upon the giver of goods. As a matter of fact, the
same dependency is basic in the ideology of the vision quest: the young
boy, who has none at all, beseeches and begs the supernatural for male
"power" as though this were a commodity. Thus male prestige among
American Indians not only depends on ability to provide and to give
generously—not to accumulate materially but to produce and distribute
goods for an intangible "spiritual" prestige—but also reciprocally influences the concept of the supernatural as a kind of reservoir of the commodity: discrete, impersonal, bestowable "power." Male personality itself
is part of an "open" system.

The "openness" of American hunting societies explains another remarkable phenomenon—the premium placed on a chief's powers of persuasion,
which rose at times to great force and quality. Whatever else they were,
great native Americans, from Hiawatha to Chief Joseph, were usually
consummate orators.[23] In few arts, certainly not in music or painting,
could Indian accomplishments bear comparison with those of many societies of equivalent complexity in the Old World. Only in ritual did Ameri-

can Indians excel; and it is no accident that their highest intellectual and artistic flights were the written word in Maya books and the spoken word in Inca dramas. Even the hieratic architecture and sculpture, impressive though scarcely beautiful, of the theocratic cultures of Mexico and Peru both derive ultimately from religious ritual. But ritual serves the agglutination of uncritical and ordinary men; thus, with little social stratification and few settled elites, authentic fine arts scarcely developed in America.

As the size of the group grew, Indian society was still "open" to a marked degree. The size of the hunting band, in various times and places in America, undoubtedly depended on the animals hunted, whether mammoth, buffalo, or deer. But everywhere the hunting band can be seen as the aboriginal form, underlying and preceding later more elaborate political structures. The Eskimo have no "state"—they are only brawling, but meat-sharing, hunters. In regions of hardly less difficult winter hunting "atomistic" family-band hunters and trappers among Algonkians in south-central Canada are barely more co-operative—though the rapid northward autumn hunting among Athapaskans to prepare hasty food-caches, used in later slow winter southing, implies co-operation in a small band.

The "state" in America was at one time no more than the strength and influence of visible men: band chiefs. In the Plains, winter hunting was still on a band level; and the whole tribe came together only for the tribal hunt at the yearly summer Sun Dance. Individual families in the Plains might attach themselves to or leave a hunting band at will, depending on their feelings toward the personality of the band chief, or on fights they may have had with other band members. This put a premium on the chief's ability to compose personal quarrels among band members. The band chief was first of all the best hunter in the group, and generosity to his dependents was the basic reason for adherence to his band. As well as constantly seeking to mute in-group aggression, he also had to protect his band from outside aggression. Significantly, at the Sun Dance, one of the men's honorary warrior societies had to be specially appointed to keep order among the assembled, proudly independent hunters, and to police the tribal hunt; and the end of the Sun Dance was an appropriate time for war-parties of men, now full of supernatural "power," to make raids on other tribes.

Group size and ecology are as clear in other areas. In the southern Plains, band chiefs formed incipient though only temporary tribal governments.[24] But among sedentary maize-growing Iroquoian deer hunters, whole sub-tribes joined into the Iroquoian confederation—important to Americans not only because it formed a shield for the infant colonies, but also because we borrowed some aspects of our "federal system" di-

rectly from the Iroquoian federation. Among maize-growing Virginia hunters and fishermen, similarly, there were confederations too, such as that
of Powhatan. Among settled Pueblo agriculturalists of the Southwest there
are permanent tribal villages. Among the Colombian Chibchans, who had
both maize and potatoes, incipient feudatory empires arose; and among
highland Andean and Mexican agriculturalists, true intertribal conquest
empires.

Thus from Comanche to Iroquois and from Aztec to Inca, these larger
social aggregates exploited their ecological potentials primarily for further
war. The ethos of American Indians was born in the necessary aggression
of hunting, and aggressive their later elaborated institutions remained. If
one major function of the chief was to keep peace among individuals
within the group, whatever its size, another remained always to be the
leader in war. American chiefs were concerned with the management
of the aggressions of more and more people living together, and the
exporting of unsubduable residues onto wild animals, other tribes or bands,
or sacrificial victims captured from the enemy. In post-Columbian times,
when hunting buffalo from horseback became too easy to indicate invidious prestige, the Plains Indians focused obsessively on the man-hunt instead. Even economically more comfortable tribes never escaped the past:
Northwest Coast potlaching aggression was symbolic but overt, though
these were a wealthy, surplus-economy group; virulent Pueblo witchcraft
was symbolic but hidden, though these were securely agricultural folk.

We will not argue that successively more civilized societies inherit from
primal hunters more raw biological aggressiveness than, for their new
purposes, they need (though this may be the case); nor make invidious
judgments of Indians compared with European and other peoples. It is
simply that obsessively male-centered Indian societies never had a spectacle of other cultural alternatives, say, some that explored more the full
round of human potential, the feminine too. Aboriginal Americans knew
only the male principle, virile power.[25] More and more collected scalps
evidenced the power in a warrior's medicine bundle. More medicine bundles proclaimed the supernatural wealth of the Blackfoot entrepreneur.
More shrunken heads from the enemy increased the male potency of the
Amazonian tribelet in constant war with its neighbors. The spirit-force of
the Aztec god was increased with each human soul he ate: more victims
were sacrificed annually to the god Xipe than died a natural death in
all Mexico; Cortez saw 136,000 skulls deposited in the great temple;
Prescott estimated a yearly toll of 20,000–50,000 human sacrifices in all
Mexico; and at the dedication in 1486 of a new temple, 70,000 prisoners of war, collected for this purpose over some years, were sacrificed

to the god Huitzilopochtli. American Indian societies have been too long romanticized. They were bloody and cruel. Having, in two over-similar continents, too few conceptual categories, the socially useful admiration of the hunter, uncorrected, ended repeatedly in this social brutality.

There was another kind of openness in aboriginal American society. Of race-prejudice, the Indians had none, being all of similar race.[26] This meant that the individual, whatever his tribal origin, was free to rise, depending entirely on his own personal qualities. Whatever the fate of power-containing grown men, in both the Americas captive children, taken from even the most bitterly fought enemy, were customarily adopted and brought up as full tribal members, with no social disability whatever—for were they too not contributions to tribal potential, especially as this may have been depleted in battle—and they could even become chiefs. This racially unprejudiced openness was extended later even to those of manifestly alien race. For example, Quanah Parker, the celebrated great chief of the Comanche, was the son of a white girl captured on a raid into Texas and married by an important brave. Indeed, the chief war god of the Aztec was yearly impersonated by a captive enemy youth who had been the bravest in the battle. In war as in hunting, and in social and political power as well, status depended on the individual's own competitive efforts or personal gifts. Sheer masculine aggressiveness was the criterion of success. Codified law to protect vested interests reached no such development in America as in the roughly comparable complex societies of West Africa. The whole tone of the hunting ethos in America suggested that each man was "on his own" and obliged to defend his rights and status with power, natural or supernatural.

Male power was obtained in several ways: through body-trophy collecting, cannibalistic incorporation, or supernatural gift. The supernatural gift of power in the vision quest, we can assert on distributional grounds, was undoubtably aboriginal in America.[27] The "power" concept is at base a most curiously naïve and mistaken explanation of the facts of life. It is true that models of manhood are witnessed culturally, and introjected or incorporated *as a pattern* from outside; but we know that the primary impetus toward manhood is intrinsic and lies biologically inside. Here, however, manhood is not considered the end-result of life forces inevitably maturing and developing inside the organism. On the contrary, virility, supernatural "medicine" or power, obviously lacking in the child, Indians think must be incorporated completely from the outside in order to make the man.

Man everywhere may "need myth" to explain himself and his world. But the consequences of myth are not indifferent or innocuously comparable. It is not too much to state that this false notion of the facts of life, the "expropriative" theory of puberty or spirit-power, is at the bottom of the most lamentable developments in New World culture, just as mistaken childhood fantasies may lie at the root of individual neurosis. Blind postulates have corollaries. Now it is true that something mysterious plainly happens to a boy at puberty. His spirit hardens, he begins to make aggressive demands on life, and as Plains Indians express it he becomes "mean." He now contains, for the first time, the male power to create life. At the same time hair appears on his body, and so hair must be connected with male procreativity and strength—his "power."

But some men possess more personality force or "power" than others do. What is then simpler than to believe that different men somehow acquire different amounts of it? A boy child is no different from a girl in that he *gets none of his food himself,* unlike other primates or herbivores, but is always *given to* by a group of powerful male hunters. What is more natural than to suppose that generalized maleness also, as well as physical growth from food, is to be sought from generalized outside supernatural power? People eat animal meat and grow bigger and stronger. Some huge and dangerous animals like the hairy mammoth and buffalo are more powerful even than men. Why not incorporate from animals their great force as well as their flesh? What is more reasonable, too, than that in a male-centered and competitive society the young male should seek to obtain the power on which his future success as a man depends? One need not eat their flesh to seek the predatory hunting power of the wolf or fox, the swiftness of a mink or marten, the hunting range of the high-flying eagle, for all these are successful hunters too. But the hairy skins of inedible predatory animals and feathers of the owl and eagle are good fetishes or containers of their "medicine" or magical powers.

The vision quest in hunting tribes is interesting in its religious individualism. The boy went out alone, to a remote and isolated place, to fast and pray for a ritual number of days and nights, remaining awake, or struggling to, the whole time. Under this induced physical stress, and the abnormal psychic state coming from social isolation and deprivation of sleep, he might hope to have a dream or visionary experience, or sign of the favor of some supernatural power. Considering the self-possession, even pride and arrogance, of the adult male among Indian hunting tribes, the peculiar psychological context of the vision quest is strikingly significant. The boy displayed himself as a have-not, a helpless child; he might weep, he might lacerate himself until he bled. He solicited the "pity" of a supernatural who might give him power in his condition of childlike weakness. Perhaps an experience would be too threatening and he would run away and lose the power: it is a testing. But usually he got some physical fetish in which the power resided, a curiously shaped stone, a fallen feather; or some small animal would run by whose skin would cover the "medicine bundle" or physical repository of this supernatural power. In this way a young man would tap the vast and impersonalized supply of "mana" or magic power in the world, each man his own shaman. This vague mana was the *orenda* of the Iroquois, the *manitou* of the Algonkians, and the *wakan* of the Sioux—quite different from the manlike individual gods of the Pueblo and Aztec, which appear only in settled agricultural societies with priestly traditions and more autocratic political authorities on which psychologically to model such gods. He must obtain the power for himself, and in himself, alone. From a richer source of power than himself he has been *given* male power. As Boas noted, the vision quest is basic to all New World religion.

But if power is outside the self, one can also aggressively *take* it as well. The second way of getting power in America was by collecting human body-trophies, especially those parts in which power was concentrated. Power was thought to reside especially in the skull or in the hairy parts, for it is clear that the skull- and scalp-collecting complex in America was part of an ancient Eurasiatic and circum-Pacific pattern of collecting soul power in such trophies.[28] Indeed, the concept of the separable and annexable soul has been as noxious historically as the Amerindian fantasy of exogenous puberty: in southeast Asia (e.g., the Wa States of Burma), in Indonesia (e.g., Borneo), and throughout Melanesia, head-hunting seems aimed mostly at collecting vital power for the whole group, as when a man must take an enemy head before he may marry and so expend the tribal sum of vital power, hence in these places life-making entails eternal inter-tribal warfare. But in North America, scalping served mainly to increase the power and prestige of the individual person (as skull-taking, among Aztecs, did of the god), though there was also some sense of group benefit in the scalp-dance, i.e., a "decontamination" ritual to depersonalize and domesticate the power for tribal use. In middle and South America, most or all of the head skin, or the head itself, or in some cases even the whole skin, was a ritual trophy. Scatteredly, the pubic scalp, or the genitals, or their parts, were the trophies, as in upper Amazonia where the Boro chief's wife ate the phallus of a fallen enemy and thus incorporated his power into the tribe. But in Amazonia head-hunting also is widespread and well-known.

Thus a third way of incorporating mana is to eat it. Gods are evidently entirely manlike in their tastes, and in Mexico gods battened in power by incorporating the souls of their victims, including that of the brave enemy youth, sacrificed to the war god after his year of "impersonating" the god, war power added to war power—surely a "racially unprejudiced" feeding of the tribal god's very essence with the impersonalized mana of the enemy! In this sense the New World lacked *intrinsically powerful* true gods: these war-spirits had to incorporate their power from outside too. Human sacrifice to gods centers in middle America and extends to the Caribs and into the interior of Brazil. Blood sacrifice, skin-fragment sacrifice, and finger-joint sacrifice (Aurignacian in antiquity in France and Spain) of living individuals to spirits is even wider spread in the Americas.

Feeding humans or even parts of them to the gods is symbolic cannibalism, and the simple manlikeness[29] of projected gods consequently implies earlier cannibalism on the part of men: but apparently the tastes of gods change more slowly than those of their worshipers. The cannibalism of ancient Eurasiatic Neanderthaloids from Krapina to Peking is well established (as also is a developed skull cult in Eurasia from the late Paleolithic onward)—and yet, though cannibalism was symbolically well preserved in American Indian ritual and religion, the actual human eating of other men was uncommon and areally quite restricted in the post-Columbian New World. Eskimo cannibalism occurred only in times of great starvation and was distinctly not an accepted or usual culture pattern. In the Northwest Coast ritual of the winter dance, human flesh was bitten off by the "cannibal" initiate, but only ceremonially and with great loathing, almost as "proof" of the initiate's insanity. North of Mexico, actual cannibalism as an established cultural practice was found only in Texas among the Tonkawa, although it has been alleged of other Indians, in particular the Caddo of the southern Plains and the extinct Calusa of Florida. The Shoshoni are said to have eaten parts of a fallen enemy if he had shown any special courage; and the Huron roasted the heart of such a foe, cut it into bits, and gave these to young men and boys (much as the Chukchi of Siberia did and the Piritú and Lenca of South America) —but otherwise even such part-cannibalistic practices were sporadic among Indians of the United States.[30]

However, cannibalism flourished in middle America and southward into Amazonia. Fierce cannibals, now extinct, once lived in the Acaxee and Xixime areas of northern Mexico; and the Aztec ate parts of the bodies of ritual human sacrifices, as did also the Maya and the Chibcha. In Nicaragua there was special breeding of persons to be eaten, with strict apportionment of body parts to the chief, the priests, warriors, trumpeters and other people. The Caranque in ancient Peru also ate the flesh of human victims whose spirits had been sacrificially eaten by the gods.

Cannibalism was strongly developed in the Colombian highlands, and among the Camanagoto, Marcapana and Palenque of Venezuela. Among the Caramanta and tribes east of the Cauca River, cannibalism mounted to a definite appetite for human flesh. Of the Andeans, the Aymara and the Araucanians cooked and ate war captives.

But Amazonia is the *locus classicus* of American cannibalism. The Tupi and Carib tribes ate captives, often after breaking their legs to prevent escape and keeping them for some time. Other tribes that ate war-captives or enemy victims were the Zaparoans of the upper Amazon, the Guiana Arawak, the Witoto and other northwest Amazonians, the Patángoro of Colombia, the Canichana of eastern Bolivia, and the Amniapa and Guaratagaja of the Guaporé River. In the Caribbean, the very word "cannibal" comes from the name of the notorious island Carib or "carribals" of that region. However, it is important to recognize that almost nowhere in the Americas was there the "epicurean cannibalism" of Africa and Oceania. Eating was almost always involved in some practical fashion with warriorly or religious spirit-incorporation; and so too the eating of dead relatives and friends by the Mayoruna and Cocoma of Brazil out of protective kindness.

Abstract "power" was sought in the Americas, then, in these three ways: through supernatural "gift" from the universal supply of outside mana, through body-trophy collecting especially of scalps and skulls, and through outright cannibalistic incorporation of parts or the whole of other human bodies. While the power concept was universal, the specific vision quest was not. The lone vision quest was characteristic of the hunting peoples primarily, though it remained fundamental in all American Indian religion ideologically. Thus the *individual* vision quest was associated with a buffalo hunting ecology in the early Plains; with the coming of the horse, mounted plainsmen became not so much hunters as wealthy pastoralists who did not have to care for their herds, and the new plains-wide Sun Dance was a kind of assembled *tribal* "vision quest" to give power now to a tribal palladium instead of to an individual medicine bundle; the subsequent Ghost Dance, though influenced by white notions of immortality and world-renewal, was an *inter-tribal* crisis cult of spirits; and, finally, peyotism was an assembled pharmacological vision quest, now become *inter-tribal* and even *international*. Only the size of the group, not the concept, has changed.

Something of the same sequence, accompanying larger socio-ecological aggregates, occurred on the aboriginal level also in American religion, quite independently of European influence. For example, in the socially more integrated agricultural and semi-agricultural tribes, there was often rather more of a *group* puberty-crisis ritual, as in the Virginia "huskinaw-ing" of boys, with the use of the Black Drink (*Ilex cassine, I. yaupon,* and *I. vomitoria*). Again, in the Pueblos, groups of masked dancers representing specific supernaturals came to whip the ritually assembled boys (the ceremonial whipping of boys at puberty is also widespread elsewhere in the Americas). As the size of the social unit changed, so too did the stature of the magic fetishes. The Sun was originally the power source merely of the royal Inca clan, but was later worshiped in the whole Inca Empire. In the Sun Dance of the Plains the tribal palladia—the Cheyenne sacred arrows, the Sacred Hat of the Arapaho, the Ten Medicine Bundles of the Kiowa, and other sacred images or fetishes—were really only *group medicine bundles* in which lay power, now of the whole tribe. It is only one step beyond tribal palladia to the power-fed images of the Aztec "gods." Quetzalcoatl, the "plumed serpent," is still the male arrow.

There are other local phrasings of the vision quest. In much of North America, most or all young men in the tribe sought supernatural visions, typically around puberty. But in Amazonia only shamans did, though here as elsewhere many tried to become shamans but failed. The exclusive focusing of "medicine power" in the shaman, who alone made the vision quest in Amazonia, is correlated with two other phenomena: the godlike grandiosity of these shamans, who could even control the weather and other natural events in the outside world; and the fact that in Amazonia the shaman often functioned as chief of the tribe—uniting in one person both shaman and chief as in the immensely antique and shadowy figure of the "divine king" who is behind both the ancient gods of Europe and the African rain king.

At first glance there would seem to be a contrast between the vision-seeker of North America and the shaman-chief of South America—as though the first were a democratized form of power-seeking by all men, or as though the latter were the exclusive specialist in power-seeking. The contrast, however, is merely superficial and a matter of divergent emphasis. With the stabilizing of individuated gods, tribal shamans in the agricultural Pueblos of North America inevitably became *rain-priests,* because weather control (now still more needed) was one attribute of the old shaman prototype among hunters; in fact the priestly hierarchy is very close to *being* the tribal government in the Pueblos. Similarly, the California shamans of world-renewal cults make quite as large claims as do the nature-shamans of Amazonia—and as do the shaman-prophets of the Indian crisis cults we are shortly to examine. Again, the trickster-transformer Coyote-Raven-Manabush figure of Indian legend is plainly a shaman, with a shaman's skills and failures, and not a "high-god" Creator, for all the trickster's shamanistic arrogance. As supernatural protector of the group, a shaman's being (like Coyote) a fertility figure and master of animals in hunting magic has no inconsistency with being a master of disease spirits also, for magic cure is an essential skill of the medicine man. The function of war-shaman to bring magic success to war parties is the same protection, conceptually, all over again.

The purpose of "power" emphatically concerns *the role of the male leader in ancient hunting.* He is concerned with the mastery of animals, that is of their *availability,* whether through hunting magic, fertility magic, or weather magic alike. And he is concerned with the protection, natural and supernatural, of his dependents in the group, whether in battles with other men or in encounters with the supernatural. Hunting success and group protection—these two roles are visible throughout. It does not matter if, later, one or many men seek power; it does not matter whether the ability he yearns for be technical or magical; and it does not matter in what many later specialized forms these two concerns become expressed. It is simply that these two concerns to provide and to protect are the inescapable male responsibilities of the ancient hunter.

All variants in later history come from the basic function of the hunter-leader as provider and protector of his group. We categorize and subdivide these functions quite differently, as male specialties have gradually become culturally more elaborated. But our pseudo-problems arise only from our own categories, and not from the unity of this original figure and his functions. As secular leader in a larger group he is a chief, a political leader, a king—and in this latter role not wholly without magic or divine attributes either. In war, he is either the war-shaman (magic, sacred) or (secular) the war-chief—nor are the roles of political leader and war leader always separated in later European Caesars and kings or American presidents, or wholly devoid of charisma or magic hocus-pocus. (Caesar was Pontifex Maximus in Rome.) As supernatural protector, the shaman is both medicine man to the individual and priest to the group—but whether modern doctor or divine he is still descended from the same shaman, and both can use a touch of paranoia in their work. Nor have church and state always and everywhere sundered their original unity, nor have Pueblo hierarchies and papacies always wholly eschewed political power.

However, only one aspect of the ancient hunter-leader will concern us for the rest of this study—his "power" and his role as supernatural protector. For it is clear that the vatic role of shaman tends to attract personalities of a special type, even though all men have at times the need to imagine or to boast of greater knowledge and power than they have. Although an Indian chief—more properly a "chief man" since a tribe may have many of them—quite manifestly has much "medicine power" as hunter and warrior, nevertheless the figures of shaman versus chief are already distinct in North America. Certainly they are more so than in aboriginal Siberia and in Amazonian South America. The Siberian shaman is still largely the leader and chief man in his little social group, which he protects from supernatural dangers through his control of the spirits, and for whom he provides through his control of the "masters of animals" (the ancient Eurasiatic shaman, we should note here incidentally, *was himself* the "master of animals"). In Amazonia either the chief has great medicine power or the shaman himself is the chief, really mere phrasings of the same thing. In North America, though many men might each have his guardian spirit animal, the shaman was distinctly *primus inter pares* with respect to supernatural forces.

The shaman was the intermediary between his group and the supernatural unknown, the intermediary between man's needs and anxieties, and the world he lives in and only partly knows. Often of unstable or abnormal type, often transvestite, sometimes even psychotic in our society's terms though not necessarily in his own, the shaman may be seen as the individual most threatened by the uncertainties of life, and perhaps also the most unable to meet them on practical secular grounds or in ordinary male terms. But at the same time it was the shaman whose autistic defenses against these threats and anxieties obtained "solutions" of which his society stood in dire need. In his own way, like the hunter and the chief, the shaman was the protector of his group, through his special "knowledge" of the unknown and adaptive "power" over the feared.

He had many "shamanistic tricks" to impress the people. He was especially a master over that mysterious entity, fire. He could juggle and swallow coals of fire with impunity. He could project foreign bodies by magical means into enemies and make them sicken or die; as doctor or medicine man he could suck out evil things and the alien objects in people that were causing the sickness. He could cause the tent to shake with invisible powers, he could summon supernaturals at great speed and from great distances to appear magically from the earth in the tent. A shaman could also himself travel under the earth, or in the air, or under the sea to distant places, there to encounter the powerful supernaturals, to overcome them or to learn their will, and to bring back intelligence from the supernatural world. In some cases, these spirits would possess the shaman's own body and speak through his mouth. When the shaman was "possessed" by these spirits, to his fellows he *was* the supernatural in its at least temporary embodiment. (It requires only a skepticism about the supernaturals to know that, in a sophisticated sense, the shaman *is in toto* the "supernatural" in belief, act, and social effect.)

It is well to keep in mind the social context of the shaman: a hunting society in which a very high premium was placed on male effectiveness, because of the life-or-death meaning of men's getting food, sometimes through killing terrifyingly huge or dangerous animals. What man with only his puny hand-weapons could face without fear a gigantic wounded hairy mammoth, or even kill on foot a raging half-ton buffalo from amid a juggernaut herd? These are terrors that not all men can manage. Some men, or all men at some times, must break and flee the sometimes total catastrophe that the ancient hunt of big game must have been. And yet the life of the whole horde depended on the mustered courage of mere men, for in glacial and late Pleistocene times there was no other food than these great beasts. It is plain why hunting societies in America are so obsessively male-centered. And the pattern remained pervasive. So basically do recent Indians assume that individual excellence and personal superiority must be masculine that women of high social dominance must inevitably be called "manly-hearted women" among the Blackfoot and the Piegan, even one who had been a pampered "favorite child" or who was now an especially esteemed wife.

Pathology throws light upon the normal. Shamans, we note, specialize in the autistic but ego-enhancing aspects of supernatural male "power." But shamans might nevertheless hunt. And some shamans, with enough power to protect the whole party, would often go with warriors on the warpath. Some shamans, though, we have noted too, were transvestite, if only temporarily in the shamanistic séance. A far graver pathology was the permanently transvestite male, the *berdache,*[31] the manifest and public "not-man" who wore women's clothes. The male-centeredness of American Indian society is nowhere more evident than in the curious phenomenon of the *berdache,* one of the almost universally encountered institutions in the New World. Hardly any contact-period explorer's account is without mention of this anomaly; it is a commonplace in field ethnography, and the *berdache* is a frequent enough figure in the memory of old Indians in every tribe.

Often enough homosexual, sometimes he might marry another man, but sometimes a *berdache* might marry and beget children. Frequently a powerful and feared shaman, he might go hunting; sometimes, as shaman, he might even accompany a party on the warpath, but only to provide the men with supernatural protection and not himself to kill.

Socially he is the "not man" and is so signalized in his woman's dress and women's economic occupations. The *berdache* is the not-man who refuses to perform the most frightening parts of the male role—to kill or be killed, to mutilate or be mutilated. He wards off this fate in reality by anticipating and accepting it symbolically. His specific anxiety is evident: so intense and so threatening are the psychic burdens placed on maleness in Indian culture that enough such men are produced to create the overt institution. And certainly there are enough alienated persons in our own consumer-oriented society for us to recognize why the culturally alienated must represent the reversed mirror image of the rejected norm.

Although everyone is aware that the *berdache* is physically a male, his specific not-man-ness is nevertheless typically rationalized in terms of the male vision quest. A usual story would be that, as every boy, he had gone out on a vision quest at puberty. However, in his vision, the Moon, when he reached out for the bow she tendered in one hand, quickly crossed over her arms, and he got instead a woman's elk-rib drawknife for tanning or some such other instrument. He did not *get manhood* at his puberty crisis. His inner unconscious has sanctioned his accepted social status, but it is rationalized as an outside supernatural compulsion.

Since he is nevertheless male, curiously his very anomaly bespeaks some strange supernatural "power," and a *berdache* might quite easily become a shaman, though by no means all shamans are transvestite. In some tribes like the Navaho, the *berdache* is supernaturally associated with wealth in animals like sheep and horses; we will encounter the frequent analog of this later. Again, since a *berdache* is, after all, male, he is expected to do even women's work better than they. A typical Plains Indian compliment would be, "She does beadwork as fine as a *berdache!*" Some *berdaches* in their "feminine protest" mimic women so far as to simulate menses, force menstrual and pregnancy taboos on their husbands, and even pretend to give birth. And finally to illustrate cultural obsession with maleness, it is not the *berdache* but his husband who suffers obloquy in such a marriage. It is not sexuality as such that preoccupies the Indians, for the *berdache* has already been "demeaned" into a woman through dress. But like an American man who marries wealth, thus not validating his masculinity by earning money directly (like a man) but getting it through marriage (in a woman's way) from the prior worth of her father or former husband—so also such a husband of a *berdache* does not even have to hunt for himself, since the *berdache* might. A *berdache's* husband is thus paradigmatically as awkward and unimpressive as an American "squaw-man" is.

Indians do not "approve of" (an alien category anyway) neither do they reject the *berdache,* but instead show a gamut of attitudes from respect to awe.[32] For who can explain the vicissitudes of the vision quest? People do not contemn and never ridicule the *berdache,* for he is not responsible for his supernatural fate, and besides the tribe may benefit from his especial supernatural power which is otherwise to be feared. Indians are at best puzzled by the spectacle of a male "not-man" and appropriately cautious toward the potentially ambivalent use of his power. Also, other men can sufficiently empathize unconsciously his basic anxieties for the *berdache* to be overtly accepted as an institution. The cultural myth is that manhood can be gained only by supernatural gift, by incorporation, or by hunt-like predation. The *berdache* is the light-ning-rod of other men's anxieties and repressed fears, as is the artist in our society. The *berdache* likewise "proves" the system as the visible social result of fated not-man-ness, hence he may also spur other men on, in the pursuit and collection of reassurance and male trophies, of the scalps and phallic feathers of male prowess. The *berdache* is, in a sense, the psychic obverse of the "Crazy Dogs," the highest-ranking warriors' society in the Plains, whose members, in suicidal arrogance, would "tether" themselves in battle to one spot by shooting an arrow into a trailing sash, and take on an entire enemy tribe to the death—an alternative way of escape from the endless male game of the Plains. Still another extreme illustrates the same basic theme: Indians found it hard to explain the outstanding or dominant female, who sometimes took on a fully male social role—so they called her a "manly-hearted woman."[34]

Civilized men are psychologically quite cut off from their ecological roots—from the herdsman's close concern for the safety and fertility of his flock, from the farmer's constant watching of weather and the growth of his crops. Still, we might abstractly expect that hunters would be generally preoccupied with animals and be knowledgeable about their ways. What is perhaps not to be anticipated is that the very structure of hunting religion should express so striking a human-ecological close-ness to animals even to a kind of oedipal "identification with the enemy" they pit themselves against. Hunters kill and eat sometimes large and dangerous animals; their own substance comes from the flesh of the animals they eat. The life they extinguish feeds the fire of their own. The hunter is the eater of life.

As a hunter, early man is not merely a predator. He is also an animal that brings to the kill the effects of his individual human ecology and peculiar species-psychology. In their fascination with animals, children are likewise natural totemists. That is, they easily project their feelings

and fears onto animals and identify naïvely with them. Frightened children and fearful hunters both easily mix up ego-anxiety and superego
anxiety, that is the real danger that may come from animals, and an
animistic-anthropomorphic guilt about them. Hunting religion must therefore cope with the anxiety of *getting* animals to eat as well as with not
getting them.

Lacking any special theological motive concerned to separate man from
the other animals, one's projection of inner attitudes onto them is as
natural as the imputation of subjective awareness to other people. Thus
one of the most ancient aspects of hunting religion, still visible in
Eurasia and the Americas alike, is a ritual attitude toward animals.
For example, the "bear ceremonialism" still found among the Paleosiberian Ainu is not merely continuous around the world in the northern
hemisphere, but goes back to the caves of southern Ice Age Europe.[35]
The Ainu completely anthropomorphize the bear, raise and suckle it with
human mothers, treat and speak to it like a human, and call it father;
in this circumpolar cult, the bear is totemically oedipalized.

Somewhat less complete and dramatic, but even more widespread,
is the ritual attitude of hunters toward their kill. If men live off the
lives of animals, they are concerned that these animals be reborn, be
fertile and be plentiful for the hunter. Thus the Plains hunter will place
the feet of a slaughtered buffalo at the four corners of a rectangle
(four is still the ritual number in the Plains), address the spirit of the
dead buffalo, adjure it to live anew and come back in the flesh of a live
buffalo again—a bone-magic very old and prevalent in Asia too. Since
no one can really believe in his own death, perhaps hunters were first
motivated to impute "immortality of the soul" to the animals they killed
but wished still to live?

The cult of the individual animal is intimately connected with a ritual
respect toward a kind of supernatural *species-representative* of the animal,
the progenitor or chief of that animal species, not the particular animal
but its platonic paradigm so to speak. In Americanist and Paleoasiatic
studies, this species-spirit is referred to as the "owner" of the animal,
perhaps somewhat misleadingly since ownership as herded property is
not implied at all but rather the hegemony a spirit has over the body,
spirit-fertility over a species, or a father-chief over his group. In hunting
magic, then, one must not only arrange that immediate animals be
available or sent to be killed, but also that the species retain its fertility
and the future supply be replenished. Let the animal "owner" be the
hunter's "spirit helper" or his "guardian spirit" animal (certainly a
curiously oedipal animism) and the hunt must then be successful! The

human hunter thus fully humanizes the magic hope that he addresses. He will "pray" in ritual formula. He may make gifts of the sacred plant tobacco to the species-"owner" or blow puffs of tobacco smoke toward the spirit of the slain buffalo.

The use of tobacco in this ritual reminds us that there is still a fourth vehicle or source of supernatural "power" in the Americas beyond the vision quest, trophy collecting, and incorporative eating of power. Not only men and animals contain "power" but also plants, in particular those plants containing psychotropic drug substances. For the American Indian, the mind-changing ability that anything imbibed or eaten may have, is proof that it contains some supernatural power—even in the case of so minimal a mind-mover as tobacco. Any subjective spirit-changer obviously contains a spirit-stuff (the mind *is* the spiritual, the mental the sacred). Even tobacco, therefore, was always aboriginally used in a sacred, never a secular context. For example, a band-chief in the Plains might four times thrust upon quarreling men a tobacco pipe to smoke; if, at one of these times, they accept, the tobacco is the supernatural sanctioner of the peace; if they refuse the fourth time, they invite the secular wrath of the chief. Among Algonkians and Siouans, smoking by chiefs of the sacred double-stemmed calumet or "peace-pipe" might even sanction a peacemaking among warring tribes. Tobacco-smoking is ubiquitous in North American religion, all the way from the old and simple hunting rite for the slain animal to warrior society rituals, and from curing or rain-making ceremonials to the contemporary peyote cult.

In America, *any* visionary or psychotropic state—whether a sleeping or waking REM-state or dream, or a sensory-deprivation hallucination in the vision-quest isolate, or a directly drug-induced hallucination—is in itself a manifest experience of the supernatural. Hence narcotic and other drugs are inextricably connected in Indian religion with dream-visions and supernatural power. What is extraordinary in the New World is the enormous number of psychotropic drugs that were used ritually—narcotic mushrooms, cacti, beans, seeds, leaves, barks and vines, and in Amazonia even a narcotic bamboo-grub. Probably no other part of the world is comparable to the region of the southern United States southward to Andean and Amazonian South America in variety and number of native narcotic and other drugs employed. And such use must have been very old, not only because of the great number of drug plants Indians discovered, but also because of the wide aboriginal diffusion of a single plant's use.

For example, ritual tobacco use was universal in every area in which this native American plant will grow, which excludes only the far north and far south of the entire New World.[36] The use of tobacco must be of great antiquity. Aboriginally it was smoked in elbow pipes east of the Rockies on to the Atlantic, and in eastern Brazil southward almost to Patagonia; in cigars, in the whole Amazonian drainage and in the Antillean islands northwestward to include Cuba; in tubular pipes and in cigarettes, from southern British Columbia in Canada southward to Panama; chewed, from Cook Inlet in Alaska southward coastally to beyond San Francisco Bay, and again in the headwaters of the Amazon westward to the Andes; snuffed, in the Antilles; and in upper Amazonia, boiled into a thick brown infusion, into which each post-pubescent male dipped his ritual spatula, and licked off the paste, in earnest of keeping the faith to a tribal consensus thus taken.

Intoxication by the narcotic fly-agaric mushroom among Koryaks was related to an immensely ancient Siberian and indeed Eurasiatic use.[37] The Mexican Chichemeca use of narcotic toadstools has been known since Hernandez, the botanist of Philip II, and the Spanish friar Sahagún of the great Florentine Codex, though early twentieth-century botanists misdoubted it. The Mazatec of northwest Mexico were rediscovered still using *teonanacatl,* the Aztec narcotic mushroom (*Basidiomycetes* spp.), in 1954; and archeological finds of some hundred "mushroom stones" indicate ritual use southward to the highland Maya of Guatemala as early as 1000 B.C. The use of hallucinogenic mushrooms is now known for the Chatino, Chinantec, Mixé, Mixtec and perhaps the Tarascan and Otomi also. Psilocybin, the active ingredient of *Psilocybe mexicana,* was isolated recently by the Swiss chemist Hofmann; it is possible that *Panaeolus sphinctrinus* and *Stropharia cubensis* contain hallucinogens also. Both the immortality-conferring *ambrosia* of the Greek gods and the mysterious sacred plant *soma* of the Vedic writings are now demonstrated conclusively to have been hallucinogenic mushrooms—a culture-historically connected use around the whole northern hemisphere, as is shown by abundant linguistic, philological, mythological, and archeological evidence.

In Virginia and the Carolinas, various holly (*Ilex*) species were used in the Black Drink of the "huskinawing" or puberty rituals; the use of another *Ilex* species reappears in the maté of Paraguay and neighboring regions. In the southern Plains, the "red bean" (*Sophora secundiflora,* misnamed "peyote bean") was in use in a bloody hazing ritual in early contact times, especially among Siouan groups; archeologically, there is conclusive proof of prehistoric Red Bean use from western Texas into northeastern Mexico.

The jimson weed or "Jamestown weed" of some Virginia huskinawing may have been a *Datura* species. In any case, the genus *Datura* had several other areas of aboriginal use in the Americas. In California, Arizona, New Mexico and northern Mexico, *D. meteloides* and *D. inoxia* (the "toloache" of Mexico) were used. *Datura* species variously contain hyoscyamine, scopolamine and atropine, and the first state of intoxication is so furious that the partaker must be physically restrained until a disturbed sleep supervenes, with visual hallucinations that are interpreted as spirit visitations. The use of *Datura* in the Southwest is for divination, prognostication, and puberty rites. Six, and perhaps seven, arboreal *Daturas* were used in the Andean region from Colombia to Chile by aboriginal tribes, including the Inca and the Chibcha. In South America, *Datura* is a medicine commonly eaten by the medicine man to diagnose disease, to discover a thief, and to foretell tribal affairs; it is also given to refractory children, whose ancestors then come to admonish and correct them.

The magico-religious use of *Datura* seems especially well developed in Colombia. Schultes of Harvard, the ethnobotanical authority on New World narcotics, believes that the Kamsá and Ingano "Indians of [the] isolated Valley of Sibundoy may possess the most intricate narcotic consciousness of any peoples of the New World" for, in addition to several species of tree-daturas and *Methysticodendron,* they recognize and cultivate several drug-rich clones of *Datura* "races" so monstrously deformed by virus infections that it is difficult to identify their original species. Perhaps so, as far as *Datura* species are concerned. But for sheer number and variety of psychotropic drugs used ritually, the Aztec must surely run them a close second. In addition to *Datura,* the Aztec had the *peyotl* cactus, *teonanacatl* mushrooms, *yauhtli* marihuana, *ololiuhqui* morning-glory seeds (*Rivea corymbosa*) and *tlitliltzen* (*Ipomoea violacea*), tobacco, several alcoholic liquors, and perhaps *Sophora secundiflora* or the "mescal bean" besides! In 1960 Hofmann found in both the *Ipomoea* and *Rivea* species the amides of lysergic and d-lysergic acids, chanoclavine and clymoclavine, hitherto known only in the fungus ergot (*Claviceps purpurea*), source of lysergic acid diethyl-amide or LSD. Both drugs are powerfully psychotropic, and scholars now credit the accuracy of the colonial writer Hernandez in stating that Aztec "priests communed with their gods . . . to receive a message from them [by] eating the seeds to induce a delirium when a thousand visions and satanic hallucinations appeared to them."[38]

Ritual drunkenness on alcoholic wines and beers (including Aztec *pulque,* the true "mescal" made of *Agave mexicana*)—though not on "firewater" or distilled brandies and whiskeys like *tequila,* which are post-Columbian—was a religious practice extending from Gila River Yumans and Athabaskans of the non-Pueblo Southwest into Mexico and Middle America, and onward into Andean and Amazonian South America.[39] Plants brewed into alcoholic drinks include yucca, mesquite beans, locust pods, wild plums, *chonta* palm fruit, *Opuntia* and "sahuaro" cactus fruits, algarroba and *Prosopis* species of beans, fruits of *Tizyphus mistol, Gourliea decorticans* and *Acacia aroma, kañawa* or quinoa-spinach seeds, and many other substances including wild honey made into mead. However, the chewed-maize *chicha* beer of the Andean region, Mexican *pulque* (fermented *Agave*-sap, still the national drink of the peasants), and the *cassava* or tapioca-beers of Amazonia are perhaps the best known. Ceremonial drunkenness was (and in some places still is) the *sine qua non* in certain aboriginal religious rites from Mexico to Amazonia—for example at Jivaro victory feasts after enemy head-taking, elsewhere in Brazil at death spirit-feasts, and in Antillean ceremonies of all kinds. The many substances and means of preparation, and the uses in religion have been summarized; and the details of Central American ritual alcohol-intoxication have been well-described.

In Hispaniola, Trinidad, and the Orinoco basin (Otomacs), Indian tribes were discovered by the Conquistadores to be using *yopo,* a snuff since identified as *Piptadenia peregrina* (though West Indies snuff powder was sometimes made of the *Acacia niopa* berry too); and ethnographers are familiar with the Y-shaped tubes the Indians used to snuff up the powder of this intoxicant plant. The chief alkaloid of *yopo,* interestingly, is bufotenin, a violently hallucinogenic drug first discovered in toad skins. In Peruvian Amazonia, the little-known *huilca* snuff has been identified as *Piptadenia macrocarpa,* a divinatory snuff of the ancient Peruvians; in central Brazilian Amazonia, a snuff known only as *rapé de los indios* was lost in specimen when Black drowned in the upper Amazon rapids, but only after he had written Schultes that *rapé* was made from the fruit of a gigantic forest tree, *Olmedioperbea sclerophylla,* of the mulberry family. The snuffs *yakee* and *parica* of the Orinoco basin are quite different in origin, being *Virola callophylla, V. callophylloidea* and perhaps also *V. elongata,* all of the Myristicacaceae, to which the nutmeg tree also belongs; the active principle is probably myristicine, a violent hallucinogen known to be common in this family.

The Mazatec of northeastern Oaxaca, and possibly also the adjacent Cuicatec and Chinantec, have recently been discovered using the leaves of a *Salvia* species as a hallucinogenic drug, in Spanish *hojas de la pastora* or *hojas de María Pastora* and in Mazatec *ska-Pastora.* The species, new to science, is now designated as *Salvia divinatorum* or "diviners' mint."

Though *ska-Pastora* is well known to the modern Mazatec, there seem to be no reports from Spanish colonial times of any use in magico-religious rites for its psychotomimetic properties. If the plant was indeed not used aboriginally, then we must postulate a continuing botanical search by Mexican Indians for psychotropic plant substances.

In the whole of aboriginal Andean America northward to Nicaragua, no Indian would think of approaching his gods without a gift of coca, or without being himself coca-inspired. *Erythroxylon Coca,* source of cocaine and early studied by Freud, is too widely known to need more than mention here. Coca has been cultivated by Andeans for so long a time that the wild ancestor of the shrub is now unknown. Dried coca leaves have been found in mummy bundles of Peru dating back 2000 years B.P. In pre-Columbian times, the use of coca was restricted to religious functionaries. But since Spanish colonial times it has become used almost universally by all Andean Indians. The chewing of coca leaves with lime has spread into the northwest Amazonian regions of Colombia and Peru, where many tribes chew it with the ashes of *Crecropia* tree leaves. The chemistry of coca is very complex, with a number of alkaloids in six groups of the tropane series. Cocaine alkaloids are among the greatest contributions of the American Indian to modern medicine; but the original use of coca was religious.

One of the least understood of American "phantastika" or hallucinogens is the drink made from the Death Vine, variously called by Indians *ayahuasca, caapi,* and *yajé,* and first mentioned in Villavicencio's geography of Ecuador in 1858. The Death Vine has an extraordinarily bizarre ability to alter the mind. On purely distributional grounds, it must have been used by Indians of western Amazonia since prehistoric times. The celebrated botanist Spruce's study of *caapi* among the Tukanoan of the Uaupés River in Amazonian Brazil was published posthumously only in 1908, denoted as the malpighiaceous *Banisteria* (now *Banisteriopsis*) *caapi.* Shamans of the upper Rio Negro use it for divination and prophecy; they also give it to young male initiates in the severely painful *yurupari* puberty ordeal (much as the Red Bean was in the bloody Siouan rituals). Intoxication by *caapi* brings, among other strange effects, remarkable visual hallucinations. In larger amounts it is said to produce frighteningly nightmarish visions and a feeling of extremely reckless abandon, though consciousness is not lost nor the use of the limbs unduly affected. After Spruce, the botany of several native psychotropic plants of the *ayahuasca-caapi-yajé* group became very confused. It presently appears that several species are involved, *Banisteriopsis caapi, B. inebrians, B. Rusbyana* (sometimes with admixture of *Maloue-*

tia Tamaquarina, a toxic apocynaceous tree), and perhaps also *Prestonia amazonica* and *Tetrapterys methystica.* The alkaloid of *B. caapi* has been established chemically as harmine, a known hallucinogen. Despite the botanical and pharmacological chaos of the *ayahuasca-caapi-yajé* group of pyschotropic drugs, all the reported uses are ethnographically consistent with what we know of Amazonian religion.

Recently Schultes has estimated that at least forty species of plants were used by American Indians for their hallucinogenic properties, as opposed to only half a dozen commonly so used in the Old World.[40] He draws attention to *huachama,* a cactus genus (*Trichocereus*) used by medicine-men in Peru; a "tree fungus" (*Psilocybe yungensis?*) mentioned as decocted by the Yurimagua of Peruvian Amazonia in late-seventeenth- and early-eighteenth-century Jesuit reports; the Thunderbird-related hallucinogenic *yurema* of the Karirí and Pankarurú of eastern Brazil, which latter also use an infusion of *Mimosa hostilis; Justicia* spp. snuffs of the Guaica; the *timora* drug (*Iresine* spp.?) of several Amazonian tribes; the Kofan use of narcotic *Brunfelsia* spp. in the Colombian and and Ecuadorean Putumayo; and several other little-known South American plants. It is probable that in much of Latin America there are psychotropic drugs, employed since prehistoric times, that we have not yet even heard of. Meanwhile, what, for example, is the milky-sapped forest liana drug of the Tanimuka of the Rio Apaporis in Colombia? The *woi* of the Yekwana of southern Venezuela? In the present rapid list we have not yet mentioned the divine Aztec seed called "food of the gods" (*Theobroma cacao*) by Linnaeus in 1737, which contains the mild caffeine-theine-like stimulant theobromine; or *cohoba,* or *pasta guarana,* or *vinho de Jurumena,* and many other lesser-known drugs used in Indian religious ceremonies. Their number is legion!

Indeed, peyotism, or the well-known contemporary cultic eating of the dried button-tops of the cactus *Lophophora williamsii,* is only one more instance of the aboriginal American preoccupation with plants having supernatural "power" potential. The peyote cult is now nearly universal among the Indian tribes of the Plains, the remnants of most Eastern Woodlands groups, the Great Basin Indians westward to the Washo of Nevada-California, southwestward to include the Navaho and other southern Athapaskans of the Southwest and Mexico, and northward to the Cree and other tribes of Canada. Peyote contains more than nine psychotropic alkaloids, one of which, mescaline, produces remarkable color visions and other sensory hallucinations. The experimental use of mescaline in producing "artificial psychoses" for research in schizophrenia, as well as the native religious use of peyote, is well known. We need only point out here that the contemporary Indian use to produce hallucinations conforms precisely with the aboriginal vision quest and is the central rationale for its use. It might even be suggested that the alcoholism so widely prevalent among Reservation Indians,[41] especially in the Plains, comes in part from the traditional high value placed on abnormal "psychedelic" states, and from the wide use of psychotropic drugs in their earlier religious culture. Modern psychedelic drug cults are not new in the New World.

NOTES

(IV The First Americans)

1. Basic modern sources on New World origins: J. B. Griffin, "Some Prehistoric Connections between Siberia and America," in J. R. Caldwell (ed.), *New Roads to Yesterday, Essays in Archaeology* (New York: Basic Books, 1966, pp. 277–301, originally in *Science,* 131 [1960] 801–12, also available in Bobbs-Merrill Reprints in the Social Sciences, A-96); G. R. Willey, "New World Prehistory," in Caldwell, *op. cit.,* pp. 302–32; *idem,* "New World Archeology in 1965," *Proceedings of the American Philosophical Society,* 110, ₦2 (22 April 1966) 140–45; C. V. Haynes, Jr., "Fluted Projectile Points: Their Age and Dispersion," *Science,* 145 (1964) 1408–13; R. D. Daugherty, "Early Man in the Columbia Intermontane Province," *Anthropological Papers* ₦24 (Salt Lake City: University of Utah Press, 1956); Ronald J. Mason, "The Paleo-Indian Tradition in Eastern North America," *Current Anthropology,* 3 (1962) 227–46; W. J. Mayer-Oakes, "Early Man in the Andes," *Scientific American,* 208, ₦5 (May 1963) 116–22, 125–26, 128; and, for the dating of the charred dwarf mammoth bone, W. S. Broecker and J. L. Kulp, "Lamont Natural Radiocarbon Measurements IV," *Science,* 126 (27 December 1957) 1324–34, p. 1324, and table on p. 1326. Recently discovered (1965) by Roald Fryxell in eastern Washington, "Marmes Man" is dated 11,000–13,000 years ago (announced at the May 1968 meeting of the Society for American Archeology in Santa Fe; see "Earliest American," *Scientific American,* 218 ₦6 [June 1968] 44–45). Newman thinks the New World was peopled "as much as 30,000 years ago from the Old World, and this takes us far back in the phylogeny of *Homo sapiens,*" but his view is not universally accepted (M. T. Newman, "Geographic and Microgeographic Races," *Current Anthropology,* 4 [1963] 189–92, p. 190; see also George F. Carter, *Pleistocene Man at San Diego,* Baltimore: Johns Hopkins Press, 1957; Douglas D. Anderson, "A Stone Age Campsite at the Gateway of America," *Scientific American,* 218 ₦6 [June 1968] 24–33, p. 29; and E. N. Wilmsen, "Lithic Analysis in Paleo-Anthropology," *Science,* 161 [1968] 982–87, p. 987).

2. For a botanist's demand for more than the old allowance of 10,000 years for the first Indians in America, see Oakes Ames, *Economic Annuals and Human Cultures* (Cambridge: Botanical Museum of Harvard University, 1939, p. 11).

3. No one accepts the theory of W. J. Sollas (*Ancient Hunters and their Modern Representatives,* London: Macmillan, 1924) in unmodified form, since living peoples can not be *unchanging* "culture fossils" of earlier times. But Magdalenian-Eskimo similarities in material culture are especially striking; both hunted some of the same animals in similar climates; and, as Boule-Vallois note, the mandibular torus of Chancellade man has no parallel except in the skulls of various living arctic peoples (Marcellin Boule, edited by Henry V. Vallois, *Fossil Men,* New York: Dryden Press, 1957, p. 304). On the other hand, *direct* Magdalenian-Beothuk Indian connections from France and Spain to Newfoundland (E. F. Greenman, "The Upper Paleolithic and the New World," *Current Anthropology,* 4 [1963] 41–66) rest on much too unspecific and only superficial similarities. Thor Heyerdahl's fantasies on Amerindian peopling of Polynesia I reject entirely; distributions indicate sporadic contacts from the opposite direction (G. Friederici, "In den vorkolumbischen Verbindung der Südseevölker mit Amerika," *Anthropos,* 24 (1929). As for the sweet potato (*Ipomoea Batatas*), I am satisfied that it is New World in origin and post-

Portuguese or post-Spanish in western Oceania, so that any problem concerning the independence of New World agriculture no longer exists (H. C. Conklin, "The Oceanian-African Hypothesis and the Sweet Potato," in Jacques Barrau [ed.], *Plants and the Migrations of Pacific Peoples: A Symposium,* Honolulu: Bishop Museum Press, 1963, pp. 129–36; but see also Ping-ti Ho, "The Introduction of American Food Plants into China," *American Anthropologist,* 57 [1955] 191–210, pp. 193–94).

4. Classic papers that still represent standard opinion: R. B. Dixon, "The Independence of the Culture of the American Indian," *Science,* 35 (1912) 46–55; R. H. Lowie, "On the Historical Connection between Certain Old World and New World Beliefs," Göteborg: *Congrès International des Américanistes, Compte-Rendu de la XXIᵉ Session,* part. 2, pp. 546–49, 1925, and "Religious Ideas and Practices of the Eurasiatic and North American Areas," in E. E. Evans-Pritchard, *Essays Presented to C. G. Seligman,* pp. 183–88. With the abundance of modern field work in South America, Lowie's judgment needs only to be extended to include that continent also.

5. Racial, linguistic, archeological, and cultural evidence grows more convincing with each decade. Racial evidence is too overwhelming to cite, and too consistent to need citing; even the identical racial components in East, West, and Central Paleosiberian tribes include an identifiable Amerindoid or American Indian physical type (M. G. Levin, *Ethnic Origins of the Peoples of Northeastern Siberia,* Toronto: University of Toronto Press, 1963, p. 27). Linguistic evidence: M. Swadesh, "Linguistic Relations across Behring Strait," *American Anthropologist,* 64 (1962) 1262–91; the American Eskimo and Siberian Chukchi languages are also related; for the connection of Muskhogean-Algonkian, see Mary R. Haas, "A New Linguistic Relationship in North America: Algonkian and the Gulf Languages," *Southwestern Journal of Anthropology,* 14 (1958) 231–64.

6. Hatt thinks there were two large cultural waves in Asia, the earlier, coastal, Eskimo, which lacked the snowshoe and hence could not conquer the vast inland areas, and the later inland wave "found fullest and most unmixed in the culture of the Tungusians, although its influence is felt from Lapland to Labrador" (G. Hatt, "Moccasins and their Relation to Arctic Footwear," *Memoirs of the American Anthropological Association,* 3, №3 [1916] pp. 248–49). But some scholars regard the Eskimo as late-comers to Alaska who formed a "plug" against further invasions over the Behring Straits.

7. For a modern view on the relative lateness of the bow and arrow in America, see C. V. Haynes, Jr., "Elephant-hunting in North America," *Scientific American,* 214 №6 (June 1966) 104–12, p. 111.

8. The "semi-subterranean house" in America extends from the Alaskan Eskimo and the central Alaskan Athapaskan *kžim* southward in western Canada and into the western United States. In Siberia, it is found in the Kyzil-Khakasy *sher ab* (p. 361), Khant [=Ostyak] of the River Vakh (p. 525), Ngansan [=Samoyed-Tavgi] (p. 576), Samoyedic Sel'kup (pp. 588, 596, 597), all Kets, anciently or in modern times (p. 615), Evens [=Lamut] until the XVIII c. (p. 676), Nanay [= Goldi] in the recent past *seroma* and *khurbu* (p. 702), the Saghalin Nivkhi [=Gilyak] still in the present century (p. 772), coastal Chukchi until mid-XIX c. (p. 816), Siberian Eskimo, earlier (p. 837), most present coastal Koryak (pp. 858, 860), Kamchadal (p. 879), and the Aleut until early XIX c. (pp. 884, 886)—all in M. G. Levin and L. P. Potapov (editors), *The Peoples of Siberia* (Chicago: University of Chicago Press, 1964).

9. I use the term "tipi" somewhat arbitrarily for the conical *skin-covered* lodge, and "wigwam" for *bark-covered* conical or rectangular houses; often these are only seasonal variants found in the same tribe. In any case, the "tipi" is found among: ancient Buryat trappers' *bukhek* (p. 217), Tuvan (both conical and rectangular in

ground plan, skin-covered in winter, p. 401), Tofalar (covered with bark in summer, smoked stag or elkhide in winter, p. 478), Nentsy *mya* (two layers of furred rein-deer skin in winter, sometimes birchbark in summer, the summer *mya* sometimes with an *amex* or long V-shaped vestibule, now with tarpaulins instead of birchbark, pp. 554, 555, 559, 560, 569), Ngansan (like the Nentsi, pp. 576, 581), northern Samoyedic Sel'kup (conical, skin-covered, for winter, p. 597), northern Kets (con-ical, deerskin, winter, and birchbark for summer) but southern Kets (inverted V of birchbark, earth-covered, winter, p. 615), Evenk [=Tungus] *dyu* (basic dwelling of eastern hunters in past, pp. 637, 639–40), Dolgan [=Yakut-Tungus] (summer and winter, p. 659), Nanay (p. 692), Orochi (temporary conical *aanga* for seal-hunting, covered with fishskin, also used in summer, p. 754), Yukaghir (March to September, reindeer-skin, p. 794), Chukchi *yaranga* (cylindrical at base, but conical at top, deerskin, p. 816), and Koryak (like the Chukchi; also a sod-covered hemispherical hut, p. 858)—all in Levin and Potapov, *op. cit.*

10. Tribes using the "wigwam" in Siberia include: Yakuts (conical summer *urusa* or *uraha*, p. 264), Altai (*alanchik* or *chadyr* also sometimes conical, pp. 314, 316), Kachin-Khakasy (conical, used by poor in winter also, but another type had a dome-shaped bark roof, pp. 352–53), Kyzil-Khakasy (p. 361), Sagay-Khakasy (conical *at ib* and domed *charga ib*, p. 363), Tuvans (both conical and rectangular bark-covered for summer, in winter both but sometimes skin-covered, pp. 398, 400), Shors (temporary conical bark-covered; double-layered and earth-strewn winter house also of poor, p. 456), Tofalars (bark in summer, skin in winter, p. 476), Khant (vertical walls, conical roof, both of bark, p. 527), Nentsy (conical, sometimes bark-covered in summer, p. 554–55), Ngansan (like Nentsy, p. 576), northern Sel'kup (summer, conical, some Narym Sel'kup also, pp. 597, 598), Kets [=Ostyak] conical *tiski* of sewn birchbark strips (sometimes with arched passageway, p. 613), Evenk (Tungus, Orochen, Birar and Manegry also, pp. 637, 638), Evens of Okhotsk region (conical birchbark *dye*, pp. 675, 676–77), Negidal (conical in summer; low willow-withe dome covered with birchbark as a temporary hunting shelter, p. 688), Nanay (four-walled *dauro*, conical *choro* and hemispherical *khomuran* or *anke* all bark-covered, pp. 692, 705), Ul'chi [=Gilyak], temporary hunting shelter (p. 725), Udegey (inverted V with birchbark strips, also conical *cholo*, p. 741), Orok (conical *aundau* bark-covered in autumn fishing, fishskin-covered in winter, p. 763), and Reindeer Yukaghir (con-ical, larch-bark covered, March–September, p. 794) in Levin and Potapov, *op. cit.*

11. Birchbark canoe, pp. 261, 633, 704, 724, 741, and 753; Koryak and Aleut kayak, pp. 863, 884, and 886, Levin and Potapov, *op. cit.;* see also F. B. Steiner, "Skinboats and the Yakut 'Xayik,' " *Ethnos,* 4 (1939) 177–83; skis, Levin and Pota-pov, *op. cit.,* pp. 331, 519, 719, 878; travois, pp. 312, 412; snow goggles, p. 663; cradleboard, p. 777. Siberian Buryat medicine bundles were much like American Indian ones (Levin and Potapov, *op. cit.,* p. 214).

12. I do not agree with Ivan Lopatin ("Origin of the Native American Steam Bath," *American Anthropologist,* 62 [1960] 977–93, p. 989) that the Finno-Scandi-navian *sauna* came to America across the Atlantic. The distribution of the Indian sweat-lodge is too much of a piece with the evidence for trans-Behring Straits traits like the tipi-wigwam and semi-subterranean lodge, from all of which indeed the sweat-lodge is sometimes scarcely indistinguishable. Krickeberg points out that the sweat bath is almost universal in North America—excluding only the Shoshone, Yuma, Pima, some coastal tribes of British Columbia and the Central and Eastern Eskimo—extending into Middle America as far south as Guatemala (W. Krickeberg, "The Indian Sweat Bath," *Ciba Symposia,* 1 [1939] p. 19, cited by R. Rizenthaler, in Iago Galdston [ed.], *Man's Image in Medicine and Anthropology,* New York: In-ternational Universities Press, 1963, pp. 327–28).

13. The sled-sledge-toboggan distribution is from an unpublished paper of my own.

The "placation of the slain animal" rite so ubiquitous in America (B. Bonnerjea, "Hunting Superstitions of the American Aborigines," *Internationales Archiv für Ethnographie*, 32, ⅜3–6 [1934] 167–84) is paralleled in Siberia among the Shor, Evenk, Goldi, Orochi, and Itel'men, among others (Levin and Potapov, *op. cit.*, pp. 464, 649, 711, 757 and 879). Turner traced reindeer-caribou hair embroidery across the northern hemisphere from western Siberia to New England (G. Turner, *Hair Embroidery in Siberia and North America,* Oxford, 1955); it may have been ancestral to porcupine quill embroidery, in turn ancestral to bead embroidery, among American Indians.

14. The basic work is G. Hatt, *Asiatic Influences in American Folklore* (København: Det Kongelige Danske Videnskabernes Selskab, Historisk-filologisk Meddelelser, 31, ⅜6, 1949). Numerous references to the "magic flight" story are found in W. Jochelson, *The Koryak* (New York and Leiden: Publications of the Jessup North Pacific Expedition, 1908=Memoirs, American Museum of Natural History, vol. X, pp. 369–70), as well as in A. Skinner and J. V. Satterlee, *Folklore of the Menomini Indians* (Anthropological Papers of the American Museum of Natural History, 13 [1915] 217–546).

15. "The Orpheus Myth in North America" has been traced by A. H. Gayton (*Journal of American Folklore,* 48 [1925] 263–93); see also Å. Hultkrantz, *The North American Indian Orpheus Tradition* (New York: Humanities Press, 1957, also Stockholm: Statens Ethnografiska Museum, Monograph Series ⅜2, 1957). Raven, as a supernatural transformer-trickster among the Chukchi, Koryak, and Itel'men of Siberia (Levin and Potapov, *op. cit.*, pp. 824, 879, 880), is indistinguishable from Raven in the Northwest Coast, often found in ridiculous situations, a transformer not held in esteem but the center of various comic and obscene stories.

16. Scalping, according to Friederici, was aboriginally confined to an area stretching from the mouth of the St. Lawrence to the lower Mississippi and Gulf regions (i.e., the Iroquoians, Muskhogeans and their neighbors), but was spread in New England, the Eastern Woodlands and Plains by scalp-bounties paid by American pioneers, to become almost universal in North America: it was limited to the Gran Chaco and part of the Guianas in South America, but head-taking is almost everywhere else there (G. Friederici, *Skalpierung und ähnliche Kriegsgebräuche in Amerika,* Braunschweig: Friedrich Viewig u. Sohn, 1906, pp. 30, 85 ff). In reverse, taking the whole head, as among the Makah (Ruth Underhill, *Indians of the Pacific North West,* Riverside: Educational Division of the U. S. Office of Indian Affairs, 1945, p. 182) sometimes replaced the characteristic scalping in North America. A typical "scalp dance" is that of the Zuñi (Elsie C. Parsons, "The Scalp Ceremonial of Zuñi," *Memoirs of the American Anthropological Association* 31, 1924). The Eastern Scythian chief in the prehistoric burial at Pazyryk in Siberia had been scalped at his death (Levin and Potapov, *op. cit.*, p. 64); these Mongolian Huns, the Chinese Yüeh-chih, were the "Massagetae" of Greek writers, who also mention Scythian scalping. Incidentally, the ancient Scythians also had the equivalent of the *berdache* in their *enareis,* known to the Greeks (Herodotus, *Histories,* I, 105).

17. M. A. Czaplicka, *Aboriginal Siberia* (Oxford University Press, 1914); on American shamanism, Paul Radin, "Religion of the North American Indians," *Journal of American Folk-Lore,* 27 (1914) 335–73; and W. Z. Park, *Shamanism in Western North America: A Study in Cultural Relationships* (Evanston: Northwestern University Studies in the Social Sciences 2, 1938). On the vision quest itself, excellent sources are G. B. Grinnell, *The Cheyenne Indians* (New Haven: Yale University Press, 2 vols., 1923); R. H. Lowie, "The Tobacco Society of the Crow Indians," *Anthropological Papers of the American Museum of Natural History,* 21 (1919) 101–200; and Ernest Wallace and E. Adamson Hoebel, *The Comanche* (Norman: University of Oklahoma Press, 1952).

18. A late Magdalenian C_{14} date in Europe would be the 11,650±200 B.P. of the Grotte de la Vache in Tarascon, France (*Science*, 126 [1957], p. 1329). But Magdalenian culture may have begun to the eastward in Eurasia, not necessarily in southern France, though the evidence remains good for the latter supposition. A good Mesolithic date would be the Maglemosian period 7500 B.C. for Star Carr in England (S. Piggott, *Approach to Archaeology*, Cambridge: Harvard University Press, 1959, pp. 61, 91); see also W. C. Gabel, "The Mesolithic Continuum in Western Europe," *American Anthropologist*, 60 (1958) 658–67. Hence presently visible American culture horizons match the Magdalenian-Mesolithic range better (as they do in culture content) than with the argued 30,000 B.P. "Neanderthaloid" range, which emphatically still needs to be proven.

19. Perhaps the *windigo* legend is to be considered a "wild-man" vision quest (cf. Tungus *olonism*, the Kwakiutl winter "Cannibal Society" rite, the wild hair and manner of the weather-shamanness and sea-animal "owner" Sedna of the Eskimo). In a letter to Ruth Benedict, Edward Sapir wrote: "Now it is not at all unlikely that the Nootka Wolf Ritual dances and the Kwakiutl Winter Feast Dances are a highly specialized or petrified form of such group-manitou performances, the individually acquired manitou being changed into a ritualized and hereditarily owned being" (M. Mead, *An Anthropologist at Work*, Boston: Houghton Mifflin, 1959, p. 52). For "windigo" sources, see notes on the Introduction to present volume.

20. For the chief as provider in North America, see V. Stefansson, *Hunters of the Great North* (New York: Harcourt, Brace and Company, 1922, pp. 143–44); for South America, C. Lévi-Strauss, *Tristes Tropiques* (Atheneum paperback, pp. 300, 304–7—although this English edition identically named absurdly omits the core chapters XIV–XVI and XXIX of the French edition [Paris: Plon, 1955] which give this thoughtful book its theoretical worth). For a detailed treatment of the "generosity pattern" in a North American tribe, see M. W. Herman, "The Social Aspect of Huron Prosperity," *American Anthropologist*, 58 (1956) 1044–57; H. Hickerson, "The Feast of the Dead Among the Seventeenth Century Algonkians of the Upper Great Lakes," *American Anthropologist*, 62 (1960) 81–107, pp. 91, 98, 101, 104. In Siberia, customary generosity among the Yakut, Shor, Samoyed, Evenk, Evens, Gilyak, Udegey, Orok, and Yukaghir sometimes verges on the compulsory (Levin and Potapov, *op. cit.*, pp. 224, 275, 460, 561–62, 637, 680, 729, 742, 764, 765, and 796). The *lisudu* of the Apa Tani is quite *potlach*-like (C. von Fürher-Haimendorf, *Himalayan Barbary* (London: John Murray, 1955).

21. On the "favorite child" see Esther S. Goldfrank, *Changing Configurations in the Social Organization of the Blackfoot Tribe during the Reserve Period* (New York: Monographs of the American Ethnological Society, #8, 1945, esp. pp. 7 ff, 17 ff, 59 ff, and 66 ff); Jeannette Mirsky, "The Dakota," in M. Mead (ed.), *Cooperation and Competition among Primitive Peoples* (New York: McGraw-Hill, 1937, 382–427, p. 404); C. Wissler, "Ceremonial Bundles of the Blackfoot Indians," *Anthropological Papers of the American Museum of Natural History*, 8, pt. 2, 1912 (the relevant portion is also in M. Mead and N. Calas [eds.], *Primitive Heritage*, New York: Random House, 1953, pp. 354–55); and Esther Goldfrank, "Linguistic Note to Zuñi Ethnology," *Word*, 2 (1946) 191–96.

22. On the trait of dependency in American Indians corresponding to chiefly generosity, see A. I. Hallowell, "Some Psychological Characteristics of the Northeastern Indians," in F. Johnson (ed.), *Man in Northeastern North America* (Boston: Papers of the Robert S. Peabody Foundation for Archeology, No. 3, 1946); G. D. and Louis S. Spindler, "The American Indian Personality Types and their Sociocultural Roots," in G. E. Simpson and J. M. Yinger (eds.), *American Indians and American Life* (New York: Annals of the American Academy of Political and Social Science, 1957); Arnold Green, "Culture, Normality, and Personality Con-

flict," *American Anthropologist,* 50 (1948) 225–37, pp. 227–28; Scudder Mekeel, "A Short History of the Teton Dakota," *North Dakota Historical Quarterly,* X, no. 5 (July 1943) 137–205, p. 176; A. F. C. Wallace, "Some Psychological Determinants of Culture Change in an Iroquoian Community," *Bureau of American Ethnology,* Bulletin 149 (1951) 55–76; and John Lawson, *History of North Carolina* (Richmond: Garrett and Massie, 1951, p. 252). On dependency and alcoholism, see B. J. James, "Socio-Psychological Dimensions of Ojibwa Acculturation," *American Anthropologist,* 63 (1961) 721–46. The striking literalness of the paradigm hunter : meat :: maleness : power is shown among the Ojibwa, among whom a youth seeks and can get in the vision quest the surplus power of male other-than-human supernaturals just as one can get from a good hunter his surplus meat (A. I. Hallowell, *The Role of Dreams,* pp. 281–82). Meanwhile, to give secular largesse one must get sacred power.

23. Louis Thomas Jones, *Aboriginal American Oratory: The Trait of Eloquence among Indians of the United States* (Los Angeles: Southwestern Museum, 1935).

24. It is significant that Indian legal institutions increase in complexity along the same politico-ecological range; see E. Adamson Hoebel, *Law of Primitive Man, passim.* Note also that religious sodalities follow the same pattern (W. J. Hoffman, *The Midēwiwin or "Grand Medicine Society" of the Ojibwa* (Annual Report, Bureau of American Ethnology, 7 [1891] 143–330); and Plains warrior societies function only when band chiefs and other important men are assembled at the summer tribal Sun Dance from their winter band hunting. Interestingly, in both Americas, the very ancient communal surround-hunt is revived when there is an especially great food requirement as at such tribal assemblies.

25. An extraordinarily complete cognitive map of the puberty–power stealing–soul collecting–headhunting–guardian spirit–narcotic drug complex is found in Michael J. Harner's fine description of the Jivaro *arutam-kakarma-natemA* concepts ("Jivaro Souls," *American Anthropologist,* 64 [1962] 258–72). A similarly elegant relating of power, sexuality, headhunting, and mastery of animals among the Mundurucú is R. F. Murphy's "Intergroup Hostility and Social Cohesion," *American Anthropologist,* 59 (1957) 1018–35.

26. The lack of racial prejudice among American Indians has redounded on them in recent times: the Wichita, among others, married their Negro slaves to a degree that they are themselves discriminated against. Ironically, with large samples of Indian Mongoloids, African Negroids, and European Caucasoids, the New World has an enormous and inevitable potential for genetic "hybrid vigor" scarcely earned socially or morally by our absurd racist attitudes.

27. The guardian spirit sought in the vision quest is found in "eastern Siberia, across the length and breadth of North America, and down into South America" (Ruth Benedict, *The Concept of the Guardian Spirit in North America,* Memoirs of the American Anthropological Association, 29, 1923, p. 9).

28. Friederici, in his *Vorkolumbischen Verbindung,* interprets the voluminous data on scalping and skull collecting as evidence of Pacific-American culture-contacts; with plentiful northern Eurasiatic data also, I would regard them as merely further evidence of the Sibero-American Mesolithic base-culture. E. M. Loeb (*The Blood Sacrifice Complex,* Memoirs of the American Anthropological Association, 30, 1923) has a similar view of the great antiquity of cannibalism and human sacrifice, which he considers ethnologically and areally related, as also is circumcision. To re-emphasize the connection of shamanic "power" with weather control, scalps of enemies, if properly treated, were potent rain makers (Elsie C. Parsons, *Scalp Ceremonial at Zuñi,* p. 6).

29. Xipe, "the flayed one," was impersonated by a priest dressed in a captive victim's entire skin, symbolizing spring and the new covering of vegetation on the earth—

remotely resembling the Ghost Dance ideology of Uto-Aztecans farther north. On Aztec human sacrifice, see Homer W. Smith, *Man and His Gods* (Boston: Little Brown & Co., 1952, pp. 133–34). Tezcatlipoca was impersonated by the sacrificial captive enemy youth; the drug *yuahtli* (marihuana) was given bound victims thrown into large fires and dragged out with hooks to have their still beating hearts cut out to feed Huehueteotl (G. C. Vaillant, *Aztecs of Mexico,* Garden City: Doubleday, Doran & Co., 1941, pp. 178–80, 200–3; also Penguin Books). Ancient Mexicans also stretched out prisoners fastened to wooden frames and shot them to death with arrows as a sacrifice to fertilize the earth-goddess Tlazolteotl, "eater of filth" and "mother of the gods." "There is no doubt that it was originally meant as an imitation of the sexual act" (Eduard Seler, "Mexicans [Ancient]," *Hastings Encyclopedia of Religion and Ethics,* 8:612–16, p. 615). The St. Sebastian legend may be a European cognate; there are ancient Celtic parallels. The god as the victim is not unknown in Europe, from prehistoric times onward.

30. For various references to cannibalism, see F. W. Hodge (editor), *Handbook of American Indians North of Mexico* (Bulletin 30, Bureau of American Ethnology, 1907–10, 2 vols.) under the headings *Attakapa, Caddo, Calusa, Mihtukmechakick, Mohawk, Ottawa, Tawakoni, Timucuan Family, Tonkawa, Tuscarora, Westo, Wichita,* and *Yscanis.* For the Middle American Acaxee and Xixime area, see A. L. Kroeber, *Cultural and Natural Areas of Native North America* (Berkeley: University of California Publications in American Archeology and Ethnology, 38 [1939], p. 128); see also R. L. Beals, *The Comparative Ethnology of Northern Mexico Before 1750* (Berkeley: University of California Press, 1932); Maya, A. M. Tozzer, *A Comparative Study of the Mayas and Lacandones,* New York: Macmillan, 1907, p. 9; Nicaraguan raising of cannibal victims, S. K. Lothrop, *Pottery of Costa Rica and Nicaragua* (Contributions to the Museum of the American Indian [Heye Foundation], 8 [1926], pp. 35, 80. For cannibalism in Florida and the Antilles, see Charlotte D. Gower, The Northern and Southern Affiliations of Antillean Culture (*Memoirs of the American Anthropological Association,* 35 [1927], p. 36). For cannibalism in South America, see Thomas Whiffen, *The North-West Amazons* (London: Constable & Co., 1915), pp. 119–123, *et passim;* Julian Steward (ed.), *Handbook of South American Indians,* (Bulletin 143, Bureau of American Ethnology, 8 vols., 1946–59, I:179, 189; V:705, 713, 722, and 736); and E. Westermarck, *The Origin and Development of the Moral Ideas* (London: Macmillan, 2nd ed., 2 vols., 1926, II:555–56, 559, 560, 563 and 569). See also Hans Becher, "Die endokannibalistischen Riten als früheste Erscheinungsform der Anthropophagie," *Zeitschrift für Ethnologie,* 92, №2 (1967) 248–53.

31. Typical early travelers' accounts of the *berdache* may be found in Jacques Le Moyne, *Narratives* (Boston: James R. Osgood & Co., 1875, pp. 7–8), and in Castañeda, in G. P. Winship, "The Coronada Expedition," (*Annual Report of the Bureau of American Ethnology,* 14 [1896] 329–637, p. 515). J. O. Dorsey (A Study of Siouxan Cults, *Annual Report of the Bureau of American Ethnology,* 11 [1894] 361–544) lists the *berdache* for the Omaha, Kansa, Ponca, Hidatsa, and the Santee-, Teton-, and Yanktonai-Dakota; for the Omaha vision of the Moon, pp. 378–79; see also pp. 467, 516. W. W. Hill, in his "Note on the Pima Berdache" (*American Anthropologist,* 40 [1938] 338–40) gives a bibliography on the *berdache* in the western United States; but the classic paper is Hill's on "The Status of the Hermaphrodite and Transvestite in Navaho Culture" (*American Anthropologist,* 37 [1935] 273–79); see also Elsie C. Parsons, "The Zuñi La'mana" (*American Anthropologist,* 18 [1916] 521–28).

32. The Navaho attitude toward their *nadlε* was very respectful, as they were believed to have been given charge of wealth in the beginning and to be in charge of it today. A family into which one was born was considered very fortunate, and

special care was taken in raising such children. As the child grew older, the solic-
itude and respect increased, not only on the part of the family but from the community as a whole. "This attitude is very real. All the older Navaho have a genuine respect for the *nadlɛ* and only in rare instances do the younger men scoff at
them. They were never made fun of and their abnormalities were never mentioned
to them or by themselves. This respect verges almost on reverence in many cases
. . . If there were no more left, the horses, sheep, and Navaho would all go" (Hill,
Status, p. 274). The attitude among the Crow varied somewhat, since the Crow put
the aggressive vigor and virility of men in profound opposition to the passivity and
weakness of women, and young men who failed the test in war raids had nothing
to do or say in any public business whatever and had to endure biting obscenities.
"The *bate,* male transvestites, were no exception. *Bate* were 'crazy' people with
whom one could have some fun, a sexual escapade perhaps, and they might be
married because they excelled women in butchering, tanning, and other domestic
tasks. But they were never honored, and when a *bate* raised a gun against the enemy, the Crow remembered it as a signal event. During the Sun Dance, when a
bate was selected to cut the first pole, he would cover his face like a woman in embarrassment, for people were inclined to laugh at him" (F. W. Voget, "Warfare
and the Integration of Crow Indian Culture," in Ward Goodenough [ed.], *Explorations in Cultural Anthropology: Essays in Honor of George Peter Murdock,* New
York: McGraw-Hill, 1964, pp. 483–509, p. 490). The Navaho and Crow bracket
the range of attitudes toward the *berdache.* Standard ethnographic sources list the
berdache for the Aleut, Arapaho, Assiniboine, Blackfoot, Cheyenne, Colorado
River Yumans, Crow, Eskimo, Flathead, Illinois, Fox, Mandan, Menomini, Papago,
Paviotso, Seri, Shivwits, Timucuan, and Southern Ute, as well as in Patagonia,
Puerto Rico and the Gran Chaco. In South America, recent summaries by Métraux,
J. H. Rowe, Tschopik, Cooper, Murra, Lévi-Strauss, Nimuendaju, Kirchhoff, and
J. H. Steward list the *berdache* equivalent for the Mbaya (Chaco), Inca, Aymara,
Araucanians, Manta, Tupi-Cawahib, Trumai, Nambicuara, Tucuna, Lache, Caquetío,
Venezuelan and Orinocan tribes, and coastal Ecuadoreans (Steward [ed.], *Hand-
book,* I:159, 324; II:187, 544, 722, 805; III:304, 337, 366, 718; IV:219–29, 363,
453, 467, 486; V:713, 723, 752; and VII, Index). General statements may be
found in Ruth Benedict, "Sex in Primitive Society," *American Journal of Ortho-
psychiatry,* 9 (1939) 570–74; R. Linton, *The Study of Man* (New York:
Appleton, 1936, p. 480, also Appleton-Century-Crofts paperback), and R. H. Lowie,
Primitive Religion (New York: Boni & Liveright, 1924, pp. 181, 210, 217, 229,
243 ff). For the connection of *berdaches* with the scalping complex, see G. B. Grinnell, "Coup and Scalp among the Plains Indians," in *Selected Papers from the
American Anthropologist 1888–1920* (Evanston: Row, Peterson & Co., 1960, pp.
650–64=*American Anthropologist,* 12 [1910] 296–310). For transvestites and
berdaches in Siberia, see Czaplicka, *op. cit.,* pp. 248–49 (among the Yakut, traditions exist of male shamans bearing children, p. 252). Adaptively, the psychiatrist
E. J. Kempf, however, considers that homosexuality indicates biological inferiority,
in his paper on "The Social and Sexual Behavior of Infrahuman Primates with
Some Comparable Facts in Human Behavior," *Psychoanalytic Review,* 4 (1917)
127–54, p. 153.

34. O. Lewis, "Manly-hearted Women among the Northern Piegan," *American
Anthropologist,* 43 (1941) 173–87; see Voget, *op. cit.,* p. 490, for such women
among the Crow; compare Steward, "South American Cultures: An Interpretive
Summary," in *Handbook,* V:669–772, page 723, on the little understood occurrence
of female warriors among many Colombian tribes. It is possible, in my opinion,
that South American "Amazons" were male transvestite war-shamans (though the
suggestion for this admittedly is a far cry areally: the shaman Orpheus accom-

panied the warrior Jason and his Argonauts on a legendary expedition into the Black Sea; the conjecture, unfortunately, does not serve to explain the classic Greek "Amazons").

35. The classic monograph on bear ceremonialism is A. I. Hallowell's "Bear Ceremonialism in the Northern Hemisphere," *American Anthropologist,* 28 (1926) 1–175. The bold insights of Hallowell on the intercontinental nature of the cult are amply confirmed; in fact, we now consider "bear ceremonialism" to reach back to the Stone Age (see reference note 1 to Chapter XIII p. 423). New ethnographic data available since Hallowell's study are voluminous; for Siberia alone, see Levin and Potapov, *op. cit.,* pp. 363, 442, 464, 591, 637, 648, 711, 730, 743, 756, 765, 779, and 868; see also N. P. Dyrenkova, "Bear Worship among Turkish Tribes of Siberia," *Proceedings of the 23rd International Congress of Americanists,* New York, 1930, pp. 411–40; Ivar Paulson, "Die rituelle Erhebung des Bärenschädels bei arktischen und Subarktischen Völkern," *Temenos,* 1 (1965) 150ff.; J. B. Casagrande, "Ojibwa Bear Ceremonialism: The Persistence of a Ritual Attitude," in S. Tax (ed.), *Selected Papers, Acculturation in the Americas,* 1952, 2:113–17; and Chiba Tokoji, "On Funeral Ceremonies for hunted Japanese Bears in Mountain Villages of the Japanese Islands, Hokkaido excluded," *Minzokogaku-Kenkyu* [Japanese Journal of Ethnology], 32, ♯4 (1968) 318–27. A modern summary of the best known ethnographic example among surviving Paleosiberian peoples is by J. M. Kitigawa, "Ainu Bear Festival (Iyomante)," *History of Religions,* 1 (1960) 95–151; the human suckling of bear cubs is fully substantiated in the standard sources for Paleosiberian peoples. The incredibly abundant evidence from the cave bear bones in the Drachenhöhle (Styria) and the Drachenloch (eastern Alps) especially, but also in the Hellmichhöhle, Petershöhle and Salzofen cave, leave no doubt of a highly developed bear cult from the early Aurignacian onward, which the Montespan clay effigy—with the heel prints of dancing adolescents near the bear skull, fallen between the front paws of the spear-scarred image—and the wall paintings in Trois Frères fully confirm (see Johannes Maringer, *The Gods of Prehistoric Man,* London: Weiderfeld & Nicolson, 1960, pp. 26–43 and 69–73). In China, quite logically (since it was originally associated with a male puberty ceremonial in the paleolithic) the bear has come to symbolize the male generative *yang* principle (P. J. Dois, "L'enfance chez les Chinois de la Province de Kanson," *Anthropos,* 3 [1908] 761–70, p. 765); in India there are also evidences of an ancestral bear cult among the Oriya, Balahi and Baloch (William Crooke, *Religion and Folk-lore in Northern India,* Oxford: Oxford University Press, 1926). Against this enormous background, I feel no temerity at all in suggesting that the traditional wearing of bear-paw gloves by dancing Isleta priests (review by Edward Dozier, *American Anthropologist,* 65 [1963] 936–37, p. 937) now suddenly emerges into significance and should be compared with the bear paws of the Dancing Sorcerer of Trois Frères himself. On unpublished detailed Kiowa evidence of shared traits (especially the ritual treatment of the buffalo skull), I have come to believe that bear ceremonialism was even a remote formative influence on the Plains Sun Dance.

36. Distribution of types of aboriginal tobacco use in the Americas: Clark Wissler, *The American Indian* (New York: Oxford University Press, 1922, p. 26). Alaskan Eskimos got a distinct type of pipe and method of smoking from Siberians only after smoking had spread around the world in post-Columbian times, not from their Indian neighbors in Alaska.

37. All sources from the very earliest note the Koryak shaman's use of the fly-agaric. "The Koryaks believed that the 'prophetic fly-agaric' led him into the next world and arranged meetings with dead kinsmen, from whom the shaman obtained the necessary instructions. On awakening from his long sleep, the shaman related his visions to the people around him" (Levin and Potapov, *op. cit.,* p. 864).

For the New World, see R. G. Wasson, "The Hallucinogenic Mushrooms of Mexico: An Adventure into Ethnomycological Exploration," *Transactions of the New York Academy of Science,* ser. II, vol. 21, #4 (1959) 325–39; "The Hallucinogenic Fungi of Mexico, An Inquiry into the Origins of Religious Ideas among Primitive Peoples," [Harvard] *Botanical Museum Leaflets,* 19 #7 (1961) 137–62; "The Divine Mushroom: Primitive Religion and Hallucinatory Agents," *Proceedings of the American Philosophical Society,* 102, #3 (June 1958) 221–23; "The Hallucinogenic Mushrooms of Mexico and Psilocybin: A Bibliography," [Harvard] *Botanical Museum Leaflets,* 20 #2 (1962) 25–73; "Lightning-bolt and Mushrooms, An Essay in Early Cultural Exploration," in *For Roman Jakobson* (The Hague: Mouton, 1956, pp. 605–12); with Roger Heim, *Les champignons hallucinogens du Mexique* (Paris: Edition du Muséum nationale d'histoire naturelle, 1958); and, with Valentina P. Wasson, *Mushrooms, Russia and History* (New York: Pantheon Books, 2 vols., 1957), and "The Hallucinogenic Mushrooms," *Garden Journal,* Jan.–Feb. 1958, pp. 1–6. More recently Wasson has demonstrated, in my opinion conclusively, the identity of the divine *ambrosia* eaten by the Greek gods to obtain immortality and the long-disputed *soma* worshiped in the Vedic songs with species of narcotic mushrooms of northern Eurasia (R. G. Wasson, *Soma, Divine Mushroom of Immortality* New York: Harcourt, Brace & World, and The Hague: Mouton & Co., 1968). The evidence for the identification, which resolves a major mystery in Sanskritic and Indoeuropean studies, is voluminous and finally convincing (see W. La Barre, Review of Wasson's *Soma* in *American Anthropologist,* 72[1970] 368-73).

38. For summaries of American Indian uses, see Weston La Barre, "The Narcotic Complex of the New World," *Diogenes,* 48 (1964) 125–38; "Le complexe narcotique de l'Amérique autochtone," *Diogène,* 48 (1964) 120–34; "El Complejo Narcótico de la America autóctona," *Diógenes,* 48 (1964) 102–12; *The Peyote Cult* (Hamden: Shoe String Press, 3rd enlarged edition, 1964, and, with a new preface summarizing recent uses, Schocken Books, 1969); Richard Evans Schultes, "Botanical Sources of the New World Narcotics," *Psychedelic Review,* 1 (1963) 145–66; "Native Narcotics of the New World," *Pharmaceutical Sciences,* 3rd Lecture Series (1960) 142–85; "The Search for New Native Hallucinogens," *Lloydia,* 29 (1966) 293–308; and "The Place of Ethnobotany in the Ethnopharmacologic Search for Psychotomimetic Drugs," in D. H. Efron, B. Holmstedt, and N. S. Kline (eds.), *Ethnopharmacologic Search for Psychoactive Drugs* (Washington: Public Health Service Publication No. 1645 [1967] 33–57); "Ein halbes Jahrhundert Ethnobotanik Amerikanischer Halluzinogene," *Planta Medica: Zeitschrift für Artzeneipflanzenforschung,* 13 (1965) 125–57; "Hallucinogenic Plants of the New World," *Harvard Review,* 1 #4 (1963) 18–32; "Botany Attacks the Hallucinogens," *Pharmaceutical Sciences, 3rd Lecture Series* (1960) 168–85; "Hallucinogens of Plant Origin," *Science,* 163 (17 Jan. 1969) 245–54; and "Fly Agaric and Men," in Efron *et al., op cit.,* pp. 405–14 and Discussion, pp. 441–46. New monographs on Indian use of snuff include S. H. Wassén. "The Use of Some Specific Kinds of South American Snuff and Related Paraphernalia," [Göteborg] *Etnografiska Museet Etnologiska Studier,* 28 (1965) 9–116; and G. J. Seitz, "Einige Bemerkungen zur Anwendung und Wirkungsweise des *Espena-*Schnupfpulvers der *Waika*-Indianer," (*loc. cit.,* pp. 118–32).

39. The Siberian Khakasy have a communal brewing and drinking of wine; the Goldi consider millet beer the "drink of the spirits"; the Koryak made an intoxicating drink of blueberries; and the Itel'men, apparently, a wine of "sweet grass" (Levin and Potapov, *op. cit.,* pp. 364, 708, 864, and 880). For America, see W. La Barre, "Native American Beers," *American Anthropologist,* 40 (1938) 224–34.

40. Richard Evans Schultes, *Botanical Sources,* p. 147; *Search for New Native*

Hallucinogens, p. 295; and *Place of Ethnobotany,* p. 36. On this question see W. La Barre, "Old and New World Narcotics: A Statistical Question and Ethnological Reply," *Economic Botany,* in press, 1970, in which I argue that American Indian religion, in particular the vision quest, gives them a cultural *preoccupation* with finding plant hallucinogens. Therefore, in spite of a larger land mass and longer human occupation of the Old World than the New, the Indian inhabitants of the New World have *discovered more,* both relatively and absolutely, of such hallucinogens. In the Old World there probably exist in nature many more hallucinogenic plants still to be discovered. For example, what mushroom was it that gave Alice Lenshina the hallucinations on which she founded the "Alice" cult in Africa?

41. Interestingly, the Iroquois have used alcohol to stimulate dreaming in the vision quest, regarding intoxication as indistinguishable from it (E. S. Carpenter, "Alcohol in the Iroquois Dream Quest," *American Journal of Psychiatry,* 116 [1959] 148–51, p. 148), and R. C. Dailey, "The Role of Alcohol among North American Indians as reported in the Jesuit Relations," *Anthropologica,* 10 #1 (1968) 45–59. But alcohol is *used ritually* like any other psychotropic substance in Middle America; see Ruth Bunzel, "The Role of Alcoholism in two Central American Cultures," *Psychiatry,* 3 (1940) 361–87; and Chandler Washburne, "Primitive Religion and Alcohol," International Journal of Comparative Sociology, 9 #2 (June 1968) no page.

V

The First Gods

EXORBITANT attention has been paid to the nature of gods, whose nature it is to be inaccessible to examination. Comparatively little attention has been paid to the impresarios of gods, their prophets, shamans[1] and priests. These persons are the *de facto* source of all our religious information and, in contrast to the gods, they are themselves available for study. The nature of deities, in default of any other empirical data, might therefore be sought in the psychic disposition of their exponents. More than this, curiously, the ancestor of the god is the shaman himself, both historically and psychologically.

There were shamans before there were gods. The very earliest religious data we know from archeology show the dancing masked sorcerors or shamans of Lascaux, Trois Frères, and other Old Stone Age caves. The worldwide distribution of functionaries recognizable as shamans—in the Americas,[2] north Eurasia,[3] Africa,[4] Oceania[5] and south Asia,[6] as well as ancient east and central Asia[7]—testifies to their antiquity. The basis of all religion in both North and South America is the shaman or medicine-man —as Boas long ago observed—so that the aboriginal New World, seen in its common essence, is a kind of ethnographic museum of the late Paleolithic-Mesolithic of Eurasia, whence came the American Indian in very ancient times. Indian religious culture is of the same date and origin as their material culture, and it is as copiously documented.

Respectable tradition, a customary belief in the objective necessity of God in our universe, and the impetus of millennia of culture history all unite to give us a sense of shock at the argument that the earliest men did not know God. But it is an error to project backward in time our own conceptual categories and social horizons. In fact, the very concept of "universe" is historically one with Hellenistic origins only, when a consciousness of many peoples in a great world gave rise to a view of a king of kings and lord of the world. And before that period we have clear evidence of multiple deity-ancestors of the tribe or clan, the god of each nation, and other religious concepts—all of which invariably match the social and world horizons of the people whose views of the supernatural these were.

It is a mistake, very certainly, to require that gods or a High God be denizens of the ancient hunter's world. For ecological and other reasons we must suppose that the earliest hominids or Australopithecine hunters effectively knew only themselves, the animals and terrain about them, and the other small groups they encountered in moving about the regions where they hunted. Their experiential "world" was a much narrower place than centuries of exploration, cumulative culture and science, astronomy and astronauts, and even jet age first-hand knowledge have made of our world. The magnitude of each experiential "world" requires a different magnitude of supernatural to match it.

The analysis of Eskimo religion shows that religion is structured on the specific inner anxieties of the group. To understand these we had best carefully learn the ecological predicaments of early man rather than foist our theology on them. The first hominids, as dimly best we can see them from the teeth and bone fragments and climatic studies of the new African paleontology, were grounded foragers, probably seeking plant foods like their ape ancestors though in drying environments, and they were at least incipiently hunters of meat food. Although they undoubtedly continued to eat plant foods (since modern man still does), simple plant gathering entails few contingencies and little anxiety, beyond concern for predators and the climatic or seasonal presence of plant foods. Hunting food-game is harder, more a matter of chance despite best efforts, and often more dangerous physically. The "aleatic area" of luck for them evidently was the hunt, on which, as African treelands gave way to grassy savannahs, they increasingly depended. In becoming men, hominids became hunters.

Preoccupied with hunting and stories of hunters' luck, the first men were needful only of a "supernatural" that would help them hunt. Mimetic ritual[8]—part symbolic gesture in the telling, play or practice, and part boast-become-magic, compelling that wish come true—must have appeared early. In Old Stone Age caves, hunting ritual appears also to have been part of the initiation of boys: at Tuc d' Audoubert, for example, smaller-than-adult heel prints, as though in ritual walk or dance, surround a clay effigy of copulating bisons; and in Montespan there is another clay effigy showing many spear thrusts, and a bear skull has fallen between the paws as though the animal's head and pelt had once been thrown over the effigy as a target; wall paintings show animals and painted weapons and wounds, animal and animal-human coitus, and animal-masked men, as though the fertility of youths and of animals and a symbolic equating of men with animals occurred also.

Early man, in short, was concerned with his own life and the mastery of animals. We can predict from Eskimo religion the general psychic pattern—but we are quite startled by the literalness of the projection that surviving evidence of early hunters' religion gives us. It is a remarkable fact that a mythic "master of animals" has survived in the religion and folklore of most of the world, in Africa, in North and South America, in Eurasia and also parts of Oceania. Later a supernatural figure, this master of animals was once simply a man, a shaman, an earlier Orpheus who charmed the animals with his magic. Some of the names given this figure by folklorists are direct translations of native terms, while others attempt to express his conceptual essence. In English he is called the *master, owner, guardian* or *lord* variously *of the animals, of game, of the woods, forests,* or *spirit of the wild.* In French he is the *maître des animaux, génie des bois, être guardien* (*surnaturel*) *du gibier, esprits-maîtres* and the like. In German he is the *Besitzer, Besitzergeist, Eigner, Eigentümer, Tierhutergeist, Busch-, Kontroll-, Patron-, Schutz-, Tier-* or *Wild-Geist, Tiergottheit, Herr* and *Vater der Tier.* Animals, it seems, had a protector, master or father just as human beings did. And early hunters projected the social structure of secular power onto the supernatural just as other groups do. The fit of myth to the social structure of a hunting band is exact. Myth anticipated no later social dispensation, for religion reflected only the then contemporary social structure.

The scholarly literature on the "master of animals" is now enormous,[9] and he has been subjected to a number of interpretations. The Finnish scholar Uno Holmberg-Harva has perhaps most comprehensively studied the religion of ancient hunters, but other high authorities are the Russian Dmitrij Zelenin and the Swede Ivar Paulson.[10] Paulson emphasizes the double function of the master of animals as protector of the game and helper of the hunter—both functions that shamans themselves exercise for men as protectors and supernatural helpers. Paulson considers that a fundamental element in the game-guardian complex is belief in the animal soul, and that the guardian of the animals becomes the animal guardian-spirit of the shaman. But before this, we believe, the master of animals is first simply the human shaman himself, who has a special affinity with them and proclaims his magic power over animals.

Only when he is dead, remoter in time and gradually given a cult, does the spirit of the shamanistic master of animals become the supernatural helper of later shamans. The supernatural is patterned simply on the human master of animals.

Faced with the obvious antiquity of this figure, Pater Schmidt[11] was forced to argue that the Master of Animals was a hypostasis, a splitting off or a "degeneration" of the "primitive High God" whose aboriginal universality he was concerned to establish. On the contrary, Raffaele Pettazzoni[12] maintains, the supernatural Master of Animals was identical with the "Supreme Being" of the first hunting peoples. With this we can agree, except that "Supreme Being" and "High God" even as terms are a projection of far later concepts onto this earliest supernatural. The idea of an animal protecting his species arose simply and directly from a social organization in which the shaman-hunter-leader fed and protected, naturally and supernaturally, his small human group. However defined, the lineaments of these "supernaturals" can none of them be seen in cosmic nature. But they are elements of human social structure, and they are psychological projections of it.

Zelenin argues that the idea of the animal guardian originated within the animal world itself, and Adolf Friedrich that the concepts of power and soul were a part of this archaic complex, with both of which Paulson agrees. Again these formulations are acceptable if one acknowledges that the will and subjective consciousness of the human self first of all gave the notions of "power" and of "soul" to man, which were partly discovered in (life, warmth, breath) and partly projected (soul) onto animals—together with other features that animals do not have (shamanistic protectors) but men did. With this proviso, one can agree with Paulson that "the animals themselves—as individual beings possessing power and souls and existing in their collective associations under the protection of the guardian spirit of the species—were probably among the oldest objects of the hunter's veneration; the game spirits and game gods were perhaps the oldest divine figures known to mankind . . . [for] the animal guardians are surely among the oldest theophanies in the religious life of mankind."[13] The rite at the hunting site,[14] given to the soul of the animal killed, was thus basic, in the sense that it was addressed to its soul-essence and the general fertility of the species—although, literally, the only theophany or "god appearance" actually here is the continuing genetic pattern of the species and motivated human wishes concerning it. Hunters eat the flesh of their kill and hope that its "life" will return again incarnate. Any supernatural shamans which animals have are mere projections of their human counterparts. Shamans address no High God, but only anthropomorphized animal "entities" much like themselves. Shamans are magicians, not priests. They control mere spirits, not world-creators.

It is striking how consistent the "master of animals" is, all over the world, wherever we find him, and none of his attributes are other than those that real shamans claim of themselves. If we stay close to a citing of ethnographic evidence, we soon get a sense of which attributes are generic, and which are only local variations of the shamanistic spirit-master. For example, the Kaulipang,[15] a Carib tribe of northern South America, say that the *keyeme* is the father of all animals, birds and game in general, and when an animal dies its soul returns to the *keyeme,* who is like a man but becomes a large water snake when he puts on a colored skin in the rainbow. (Though the rainbow-snake too is very old in both hemispheres, it is not specific to the master of animals, but only a local guise.) The Quiché of Guatemala[16] say the wanton killing of animals is an offense to the God of the Mountain, who has charge of the animals inside the earth and knows the exact number of each kind. (Again, the idea of animals in the earth-womb is widely known in North and South America and also in ancient Europe, but it is not universal to the concept of "master of animals".) The Neskapi Indian[17] "Master of the Reindeer" is manlike and white-skinned, but wears dark garments like an animal. (Here, the master of a single species is not the master of all, but both are common variants of the basic idea of "owner," as is also man-animal metamorphosis). Sedna of the Eskimo was once a human being, and now controls all sea mammals and lives on the bottom of the sea; but Sedna, though producing sea mammals and controlling the weather, is a female—like the *pótnia therón,*[18] "Mistress of the Animals" and Magna Mater of the Near East. (The sex of the animal-owner, then, like that of the shaman, is sometimes female—Diana the huntress and Mistress of the Animals is a feminine doublet of Dion-Apollo, hunter and Wolf and Lord of the Animals—and sometimes the sex, as of shamans, is ambiguous, as in the case of the misogynous Orpheus).[19]

However, as Jensen remarks, "we are told neither that the Master of the animals created the world nor that he is omniscient and omnipotent; he lacks the characteristics of a first cause so dominant in the idea of a Highest Being."[20] Any Creator among ancient hunters is at best a simulacrum of the human father, but his protection and paternity are imputed only to other animal species, not to the physical world. The shaman-like intervener or outwitter of fate, such as the Legba figures of West Africa, is not necessarily an ethical god either. At best he is a world-transformer or a trickster like Coyote or Raven, both of whom resemble species-representatives, are not notable for their morality, and have only fallible powers like human shamans. In early religion, apparently, the physical world is simply accepted as self-existent. But it is much animated by spirits, and shamans manipulate only these changing "vital" features in it, such as the weather and soul-movements in men and animals in life and death. It is only later philosophers, with a different world-scope, who are concerned with the First Cause, the *Anima mundi* or soul of the world supposedly "behind" total existence, Himself modeled on these earlier nature spirits.

A supernatural "master of the animals" that preserves peculiarly well its origin in a human shaman, is that of the Eskimo.[21] All Eskimo groups have a concept of many supernatural "owners" in nature, for example of flint- and soapstone quarries and the like, whom they placate with small gifts when they appropriate these commodities. The term "owner" must not be supposed to connote advanced property concepts as in modern capitalism; it means ownership only in the sense that soul or life possesses the body—here imputed to physical portions of nature supposed to have *anima*—or to the life spirit or genetic essence of an animal species. Indeed, for these coastal people who depend on sea hunting in winter, the most important one is the "owner" of the sea mammals. Of the Eskimo groups stretching from Cook Inlet in Alaska to southern Greenland and coastal Labrador, perhaps the Central Eskimo have the most typical supernatural "owner" of sea mammals. As we have seen, "Sedna" is a special locative pronoun meaning grammatically "that one down there [in the sea]" which refers only to this supernatural. Sedna was once a young girl who lived with her widowed father. She refused all suitors until a fulmar petrel came promising a fine home, and she married him. But the fulmar had deceived her. It was a wretched house, and when her father came to visit them and saw it, he angrily killed the fulmar and set out for home with his daughter. But the other fulmars found the dead one and stirred up a great storm. To save himself, the father made a Jonah of his daughter and threw her overboard. As she clung to the gunnels of the boat, he chopped off first her fingernails, and then her joints in turn. These became successively whalebone, whales, seals and ground seals. Then the storm subsided, since the fulmars now thought her dead. Her father let her back in the boat where, unforgiving, she allowed the dogs to gnaw off his hands and feet as he slept. Her father cursed her and the earth swallowed them all up.

Sometimes the *angakoks* or shamans visit her in her house in the sea, which is a very fine one. But the dirt from men's sins sinks down into the sea and becomes tangled in Sedna's hair, which (like a seal's flippers), not having any fingers, she cannot comb. Angered, she withholds the seals and sends storms so the men cannot hunt. The shaman must thereupon make a dangerous journey to the bottom of the sea to cleanse and appease her, so she will send animals to the starving people. (In some other groups, and in Siberia, the shaman "harpoons" her as she emerges from the floor of the hut at his magic call; the Pacific Eskimo have her counterpart in Nunam-shua, mistress of the land and mountain forests and owner of the land animals, who wears a coat of furs of all the animals and beams with a dazzling light.) Sedna cannot abide deer, and she will not have them about her—the full paradigm would be that her mutilated father became master of land-animals (who lack human hands and feet)—for one sin that enrages her to wild-tangled hair is the cooking of land- and sea-animal meat together. Since hunting of land animals is less anxiety-laden than winter sea ice hunting, the father of Sedna was evidently of less cult importance—though we would not be surprised to encounter an Eskimo myth one day that completed this logic.

The Copper Eskimo call her "the big bad woman," the origin of all taboos, and of all spirits she is the most feared, since she is sovereign over all sea beasts. She is especially touchy over women's uncleanness; if her taboos are broken she covers the seals with women's sewing things so that they cannot get out to be hunted. The shaman then calls her with magic songs, and when she possesses him the men hold him tightly, while the others in the hut tumble over one another to confess their breaches of taboo. Gradually her hair becomes smooth again, she leaves the body of the shaman, sinks to the bottom of the sea, turns her soapstone lamp upright again, the storms abate, and the animals come back to the hunters. But for four days after she has been called, no woman sews, and no man works. If a man goes out to a seal breathing-hole, he must walk, not ride his sled. If he catches a seal, he may not eat the liver while out on the ice, which is otherwise the custom. Other animal rites and taboos are enforced. When a caribou is cut up, a bit of groin skin is hid under a stone with the formula, "Here is something that can be nearest your body soft and warm; give me instead [another] caribou that I can bring down." A hunter must not cut around the eyes or the aperture of a seal's penis either, lest it be ashamed and bring bad luck to the hunter. The genitals are evidently the mysterious generator of new animals. Nor may one cut skin from the end of a muskox tail; nor can a dog eat the head of a caribou.

Netsilik Eskimo men must cut up all caribou, while the women cut the seals. The chief spirit of the Netsilik is *Nuliajuk,* mother of animals and mistress of both land and sea. She rules through *to·nrät* or spirits, much like a shaman, making storms, and making animals visible or invisible. Nuliajuk had once been a human girl, neglected and despised. Once on a trip over the sea, her knuckle joints had been successively cut off to become sea animals; she sank to the bottom, the mother of animals. In another version, her father told her to marry a dog and she became the mother of Eskimo and Indians; later she had them kill her father, but her children cut off her finger joints. When animals are scarce, the shamans call and hook her to the house door, and only when she promises to send seals do they let her go. But she has a *to·nrät* who records all breaches of taboo, and she is often angry with her children.

Enough variants have been presented to give a sense of the range of Eskimo stories of the "mistress of the animals." Sedna, like the others, is connected not only with food but also with sexuality. During one twenty-four hour period, Eskimo men and women pair off unconventionally, which is thought to please "the mother of the sea," "the dear wife," or "the old majestic one," as she is variously called. In some myth versions, Sedna had refused incest and had jumped or been thrown from the boat to have her finger joints chopped off by her father—an allusion to the one sexual sin in the isolated male-dominated family about which the Eskimo apparently have any conscious anxiety. But other sins, sexual and non-sexual, are implicated in her cult. Why should this be?

As all who hunt and fish know, these pursuits are attended with a large element of the "aleatic"—the contingent, unpredictable, unknown aspect of things, in a word, "luck." Some potent fetish, an old hat, a favorite pipe, a lucky arrowhead, we know, will surely help: my wish is a *power,* living in my lucky piece. This magic notion is psychologically more primitive than the developed animism of some primitive men! Quite apart from history and from ethnology, *psychologically* animal masters are simple anthropomorphic projections. A man knows what he wants, to get animals in the hunt, and he has practiced means and confident strength toward this technical end. How easier to explain unaccountable failure, then, than to suppose that there are other prepotent "supernatural" wills in these events—not unlike his own, but outside and more powerful, like a father's or a stronger man's will. In a power struggle he needs power, either impersonal mana, positive good luck, or the good will of a greater power—or magic power over him—it does not matter, just so his own wish prevails.

In simple narcissism the animist believes all events in the world, in the last analysis, depend upon himself and his actions. What have *I* done to influence events in the outside world—even the weather? As the manifest center of things, what I have done or not done has unwittingly but still inexorably created the result. In aboriginal America, as elsewhere, the "explanation" comes through a confusion of real or ego-anxiety with cultural or superego anxiety. My morality has affected physical reality. The way to correct mishap is universal in native America: the confession of sins.[22] If we lack luck in the hunt, plainly we have broken some taboo. Supernaturals, like parents, are offended at such sins. They will withhold their goodwill until we make just amends. Perhaps we have not treated some slain animal with enough respect, or some camp dog has been carelessly allowed to eat the heart or some other sacred part. Let us remember to put the four feet of our prey on the ground, placed as in life, ritually undo our killing, confess the misstep to the master of animals, and then perhaps he will send his animals again to the hunter.

It should be noted that the Sedna cycle has many features of the vision quest or puberty ordeal. For example, as the result of her suffering, she obtains a shaman's power over the weather, as it were from her spirit-familiar or bird husband; and she magically creates the animals over whom she has a shaman's powers. The main theme of the Sedna story deals with storms, seals and sin, in a context of sexuality and female fertility. But as in male coitus and hunting, body image has been confounded with the world's body. Somehow in her legend other human anxieties have become entangled. Real fears about food from the outer physical world (ego anxiety) have become mixed with fears about sexuality in the human world within (superego anxiety). And somehow her story mixes feelings within persons with powers outside, anger with storms; and one need with another, sexuality and food; and the physical world with parents, father or mother. The Eskimo supernatural is a conglomerate projection of all these concerns. Sedna is an "owner," an animal- and weather-controlling shamaness, and an adolescent in a supernatural power ordeal all in one. But the Sedna-animal to be killed can be a sexual Sedna (whether mother or daughter) likewise only in non-tabooed ways.

Notable about shamanistic power, and "supernatural" power in general, is the association with adolescence, though far predominantly that of males, and among hunting peoples the first acquisition as the boy becomes a man. Psychologically, supernatural power is an answer to the *need* of the boy approaching manhood. It is a fusion of male aggression and sexuality—a north African drawing leaves no doubt of this, since a line connects the hunter's weapon with his wife's pubic region; a wife's behavior at home affects the hunter's luck in a magic way; and the Indian hunter aims an arrow at a legendary deer only to find her turning into a beautiful woman. Sexual aggression and hunting, body image and weapon, are very early fused in the human-animal coition and hunt scenes of the ancient caves, as Leroi-Gourhan has shown.[23]

The aggressive weapon-phallus, life-making and life-destructive, form a symbolic pair still in Almighty Zeus, creator and bolt-hurler, beneficent skyfather, owner of Promethean fire-life and lightning-death alike. Symbolically, the father is master of life and death. His ambiguous nature is the result of ambivalence toward him. But the gods of these later Neolithic men have changed: it is now more important to control weather for the cultivated crops through sky-gods and rain-bulls, and the domestication of animals is a *direct* technical mastery that makes the "master of animals" among hunters recede behind the neolithic god, shaped though he is by his paleolithic predecessor. Besides, for our understanding, the more immediate symbolisms and cultures of Mesolithic hunters are plentifully available—even similarly cold climates in post-Wurm Europe, late Wisconsin America and Siberian Asia, a vast ecological continuum even to identical animal species hunted. Perhaps the individual vision quest is logically simpler, too, than the acquisition of manhood *en bloc* in the group initiation ordeal; certainly it is the more to be expected in an ecologically small hunting band than in a denser agricultural population. Ethnographic data would consequently best be sought among sub-boreal peoples who are still hunters in small bands, and whose culture has not undergone great ecological change since the ancient past.

Seventeenth-century maps, drawn when imperialist Russia began spreading to her wild east, show the Tungus occupying the vaster part of Siberia, all the way from Lake Baikal northward to the Arctic Ocean, and from the Yenesei region eastward to the Pacific.[24] Gudmund Hatt considers that the inland culture of Siberia "is found fullest and most unmixed in the culture of the Tungusians, although its influence is felt from Lapland to Labrador."[25] Long before the relatively late Siberian domestication of the reindeer, this old inland culture was based on the winter hunting, on snowshoes, of moose and reindeer. Without snowshoes inland winter hunting is impossible, and the great variety of snowshoe types and associated footgear within an enormous tri-continental range argues a very considerable age for this old inland boreal culture. Other diagnostic traits are the conical lodge, the birchbark canoe, and the cradleboard.

Very fortunately we have a superb account by Shirokogoroff[26] of Tungusic shamanistic culture, which is so detailed that it explains otherwise baffling elements even in North American myth and ritual. Originally all Tungus were hunters of reindeer, and all Tungus are still dependent on them. Some poorer groups in eastern Siberia still ride the few reindeer they own, in order to cover the large territories over which they hunt, and some use them as decoys in hunting. But the "Reindeer Tungus" have sometimes quite large semi-domesticated herds, which constitute their main wealth. Personal power and prestige depend on ownership of reindeer, and there is consequently marked difference in power and prestige between man and man, and between fathers and sons. The mastery of reindeer takes active strength and aggressive vigor, and Tungus society is markedly male-centered and patriarchal. Weather is also a critical factor, for on weather depends the finding of forage or the loss of one's whole property and prestige in a prolonged or especially severe storm. Tensions between men, tensions between the generations, and severe anxieties about nature are all evident in Tungusic society.

It is not a personal god the young Tungus man seeks, as it were a loving father. It is raw supernatural power. This power is male and quasi-human, but it comes from remoter sources. Notable in Tungus prayers and summonings of spirits is a stereotyped language of self-deprecation and self-depreciation, much as in the North American vision quest. The Tungus petitioner continually speaks of his stupidity, unimportance and helplessness, as if he were a dependent herdsman addressing an owner or a child beseeching powerful persons. Food, power and skill on which the life of all depends, all reside in some powerful other; and, in this respect, the young man is like women, children and the aged in earlier hunting groups. These religious communications are directed to the generalized ancestral spirits of the clan. On the whole, these supernaturals are somewhat inimical and often bring harm to the people—a view indicative, perhaps, of feelings that Tungus have-nots harbor toward the haves in everyday life. The psychic origins of Tungusic sacred culture are thus quite clear in reflecting secular anxieties.

The premise of Tungus religion is simple animism. Spirits separable from the body exist. Alien spirits may invade the body of a person. And while there, these alien spirits may act through the body in a strange manner. In Tungus theory, spirits show themselves in two closely related ways: in *arctic hysteria* and in *olonism*. "Arctic hysteria"[27] is characterized by a state of intensified suggestibility or quasi-hypnosis, during which the victim suffers an induced echolalia and echopraxia. That is, he may be compelled "against his will" to copy the words and acts, often obscene, which bystanders force upon him for their amusement. Tungus society is brutal and pitiless. Preoccupied as the Tungus are with invidious power, the forcing of words and acts on the suggestible and helpless "arctic hysteric" is almost a paradigm of human relations among them.

Arctic hysteria can occur in a single individual, as in one man whose specialty it was to be forced by imitation to stuff his mouth with mush uncontrollably until he could no longer eat. Or it may occur as a kind of mass hysteria in a whole group, as when a group of Tungusic soldiers once fell into a fit of repeating the commands of their Russian officer, and even his curses, but did not obey him except in this distorted verbal way. One source of this echolalia may be the practice, during shamanistic seances, for those present to repeat the last words or phrases of the ecstatic shaman. There is thus a psychic resonance between the shaman and his clientele, between the voice of the spirit in him and the half-hypnotized antiphonal response of the communicants, as if mass assent were spread by psychic contagion. Whatever the religious rationale of the Tungus may be in terms of supernaturals, the origin of arctic hysteria seems plainly to be in the human influence of persons on persons.

Arctic hysteria and olonism are two sides of the same coin. But they are critically distinguished in Tungusic thought. Arctic hysteria is a *passive* state of possession, during which the person is helplessly exploited by the spirits or the people about him. Olonism, on the other hand, is an *active* and self-induced state, during which the person so to speak *possesses* the spirits transitively, masters them, and exploits the spirits and the people about him. The distinction is a matter simply of whose force masters whose spirit. In the olonistic state the person may relax, weep, or loudly express himself, either directly or as the supposed *porte parole* of the spirit. Spirits often say things that ordinarily could not be said either before the elders or before children. They represent a naïve "return of the repressed"; the cult is the therapy of the culture.

Thus, typically, a young person might express a secret sexual wish openly and without fear of consequence. (The shamanistic dream-vision elsewhere often proposes sexuality with a succubus animal, a spirit marriage, or some other "forced" choice, which if disobeyed will drive the initiate mad.) When holding a spirit, the olonist may require personal attention, sacrifice, prayer to himself or herself, express sexual desire for a named individual, either directly or in conventionally understood symbols, or otherwise break the usual taboos on behavior, without personal blame. Afterward he will come out of the olonistic state, and calmness and satisfaction may reign for a while. Like arctic hysteria, olonism is also rationalized as being due to "spirits." But, again, it is easy to see the origin of olonism in the enculturational and other psychic pressures by other people on the individual. The Tungus say well that the influence of "ancestors" is still culturally alive in their spirits.

In western terms, the whole performance has an inevitable tone of chicanery, of naïve disclaimer of psychic responsibility for one's own wishes and acts. However, given the premises of animism, the belief in such spirit behavior is entirely sincere, however it is exploited. Animism not only explains but justifies here psychic phenomena we would describe as the temporary abdication of the ego, and disenthronement of the superego, in order to hear the pure voice of the id. The context is significant. Olonism is not usual when one is alone, or with nobody of consequence about, such as young children or old people only. The chance of its occurrence is still less when one is traveling, or in some other responsible or difficult practical situation.

Even so, an attack may come at any time, as long as others are present to receive the protest, conscious or unconscious, against the psychic hardships caused by other persons. Both the witnesses and the person affected will hold the spirit responsible. Olonism often comes during the hours of darkness,[28] when self-absorption is easier and the outside world less distracting—that is, in conditions of relative social isolation, sensory deprivation, or the hallucinatory dissociation of dreaming. Thus, in daytime, the olonist may close his eyes or partly cover them with his wildly disheveled hair (a convention of this state), though as Shirokogoroff says he is not averse to opening one eye, now and again, to observe the effect of his behavior on his audience. Sometimes, more spectacularly, he may "run away into the forest" and thrust himself into branches or clefts in the rocks. Since he has been sure to leave behind easily visible signs of his flight, as soon as they notice it the people follow him helter-skelter to "bring him home," either with admonitions, promises to give him his wish, or sometimes by force. In some ways, olonism looks like a stylized "temper tantrum."

Although persons suffering from arctic hysteria are semi-hypnotic, passively suggestible, and not in control of themselves, the question arises with olonists, "Are they fully conscious of their acts?" In the opinion of Shirokogoroff,

this question can be answered by saying in a sense that they are conscious, but they do not want to be so, and after and before the performance they do not act "logically," i.e. going from fact to fact, making slow inferences, acting step by step, etc. but they act quasi-unconsciously. In this condition, if they wish, they can forget everything, but their forgetfulness is not "sincere" for the next time they may introduce corrections into the performance if the latter was not "correct," and they do remember, when necessary, all details, even in a "normal" state.[29]

The reciprocal to this behavior is of course the attitudes of other people. They do not disapprove of the olonist but instead pay special attention to him, for he is marked by a distinction. People are interested in the olonist, they gossip about the attack and spread information about the affair to the neighbors. From having suffered real grievances, such individuals may for a time become significant members of the community, as persons through whom spirits speak.[30] Indeed, it is from among olonists that shamans emerge.

With spirits so promiscuously about, the constant threat is that they may overwhelm the people in mass arctic hysteria. For this reason the shaman is particularly necessary to master the spirits, and so preserve some psychic equilibrium in the community. The majority of Tungus are susceptible to these spirit attacks, women perhaps more so than men, but young children are never and old people only rarely affected. The most vulnerable age is shortly after puberty. Being persons of secondary importance, the youthful can more safely be allowed to succumb to spirit visits than in the case of responsible persons in authority, to whom visits occur more rarely. For an adult, the shaman is speedily summoned to exorcize the spirit. Hence an important hunter, or a young mother with several children to care for, would be promptly attended to.

Another reason for a less interventionist treatment of the young is the belief that spirits are constantly looking for a young person who may become their "master," i.e., a shaman. One might say that, insofar as a shaman-to-be reflects typical culture pressures (to which others make response in their "reasonable" treatment of him), the olonist in a sense is the person "chosen" by people to be sick for them. But to the degree that the olonist's responses are idiosyncratic, culturally untypical, or really unacceptable socially, he is in society's terms individually "sick" and he is scolded or is apprehensively considered in need of cure. Many persons may claim to have shamanistic powers after an olonistic attack. But the significant fact is that only social recognition makes them officially shamans. There is thus a delicate homeostatic balance in the situation. Society can accept minimal (and socially wished) change, on the "authority" of the shaman as a charismatic culture hero. But excessive "acting out" must be cured by social pressure and disapproval, or by direct individual treatment by established shamans. In this way society constantly achieves its own therapy, though sometimes at the expense of the individual they decide is "sick." So thin a line there is between the martyr and the heretic.

In one sense, arctic hysteria is a psychosis that may spread epidemically, if unmastered spirits invade enough members of the group. Hence the olonist-qua-shaman is the individual on whom rests the psychic health of the whole people. If spirits are free, whether by reason of a shaman's recent death, or his abstaining from or inability to control them, then spirits enter people freely and cause many harmful acts by them. If the shaman-master is alive and active, though, he can expel the spirits. If he is not, society is overwhelmed by mass arctic hysteria. An active hunter would not be able to kill animals, because the spirits would turn his gun down or aside at the moment of firing, and so interfere with his potency as a hunter. His family, dependent on his hunting, would then starve. The anxiety produced would reverberate throughout the whole group, and other hunters would also be "caused" to fail in hunting. The effects of mass arctic hysteria would be disastrous.

Some of the young men would lose normal sleep, would sit upon their beds, speak and sing in a half asleep state and thus would not have the necessary rest; their thoughts would be concentrated upon the spirits that haunt them; they would be distracted, and absent-minded; they would neglect or miss their duties in the family work and would gradually be disabled altogether. Some other clansmen might "run away into the rocks or forests" where they would remain for days without food and even some of them would perish. Others, who are inclined to "olonism," might become dangerous during momentarily uncontrolled states; they might throw various utensils, burning wood or hot water, on those supposed to induce reflexes; they might even use weapons, like knives, axes and rifles and so the most harmless and amusing olon, become *kōdu* [psychotic]. Other clansmen would have "nervous attacks" at moments of great responsibility, e.g. during the crossing of rivers, keeping in their arms children, handling hot water and fire. Accident after accident would follow and several persons might perish altogether. This would be a case of a real mass psychosis which might put the clan into a state of complete social and economic paralysis threatening the very existence of the clan.[31]

If the evil comes from ancestral spirits only, then only the clan itself will be affected. But if the epidemic is of alien spirits as well, then the whole ethnic region might become infected by a mass psychic breakdown, and the whole area be affected (as if by stressful alien acculturation and consequent "Hellenistic despair").

The paraphernalia of the accredited Tungus shaman include his shamanistic costume, special headdress, staff or baton, mirror, singleheaded drum or tambour, and other musical instruments, as well as various "placings" for the spirits independent of other offerings, in a sense bait-traps or fetishes, the temporary physical locus of the spirits. Curiously, the shaman's headdress contains "snakes" although snakes are neither usual nor important in many areas of northern shamanism. The symbolic adhesion of snake and shaman must be older and from elsewhere.[32] The paleoasiatic center of this trait is southwest of Lake Baikal, the archeological connection being with magic snakes drawn in late paleolithic caves of Europe. Tungusic shamans' staves and batons remarkably resemble the so-called "bâtons de commandement" of Solutrean-Magdalenian Europe. The pattern must in any case be very old, since Okladnikov reports figurines of women and birds in mammoth ivory and engraved drawings of mammoths and serpents in the Siberian upper paleolithic, which he regards as offshoots of the art of glacial Stone Age hunters of Europe.

There are two kinds of shamans, bird shamans and reindeer shamans. Bird shamans not only dress in bird skins and in costumes imitating birds but, conceptually, they *are* birds. Yakuts shamans, especially, can imitate remarkably the cries of birds, as a kind of "secret language" for use with supernaturals. Shierozewski reports that during shamanistic performances of Yakut shamans, "Mysterious noises are audible sometimes from above, sometimes from below, sometimes in front of, sometimes behind the shaman . . . you seem to hear the plaintive call of the lapwing mingled with the croaking of a falcon interrupted by the whistle of the woodcock, all that is the voice of the shaman, varying the intonations of his voice . . . the screaming of eagles mingled with . . . the refrain of the cuckoo."[33] Many Siberians say the first shamans were birds, and both Yakuts and Tungus have a belief in soul-birds, a very widely distributed and ancient notion, as though birds were the quintessence of angelic spirits. The eagle in particular plays an important part in the shamanistic mythology of the Buryat, the Yakut, and other Siberian peoples, as well as of the Indoeuropeans, the Finno-Hungarians, and the Huns.

The most complex of the bird costumes are found among the Yakuts; of the reindeer, among the Buryat. The "bird" costume is used for shamanizing to the upper world, primarily for the cure of sickness, sometimes accompanied by the sucking out of various "foreign bodies" from different parts of the patient's body, and sometimes by the sacrifice of a boar or pig. In the old days these shamans could kill people, make trees and rocks fall down, produce thunder and lightning, and even in summer send snow that would not melt for days. Bird shamans are thus particularly connected with cosmic forces, the weather, and disease.

The headdress of the Siberian reindeer shaman always includes the antlers of a reindeer (like his European counterpart from the "reindeer shaman" of Trois Frères down to the deer "horned god" of animal fertility and wealth, the Celto-Roman Cernunnus). The "reindeer" costume is for shamanizing to the lower world, to search for the lost souls of living people or to settle the souls of dead ones. That is, the shaman finds souls and manages them in this world, sends them to the lower world and manages them there, or brings back souls from the lower world. The reindeer shaman neutralizes the malevolent activity of ancestral shamans as well, as a natural extension of this power.

The division of Siberian shamans into reindeer and bird, earth and sky, has very ancient analogues. At Lascaux, for example, we have a reindeer shaman in the Dancing Sorcerer, plentifully associated with game animals and literally underground in a cave, as well as a bird shaman in the bird-headed man with a bird-headed shaman's staff, both in the same cave though of somewhat different date. Birds carved on mammoth ivory of Solutrean-Magdalenian date are found in the upper paleolithic of Siberia itself. The Siberian earth/sky dichotomy of spirits is intercontinental in spread elsewhere, as well as very old. Chafe,[34] for example, found that Seneca spirits fell naturally into two classes, terrestrial and celestial.

The familiar Greek chthonic/Olympian dichotomy is only one example of the ancient shamanic dualism of Indoeuropeans, especially elaborated in the Iranian light/darkness dichotomy, this last perhaps in possible association with the Sinitic sky/earth, light/dark, male/female, yang/yin, bird/reptile (phoenix/dragon) dualism. Pater Schmidt[35] divided Siberian shamans into the ecstatic "black shaman" who goes to the land of the dead, and the "white shaman" or *Himmelsdiener* who only shams ecstasy and tends toward the priest. But Eliade[36] does not accept a dichotomy in these terms into black and white, mystic and actor. With this we can only agree: the fundamental distinction is into earth and sky, animal and bird shamans, as though old stone age men recognized in nature two major *kinds* of creatures, animals and birds, which they associated with two distinct realms of nature, earth and sky—and hence had two kinds of shamans to deal with them. Schmidt has added, for polemic reasons, a necessarily much later discrimination we make between shamans and priests. But Siberian animal and bird shamans both use black and white magic, are both mystics and actors, hysterics and histrions, and both are equally *shamans* ranging from "natural" ecstatics to dissimulators. We find again the same simple division into "departmental" deities of nature in Zeus and Dis, rulers of sky and underworld realms. Russian authors have recently added considerable ethnographic evidence on bird/reindeer, sky/underworld shamans among the Buryat, Yakuts, Altai, and Sel'kup tribes of Siberia.[37] Formerly, Siberian shamans were often also smiths, and iron is still a sacred shamanic substance; interestingly also, dead Yukaghir shamans themselves became objects of worship, and parts of their bodies were kept as relics.[38]

In one sense, the bird shaman is oriented to the "outer" cosmic world (the sky, the weather, and invading disease spirits), the reindeer shaman to the "inner world" of human or once-human spirits (to ancestors, to spirits of the dead, and to animal-human fertility), but otherwise cosmic *mana* and living *anima* pass easily into one another. As among other Paleosiberians, the Tungusic shamanistic costume is of two kinds, covered with bird[39] and animal[40] pictures and cosmic symbols of the sun, moon and stars, but distinguished according to the realm of spirits mastered by the shaman.[41] In many Paleosiberian tribes, another prime function of the shaman is to control the "masters of animals" or supernatural "owners" of the animals on which people live. But this function is not important among the Tungus, who themselves control their semi-domesticated herds, if not the weather.

Among the Manchurian Tungus, a shaman may be selected and educated in shamanism as a child. One day such a candidate runs away to the mountains, living there for seven days or more on animals he is said to catch directly with his teeth, like a wild animal. When he returns or is brought back, he is dirty with blood, his clothes are torn, and his hair is disheveled like a wild man's. After ten days he begins to speak incoherently a few words, which an old and experienced shaman carefully listens to, meanwhile cautiously asking questions. The spirit (candidate) may at times become angry and designate another shaman, who conducts an elaborate ceremony over the candidate, ending in much animal sacrifice and feasting. The runaway child is now being dramatically attended to.

The aims of shamanistic ceremonies in general are several: divination of the causes of various troubles, discovery of the future, curing the sick, transporting souls back and forth from the underworld and managing them there, sacrifice to spirits, including those of "animal masters," and initiating new shamans. Some shamans interpret dreams. Others, when asked about a problem, will "dream on it" themselves and supply the answer later. Some shamans eat narcotic mushrooms (*Amanita muscaria*), and in their hallucinations visit the world of spirits, where they get the answers to questions posed them. Some, like the Chukchee, preside over group mushroom-intoxication, each man in turn drinking the urine of another to extend the action of the precious narcotic spirit-substance. All shamans have various shamanistic tricks, such as cutting the stomach open with a feather, with much effusion of blood, after which a short time later the skin may be seen to be without a scar. Many can cause the spirits to shake the tent violently, or they may juggle with, or swallow hot coals of fire. Shamans are sometimes rivals, and feud with one another through their supernatural familiars, but most shamans in social terms are "good." At death, the shaman's magic trident spear is always buried with him (a form associated with a late-Magdalenian period fish spear, which Neptune still carries but in altered form).

As individuals, shamans vary widely. Though some are given great feasts, some are poor or economically marginal. To European eyes they vary from apparent "normality" to the clinically insane, from naïve believers to conscious manipulators, from those with limited knowledge to those in complete possession of the lore of the local shamanistic complex, from egocentrism to a perfect fusion with the social milieu, and from clumsy technicians to erudite masters. Some shamans first treat their individual patients as children and then carry them throughout their lives, building up a clientele of patients who organize into strong partisans of the shaman. In fact, one might hesitate going to a very old shaman because he might die soon and leave one stranded.

Although Paleosiberian shamans ordinarily wear the picture-covered costumes symbolic of their power, certain especially potent spells require nudity. In "black" magic the Chukchee shaman strips naked outdoors on a moonlit night and casts a spell:

"O moon! I show you my privy parts. Take compassion on my angry thoughts. I have no secrets from you. Help me on suchandsuch a man!" Saying this, the shaman tries to weep in order to win the compassion of the moon. He also makes peculiar movements with his mouth, as if catching something, and drawing it inward. This symbolizes his desire to catch and eat up the victim.[42]

Bogoras wrote that at Mariinsky one shaman crawled on all fours wearing only a shamanistic cap when invoking the moon. The shaman Scratching Woman also made some of his magic thus lightly accoutered. A similar charm mentioning the genitals was used by Chukchee reindeer hunters, and in some yearly family rituals the shaman performed naked, singing songs to his animal familiars that mention genital parts. The moon appears repeatedly in the special transvestite form of Chukchee shamanism.

In this form, there is a shamanistic transformation of sex into a "soft man being" at the behest of the *ke'let* or familiar spirit, "usually at that critical age of early youth when shamanistic inspiration first manifests itself," that is, the "supernatural" (oedipal) Other demands change of sex. This was much dreaded, and in most cases of suicide of young initiates in preference to accepting shamanistic power, change of sex had been demanded. There are several stages in the transformation. First, at the call of the spirits, the shaman braids his hair like a woman—but shamans often enjoin women's hair-style upon sick men, to change their appearance so as to be unrecognizable by malignant spirits. The second stage is marked by the adoption of women's dress, ordered by a spirit in a dream—but transvestitism is also sometimes prescribed by the shaman for medico-magic reasons to cure some congenital diseases.

The third stage of transformation is more complete. A young man who is undergoing it leaves off all pursuits and manners of his sex, and takes up those of a woman. He throws away the rifle and the lance, the lasso of the reindeer herdsman, and the harpoon of the seal-hunter, and takes to the needle and the skin-scraper. He learns the use of these quickly, because the "spirits" are helping him all the time. Even his pronunciation changes from the male to the female mode. At the same time his body alters, if not in its outward appearance, at least in its faculties and forces. He loses masculine strength, fleetness of foot in the race, endurance in wrestling, and acquires instead the helplessness of a woman. Even his psychical character changes. The transformed person loses his brute courage and fighting spirit, and becomes shy of strangers, even fond of small talk and of nursing small children. Generally speaking, he becomes a woman with the appearance of a man . . .

The most important of the transformations is, however, the change of sex. The "soft man" begins to feel like a woman. He seeks to win the good graces of men, and succeeds easily with the aid of "spirits." Thus he has all the young men he could wish striving to obtain his favor. From these he chooses his lover, and after a time takes a husband. The marriage is performed with the usual rites, and I must say that it forms a quite solid union, which often lasts till the death of one of the parties. The couple live much in the same way as do other people. The man tends the herd and goes hunting and fishing, while the "wife" takes care of the house, performing all domestic pursuits and work . . .

The state of the transformed man is so peculiar that it attracts much gossip and jests on the part of the neighbors. Such jests are of course only interchanged in whispers, because the people are extremely afraid of the transformed, much more so than of ordinary shamans . . . Moreover, each "soft man" is supposed to have a special protector among the "spirits," who, for the most part, is said to play the part of a supernatural husband, ke'le-husband, of the transformed one. This husband is supposed to be the real head of the family and to communicate his orders by means of the transformed wife . . . The ke'le-husband is very sensitive to even the slightest mockery of his transformed wife, because he knows that the "soft man" feels exceedingly "bashful," and also because he is doubtless conscious that the position of the latter is ridiculed on account of his obedience to his own orders.[43]

Some shamans may even have a ke'le-wife. "Soft men" are supposed to excel in all branches of shamanism, including ventriloquism, which ordinary women cannot do.

"Soft men" also show their great bashfulness in retiring from ordinary shamanistic rivalries. But they are dreaded even by untransformed shamans, because their supernatural protector-husbands will retaliate upon aggressors. Tulu'gi, who was married to a man, admitted to Bogoras that he had not been physically transformed, but in appearance and behavior he was otherwise entirely a woman. E'chuk, however, another shaman of transformed sex, claimed to have borne sons from his own body, fathered by his *ke'le* spirit. Another transformed shaman, Kee'eulin, was first married to a wife who bore him several children, and then he was married to a man for over twenty years. Bogoras knew two other young shamans who kept the whole camp upset in their rivalry with girls for male lovers. Still another among the Yukaghir was called Supan, after the Kamchadal word for winter-hut door, tabooed to men but used by women and transformed men.

Jochelson[44] found traditions of *qev'eu* among the Koryak, said to be not uncommon in ancient times. Earlier, Krasheninnikoff[45] wrote of Koryak traditions of *ke'yev* concubines, whom he compared to Kamchadal transvestite shamans and dream interpreters. Sumner[46] described in detail a transformed Yakuts shaman named "The-man-who-fell-from-heaven" who had a Russian male spirit who called for vodka and women; he also had a spirit's daughter and a Tungusic male spirit as familiars, both of whom unceremoniously asked people present in a group if they had pudenda, an affirmative answer bringing mutilation of the men by the female spirit, and of the women by the Tungus spirit. One shaman was said to have given birth several times, once to a fox; another, to a raven, but nearly died of the difficult birth; still others gave birth to gulls, ducks, and puppies. The songs of Yakuts shamans are full of sexual references; and their dances, of indecent gestures and movements.

There are repeated striking similarities in Siberian and American shamanism, even to small arbitrary details, that argue unmistakably for their ethnographic continuity—the "wildly tangled hair" of Sedna, Tungusic olonists and Manchurian shaman-candidates; shamanistic juggling and swallowing of live coals of fire; visionary weeping and beseeching "pity" of the spirits; doctoring by sucking out foreign bodies; shamanistic use of narcotics; the shaman's staff or trident; connection of the moon with vision-commanded transvestism; the frequent relation of shamanism with *berdache*-transvestism and change of sex; shamanistic tent-shaking; the rain- and rainbow-snake; the Eagle as thunder bird[47]; shaman-like animal "Tricksters" (Raven is both Northwest Coast and Chukchi); and the like. There are other more general parallels too, in arctic hysteria, windigo-madness and the stylized "running away into the forest" of the Tungus olonist and the Kwakiutl cannibal-spirit-possessed candidate in the winter dance, the need of the initiate to relearn human speech, rivalry in shamanistic tricks (a kind of "medicine show" in Algonkian *midewewin* societies), and the organized clientele of the Siberian shaman and American Indian "medicine societies" of persons cured, say, by the same bear-doctor of the same disease.

The bird-shaman in Siberia and the widespread specific connections of feathers and medicine-power in America should not pass unnoticed either. The nature-mover and weather-shaman in South America and Siberia, and the North American nature-transformers and world-renewers shortly to be described, are all surely from the same mold. Some features, of course, like bear ceremonialism, are more than merely Sibero-American; these should be treated strictly as the intangible religious counterparts of such widespread features of tangible material culture as the conical lodge, sleds, skis, snowshoes and circumpolar footgear. There are many other close Siberian-American parallels such as spirit-possessed ecstatic shamanism itself, the supernatural group-protecting function of the shaman, the shamanistic "mastery" over animals with "power" mere secular huntsmen lack, human-animal metamorphosis, coitus and marriage with animals, and the general sexual nexus between the shaman and his familiars, human or animal and male or female—but all these particular features are not merely specific to Siberian-American but to ancient Old World shamanism at large.

In this whole complex, the "first god" we can discern is only selfconsciousness of vital spirit—the *mana* power or will man thinks he sees in nature, the *anima* or soul he is sure comes and goes in the bodies of men and of animals. Mana and anima are close, and both are manmade in the shape of man, the difference depending only on the degree of personalization, on the stage of ego perception one projects out into the world. The closeness of mana and anima makes the line between men and animals thin and imprecise and even nonexistent. The shaman *is* his animal familiar when the man is thought to change into an animal and back again: the spirit stuff is the same, whether inside him or out, the shaman possessed or the shaman "outside himself," and the living shaman or his spirit-life outside the dead or inanimate dream-body. The shaman as the master of animals is identical with the Master of Animals as the shaman's animal familiar. The first god is his animal self, the life he consumes and that is his life.

The archaic indistinction of this primitive view of self and world has the same psychic fuzziness as the self-involved preoedipal child's view. The first possible "objectivity" is subjective emotional assent to the dim unwanted otherness of some Other, food or mother, father and moral humanity. The specific psychological *humanness* of shamanism is quite inescapable. It represents the paranoid stance of preoedipal magic in a uniquely neotenous animal. Shamanism reacts to the imperfect omnipotence of the hunter, to his secular failure, to the human failure of fathers and all other men—and then imagines a recaptured sacred omnipotence at the vague ego boundaries.

Even the "fatherhood" of the shaman to his group is a paranoid and vatic one, often expressing a basic infantile and paranoid unmanhood and fear of secular virility. It replicates only a child's vision of fatherhood. To a frightened clientele he must seem a father, because a father is what others seek in the shaman. If he is too frightened and too childlike, like themselves, they reject him as inadequate, sick, a passive spirit-exploited child. The shaman is the artist of feeling, the autoplastic sculptor of himself, the god-maker. His vision quest is a quest for an identity-vision of himself—another reason why olonism is so like the self-impresarianism of adolescence. The shamanist is above all a self-drama-tist, but often seems only to half-believe in himself and in his role. He dreams, he hears voices, he orders and is "ordered," half man and half child. He is a "Little Hans" totemist, he has sexuality with oedipal "super-naturals" and their animal stand-ins, he is the fertility of animals and the unique grandiose Adam of all men.

Hence we find the curious quality of cozening and of adolescent "acting out" in olonism and arctic hysteria. "Spirits" seem far too often to express the subject's personal wishes. If, for example, one likes the luxury food, grain mush, or dislikes a commanding officer, or desires some forbidden sexual object, surely it is the accomplishment of one's own wish "uncon-trollably" to stuff in mush, to deride the officer, and to demand the woman? The provocation of obscene mimicking in arctic hysterics seems much too close to the provocative behavior of olonists. In the frank "return of the repressed" both arctic hysteria and olonism seem to object directly to the restraints of culture. But is culture concerned to set up taboos only to circumvent them? Is the purpose of culture only to control the surge of animal energies at adolescence? Are taboos merely adult ways to cope with and defend against adolescents?

Arctic hysteria and olonism are both shadows of intergenerational con-flict, compounded by the controlling Tungusic use of reindeer as prop-erty, since a youth cannot get status till he gets some of his father's reindeer, after a son's exploited long hard herding of reindeer, and from a reluctant physically failing father. Certainly in the "spirits" we can see a masked conflict of group culture and individual biology, everywhere especially acute at adolescence. And Tungus "ancestors" seem much in the service of adolescents' derision of the adults they are soon to be. Indeed, the psychic tone of the arctic hysteric and the olonist seems close to that of the shaman-trickster: Raven and Coyote hilariously do everything the culture forbids.[48] The tone is unmistakable and deep in Siberian-American religious culture: for example, the mud-clowns in staid Pueblo ritual do everything provocatively obscene and filthy or ritually backwards, and Iroquois Long House ritual is half slapstick horseplay. Do ritual and humor both "let off steam"? Is religion a dramatized vacation from the duress of the secular, as the dream is from waking life? Must there not be some "give" at adolescence, between child and adult, to the absurd recalcitrancy of culture? Is the sacred a dream that must fluctuate to fit secular vicissitudes?

NOTES
(V The First Gods)

1. The word shaman comes from the Tungusic, although a connection with Sanskrit has been implausibly argued (Berthold Laufer, "Origin of the Word Shaman," *American Anthropologist*, 19 [1917] 361–71; N. D. Mironov and S. M. Shirokogoroff, "Śramana-Shaman: Etymology of the Word 'Shaman,'" *Journal of the Royal Asiatic Society, North-China Branch* [Shanghai], 55 [1924] 105–30; Paul Roux, "Nom du chaman dans les textes prémongols," *Anthropos*, 53 [1958] 133–42; and Julius Németh, "Über den Ursprung des Wortes Šaman und einige Bemerkungen zur türkischmongolischen Lautgeschichte," *Keleti szemle* [Budapest], 14 [1913–14] 240–49).

2. Basic papers on American shamanism: Clark Wissler, "General Discussion of Shamanistic and Dancing Societies," *Anthropological Papers of the American Museum of Natural History*, 11, pt. 12, 1916; W. Z. Park, *Shamanism in Western North America;* R. H. Lowie, *Religious Ideas and Practices;* Alfred Métraux, "Religion and Shamanism," in J. H. Steward (ed.), *Handbook of South American Indians*, 5:559–99; A Métraux, "Le chamanisme araucan," *Revista de l'Instituto de Antropologia de l'Universidad Nacional de Tucumán,* 2 (1842) 309–62; and W. Thalbitzer, "Shamans of the East Greenland Eskimo," in A. L. Kroeber and T. T. Waterman (eds.), *Source Book in Anthropology* (New York: Harcourt, Brace and Company, 1931, and Johnson Reprint Corporation, 1965).

3. Henry N. Michael (ed.), *Studies in Siberian Shamanism* (Toronto: University of Toronto Press, 1963) is especially valuable for translations from Russian sources; a stimulating and valuable monograph is by Georg Nioradze, *Der Schamanismus bei den sibirischen Völkern* (Stuttgart: Strecker und Schröder, 1925); see also V. M. Mikhailovskii, "Shamanism in Siberia and European Russia," *Journal of the Anthropological Institute of Great Britain and Ireland*, 24 (1895) 62–100; and Carl-Martin Edsman (ed.), *Studies in Shamanism* (Stockholm: Almquist & Wiksell, 1967); but the major work on Siberian shamanism is Hans Findeisen, *Der Schamanismus, dargestellt um Beispiel der Bessessensheitspriester nordasiatischer Völker* (Stuttgart: W. Kohlhammer, 1957). The best general source in English is, of course, Mircea Eliade's *Shamanism, Archaic Techniques of Ecstasy* (New York: Pantheon Books, 1964, revised and enlarged from the original, *Le chamanisme et les techniques de l'extase*, Paris: Payot, 1951). Wilhelm Schmidt devoted to shamanism the last four volumes of his monumental *Ursprung des Gottesidee.* For European shamanism, besides Mikhailovskii and Eliade, cited above, an important source is N. Lid, "North European Shamanism," in A. F. C. Wallace (ed.), *Men and Cultures: Selected Papers of the Fifth International Congress of Anthropological and Ethnological Sciences* (Philadelphia: University of Pennsylvania Press, 1960, pp. 305–8). The shaman's (or, before battle, sometimes a special warrior's) ecstatic trance and metamorphosis into a bear, in ninth-century Norse poems, is the origin of the *berserk* and his "berserker rage" (p. 305), attested to by Swedish rock carvings of about 4000 years ago. "One of the White Sea carvings (Figure 6) contains [three] nude skiers on a cross-country run, with ski poles. Their faces are peculiar. If you consider all the symbolism in these carvings, and especially all birds depicted there, you may interpret them as birds' faces! A birdlike appearance is quite common in shaman tradition as symbolizing his

spiritual flight" (p. 308), and Lid thinks the boats and skis in rock carvings are also associated with the shaman's ecstatic journey, Peter Buchholz also emphasizes the animal metamorphoses of a shamanistic "god" like Óðinn ("Schamanistische Züge in der altisländischen Überlieferung," Doctoral dissertation, University of Münster, 1968). He writes that "among attributes [of Óðinn are] not only the animals escorting him but also those that he becomes through metamorphosis. Names like Jálkr, Hrosshársgrani, Geirloþnir, Ólgr, Ginarr, Arnhofþi, Qrn, Viþhrímnir, Sváfnir, Ófnir, Jalfaþr, Bjorn, Hrjótr, Jormunr, Qlgr, Sviour, Sveigþir, Grímr, and others are not at all proof that the god was worshiped in the shape of such and such an animal, but they do testify to his changeability. Real background is probably cult masquerade. Óðinn is the disguised god par excellence . . . Óðinn's changing into animals and his relations with warriors' societies and initiation customs are strongly reminiscent of certain traits of North Eurasian shamanism" ("Perspectives for Historical Research in Germanic Religion," *History of Religions,* 8 [1968] 111–38, p. 133). On these last points, see Dag Strömbäck, *Sejd Textstudier i nordisk religionshistoria* (Stockholm: Geber, 1935, p. 21), who likens this to Lapp shamanism; and Laszló Vajda, "Zur phaseologischen Stellung des Schamanismus," *Ural-altaische Jahrbücher,* 31 (1959) 456–85.

4. "Shaman" should always be used in the strict sense of Eliade to mean ecstatic possession of a human practitioner by a (supposed) alien spirit or power; in this sense Eliade states that the only continent where shamanism is a rather rare phenomenon is Africa ("Recent Works on Shamanism: A Review Article," *History of Religions,* 1 [1961] 152–86, p. 153). But note the numerous examples of African spirit-possession, trance, and spirit-trance mapped by Erika Bourguignon, in Raymond Prince (ed.), "Trance and Possession States," *Proceedings Second Annual Conference R. M. Bucke Memorial Society.* Montreal, 1966, 3–34, p. 19. Moreover, in the African "divine king" or "rain king" who embodies all the fertility of animals and men, is connected with the ancestor cult, and has supernatural political charisma, we have all the usual features of the shamanism of hunting and gathering peoples *except* ecstatic possession. With the officially announced demise of the Viennese *Kulturkreislehrschule,* which insisted on finding everywhere the true and only primitive High God, the pre-theistic shamanism of primitive hunting peoples now becomes increasingly visible. Indeed, Africa also unarguably has true shamanism as well as the rain king (S. F. Nadel, "A Study of Shamanism in the Nuba Mountains," *Journal of the Royal Anthropological Institute,* 76 [1946] 25–37; see also Adolf Friedrich, *Afrikanische Priestertümer,* Stuttgart: Strecker und Schröder, 1939, pp. 292–325; and E. M. Loeb, "The African Divine Kingship: Its Function and History," Paper presented at the Annual Meeting of the American Anthropological Association, San Francisco, 1963). Loeb thinks this politico-religious complex is derived from the ancient Mediterranean cultures and southwest Asia, perhaps in the late Neolithic. The possession-ideology of African magicians should be re-examined from Nadel's point of view in the light of the classic works of social anthropologists (e.g., E. E. Evans-Pritchard, *Witchcraft, Oracles and Magic of the Azande,* Oxford: Oxford University Press, 1937).

Deursen revives Breysig's earlier notion of the religious position of the culture hero and considers him a mediator between God and man, but not a figure of veneration, but rather one who originated in an historical hero, chief, medicineman or prophet (A. van Deursen, *Der Heilbringer: Eine ethnologische Studie über den Heilbringer bei den nordamerikanischen Indianern,* Groningen: J. B. Wolters, 1931; see also Åke Hultkrantz, *History of Religions,* 7 [1967], p. 145). In my opinion trickster, culture hero, and spirit-mediator are all related *via the purely human shaman.* It is a matter of emphasis only. For example, Hermes is only weakly a culture hero until Hellenistic Gnosticism, and classically very much a shamanic spirit-mediator; Prometheus is very much a culture hero, but hardly a god-chosen mediator or messenger like Hermes; Apollo is at once a master of animals and lord of fertility, a culture hero as well as a god and patron of the muses; Zeus is a trickster-figure, a fertility-god, and greatest master of animal-metamorphoses of them all; while the American Indian culture hero, scarcely an omnipotent god, is very conspicuously a shaman-trickster. Gösta Kock attacked van Deursen's view of the culture hero as a mediator, and thought it plausible to derive the culture hero from the master of animals (Gösta Kock, "Is 'Der Heilbringer' a God or Not?" *Ethnos*, 8, nos. 1–2 (1943) 61–77; *idem*, "Der Heilbringer, Ein Beitrag zur Aufklärung seiner religionsgeschichtlichen Voraussetzungen," *Ethnos*, 21, nos. 1–2 (1956) 118–29). The whole picayune argument over subjective taxonomies is concerned with a bogus problem: for all these figures derive simply from the human shaman who is all of them, and the "problem" arises from our separating and over-categorizing his traits. Thus van Deursen is right (the culture hero *is* a mediator between his "spirit" and his people, and he *is* human)—and so is Miss Kock (the "Owner" or "Master" *is* a helper and *is* a familiar or double *of the shaman*).

5. It is important to note the case for shamanism rests not only on ecstatic spirit-possession but also on persistent arbitrary motifs: the "bird-man" of Easter Island and the spirit-possessed *etua* of the Marquesas, in the most far-flung islands of Polynesia, are still specifically shamanistic. Again, Toradja shamanism in Celebes embodies *mejapi* withdrawal into the woods, head-hunting and "muellos" ideology, transvestism, and the shaman's ascent to the spirit world (J. Van der Kroef, "Messianic Movements in the Celebes, Sumatra, and Borneo," in Sylvia L. Thrupp [ed.], *Millennial Dreams in Action: Essays in Comparative Study* [The Hague: Mouton and Co., 1962, 80–121], pp. 89–90; see also his "Transvestitism and the Religious Hermaphrodite in Indonesia," *Journal of East Asiatic Studies* [Manila], 3 [1954] 257–65 for other specific similarities of mainland Asian and Indonesian shamanism). For the specific shamanistic mastery over fire, see M. Eliade, *Forgerons et alchimistes* (Paris: Flammarion, 1956, pp. 81ff); *Patañjali et le Yoga* (Paris: Editions de Seuil, 1962, pp. 330ff); and *Myths, Dreams and Mysteries* (New York: Harper, 1961, pp. 92ff).

6. In a well-documented area like India, not only can an impressive continuity be shown from the dancing sorcerers or hunters of the Mesolithic rock paintings of the Mahadeo Hills (D. H. Gordon, *The Prehistoric Background of Indian Culture*, Bombay: N. M. Tripathi, 1958, pp. 26, 104) to the horned bow-carrying shaman or "Lord of the Beasts" of two Indus copper tablets (H. P. Sullivan, "A Re-Examination of the Religions of the Indus Civilization," *History of Religions*, 4 [1964] 115–25, fn 54) and the Harappan "Master of the Animals" to the modern Hindu Shiva as Pašupati—but also surviving present-day shamanism. For example, Elwin describes the shamanism of the primitive Saora of Orissa, who preserve such classic details as the visit by a spirit, proposal of marriage, resistance and acute crisis, resolved on marrying the spirit-spouse from the underworld (Verrier Elwin, *The Religion of an Indian Tribe*, Oxford: Oxford University Press, 1955, pp. 128–71). Shamanism is also found among the Munda or Kolarian-speaking Santal, Korku, Munda, Birhor, etc.; the Dravidian-speaking Oraon, Khond, Gond, etc.; and the Aryan-speaking Bhuiya, Baiga, and Bhil (Rudolf Rahmann, "Shamanistic and Related Phenomena in Northern and Middle India," *Anthropos*, 54 [1959] 681–760); see also Josef Haekel and C. B. Tripathi, "Eine Bessessenheit-Séance der Rathva-Koli in Gujerat (Indien)," *Oesterreichische Akademie der Wissenschaften, Philosophisch-Historische Klasse, Sitzungsberichte, 248, Band 5, Abhandlungen Veröffentlichen der Ethnologischen Kommission, Heft I*, Vienna: Hermann

188   THE GHOST DANCE

Böhlaus Nachf., 1966; and Edward B. Harper, "Shamanism in South India," (*Southwestern Journal of Anthropology*, 13 [1957] 267-87).

7. Of the essential shamanism of the whole of ancient east Asia there can be no question. For example, in the Shang dynasty (1766-1122 B.C.), *wu* were ecstatic singing and dancing shamans who brought rain, exorcized disease spirits, and acted as mediums for ancestor-spirits; they were often mentioned in texts of the Han and later dynasties (H. J. T. Johnson, "Priest, Priesthood [Chinese]," *Hastings Encyclopedia of Religion and Ethics*, 10: 290–93; L. C Hopkins, "The Chinese Wu: His Inspired Dancing and Versatile Character," *Journal of the Royal Asiatic Society*, 1–2 [1945] 3–16; (Heimo Kremsmayer, "Schamanismus und Seelenvorstellungen im alten China," *Archiv für Völkerkunde*, 9 [1954] 66–78); and Eduard Erkes, "Der schamanistische Ursprung des chinesischen Ahnenkultus," *Sinologica*, 2 [1950] 253–62). The dragon and phoenix of Taoism suggest comparison with the serpent and bird of palaeoasiatic shamanism; note also that "The whole animal world is affected by the character of a benevolent ruler" (H. F. Rudd, *Chinese Social Origins*, Chicago: University of Chicago Press, 1928, p. 107). On the shamanistic origin of Japanese *shinto*, see William P. Fairchild, "Shamanism in Japan," *Folklore Studies* [Peking], 21 (1962) 1–122; and Matthias Eder, "Schamanismus in Japan," *Paideuma*, 6 (1958) 367–80; see also Yuji Sasaki, "Psychiatric Study of the Shaman in Japan," *Transcultural Psychiatric Research*, 4 (1967) 15–17. Paleosiberian shamanism, indeed, is strongly suggested in the origin legend of Japanese Shintoism (e.g., the "frenzy" and sulking of Amaterasu o Mikami, and the mirror as one of the "sacred treasures"). The Tungus shaman's mirror is of *bronze*, but some of his paraphernalia are of *iron*, still a sacred substance in Siberia; formerly shamans were often smiths also, and the worship of iron and of iron objects was associated with the "idolization" of the smith's trade (Levin and Potapov, *op. cit.*, p. 214). Compare the special position of the smith in Negro Africa. A smith-scope-shaman association is found also in archaic Europe and north Africa (see M. Eliade's monograph on *Forgerons et alchimistes*, and his "Smiths, Shamans and Mystagogues," *East and West* [Rome], 6 [1955] 206–15; and Findeisen, *Schamantum*, pp. 94ff), and singing artificer-priests in the *tuhungas* of Oceania. For copious documentation of shamanism in Tibet, China, Mongolia, Korea, and Japan, see Eliade, *Shamanism*, pp. 428–65, and *Recent Works*, pp. 176–82; for India, pp. 403–27 and pp. 174–76 respectively; Southeast Asia and Oceania, pp. 337–74 and 168–69; North and South America, pp. 288–336; Indoeuropeans, pp. 375–427 and 172–76; *Recent Works* on the shamanism of Lapps, Finns, and Estonians, pp. 170–71; and Huns and Magyars, pp. 171–72.

8. The aspect of showmanship and entertainment in shamanism has perhaps been neglected; see Lucille Hoerr Charles, "Drama in Shaman Exorcism," *Journal of American Folklore*, 66, #260 (1953) 95–122; and M. Eliade, *Recent Works*, p. 186; see also Donald W. Hogg, "From Religion to Theatre: A Case of Cult Development in Jamaica" (Paper delivered at the Annual Meetings, American Anthropological Association, San Francisco, 1963) for a striking parallel. It should of course not be forgotten that the ritual of the priests of Dionysus was actually the origin of classic Greek drama; and shamanistic rivalry seems to have survived directly in Roman opera, in "a kind of insulting repartee between two performers known as Fescinnine verse" (T. A. Cole, "Opera in Ancient Rome," *Ventures*, 7 #1 [Yale University, Spring 1967], 35–39, p. 37). The shamanistic origin of music and religious art in paleolithic Europe is also quite plain. Regarding artistic "inspiration," a useful work of somewhat different scope than Eliade's is T. K. Oesterreich, *Possession, Demoniacal Or Other, among Primitive Races in Antiquity, the Middle Ages, and Modern Times* (London: K. Paul, Trench, Trubner & Co., and New York: R. R. Smith, 1930); see also Irving I. Zaretsky, *Bibliography on*

Spirit Possession and Spirit Mediumship (Evanston: Northwestern University Press, 1966). Artistic metaphor still profusely reflects the inspiration-possession theme (e.g., by Apollo's Muses) derived from archaic shamanism, though nowadays we think that artistic inspiration comes from outside (the conscious mind) only in coming from the artist's own unconscious.

9. There are compendious regional studies of the Master of Animals. For Africa: Leo Frobenius, *Die reifere Menschheit* (Hannover: Gebr Jänecke, 1902, pp. 163–212; *Kulturgeschichte Afrikas* Zürich: Phaidon-Verlag, 1933, pp. 70–79); and H. Baumann, "Afrikanische Wild- und Buschgeister," *Zeitschrift für Ethnologie*, 70 (1938) 208–39. Songhai "owners" have been assimilated to Arabic *jinn* (E. R. Parrinder, Review, *American Anthropologist*, 65 [1963] 474–76).

For North America: Åke Hultkrantz, "The Owner of the Animals in the Religion of the North American Indians: Some General Remarks," in Åke Hultkrantz (ed.), *The Supernatural Owners of Nature: Nordic Symposium on the Religious Conceptions of Ruling Spirits (Genii Loci, Genii Speciei) and Allied Concepts* (Stockholm: Almquist & Wiksell, for *Acta Universitatis Stockholmiensis*, 1 [1961] 53–64) and "The Masters of Animals among the Wind River Shoshoni," *Ethnos*, 26 (1961) #4.

For Central America: Otto Zerries, "Wildgeister und Jagdritual in Zentralamerika," *Amerikanistische Miszellei-Mitteilungen aus dem Museum für Völkerkunde in Hamburg*, 25 (1959) 144–50; Joseph Haekel, "Der 'Herr der Tiere' in Glauben der Indianer Mesoamerikas," *ibid.*, pp. 60–69.

For South America: Otto Zerries, *Wild- und Buschgeister in Sudamerika: Eine Untersuchung jägerzeitlicher Phänomene im Kulturbild südamerikanischer Indianer* (Wiesbaden: Franz Sterner Verlag, 1954); Henry Wassén, "Contributions to Cuna Ethnography," *Ethnologiska Studier* 16, Göteborg: Etnografiska Museet, 1949; Herbert Baldus, "Supernatural Relations with Animals among Indians of Eastern and Southern Brazil," *Proceedings of the 30th Congress of Americanists*, Saõ Paolo, 1955, pp. 195–98; for other "owners" in specific tribes, see Steward, *op cit.*, 1:102–3 (Yahgan), 2:520, 525, 559 (Aymara), 3:145 (Tenetehara); and for a South American summary, A. Métraux, "Religion and Shamanism," in Steward, *op. cit.*, 5:565–66.

For North Asia: Ivar Paulson, "Schutzgeister und Gottheiten des Wildes (der Jagdtiere und Fische) in Nordasien: Eine religionsethnographische und religionsphänomenologische Untersuchung jägerischer Glaubensvorstellungen," (Stockholm: *Acta Universitatis Stockholmiensis*, 1961); Hildegard Wozak, *Herr und Herrin der Tiere in Vorderasien* (Doctoral Dissertation, University of Vienna, 1966); Levin and Potapov, *op. cit.*, pp. 225–27, 280, 358, 364, 435, 464, 479–80, 564, 578, 601, 711–12, 730, 743, 757, 764, 778, 823, and 845; and Eveline Lot-Falck, *Les rites de chasse chez les peuples sibériens* (Paris: Gallimard, 1953).

For Finno-Ugric peoples: Uno Holmberg, "Die Wassergottheiten der finnischugrischen Völker," *Mémoires de la Société Finno-Ougrienne*, 32, Helsinki, 1913; "Die religiösen Vorstellungen der altaischer Völker," Helsinki: *Folklore Fellows Communications*, No. 127, 1938; and Géza Róheim, *Hungarian and Vogul Mythology* (New York: Monographs of the American Ethnological Society, 23, 1954). Róheim has interesting psychoanalytic comments on "Der Wilde Jagd" in *Imago*, 12 (1926) 465–77.

For Europe: A. Dirr, "Der kaukasische Wild- und Jagdgott," *Anthropos*, 20 (1925) 139–47; Leonard Schmidt, "Der 'Herr der Tiere' in einigen Sagenlandschaften Europas und Eurasiens," *Anthropos*, 47 (1952) 509–38; Lutz Röhrich, "Europäische Wildgeistersagen," *Rhenisches Jahrbuch für Völkskunde*, 10 (1959) 79–162; "Die Sagen vom Herrn der Tiere," *Internationaler Kongress der Volkser-*

zählungsforscher in Kiel und Kopenhagen, 1959, Berlin, 1961, pp. 341–49; and Edmund Mudrak, "Herr und Herrin der Tiere," *Fabula,* 4 (1961) 163–73.

10. A fine modern summary of the "Master of Animals" is Ivar Paulson's "The Animal Guardian: A Critical and Synthetic Review," *History of Religions,* 3 (1964) 202–19—but his term "animal guardian" for the Master as *guardian of the animals* is misleadingly like the "guardian animal" as the *animal familiar of the shaman* or hunter; hence, although the Master *can be* the shaman's familiar, I prefer to keep both established Americanist terms, "Master of the animals" and "guardian spirit" [="guardian animal"]. On the latter the classic work is, of course, Ruth F. Benedict. *The Concept of the Guardian Spirit in North America.* On the religion of ancient hunters, important works are: Uno Holmberg (since 1927, Harva), "Über die Jagdriten der nordlichen Völkers Asiens und Europas," *Journal de la Société Finno-Ougrienne,* [Helsinki], 61 (1925) 1–53; Dmitrij Zelenin, *Le culte des idoles en Sibérie* (Paris: Payot, 1952); Adolf Friedrich, "Die Forschung über das frühzeitliche Jägertum," *Paideuma,* 2 (1941) 20–43; Carl-Martin Edsman, [Referat:] "Studien zur Religion des Jägers," to "Studier i jägarens religion," *Annales Academiae Regiae Scientiarum Upsaliensis, Kung. Vetenskapssamhällets i Uppsala, Årsbok,* 2 (1958) 33–94; Andreas Lömmel, *Die Welt der Frühen Jäger;* and Burghard Freudenfeld (ed.), *Völkerkunde: Zwölf Vorträge zur Einführung in Ihre Probleme* (München: Verlag C. H. Beck, 1960).

11. For Pater Schmidt's degenerationism: W. Schmidt, *Handbuch der vergleichenden Religionsgeschichte: Ursprung und Werden der Religion* (Münster: Aschendorffsche Verhandlung, 1930, pp. 254ff).

12. Raffaele Pettazzoni, *The All-Knowing God: Researches into Early Religion and Culture* (London: Methuen, 1956, pp. 441–42); "The Supreme Being: Phenomenological Structure and Historical Development," in M. Eliade and J. M. Kitigawa (eds.), *The History of Religions: Essays in Methodology* (Chicago: University of Chicago Press, 1959, p. 65).

13. Paulson, *Animal Guardian,* p. 219.

14. Excellent sources on the animal-bone cult of northern hunters are: Ivar Paulson, "Die Tierknochen im Jagdritual der nordeurasiatischer Völker," *Zeitschrift für Ethnologie,* 84 (1959) 270–93; "Zur Aufbewahrung der Tierknochen im nordlichen Nordamerika," *Amerikanistischen Miszellen-Mitteilungen aus dem Museum für Völkerkunde in Hamburg,* 25 (1959) 182–88; Adolf Friedrich, "Knochen und Skelette in der Vorstellungswelt Nordasiens," *Wiener Beiträge zur Kulturgeschichte und Linguistik,* No. 5. 1943; F. Gahs, "Köpf-, Schadel- und Langbeinknochenopfer bei den Rentiervölkern," in W. Koppers (ed.), *Publication d'hommage offerte au P[ère] W. Schmidt* (Wien: Mechitharisten-Congregations-Buchdruckerei, 1928, pp. 231–68; B. Freuenfeld, *op. cit.;* and Lömmel, *op. cit.* For American parallels, see B. Bonnerjea, *op. cit.*).

15. Kaulipang: Koch-Grünberg, in Jensen, *op. cit.,* p. 138.

16. Quiché: L. S. Schultze-Jena, *Leben, Glaube und Sprache der Quiche von Guatemala* (Jena: Gustav Fischer, 1933, p. 20). The mountain-womb of the Quiché has a Zinacantecan parallel (E. Z. Vogt, "Structural and Conceptual Replication in Zinacantecan Culture," *American Anthropologist,* 67 [1965] 342–53, p. 350).

17. Neskapi: F. G. Speck, in Jensen, *op. cit.,* p. 137.

18. The "Mistress of the Animals" is found especially in the eastern Mediterranean; see W. Dorstal, "Uber Jagdbrachtum in Vorderasien," *Paideuma,* 8 (1962) 85–97; also Röhrich, *Europäische Wildgeistersagen,* pp. 150ff. In Anatolia, the "Mistress of the Beasts" was the earth-goddess Cybele, associated with flanking lions (as in the Gate at Mycenae in Greece), a feature that even passed over into 5th-century iconography of the Virgin, in the Adana Reliquary (Michael Gough,

The Early Christians, New York: Praeger, 1961, p. 30); in Anatolia, Cybele's primitive cult has "owners" for mountains, trees and stones, as well as for separate animal-species. A case might be made that the use of animals in heraldry derives ultimately from ancient hunting religion and magic.

19. For so ubiquitous and antique a figure as the Master of Animals we must of course expect traces in our own cultural tradition. For another example, Proteus, the god of many metamorphoses, who lives among the seals and counts them, is probably a survival of a "Master of seals" (Homer, *Odyssey,* iv, 450; cf. xvi, 5); he is also a soothsayer to Telemachus and servant of Poseidon, god of the trident, both of which increase his shamanistic associations. The many animal metamorphoses of Zeus (fertility figure and weather mage as well) show a high shaman's many animal familiars. By contrast, the Hindu high god Shiva as *Paśupati,* "Lord of the Beasts," probably harks back not to an Indoeuropean but to a Harappan prototype, in which an ithyphallic figure, seated cross-legged, is surrounded by an elephant, tiger, rhinoceros, and buffalo; this Indus deity is also the source of Shiva's important emblem, the *triśula* or trident. Jean Przyluski sees in a figure with two tiger attendants, on a Mohenjo-daro seal, "la plus ancienne représentation indienne de la Maitresse des Fauves" (in H. P. Sullivan, *Religion of the Indus Civilization,* p. 117; for Shiva's prototype, see pp. 118–19). It is interesting that the Biblical injunction to "Be fruitful and multiply" (Genesis, ix, 1) is immediately followed by the statement that mankind should have dominion over the animals, whence it is suggested that Noah has some attributes of an old Master of Animals. In early Christian iconography, in which he is assimilated to Apollo, Christ also has attributes as a master of animals, with whom he is surrounded (cf. the animals of the Gospel-writers); again, the resurrection of Christ is assimilated to the festival of a Germanic goddess of Spring (Anglo-Saxon *Eástra*) notable for her association with the symbolic fertility of plants, animals, and birds. Eric Wolf even compares St. Nicholas to a shadowy North European spirit emergent from the underworld at Christmas time, compounded equally of the Roman god of the winter Saturnalia and the Germanic Knecht Ruprecht, *rauhe perchta,* "wild demon" or Woden, wild master of the wild hunt (Eric Wolf, "Santa Claus: Notes on a Collective Representation," in R. A. Manners [ed.], *Process and Pattern in Culture, Essays in Honor of Julian H. Steward,* Chicago: Aldine Press, 1964, 147–55, p. 148). That presents are given in this winter festival also recalls the underworld Cernunnus-Pluto god of wealth and shamanistic ruler of spirits of the dead in the Old Religion.

20. Jensen on the dissimilarity of the Master of Animals to a "High God," *op. cit.,* p. 140.

21. Boas gives a number of Sedna and cognate myths in various Eskimo groups (Franz Boas, *The Central Eskimo,* Annual Report, Bureau of American Ethnology, 6 [1888] 399–699, pp. 583ff). Further variants: Knud Rasmussen, "Iglulik Eskimos," *Report of the 5th Thule Expedition 1921–1924,* vol. VII, no. 1, Copenhagen, 1929; "The Netsilik Eskimo," *loc. cit.,* VIII:173, 224–28; "Intellectual Culture of the Copper Eskimo," *loc. cit.,* IX:24, 39; E. M. Weyer, *The Eskimos* (New Haven: Yale University Press, 1932, Ch. XXI, pp. 349–64); and Kaj Birket-Smith, *The Eskimos* (New York: Dutton, 1936, p. 165). The Siberian Chukchi cognate, *keretkun'a,* is the "master spirit of the sea" (Levin and Potapov, *op. cit.,* pp. 802–3).

22. On aboriginal confession of sins among American Indians, see W. La Barre, "Primitive Psychotherapy in Native American Cultures: Peyotism and Confession," *Journal of Abnormal and Social Psychology,* 24 (1947) 294–309 [=*Bobbs-Merrill Reprints in the Social Sciences,* 1965]; and "Confession as Cathartic Therapy in American Indian Tribes," in Ari Kiev (ed.), *Magic, Faith, and Healing* (New York: Free Press, 1964, pp. 36–49); see also H. S. Darlington, 'Confession of Sins," *Psychoanalytic Review,* 24 (1937) 150–64.

23. For the association of hunting and coitus, see André Leroi-Gourhan, *Préhistoire de l'art occidental* (Paris: Éditions d'Art Lucien Mazenrod, 1965).

24. Seventeenth-century distribution of the Tungus, Levin and Potapov, *op. cit.,* Map, p. 5.

25. On Tungus representativeness, see Gudmund Hatt, *op. cit.,* pp. 248–49.

26. S. M. Shirokogoroff, *Psychomental Complex of the Tungus,* pp. 255, 264.

27. David F. Aberle, "'Arctic Hysteria' and Latah in Mongolia," *Transactions of the New York Academy of Sciences,* Ser. II, vol. 14, no. 7 (May 1952) 291–97. On the connection of arctic hysteria and shamanism, see W. Mühlmann, *Hyperboräische Eschatologie,* pp. 210–19. In the Shango cult of Trinidad, "Perhaps the most striking pattern of behavior during possession is that in which the possessed controls the activities of those around him" (Walter and Frances Mischel, "Psychological Aspects of Spirit Possession," *American Anthropologist,* 60 [1958] 249–60, p. 254). The same principle has been noted in possession states in many other parts of the world; one might add that not only the heightened narcissism of the medium and its "fascination" for others (Olden) in the possession state, but also the access to "primary process" material via the shaman, constitute part of the exciting and seductive charisma (Weber) implicated in the group psychology and ego-abdication (Freud) of the shaman's clientèle.

28. The Tibetan lamaist "chöd" is a visionary ordeal closely cognate with Tungus "olonism." In *chöd* the candidate seeks at night a wild and lonely site, a cemetery or a place associated with a terrible legend or recent frightful tragedy, and there seeks actively to hallucinate demons (Jacques Schnier, "The Tibetan Lamaist Ritual: Chöd," *International Journal of Psycho-Analysis,* 38 [1957] 402–440). In the possession-shamanism of the Bare'e Toradja of Celebes, *mejapi,* literally "to hide oneself," or withdrawal into the woods of an angry person, has a marked psychological similarity to olonism (J. Van der Kroef, *Messianic Movements,* p. 80). Again, the original Hiawatha was a Mohawk (or Onondaga) sachem who, recently bereaved, wandered alone in the woods in a state of agitated depression, with "the delusion of being a cannibal monster named Atotarho with a crooked body, snakes in his hair, and great and destructive powers" (A. F. C. Wallace, "The Dekanawideh Myth analyzed as the Record of a Revitalization Movement," *Ethnohistory,* 5 [1958] 118–30, p. 123). This Iroquois legend bridges the Algonkian "windigo psychosis," Kwakiutl Winter Dance "cannibalism" and Asiatic olonism-chöd in a striking fashion.

29. Shirokogoroff, *op. cit.,* p. 255.

30. For psychological parallels in which the "possessed" person exploits those about him, see the *saka* complex among the Taita (Grace Harris, "Possession 'Hysteria' in a Kenya Tribe," *American Anthropologist,* 59 [1957] 1046–66); also Louis Mars and George Devereux, "Haitian Voodoo and the Ritualization of the Nightmare," *Psychoanalytic Review,* 38 (1951) 334–42. In both instances, the "possessed" is a low-status person who acts out ordinarily forbidden wishes. Olonism represents a kind of institutionalized "adolescent turmoil" in aboriginal America as well as in Asia. Devereux has acutely remarked that "the broad pattern of shamanism is, from the viewpoint of a disturbed youngster, a socially tendered and culturally prepatterned general bromide for his 'subjective headache'" (George Devereux, "Dream Learning and Individual Ritual Differences in Mohave Shamanism," *American Anthropologist,* 59 [1957] 1036–45, p. 1043). In Tungus olonism, since young unmarried persons are not restricted sexually, Shirokogoroff considers that, rather than sexuality, "social oppression" by seniors of juniors is the major theme (*op. cit.,* pp. 257–58). The artificial and meretricious element in olonism suggests that it is a kind of malingering, a stylized "ethnic psychosis," or mimicking of a cultural preconception of the "proper way of being insane" (e.g., the Amer-

ican layman's wildly erroneous notion of what "hysteria" is). Compare the Ganser syndrome and prison psychosis (George Devereux, "Normal and Abnormal: The Key Problem of Psychiatric Anthropology," in J. B. Casagrande and T. Gladwin [eds.], *Some Uses of Anthropology: Theoretical and Applied,* Washington, D.C.: Anthropological Society of Washington, 1956, pp. 3–32).

31. Shirokogoroff, *op. cit.,* p. 264. The *protective* function is central in New World shamanism also. "The first place in Tapirapé society belongs to the person who defends the community against the ever terrible dangers of the supernatural world" (Herbert Baldus, "The Fear in Tapirapé Culture," in A. F. C. Wallace, *Men and Cultures,* 396–400, p. 397). "Without our pančé, all we Tapirapé die" (Charles Wagley, "Xamanismo tapirapé," *Boletim do Museu Nacional* [Antropologia] 3 [1943] 79).

32. On the snake and shamanism (Siberian paleolithic): Okladnikov, in Levin and Potapov, *op. cit.,* p. 21. In America the snake is only one of many sources of power, e.g. the Penobscot strike the head of the serpent to bind him as a familiar (Ruth Benedict, *Guardian Spirit,* p. 41). But in North America, and especially in Mexico, the thunderbird (eagle) and lightning (snake) of ancient Eurasia are still closely associated; and in the Southwest, especially, rain-priests still invoke snakes to control the weather (the rain snake is of course also archaic-Semitic and African; see W. La Barre, *They Shall Take Up Serpents: Psychology of the Southern Snake-handling Cult,* Minneapolis: University of Minnesota Press, 1962, and Schocken Books, 1969, pp. 54–64).

33. W. Shierozewski, "Du chamanisme d'après les croyances Yakoutes," *Revue de l'Histoire des Religions,* xlvi, 1902, in Eliade, "The Yearning for Paradise in Primitive Tradition," *Diogenes,* 88 (1959) 255–67.

34. W. L. Chafe, *Seneca Thanksgiving Rituals* (Washington: Bureau of American Ethnology, Bulletin 183, 1931).

35. Wilhelm Schmidt, "Synthese der Schamanismus der innerasiatische Hirtenvölker," in his *Ursprung des Gottesidee,* vol. 12, pp. 615–71.

36. M. Eliade, *Recent Works,* p. 156.

37. Levin and Potapov, *op. cit.,* pp. 227, 279, 325, and 601.

38. Levin and Potapov, *op. cit.,* p. 796; cf. pp. 281 for Yakut and 714 for Naney-Goldi parallels. This is a precise instance of the dead shaman's spirit becoming a cult-worshiped "god" (in the living shaman's "medicine society" of his cured clients, he was already a *leader* of a cult), as I have argued elsewhere. Again, since birds are so commonly the shaman's spirit-familiar, we should not be surprised to encounter the deity-as-bird: unknown until 1956–57, pictured bird-headed "goddesses" from Jabbaren in the remote Saharan Tassili Mountains show resemblances to those on XVIIIth Dynasty Egyptian monuments of about 1200 B.C. (André Lhote, "Saharan Rock Art," *Natural History,* 69 ≹6 [June-July 1960] 28–43, p. 33).

39. For the bird-symbolism of the shaman's garb, see Mircea Eliade, *Le chamanisme,* pp. 141–167; for elaborate bibliographic references, see H. Kirschner, "Ein archäologischer Beitrag zur Urgeschichte des Schamanismus," *Anthropos,* 47 (1952) 277–86. Karl Hentze has repeatedly emphasized the shamanic symbolism of ancient monuments of China and northern Asia ("Eine Schamanendarstellung auf einem Han-Relief," *Asia Major,* 1 [1944] 74–77; "Schamanenkronen zur Han-Zeit in Korea," *Ostasiatische Zeitschrift,* 9 [1933] 156–63; "Eine Schamanentracht in ihrer Bedeutung für die altchinesische Kunst und Religion," *Jahrbuch für prähistorische ethnographische Kunst,* 20 [1960–63] 55–61), as well as the shamanistic significance of birds ("Le symbolisme des oiseaux dans la Chine ancienne," *Sinologica,* 5 [1957] 65–92). See also A. J. Wensinck, *Tree and Bird as Cosmological Symbols in Western Asia,* Amsterdam: Verhandlingen der Koeniklige Akademie van Wettenschappen, 1921. On the shamanistic "traveler" Aristeas' journey as a

bird (Herodotus, *Histories*, 4.15.2; Pliny, *Natural History*, 7.174; see also E. D. Phillips, "The Legend of Aristeas: Fact and Fancy in Early Greek Notions of East Russia, Siberia, and Inner Asia," *Artibus Asiae*, 18, 2 [1955] 161–77). On Yakuts and Tungus soul-birds, Siberian bird-costumes, and the belief that the first shamans were birds, see references to Holmberg, Chadwick, Nioradze, and Nilsson in E. R. Dodds, *Greeks and the Irrational*, p. 162, n. 38). At a curious séance in the Iseum in Hellenistic times, the presence of birds puzzled Dodds and other scholars (pp. 289–91). Dodds finally decided they were apotropaic, to protect the operators from attack by evil spirits (p. 291). This may well be true. But why not accept the birds simply as shamanistic familiars or guardian spirits? Plutarch, incidentally, noted that the hero Theseus, long before this, introduced in Delos a crane dance performed around an altar—a bird sacred to the sky-god Apollo and master of animals.

40. With regard to the "reindeer shaman," a characteristic shaman's costume is that of the Evenk, which symbolizes the bear or the reindeer; west of the Lena, the shaman's headgear is a "crown with reindeer antlers" (Levin and Potapov, *op. cit.*, p. 648; cf. p. 641). V. Diószegi believes that ancient Hungarian shamans fought specially in the form of reindeer ("Die Überreste des Schamanismus in der ungarischen Volkskultur," *Acta Ethnographica*, 7 [1958] 97–134, pp. 127–129). The rock pictures at Saymali Taš (First Millennium B.C.), in what is now Kirghiz territory, show shamans opposing one another as reindeer (L. Vajda, *op. cit.*, p. 472, n. 5). Diószegi also pictures shamans' headdresses with deer horns (especially Figures 1, 3–4, 6, 9–11, and 22–23) in a significant study on Nennish or Goldi shamanism ("Golovnoi ubor nanaiskh [goldskikh] šamanov," *A Néprajzi Értesitö* [Budapest], 37 [1955] 81–108, pp. 87–89). Reindeer remains are found in upper Lena tombs dated seventh-fifth centuries B.C. by A. P. Okladnikov. On a late Chou ceremonial bronze vessel found at Ch'ang-sha, Salmony recognizes shamans in two dancers wearing antlers (Alfred Salmony, *Antler and Tongue: An Essay on Ancient Chinese Symbolism and its Implications*, Ascona: Artibus Asiae 1954); in a review, Robert Heine-Geldern accepts this interpretation (*Artibus Asiae*, 18 [1955] 85–90), noting that Waston had earlier come to the same conclusion (W. Waston, "A Grave Guardian from Ch'ang-sha," *British Museum Quarterly*, 17 [1952] 52–56). In Korea, shamanism is documented as early as the Han period (Hentze, "Schamanenkronen"), when the presence of staghorns on shamans' headdresses indicate Paleosiberian connections with an ancient Turkic stag cult (W. Eberhardt, *Lokalkulturen im alten China*, Peking: Monumenta Serica, Monograph Series 3, 1942, vol. II, pp. 501ff). On reindeer-antler as magic substance, see Chapter XIII.

41. In the fantastic art of the eastern Scythians (Mongolian Huns or "Massagetae" of the Greeks) found at Pazyryk in Siberia, birds are shown at the ends of reindeer antlers, beasts of prey with birds' wings, birds with mammalian ears and horns, deer or predatory animals with birds' beaks, and tails of monsters ending in a bird or snake head (Levin and Potapov, *op. cit.*, p. 64). Since this celebrated "animal style" of the Scytho-Hunnic peoples so conspicuously mixes birds and animals into composite monsters, one wonders whether this central Asian style might not have found inspiration in Paleosiberian shamanistic costumes. The art of ancient hunters (Altamira, Lascaux) is notable for its realism, as we might expect from their ecological interest in and close observation of wild animals; but the fantastic composite creatures of the later "animal style" is not inconsistent with narcotic mushroom visions of northern Eurasiatic shamanism. And, like the use of narcotic mushrooms, the "animal style" is a further Eurasian and Asiatic-American intercontinental trait (Franz Hančar, "The Eurasian Animal Style and the Altai Complex," *Artibus Asiae*, 15, [1952] 171–94); and Carl Schuster, "A Survival of the Eurasiatic Animal Style in Modern American Eskimo," in Sol Tax (ed.),

The First Gods   195

Selected Papers of the 29th International Congress of Americanists, Chicago, 1952, III, pp. 34–45. Ideologically, of course, there would be no reason why a shaman might not have several sources of power.

42. Nudity of the Chukchi shaman: W. Bogoras, The Chukchee (New York: Memoirs of the American Museum of Natural History, 11, 1904, p. 449). The mouth-movements forcibly recall certain REM states.

43. Change of sex, Bogoras, op. cit., pp. 450–52.

44. W. Jochelson, The Koryak, pp. 754–55.

45. S. P. Krasheninnikoff, The History of Kamtschatka and the Kurilski Islands, London and Glocester: T. Jefferys, 1764, pp. 114, 122.

46. W. G. Sumner, "The Yakuts," Journal of the Anthropological Institute, 31 (1901) 65–110, pp. 102–4. Cf. M. A. Czaplicka, Aboriginal Siberia, pp. 252–53). At the same time we should remember that paleo-European shamans also performed naked (Trois Frères).

47. The eagle is a shamanistic bird from Indoeuropean north Europe (e.g. Zeus) and among the Semites (for the eagle-Baal connected with lightning-rain-thunder, see John Gray, The Canaanites, New York: Praeger, 1964, pp. 129, 131), and across Siberia into North America (H. Findeisen, "Der Adler als Kulturbringer im nordasiatischen Raum und in der amerikanischen Arktis." Zeitschrift für Ethnologie, 81 [1956] 70–82; and Leo Sternberg, "Der Adlerkult bei den Völkern Siberiens: Vergleichende Folklore-Studie," Archiv für Religionswissenschaft, 28 [1930] 125–53). For the eagle in shamanistic myths of the Buryat, Yakuts, and other Siberians, see L. Sternberg in Eliade, Le chamanisme, p. 77; among the Huns, J. Werner in Eliade, loc. cit., See also Géza Róheim, "Hungarian Shamanism," in G. Róheim (ed.), Psychoanalysis and the Social Sciences, III, New York: International Universities Press, 1951, 131–69. Róheim considered that the "flying dream is an erection dream . . . the flying dream is the nucleus of shamanism" (p. 154) —a hypothesis made all the more plausible by the new phenomenology of the dream, as well as by the shamanistic succubus, "marriage" with the spirit familiar, and the like. Shamanistic journeys are consequently dream journeys. (For the connection of shamanism and sexuality, see also Derek Freeman, "Shaman and Incubus" [Australian National University, Mss., 1965]; cf. also D. Zelenin, "Ein erotischer Ritus in den Opferungen der altaischen Tuerken," Internationales Archiv für Ethnographie, 29, 4–6 [1928] 83–98.)

48. The puzzling character of the Asiatic-American "Trickster" as a mixture of clown, culture hero and demigod, comes only from the procrustean attempt to force our categories on the clear and consistent aboriginal data. Brinton, influenced by Max Müller's degradationism, tried to argue that the trickster elements in the Algonkian Manabozho or Hare were late and foreign accretions on an original high god of light; but Boas acutely asked, Why then did the same fate come to all such American Indian tricksters? To which we might add "And to old Eurasiatic ones too?" It is a pseudo-problem, resolved simply by seeing the trickster as the animal form or familiar of the shaman himself. The great antiquity of the trickster should be suggested first of all by his being much the same in both Paleosiberian and American hunting tribes; and again by the fact that the more a tribe has been influenced by agriculture in America, the less important he becomes in the total tribal mythology as compared with his pre-eminence among both Siberian and American hunters. Indeed, he still remains in the religions of agriculturalists like the Zuñi and the Iroquois as a religious performer. Ricketts is unquestionably correct in considering that the trickster is "an extremely archaic figure, belonging to the culture of primitive hunters and gatherers . . . that the trickster and culture hero are, from earliest times, combined in one figure . . . [and] that the trickster-transformer-culture hero is in origin a unitary figure, despite his complexity" (Mac Linscott Ricketts,

"The North American Indian Trickster," *History of Religions*, 5 [1966] 327–50, pp. 328, 330, 334). Ricketts thinks (p. 338) that trickster stories are told to ridicule the shaman, a not implausible hypothesis, considering the encompassing power of the ancient shaman. Still, we must not forget the element of *entertainment* in Old World shamanism: were tales of the erotic escapades of eagle-Zeus once told in the same tone of voice as those of Sibero-American Raven? And did not shamanistic rivalry develop into both the Dionysian bard-contests of Greek drama in the Old World and into *midewewin* medicine-shows in the New? As for that, have modern medicine-men entirely lost the old shamanic self-dramatization?

On the peculiar "contrary behavior" of Eurasiatic-American shamans, see E. C. Parsons and R. L. Beals, "The Sacred Clowns of the Pueblo and Mayo-Yaqui Indians," *American Anthropologist*, 36 (1934) 491–516; J. H. Steward, "The Ceremonial Buffoon of the American Indian," *Michigan Academy of Science, Arts and Letters*, 14 (1930) 187–207; V. F. Ray, "The Contrary Behavior Pattern in American Indian Ceremonialism," *Southwestern Journal of Anthropology*, 1 (1945) 75–113: Paul Radin, *The Trickster: A Study in American Indian Mythology* (New York: Philosophic Library, 1956).

The European court jester retains many traits of the trickster. See Enid Wilsford, *The Fool: His Social and Literary History* (New York: Farrar & Rinehart, and London: Faber and Faber, 1935; Garden City: Doubleday-Anchor Books 1961, reprinted in hardback Gloucester [Mass.]: P. Smith, 1966, and London: Faber and Faber, 1968) suggests the similarity of royal sceptre to magic wand to the (ancient shamanistic) *phallos*. Hence both sceptre and crown of the king are shamanistic, charismatic. On sceptre-wand-phallus, see S. Tarachow, "Circuses and Clowns," in Géza Róheim (ed.), *Psychoanalysis and the Social Sciences* (New York: International Universities Press, 1951, III: 171–85); H. J. T. Johnson, "Regalia," in *Hastings Encyclopedia*, 10:632–39, section "5. Sceptre," pp. 635–36.

William Willeford, *The Fool and His Sceptre* (Evanston: Northwestern University Press, 1969) remarks on the arbitrary and otherwise incomprehensible connection of fools with birds, sexuality, genitalia (as a Terminus or Hermes), transvestitism, and ambiguity of sex (e.g. Harlequin as Diana, goddess of the chase), Harlequin as half-man, half-woman—interpreted by Willeford in fuzzy Jungian and pretentious Lévi-Straussian terms—but these are merely the normal and quite comprehensible attributes of the cultural descendants of the shaman. Synchronic social anthropology is repeatedly imprisoned in fatuous and absurd etics when it neglects the plain emics of ethnographic history.

VI

The Culture Heroes Return

WHATEVER else crisis cults may be, their phrasing is conditioned universally by two specific traits of human beings, the articulate consciousness of an intricate subjective life in consequence of a big brain, and a biological experience of extended early security that is inveterately sought again when later adaptations go awry. The complex, learned consciousness of the self is projected, in part legitimately into other persons and animals, in part not, into physical objects, in a naïvely animistic world view. Animism is not alone a human cultural phenomenon, it is also re-encountered in every human childhood. Furthermore, the fact of biological childhood means that the traits of the parent-helper and protector will inevitably be refound when need becomes overwhelming, and found both in the charismatic human culture hero who is the agent of help, and in the parental after-image seen in nature from whom the culture hero borrows his charisma. Both the arbitrariness and the inevitability of our projective systems will be made apparent by suggesting that *with a different biology* we would have a different supernatural world, or none at all. What is the god of an oyster like? An ostracoderm? A coelocanth? There is a specific biological subjectivity of man encountered in his institutions.

Mind and family. The shaman, very simply, has a powerful spirit and can therefore dominate the other spirits that flock around him in the world. And because by need-definition he must be powerful, he will define himself, and be seen by others, in archaic parental terms. His powers will be commensurate with needs, not realities. A shamanistic rain-maker is not a cosmic being. He is merely a man with magic power to make rain. That is all.[1] It is our own sense of the scope of the universe that makes us gasp at the primitive shaman's megalomaniac pretense—

and insist on substituting instead a superhuman entity whose paranoiac power will be commensurate with the universe we see. The shaman is the first "god," only in a very little world. But he is not a God in our sense, because his world and ours are of different magnitudes. Only when our sense of cosmos enlarges, do we suspect that human power cannot be commensurate with this cosmos. It is nevertheless startling how often a human messiah or culture hero is mistaken for this very God—and how much this God is like an omnipotent human shaman. Only for a few, crushed with mind-staggering evidence of its magnitude, does the cosmos outgrow all anthropomorphic explanation entirely, a difficult piety.

The distinguished prehistorian Narr[2] makes a quite mistaken projection of a "supreme being" backward in time to paleolithic peoples who had no secular model (king or emperor) for it. He is then concerned whether they were intellectually capable of so "lofty" an idea. And finally, finding only shamans and the Master of Animals in the Old Stone Age, he invokes a "supression" of a supposed awareness of the Supreme Being, the "true and pure idea of God." In Stone or Atomic Age, however, it is not so much a matter of intellectual ability as it is of discernment of the secular and psychological sources of what one rationalizes and why. Nor is one free to discover if one is motivated to find.

In this task, therefore, the Truth is less useful than an informed sense of psycho-ecology and paleo-ethnology. There exists still, in the remoter parts of South America, the kind of shaman who, on wide comparative grounds, unites the traits of his ancient prototype. Primitive Amazonia, to be sure, is very remote in time and place from paleolithic Europe, and yet in social structure and general ecological context far closer than we are to either; on paleohistoric grounds we even consider them both to be part of the same shamanistic continuum.

At the time of discovery, the *carai, cara-ìbe,* or *pagé* (Thevet says this word means "demi-god") was a kind of man-god, found all the way from the mouth of the Orinoco in Venezuela to the Rio Plata in Argentina. This constitutes almost the whole of the Atlantic seaboard of South America—and we have since found this man-god in the vast interior behind the coast, which is to say everywhere in South America, except in the high agricultural societies of Colombia and Andean America where he reappears as a divinized monarch, and among the archaic peoples of Patagonia. As may be seen subsequently, cognates of the shamanistic man-god are found nearly everywhere in North America also.

In ceremonies, the *cara-ìbe* held in each hand a *maraca* or gourd rattle containing the spirits that spoke to him. He was sumptuously dressed, with

a large colored feather head-dress and feather armlets as though he were
a bird, and he was accorded quasi-divine honors and deference.

The influence of the Caraibes over the people was paramount. They
were medicine-men, wise-men, astrologers, prophets, sorcerers, and devil-
propitiators . . . The sun, moon and stars obeyed their orders, they
let loose the winds and the storms . . . the most ferocious beasts of the
forests were submissive to them, they settled the boundaries of hunting-
grounds, interpreted dreams and omens, were entrusted with all secrets,
were father confessors in all private matters and . . . held life and death
at their disposal.[3]

This god-man seems grandiose indeed. We are shocked anew at his
godlike claims—which are those we would ascribe only to a veritable
High God. But he is in all accounts specifically a living man. He is not a
high god. He is a primitive shaman.

The war gods, the rain gods of the agricultural societies in those areas
excluded above, were, we believe, historically developed from these living,
shamanistic man-gods. In Mexico, the war god was still impersonated by
a living, courage-laden man. In Peru, the Great Sun was only the living
Inca. In the Pueblos, the rain gods and *kachinas* are still impersonated by
dancing men. Given the animistic ideology of spirit-substance or soul,
all that is needed to make a "god" is for a man-god (or power-laden man)
to die and his cult to continue. These were the only "gods" that the
aboriginal New World knew—shamans, "owners" of animals, "transformer" demiurges and magicians, culture heroes and tricksters.[4] And
even Montezuma and the Incan Great Sun remained living men.

The Creator is not among them: Earth-Diver made land by diving
deep into primordial waters and bringing up dirt which he magically made
grow. He is a figure in etiological myth, not religion. He is not prayed to,
gets no sacrifice, and has no cult. He may have great magic power, he
may be a culture-hero who brings men new arts, he may juggle and
swallow coals, the master of fire—but he is at best Prometheus, not Zeus.
The transformer-demiurge is no ethical high god either, no sternly moral
Yahweh of the Old World. On the contrary, the trickster is beyond cultural
good and evil. A projective safety-valve, he is the obscene funster who
lets the cat out of the bag of each society's repressions; he is the automatic
olonist in each morality. Nor is his magic omnipotent. Often, too clever
by far, he comes a cropper. The trickster-fixer has no dignity. He has
no ethics. He has only great shamanistic power.

The culture hero is the innovator who first brought fire, who taught
sexuality to men, a new art like ironworking or agriculture, or some new
technique like writing. As the shaman is the supernatural mediator, so the

culture hero is the secular intermediary between men's needs and the world he lives in. But the culture hero, like the shaman, may depart the here and now; to the degree that natives do not discriminate them, the culture hero could well be a dead shaman, or his spirit after death. Very often the culture hero is a protector, champion, or some great war hero of the past. Having helped men, he has now departed. But he is not dead. At some crucial time of great stress in the future, when enemies come to destroy the tribe and its way of life, he will come again to help the people. The "Barbarossa" motif of the undying hero is very common in crisis cults—so common that it must rest on generic animism and hero worship, on the need for powerful helpers and human fathers, and not on technical diffusion.

Native American messiahs and prophets of crisis cults are all cast in the mold of the old Indian shamanistic god-men and culture heroes; indeed, one Shawnee messiah claimed he was the culture hero himself, Manabush the Hare, incarnate. Perhaps the earliest and best known of these are Viracocha of Peru and Quetzalcoatl of Mexico. Viracocha was a bearded, white-skinned culture hero of the Inca. (Does he represent, in his un-Mongoloid appearance, prehistoric Caucasoid Polynesian culture bringers?—for conservative scholars like Nordenskiöld have collected considerable evidence of Oceanic traits in the Americas—however, much the same legend is found in Colombia as in Mexico and Peru.) Angered by a falling away from the customs he had taught the people, he left them, some say walking on the waters.

When Pizarro came to Peru, and Cortez to Mexico, they were at first mistaken for the returning culture heroes.[5] Here were supernaturals indeed! They rode giant spirit-dogs and wore rock-hard detachable skins that shone like the sun and were invulnerable to arrows. They carried thundersticks that spat lightning-fire and death. Oddly, however, these culture heroes did not seem really to understand Indian culture. Every Aztec knew that war is intended to get victims for the gods, hence there was little amiss in the gods' directly claiming their own. But the Spaniards did not stop even with armies of victims they killed on the spot without proper ceremony and pressed forward still to the great Montezuma's throne.

Much the same happened in Peru. Here Atahuallpa and Huascar were disputing the Great Sun's throne; and everyone knows the rest, the fabulous roomful of ransom in silver and gold, and the treachery and murder by Pizarro and his men. True enough, the Spaniards sought gold. But these "feces of the gods," as the Indians called gold, were from Mexico through Nicaragua, and from the Chibchan to the Inca country, the prerogative of kings and nobles, and fit sacrifice or gift to the gods. The

Spaniards also brought *berdache* shamans with them. But these transvestites laid hands on the Indians' holy things to destroy them and the
right worship of gods, and religion was once again outraged, as it had
been in the treatment of the sacred persons of their kings. Soon they
knew well enough that the Spaniards were not gods but a new and terrible
pestilence. It was too late. With a mere handful of men, and with comparative ease, the Conquistadores put their Iberian feudalism on top of
the pyramided power structures of these aboriginal autocracies and ruled
them in cruelty and carnage. Today, on the Titicaca plateau, the correct
form of address, "Viracocha," falls ironically on the white man's ears.

The political conquest was not without deep cultural upheaval however.
The Spanish tried zealously to Christianize the Quechua. But in 1565
came a great religious revolt under the young Inca, Tupac Amaru, and
the revival of worship of the *huaca,* place spirits crushed into the earth
by the Spanish Conquest. Now they had come back to life from the
body of Pachamama, the Earth Mother.[6] Huaca spirits had sowed worms
that would eat the hearts of the Spaniards, of their horses, and of
Christian Indians. The place spirits would enter the bodies of the faithful in a kind of trance. (Molina, the chronicler of Cuzco, said this
was like a Biblical possession by alien demons, but it could just as
well, and more probably, have come from Indian spirit-familiars). Believers were to renounce baptism, and cleanse themselves by fasting and
avoiding all Spanish articles and customs. The huaca revival spread
widely from its center in Vilcabamba under Titu Cusi, into the provinces
of La Paz, Cuzco, Huamanga, Chuquisaca, Arequipa and Lima, taking
in even the old enemies of the Quechua, the Aymara around their ancient
cult center of Tiahuanaco, and including both *hatunruna* finca serfs and
city *yanacona.* The revolt was crushed only in 1572, with the sack of
Vilcabamba and the execution of the new "Inca," Tupac Amaru.

A remarkable messiah led the Inca to a new revolt in 1742. He was
born an Inca Indian in Cuzco, but had gone to Spain. Returning, he
called himself Juan Santos Atahuallpa Apo-Inca, son of God and descendant of the last Inca Emperor.[7] He had the wisdom of Solomon and could
make mountains fall. God had sent him to restore His Kingdom. This messiah, as so many others, often seemed to waver across the thin line that
divides the prophet of God from God himself, perhaps because he was in
the great line of Inca god-men himself. His revolt, extirpated in blood and
slaughter, is still dimly remembered in the legends of the Indians. In 1938
the present writer heard of a great shaman-chief still alive in some remote
part of the vast Titicaca plateau, but much travel never discovered him
in person. Many revolutions in Bolivia have drawn strength from the

belief of Aymara miners and finca serfs in their perennial native messiahs and returning culture heroes.

Thus the Andes. In the tropic lowlands, the Cario,[8] a Guaraní group,
understood the Spanish lust for gold and, hoping to make them allies on
their own accustomed raids, were solicitous of the Spaniards and gave
them food and women. From then on they were janizaries and porters
on all Spanish looting raids, to the Gran Chaco or the distant Andes alike.
In 1540, ten thousand Guaraní gathered at Tapuá to aid Alvar Nuñez
Cabeza de Vaca in the battle against the combined Mbaya and Guaicurú;
two thousand Guaraní went with Domingo de Irala in 1548, and even
more with Nufrio de Chaves in 1558. But what began as a brotherhood in
arms ended in quasi-serfdom. In time, the Guaraní tried to resist the
ruthless exploitation by the Spaniards. But they lacked unity and decision, and their disorganized revolts were easily routed by the Spaniards.

In Paraguay[9] the Jesuits almost succeeded in setting up a theocratic
state, through their custom of gathering Indians into missions and teaching them new material arts, as proper culture heroes do. (The native
contribution to this culture was the ready Indian dependence on their earlier shamanistic god-men.) But this powerful order felt the repercussions
of Spanish-Portuguese struggles in Europe. Also, the private enterprise
of local haciendados did not tolerate the loss of labor to the communism
of Jesuit rule. In 1630, the rich missions of El Guiará were sacked by the
dreaded *mamalucos* or slave raiders from São Paolo, who killed all they
could not capture, and burned all they could not carry off. It is
conservatively estimated that they killed or enslaved 300,000 Guaraní
in a few years; in the three years 1628–30 they took 60,000 Jesuit
mission Indians to the slave markets of São Paolo alone. In 1631,
the renowned apostle to the Indians, Ruíz de Montoya, abandoned the
last two missions that survived in El Guiará and led 12,000 Indians on a
heroic anabasis through the wildernesses of South America. Only 4000
survived to reach the Paraná River.

In Brazil, the Portuguese easily defeated and drove back the Tupí tribes
near the coast.[10] Around 1540, some thousands of Tupinamba fled westward in search of the legendary "Land of Immortality and Perpetual
Rest." They traveled nearly across the continent, and nine years later they
reached Chachapoyas in Peru, which is not this Land. Unfortunately it
transpired that they had passed through gold-rich lands, which led the
Spaniards to make several expeditions through their territory to find El
Dorado. In 1605, another group of Tupinamba left Pernambuco, following a prophet whom they treated as a god, on a quest for his "Land of
Immortality" to which the culture hero had retired from his doings on

earth. On the way, they invaded the territory of Maranhão, then French, where they were defeated by the combined forces of the French and the Portiguara tribe. Earlier, some of the Portiguara themselves had journeyed off on a hunt for the "Earthly Paradise," at the behest of a shaman who said he was a resurrected ancestor. The Tupinambarana,[11] who gave their name to the great Amazonian island, were also Tupinamba who had fled Pernambuco to escape Portuguese cruelties. They went far up the Amazon and then up the Madeira, only to encounter Spanish settlements in eastern Bolivia. Turning again on their path, they went down the Madeira to its mouth on the Amazon and settled on the large island there. But in seeking the earthly paradise, their fortunes declined still further after the Guayarise invaded their land.

Among the Guaraní, some shamans were greatly feared for their enormous supernatural powers. These shamans would go into the jungle, eat celestial food there (some psychotropic drug?), and by constant dancing nourish the *ayvucué* or resurrected butterfly soul,[12] until it could fly to the Land Without Evil. These shamans could kill with their spittle, and their power could drag a whole tribe across a wide river. Some ruled the sun and moon and stars, and their bones were kept in rich hammocks in sacred houses, and consulted as oracles after the shaman's death. Their political power was absolute. Any series of bad happenings was owing to sorcerers, and when the shaman-chiefs infallibly pointed them out, the sorcerers were killed with suitable torture.

All through contact times, the Apapocuva Guaraní[13] have been haunted by a fear of impending world destruction—a supernatural symbol, perhaps, of their concurrent secular fate, though this same fear was indigenous among Pacific coast Indians of the present United States also. Their shamans rescued them from these fears again and again, teaching them dances that would bring believers to an earthly paradise. Guaraní shamans gave themselves out as Lords of the Universe, a grandiose claim no doubt, but only commensurate in magnitude with the world catastrophe they repeatedly averted. Some shamans led holy wars against the Spaniards, whose rule they announced had ended; and some led the tribe from its home territory to seek the legendary Land Without Evil. Some of their messianic ideas seem to be borrowings from Christianity, and the naïve directness of their faith sometimes seems to caricature our own. Most of the Apapocuva shamans said the sacred land was to the east, beyond the sea, and so these Guaraní went to the Atlantic coast, where contact with the white man was speedily disastrous. Shamans exhorted the people to dance day and night, in order to reach the land of abundance and eternal life. Some Apapocuva were still dancing in 1910, so as to lose weight and fly across the ocean. Despite repeated failures, the Apapocuva, the Tanyguá and the Oguauíva, all Guaraní tribes, tried desperately time and again to reach the promised land. They had believed the missionaries' and their own old myths.

The Chiriguano,[14] on the eastern slopes of the Bolivian Andes, are the descendants of other Guaraní who migrated in waves across the continent, partly seeking the now half-legendary loot of the Inca, partly following the old dream of the Great Ancestor's home, and partly fleeing real catastrophe in their old lands to the east. Some came from Paraguay clear across the Gran Chaco, stopping only when like waves they brushed the *montaña* or foothill *yungas* of the Andes—the Ultima Thule, in fact, of their ecological adaptation as Tropic Forest tribes. One half-mythical figure is Candir,[15] a Guaraní term applied in 16th century documents to the far-off Inca emperor. But to others Candir is a god, like Tamoi the Great Ancestor, or a culture hero who brought men agriculture and the making of *chicha* maize-beer. For his sake many Guaraní fasted in long seclusion until, seized with fits of frenzy, they ran through the thorny forest oblivious of wounds and pain. Many times again in the early 1800s, the Guayarú gathered in their dancing houses to the rhythm of their rattles and hollow stamping tubes, singing in the hope that Tamoi, the Great Ancestor, would take pity on their persistence and remove them to his heavenly home. In 1886, still another messiah roused the Chiriguano against the oppression of the Bolivians. They had nothing to fear, since the white men's guns would only "spit water."[16] But the messiah, together with his entourage, was decisively defeated near Cuevo, when the Bolivian bullets did not behave as promised.

The messianic movement of the Tucuna is reported by a remarkable ethnographer, who lived for decades among the Indians and took a native surname, Curt Nimuendajú. He writes that

The Tucuna messianic movement springs from a consciousness of having offended Dyaí, the culture hero, by corrupting their ancient spiritual (not material) culture under the influence of the civilized people, and from a fear that the cataclysms of former times would be repeated. It also involves the tendency of immortals to appear during a person's puberty. In repeated visions, a pubescent man or woman in seclusion sees and talks with the immortals (má/gita), who sometimes may carry his soul (naáe) to their abode and keep it there for a time. The immortals foretell an imminent cataclysm, which threatens to destroy civilized people, and instruct the Indians to save themselves by gathering at a sheltered place and performing certain ceremonies. As soon as the Indians assemble, the civilized people quash the movement, fearing a threat to their interests. This happened in 1941, when the Tucuna met in Taivegíne, following the visionary instruction of a thirteen-year old boy named Naráne.[17]

Messianic movements in South America, therefore, still continue into our own time.

In North America, one of the earliest Indian uprisings came in an area earliest influenced by massive contact with Europeans. The peaceful Pueblo tribes, settled in their agricultural villages of the Southwest, had at first welcomed the Spaniards, glad to have aid against maurading Apache. But the Pueblos, whose intense and codified religion is adapted to the magic getting of that greatest local contingency and their greatest need, rain for their crops, soon found the Spanish padres bent on destroying all these sacred and necessary rites, and imposing an outlandish new belief in a murdered god one ate, but with no special power at all for making rain. The new cult was a threatening assult on compulsive defenses against anxiety in their rituals, and they reacted with typical compulsive explosiveness.

Among the Tewa,[18] in 1690, arose the medicine man Popé, who claimed to have come back from the far north on a visit to Shipapu, the mythic lake of origin of the Tewa, and the place to which spirits of the dead returned. Great marvels appeared at his call. The *kachina* spirits came swiftly under the earth from the sacred water, and reappeared in the underground *kiva* sanctums in the form of fire, to tell them what they all wanted to be told, to revolt. Knotted yucca-fiber cords were sent to all the Pueblos; each day the chief was to untie one knot until the time when all Pueblo tribes would rise at once together. In August 1690, from Pecos to Zuñi and the distant Hopi mesas, the sudden insurrection came. Spanish soldiers and padres alike were slaughtered, or fled, first to Santa Fe and then even to El Paso, until in October there was not a single Spaniard alive in the whole of Nueva Mejico. In the two centuries since, the white men have irresistibly returned to these semi-arid lands. But the Pueblos still practice, in fanatic faith, the compulsive rites they believe bring rain. Until mightier men build dams, or seed clouds from thunderbirds for rain, it will doubtless always be so, as long as there are Pueblos.

Farther north and somewhat later, Indians of the eastern woodlands began to be caught between the rival imperialisms of France and England. The English, pressing from the Atlantic, were a new kind of threat. If the English did not enslave them or seek gold as insatiably as did the Spaniards, they nevertheless dealt just as fatal a blow to the Indians. To build their cabins and grow their corn, these men cut down the forests, and by fair means or foul they took the lands that had made up the old family-band hunting territories of the Algonkians of northeastern America. By contrast, perhaps because the hardy young French *voyageurs* married into their tribes, and also because the trading of their furs for new trinkets disrupted the old tribal life less than did British settlements, many Algonkians allied themselves with the fur traders during the French and Indian War. It was only because the powerful League of the Iroquois (after a smarting defeat dealt to Antoine Lefebvre de La Barre, governor of New France) became a shield to their expanding frontier, that the colonizing British survived and pushed still farther west beyond the Alleghenies.

This time it was to the Delaware,[19] displaced from their woods in eastern Pennsylvania and New Jersey, that a new culture hero came. At Tuscarawas on the Muskingum, a new prophet appeared in 1762. Eager to know the "Master of Life" in these trying times, the Delaware Prophet one night dreamed he could journey to meet this supernatural personage. Next morning he took his kettle, his gun and ammunition, and began to travel. One night he built his fire by a stream near three paths, and he was astonished to see the paths grow brighter as night came on. Although frightened, he recalled his dream and stayed the night. Next day he took the widest path, only to be barred by a great wall of fire rising from the earth. He went back, terrified, to take the next largest path, but here too there were flames that flared still higher as he approached. On the third and straightest path he walked until he came to a dazzling mountain, up which there was no way.

He was in despair. But then he saw a beautiful woman dressed in white. She told him to take off all his clothing, bathe in the river, and climb the glass-slippery mountain naked, using only his left hand and left foot. Arrived at the summit he saw three villages, but he has ashamed to go on because of his nakedness. Then a voice said that because of his river bath he might go on without fear. Next he met a handsome man, also dressed all in white, who led him into the presence of the Master of Life, and there he saw many marvelous and beautiful things. The Master of Life gave him a gold-bordered hat for a seat. He hesitated to sit on it, but did as he was told and listened to the instructions of the Master of Life.

The animals had been taken from the woods, the Master said, because of the wickedness of the Indians in their new ways—using bad-smelling gunpowder, for example, instead of bow and arrows when they hunted. But if all the Indians would unite and drive back the whites to the land appointed for them, then the Great Manitou would send game animals again in great plenty. He gave the prophet a stick engraved with strange signs which were his commands: drink water only once a day, or at most twice; give up the old custom of having many wives and take only one; do not fight other Indians; do not sing the old medicine songs, for they are addressed to the evil spirit; do not buy and sell food, but share it as freely as it was given to them by the *manitou;* and unite with other Indians to drive all the white men from the land. These commandments were sent by the Master of Life to the Indians, to recite morning and evening on the prophet's return to the earth.

This revelation, beyond its interesting psychiatric content, is a strange mixture of the old "vision quest" and Christianity, whose new Moses the prophet was, with his fires and mountain and table of the law, though from a god become more personal perhaps than the old Indian "Master of Animals." The commandments also are a synthesis of the old and the new: to bring back the old days they must give up the old medicine songs and the old custom of polygyny. But this is reasonable. If old behaviors let us down, then evidently we must change them. However, as it turned out, there was no causal relation between gunpowder and polygyny, and no historic effect on Manifest Destiny to come from abandoning the old medicine songs.

Culture fantasies protect men from clear knowledge of their predicament at all times. But that is the function of sacred culture. We do not hunt alone, we have guardian spirits, there are masters of animals to give us game! Sedna will send seals! Our fields are dry, but we can make rain! When such fantasies are threatened, men are thrust back, shorn of defenses, to the same old anxieties and unmastered problems, and new dream work must be done by culture heroes. They must mend the old fabric with new threads. The Delaware Prophet stood between two compelling culture worlds and engaged them both; he strove mightily to dominate both the native and the alien "spirits." But as William James noted,[20] for all their contact with omniscience, mystics strangely give us only the contemporary. And the mystic who is listened to, at best expresses only a current consensus. He dives deep, only to meet his own mind and the common problems of all.

It is in this fact that Devereux[21] finds the crucial difference between the "neurotic" shaman and the "private" hysteric or recognized psychotic. The conflicts of the successful shaman are located in the unconscious segment of his common "ethnic personality" (his "culture"), not in the idiosyncratic part of his unconscious. That is, the shaman is ill for conventional reasons, and in a conventional way characteristic of many others. In the specific sense, he is the "neurotic personality of his time." For this reason, his symptoms (ritual acts), evolved as defenses for him, are found to be reassuring to his fellows. What the shaman does is "uncanny"—something, as Freud has shown,[22] mysteriously and unexpectedly familiar, unlocking some forgotten dream, thus strangely *déjà vu*. Shamans make phatic communications of this sort, not psychiatric insight-cures. And for this very reason, whereas the meddling and un-welcome psychiatrist is combated violently for his *examination* of our "personality" defenses, the shaman is beloved for his *support* of "cultural" solutions or "cures." The uncanny appositeness of his communication (congruence with each unconscious) is proof enough of his charisma or "supernatural" charm. He clearly comes from god (one's own uncon-scious). He tells us what we want. By contrast, the psychotic tells us of the content of his untypical or idiosyncratic unconscious. He tells us what we fear.

In the narrative of John McCullough,[23] captured as a boy of eight and adopted by a Delaware family, we read that the principal doctrine of the Delaware Prophet was to purify oneself from sin by taking emetics and by abstinence from sexual intercourse. Although the injunction to take emetics is an old Indian "ethnic" one, the forbidding of sexual intercourse is an "idiosyncratic" one, or at least one alien to the old Indian culture if borrowed from the whites, and not from the prophet's own disturbed unconscious (there is of course no reason why a prophet's message cannot be a mixture of all three, public and private and alien). One minor ritual is a clear syncretism of the old and the new. Indians were to shake hands, but with the *left* hand, to signify that they gave the heart along with the hand, not like those pretending friends, the whites, from whom this trait was borrowed. The determined sinistral trend in the Prophet's symbol-isms (compare his mode of climbing mountains) will interest students of psychopathy.

The Delaware Prophet's teaching spread to all the Algonkians of the Ohio Valley and the Great Lakes. But the real conflagration of his teach-ing came when it was taken in hand by Pontiac, the celebrated Ottawa chief and shaman of the Midewiwin Grand Medicine Society. In April 1763, Pontiac called the chiefs to a great council near Detroit, and soon all the important Algonkian tribes were allied, together with the Iroquoian Wyandot and Seneca, and the Siouan Winnebago. All were to strike at once on the five hundred miles of wilderness frontier between Fort Pitt and the Straits of Mackinaw. Of the later events in the "Conspiracy of Pontiac" anyone may read in Parkman's brilliant and romantic account[24] —the warning by the Indian girl, the ball play at Mackinac on the king's birthday and the ensuing massacre, the siege of Fort Pitt and the bloody battles of Detroit and Bushy Run. But the realistic actions of the military genius Pontiac, supported psychologically though they were by the teach-ings of the Delaware Prophet, did not muster enough secular strength to win the struggle, and Pontiac was eventually assassinated by an Indian renegade.

In 1768, colonial treaties with the Iroquois, and also the Cherokee, broke the last power of any considerable tribe east of the Alleghenies. The Revolution came and went, during which many of the tribes understandably allied themselves with the British, and still the Americans pushed westward to the frontier, now in Kentucky. For twenty years, under Little Turtle and other chiefs, the Indians bravely fought the whites until their final defeat by Wayne at Fallen Timbers, and the 1765 Treaty of Greenville, which signed away virtually the whole Ohio Valley and their favorite hunting grounds in Kentucky. The Delaware, Wyandot, and Shawnee (of whom we are to hear more later), their bravest warriors slain, their cornfields and villages burned, and their hunting territories now lost to them, became dispirited and broken refugees among the Miami.

Among the Iroquois, the fifteen hundred Seneca made an historically wrong choice. The most powerful tribe in the Indian confederacy—whose "League of the Iroquois" Benjamin Franklin urged as a federal model for the Colonies—the Seneca had defeated most of the tribes in the present states of New York, New Jersey, Pennsylvania and Ohio. In the French and Indian War they had held the balance of power between the French and English. But in the Revolution, the Seneca joined the British. In 1779, General Sullivan's punitive raiders devastated their villages and cornfields. Still fighting in 1783, they were abandoned by their allies, in the separate peace of the British with the Americans. The next year at Fort Stanwix, Seneca delegates signed away their lands in western Pennsylvania and Ohio. And in 1797, the chiefs, plied with rum and bribes, sold all the remaining territories west of the Genessee River, leaving only small reserved islands in a sea of white pioneers.

With their hunting grounds and cornfields gone, deserted by both allies and subordinate tribes and defeated in the war, theirs was a generation of despair. Mutual accusations of witchcraft were rife, and the proud old way of life was gone with the wind. Their white neighbors condemned them with mixed pity and hatred. Many drank to excess, and families split bitterly on the issue of following the Indian's or the white man's road. Western tribes beyond the frontier were contemptuous of one Seneca faction under Cornplanter, who sought peace with Washington and made treaties for their lands for as long as grass should grow and waters flow.

An older half-brother of Cornplanter was Handsome Lake,[25] a man in his middle fifties at the time. Handsome Lake had served against the Americans in the Revolutionary War, and he was now one of the fifty-nine chiefs of the Great Council of the League. But by 1779 he had almost drunk himself to death—bed-ridden, brooding over the deaths of his wife, his favorite son and favorite niece, Cornplanter's daughter, and his abandonment by another son. Fearing death himself, from sickness or from witchcraft, he drunkenly sang the old *Ohgiwe,* sacred songs to be sung only by the Chanters for the Dead. When he sobered, he felt guilty for this sin, which only added despair to his drunken way of life. He was a broken man.

In June 1799, Handsome Lake had a vision or dream. Three angels came from heaven to explain that his illness was from too much drinking—all the Seneca, in fact, drank far too much liquor and wrought too much witchcraft, and these were the cause of their present state. The angels conducted him on a tour of heaven and hell, and they told Handsome Lake the Good Spirit said he was to instruct the Seneca in the right way of life. He came out of his trance just as his family was preparing him for burial. Fortunately, a nearby Quaker preacher wrote down an English version of his revelations, and his brother Cornplanter brought the people round to hear his words. After several other visions, Handsome Lake felt better, left his bed, and began his preaching career.

His code was austere and largely negative, forbidding liquor, fiddles, dancing and card playing; witchcraft, adultery and wife-beating; gossip, greed and the sale of land. The world would be destroyed in flames, and the wicked go to hell, where they would suffer in specific ways recalling the old Iroquois torture of war prisoners. No white man would go to heaven with good Seneca. Even George Washington, the best of these, hung in a halfway house between heaven and hell. Some Seneca should learn to read and write English. Others should farm like the whites, with plows, fences and frame houses, and—most revolutionary of all in a land of female agriculture—males should farm, as they did among the whites. Certain old rituals should be stopped or changed, others kept and strictly followed. The teachings of Handsome Lake spread widely, probably helped by three Quaker missionaries who had arrived in 1798 the year before. His doctrine was a mixture of the old and new, in part harking back to the good old days of the past, in part a practical and drastic accommodation to new times. Several women were cruelly executed as suspect witches, but then witches had never been socially admired before among the Seneca anyway. Some students have suggested that Handsome Lake had alcoholic or paranoid delusions of persecution. In any case, his injunction of male agriculture was momentous.

The effect on the Seneca of Handsome Lake's teaching was deep and lasting. Indian traders were startled to find their rum refused and sugar water asked for instead. Men took on erstwhile women's work, fenced, plowed, planted, and raised pigs and cattle. Indian children went to frame schoolhouses to learn white ways, with one remarkable result that the Iroquois young men are nowadays famed "high steel" workers on American skyscrapers.[26] From being a frontier slum folk, the Iroquois became the best adapted and most populous Indian group in the East. Several decades after his death, the Old Way of Handsome Lake, as it was now called, changed from a sect to a church. His gospel is now codified. A sort of mother church at Tonawanda licenses itinerant preachers, and male and female Keepers of the Faith are the deacons of the congregations, each with its own Longhouse for meetings. Some Longhouses still exist today on the Iroquois reservations in New York and Ontario. Fitly, too, Cornplanter is to this day one of the proudest family names among the Iroquois, for his policy led his faction to a better adaptation than the more traditional Seneca policy of continued war against the whites. In the new context, hate and fear of other men was a lethal culture trait; the borrowing of white farm-technology and new occupations for warriors was adaptive.

The close time relationship between cultural chaos and revelation is shown again in the case of the Shawnee. Like the Iroquois, the Shawnee had lost most of their territory at the Treaty of Greenville in 1795. In 1805, one Lauliwasikaw (named from the shaman's sacred rattle) began his career as the famous "Shawnee Prophet."[27] It is said that Lauliwasikaw, previously noted only for his stupidity and drunkenness, was lighting his tobacco pipe one day in his cabin, when he fell back apparently dead. His friends gathered for his funeral, so goes this now-cliché, when he rose from his trance, or alcoholic crisis, and announced he had been led by two young men to the border of the spirit land and allowed to look in. There he was given a new revelation from the Master of Life. All the old shamanistic jugglery and medicines were to be given up; the young should aid the old and handicapped (the Shawnee Prophet had but one eye); intermarriage with whites was forbidden; the white man's flint-and-steel and clothing should be discarded for the Indian firestick and buckskin; and the firewater of the whites was pronounced an accursed poison, to be given up lest eternal flames issue from the drunkard's mouth in the afterworld. As proof of his visionary visit, he had received power to cure all sicknesses and to overmaster death, on the battlefield or elsewhere.

Lauliwasikaw's words created great excitement, the most immediate effect of which was the burning of medicine men and suspected witches. The first victims the Shawnee Prophet designated were Delaware, including one old woman whom they roasted over a fire four days until, dying, she recalled that her grandson, then out hunting, had her medicine bag. When captured, he freely admitted that the medicine had helped him to fly over Kentucky to the Mississippi and back in one day. But he insisted that he had returned the medicine bag, and he was set free. Next came a venerable chief, Tatepocoshe, whose death was deliberated in council. Dressed in his bravest regalia and awaiting his death, out of respect the old chief was first tomahawked before being burned. The next day, an old Indian preacher called Joshua was also burned to death, and likewise the chief's nephew, an irreproachable young man who died singing and praying in the flames. Preparations were being made to burn Chief Tatepocoshe's wife, when suddenly her younger brother, a boy of twenty, stood up, and, taking her by the hand, led his sister out of the council house. "The devil has come among us, and we are killing each other," this young agnostic said, when he came back and courageously sat down again in the midst of the crowd. His brave act stopped the burnings, and for a time greatly checked the influence of the prophet, at least among the Delaware.

The Shawnee Prophet now styled himself Tenskwatawa, or "Open Door," to symbolize his new status and his power over death. Still, some doubters remained. Then Open Door learned, in some manner, of a coming eclipse of the sun, for the summer of 1806, and predicted it would take place as a result of his supernatural power over the sky. When the eclipse did in fact occur on schedule, his fame spread widely by word of mouth, until it reached all the way from the Blackfoot of Saskatchewan to the Creek in the Everglades of Florida. Open Door now claimed he was Manabozho, the First Doer and Hare trickster of Algonkian myth. In anger at the Indians' taking over wicked white ways, he, Manabozho, had called in all the game from the forests and shut it under the earth, until the Indians would give up their evil sorcery and sacred calumet-pipe dance. They should keep but one dog to a family, and the First Doer would give them new medicine. Then, after four years, he would cause a two-day darkness, during which he would free the animals in the earth, and restore all the dead Indians to life.

The doctrine of the Shawnee Prophet varied somewhat as it spread to other tribes. The Cherokee learned from the Creek, about 1812, that a terrible wind would come, with hailstones as big as hominy mortars that would kill both whites and unbelievers alike. Those who would be saved must flee to the Great Smoky Mountains. Full of these beliefs, many Cherokee in Alabama and Georgia abandoned their beehives, orchards, slaves, and everything else they had got from the white man, and in spite of the pleas and remonstrances of friends who did not believe, many took up a toilsome march to the mountains of North Carolina, where most of the Cherokee still live today.[28]

From the opposite diagonal of the Shawnee Prophet's enormous area of influence comes the account of John Tanner,[29] who was captured as a boy in Kentucky and brought up among the Ojibwa Indians of Lake Superior. Tanner wrote that a strange man brought a message from the Shawnee Prophet, saying that they must keep perpetual fires in the lodges, kill all their dogs, and throw away their medicine bundles. They must not drink, steal, lie, or strike any man, woman or child. Two young men attended a mysterious palladium under a blanket, and made a bed for it like a person. In time this was disclosed to be four strings of moldy and discolored beans (narcotic *Sophora secundiflora* "mescal beans"?). The ritual of "shaking hands with the Prophet" consisted in pulling these strings of beans through the hands like a rosary, and this symbolized a solemn promise to keep his commandments.

Though the white traders ridiculed the notion of a new revelation of the Divine Will, and other whites scouted the notion that this could be given to a poor and lowly Shawnee, the Indians continued to believe. In 1808, one hundred and fifty canoe loads of Ojibwa set out in a body to visit the new Master of Life in Detroit, one family carrying a dead child to be brought back to life by him. On the way, however, they were met by a trusted French trader who gave them the news of starvation at the Prophet's camp. The Indians there had given away all their food to the many visitors, and had been so busy with ceremonies they had not gotten around to planting any corn.

Dreamers and culture heroes are troublesome enough as the figure-heads of culture change. But when they enlist the aid of movers and shakers, even history is forced to take notice of them. The one-eyed Shawnee Prophet had a brother, six feet tall and handsomely built, who bitterly hated the whites. His father had been killed in a battle with Virginians in 1774, his favorite eldest brother had been lost attacking a southern frontier post, and still another brother had been killed at his side in Mad Anthony Wayne's victory of 1794. This man was Tecumtha or Tecumseh,[30] an untranslatable oblique reference to a "Panther Crouching in Wait" or to a celestial panther, "Meteor" or "Shooting Star." He was all of these in American history, for even Tecumseh's command village at Tippecanoe is remembered, and out of the ensuing campaign came another of America's usually mediocre general-presidents.

Primarily a warrior and a shrewd diplomat, Tecumseh was nevertheless not incapable of shamanistic tricks, like those of his brother the Shawnee Prophet. On one visit to the Creek town of Tuckhabatchee, Tecumseh found only lukewarm support and sympathy. Angrily he said he would go straight to Detroit—they should count the days of his journey—and when he arrived, he would stamp his foot on the ground and shake down every house in Tuckhabatchee. On the morning of his computed arrival at Detroit, there was indeed a great rumble and a mighty shaking of the earth, so that all the houses in Tuckhabatchee were tumbled down. So powerful were ancient Indian nature shamans. It was the New Madrid Earthquake on the Mississippi.

Tecumseh had ordered his brother to keep the uneasy peace with Governor Harrison of Ohio until he, Tecumseh, proceeding through Missouri, Iowa and Illinois with ever more accession to his confederated power, should return to renew negotiations with the President. But the attack was prematurely made, largely at the hands of the overconfident messiah, who lacked his brother's military genius, and from then onward the campaign was a shambles. There was an unusually large proportion of wounded among the confederated Indian troops, probably because of promises of the Prophet that the whites' bullets would fall harmless at the Indians' feet. But the bullets did not do this. The Indians were routed in complete defeat, and Tippecanoe was abandoned. The Shawnee Prophet was a deflated messiah who thenceforth ended his days in obscurity. In the War of 1812, Tecumseh was regularly commissioned a brigadier general in the British Army. But at the Battle of the Thames, which he knew would be his last, he gave his British sword to friends for his young son, took off the British military dress for his deerskin hunting clothes, and was killed in an onslaught of American cavalry, still disputing the Greenville Treaty boundary of his tribal hunting lands.

But American pioneers still continued to press westward. In 1819, the Kickapoo were forced to give up all their lands in Illinois, nearly half the area of the later state, in exchange for a guaranteed possession of rugged hill country in Missouri. Even after the treaty, however, many Kickapoo showed a reluctance to leave their villages and rich lands for new territory. "This may have been due to the innate perversity of the savage," wrote the old Indian hand Jim Mooney, "or possibly to the fact that the new country guaranteed to them was already occupied by their hereditary enemies, the Osage, who outnumbered the Kickapoo three to one."[31] In fact, by now, Indians were so distrustful of American guarantees that half the Illinois Kickapoo moved south *en masse* and did not stop until they reached Mexico, where they still live.

Känakûk[32] was the chief of the remaining Kickapoo. In a conciliatory manner, he besought the whites to let the Kickapoo live peacefully among them. He had had a vision and preached a new doctrine (though the traders said he got it from a Methodist preacher in those parts) telling his people not to steal, to lie, to murder or to quarrel, and to throw away their medicine bags. Drunkenness and witchcraft also must be given up. He explained his doctrine by means of a peculiar map or symbolic diagram, as had earlier Algonkian prophets before him, and each Kickapoo had a carved maple stick made and sold by the prophet. Catlin, who painted his portrait and heard him preach, thought Känakûk a speaker of great ease, grace and eloquence. Känakûk preached on Sundays, in the white fashion. On Fridays, the Kickapoo met for confession of sins in the aboriginal way, after which certain appointed persons gave each penitent strokes with a hickory stick, moderated and numbered according to the seriousness of his sins. But despite the eloquence of their chief's appeals, the Kickapoo were forcibly removed to Kansas. Känakûk died there of smallpox in 1852, after predicting he would rise again on the third day. In anticipation of this event, his followers gathered around his dead body. He did not rise. But many of them caught smallpox, which so decimated the tribe that today there are only a few hundred Kickapoo left in Kansas and Oklahoma.

In the same year of 1852, a Winnebago Indian named Pátheske,[33] of Turkey River in Iowa, had a vision for a new dance which he taught his people, having seen the spirits dance it when he fasted several days. The Winnebago were to dance it at intervals for a year, and in the spring they were to make war upon the Sioux, when they would take many scalps. The dance was faithfully performed, but in the spring he announced a new revelation forbidding them the warpath. When his chief follower was killed accidentally soon after this, and when Pátheske himself died on an embassy to Washington, the Winnebago knew that all this came from failure to accomplish his first prophecy.

In the middle of the nineteenth century, gold was discovered in the Far West, and the frontier leaped the Rockies—as these Indian crisis cults were promptly to do likewise. The impact of the Gold Rush was to shake the Indians of the region most profoundly. Only since Mooney's great study of the Ghost Dance have anthropologists learned the beginnings of the earlier Prophet Dance,[34] in the smaller and less studied tribes of the inland plateau of the Northwest and California. The Prophet Dance seems now to have been the origin of many later messianic Indian cults, even of some that spread eastward in a backwash, fomenting great military clashes in mid-continent and the final catastrophic end of Plains Indian culture. The Prophet Dance of the northwest had five offshoots: the Smohalla ritual of the Sahaptan tribes, the Messiah Cult of the Mackenzie Athabaskans (still scarcely known), the Puget Sound Shakers, and the two "Ghost Dances" proper. We will treat each of these in turn.

Among the peoples of the Plateau, there was an aboriginal belief in the imminent destruction and renewal of the world. At the renewal, all the dead would return again. Indeed, from time to time, individual men did just this, "died" and returned with new knowledge of that world. All the cataclysms of nature that grown people could remember were only small portents of the time to come. Visionaries taught the dances of the dead they had witnessed in the other world. If living men performed these dances, they would hasten the renewal of the worn earth.

Near the center of the area over which the Prophet Dance later was to spread, lived the Southern Okanagon. This apprehensive tribelet believed that falling stars, earthquakes, and other anomalous events in nature were all signs of the coming destruction of the world. Some men dreamed they had talked with the Transformer. Others went to the land of the dead and came back preaching domesday, when death itself would die and the dead rejoin the living—if the living would reform and live good lives. Some non-shamans also had these dreams, but these were mere revelations with no curing power. Dreamers called others to their houses in the evenings and told them of their experiences. At a sign of the end of the world, usually a low-flying double-headed goose or some other messenger bird, they were to begin the dance, each standing in one spot in a circle around the dreamer, singing songs he had taught them.

The dreamer would exhort them not to lie, not to fight, rape or steal. No one ate in the daytime during a dance period, and no one hunted, fished or gathered berries while it lasted. The Okanagon danced for indefinite periods, sometimes through the spring and summer into the fall. At one famous time, some "dry snow" fell from the skies—volcanic ash of an eruption early travelers date about 1790—and they stopped their summer food-gathering to perform the dance, later starving in the winter that followed. One old woman, past seventy in the 1930s, said a four-legged double-headed goose came flying in her grandmother's time and predicted the direction of the coming of the whites. The Okanagon lived in a perpetual age of anxiety. They believed that in time the rivers would undercut the earth and set it afloat like an island, as it had been in the time of Earth Diver, and then the Trickster would return to make the happy world that once was. The Okanagon thought the whole world, just as men do, would die and be reborn.

Aboriginal also in this tribe was the old "Confession Dance," performed at any strange event in nature. At such times the tribe gathered around the chief in his house. There the chief first of all confessed his sins, and after this all the rest, young and old, confessed theirs, swaying in a rhythmic circle around the chief. This went on, with short rests, sometimes for two or three days and nights, until nature came to rights and their panic subsided. Some years after the "dry snow," a Sanpoil Indian named Michel had a dream in which he predicted the coming of the whites. Another Sanpoil named Skolaskin,[35] who had been lame from birth and had been abandoned as an orphan and left for dead, miraculously came back to life to preach a religious life lest they all turn into birds and rocks. At another time he had people build a big boat, to escape a flood to come. But his own life was less righteous, for "quite unlike his virtuous predecessor, he inveigled young girls into illicit relations with him on the pretext that only thus might they enter heaven." Skolaskin was arrested and deported in 1889 by officials, at the instigation of Chief Moses.

Suipuken, the last chief of the Kartar band, dreamed the coming of the priests and warned the people against them. Strangely enough, though, he himself made the sign of the cross in his rites, believed in the resurrection of the dead, and told parents to leave dead children unburied for three days. But he, too, seduced young girls. These personal failings of Skolaskin and Suipuken must be mentioned, since Spier thinks such sexuality was patterned among some Plateau seers. In fact, the Shuswap prophet promised that all who remained celibate against his commands would become animals at death. Suipuken may be the same individual Gibbs met in 1853, "a religious personage, who sported the title of King George, and persecuted us nightly with family worship."[36]

The Modoc greatly feared the world's end. Every year in the fall they danced at the coming of the aurora borealis. This was the sky on fire, set by Kumukámts the Creator, his son, and Red Fox. Its smoke or flames would cause incurable sickness, and on this account they took shouting to the water, to beat about and bathe in it to avoid the sickness. Then they danced to ward off the great burning of the world, lest the earth catch flame from the sky at the edge of the world, and make deep fires to consume them all from beneath the ground. The Modoc also greatly fear the dreams that come in their anti-sunwise shuffle dance, and sometimes faint from these dreams. But they must dance on to prevent the world's end.

Some Indians thought to see their culture hero coming back. The thoroughly mundane David Thompson, the first white man to descend the Columbia River (in July of 1811), was apparently mistaken for a kind of angel of the apocalypse. This most sober of explorers was acclaimed a miracle everywhere he went. The Salish were "at a loss what to make of

us," and passed their hands over him to discover what manner of man he
was. Near the mouth of the Snake, another group "sent forward two
very old Men, who lay flat on the ground in the most pitiful manner;
crawling slowly, frequently lifted their heads a little as if imploring
mercy; my Native Interpreter would not speak to them, and all the signs
I could make gave them no confidence; close behind the men three
women crawled on their knees; lifting up their hands to me as if supplicat-
ing for their lives."[37] Perhaps the Indians were more right than they
knew. For the coming of the white man was the end of their world.

The tribes on the Columbia who followed chief Smohalla,[38] some two
thousand strong, had never made treaties giving up their rights to fish
salmon on their rivers, or to dig *kamas* root in the swamps. Nevertheless the settlers constantly encroached upon them. Money promised
the Indians by the government never came. The chiefs of the Cayuse, the
Wallawalla, and the Umatilla all made eloquent pleas which have been
recorded. The young Umatilla chief said:

I have only one heart, one tongue. Although you say, Go to another
country, my heart is not that way. I do not wish for any money for my
land. I am here, and here is where I am going to be . . . I will not
part with my lands, and if you come again I will say the same thing. I
will not part with my lands.[39]

Smohalla "the Preacher," born sometime between 1815 and 1820 was
the chief of a small Sahaptan tribe on the Columbia; he was also sometimes called "Shouting Mountain" from an element in his theology. He
was a short, bald, thickset, almost hunchbacked man. A finished orator,
he held the tribes spellbound. In his youth, Smohalla had frequented a
Catholic mission among the Yakima, and as a young man he had been a
famous warrior. He would go into rigid trances of some duration, and
while he was in this state people would stick needles into his flesh and
cut him bloodlessly with knives, showing he was surely dead.

Smohalla began to preach about 1850, but his doctrine was modified
by events that occurred around 1860. As a shaman, he had been making
medicine against his great rival Moses, chief of an up-river tribe. In a
fight provoked by Moses, Smohalla was wounded and left for dead.
Alone, reviving, he managed to crawl to a boat and be carried down-river,
where he was rescued by white men, and among them he slowly recovered. Ashamed to return, he now began his great odyssey—to the
Pacific coast, south to Oregon and California and into Mexico, and then
through Arizona, Utah and Nevada to his former home on the Columbia.
There the people were amazed and received him as a messenger from the
world of ghosts.

Smohalla told them that Sághalee Tyee, the Great Chief Above, was angered at their ways. He had a book with mysterious characters, some like the letters of our alphabet, which he said recorded his adventures and doctrines. Kotaíaquan, an early disciple among the Yakima, may have added to these doctrines. Smohalla had an elaborate anthropology, evidently influenced by Mormonism, according to which the Indians were made by the creator first, then the Frenchmen, the Boston Men (in Chinook Jargon, "Americans"), King George Men (the British), and lastly black men and the Chinaman with a tail. The earth maker and culture hero first made men and women with wings like birds, and the fish and animals besides. But the quarreling of the people made Tyee take away their wings; the bones of these first people may be found in the earth. And now the new invaders were inviting them to further sins.

> You ask me to plow the ground! Shall I take a knife and tear my mother's bosom? Then when I die she will not take me to her bosom to rest.
> You ask me to dig for stone! Shall I dig under her skin for her bones? Then when I die I can not enter her body to be born again.
> You ask me to cut grass and sell it, and be rich like white men! But how dare I cut off my mother's hair?
> It is a bad law, and my people will not obey it. I want my people to stay with me here. All the dead men will come to life again. Their spirits will come to their bodies again. We must wait here in the homes of our fathers and be ready to meet them in the bosom of our mother.[40]

One day Sághalee Tyee would overturn the earth. And the spirits, living now in the mountains, where they echo back their names when we shout them, will come down and reinhabit their bones, as do animals in the hunt when men respect their bones. Smohalla not only opposed all agriculture. He would also have no domesticated animals of the whites anywhere about him. He said Indians took the gifts of the earth, freely given as to a baby at its mother's breast. But the white man's endless working hardened his heart even to ravage his mother Earth Woman's body. Smohalla was deeply offended at the lack of Indian generosity patterns among the whites. "My young men shall never work," he said. "Men who work can not dream, and wisdom comes to us in dreams." His much ritualized cult, however, with flags and bells and calisthenic exercises, was borrowed both from the Catholic mass and from drill behavior on the military posts, rather than wholly from his own dreams.

The "Dreamers" on the Columbia River arose among small, often internally squabbling, Sahaptan tribes. But the doctrine that the dead, when they returned, would make them populous indeed and help them overcome the whites—this doctrine gave history a different turn among the

Nez Percé,[41] the most powerful of all the Sahaptan tribes. The sequence of events began when some lawless whites encroached upon their lands in southwestern Oregon. Since the Nez Percé were by all accounts a proud and honest, brave and upright group, and acknowledged leaders in the Plateau, the government sought to deal with them. In 1843, the chiefs assembled to hear the government's expression of good intentions to protect their lands against white renegades; in 1855, the Nez Percé, under pressure, gave up a large part of their territory, on the strength of immutable guarantees of the rest; in 1860, gold was discovered on their reservation. Then, in defiance of all agreements, the site of Lewiston was brazenly laid out on Indian land, and a new treaty in 1863 gave the whites what they had already seized. Next, an Indian of Chief Joseph's band was murdered by the whites. Despite all provocation, this brave and honorable man nevertheless restrained his warriors and consented to meet government agents in a conference, where the dreamer Toohulhulsote was the chief spokesman. At this conference they agreed to leave their lands again for the smaller Lapwai Reservation.

But in 1877, as they were gathering up their stock to move to Lapwai, a band of white rustlers attacked them, ran off their cattle, and killed another Nez Percé. Chief Joseph could restrain his braves no longer. The Nez Percé War had begun. Then began the most brilliant generalship of many brilliant Indian wars. With a mere hundred men, and impeded by three hundred and fifty women and children, Chief Joseph led a masterly movement over a thousand miles, meanwhile meting out smarting defeats to overwhelming numbers of government troops. But fresh armies and more armies came up, killed Chief Joseph's brother, and partly cut off their retreat. Chief Joseph had to choose surrender or the abandonment of his wounded and the women and children. The ancient male burden of the band chief to protect all those dependent on him held him fast. The surrender speech of Chief Joseph is a part of American literature.[42]

I am tired of fighting. Our chiefs are killed. Looking Glass is dead. Toohulhulsote is dead. The old men are all dead. It is the young men who say yes or no. He who led the young men is dead. It is cold and we have no blankets. The little children are freezing to death. My people, some of them, have run away to the hills and have no blankets, no food. No one knows where they are—perhaps freezing to death. I want to have time to look for my children and see how many of them I can find. Maybe I shall find them among the dead. Hear me, my chiefs! I am tired. My heart is sick and sad. From where the sun now stands I will fight no more forever.

The greatest warrior of his time was abandoning the core of Indian culture, the proud manly game of war.

The "Prophet Dance" of the Plateau also spread deep into wilderness Canada, among the Athabaskans of the northern lakes. The doctrine arrived with a remarkable Kutenai woman, a transvestite. She had lived at the North West Company's post on the Columbia, her husband being a servant there. Then one day she suddenly put on male clothing, got a horse and weapons, and joined a war party. She was known thereafter as Manlike Woman, and took as wife another woman as the result of her supernatural experiences. About 1812, she began to preach among the Mackenzie River Athabaskans of the coming end of the Indians in a great plague, and of the devastation of the world by two supernaturals of enormous size. She predicted a new golden age, after the whites had been destroyed, and seems to have spoken of one who would revive the dead. They should kill their dogs in order to bring back the ancestors and perhaps too the great hero who had once traversed the earth. Little more is known of this Messiah Cult of the Mackenzie, except that it came to the Beaver, Slave, Sekani and Chipewyan, and even to the Satudéné, the Caribou Eaters, the Dogrib and the Yellow Knives of the far north.

The Prophet Dance had still another offshoot in Indian Shakerism.[43] John Slocum was the founder of the Shakers. Born about 1838, he was a Squaxin Indian, a small Salishan group on Little Skookum Bay in southwestern Puget Sound. In his youth he had been to the Protestant mission among the Skokomish, and he was an ordinary sort of man except for a mild addiction to liquor and pony racing. One morning about daylight, in 1882, when he was in his early forties, Slocum "died" or fell into a trance which lasted until late afternoon. His brother went to Olympia to get a coffin, and a grave had already been dug (precipitancy in burial is characteristic of the region). But on waking, he announced that he had been to heaven. There, however, angels barred the way, because of his sins on earth. Given the choice of hell or returning to earth and telling people how to get to heaven, he chose the latter.

Slocum's followers built a church for him. Here he promised to turn four women into angels with restored wings, raise the dead, and perform other shamanistic miracles, if other tribes on the Skokomish reservation would attend his services. The first meeting lasted a whole week. Meetings often ran from six o'clock until midnight, during which the Indians wore candles on their heads in a kind of cedar-bark crown (coal-oil came from Satan and was barred from meetings) while Slocum harangued against sin. Because of their peculiar rapid nervous twitchings, somewhat in the fashion of their old "black *tamahnous*" winter rituals when they were possessed by guardian spirits, the people of his sect became known as "Shakers." The agent and his missionary brother persecuted the sect with some violence, once trussing up a number of them in chains. But a juridical decision that land-holding Indians were American citizens, and thus beyond the jurisdiction of the agent, soon removed this source of annoyance. Many ridiculed and inveighed against the shaking. But this was believed to be as "catching as the measles" and some scoffers stayed to shake and become pillars of the church. The Shakers also had a practice of brushing or messaging sins off one another, which at times reached questionable extremes, and ringing bells to cure sickness, and the like. They also had a habit of shaking hands and of making the sign of the cross many times during the day, as a kind of apotropaic compulsion to hold off evil.

When an order came from Washington to stop all the old magic curing of illness, the medicine men, at first opposed to the sect, joined it, and thereby strengthened its prestige. Mud Bay Louis, a tall raw-boned Indian, became the chief organizer of the church. He fully conceded Slocum's leadership as the man who went to heaven, but he took over building churches and sending preachers to other tribes, with the result that the sect has now spread over all western Washington. His brother, Sam Yowaluch, became head of the faith cure department in the church. One Indian claimed to be Christ, and he rode through the streets of Olympia with his arms outstretched as on a cross. But both Indians and whites laughed at him, and he subsequently cut down his claim somewhat to mere personal visits to heaven. Several people prophesied the end of the world, generally scheduled for the Fourth of July. At this, many gave up gambling, drinking, and horse-racing. Over the years, with further acculturation, the sect has become more and more correctly Christian. It has been endorsed by the Presbyterian Church, and is now fading into the complex tangle of indistinguishable Protestant American sects.

Why do men fear the death of the world? Why do some men believe that they dominate the skies like gods, while others join in the belief that these god-men can master death and bring back the living spirits? Why do men confess their sins to the winter seas, or tell the flaming sky that they are sorry? Why do they fear to ravage Mother Earth? And why should new abnegations and discipline of their appetites concern the cosmos?

Every ritual designed to coerce the outside world is founded finally on the inner animistic faith that human will can magically command and influence the outside world. And every ritual, in the last analysis, begins in the compulsive defense of some individual human being, but now given social currency to the degree it has contemporary fit with the anxieties of others. When the ego-adaptations of adult men, as individuals or in societies, fail to cope with the austerities of an inhuman universe, then the means they use will naïvely borrow from their own emotional prehistory, from the more archaic adaptation to other people whom they would command or placate in the childhood family, to which, when under stress, all men regress.

Every cosmos peopled with human-seeming personages merely replicates the persons who ministered to the child's dependency and need in his earlier world. No secular search, however yearning or prolonged, has ever found again these supernatural persons in the outer world. But, for good reason, every sacred sect manifests them, resurrected from the inner universe of men's minds and needs. Born in stress, sacred culture is nourished endlessly by new stresses. Culture is part of the human defense, for it is communicated belief in which others join us. The cult of our fathers, living still, defends us; borrowed cults of stronger races sometimes serve; new cults may need to be dreamed. In the mapping of these successive New World cults, the salient fact is that, everywhere the white man came, there was soon to be a rebirth of old Indian culture heroes, mixed with borrowed revelation. It is not so much that shamanism is the root of all religion as that all religion is in sober essence shamanism. And human need is so much the same, it is no wonder that these simple shamans thought they were like the great Master of Life of white men.

NOTES

(VI The Culture Heroes Return)

1. The naturalistic origin of religion in the shaman is a concept I owe to Gilbert Murray, *Five Stages of Greek Religion*, p. 48. That sacred social structures are a projection of the secular is a long-accepted insight of Emile Durkheim, in his *Elementary Forms of the Religious Life*. Recognition of the importance of individual ontogeny in the process comes from Freud and Abraham; of cultural "phylogeny," from Ferenczi and Róheim; and of the species-specific nature of human nature from my own synthesis of these with human biology as I have elsewhere described it (*Human Animal*, Chs. 9, 12–13).

2. On *Urmonotheismus*, Karl J. Narr, "Approaches to the Religion of Early Paleolithic Man," *History of Religions*, 4 (1964) 1–22. Although his own subject matter has a tempting near-universality, James states forthrightly that "There is no convincing evidence that in prehistoric or protohistoric times one sole Supreme Deity was believed to have existence to the exclusion of all other divine beings" (E. O. James, *The Worship of the Sky-God*, London: Athlone Press, 1963, p. 21).

3. On the *cara-ìbe* shamans, G. E. Church, *Aborigines of South America* (London: Chapman and Hall, 1912, pp. 31–32). Ackerknecht supposes that divination by drugs is specific to South American shamans (E. H. Ackerknecht, "Medical Practices," in J. H. Steward [ed.], *Handbook of South American Indians*, 5:625), but it is certainly characteristic of much of the New World (La Barre, *Narcotic Complex*), and often also of ecstatic shamanism elsewhere in the world.

4. Paul Radin, *The Trickster: A Study in American Indian Mythology* (New York: Philosophical Library, 1956); Mac Linscott Ricketts, *North American Indian Trickster*, pp. 327–50. The monograph of Harry Tegnaeus, *Le Héros civilisateur* (Uppsala: Studia Ethnographica Upsaliensia, 1950) is on culture heroes in Africa. For South America, an important work is by Alfred Métraux, "Les Hommes-dieux chez les Chiriguano et dans l'Amérique du Sud," *Revista de l'Instituto de Antropología de l'Universidad Nacional de Tucumán*, 2 (1942) 61–91.

5. W. H. Prescott, *History of the Conquest of Mexico* and *History of the Conquest of Peru* (New York: Modern Library, n.d.). On Viracocha, W. La Barre, *The Aymara Indians of the Lake Titicaca Plateau, Bolivia* (Memoirs of the American Anthropological Association, 68, 1948, pp. 22, 42n, 203, and 207). On the possibility of Caucasoid Polynesians in America, see Aleš Hrdlička, "The Peopling of America," *Journal of Heredity*, 6 (1915) 79–91; and G. Friederici, *Vorkolumbischen Verbindung*. On the Hero as Barbarossa, see Chapter VIII, fns. 37 and 40.

6. The *huaca* cult of Tupac Amaru, G. Kubler, "The Quechua in the Colonial World," in Steward, *op. cit.*, 2:331–410, pp. 406–7.

7. Juan Santos Atahuallpa Apo-Inca, J. H. Steward, "Tribes of the Montaña: An Introduction," in Steward, *op. cit.*, 3:507–33, p. 512. See also A. Métraux, "A Quechua Messiah in Eastern Peru," *American Anthropologist*, 44 (1942) 721–25; and his "Messiahs of South America," *The Inter-American Quarterly*, 3 (1941) 53–60.

8. Cario: A. Métraux, "The Guaraní," in Steward, *op. cit.*, 3:69–94, pp. 76–77, 93–94.

9. Guaraní of Paraguay, *loc cit.*, pp. 78–79; see also Egon Schaden, *Aspectos Fundamentais da Cultura Guaraní* (São Paolo: Boletin 188, Universidad de São Paolo, 1954).

10. Tupí-Tupinamba: A. Métraux, "The Tupinamba," in Steward, *op. cit.*, 3:95–133, p. 131.

11. Tupinambarana, Métraux, *loc. cit.*, pp. 98–99.

12. On the butterfly soul: Métraux, *Guaraní*, p. 92.

13. Apapocuva Guaraní: R. H. Lowie, "The Tropical Forest: An Introduction," in Steward, *op cit.*, 3:1–56, pp. 42, 47.

14. Chiriguano: A. Métraux, "Tribes of the Eastern Slopes of the Bolivian Andes," in Steward, *op. cit.*, 3:465–506, pp. 465–66.

15. On "Candir," A. Métraux, "Tribes of Eastern Bolivia and the Madeira Headwaters," in Steward, *op. cit.*, 3:381–454, pp. 436–37.

16. On the Chiriguano messiah's promise that white guns "spit water," Métraux, *Tribes of the Eastern Slopes*, p. 468.

17. C. Nimuendajú, "The Tucuna," in Steward, *op. cit.*, 3:713–25, pp. 724–25; see also "The Tucuna," *University of California Publications in American Archeology and Ethnology*, 45, 1952, for the apparition of "immortals" to pubescent boys and girls.

18. Popé of Tewa Pueblo: James Mooney, *Ghost Dance*, pp. 659–60.

19. Delaware: Mooney, pp. 662–69; A. F. C. Wallace, "New Religions among the Delaware," *Southwestern Journal of Anthropology*, 12 (1956) 1–21. The Delaware Prophet's encountering two blockades before safe passage is like the "magic flight" legend in reverse.

20. William James, *Varieties of Religious Experience;* cf. J. H. Leuba, *Psychology of Religious Mysticism*.

21. George Devereux, *Normal and Abnormal*, pp. 3–32.

22. S. Freud, "The Uncanny," *Collected Papers* (London: Hogarth Press, 1934, 4:368–407; also Rieff edition, New York: Collier Books AS583V, 1963, pp. 19–60).

23. John McCullough, in Mooney, *op. cit.*, p. 668.

24. Francis Parkman, *The Conspiracy of Pontiac* (Boston: Little, Brown & Co., 10th ed. rev., 2 vols., 1886).

25. A. F. C. Wallace, "Cultural Composition of the Handsome Lake Religion," *Bulletin, Bureau of American Ethnology*, 180 (1961) 139–57; M. H. Deardorff, "The Religion of Handsome Lake: Its Origin and Development," *loc. cit.*, 149 (1951) 79–107; and A. C. Parker, "The Code of Handsome Lake," *New York State Museum Bulletin* 163, Albany, 1913. On Hiawatha as a visionary, A. F. C. Wallace, *Dekanawideh Myth*.

26. On the Mohawk as "high steel" workers, Morris Freilich, "Cultural Persistence Among the Modern Iroquois," *Anthropos*, 53 (1958) 473–83.

27. Mooney, *op. cit.*, pp. 670–80.

28. James Wofford, in Mooney, *op. cit.*, pp. 676–77, on the Cherokee movement to the Great Smokies.

29. John Tanner, in Mooney, *op. cit.*, pp. 677–79.

30. Mooney, *op. cit.*, pp. 681–91.

31. Mooney, *op. cit.*, p. 692.

32. Mooney, *op. cit.*, 692–700.

33. Mooney, *op. cit.*, 700–1.

34. L. Spier, *The Prophet Dance of the Northwest and its Derivatives: The Source of the Ghost Dance* (Menasha: General Series in Anthropology, 1, 1935); "The Ghost Dance of 1870 among the Klamath of Oregon," *University of Washington Publications in Anthropology*, vol. 2, no. 2, 1927; A. H. Gayton, "The Ghost Dance of 1870 in south-central California," *University of California Publications in American Archeology and Ethnology*, vol. 8, no. 3, 1930; D. F. Aberle, "The Prophet Dance and Reactions to White Contact," *Southwestern Journal of Anthropology*, 15 (1959) 74–83. See also Jaime de Angulo and L. S. Freeland, "A New Religious

Movement in North-Central California," *American Anthropologist,* 31 (1929) 265–72; Cora Du Bois, *The Feather Cult of the Middle Columbia* (Menasha: General Series in Anthropology, 7, 1937); R. F. Heizer, "A California Messianic Movement of 1801 among the Chumash," *American Anthropologist,* 43 (1941) 128–29; E. M. Loeb, "The Western Kuksu Cult," *University of California Publications in American Archeology and Ethnology,* 33, ❋1, 1932; *idem,* "The Eastern Kuksu Cult," *loc. cit.,* 33, ❋2, 1933; Philleo Nash, "The Place of Religious Revivalism in the Formation of the Intercultural Community on Klamath Reservation," in F. Eggan (ed.), *Social Anthropology of North American Tribes* (Chicago: University of Chicago Press, 1937, pp. 375–449); Wayne Suttles, "The Plateau Prophet Dance among the Coast Salish," *Southwestern Journal of Anthropology,* 13 (1957) 352–96; and T. Stern, "A Umatilla Prophet Cult: An Episode in Culture Change," in A. F. C. Wallace, *Men and Cultures.*

35. V. F. Ray, "The Kolaskin Cult, a Prophet Movement of 1870 in Northeastern Washington," *American Anthropologist,* 38 (1936) 67–75.

36. On Suipuken, George Gibbs in Spier, *Prophet Dance,* p. 9. Such shamanly sexuality, on the evidence of the Cogul Dance and all the shamanistic fertility figures of the Old World, may be very old indeed, since they appear in Africa, Europe and Asia, and even in Oceania as a pattern.

37. Modoc, David Thompson in Spier, *Prophet Dance,* p. 18. This Pacific Coastal region, of course, is one of the major earthquake regions of the world, which may account in part for Okanagon and Modoc apprehensiveness.

38. Smohalla, Mooney, *op. cit.,* pp. 708–11, and 716–31. Another view of the Smohalla-Chief Moses conflict is to be found in R. H. Rusby and John A. Brown, *Half-Sun on the Columbia: A Biography of Chief Moses* (Norman: University of Oklahoma Press, 1965).

39. Mooney, *op. cit.,* pp. 708, 710.

40. Mooney, *op. cit.,* pp. 716, 721.

41. Chief Joseph and the Nez Percé War, Mooney, *op. cit.,* 711–15.

42. Mooney, *op. cit.,* p. 715.

43. On the "Messiah Cult" and the Shakers, Spier, *Prophet Dance,* pp. 14, 30–49. See also H. G. Barnett, *Indian Shakers: A Messianic Cult of the Pacific Northwest* (Carbondale: University of Southern Illinois Press, 1957); Marian W. Smith, "Shamanism in the Shaker Religion of Northwest America," *Man,* 54 (1954) 119–22; J. Collins, "The Indian Shaker Church: A Study of Continuity and Change in Religion," *Southwestern Journal of Anthropology,* 6 (1950) 399–411; and Erna Gunther, "The Shaker Religion of the Northwest," in Marian W. Smith (ed.), *Indians of the Urban Northwest* (New York: Columbia University Press, 1949, pp. 37–76).

VII

The Ghost Dance

THE TWO Ghost Dance movements represent the final catastrophe of Indian cultures in the United States.[1] Both were part of a returning wave of crisis cults spreading eastward from the Prophet Dance of the Far West. The first Ghost Dance, that of 1870, came with Tävibo[2] or "White Man," a Paiute (Paviotso) from Walker Valley, south of Virginia City, Nevada. White Man was gifted with invulnerability to weapons. He also had visions, and for this reason he was visited by many Bannock, Shoshoni and other tribes of Nevada, Oregon and Idaho. Earlier he had gone into the mountains, where he met the Great Spirit, who told him all the whites would be swallowed up in a great earthquake, leaving, however, all their houses, goods and stores. When many people scoffed at the notion of so discriminating an earthquake, he went up the mountain again for further revelation. This time he announced that both Indians and whites would be engulfed, but after three days the Indians and the game, the fish and the pine nuts would all come back, though the whites would be gone forever.

Some people still did not believe. So, after fasting, he went up the mountain a third time. The Great Spirit, incensed at the unbelief in his prophet, would now resurrect only the faithful, leaving unbelieving Indians to be damned with the whites. Some Utah Indians heard of the excitement and took Tävibo's dance home with them. They performed it properly, in a circle round a central fire, but their eschatology stated that all the reborn dead would have white skins. Another faith in Utah modified their theology somewhat. Mormons have a doctrine that Indians are descendants of the "Ten Lost Tribes" of the Hebrews, some of whom were still held icebound in the far north, but would some day rejoin their brethren to the south. Hearing the Indian revelation, and believing it to be an imminent fulfillment of Mormon prophecies, Orson Pratt preached a famous sermon, urging believers to set their houses and affairs in order so as to be ready to receive the promised wanderers. At the same time, many Bannock were induced by promises of the free rations to leave Idaho, join their new protectors, and be baptized as Mormons in Utah. In this way two revelationary sects were syncretized.

With the Gadsden Purchase in 1853, the Americans were filling out the last corner of their country. In a now almost predictable response, in early 1881, an Apache shaman named Nakaídoklíni[3] began his mission in southern Arizona, which was part of the Purchase. He communed with the spirits and could raise the dead. He predicted that the whites would be driven from the land. His dance was novel. In eight radial lines, the dancers wheeled around a hub where the prophet stood and sprinkled them with sacred pollen, the latter in the old pattern of the Southwest. In the summer of 1881, Nakaídoklíni said, he would bring back two chiefs, killed a few months before, if he were given enough blankets and horses for his efforts. The Apache eagerly made these gifts. But even after much dancing the dead chiefs did not return. Their spirits were angry at the continued presence of the whites; however, the whites would leave at corn harvest time. Hearing about these prophecies, the Indian agent, somewhat alarmed, arrested the unresisting prophet in his camp. In a skirmish that occurred while he was returning to Fort Apache, many Indians were killed, Nakaídoklíni at the first shots fired. With this event began the Apache wars that lasted into the present century.

In 1883, a Potawatomi prophet,[4] visiting with some Winnebago and Ojibwa from Wisconsin, taught the Kickapoo and Potawatomi in Kansas a new cult, which later spread also to the Sak-and-Fox, Kickapoo and Potawatomi of Oklahoma. The Potawatomi prophecy was in part a revival of the Känakûk Cult of half a century earlier. But since it taught a morality not unlike the Ten Commandments—together with a prohibition of liquor, gambling and horse racing—and made the Indians cleanly, chaste and industrious, the agent did not interfere. These four Algonkian tribes, long in contact with the whites, were now slowly adapting to them culturally.

Not so easily did the warlike Crow of thinly populated Montana. In 1887, a Crow medicine man named Cheeztahpaezh[5] showed such fortitude in the tortures of the still-practiced Cheyenne Sun Dance that his hosts gave him a red-painted medicine saber. In sign of this honor, he then took the name Sword Bearer, claiming invulnerability to bullets. After he had made some threatening demonstrations, he was ordered arrested by the military. Theodore Roosevelt has told the dramatic story.[6] As the two armies approached one another, a sudden thundercloud appeared, and a single Indian in full regalia dashed out to ride solemnly twice around the mystified white troops. It was Sword Bearer, who had promised the Crow to bring a rain and turn the whites' hearts to water. A cloudburst came, and the whites retired to their camp. At the next encounter, to the intense annoyance of the white troops, Sword Bearer began his magic ride again. But some young Indian warriors could not be held back from provocative firing. The white troops replied instantly, and the fighting was over in a minute or two, with the Indians fleeing dispirited in all directions. Cheeztahpaezh had fallen. He was not invulnerable.

It was the Great Ghost Dance of 1890, however, that provided the crashing climax to the collapse of American Indian culture. Tävibo, the messiah of the Ghost Dance of 1870, is said to have left a son when he died, a boy named Wovoka, "The Cutter."[7] Some students doubt the relationship, but the two messiahs did come from the same area. As an adolescent boy, Wovoka is thought to have witnessed the ceremonies in Tävibo's tule reed wickiup, and he certainly saw the many visitors from all over the West who came reverently to hear the prophet's revelations. Like many other Paiute, Wovoka worked for the white ranchers of Mason Valley in Nevada. He became attached as a ranch hand to the very religious family of David Wilson, from whom he learned some English and at least a smattering of Christian theology. He also got from them the name Jack Wilson,[8] under which he had an almost legendary fame all over the West. Even far-off tribes knew he was omniscient, spoke all languages, was invisible to white men, and was a direct messenger from the Great Spirit.

While still a young man, Wovoka became sick with fever in 1889. At this time "the sun died" in a total eclipse, and in a delirium or trance Jack was taken to see God. All the people who had died long ago were there in heaven, busy with their games and occupations, happy and forever young. God told him to preach goodness to his people and to practice war no more. They should dance a ceremony that God taught him, to hasten the reunion with the dead. God gave him charge of the West, while "Governor Harrison" would take care of the East, and God look after heaven. Finally he got five songs by which he controlled the weather, one each for mists, snow, showers, storms, and clear weather. He then had a letter drawn up for the President, stating his powers, and promised to keep the West informed of the latest news from heaven. He also agreed, for a small regular stipend, to furnish rain when needed. Jesus, he told the Arapaho and Cheyenne, was now back on earth. They should not fear the earthquake of the new world when he came like a cloud, either in the spring of 1891 or on the Fourth of July. His command was exact and exacting: Do no harm to anyone, Do right always.

At the news of the messiah, various tribes reacted variously. Since they would soon rejoin the dead, the Arapaho gave up shooting their horses and gashing their arms in mourning when someone died. To escape the flood, they should go to high mountains, leaving skeptics behind to turn to stone and the whites to be covered. On the new skin of the earth, game would once again abound. The Cheyenne said the Earth was getting old, grass and trees were worn out, and the people getting bad. Besides, the Earth was too small, so God was going to do away with heaven and remodel a bigger Earth for both living and dead. The Shoshone said a deep four-day sleep would come over all believers, and they would awaken on the fifth to a new world. Kiowa thought the new earth would slide from the west over the old one, bearing buffalo and elk upon it, and their sacred dance feathers would lift the faithful up onto the new world. Some Arapaho spoke of a wall of flame that would drive the whites back to their own country; sacred feathers would lift them over the fire and a twelve-day rain would subsequently extinguish it. The Walapai awaited a hurricane, the thunder of which would kill the whites and unbelievers. All these tribes believed the whites would be eliminated through supernatural means, and they bitterly blamed the warlike Sioux for later taking naturalistic means to this same end.

In 1890, the Sioux, under the influence of the medicine-man Sitting Bull, were greatly excited at the coming "return of the ghosts." The Great Spirit had sent the white man to punish the Indians for their sins. The Indians had now been punished enough and deliverance was at hand, but the whites had been bad ever since they had killed Jesus. Dancing would preserve the Indians from sickness, and the white man's bullets could no longer penetrate Indian skins. Red paint from the Paiute messiah was also widely used for this same protection. A deep landslide would hold the whites down with sod and broken timber, and any who escaped would become fish in the rivers.[9] The earth would tremble with the avalanche or flood. They must wear "ghost shirts" painted with the sun and moon and stars.[10]

Some Sioux danced around a sacred bow and arrows tied to an evergreen cedar in the center of the circle, in a fashion not unlike the old Sun Dance ceremony that the white men had suppressed in the Plains because of its common connection with war. Sweat baths were taken for medicine purity before dancing. No white men's clothes or decorations were allowed, not even metal ear-rings; trade beads, however, were equated with the old shell wampum or porcupine quill embroidery, and were not disallowed. Short Bull, who had been sent to visit the messiah, gave the revolutionary doctrine that men and women should dance naked, without shame. Other Sioux regarded it as innovation enough that men and women, placed alternately, should hold hands and dance together in the same circle. In fact, some conservatives held onto the diagonal ends of insulating handkerchiefs and did not touch hands, for in the old Plains rituals men and women danced in separate concentric circles.

The Sioux were the largest and strongest tribe in the United States, still numbering 26,000 in 1890. But they too had suffered from the coming of white pioneers. In 1868 they gave up by treaty all their vast territories west of the Missouri, except for a portion of the Bad Lands in South Dakota which was to be their reservation. But the great buffalo herds[11] were now vanishing under the guns of builders of the transcontinental railroads. Next, gold was discovered in the Black Hills, on their reservation, and they were promptly overrun by lawless white desperados. The result was the Battle of the Little Bighorn and the massacre of Custer's command. In 1876, they again lost a third of their remaining land, including the Black Hills. After this, one catastrophe after another came in swift succession. Within eight years the buffalo were gone. In 1882, a white corridor was desired through the heart of their reservation, and the offer of eight cents an acre was so outrageously unfair that even Congress objected. In 1886, an experienced Indian agent, a doctor, was replaced by an incompetent political appointee whom the Indians came contemptuously to call "Young-Man-Afraid-of-Indians."

In 1889, the Sioux surrendered 11,000,000 acres, about half of the dwindling land they had left. But payments for the ceded lands did not arrive. Seed and rations were promised that never came. Congress still failed to repay friendly Indians for horses requisitioned fourteen years before. In 1888, "black leg" among the cattle diminished their limited livestock. In 1889, crops were a failure, and there were terrible epidemics of measles, influenza, and whooping cough, all usually fatal to Indians. In the drought of 1890, crops were again a complete failure. At Pine Ridge all their chickens were stolen. After the treaty, and against express promises, beef rations were halved by Congress, two million pounds being withheld at Rosebud Agency, and one million at Pine Ridge. The dispirited, sick, and cheated Indians now faced starvation. The calamity was complete.

At the end of these disasters a colorful psychotic, Albert Hopkins, claiming to be the Indian Saviour, appeared at Pine Ridge with the "Pansy Banner of Peace." Nevertheless, frightened by the continued dancing of the Ghost Dance, some agents called for troops. When the unexpected troops suddenly appeared, the Indians became alarmed in turn. Short Bull and Kicking Bear led a large group from the southern reservations on an escape, or a stampede, to the Bad Lands, on the way to which they destroyed some loyalist Indian houses and captured agency beef. Sitting Bull, unreconcilable, sulked in his camp on Grand River. Sitting Bull was a shaman and chief of the Hunkpapa band of the Teton Dakota Sioux, and he had been a participant in the Custer Massacre. His group, almost alone now, still stubbornly continued the Ghost Dance. Buffalo Bill was summoned to induce Sitting Bull to come in peacably to Fort Yates at Standing Rock. But when Buffalo Bill arrived, this plan was countermanded by the military.

Sitting Bull was among those killed in the sharp skirmish that broke out when the white troops came to arrest him. Yellow Bird, a firm believer in the protection of the "ghost shirts," led a hopeless revolt in late December, and in a few minutes Hotchkiss guns killed two hundred men, women and children. The Battle of Wounded Knee was a vengeful massacre. Fleeing women were shot down, pregnant and with children in their arms, miles from the encounter and after their men had been killed. A few escaped, wounded, only to freeze to death later in a savagely cold Great Plains blizzard. Some half dozen babies, wrapped in shawls beside their mothers' bodies, survived. One of them was still nursing at his dead mother's breast.

This was the last time that any considerable body of Indians in North America ever sought to threaten their new masters. By the turn of the century the white man was everywhere, and the old Indian cultures were either disintegrating or gone. The basic sameness of "Ghost Dance" movements everywhere in the Americas is quite remarkable. The repeated similarities in New World movements may be ascribed to four causes: to contact-borrowing of the same European elements of belief, to old culture traits common in both Americas, to a diffusion of traits of specific cults, and to the general psychic characteristics of a basic human nature.

As to borrowing, in several cases there was explicit identification of the shaman-prophet with Christ, or at least colorings of the prophets' doctrines by Christianity—for example, the appearance of God to his prophets, the Mosaic commands, the prophet's death and resurrection, the apocalyptic end of the world and a new Heaven on earth. But these interpretations must be made with caution. Why, so often, were just these elements borrowed?—for, in general, alien non-material culture is borrowed rarely, with difficulty, and only after long contact. Further, a mechanical borrowing should not be too easily assumed here—for the shaman's contacts with the spirit world, the aboriginal concept of culture heroes, and the world-renewal beliefs in the Plateau and Amazonia, and perhaps elsewhere, might account just as well for some of these common elements.

As for trance and dreams and human nature, there are many questions to be asked first. What are the conditions, individual and social, under which these dreams occur and achieve historical group-currency? What is their psychological content, rationale and meaning? Why do these individual dreams affect group behavior as they do? And what are the personalities of these new culture heroes like? In many instances we do not have sufficient information to answer these questions properly. Although the New World movements afford many instances of similarities out of which some limited generalizations can arise, we need some additional test cases outside the New World for perspective first, before further discussion of general "Ghost Dance" phenomena.

A striking parallel to the Ghost Dance is found in South Africa, with of course no possible suggestion of influence by American Indians. One morning in May in 1856, a young Xosa[12] girl went to draw water at a stream, and there she met some strangers from the spirit world. She later took her uncle, Umhlakaza, to the place and he spoke to these same spirits there too. They announced that they had come to help the Xosa drive the English from the country. Many cattle must be killed as offerings to the spirits. To obtain the much-desired end, the disappearance of the English, Umhlakaza sent an order to his tribesmen to kill every animal in their herds and to destroy every grain of corn in their granaries. If these things were done, an earthly paradise would come. Flocks of fat cattle would rise from the earth, and millet fields would spring up ready for the harvest. The old heroes and wise men of the tribe, reborn, would come back to guide them and to share in the new general happiness. Sickness and troubles would be gone, and the aged would become young and beautiful again. Umhlakaza's order was carried out, and some two thousand cattle were slaughtered for the spirits. But the vision was false. In the famine following, so many people died that the Xosa tribe for a time almost ceased to exist.

Another striking case comes from another far corner of the world. At the end of August 1934, a Maori of the village of Waitarata, in New Zealand,[13] dreamed that the world was coming to an end. For a week the whole village prepared for the cataclysm which would send them to their ancestors. The dreamer who had seen the angel and heard its message was a hero to his people. His daughter felt the spell too, and announced she was the vessel of the newborn Holy Ghost, come to give them back the lands that the whites had taken from them. In the village of Waitarata, the Maori refused to do any work, and sat around for days, chanting, without food. Some threw away their money and would take no payment for goods. Some gave away their motorcycles, and even motorcars. Police investigation followed. Children were found naked and unfed and the people in a state of great excitement. Finally the visionary was declared insane and was sent away to a mental hospital, while a Presbyterian minister attempted to pacify the natives. It took two days to disperse the crowd that had come from fifty miles around to witness the world's end.

Still another instance comes from remote interior Asia. In July 1904, Chot Chelpan, an Altai Turk of mid-Siberia, had a vision. A man in white came riding on a white horse and spoke to Chot in an unknown language. Two riders with the spirit translated him thus: "I was and will be forever and forever. I am the chief of the Oirots, which I proclaim to you, for the time is near. Thou, Chot, art a sinful man, but thy daughter is innocent. Through her I shall announce to all Altaians my commandments."[14] Then, as his fourteen-year-old adopted daughter Chugul watched the flocks, two young women came, saying she must cause her family to leave the *yurt* that night, when they would come again. She told no one, but that night, nevertheless, her adoptive father felt a great urge to visit neighbors. Then two rainbows came to her and again the two young women, telling Chugul to make prayers to the household idols. But this she could not do, because of female disability in ritual among the Altai, whereupon the young women caused the idols to topple into the fire. When she told of this, the neighbors thought Chot's daughter mad.

But in a thunderclap the supernaturals returned, promised punishments on unbelievers of the sign, and foretold the imminent return of the ancient Oirot Khan. Chot then preached political unity under the new god Bur-khan to the Altai local groups. The missions of the Russian Orthodox Church had discovered Altai grazing lands were good for farming, with the result that many Altai, and especially those who refused conversion, lost their land through legal means or through outright seizure. Chot's formal prayer makes clear their feeling. "Thou art my Burkhan dwelling on high, thou my Oirot descending below, deliver me from the Russians, preserve me from their bullets." Because they feared an uprising, the Russians sealed the border with Mongolia, under rumors that thirty thousand Chinese troops would invade the Altai.

Chot's commandments are instructive. Do not smoke; but if you must, mix in two parts of birchbark. This injunction was influenced by the rigid Old Believers who came in the nineteenth century, but it was also directed against the Russian traders, to whom the Altai were chronically in debt. Kill all cats in the *yurts*—an oddly un-Buddhist act, but clearly turned toward pets, still rather rare, of Russian origin. Do not chop down living trees, and do not swallow the blood of animals (both old shamanistic rules). Every night and morning, sprinkle milk to the four points and to the sky. Set up four birches and juniper censers in the *yurts;* give a sprig of juniper in greeting, in place of the Russian offer of a pipe, saying *yakshi,* "It is good," not "What is new?" as Russians do. Burn the shamans' sacred drums, for they come from Erlik, judge of the dead in the west, here posed against Burkhan, after the old shamanistic dualism of east and west, birth and death, light and dark, good and bad spirits. Sup not from the same pot as a Christian or a converted Altai; call no Russian friend, but refer to them as *chichke put* or "thin legs." Bend your heads again to the northern white mountains as of old, for a day will come when you have a new lord. Once the Oirots ruled us; now they will join us to destroy the Russians. "Soon their end will come, the land will not accept them, the earth will open up and they will be cast under the earth." Spend all money on shot and powder, even Russian wares; and what is left, bring it to me. The sun and moon are both our brothers. Hang on birch trees five different-colored ribbons, symbolizing the five chief peoples and the five chief religions of the earth. Do not hide a kopeck from me; those who do will sink into the earth with the Russians.

At one time four thousand Altai came together to pray to the White Burkhan, with a great burning of drums and shamans' transvestite clothing. When the Russians came later to arrest Chot's family, he was gone, but they found three thousand natives facing east in prayer. Chot's *yurt* was razed, and he was later captured. His *yarlikchi* or disciples moved eastward to Mongolia, but for years the Altai shamans still feared the Burkhanists. The Altai even gave up vodka, using instead only *kumiss* or fermented mare's milk. Czarists still feared the movement in the 1905 revolt. The Soviets later regarded the movement as "revolutionary" until, in 1930, it was attributed as before to Japanese agents working through Mongolian lamas. Even in World War II, the western allies kept the Dilawa Gegen Hutukhtu, the Living Buddha of Mongolia, in Chungking for safekeeping, still apprehensive of the politico-religious movements in Mongolia. The fear is not yet abated as two politico-religious sects face one another at the Sino-Russian frontier.

Remarkable parallels to Ghost Dance movements come from still another historically discrete region, the Melanesian islands of Pacific

Oceania.[15] By the third quarter of the nineteenth century, Fiji, once the notorious "Cannibal Isles," had been nominally Christianized through the intensive work of Wesleyan missionaries. Meanwhile, the notorious "black-birding" for indentured labor had also largely broken up the old village social life and native economics, and had set the moneyed journey-proud "finish-time boys" against the village elders. Resentment against white exploitation and low wages was also rife, though at the same time the Fijians envied European goods and power. The ensuing Tuka ("immortal thing") cult of the 1870s and 1880s was led by Ndugumoi, whose spirit could leave his body and wander about the country. He took the title Navosavakandua, "He who speaks once," a native term for the white Chief Justice of Fiji, and announced the world order would shortly be reversed, with whites serving blacks and chiefs the commoners.

Navosavakandua's troops of men with blackened faces, wearing native cloth robes and led by "destroying angels," understandably alarmed the colonial whites. Navosavakandua said the ancestors would soon come again to Fiji, when the Mouroto Kula or "Glorious Paradise" would begin. Ancient lands and native rule would be restored, the old would become young and beautiful and everyone immortal, shops would fill with calico and canned salmon and other goods for the faithful. Unbelievers would die or serve believers or go to everlasting hell, and the whites—traders, government and missionaries alike—be driven into the sea. The twin hero gods, sons of the divine snake Ndengei and opponents of Jehovah, would return. The visionary prophet meanwhile sold holy water from the Fountain of Life, conferring immortality on his followers for a price ranging from ten shillings to two English pounds. He also assembled young girls into his Yalewa Ranandi, saying the holy water would keep them virgin there, though their parents later disputed this in tales told to the police (the seer earlier had been accused of molesting nuns). The Tuka leader was forthwith banished to Rotuma Island by the British, and his village was later razed to the ground.[16]

In these same years arose the Luve-ni-wai or "Water Babies," a group of young people who "made" food and did other tricks, through powers given them by guardian spirits from the forests. They drank kava, a narcotic root formerly reserved for the upper classes and the old, danced and sang, and when possessed by a spirit each took a flower name. In 1884, the leader Pita and forty-four others were seized at Serea and flogged. In 1890, some were sentenced to hard labor. The governor of Fiji started cricket clubs as an alternative youth activity, but these rapidly became ritualized, with "elders of the guild," a "Home

Secretary," and "Lord High Admiral," and with great stress on signals, books and codes and registers. This was not cricket!

New Guinea,[17] largest island in the world and still one of the least explored, is another laboratory for our study. In 1893, Tokeriu, of the village of Gabagabuna on Milne Bay, went to *Hiyoyoa,* the other world. When he returned, he prophesied a tidal wave that would swamp Wagawaga and other coastal villages, but believers would be saved if they banned tin matchboxes and pocket knives, and returned to stone tools and native ways. If they moved their villages inland, away from the whites, the southeast harvest wind would blow continuously, producing endless taro, yams, and other foods. A huge ship with spirits of the dead would come, and the faithful would be united with their dead kinsmen. Hundreds of pigs—the major source of prestige and native wealth—were killed and no work done, since of course easy abundance would soon reign. But after much unrest and disappointment, the Government imprisoned Tokeriu for two years in Samarai.

The "Baigona Men" of 1912, in northwest Papua, were led by a man named Maine. He had been captured by Baigona, sacred snake of the Keroro mountain, taken there, his heart extracted and smoke-dried, after which the snake returned his heart, taught him many mysteries, and sent him back to his village. The Baigona Men massaged the evil immaterial sicknesses out of men, not the old stones and splinters of former native cures. They had many taboos and had animal familiars, especially ancestor-spirit snakes. They could make rain, had trances and spirit possession, and spoke with tongues—often bitterly, it is said, against the whites, some of whom they killed by magic. The Baigona cult arose primarily in reaction to poor black-white relations after gold was found in Mambare, and its open rituals at least were stamped out by 1914.

In 1914, on the lower Mambare River, a native named Buninia[18] became possessed by the spirit of the Taro and announced a new ritual and easier agriculture. Men put their digging sticks and axes against his body to absorb power, and the hardest work afterward would be purely liturgical. Taro cultists got *jipari,* or shaking fits with clenched fists and jerking heads, received spirit messages, and did doctoring. These "Taro cults" arose again and again, despite constant repression. The British anthropologist Marett wrote dryly, "With the unfortunate precedent of Pontius Pilate, Government should be wary of applying police methods to new movements in religion."[19]

The Kekesi cult of Bia, "a notorious sorcerer and a most plausible rogue," began in the same year. Bia was possessed by the spirit of

Kekesi, who controlled the growth of food and lived at Mitre Rock near where Bia had his vision. *Kesi* was the name of Kekesi's steamboat, which would mysteriously bring them much white goods from overseas. This last feature—also present in the Manau, the "German Wislin" (Wesleyan), and other cults—has led to these New Guinea movements being called in general the "Cargo Cults," forms of which continue in the present time over post-war Oceania.

The importance of cargo ships in the Pacific islands cannot be exaggerated, for they are the main link with the outside world. Everyone becomes excited on the remote islands when at rare times a ship ties up at the sleepy ports to break the endless monotony of labor in the tropics, especially now that the inspiriting periodical native ceremonials have been suppressed and they have only the dour and cheerless cults of ascetic missionaries to solemnize. If alligator gossip is stale, and there is no new exciting news of sorcery, even the Government yacht is a subject of endless conversation and speculation. It goes everywhere, now to dash down the coast to punish a cannibal raid, and again to chase a Japanese schooner poaching on the pearl fisheries, to take stores to some far-off station, to lay buoys in the dangerous passage through the coral reef, to run suddenly to another island with despatches, and to bring in explorers and anthropologists to their jumping-off place to bid them good luck and good-by. The yacht is man-of-war, cargo tramp and passenger steamer, a court of justice and a Government House—for trials are held in her sleek saloon, and meetings of the local parliament are also held there. Indeed, the Australian Governor spends more time on the ship than in the Government House at Port Moresby. Her comings and goings are the subject of endless interest and gossip. Even the mail boat from Australia brings contact with the outside world only once every three weeks.

But the great cargo ships arrive mysteriously and unscheduled from far away romantic places. Black boys have been to some of the other islands, but never to the place where white goods are made, a homeland like heaven that sometimes the white people talk about with nostalgia and reverence. The great wealth and power of the whites is a mystery to Melanesians.[20] As far as they could see, whites did no work at all and made no artifacts, and yet got great stores of goods merely by sending out bits of paper, though meanwhile blacks must labor to produce gold and copra. The beings who made these goods became "the secret of the Cargo," for surely they could not be idle white men—perhaps the spirits of their ancestral dead in some unknown land. The cargo ships were their link to that mysterious country and the obvious secret of their power.

Sometimes cargo cult revelations were hostile to the whites. In the Sepik River region, around 1935, rose an anti-mission cult, with apocalyptic rumors of a Black King in the interior who had many hands and a skin of iron and stone.[21] One Marafi went to Satan in a dream into the bowels of the earth and saw the spirits there. They should worship Satan, for he would send an earthquake and a rain of burning kerosene to destroy his enemies, the whites. The blackfellows should build large refuge houses, for after the holocaust they would find their own dead returned with many cases of canned meat, tobacco, loincloths, lamps and rice, and rifles bigger than the whites'. No more gardening need be done. Marafi's Satanism smoldered under the police as late as 1936.

The most famous cargo cult, however, is the "Vailala Madness."[22] At the end of 1919, near Vailala in New Guinea, there began a spectacular new cult called *kavakeva* ("Madness"), *iki haveve* ("belly-don't-know") or, in Pidgin, "Head-he-go-round." This cult spread in the coastal villages of the Coral Sea, from Nomu to Oiapu and for sixty miles inland, with the swiftness and certainty of an epidemic disease. Whole villages were affected by it, even little children, and when it died down, as in the delta at Kerewa, an airplane flying over was enough to set it off again. Cult behavior was spectacular. An eyewitness of the "Vailala Madness" said the natives would take "a few quick steps in front of them, and would then stand, jabber, and gesticulate, at the same time swaying the head from side to side; also bending the body from side to side from the hips, the legs appearing to be firmly held." One young man continually rolled his eyes and uttered cries which the onlookers said were unintelligible to them. He would peer up into the *eravo* roof and perform other antics; he was not ridiculed, but was the object of a silent and rather frightened interest. One old man, reputed to be a diviner and sorcerer, "moaned and shuddered continually in a way suggestive of teethchattering." Another highly excited man shouted at the top of his voice like a missionary, and struck himself repeatedly on the chest, while his right leg trembled violently as if uncontrollable. One man, apparently hilarious, walked up and down panting, as the people watched him with a kind of gloomy uneasiness. The natives themselves described the Vailala Madness as "all-a-same whisky." In the little-known central highlands one student has found a narcotic "mushroom madness" and another a degenerative recessive-gene or virus psychosis, but the coastal "Vailala Madness" is entirely a psychic contagion, so far as is known.[23]

Evara of Iori, on the lower Vailala, a small brisk and intelligent person, was the first of the "Head-he-go-round Men." Evara seems to have been subject to epileptic episodes or trance states. One day, alone in the bush, he was hunting for birds with bow and arrow. His son Kivavia said Evara must have fallen unconscious, for he was gone four days, during which the villagers searched for him in vain, but at length he came to consciousness by himself and returned home. People thought that perhaps a *puripuri* witchman lurking in the bush had fallen upon him and magically ripped his belly open (wisdom and thought, in this area, come from the stomach, sometimes from ancestors, although the head can become dizzy). Many years ago, when his father died, he had had his first experience of the *iki haveve* or "belly-don't-know" sickness, but he lay on the floor of his hut and told no one then. Later, when he was much affected by his younger brother's death, the madness came on again. This time he told others in the village, and they all got *iki haveve* also. There was much bustle and brouhaha, and the news spread rapidly. When visitors flocked to see these happenings, they got *iki haveve* too.

The ideology of the cult seems to have grown by accretion. Much talked of early was an airplane that dropped message papers from the sky. One of these turned out to be an English pulp novel, *Love and the Airplane* and another was an advertisement of a well-known soap, the figures on which Evara identified as his father, deceased elder brothers, and his own dead son. The chief tenet of the cargo cult was that the ancestors and dead relatives were to visit them soon in a large steamship loaded with gifts of tobacco, axes, calico, knives, foodstuffs and the like. They were meanwhile to gather coconuts and sago to feast the ghostly crew, while the message was sent widely around. In early versions of the belief, the boat was filled with rifles, to be used to drive the white man out of Papua. Also current at the time were some vague ideas of "Papua for the Papuans," which the alarmed Europeans recognized as an absurd enough idea in itself.

In some places the ghosts were expected to be white. Chinnery and his party were taken for these ghosts when they entered a new village in the Kunimapa Valley. In several other cases, no doubt greatly to their embarrassment, white men were warmly greeted by a native as "father." Again, Laiva of Wamai said his father came back down from the sky, "hit his head" and knocked him senseless, and when he came to, there was his father standing as a white man. Other elements seem fathered by white men also. Some villages had a special hut called the "office" or *ahea uvi,* "hot house"—a "hot" man was one inspired by the Vailala

Madness—which was the rendezvous for cultists and the ghosts. In these "offices" they got messages from "Goss." Some also got messages down the village flagpole into their bellies, and thence out through their mouths. One trader saw a pumpkin placed on a flagpole and was told it was to be radioed to the ghosts in this manner as a gift. More recently, a visitor has taken movies of a large rickety airplane frame built of sticks and leaves, placed in a clearing on a hill as a decoy to attract its mate, a great plane loaded with cargo.

A major motif of the early movement was a tremendous interest in the dead. Indeed, the chief ritual was the making of mortuary feasts for them. Wooden benches and tables were set up for the feast and decorated, in imitation of white tables, with a clean loincloth table cover, neat beer-bottle vases and vivid croton leaf "flowers" in them. These feasts are obligatory to cultists, lest the ghosts visit sickness on them. Some say these meetings were not so much in imitation of the whites as a magic means and symbol of reversal of white-black roles. Some natives used as tablecloth their village flags, given them by the London Missionary Society to hoist on Sundays. In one place, a faded but still martial portrait of George V was displayed as *Ihova Yesu-muovaki,* "Jehovah, younger brother of Jesus." *Ihova* was the chief in heaven, and under him were *Noa, Atamu,* and *Eva* wife of *Atamu,* as well as their daughter *Mari* and *Ihova's* sons *Areru* and *Maupa.* Heaven was much better than this earth, with fine dirt houses and much white-man's-food like limes, oranges, sugar cane, watermelons and bananas, as well as sheep and *arivari,* a strange pig-cow-horse animal, probably modeled on a water-buffalo seen in Port Moresby. Everyone in heaven wore long ladies' dresses like the Catholic priests on Yule Island.

Kori of Nomu was the Paul of Papua, "more than usually keen and alert, perhaps more than usually cunning." He seems to have made certain innovations in Evara's cult of the dead. According to an old belief, the dead sent sickness, and to cure it diviners accused the sick of sins, which they then had publicly to confess. Taking the initiative himself, Kori went around to sick people in the villages and sharply accused them of adultery, stealing, or some other sin in turn until the sick man, discovered, confessed and killed the traditional pig in expiation. Some imitated the close-cropped hair of white men, and also the "fall in" of indentured-labor plantation-gangs and police lines; one dance which particularly frightened the whites was regulated by whistle blasts. Kori became a militant enthusiast and led groups to Maipuan villages even as far as Kaimara, where the overawed inhabitants looked on helplessly as he dragged out sacred objects from the *ravis* and heaped them on bonfires like a new Savonarola. A Moriavi man stated Kori's doctrine succinctly, "Throw 'em away, bloody New Guinea somethings!" Lai, a Christian *kavakevi* man of Motu-motu, was told by dead ancestors in visions that "the first-time men were bloody fools—no savvy anything," a clear enough doctrine, perhaps, but puzzling when submitted to the higher criticism of internal self-consistency, since the ancestors were the first-time men, now made equally fallible authority for new dogma.

All the sacred masks—made with "a wealth of skill, art and humour" the ethnologist Williams lamented—were destroyed. When he asked the reason for this astonishing behavior, the answer was this: the Head-he-go-round Men had said to do it, the missionaries had condemned their ritual paraphernalia, and nowadays there was too much work to do for the white man to have time for ceremonies anyway. They had a dull and drab prisonlike life now, a cult of ascetic puritanism. The old dances were "wicked" and some people even gave up their shell and feather nose and ear ornaments. Williams, sympathetic with the New Guinea blackfellow, wondered "whether he is not sometimes hustled by the scruff of the neck up the wrong path of righteousness." He felt that the routine and almost lethargic Purari Delta life needed punctuation with vivid ceremonies, and he criticized the plantation owners' suppression of the old dances:

. . . hold down or stifle these purely natural activities and you may have to deal with an objectionable case of collective hysteria . . .
One essential, at least, toward preventing further ebullitions of the Vailala Madness, or similar abnormalities in other parts of the Territory, is to give the natives some other or more wholesome means of satisfaction; and for this purpose it appears that, generally speaking, nothing can be more suitable than their own ceremonies.
There is no doubt that the Vailala Madness has been the principle direct agent in the destruction of the Gulf culture . . . Where it has touched it has made a clean sweep of the ceremonies, and has destroyed almost every treasure of religion and art. This is undoubtly the serious feature of the disturbance: compared with the wholesale destruction of native practice and tradition, the collective nervous disorder is [a] matter of small and transitory importance.[24]

White influence had been felt longest in the Port Moresby region. The majority of the Head-he-go-round Men had been indentured laborers and had thus had more contact with whites, as shown in cult theology. At the same time, the contempt of white colonials soon became contempt for their own native culture. Williams was deeply disappointed to find the cultural devastation that the Madness had left in its wake in village after village. He listened with disgust and amazement to the condemnation of old customs on all sides, finding it incredible that old men taught to think their main duty was to pass on old ceremonies to young initiates should come to despise and abandon them, and yet the demoralized old men would none of them defend the dishonored tribal customs.

It was a time of acedia and anomie, of truly Hellenistic despair and ennui. Bizarre innovations were conspicuous in the Madness. For one thing, women now feasted with the men, and their former disbarment from ceremonies was now regarded as bad and thoroughly out of fashion. Another item was a large and heavy pole, up to thirty feet long and six inches in diameter, with a knob at the end, used as a kind of vigilante battering ram of righteousness. This knob represented the head of a snake; in the Central Highlands at Kainantu some people had seen the ancestors emerge as white men from the belly of a giant bird and send snakes into the vulvae of native women to kill them. The snake-pole was kept on the porch of the *ahea uvi* "hot house" or inside the "office." Carried on the shoulders of the men, the pole moved of itself, like an ouija planchette, for the men merely went where the snake took them. It was infallible in detecting crimes like stealing, and it would batter at the timbers of a culprit's house until he paid the customary pig. The pole was treated like a person, spoken to, and exhorted on its way with cries of "Come on boy! Come on boy!" One inquiring white man experimented with the snake "pole's" ability to find hidden tobacco, but its success was indifferent. When the pole threateningly barred his party's way, however, it immediately obeyed his order, given on advice, to "go to bed." The use of the snake-pole against accused natives gave the Head-he-go-round Men much power in the villages. It was possibly inspired in part by the old *Baigona* python cult to the north, which also had a sin-discovering battering-ram.

White elements in the cult, such as the names of personages in heaven, are conspicuous too. Indeed, these easily recognizable elements may lead us to neglect the less known old native sources. In the ancient *sevese* ritual, for example, masked figures representing the dead were given great heaps of food, after which the masks and food were piled together on a fire lit by the maternal uncles of the dead, in a farewell to their ghosts. Though it was a mortuary ceremony and a feasting of the *ove* ghosts, its tone was gay, not sad. It was not only a religious rite but also an intentionally brilliant and artistic pageant, full of lavish hospitality, graciousness, and occasions for good will.

Another old cult was the *harisu,* half initiation rite, half fun-making game. Each harisu had a personal name and was a familiar figure that had appeared many times before. The *hahoedas,* hereditary makers, were rewarded with pigs by the *harisoas,* hereditary owners of the harisu masks, in this way stimulating both art and generosity. The invasion of the village by masked harisu is by prearrangement between the harisoas and the hahoedas, usually when a large enough batch of young men want to learn the harisu secrets. Some pretext for a demonstration is quickly found, usually by picking a sham quarrel. At this signal there is much bustling about, and in enclosures made in the bush the preparation of sheets of coconut fiber, sewn into headpieces with eyeholes burned in them. The young men collect banana leaves for clothing, and betel nuts for the old men. Then follows a kind of hilarious mock raid by the masked figures—the same young men who had told their wives before that they were going on a journey, and who afterward profess disappointment at missing the exciting visit of the masked figures. Then village criers announce the young men who have "seen the harisus," at which the women are alarmed because they think their men are doomed. But the initiates explain that although they did see harisus retiring into the bush, the payment of a pig will take care of the problem. "Seeing" means that the initiates have seen the harisu masks being made in the bush, the essence of initiation being the discovery that harisu are people wearing masks and not strange beings from the bush.

The harisu rite was a kind of masculine horse-play, frightening only the naïve and reassuring the sophisticates. It is evidently an old initiation ceremony transformed into a distribution of surplus food, about as dangerous as a reverse Santa Claus or Easter Rabbit make-believe, for the young men load the old men mask-owners for the fun of it with extravagant amounts of food and other gifts until the old men stagger comically under the wealth, and then they all feast on the donated pig. Another function of the harisu rite was to patch up petty but real quarrels by giving the ceremony, for at one point during it the supernaturals announce to men that they must give up private feuding. The women and children are supposed to believe in the bush spirits; however, women everywhere are generous and pretend to believe male nonsense, if it is fun. Williams thinks there is some confounding of *harisu* with *karisu,* the more or less malignant and fearsome remains of dead men, sometimes seen in human form flying about the villages or the graves. If this conjecture is correct, then the cult is not merely a guardian of morality and a fomenter of generosity and good will, but also an exorcism of ghost fear through boisterous make-believe.

But the Acting Resident Magistrate of the Gulf Division would have none of the Vailala nonsense. In one village he saw decorated flagpoles, and tables in the clearings ornamented with flowers in bottles, and, seated on the benches, with their backs to the tables, were numerous men dressed in clean *ramis* and singlets, some even in new suits of European clothing.

They sat quite motionless and never a word was spoken for the few minutes I stood looking at them. It was sufficient to raise anybody's ire to see them acting in such an idiotic manner: a number of strong able-bodied natives, in mid-afternoon, dressed in clean, new toggery, sitting as silently as if they were stocks and stones instead of being at work or doing something else like rational beings. They appeared to be fit subjects for a lunatic asylum; but they were breaking no part of N.R.O., and I simply dispersed their meeting with instructions to act like sensible beings in future.[25]

This was an odd attitude to take. For they were only imitating British colonials at tea.

It was not until 1937, however, that the Mambu movement[26] in the Madang District finally solved "the secret of the Cargo." The revelation of the Mambu cult was that it was their native ancestors, living in a volcano on Manum Island, who "made the Cargo." There the spirits worked hard, making things for their descendants, loincloths, red dye, bush-knives and mirrors, axes, flashlights, and all the other goods. But the whites had deceived the native people; the scoundrels took possession themselves of the cargo when it reached Rabaul. Mambu, who claimed invulnerability among his other powers such as getting rice magically by air, took the title "King long ol kanaka" or "Blackfela King," and a ceremonial feast of "Gudbai King" was given when he left any village he visited. He also collected "tax."

At thirty Mambu was still unmarried, "all-same mission-sister," though he had earlier been accused of invading a nun's bedroom at night (perhaps in the old Oceanic pattern of premarital "sleep-crawling"). Prayers for money were offered at ancestral graves, and village temples were set up. Baptism, however, was performed in Government rest houses, to symbolize the assumption of white men's privileges. Men and women initiates entered the rest house in pairs, where the woman's grass skirt and the man's loin covering were cut away, and their genitals washed or sprinkled with water.[27] Thenceforth only European-made loincloths and long "Mother Hubbards" were to be worn. The "nogud" traditional clothes kept the ancestors away, so these were discarded, heaped into two piles, and, after Mambu made the sign of the cross over them, ritually buried in the ground. Mambu was arrested in 1938, exiled, and sentenced to six months' imprisonment, but his movement broke out several times later.

The Mansren[28] myth of the *konor,* shaman or redeemer, of Geelvink Bay in Dutch New Guinea, began in 1867 and spread in several versions as late as 1942. Long ago, Manamakeri, "he who itches," was a wrinkled old man, his skin covered with sores, who loved *mareš*-tree wine. Daily, despite his age, he climbed the trees to change the bamboo cups and collect the sap. One day he found a thief had been stealing the cups. So he lay in wait and at length caught the thief—it was Kamuséri, the Morning Star! Much ashamed, the Star offered successively for his release a fish-producing wand, a wealth-tree, and a fruit that when thrown between the breasts of young girls would make them pregnant. But only when the Star also gave him a wishing-stick did Manamakeri release the thief. The beautiful girl Insoraki, surprised while bathing, became pregnant of his fruit, and a miraculous son was born who spoke at birth. Her kin tried every means to find the father, until at the age of three weeks the baby answered this himself. Horrified, the villagers abandoned them and moved away.

One day Insoraki, vexed by the hungry child, cried out, "Go ask your father for the flakes of his skin for food!"—and the magic staff filled the house with food. Manamakeri began to feel he did not suit his young wife, so he made a large fire and stood in the flames. His old skin fell off in the form of valuable brass gongs and armlets. But his skin color was too light, so he stepped back into the fire until the color pleased him. His wife was astonished at the handsome youth who came, and ran away saying she was married, but finally he convinced her that it was Manamakeri himself. He drew a *prau* on the sand, stamped his foot, and in this boat Mansren, "the Lord" as he was now called, voyaged widely with his family, creating many islands whenever the little boy wished to play on land.

Mansren cured everyone, but one mother doubted his ability to cure her dead child. Furious at this lack of faith, Mansren departed in his magic *prau* and has never been seen again. But the *koreri* era, "skin sloughing" as of snakes, would come with his return, the old become young, the sick well, and the dead return with much food, many women and ornaments. The Dutch Company would go away, taking with them forced labor and taxes and all work from the land. It was the hope of this millennium that inspired the many Mansren cults in later Melanesia. The anthropologist Moszkowski was once taken for Mansren because he doctored natives![29] The linguist Cowan has shown in detail the relationship of "snake" in Melanesian languages with words for "reborn," "revived," "alive" and "living" and the like.

The "Naked Cult"[30] of 1948, in Espiritu Santo in the New Hebrides, like several others, embodied phallic elements. It was also openly anti-white. Its leader, Tsek, preached a violent doctrine of no working for whites, the destruction of all European goods even if native-owned, the destroying of native artifacts, hut burning, and the killing of all pigs and other livestock. Two large communal huts would be built in each village, one for men and one for women, and each with a communal kitchen. All clothes and ornaments were to be cast away. Marital co-habitation at night was banned, and the sexual act would take place by day in public, such would be their purity of heart. Husbands should show no jealousy at open sexual affairs, and lineage endogamy (a form of incest in these lineage-exogamous groups) would be permitted. One authority has written that the Naked Cult deliberately cut across all family and totemic lines, since it was intended to break all existing social ties in order to unite people on the exclusive basis of the cult. When the cultist Ronovoro's wife died in the middle of a "sing sing," he accused a deaf old planter Clapcott of causing this. Five men then shot the planter, mutilated his body, and ate parts of it. In retaliation, the warship HMS *Sydney* shelled the bush, and seventeen natives were tried and six condemned to death, including Ronovoro, who died fear-lessly in the belief of his invulnerability.

John Frum,[31] of Tanna in the New Hebrides, announced in 1940 that he was the god *Karaperamun* of Mount Tukosmeru. Frum prophesied a cataclysm in which the volcanic mountain would fall flat into fertile river beds, Tanna be joined with Eromanga and Aneityum into one new island, and a new reign of bliss and plenty be restored. The whites would go and sickness vanish. There would be no need to care for trees or pigs or gardens, and kava-drinking and dancing would return. In the later form of the cult, young girls and boys, dedicated to new gods, lived together in a common hut, ritually bathing by day and dancing by night. John Frum was jailed for three years. His movement nevertheless diffused broadly, becoming later much confused with the coming of the Japanese invasion, and the final landing of the Americans with their fire-snorting earth-movers and their incredible piles of stores, both con-firming his prophecy.

The "Chair and Rule" movement[32] of the 1930s, in San Cristoval and Santa Ysabel of the Solomons, though aided by a friendly missionary (later deported by the white authorities), was much more secularized in its means and goals than were most other movements. It sought representation on the Advisory Council, increased wages, and Native Courts. The "Massinga ['Brotherhood'] Rule," erroneously called the "Marching Rule" or the "Marxist Rule," was increasingly an incipient political party, as the natives learned more about what was happening to them socially and economically. Not vain hope of "Cargo" but black political participation was to be the new "Rule." Under post-war American pressure, many erstwhile colonial Pacific islanders are gradually turning toward a native rule of their own destinies, and quickly learning new white symbolisms and institutions for the accomplishment of this goal. There are many fine points, perhaps, that they still need to learn about Caucasian categories, such as that beer bottles are not quite flower vases, nor loincloths quite tablecloths. But when at times their behavior seems bizarre, and even ludicrous, it is edifying and salutary to remember it is the white man that, in all earnestness, they ape.

NOTES

(VII The Ghost Dance)

1. On the Ghost Dance of 1890, in addition to Mooney, the major contemporary sources are W. K. Moorehead, "The Indian Messiah and the Ghost Dance," *American Antiquarian*, 13 (1890) 161–67, and "Ghost-dances in the West," *Illustrated American*, 5, no. 48 (1891) 327–33; Lieutenant N. P. Phister, "The Indian Messiah," *American Anthropologist*, 4 (1891) 105–7; G. B. Grinnell, "Account of the Northern Cheyenne Concerning the Messiah Superstition," *Journal of American Folk-Lore*, 4, no. 13 (1891) 61–69; Alice C. Fletcher, "The Indian Messiah," *loc. cit.*, 4, no. 12 (1891) 57–60; J. O. Dorsey, "The Social Organization of the Siouan Tribes," *loc. cit.*, 4, no. 14 (1891) 257–66; and Alice F. Chamberlain, "New Religions among the North American Indians," *Journal of Religious Psychology*, 6 (1913) 1–49. There are eighty-two post-Mooney references to the Sioux Ghost Dance in J. S. Slotkin, *The Peyote Religion* (Glencoe: Free Press, 1956, in his note 5 to Ch. II, pp. 100–3. Important for its context in non-Plains tribes: W. W. Hill, "The Navaho Indians and the Ghost Dance of 1890," *American Anthropologist*, 46 (1944) 510–13; and Alice B. Kehoe, "The Ghost Dance in Saskatchewan," *The Plains Anthropologist*, 13–42, Pt. 1 (1968) 296–304, has a new theoretical approach; see also A. Lesser, "Cultural Significance of the Ghost Dance," *American Anthropologist*, 35 (1933) 108–15. For its relation to another old Indian institution, see A. Lesser, "The Pawnee Ghost Dance Hand Game," *Columbia University Contributions to Anthropology*, 16, 1933; and for informed sympathy with native "culture shock," Ruth Hill Useem, "The Aftermath of Defeat: A Study of Acculturation among the Rosebud Sioux of South Dakota" (Ph.D. Thesis, University of Wisconsin, 1947), and Gordon Macgregor, *Warriors Without Weapons* (Chicago: University of Chicago Press, 1946). A minimal sampling of later Ghost Dance-influenced cults in non-Plains tribes would include S. A. Barrett, "The Dream Dance of the Chippewa and Menominee Indians of Northern Wisconsin," *Bulletin of the Public Museum of the City of Milwaukee*, 1, no. 5, 1911; H. F. Dobyns and R. C. Euler, *The Ghost Dance of 1889 among the Pai Indians of Northwestern Arizona* (Prescott: Prescott College Press, 1967); W. N. Fenton and Gertrude P. Kurath, "The Feast of the Dead, or Ghost Dance at Six Nations Reservation," *Bureau of American Ethnology, Bulletin 149*, 1951. And see also Milton Lott, *Dance Back the Buffalo* (Boston: Houghton Mifflin Company, 1959). David H. Miller, *Ghost Dance* (New York: Duell, Sloan & Pearce, 1959), is a popular work, not by a professional anthropologist, but it has the merit of being based on numerous conversations with old Indian informants.

2. For an account of Tävibo, see Mooney, *op. cit.*, pp. 701–4. Basic modern works: L. Spier, *Ghost Dance of 1870*, and Cora Du Bois, *The 1870 Ghost Dance* (Berkeley: University of California Anthropological Records, vol. 3, no. 1, 1939).

3. On Nakaídoklíni, J. G. Bourke, "The Medicine-men of the Apache," *Bureau of American Ethnology, Annual Report*, 9, 1892; and Mooney, *op. cit.*, pp. 704–5.

4. On the Potawatomi Prophet, Mooney, *op. cit.*, pp. 705–6.

5. Cheeztahpaezh, Mooney, *op. cit.*, pp. 706–7.

6. Theodore Roosevelt, "In Cowboy Land," *Century Magazine*, 46, no. 2 (June 1893) 1–283.

7. For Wovoka, see Mooney, *op. cit.* pp. 764–85; the Ghost Dance doctrine in various tribes, pp. 785–91; the Mormons and the Indians, pp. 792–96; the Ghost

Dance ceremony, pp. 915–27; songs and tribal sketches, pp. 953–1103; the Sioux Ghost Dance, pp. 796–801, 816–24; causes of Sioux outbreak, pp. 824–42; Sitting Bull and the Battle of Wounded Knee, pp. 843–86. For an important influence on public opinion, see Helen Hunt Jackson, *A Century of Dishonor* (Boston: Roberts Brothers, 1885).

8. Jack Wilson of the Paiute Ghost Dance is not the same man as Jack Wilson the promulgator of peyotism. The confusion comes from the fact that the latter, Nishkuntu or "Moonhead," a Caddo-Delaware, brought both Ghost Dance and peyotism to the Kiowa about 1890. On Nishkuntu, see references to John Wilson in La Barre, *Peyote Cult*, p. 260; F. G. Speck, "Notes on the Life of John Wilson, the Revealer of Peyote, as recalled by his nephew, George Anderson" *General Magazine and Historical Chronicle*, 35 (1933) 539–56; and Mooney, *op. cit.*, pp. 903–14.

9. That the whites would become fish has a peculiarly pejorative tone for the northern Plains tribes, many of whom had a disgust for fish-eating and a water phobia (David McAllester, "Water as a Disciplinary Agent among the Crow and Blackfoot," *American Anthropologist*, 43 [1941] 593–604).

10. On "ghost shirts," see Mooney, *op. cit.*, p. 789 and references p. 1118; the ghost shirt may have been influenced by the Mormon "endowment robe," conferred invulnerability, but was specifically repudiated by Wovoka.

11. Buffalo, which once reached as far east as the Alleghenies in the early 1800s, had already begun to recede in 1829 (Alexis de Tocqueville, *Democracy in America*, New York: Vintage Books, 1954, 2 vols., I, pp. 350–51); see also Mooney, pp. 149–50. For old warriors' imputation of the parlous Indian state as owing to the change from hunting to agriculture, see de Tocqueville, *op. cit.*, I:356, n. 12.

12. Xosa Revival, G. M. Theal, *South Africa* (New York: G. P. Putnam's Sons, 1894); see also W. M. Macmillan, *Bantu, Boer, and Briton: The Making of the South African Native Problem* (London: Faber and Gwyer, 1929, pp. 294–95).

13. Maori of Waitarata crisis cult, *New York Times*, 29 August 1934, despatch from Wellington, N.Z. See also F. Keesing, "Maori Progress on the East Coast (N.Z.)," *Te Wananga* [Wellington: Board of Maori Ethnological Research Journal] 1–2 (1929). "The Changing Life of Native Peoples in the Pacific Area," *American Journal of Sociology*, 39 (1934) 443–58; and "Aftermath of Renaissance: Restudy of a Maori tribe," *Human Organization*, 21 (1962) 3–9.

14. On Chot Chelpan, see Lawrence Krader, "A Nativistic Movement in Western Siberia," *American Anthropologist*, 58 (1956) 282–92; also Berthold Laufer, "Burkhan," *Journal of the American Oriental Society*, 36 (1917) 390–95. The "Big Candle" *Kugu sorta* is a similar movement (T. A. Sebeok and Frances J. Ingemann, Studies in Cheremis: The Supernatural (*Viking Fund Publications in Anthropology*, 22, 1956, pp. 320–37); Fred Adelman has a doctoral dissertation on a related Kalmyk Mongol "cultural renewal" (*Mss.*, University of Pennsylvania, 1961) to be published in the Sebeok series. That Chot Chelpan exhorted his followers to mix costly tobacco with birchbark reminds one of the American Indian *kinnikinick* mixture with willow or sumac bark.

15. The best summary of cargo cults remains that of Peter Worsley, *The Trumpet Shall Sound, A Study of "Cargo" Cults in Melanesia* (London: Macgibbon & Kee, 1957; also New York: Humanities Press, 1961) and his "Millenarian Movements in Melanesia" (*Rhodes-Livingston Institute*, 21 [1957] 18–31; also in *Bobbs-Merrill Reprint Series in the Social Sciences*, A-248).

16. On the Fijian *Tuka* cult of Ndugumoi or Navosavakandua, see Worsley, *op. cit.*, pp. 20–21; also A. B. Brewster, *The Hill Tribes of Fiji* (London: Seeley Service, 1922); A. C. Cato, "A New Religious Cult in Fiji," *Oceania*, 18 (1947) 146–56; and B. Thomson, "The Kalou-Vu (ancestor-gods) of the Fijians," *Journal of the Anthropological Institute of Great Britain and Ireland*, 24 (1895) 340–59.

17. The first report of Papuan crisis cults is that of E. W. P. Chinnery and A. C. Haddon, "Five New Religious Cults in British New Guinea," *Hibbert Journal,* 15 (1917) 448–63; these include the prophet Tokeriu of Milne Bay, the Baigona Men, *Kava keva, Kekesi,* and the "German Wislins."

18. Buninia's "Taro Cult" is reported by F. E. Williams in *Orokaiva Magic* (London: Oxford University Press, 1928, pp. 12–16, 30, 74); cf. Worsley, *The Trumpet Shall Sound,* pp. 22, 63.

19. R. R. Marett on Pontius Pilate, Worsley, *op. cit.,* p. 98.

20. "When your boots are obviously regarded as a miracle, your hat as a piece of magic—when a stray button from your clothes is cherished like the relic of a saint, and the back of an old letter out of your pocket is accepted with trembling joy—when your lordly munificence is giving away halfpenny sticks of tobacco, and your splendid generosity in bestowing inestimable fourpenny knives seem to drive the beneficiaries half out of their minds, it is hard not to feel that you are great and good to a degree that even you yourself had not previously suspected" (Beatrice Grimshaw, *The New New Guinea,* London: Hutchinson & Co., 1911, p. 252; see her pp. 204–5 on the emotional importance of the cargo boats).

21. On the "Black King" Marafi of the Sepik, Worsley, *Trumpet,* pp. 101–2.

22. The original classic is F. E. Williams, *The Vailala Madness,* supplemented by *The Vailala Madness in Retrospect,* in E. E. Evans-Pritchard, *et al.,* pp. 369–79. Important later works on the cargo cult include: R. M. Berndt, "A Cargo Cult in the East Central Highlands of New Guinea," *Oceania,* 23, nos. 1–2 (1952–1953) 40–65, 137–58, 202–34; and "Reaction to Contact in the Eastern Highlands of New Guinea," *Oceania,* 24 (1954) 190–228, 255–75; G. Hoeltker, "Der Cargo-Kult lebt noch," *Nouvelle Revue de Science Missionaire,* 18 (1963) 223–26; Peter Lawrence, "Cargo Cults and Religious Beliefs among the Garia," *International Archives of Anthropology,* 47 (1954) 1–20, "The Madang District Cult," *South Pacific,* 8 (1955) 6–13, and *Road Belong Cargo: A Study of the Cargo Movement in the Southern Madang District, New Guinea* (Manchester: Manchester University Press, 1964); G. Oosterwal, "A Cargo-Cult in the Memberamo Area," *Ethnology,* 2 (1963) 1–14; W. E. H. Stanner, *The South Seas in Transition* (Sydney: Australasian Publishing Co., 1953); and Helga Uplegger and W. E. Mühlmann, "Die Cargo-Kulte in Neuguinea and Insel-Melanesien," in W. E. Mühlmann (ed.), *Chiliasmus und Nativismus, Studien zur Psychologie, Soziologie und historischen Kasuistik der Umsturzbewegungen* (Berlin: Dietrich Reimer Verlag, 1961) pp. 165–89.

23. The ethnopsychiatry of interior New Guinea is complex, and at least four factors appear to be present, cultural, pharmacological, viral and perhaps genetic; see L. L. Langness, "Hysterical Psychosis in the New Guinea Highlands: A Bena Bena Example," *Psychiatry,* 28 (1965) 258–77; Roger Heim and R. G. Wasson, "The 'Mushroom Madness' of the Kuma," [Harvard] *Botanical Museum Leaflets,* 21, no. 1 (1965) 1–36; *idem,* "La folie des Kuma," *Cahiers du Pacifique,* 6 (1964) 3–27; Marie Reay, "Mushroom Madness in the New Guinea Highlands," *Oceania,* 31 (1960) 135–39, "Mushrooms and Collective Hysteria," [Canberra: Department of Territories] *Australian Territories,* 5 (January 1965) 18–28; and D. C. Gajdusek, Vincent Zigas, and Jack Baker, "Studies on Kuru III. Patterns of Kuru Incidence: Demographic and Geographic Epidemiological Analysis," *American Journal of Tropical Medicine and Hygiene,* 10, no. 4 (July 1961) 599–627, for a brilliant use of lexicostatistics to solve an essentially medicobiological problem. The best summarizing article is D C. Gajdusek and V. Zigas, "Kuru: Clinical, Pathological and Epidemiological Study of an Acute Progressive Degenerative Disease of the Central Nervous System among Natives of the Eastern Highlands of New Guinea," *American Journal of Medicine,* 26 (1959) 442–69; Gajdusek and Michael Alpers printed a "Definitive Bibliography on Kuru in New

Guinea" in 1966. See also R. Rodrigue, "A Report on a Widespread Psychological Disorder called Lulu seen Among the Huli Linguistic Group in Papua," *Oceania,* 33 (1963) 274–79; P. Newman, " 'Wild Man' Behavior in a New Guinea Highlands Community," *American Anthropologist,* 66 (1964) I–19; E. Cook, "Conflict Resolution and Hysteria: Another Instance of 'Wild Man' Behavior from Highland New Guinea," Paper delivered at the 34th Annual Meeting of the Southwestern Section, American Anthropological Association, Davis, California, 1966; R. Salisbury, "Possession in the New Guinea Highlands: Review of Literature," *Transcultural Psychiatric Research,* 3 (1966) 103–8; L. L. Langness, "Rejoinder to R. Salisbury," *loc. cit.,* 4 (1967) 125–30; and "R. Salisbury Replies," *loc. cit.,* 130–34.

24. Williams, *op. cit.,* pp. 2, 39, 57; also p. 40.

25. Williams, *op. cit.,* pp. 68–69.

26. The fullest source on this movement is K. Burridge, *Mambu: A Melanesian Millennium* (London: Methuen and Co., 1960), notable for its comprehensive bibliography. Very useful also is Ida Leeson's *Bibliography of Cargo Cults and Other Nativistic Movements in the South Pacific* (South Pacific Commission, Technical Papers, No. 30, 1952). For a world survey of crisis cults and theories about their causes, see W. La Barre, "Materials for a History of Studies of Crisis Cults: A Bibliographic Essay," *Current Anthropology,* 1 (1970) in press.

27. On Mambu genital-washing "baptism," Worsley, *Trumpet,* p. 106.

28. H. Pos, "The Revolt of 'Manseren' " *American Anthropologist,* 52 (1950) 561–64; and D. A. ten Haaft, "De Manserenbeweging op Noord-Nieuw-Guinea, 1939–43," *Tijdschrift Nieuw-Guinea,* 8 (1948) 161–65 and 9 (1949) 1–8.

29. On Moszkowski's being taken for Mansren, Worsley, *Trumpet,* p. 133; on Mansren, see also Worsley, pp. 126–27.

30. J. G. Miller, "Naked Cult in Central West Santo," *Journal of the Polynesian Society,* 57 (1948) 330–41; on naked cult coitus, Worsley, *Trumpet,* pp. 150–51.

31. On the John Frum cult, Worsley, *Trumpet,* pp. 154–55.

32. On Chair and Rule, Worsley, *Trumpet,* p. 171; on Masinga Rule, pp. 22–23 and 173, for which last see also C. H. Allen, "Marching Rule: A Nativistic Cult of the British Solomon Islands," *Corona,* 3 (1951) 93–100; and C. S Belshaw, *Changing Melanesia* (Oxford: Oxford University Press, 1954).

VIII
Crises and Cults

To LIMIT our study to Ghost Dances and Cargo cults alone is to risk generalizing only those traits these may accidentally hold in common. To find larger regularities we must seek further data, if we would wrestle with the problem of just how—given their spectacularly unrealistic and bizarre beliefs—such crisis cults could arise. If we judge correctly that crises cults rest on certain basic aspects of human nature, then they will not be confined to two mere culture traditions in America and Oceania, but must occur universally among men. Though Mooney, student of the Ghost Dance of 1890, elaborated no explanatory theory (beyond noting the economic débacle and hence realistic malaise of Plains Indian culture), he did have a lively sense of what constituted such reactive social movements historically. He shrewdly noted "parallels" elsewhere, in the Biblical period, Mohammedanism, Joan of Arc, the Dancers of St. John, the Flagellants, the Ranters, Quakers and Fifth Monarchy Men, the French Prophets, the Jumpers, Methodists, English Shakers, Kentucky Revivalists, Adventists, Beekmanites, Patterson-and-Brownites, Wilderness Worshipers, and the Heavenly Recruits.

Mooney's suggestion that Ghost Dance-like phenomena might occur also in the European tradition has been pursued in recent years. Coates, for example, saw in the English "Diggers" of the seventeenth century another movement like those Mooney had so astutely pointed to, and Kaminsky also perceived the Hussite Rebellion in this guise, as did J. L. Talmon social prophetism in nineteenth-century France.[1] Indeed, in a broad sense, the whole Reformation was a massively nativistic return to biblical Christianity, as well as a struggle for political autonomy. Wallace early argued[2] that in fact "all organized religions are relics of old revitalization movements, surviving in routinized forms in stabilized cultures, and that religious phenomena per se originated . . . in visions of a new way of life by individuals under extreme stress."

Indeed, to take a firmly secular view of it, Christianity itself was a crisis cult. Initially it was an ordinary politico-military revolt in the traditional Hebrew mold of secular messiahs, one of whom the Roman governor Pilate straightforwardly regarded as a rebellious would-be King of the Jews of the Davidic line, and executed in a usual fashion between two *lestai* or "brigands" as the Romans called the Zealot resistance fighters.[3] The alleged crucifixion of their messiah by the Jews themselves is historical nonsense, indeed quite non-textual, and obviously a tendentious later distortion by Christians. The fact has been obliquely but officially recognized as such in 1966. With a long tradition of secular messiahs, the Jews simply never accepted a supernatural Hellenistic one. But in subsequent centuries the failed secular messiah was transcendentalized in a new heresy of Judaism, Christianity, and the messiah blasphemously made God. This heresy drew also from a Neolithic vegetation spirit, the "dying god" of the Near East, the paschal scapegoat in a tradition going back to Abraham, and from the Essene sect as many Dead Sea Scrolls have shown. Christianity is the still cognitively troubled and imperfectly melded Hellenistic "ghost dances" of the Hellenic and Semitic peoples crushed by Rome. As Fokke Sierksma has pointed out, Christianity was a standard messianic movement in an acculturative context, with a royal court adopting an alien culture under the Roman occupation, with the usual gamut of conservatives, pacifists, progressives and revolutionaries, and with a typical prophet predicting the destruction and renewal of the world. "The religion of his followers was a typical *Plebejereligion* with social, political and religious aspects. Jesus standing before Pilate is just another messianic prophet standing before a District Officer."[4]

Within Mooney's generously conceived pattern, a great many other movements in our own tradition can be seen, by historical hindsight, to have been crisis phenomena. For example, the seventh chapter of the *Book of Daniel*, composed about 165 B.C. at the peak of the Maccabean Revolt, prophesies that Israel will overthrow the Greek empire and thenceforth dominate the whole world for all eternity—characteristically, of course, received in a dream-vision. Again, the *Apocalypse of Baruch*, written during the struggle of the Jews against Rome between 63 B.C. and 72 A.D., foretells (as do many such apocalyptic writings of the time) that the messiah will crush the power of Rome and of all other nations that had ever dominated Israel. He would establish an everlasting kingdom in which pain and disease, untimely death, hunger and want, strife and violence would vanish, and the earth yield tenthousandfold. The later sectarian Zealot Revolt of 131 A.D. had similar millenarian inspiration.

Adventism, the belief in the imminent return of Christ, was powerful in the Church as long as Christians were a persecuted minority. But the millenarian trend disappeared when cult and establishment merged in the Fourth Century, and Christianity became the official religion of the Empire—tensions only to reappear later, in more complex form, as heresies in explicit opposition to official doctrine. The great heresies were by no means the picayune hairsplitting of a few crabbed theologians, as they sometimes appear to the modern reader. The heresies symbolized and turned upon great political and social issues, and ordinary people not only were well familiar with the arguments but followed them with avid concern. Most interestingly to the psychiatric ear, the great heresies usually argued the metaphysical relationship of the Son and the Father, and the obliquely approached goals of many heresies have since been politically and socially accomplished despite still-official dogma.

The Crusades also contained some features of the crisis cult. The areas swept by mass hysteria in the First Crusade of 1095 had suffered ten preceding years of drought and famine, and five years of plague. Famines also preceded the Crusades of 1146, 1309, and 1320. Actually, famines were not normal in the fertile Low Countries and the lower Rhineland. Only three occurred in the eighty-four years between 1225 and 1309, and each of these was accompanied by a crusade or other popular mass movement.[5] Indeed, the Church itself, in Gibbon's eighteenth-century view, was a ghostly revival of the corpse of the Roman Empire, though grievously rivaled by another ghost, the Holy Roman Empire. And, in Italy at least, the Renaissance as well had many nativistic features in its fervent revival of the classic past, though the Humanist revival more often served the ends of secular than sacred culture.

The Savonarola movement in Florence, birthplace of the Renaissance, is an instructive example in our quest for understanding. The weak and unwise Piero de Medici had not followed his father's established policy of friendship with the French, whereupon Florentine merchants were expelled from France in reprisal. In the late summer of 1494, the French king invaded Italy. When Charles VIII reached the border of Tuscany, Piero lost his nerve and, in an attempt at appeasement, surrendered pivotal Florentine ports and fortress towns. The Florentines, who had long regarded themselves as a chosen people, were enraged at this humiliation and calamity. Their revolt, at first political, took a nativistic cult turn with the fanatic and ignorant monk Savonarola. The French invasion, he said, was the opening of the "fifth age" of the world, with the appearance of Anti-Christ in the person of the French ruler, and a coming conversion of all peoples to Christianity.

Savonarola preached that Florence, the center of Italy, was a chosen city where culture and piety abounded more than elsewhere. A new Charlemagne would come to rescue them—Charlemagne, of course, because the voluntary coronation in Rome of this medieval German emperor had laid the groundwork for papal pretensions, as well as for the long subsequent struggle of the Papacy with the Holy Roman Empire, both harking back to classic times. To his disciple Nesi, Savonarola was a moon-born seer, the god-man Thoth-Hermes, or the magic shaman of Gnosticism returned. The doctrine became loaded with the most recondite symbols of Christian millenarism now suddenly revealing themselves in Holy Writ, together with resuscitated Neo-Pythagorism, Neo-Platonism, and the Kabbala of Jewish mysticism. To this, Ficino added oracles of the Chaldeans, Hermes Trismegistes and Zoroaster, and the preposterous mélange became as confused as the later secular events of the revolt.[6] Savonarolism was far more than a simple political event. It was a churning up of a mass of antique autisms in the attempt to meet new crises.

One of the most extravagant movements in Eastern Orthodox Christianity came with the religious reaction of the plebian Raskolniki, "Old Believers" for whom the Czar became regarded as the Anti-Christ who had ruined the church as the vehicle of salvation. Like many other Russian sects, the Skoptzi also were millenarian. The roots of Skoptzi doctrine reached far back to pre-Christian mother-goddess cults of Attis-like gods in Asia Minor, perhaps also to Scythian shamanism in southern Russia. The teaching in the secret but highly efficient sect of the Skoptzi was that all men be castrated and all women lose their breasts. Selivanov, the messiah of the cult which ultimately numbered in the tens of thousands, was considered a reincarnation of Christ—and also of the long dead Czar Peter III, somehow mysteriously saved ex post facto from his assassins. The Christ-Czar would bide his time till he mounted the throne, presided over the Last Judgment, and ruled a worldwide kingdom of holy sexless beings. The Skoptzi can hardly be considered an instance of simple Marxian class conflict, for members of the sect included noblemen, state officials, army officers and rich merchants, as well as peasants, scattered all over Russia. It was in significant measure a revival of millenia-old self-castrating cults, only autistically connected with contemporary crises.

Nor was the Mazdak movement merely a reaction to severe economic conditions in the fifth-century Sassanid Empire, as a cliché of earlier scholarship would have it. Müller[7] has shown that its main dynamic was religious, in which Neo-Platonism joined with and revived still powerful Manichean forces in the region. Historians of religion appear sometimes to have a misleading bias toward discerning only majority-culture, perhaps because to believers the more conspicuous surviving culture is, by that token, unconsciously assumed to be simply "right." But even the most rigorous and relentlessly tyrannical orthodoxies do not make deeply entrenched prior cultures simply disappear—and Manicheism had been a powerful though repressed religious force, active from Spain to China, and one that influenced Eurasia for at least twelve centuries.

Manicheism is an ultimately Iranian dualism of light and darkness, spirit and matter, a dualism of at least Bronze Age Indoeuropean antiquity, which in the Iranian form holds that the material world is evil. Its influence is multiple and complex, and Mazdakism is often classed as a sect of Gnosticism, the bitter enemy of early Christianity. However, the Church, in being platonic, itself incorporates a subtle Manicheism that exalts the ideal above the real. At the same time, the Reformation attack on the Church is also in effect an overt neo-Manicheism in holding that the Establishment was intrinsically evil. Meanwhile, the repressed traditional Manicheism of the Bulgarian Bogumili, the Patarenes of northern Italy, and the Albigensians of southern France had stayed alive, even under the bloodiest persecutions and determined genocide, as a source of recurrent nativistic minority crisis cults, many of them with clear socio-economic and political components. There is also a Manicheist element in all the "Old Evangelical" pre-Reformation movements such as the Cathari, Waldensians, Hussites, Beghards, Beguines, and Anabaptists.

The Enthusiasts of the fifteenth century represented the last intellectual upsurge of Manicheism before the Reformation. Manichean ideology was especially well entrenched at a late date in the Scheldt and Meuse districts. During the time of the armed rebellion of the Anabaptists in Münster in 1534–35, a mass psychosis broke out in which people stared at the sun, in the quite Manichean belief that the Father sat literally in the sun. For a time, in fact, some Protestants feared that the Enthusiasts and the Anabaptists would absorb into themselves the whole Reformation, and take over the Lutheran inheritance entire.

In each new Church, Christianity, originally a religion of the oppressed against the state, is forever in a poor moral and intellectual position to oppress in the manner of a state. In arguing the pre-eminence of the ideal over any actualization, the built-in Platonist-Manicheist dogmas of the Church (themselves sufficiently absolutist) are, ironically, the eternal enemy of establishmentarianism as such. The philosophical-religious argument falls strangely otiose on modern ears, which listen to different myths. Nevertheless, "religion" was unquestionably the effective social language of these earlier centuries, an historic fact hard to credit when our equivalent myths are so obsessively economic and political. We have our own kind of holy wars, quite prepared to commit pious genocide for the sake of democracy and freedom. And some twentieth-century enthusiasts would willingly annihilate our species to procure the triumph of a preferred politico-economic religion. For that is what crisis cult thinking is like. And certainly some human sacrifice of innocents in holy war is noble and necessary for the transfer of power in each political revolution, not alone in Africa and Asia, for that is what power is about.

Crisis cults are by no means exclusively a phenomenon of western Christian societies. For instance, the revolt of the secret brotherhood of the "Red Eyebrows" in the Han dynasty was in part a religious movement incidental to land reforms. In the revolt against the Mongol dynasty, the cult of the "little Bright King" was a similar phenomenon. In the Manchu dynasty, the Taiping Rebellion and the Boxer Uprising were clearly crisis cults. It should be noted in passing that Sun Yat-sen, father of the Chinese Revolution against the Manchus, in his youth was in close contact with groups of Taiping Rebellion origin.[8] The Maoist "Red Guards" of contemporary Communist China, though as yet little studied or understood, appear to have cult elements in their movement as well.

Nor are crisis cults characteristic only of troubled modern times. In the Egyptian XIIth Dynasty (2000–1788 B.C.), a curious shamanistic prophet named Ipuwer delivered before the Pharoah a grim prophecy of coming political and social ruin, foreign invasion, and other calamities. But he also promised a saviour who would smite the evil about him, and be like a shepherd to the people. Other examples of this remarkable genre of Egyptian literature are common enough for Breasted[9] to suggest ultimate influence upon Hebrew prophecy and the messianic tradition of the Jews.

An ancient crisis cult is discernible in early Greece as well. Scholars are agreed that the aristocratic families in Greece were probably derived from the invading Indoeuropean warriors, the agricultural peasants and helots being relicts of autochthonous "Pelasgians." As a later reaction, the Draconian Law of 624 B.C. was codified from the repressive precedent-decisions of the aristocratic *boulé*-assembly of the archons, elective dignitaries who in 683 took over power from the archaic kingship. The mass of peasants suffered greatly under the regime of the noble Eupatrid families, and some of them even sold their children into slavery to repay loans. In 612, a popular athlete of the Olympic games, Cylon by name, led a politico-military revolt that failed, ending in his arraignment and severe punishment by the archon Megacles, of the Alcmaeonid family. The Eupatrids thereupon appeared still more odious; the people even considered the Alcmaeonidae an accursed stock. The whole country needed to be supernaturally purified. So they sent to Crete for Epimenides of Knossos, a holy man of the ecstatic type already familiar to Cretan families in Greece, to purge the curse on the country. Epimenides came and held excited gatherings not unlike modern revivalist meetings. These comforted the people to a degree, but left the severe Eupatrid rule unchanged. It was not, in fact, until Solon of the Neleid, probably Cretan, family became archon in 594 B.C. when the laws were reformed, land-secured debts canceled, and the coinage debased by 27 percent, that the worst abuses were largely removed. Greek history from Draco to Solon well shows the socio-legal situations of which crisis cults are so often a part.

Considering the conservatism of the dour and sober Romans of the Republic, it is remarkable that an alien oriental cult—and the most orgiastic of them all, that of the Phrygian Cybele, Lady of the Beasts— should be borrowed, the first to be borrowed, and officially into the bargain. At the end of the third century B.C., during the Second Punic War when Hannibal was still on Italian soil, the ancient Sibylline shaman-esses put forth the prophecy that only the presence of the Mighty Mother in Rome would end the lengthening list of omens that terrified the people. Perhaps it is not surprising that shamanesses would summon the Mistress of the Animals (*Potnia theron*), though it is less to be expected they would be obeyed in this severely patriarchal society. But an emer-gency is an emergency, and drastic measures were needed. After some negotiations, and for a price, Attalus I of Pergamum was persuaded to send from Pessinus the black meteorite in which the Earth Mother dwelt. When in due course the Carthaginian menace was averted through victory in the Punic War, the Romans built a temple to Cybele on the Palatine Hill itself, and every April thereafter celebrated the Megalensia to honor the anniversary of her arrival.[10]

The legendary German *Götterdämmerung* also resembles the Ghost Dance phenomenon, even to its ideology of the old age of the earth and the passing of pagan deities. The Twilight of the Gods was ultimately a nativistic legend echoing the coming of Christianity to northern Europe. Nor need the same ethnic group necessarily evolve a crisis cult once only; the more chauvinist a people, the oftener its narcissism is piqued. Erich Heller[11] writes nostalgically of the Götterdämmerung of the Germanic Holy Roman Empire itself, the decline and fall of the vast, untidy and baroque Austro-Hungarian Empire, corrupted by its sense of drama, essential *Schlamperei,* and childlike faith in its own eternity —preparing the scene for an activist Hitler, unprincipled exploiter of the moral relativism revealed. In the retrospective eye of history, Nazism was yet another nativistic cult, complete with xenophobic myth and a paranoid messiah. What is not widely known in America, though, is the *Welteislehre* or "World Ice Doctrine" of the Austrian engineer Hanns Hörbiger. This archaistic psychotic system was actually offered to Hitler to be the official "Nordic" science of cosmology.[12] The Führer, however, sharply rebuffed the suggestion. The same ground was already occupied functionally by his own autism, and evidently one Austrian messiah at a time was enough.

Perhaps the intense chauvinism and extreme xenophobia of post-war France, its hint of messianism, and its attempt to recapture the *gloire* of the vanished past would place *degaullisme* among those movements that Linton has called "nativistic."[13] The traumata of 1870, 1914–1918, and the capitulation to Vichyism are of course part of this too. Somewhat similarly, post-Revolutionary Russia went through a long paranoid period of suspiciousness and exclusiveness, from which Russia happily now gives some signs of emerging. And, not to be jingoistically invidious, more than one American critic has suggested that our own country sometimes seems to have a view of its role and destiny that partakes of the nativistic and the messianic.

Many of the terminologists and most of the taxonomists noted in my summarizing article on crisis cults in the February 1970 *Current Anthropology,* by implication at least in their very terms and typologies, have contended with the complex problem of causality. In keeping with contemporary constructs, the preferred etiological myth is political. Lanternari,[14] for one, would see all crisis cults as protests against European colonial imperialism. But peyotism, which he lists, was never an antigovernmental uprising or separatist national movement. Admittedly, political elements are often prominent in the Congo cults, the Nyasaland millenia, the later Melanesian cargo cults, and in some Indonesian movements.[15] Similarly, the "Islam" movement has been seen by some in the guise of "religious nationalism" although its more important dynamic is surely the grave socio-economic deprivation of the Negro Amer-

ican. Again, the Jamaican *Ras Tafari* movement[16] was significantly political, since the "living god" Haile Selassie, the "invincible Emperor" of
the "heaven" of Ethiopia, was to receive the black "Israelites" exiled to
the West Indies (as earlier in Egypt and Babylon) for their transgressions,
and the wicked white men of the Jamaican "hell" would then be dominated by the racially "superior" blacks. But the very description shows
this to be more than merely political. Sometimes it depends only on what
one is accustomed to consider more "real," politics or religion.

If causality were purely political, then crisis cults would be simple
secular activity within the establishment. But this oversimplifies too. As
a case in point, the *Pau Cin Hau* movement[17] in the northern Chin Hills
of Burma was an apparent response to British political domination. But
in origin it antedated even the first missionary penetration. Its dynamic,
in fact, is curiously endogenous. Pau Cin Hau is based almost entirely
on indigenous religion, and yet it modified the chief feature of Chin
social structure, the achievement of status through expensive feast giving
—surely an internal economic matter rather than an external political
one. Again, the Karen had a strong "national" selfconsciousness and
hoped for a Karen king to liberate them from Burmese domination,
and even to a degree from their most useful allies and protectors, the
British. One prophet was even a sort of quisling just before the Japanese
invasion. But those who heeded him were actually the least affected
politically, the more primitive Karen in the Toungoo Hills and the
remoter parts of the Irrawaddy delta. The *Telakhon* sect drew mainly
on traditional Theravada Buddhist doctrine, and despite the *Klipobah,
Ko San Ye, Saw Johnson Po Min* and other movements, most Karen were
strongly loyal to the British government. So political causality can
scarcely be primary here either.

The rebellious Maya, it is true, aimed to restore the absolute rule of
their native *caciques,* with revived memories of their first revolt in 1540
against the conquistador Montejo. In fact, politically they were finally
successful since, in the peace settlement, Indian leaders were given
complete control over the East Central Territory of Quintana Roo—but
only because, in an earlier moment of near defeat, the "returned Christ"
Juan de la Cruz of Xocen, a Maya priest with the same given name
as the famous sixteenth century mystic, revealed the "Talking Cross"
which inspired them to fight on for fifty years more. "Hoax" it may have
been from a churchly point of view,[18] but at last in 1914 the Maya
won the war, and their religion has remained to the present day. A
significant point is that the Maya had talking idols from pre-Columbian

times. It was on the basis of this critical and indispensable nativistic ideology that the political battle was won.

Chanjiri, the Chikunda prophetess of 1907, said that white men would have to leave her country and no more taxes need be paid. The later uprising of John Chilembwe in 1915 even tried directly to overthrow British power. But some at least of the ideological impetus came from the preaching of "Watchtower" Russellites or Jehovah's Witnesses that "gentile times" would end in 1915, for example in the Tonga tribesman Kamwana's adventist evangel in 1914 that self-government would come as the whites disappeared from Nyasaland.[19] Various interpretations sometimes depended only on the degree of literalness with which Africans took the chiliastic revelations of Christianity. In another case, the Father Cicero movement of Brazil at first challenged the Church hierarchy and then the political power of the state.[20] But it began only after a drought had drawn great numbers of sick and starving Indians to his shamanlike protection in the environs of his remote village—an economic factor before it became a political one—and Father Cicero himself seems merely to have been an earnest priest who took primitive Christian teaching too literally for the comfort of the hierarchy.

Worsley,[21] while not neglecting the traditional elements in Melanesian movements, provides a modulation of overly *simpliste* political causality. He observes that in the later stages mainly of Oceanic movements the rational politico-economic themes tend to overshadow the magical: on Biak, the liberation from alien rule, whether Dutch or Japanese, Chinese or Indonesian; on Santo, refusal to work for Europeans and hostility to missions; and on Malaita, demands for better social services, more self-rule, higher wages, and the like. The same is true in Africa, as evidence in Andersson and Shepperson would indicate. Fernandez also has emphasized the connection of politics and prophecy in new African religious sects, but he has been equally sensitive to the rich traditional symbolisms in the Fang *bwiti* cult, which includes the use of the drug "eboga" (*Tabernenthes eboka*) "to make the body light and to enable the soul to fly."[22] The German scholars around Mühlmann of Heidelberg see nativistic cults as only one kind of political revolution (*Umsturzbewegungen*); in part, also, do Justus van der Kroef and Norman Cohn, while Köbben sees prophetic movements as expressions of social protest, and Boardman as a complex of political history and psychology.[23]

Some "realists" profess to see crisis cults only as the adventitious trappings and superstitions surrounding the ultimate stern reality, war. But war may be viewed as the breakdown of political process on various levels, or as a mere extension of the power-seeking trend of politics. However, whether civil or international, war must have its energizing rationale in ideology, since war is ultimately the crass conflict of ideologies, or, more precisely, war is an attempt to annihilate an ideology by the simple means of killing off people who hold it. That militarists can see only one "right" ideology does not militate against the fact of its being an ideology—though militarists are often uncomfortably more right than we would like, when protesting their innocence of ideas. Again, for any ideology effectively to convince and propel men, it must have a secure base in (however unexamined) established culture complexes. Ideology does not appear on fiat like a military order, nor can it be plotted "rationally" like a military campaign. In any case, one might hesitate to kill people unless he knew it was for their own good.

The obsession with command power in war blinds such theorists to the prepotent encompassing power of culture, as an already "prepared position." For example, the Pueblo Revolt of 1680 was certainly successful in the military sense, since within a few months all Spaniards in Nuevo Mejico were slaughtered or driven out—but only because the medicine-man Popé made a successful social invention, intertribal co-operation, a political "technology" based on Pueblo structure perhaps, but otherwise new to the region intertribally. Again, Chief Joseph of the Nez Percé and Sitting Bull of the Sioux both had resounding military successes initially. But in the long run they failed precisely because their politico-economic base was competitively inferior to that of the young United States.

The Xosa prophetess announced that the spirits of the ancestors would join rank with the living warriors to drive the English from the land. But the military aspect of this movement lost itself in fatal autism. Every animal in the herds and every grain in the storehouses had to be destroyed before the earthly paradise would emerge, the land filled with beautiful new cattle and selfsown millet, the ancient heroes and counselors return, eternal youth be restored to the old, and trouble and sickness come no more. But in the subsequent famine, the tribe for a time almost ceased to exist. A point to remember is that, in purely military terms, Chaka of the Zulu had been sufficiently powerful to dominate most of the eastern half of Africa. But his system did not embody Xosa economic autism, and he exploited astutely a cultural potential, the partly military age-class systems of the east Africans. The "Marching Rule" of the British Solomons also clearly passed into a politico-military movement. But it was initially acculturative and syncretic rather than antagonistic, with an almost ludicrous imitating of the British bureaucracy and military structure. The "Massinga Rule" was neither "marching" nor "Marxian" (as the European planters feared) but came from the Ariari *masia,* "brother" or "young shoot of the taro," (as Worsley believes),[24] in any case ecumenical or economic, not military.

A recurring irony in some military skirmishes is white misunderstanding of native misunderstanding of European religion. In Buka, for example, the native Pako renounced paganism and magic, built himself a European-style house, and embraced Christianity. He preached that Melanesian blacks were to be the Christian equals of colonial whites, and that human spirits were immortal—only to have the reverential ancestor-cult, focused on village burial grounds, rigorously repressed. The government exiled Pako and two others to Rabaul, where he later died. The natives insisted, despite the missionaries, that his immortal spirit had returned to his old house at Malasang, burned to ashes by the authorities. Evidently Christian egalitarianism and immortality were not meant for the blacks, or at least they should not take it so literally.

Only then did assiduous drilling with sticks begin, to be used until better weapons came. The earlier Mandate Germans would return and teach the cargo-secrets kept from them by the missionaries and the government—but at this moment, such is the unpredictablity of history, the Japanese invasion came instead. Earnest syncretizing continued resilient. The ancestor cult of the Japanese was found to be more compatible with the Melanesian one than Christianity had been. The military shipments of the Japanese even confirmed the arrival of "cargo." In time, however, cross-cultural misunderstanding was renewed. The Japanese captured and tortured the leaders, three of whom were executed and the rest imprisoned.[25]

Certainly the *ngunzism* of Kimbangu in the Congo contained militaristic anti-white trends. But these seem not to have been present originally. They were in part elicited by the whites' alarm at the "militant phraseology" of the Salvation Army-inspired blacks, including their interpretation of "Onward Christian Soldiers." Police confiscated from the Bembe several man-loads of *cinqui,* small coins worth about a quarter, out of the distorted notion that these were to be melted down for German cannon. But these were merely individual fees collected in a Bembe purification ceremony. Other punishments also seem unduly severe. In the Sundi-Ladi movement under Matswa André, four men got three years imprisonment and ten years exile—but the money they collected was intended merely to aid African students then in economic difficulty in Paris. After this, the exasperated people tried to storm the court buildings, but they were put down.[26]

Tribesmen flocked to the English-Baptist Kimbangu, who had "found the god of the blacks," originally because of his awesome reputation for faith-healing learned from the whites. His harsh treatment by the authorities and deportment to Katanga in 1921, after a military affray in which a child on its mother's back was killed, doubtless stimulated anti-white resentment, as well as did the rumor that Kimbangu himself had been shot. In the 1930s, perhaps understandably, Yoane Mvubi, after a three-day visit to heaven, preached that prison doors, then confining many native leaders, would open at the same time that ships bearing new kings came to Kinshasa from America.[27] Governmental and police officials seem particularly prone to scent military significance in native cults, sometimes because their own acts produce self-confirming prophecies. But it must be agreed that the Hauhau, Te Whiti, Rua and Kingites of the Maori New Zealanders might have generated military potential in time, as also in the case of the revolt of Mansren, the Runovoro outbreak in the New Hebrides, the later Marching Rule, and many Salvation Army movements in Africa.

One must admit that real revolutionary potential may lurk behind the smokescreen of cult ambiguities. In the Jamaican "Ras Tafari" movement, there was much noise among members and nonmembers of Locals of the Ethiopian World Federation, Incorporated; literalists about the Emperor of Ethiopia, and those who saw only racial-political slogans and symbols; those totally alienated from Jamaican society, Marxists and Nyabini violent activists, and pacifist opponents of them all; those with beards and long hair or plaited hair, and those with none of these; cult users of the drug *ganja* (hashish or marijuana), and abstainers; with further cleavages among the rural and urban, older and younger, employed and unemployed, and organizers versus laissez-faire passivists. In 1959, in what seemed to be a strictly commercial transaction, the Reverend Claudius Henry, of the African Reform Coptic Church of God in Christ, the First Fruit of Prayer, God's Army Camp, urged his followers and sympathizers to sell their possessions, come to Kingston, get a card and board a free ship back to Africa (legend had it that £23,000,000 were available for repatriation). Hundreds came, but when no ship appeared, the Rev. Henry blamed the Jamaican government. When it seemed likely that verbal violence might take other forms, police made two raids on the Reverend Henry's church, arresting him with fifteen of his followers. In the headquarters of God's Army Camp, security officers seized revolvers, shotguns, dynamite, detonaters, machetes, and a letter addressed to Fidel Castro. In October 1960, Rev. Henry and his followers were charged with treason and jailed on sentences ranging from three to ten years.[28]

Older writers like Christian, Thurston and Theal tended to see native movements mostly as insurrections, though sometimes with sufficient cause, as in the case of the 1900 "riot" at Karravanivasala in the Vizagapatam district of India.[29] Korra Mallayya, of the Konda Dora or hill cultivator caste, had an ecstatic vision at the turn of the century and gradually collected a camp of four or five thousand people about him. At first his cult seemed harmless enough, until he announced he was the reincarnation of one of the Pandava. These five brothers were the heroes of the *Mahabharata,* the interminable epic of endless battles in ancient India. This military note would have been the more alarming were it not that the Konda Dora had always declared themselves in the Census as *Pandava kulam* or Pandava castes and had long worshiped the Pandava brothers, epic companions of Krishna. Next, but in a genealogically somewhat confusing fashion, Mallayya revealed that his infant son was the god Krishna, come to drive out the English and to rule the country himself.

To do this, bamboos were to be cut to resemble guns, and the Swami drilled his camp thus armed. Later, he would turn the bamboos by magic into guns, and the weapons of the English into water. When he announced he would loot Pachipenta, two constables came to look into things, but were beaten to death. Local police tried in vain to recover the bodies, whereupon the district magistrate collected reserve police to arrest the Swami. Resisted by the mob, the police were obliged to fire. Eleven rioters were killed, others wounded or arrested, sixty were tried for rioting, and three, including the Swami, for murder. Of these, the Swami somehow died in jail, and the two others were hanged. When the god Krishna also died, the trouble ended.

The Taiping ("Great Peace") Rebellion was overtly a military movement. But its leader, Hung Hsiu-ch'üan, had been much influenced by the tracts of Protestant missionaries. On his third failure to pass the government examinations, Hung had a psychotic episode, with confused visions of God, Jesus and Confucius, who commanded him to set up a new order in China to replace the Ch'ing emperors.[30] He collected destitute and desperate farmers, in the beginning especially Hakkas and Miaos, non-Chinese minorities in Kwang-si who had suffered even more exploitation than the other peasants. Hung and other leaders, who soon vied in out-trancing one another, moved with a swelling horde of rebels northward to the Yangtze, took city after city, and for a time it looked as though they would overthrow the dynasty of the Manchus. But the confused part-Western ideology of the Taipings[31] failed to enlist the scholar-officials and Confucian intellectuals; their fanatic destructiveness and partly un-Chinese origin aroused bitter resistance among farmers through whose regions they passed; and the "Great Peace" war ended in defeat.

The main strength of the Taiping Rebellion was its economic impetus, mobilized by the largely psychic deprivation of its founder. Economic causality alone appears to dominate the thinking of many theorists. It is of course not arguable that economic factors loom large in nearly all European religious mass movements, from primitive Christianity to the medieval and Renaissance Church, the great heresies and the Crusades, and perhaps even to the smallest sectarian movement of later times. But it is equally indisputable that the economic, like the political motives were contained within a larger and then prepotent framework, that of religion. On the tribal level, Jomo Kenyatta, as might be expected from his Marxist sympathies, links the Kikuyu *maumau* with economic factors, including greatly reduced rainfall in Kenya. But even he properly notes that the Kikuyu linked this misfortune with their ancestor religion, and *maumau* was as much religious as economic.[32]

Certainly no Melanesian specialist would ever deny the enormous economic (and emotional) impact of the periodic appearance from nowhere of cargo ships, and the multiple mysterious functions performed by the government steam packets bringing mail and other paper-magic, when the slow round of tribal life in the sleepy tropics is temporarily electrified into frenzied activity. "Cargo" did indeed stimulate an extravagant appetite for foreign goods, certainly an economic phenomenon. But the economic myth that "explained" the appearance of cargo from faraway ghost-ancestors was preposterous and drew on the native, noneconomic, religious past. Economically, the Melanesian was as unrealistic as the African cultist who wants an electric lamp or radio, but does not dream of the enormous, and necessary, economic complex behind the light-plug or the radio commercial. A "total" economic rational explanation must operate with a realistic economic whole. "Cargo" ideology was not rational-economic but irrational-religious.

The economic component of many if indeed not most modern African cult movements is plain, even though the cult content itself is largely that of the Jehovah's Witnesses, the Salvation Army, or other (though, in being closer to our class faiths, less exotically conspicuous) evangelical sects, mixed with older native religions. The Nyasaland millennium, for example, would come with the invading Americans, not in military but in economic guise. The Nyasaland cultists thought that all Americans were Negro, like the distinguished Negro emissary, Dr. James Emmon Kwegyir Aggrey, a Columbia-educated native of the Gold Coast, who had taught

Negroes in North Carolina before he came to Africa with the Phelps-Stokes Commission. The new economic messiahs would order merchants to sell their goods cheaply, or to give them away, as Americans do. It must be admitted that the "foreign aid" religion had a basis in fact. The Nyasaland Tonga, Tom Nyirenda, leader of the Mwana Leza, promised the Redeemer would arrive in an airplane laden with motorcycles and bales of calico.[33] Who can blame Africans for mistaking foreign aid for "cargo"?

As to economics, one Ngunza prophet prohibited all work, no food crops could be planted, and nothing was to be eaten except weeds and wild grass seeds. Tax-paying would be abolished, he promised, and God would send firearms from heaven to annihilate the whites (Europeans only). As a result, not accustomed to our latter-day taking of adventism with a certain tentativeness, the faithful villagers of Kikenge, one day in July 1921, matter-of-factly set out on the road to meet Jesus Christ, who was coming back, the prophet said, at two o'clock that afternoon.[34] And who was to gainsay them, since Russellite missionaries told them that Christ already earlier had returned invisibly to the earth in America in 1874?

Indeed, some European theorists seem to believe that all native messianism must be patterned on a naïvely misunderstood but earnest New Testament Christianity since there has been but one authentic messiah historically. Margull would appear to propose, Werblowsky says,[35] that all native messianisms, like everything else, are to be interpreted in terms of the new German Protestant theology. Of course it is true that a number of native prophets, as missionary preaching seemed to urge, have identified themselves in great simplicity with Jesus Christ. An American example that comes immediately to mind is the peyote prophet, Jack Wilson or "Moonhead," who shaped his earthen altar-moon in the cult tipi into his own divine face, and who dressed his hair like the traditional pictures of Jesus. Indeed many Indian messiahs assimilated themselves to Christ, and so did many messiahs elsewhere in the world. But it is fatuously and absurdly ethnocentric to suppose that every native messiah is necessarily patterned on a European Christ. The fact is not so much that all native messiahs derive historically from the only genuine messiah, as that Christ himself is one example of a culturally very common type.

Even when the messianic Christian pattern is historically available through culture contact, the new revelation may take a non-historic turn in some individual vatic personalities. "Father Divine" taught that he was the incarnation of God himself, bringing back literal earthly "Heavens" by economic miracle in a Great Depression cult in Harlem of the 1930s and 1940s. "Daddy Grace" was another example of this type. Or white men may be regarded in messianic terms, the ideological independence of which is guaranteed by their occurring in first-contact times. Pizarro was welcomed in Peru as the returning culture hero Viracocha, Cortez in Mexico as Quetzalcoatl. Captain Cook was regarded by some Polynesians as a native deity reappeared. Returned gods are commonplace, and as real as David Thompson or Dr. Moszkowski.

Quite different was the "Johnson Cult" that began in 1964 on New Hanover Island in the southwest Pacific. Its leader, one Bosmailik, collected nearly $83,000 in order to buy Lyndon B. Johnson as their leader. More than 150 believers were jailed for contributing their money in this way instead of paying local taxes. In April 1965, an assembly of five hundred natives jeered an American member of the visiting UN Trusteeship Commission, who felt obliged to state that the President had no intention of becoming their leader. It should be noted that the Johnson Cult antedated the several visits of the President to the Pacific, although not to this region.[86] In October 1966, the Mindanao messiah who called himself God was causing much trouble with the Philippine police. His sect was a hodgepodge of Christian and Moslem beliefs; the long-bearded leader, subsisting on banditry, maintained that no bullet could kill him. There are a number of other messianic possibilities. In a Gilbert Islands cult of the 1930s, for example, a native pastor had a revelation of a certain originality. He stated that he was "the father of God."

In our own western tradition there is still a lingering disposition, among some, to believe in divine intervention in human affairs. As the secular present sickens unto death, a real deity or his certified representative, imbued with authentic charisma or divine *mana,* stands on this very earth to rearrange events or to end history. A partly secularized version of this mystique is the belief in the divinity of kings or the charisma of culture heroes. Still baser coin is the cliché of the "personal magnetism" of purely human heroes and leaders. All these, of course, are follower-attitudes, and the amount of charisma depends on the degree of need, naïveté, awe and ego-infantilism of the cultist himself. We are oedipal animals. Freud too refused to explain "genius" ultimately by his technique.

In any case, to cultists themselves their leaders are quite simply divinely sanctioned (i.e., by themselves). The cultist view of events is that the godhood of the leader explains all "causality" in the situation, and there is nothing else to explain. History is powerless before the hero, the genius, or the god. However, the ethnographic observer of the crisis cult, viewing the impressively irrational event, must not be seduced by suggestion or empathy into even an attenuated version of this attitude to explain the phenomenon. In the presence of the compellingly irrational, he must still hold on firmly to his rational ego and coolly call men men. Of course this becomes uncannily difficult when the man invokes our own deep admiration as an oedipal model, our gratitude or hope (has one yet forgiven history for the death of John Kennedy?) and when personal childhood becomes entangled with the historic past. History itself in time confers charisma, as we idealize the past through the polarized lens of memory.

For this reason, ubiquitous in new crisis cults is the "Barbarossa" legend that the historic hero or king never died but still lives, one day to return and lead us. Somewhere the hero only sleeps, and in catastrophe will awaken to change chaos into utopian order. Frederick I, twelfth-century ruler of the Holy Roman Empire—the remembered red-bearded conqueror of Henry the Lion and antagonist of the papal Lombard League—was drowned, historians say, while crossing a river in Asia Minor leading an army to the Third Crusade. But Germanic folk say he will awaken to champion his people in some new crisis; King Arthur, Charlemagne and the Seven Sleepers are other cognates of Frederick Barbarossa. Chambers[37] finds them in every western nation, hence it might be argued that the Barbarossa myths take their pattern from the Pentecostal Christ. But this is an inadequate explanation that also leaves Christ unexplained. The early Christians themselves invented the Resurrection out of a far wider need of mankind, and on patterns of the spring-resurrected dying god earlier and ubiquitous in the Neolithic Levant. The emotion some feel on the resurrection of Christ borrows from the history of one's own mind.

And surely Jesus of Nazareth is not in mind in at least some instances of "Barbarossa" belief. Hitler escaped death in the flaming bunker in East Berlin, was spirited away by submarine, and still lives in Argentina, as one fantasy has it. Many refused to believe in the death of Lawrence of Arabia, T. E. Shaw on his racing motorbike, and stories of his alleged activities are found in both British and German propaganda of World War II.[38] Another hero, the young James Dean, was not killed in the wreck of his Porsch by the improbable Mr. Turnipseed; somewhere he still lives in seclusion, while plastic surgeons slowly and painfully restore his broken body and ruined face. These imaginings have quite nothing to do with the Pentecostal legend. They are simply refusals to believe in the death of identity-figures; the intense narcissism of Lawrence and Dean speaks to one's own.[39]

As with self-identified narcissistic, so also with anaclitic parental figures. When Peter III was assassinated and the alien empress Catherine the Great ascended the throne of all the Russias, many peasants refused to credit his death. Also widespread in Russia was the belief that Alexander I did not die in 1825 in Taganrág, but retired secretly to Siberia, there to live on as a recluse—a belief greatly strengthened when his sarcophagus was opened in 1927 and found to be empty. Likewise, Brazilian "Sebastianismo" cultists believe in the still-living Portuguese prince who died centuries ago fighting the Moors of north Africa. The Czech hero Oleksa Dovbush sleeps while his buried ax moves each year the thickness of a poppy seed nearer the surface of the earth, and when it emerges another hero will arise, a champion of justice for the people against their oppressors.[40] The list is endless. There is no single source, there is no Barbarossa archetype in any folk-unconscious. It is simply that, on occasion, many people wishfully deny death, a proposition sufficiently established by other evidence.

Because of the known influence of Christianity in certain non-European areas, Belgian historians of religion nevertheless still insist, with some credibility, that resurrection myths in these places always originate in the European Christ, just as all messiahs did. History declares that Matswa André died at Mayama Government Post in the Congo in 1942, but legend claims he is alive and will come back. Lenshina, leader of the "Alice" movement, even seemingly fulfilled the legend. She claimed to have risen again after her "death" in 1953, when she brought back from Heaven the message that Christ, having left on a white cloud, would return at the Last on a black one. The "Negro Christ" of many prophetic religions in Black Africa also, in many cases, seems to implicate the resurrection of once-living messiah-prophets. Even when Isaac Shembe[41] died, the founder of South African Zionism, a tradition that eschews the supernatural messiah, rumors spread that he would rise again. As in missionized Africa, so also in Christian America. According to popular belief, Macandal, the Haitian hero of national independence, escaped from the flames of the stake when he was burned alive. Jamaican "Bedwardism" embodies in the theology of Alexander Bedward the awakening to real life of real persons, including himself. João Maria and Padre Cicero of Brazil will also return some day to fulfill their prophecy of peace. It must be conceded, too, that on occasion Indian ghost dance prophets in North America patterned themselves, in part, on a syncretized Christian model, although there are enough messianic models in quite aboriginal shamanism in the Americas.

However, just as the ethnocentric fiction that the only true Messiah gave rise to all false ones must be abandoned, so also as we get farther and farther away from any plausibility of Christian influence, the insistence that all Barbarossa figures be Christian must be abandoned too. A clear case exists in Asia. In the *Burkhanism* of the Altai Turks of Siberia in 1904, Chot Chelpan had a vision of "Oirot Khan" and preached the re-establishment of this mythical hero's kingdom.[42] It does not matter that there never was an "Oirot Khan" with whom Chot could have conversed, but that the Altai Turks, rather, had been subjugated by the Oirat Federation; the significant point is that "Burkhan" comes from the native word for the Buddha and, although the cult was messianic, it was quite specifically not Judeo-Christian.

More commonly, nativistic cults call for the return of the natives' own ancient heroes, or great kings, or supernatural shamanistic helpers. In a Javanese movement of 1920–1922, Tumenggung Badar assumed the title *Kakah Gajah* or "Great Grandfather." This revived the Samarikung myth of the hero-shaman Moung Munur, who had a supernatural gong which "cured death" and would bring back souls of the dead from Bukit Lumut to their respective villages—all identifiably indigenous motifs.[43] Javanese prophetic movements often included the messianic expectation of Ratuadil or "Prince of Justice" and the return of Diponegoro was commonly expected by many Indonesians. In 1767, the Batara Gowa was exiled by the Dutch to Ceylon, where he died in 1795, but every messiah ever since in the southern Celebes claims to be the Batara Gowa or, for greater plausibility perhaps, his son or grandson. The last Malawi hero, Chief Kankhomba, when overwhelmed by the Yao tribe, retreated to Soche Hill in east Africa, and there he still lives in a cave to come again when the Malawi need him[44]—a classic Barbarossa legend, but quite certainly having no connection with the European one. And, finally, in all its details apparently aboriginal, the Sauk Indians have a myth that the brother of the culture hero waits in a northern region of ice and snow, but when the world comes to an end the brothers and all the Sauk will rejoin one another.

The omnipresence of a leader, sacred or secular, in every crisis cult—together with an uncritical acceptance of the nature of his "charisma"—has led inevitably to a "great man" theory of movements. But the notion of the "innovative genius" who carries everything before him entails a kind of psychological explanation just as monolithic as the single-cause political, military, economic, or other theories reviewed above. Of course leadership is a necessary part of every movement. In fact, Edmonson[45] has listed some hundred and ten cases of "Indian Resistance Movements" in the Americas between 1510 and 1941, and despite the lacunae common in such marginal and early native history, he was able to name forty known leaders. Cohn notes that European millenarian revolts never formed save round a prophet—John Ball in England, Martinek Hauska in Bohemia, Thomas Müntzer in Thuringia, and first Jan Matthys and then Jan Bockelson at Münster—to which we might add, for still larger movements, Martin Luther, Calvin, Zwingli, and the Wesleys.

As a matter of fact, in many aboriginal crisis cults there commonly appears a second leader too, a secular "organizer" at the side of the sacred-charismatic prophet-founder—in Homer Barnett's lively metaphor the "inventor" and the "salesman"—as in the Joseph Smith–Brigham Young pair of Mormonism. And Sierksma properly notes that the Yaruro leaderless exception confirms the rule, for Yaruro messianism is "static," that is, there is no social "movement" among them. There are a sufficient number of instances of the "failed messiah" that tend to cast doubt on the "Great Man theory" of the Romantic and early Victorian period. Of course only people make history. But not only the leader. To varying degrees, all people do. Indeed, the religious "genius" is a psycho-social phenomenon as a shaman-messiah (and not a psychotic or criminal or some other social category) only if and when he is dynamically relevant to and functioning in his proper socio-cultural context. This is a far more complex and instructive naturalistic phenomenon than mystic charisma, alleged by cultist and accepted in faith by the historian of religion.

NOTES

(VIII Crises and Cults)

1. Willson Coates, "A Note on the Diggers," in Thrupp, *op. cit.*, pp. 220–21; H. Kaminsky, "The Free Spirit in the Hussite Rebellion," *loc. cit.*, pp. 166–86. J. L. Talmon, "Social Prophetism in 19th Century France," *Commentary*, 26 (1958) 158–72. See also N. Cohn, "Hysterical, Superstitious, and Apocalyptic Mass Religion," in Norman F. Cantor and Michael S. Worth (eds.), *The History of Popular Culture* (New York: Macmillan, 1968), pp. 102–7.

2. Wallace, *Revitalization Movements*, p. 268.

3. S. G. F. Brandon, "The Zealots: the Jewish Resistance against Rome A.D. 6–73," *History Today*, 15 (1965) 632–41; *Jesus and the Zealots* (Manchester: Manchester University Press, 1966); and "The Trial of Jesus," *Horizon*, 9 (1967) 5–13.

4. Sierksma, review of Lanternari, *Current Anthropology*, 6 (1965) 455–56.

5. Norman Cohn, *The Pursuit of the Millennium: Revolutionary Messianism in Medieval and Reformation Europe and Its Bearing on Modern Totalitarian Movements* (New York: Harper Torchbooks, 1961), also "Medieval Millenarism," in Thrupp, *op. cit.*, pp. 31–43.

6. Donald Weinstein, "Millenarianism in a Civic Setting: the Savonarola Movement in Florence," in Thrupp, *op. cit.*, pp. 187–203.

7. Werner Müller, "Mazdak and the Alphabet Mysticism of the East," *History of Religions*, 3 (1963) 72–82. See also R. A. Nicholson, "Mazdak," *Hastings Encyclopedia*, 8:508–10.

8. E. P. Boardman, "Millenary Aspects of the Taiping Rebellion," in Thrupp, *op. cit.*, pp. 70–77; J. R. Levenson, "Confucian and Taiping 'Heaven': The Political Implications of Clashing Religions Concepts," *Comparative Studies in Society and History*, 4 (1962) 436–53; W. J. Hail, *Tseng Kuo-fan and the Taiping Rebellion* (New Haven: Yale University Press, 1927). K. S. Latourette, *The Chinese: Their History and Culture*, 2nd ed. rev., 2 vols in one, New York: Macmillan, 1943 (Red Eyebrows, I:124; Taiping, I:376–88; Boxer Rebellion, I:412–19; on Taoists as Chou Dynasty crisis-cultists, I:76–78; on Chinese politico-religious cults, II:181). See also Victor Purcell, *The Boxer Uprising* (Cambridge: at the University Press, 1963).

9. J. H. Breasted, *A History of Egypt* (New York: C. Scribner's Sons, 2nd rev. ed., 1921, p. 205). Wallace, *Revitalization Movements*, p. 264, for the suggestion that Ikhnaton and the Mahdi involved crisis cults.

10. Michael Gough, *The Early Christians* (New York: Praeger, 1961, pp. 29–30) for the origin of the Roman Megalensia. W. Crooke suggests that the Muslim invasion greatly affected new sectarian movements in Hinduism ("Hinduism," *Hastings Encyclopedia*, 6:704).

11. Erich Heller, *The Disinherited Mind* (Penguin Books, 1961, pp. 213–14).

12. Willy Ley, *Watchers of the Skies* (New York: Viking Press, 1966, pp. 514–17).

13. For a psychological understanding of French xenophobia, see the felicitous and charming book by Lawrence Wylie, *Village in the Vaucluse* (Cambridge: Harvard University Press, 1957). For the centripedal trend of the French family (likewise village and state, in Wylie's thesis), see also Margaret Mead and Rhoda Métraux, *Thèmes de "Culture" de la France: Introduction à une étude de la communauté française* (Le Havre: Institut havrais de sociologie économique et de psychologie des peuples, 1957).

14. Vittorio Lanternari, *The Religions of the Oppressed: A Study of Modern Messianic Movements* (New York: Knopf, 1963; also in Mentor Books, 1965). "Reli-

gione, società, politica nell'Africa Nera avanti e dopo la indipendenta," *Nuovi Argo-menti* [Roma], 1964, 69–71; "Profeti Negri e movimento di liberazione in Africa," *Sapere* [Milano], Dec. 1964, pp. 689–95; and "L'acculturazione dei populi ex-colo-niali," *Sapere*, April 1964, pp. 201–7.

15. For Africa, Efraim Andersson, *Messianic Popular Movements in the Lower Congo* (Uppsala: Almqvist & Wiksells Boktryckeri [Studia Ethnographica Upsaliensia 14], 1958); and George Shepperson, "Nyasaland and the Millenium," in Thrupp, *op. cit.*, pp. 144–59); David B. Barrett, *Schism and Renewal in Africa: An Analysis of Six Thousand Contemporary Religious Movements* (Nairobi, Addis Ababa, Lusaka: Oxford University Press, 1968). Melanesia, P. M. Worsley, "Millenarian Movements in Melanesia," *Rhodes-Livingston Institute*, 21 (March 1957) 18–31, also *Bobbs-Merrill Reprint Series in the Social Sciences*, A-248; and Indonesia, J. Van der Kroef, *The Communist Party of Indonesia* (Vancouver: University of British Columbia Press, 1965).

16. George E. Simpson, "The Ras Tafari Movement in Jamaica in Its Millenial Aspect," in Thrupp, *op. cit.*, pp. 160–65; "The Ras Tafari Movement in Jamaica: A Study of Race and Class Conflict," *Social Forces*, 34 (1955) 159–71; M. G. Smith, R. Augier and R. Nettlefold, *The Ras Tafari Movement in Kingston, Jamaica* (Jamaica: Mona, 1960); S. Kitzinger, "The Ras Tafarian Brethren of Jamaica," *Comparative Studies in Society and History*, 9, no. 1, October 1966; and Donald Hogg, "Statement of a Rastafari Leader," *Caribbean Studies*, 6 (1966) 37–40.

17. E. Pendleton Banks, "Pau cin hau: A Case of Religious Innovation among the Northern Chin," in C. R. Riley and W. W. Taylor (eds.), *American Historical Anthropology: Essays in Honor of Leslie Spier* (Carbondale: Southern Illinois University Press, 1967, pp. 37–59).

18. Charlotte Zimmerman, "The Cult of the Holy Cross: An Analysis of Cosmology and Catholicism in Quintana Roo," *History of Religions*, 3 (1963) 50–71. Middle American syncretism with Catholicism may be overstated by Zimmerman and the Tulane group. For the Nagualists, a mysterious sect or secret society, had for its object the total destruction of Christianity; Jacinto Can-Ek, who led the Maya revolt at Valladolid, Yucatan, in 1761 prophesied the destruction of the Spaniards; and the Indian girl Maria Candelaria led a similar revolt and prophesied the Spanish downfall [Louis Spence, "Prophecy (American)," *Hastings Encyclopedia*, 10:381–82, p. 382].

19. Shepperson, *op. cit.* pp. 145–48; G. Shepperson and T. Price, *Independent African: John Chilembwe and the Origins, Setting, and Significance of the Nyasaland Rising of 1915* (Edinburgh: Edinburgh University Press, 1958); and Andersson, *op. cit.*, pp. 48–57, 115–24, 135.

20. René Ribeiro, "Brazilian Messianic Movements," in Thrupp, *op. cit.*, pp. 55–69.

21. P. M. Worsley, *Millenarian Movements*, p. 24.

22. J. W. Fernandez, "Politics and Prophecy: African Religious Movements," *Practical Anthropology*, 12 (1965) 71–75; "Symbolic Consensus in a Fang Religious Movement," *American Anthropologist*, 67 (1965) 902–9.

23. Mühlmann, *et al., Chiliasmus und Nativismus;* Van der Kroef, *Communist Party;* Cohn, *op. cit.;* A. J. F. Köbben, "Prophetic Movements as an Expression of Social Protest," *International Archives of Ethnography*, 49, pt. 1 (1960) 117–64; and E. P. Boardman, "Millenary Aspects of the Taiping Rebellion," in Thrupp, *op. cit.*, 70–79.

24. P. M. Worsley, *The Trumpet Shall Sound, A Study of "Cargo" Cults in Melanesia* (London: Macgibbon & Kee, 1957; also Schocken Books, 1968, p. 173).

25. In Biak, startlingly, "the great miracle had happened; not one ship, but hundreds arrived with supplies which the Americans actually landed on Meok Wundi, the island where the myth said the Messiah would return. . . . The entire island became a stock pile and the islanders screamed themselves hoarse in the first amazement.

. . . The Koreri (Promised Age) had come" (F. C. Kamma, *Die messiaanse Koréri-bewegingen in het Biaks-Noemfoorse Cultuurgebied* [Den Haag, 1954, pp. 182–83]), in Köbben, *Prophetic Movements*, p. 128. Compare Hans Fischer, "Cargo cults and the 'Americans,'" *Sociologus*, 14 ½1 (1964) 17–29.

26. Ngunzism of Kimbangu, pp. 48–57; Bembe *cinqui*, p. 135; and Matswa André's "Sundi Ladi" movement, pp. 115–24, in Andersson, *op. cit.*

27. Andersson, *op. cit.*, p. 99.

28. G. E. Simpson, in Thrupp, *op. cit.*, pp. 161–62.

29. Edgar Thurston, *Omens and Superstitions of Southern India* (London: T. F. Unwin, 1912, pp. 265–66).

30. On Hung Hsiu-ch'üan's psychosis, see Theodore Hamberg, *The Visions of Hung Siu-Tsuen and the Origins of the Kwangsi Insurrection* (Peiping: Yenching University Library, 1935, p. 22); and Dr. P. M. Yap, "The Mental Illness of Hung Hsiu-ch'üan, Leader of the Taiping Rebellion," *Far Eastern Quarterly*, 13 (1954) 287–304.

31. E. P. Boardman, *Christian Influence upon the Ideology of the Taiping Rebellion* (Madison: University of Wisconsin Press, 1952).

32. Jomo Kenyatta, "Kikuyu Religion, Ancestor-worship and Sacrificial Practices," *Africa*, 10 (1937) 308–28.

33. Shepperson, *op. cit.*, pp. 144, 157.

34. Andersson, *op. cit.*, pp. 76–77.

35. R. J. Zwi Werblowsky, "A New Heaven and a New Earth: Considering Primitive Messianisms," *History of Religions*, 5 (1965) 164–72; cf. E. M. Mendelson, Review of A. Abel *et al.*, *American Anthropologist*, 67 (1965) 1298–1300, p. 1299.

36. "Johnson Cultists Jeer American in U. N. Group," *New York Times*, 4 April 1965; "Cult That Tried to 'Buy' Johnson End Tax Revolt in New Guinea," *loc. cit.*, 28 June 1964; and "64 Lyndon Johnson Cultists Arrested by Australians," *loc. cit.*, 9 August 1964. See also D. S. Jhabvala, "The Cargo Cultists' Bid for Johnson," New York *Herald Tribune*, 13 June 1965; and "What Price LBJ?," *Newsweek*, 22 June 1964, p. 47.

37. On Barbarossa figures in Europe, see E. K. Chambers, *Arthur of Britain* (London: Sidgwick & Jackson, Ltd., 1927, pp. 217–32).

38. David Garnett, *The Essential T. E. Lawrence* (Penguin Books, p. 25).

39. Christine Olden, "About the Fascinating Effect of the Narcissistic Personality," *American Imago*, 2 (1941) 347–55.

40. On Peter III and Alexander I as Barbarossa figures, see notes by the translator, Aylmer Maude, in Leo Tolstoy, *War and Peace* (New York: Simon and Schuster, 1942, pp. 802, 1263); on Sebastianism, Ribeiro in Thrupp, *op. cit.*, p. 58, and J. Lucio de Azevedo, *A Evolução do Sebastianismo* (Lisboa: Livraria Clássica, 1947); on Oleksa Dovbush, see E. J. Hobsbawn, *Primitive Rebels, Studies in Archaic Forms of Social Movement in the 19th and 20th Centuries* (Manchester: Manchester University Press, 1959). See also La Barre, *Crisis Cults*, on Barbarossa figures.

41. B. G. M. Sundkler, *Bantu Prophets in South Africa* (London: Lutterworth Press, 1948; 2nd ed., London: Oxford University Press, 1961, pp. 111, 126.

42. Krader, *op. cit.*, p. 283.

43. Kakah Gajah, pp. 109–10, Batara Gowa, pp. 118–19, in Van der Kroef, in Thrupp, *op. cit.*

44. Shepperson, *op. cit.*, p. 147; compare the legend about Matswa André, Andersson, *op. cit.*, p. 124.

45. M. S. Edmonson, "Nativism, Syncretism and Anthropological Science," in *Nativism and Syncretism* (New Orleans: Middle American Research Institute, Tulane University, Publication 19, 1960, 183–203, pp. 186–88).

IX
Culture and Acculturation

CRISIS cults have been repeatedly observed to occur in contexts of acculturation. Is acculturation, then, the *cause* of crisis cults? The acculturational theory might be called a kind of "anthropological explanation" of causality, in parallel with the political, economic, and other attempted explanations. In this view, some sort of "culture clash" is responsible for engendering the crisis cult. There is a "cognitive dissonance"[1] between competing systems which the syncretic cult somehow resolves. Cultural thesis and antithesis breed Hegelian synthesis. In this simple form, the culture-contact theory is as inadequate as it is anthropomorphic. Cultures do not make love, and they breed nothing. Neither are cultures platonized entities that stand eyeball to eyeball and slug it out like some sort of superorganisms. Concretely, only a person can be in conflict within himself over alternative cultural beliefs and behaviors, only people in society in conflict with one another, and only societies of people in conflict with one another.

Acculturation is not the cause of crisis cults, but only one very common *arena* for human ambivalence about culture (including one's own) and for cultural "identity crisis"—but always of individuals and groups of individuals, and always in the psycho-biological context of human learning of culture. Even when long continued, mere social contact may foment only simple antagonism of peoples, ending in war, economic competition, and many forms other than crisis cults. European nationalism itself is one reaction to the continuing contact of differences. Cultural polarization and compulsive loyalty may increase in this way on continued contact; alternatively, various degrees of conscious and unconscious syncretism of culture may also result. Besides this, many European crisis cults do not seem to exemplify the clash of two ethnographically distinct or alien cultures at all, inasmuch as the conflict is socially endogenous. Thus both sides in a class conflict might have a fairly clear sense of who gets what, economically and politically, and yet have commonly shared cultural assumptions. They might in fact exploit these assumptions polemically against the other side in their propaganda. But propaganda succeeds only because it appeals to beliefs already held. That is, both sides may appeal to traditional culture as the undisputed sanction for each side's rightness, and the arguments have compelling force only because common cultural assumptions are made. In this sense, a great many crisis cults in Europe are specifically "nativistic" in their appeal to primitive Christianity, but are nonetheless socially internal class crises, not intercultural clashes between nations.

Again, and notoriously, cognitive dissonance need not produce, nor does it prevent, autistic innovation; nor does it modify such an innovation once made. When prophecy fails, belief may continue unabated.[2] Such "cognitive" systems are often causally secondary to belief anyway, that is they are rationalizing ways of distorting experience to preserve preferred beliefs—in a concrete situation poorly apprehended cognitively, irrelevantly reacted to, and left unchanged by magic cult belief or behavior. A good example of this is the typical "Doomsday Cult" described by John Lofland,[3] in which conversion, proselytization, and maintenance of faith had almost no relevance rationally to economic, political, or historical facts. The protectively needed belief is causally prior to the elaborated and distorting "cognitive" system that results.

A salient feature of minority cults, in fact, is their striking cognitive dissonance with majority culture, available for the asking to set the minority right, or forcibly proffered. In terms of the cognitive success-techniques of majority culture, the minority is epistemologically underprivileged. Such a crisis cult creates cognitive dissonance, and does not necessarily result from it. Further, many minority systems are so bizarre—the snake-handling cult for example—that one wonders, "How on earth can people believe such obvious nonsense!" or invokes a conscious make-believe and self-deception in communicants or a clever hypnotic charlatan leader. But this is unfair to faith. Believers do believe. And the fact is that any system can rationalize any apparently untoward event or secular disproof of prophecy and still sail on undeterred. One's shock at the spectacle is merely the measure of one's own cognitive distance from the system being studied.

Thus, whether ethnic or class, mere cognitive dissonance makes no difference to the presence or absence of crisis cults. And as far as acculturation is concerned, the notion that rational beings operate with rationally accessible alternative cultures is simply not the case. Cognition without affect toward what is "known" engenders no crisis cult, otherwise anthropologists and other professional travelers would be the main source of new crisis cults, which they are not. Instead, the innovator's ambivalence toward his culture, his tribe's ambivalence toward either native or alien culture or both, the crisis of cultural faith, and the psychological relationship of innovator and group are all essential. In both prophet and group, mere cognition of culture difference must in some way also involve emotional stress. Cognition and Culture are bloodless; cults are always of people, by people and for people.

The simple state of "culture contact," then, does not eventuate necessarily in crisis cults. There are many alternative situations. One type of reaction to culture contact may be almost purely nativistic, e.g. the Maori "Kingites" thought simply to encapsulate themselves culturally by geographic removal and isolation from foreigners. Possibly eighteenth-century China and nineteenth-century Japan, perhaps even early twentieth-century Russia as well, all represent similar cases. We find the withdrawal reaction on a smaller scale among Mennonites, Doukhobors, Mormons and others, including primitive Christians who would remove themselves from "the world."

Many primitive cults are almost wholly nativistic. The Fijian *kalou vu* were simply ancestor gods "revitalized." The *buriti* cult of northern Gabun and Spanish Africa was a reworking of the old Fang ancestor cult; the *bieri* cult, curiously, a borrowing from the northwest Bantu whom, historically, the Fang were replacing—an atypical direction of acculturation. In the New Guinea highlands, open only since the 1930s, millenarian movements were in full swing even before the white people reached them. The cults first appeared in areas under administrative control for only a few years, and then spread rapidly to aboriginal tribes before white contact. And the Orokaiva "taro cult," Belshaw insists,[4] was based entirely on old Melanesian garden magic and borrowed nothing from outside. Some movements have an ambiguity that is the bane of "pure" typologies and monolithic causal explanations. For example, the "Talking Cross" of the Maya borrowed perhaps more from native tradition than from Christianity. The same is true of the Chinese Boxer Rebellion and Taiping Revolt.

Some cults are really in a sense "anti-nativistic." The visionary *Pau Cin Hau* cultists in Burma were to give up the old *nat* worship and to cease keeping the dead in the house, as was the old custom. At the height of Kimbangu's *ngunzism,*[5] the people in some Congo villages collected native fetishes in order to destroy them. Almost all the masks and other rich ceremonial paraphernalia were thrown away in some Melanesian cargo cults, to the dismay of ethnographers like Williams.[6] Some early peyotists threw away their medicine bundles on joining the new religion; and in one pre-Ghost Dance movement, Indian "witches" (shamans) were burned alive. The *Mwana Leza* movement was anti-witchcraft, and so were several other African cults.[7] The "Alice" movement of the Mulenga prophetess Lenshina produced fantastic heaps of witchcraft charms discarded by her followers.[8] And Savonarola's order to the Florentines to burn their vanities, even priceless Renaissance paintings, resembles this selective rejection also—although the Savonarola movement was otherwise "nativistic" both in intent and ideology.

Some cults are accommodative-Christian at the same time they are anti-white, notably those in Africa. Again, the Menomini "Dreamers" flatly proclaimed that the heads of all whites would be severed from their bodies as the scythe cuts their wheat, and the country would be restored to the Indians. By contrast, according to one Congo "Salvation Army" cult, only white garments were to be worn, in order to get a better seat in heaven. Perhaps a majority of movements based on acculturation actually occupy varying positions on a continuum between the purely nativistic and the accommodative. The Buka movement rejected native magic and in-law taboos, but also monetary wealth, at the same time it took over the alleged racial and social egalitarianism of European Christians. Africans and Indians and Melanesians often want the white man's superior magic and material goods—but sometimes without the white man.

Some movements have been the cultural syncretism of two separate oppressed and persecuted minorities, such as the mass takeover of Mormonism by the South Carolina Catawba.[9] The Russellites too were made up of underprivileged and confused "little people" who were distrustful of the parlous state of their world and hopeful for an Armageddon which would bring a better morrow—an ideological commodity that also found ready buyers among African tribesmen displaced by industrialism.[10] HUAC, KKK, and SNCC "black power" all represent "little people" whether motivated, meretriciously and dubiously in each case, by Legion "Americanism," by "Christian" or by "Marxist" doctrines. The *modekgnei*[11] theology and liturgy in Palau, that arose and was suppressed during the Japanese occupation, was a conscious and openly acknowledged mixture of traditional protective shamanism and Christian ideology. In fact, since Christianity itself arose among the oppressed—and its messianism out of still earlier traditional oppressions of the Jews—Christianity contains many scriptural messages in a sense preadapted for appeal to later oppressed peoples everywhere. Ras Tafarist "Israelites" in fact borrowed from both Judaism and Christianity, and "Black Muslims" from both Christianity and Islam.

Another alternative in acculturation is peaceful, viable, and fairly complete syncretism of two cultures. In Attic Greece at least, the amalgamation of north European and Mediterranean deities was sufficiently complete that Hesiod later was hard put to rationalize theologically what he did not know were two diverse systems; and Athena, a non-Indoeuropean goddess, became the patroness of the very conquerors' city. Some cults like the Indian "Shakers" of Oregon have been successfully and almost completely accommodative.[12] Again, modern peyotism,[13] legally incorporated in a number of states as the "Native American Church," not only has an authentic pre-Columbian native core and an intertribal "ecumenical" syncretism of residual Indianisms—together with a patina of Christianity among some northern Siouans and Utes—but also shows great skill in manipulating white mechanisms like appeal to Washington and to the American Civil Liberties Union, as well as to sympathetic anthropologists strongly nativistic concerning their Constitution's guarantee of freedom of religion. The Tulane anthropologists see Middle American religion from Mexico to Yucatan as a successful syncretism of Catholicism and indigenous cults. Culture contact does not always bring crisis: for example, the Spanish horse, gone wild (more properly, feral) in the Plains, was splendidly adapted for buffalo hunting. After incorporating Spanish horse furniture entire, Plains Indian culture took on a magnificent new vitality and power, and even elaborated and spread the new Sun Dance before white power caught up and crushed a hunting technology.

An important non-acculturational theory of magic and ritual is that of Malinowski.[14] He points out that ritual and magic are not needed and do not occur in Trobriand inner lagoon fishing, which is easy and safe and sure of result, especially if an empirical technique like fish poison is used. By contrast, open sea fishing is physically dangerous and uncertain of success; and only in this kind of fishing has magic ritual been elaborated. As a pious but really rather cynical cliché would have it, "There are no atheists in the foxholes." Both formulas imply that men call for supernatural help only in situations of anxiety and stress.

Psychological stress, we must agree, is always a necessary cause but not a sufficient cause of crisis cults. Any adequate theory must somehow also explain negative cases—such as Lessa's,[15] of the terrible typhoon Ophelia which virtually destroyed Ulithi atoll, and yet provoked in the Ulithians not a "crisis" reaction but only a rationalist-secular response. Some Ulithian psychotics seemed actually improved by the reality "shock therapy" of the typhoon. Other marginal individuals suffered *ruschealokh* or stress-disorientation, but not the group as a whole. In fact, *serawi* (typhoon magicians) and *tolo* (wave magicians) were permanently put out of business by this natural disaster.

Simple theories of stress, however, fail to predict anything about the quality of the response. And the negative instance must be accounted for by any scientific hypothesis. *It is not stress as such but the psychic style of reaction to it that is important.* We must view "stress" in the special physiological sense of Selye[16]—as a pathological "decompensation" of normal homeostatic devices in the body—and in the precise Freudian sense of "regression" or psychological decompensation.[17] Like the dream and the ecstatic vision, regression is a decompensation of ego functions, especially to be found in an animal species with the peculiar psychic ontogeny of *Homo sapiens*. Regression is a return to an earlier life-historical stage of adaptation, once *experienced* as successful, but now incompetent and irrelevant in a new situation. Thus the magic cry may indeed summon the mother, and words still coerce people *but not things;* suffering and guilt may placate a moral father *but not the physical universe.* Hence it is inapposite to try magically to control weather and waves with the verbal techniques earlier successful with persons; it is ineffectual to attempt to move stars with techniques once successful in human relations. Nevertheless the conviction of a "deeper truth" in these styles comes from an earlier experience of their successful use, and from this earlier experience only.[18] But these old styles are irrelevant in the new stress situation when later ego techniques "decompensate" in regression.

Now, psychological regression is sometimes in the service of the resilient ego.[19] Perhaps regression in dreams is such for the individual. However, though similar in style to the dream, wide-awake schizophrenia is a massive decompensatory regression that is maladaptive when chronic. Similarly art, like the dream, may refresh the day-worn mind; but music and poetry do not grow corn or repair a truck. Id- and ego-analysis apply to the individual, but in some sense a "superego analysis" is required to deal with a society. The French sacred and secular formulation is needed to study society, whose codified behaviors encompass both the moral and the material adaptations of its past that need to be discriminated in their locus and effects. Secular ego-techniques and technologies to meet animal id needs snowball up cumulative human cultural adaptations, which techniques and technologies evolve like all other animal adaptations of a species.[20] But sacred superego-assuaging behaviors are often re-gressive and do not evolve at all, but only change; they adapt not to an outer but an inner world whose cultural tensions change. In this sense, the sacred is relevant to the psychic ontogeny of the individual, the secular to the phylogeny of material-culture adaptation of the society or of the species. The relation of the prophet shaman as group-dreamer to a society of persons similarly under stress must be studied too, and any adequate theory of crisis cults must examine as control cases those of the "failed messiahs" (see Appendix, *The False Messiahs*).

Simple stress theory as a single-cause psychological explanation of crisis cults cannot predict the nature of response also because it concentrates too largely on the "outer" stressor realities of history, economics, politics and war. And it has too wooden a notion of what "objective" culture is, especially in the context of acculturation. The objectivism of such culturology forgets where culture is, in people, and forgets what culture is for, human beings. The failure of the political and economic and other explanations of causality lies not so much in their being wrong as in their being incomplete, for political and economic behaviors are only departments of total culture in any society, and as such are very likely all to be partly correct, but only partly.

Just the same, the total-culture "explanation" of anthropology will be incomplete too, if it neglects the human animal whose biology culture serves. If explanation of any human behavior is unsatisfying, it is because it does not include enough. In the quest for understanding we must avoid the "disciplinary cult" of each social science, anthropology included. And here, even in the total-culture holism of causality in crisis cults, we must be careful not to be blind as to what culture, dynamically, is and is for. False objectivism about culture forgets its only home, man.

The cultural includes the intellectual and the scientific as well. The "cultic" we define as the indisposition to accept either disruptive feedback or the case-hardened ego's critique of experience; the cultic is the indulgence instead of an appetite to believe and to belong. This definition includes on occasion, of course, any school of scientific thought that betrays a stubbornly nationalistic or disciplinary limitation of cognitive response—the "culturologist" denial of psychology and human biology, the "social anthropologist" exclusion of diachronic history and diffusion in the obsession with synchronic function, etc. And belonging should not be the first appetite of the scientist, as for good citizens it often is. Whatever a crowd does is uncritical and therefore suspect, and, if not potentially dangerous, at least intellectually stultifying. Magic ritual is required to create specifically what-is-not—an educated man at Commencement, a holy one at baptism, blood brothers of unrelated men, a scientist of a conformist—hence we should shun intellectual ritual too. For "methodology" is the magic ritual of scientism. No crowd's—or coterie's—solemn rituals create truth, and each fundamentalism is intellectual lobotomy.

Cognitive dissonance as such, we saw, need not cause stress; but consciousness of it can. Authentic psychological stress is a component of scientific thinking as well as it is of religious feeling, and crisis cult theory must be able to account for the diverse directions taken. In a sense, scientists actually cultivate cognitive dissonance through their constant collection of theory-testing empirical data. As a result of their own efforts they repeatedly encounter, or create, epistemological crises of knowledge; and there is a human touch of the cultist "believer" in every theorist that he must struggle against as being unworthy of the scientist. Some of the greatest men of science have publicly repudiated a theory which earlier they hotly defended. In this lies their scientific temper, not in the scientistic defense of theory.

The usual view of science is of a steadily growing mass of information and insight—or anyway of "hard" unerodable data, since admittedly some theory does not last but is junked in the storeroom of past errors called "the history of science." Worse yet, "data" themselves fade away with discarded insights. For example, shelves of patiently collected craniometric tomes became waste paper when Boas showed that anthropometrists were measuring what is not there genetically, in his famous study of the cephalic indices of immigrants to New York and their children.[21] Similarly, sociology "verifies" with rigorous methodology what is really only our own unwittingly and laboriously undiscovered contemporary folklore, built into naïvely culture-bound "hypotheses"—though it will take as much as a half-century of culture change to show this folklore up as such in later perspective.

In any case, if data do accumulate, Kuhn[22] has shown that what also accumulates are anomalies contravening a current "normal science" paradigm. At first, an accommodation of these anomalies to current theory-consensus is sought. But after a period of increasing dissatisfaction and confusion, a crisis, a scientific "revolution," occurs. The psychological illusion of continuity comes from the fact that scientists are never without a theory, because no theory is really relinquished until another is ready to replace it. Thus Aristotelian cosmology is replaced by Galilean, then by Newtonian, and this in turn by Einsteinian—and these are all *disjunctively different*.

Since textbooks and teaching are orderly statements of the rationale and procedures of a current "normal science" accumulation of data within a consensus paradigm, the basic historical fact of *change of paradigm* tends to be minimized. But there is real cognitive disjunction between theories of phlogiston or ether and the currently accepted equivalent paradigms of explanation. Working scientists tend to be functionally blind to the *history* of their science—to think earlier theories simply wrong "in the light of new data" though they "well explained what was then known," and the current theory obviously correct. Only in a crisis of paradigms do we recognize their ephemeral nature. Nor do working scientists, any more than any other journeyman symbol-pushers, have a sufficiently Whorfian sense of the shaky contingency of symbolic scaffolds that their own mathematical logicians warn them about.[23] It is therefore entirely appropriate that Vasco Ronchi should call his book *The History of Light,* since different light-worlds were apperceived via successive paradigms. *Scientific theories are in this like alternative cultures.*

To see scientific development as serenely linear rather than disjunctive is perhaps understandable in a discipline so honorably motivated and ready to discard hypotheses that no longer serve intellectual peace of mind. But it is difficult for the student and the young mind without perspective of style-graveyards not to feel that what we believe *now*— and on authority!—is simply true. The oedipal animal has simply not yet discovered the limited contingency of mere intellectual manhood. To construe Freud, not unfairly, he suffers an over-evaluation of the paradigm. (The awesome responsibility of the scientist was first borne in upon me on discovering that authoritative dogma for the founding of new Indian peyote churches was being taken from my—conceivably fallible?— doctoral dissertation of a third-century ago. And how many grave authorities on one bone fragment does it take to make a current paleontological truth?)

The irony of "social scientists" appetitive of the prestige of physical scientists is that they have failed to discern changes of paradigm in the physical sciences themselves. Thus "social scientists" imperceptive of the Einsteinian relativity of the observer that both Freud and anthropology would enforce upon us, still solemnly manipulate their data in a world of innocently Newtonian mechanics, unaware of the critical importance of the relativists' subjective position and their "countertransference" to their "data."[24] Without ethnologic perspective all social science is hopelessly pre-relativistic—and some, like economics and political science, have scarcely begun to pay even the preliminary lip-service to ethnology that psychology and sociology piously do. The human universe has ethnographic space and historic time too! The student of society as chastened humanist we can still admire, but the sociologist as computer-scientist would make the angels weep. A subtler and undiscerned computer, his unacknowledged time-serving and symbol-laden brain has already programmed his "computerized" cultural results before they are fed to the Truth Machine. Their "data" go in, and come out, untouched by human mind. Or so they think.

Of course the predicament of symbol-using culture-animals is dis-comfiting. But if this is our psycho-cultural epistemological predicament, let us state it as clearly and honestly as we can. To speak of the psychotic, the culture hero, and the scientist as brothers is not an idle or irresponsible extravagance. Men did literally call Copernicus mad when he proclaimed that the obviously static and stolid earth does move. Is not Freud insane to say a man does not know his own mind? And what of Einstein who insists that existence does not exist *now* in three easy experiential dimensions but only in the space of time? Commonsensical Euclidean space, we all know, is linear, homogeneous, and decently isotropic; but Einsteinian space is outrageously warped and curved by matter and has four unimaginably disposed but indispensable dimensions, including the greatest mystery in the universe, time, without which even space, which is nothing, cannot be. Unless, of course, space is only the speed of light in disguise, light really being only space-warping matter!

"Common sense" is merely the unexamined consensus of our day, unaware of the fact that, by drastic steps, consensus changes radically in time—and that the very language we express consensus in, by im-perceptible linguistic steps changes into the unintelligibility of a "foreign" language, in a few centuries, in a few hundred miles. Indeed, consensus is our only sanity, and non-consensus our first measure of psychosis. Science is only a more systematically sought supra-tribal consensus, on this matter a difference in degree, not in kind. The questions we hold steadily in view here are, What is thinking for? and what does culture do for us? Scientific endeavor is homeostasis-making too. But the critical point is, at what price of further adaptation to the environment is an inner homeostasis purchased? To what culture-evolutionary specialization does it commit us? And what proportions of self-serving Pleasure Principle and adaptation-loyal Reality Principle enter into the "solution"? For organisms *invent* reality as they evolve.[25] They discover new *potentialities* of matter.

The motivational aspect of belief is demonstrated in a recent study[26] showing that disconfirmation of a prophecy may only increase the in-tensity of religious proselytizing—no doubt growing out of a naïvely democratic epistemology which holds that the more believers, the higher the truth value of the belief. In "Lake City" not long ago, Mrs. Marian Keech began to get messages from outer space, from Sanandra of the planet *Clarion* she said, predicting the end of the world by flood. Others joined her cult, including a potential rival through whom not only Sanandra but "one who knows" (the Creator himself) spoke and prophesied. But grave disconfirmation of the All-Knowing One's prophecies ensued. In particular, the predicted flying saucer never arrived to rescue them, though the cultists had obediently quit their jobs, fasted, abstained from mending household appliances, and otherwise prepared themselves quite like pious Xosas. With failure of the prophecy, the cultists did not shun but instead began zealously to seek publicity in the press, as if a larger clientele increased prophetic apodicity. The Sanandra cult shaped a bona fide sub-culture. Nevertheless, the psychiatrist might make relevant remarks on the characteristic impermeability of paranoia to cognitive feedback.

Prophetic movements seem especially common among socially, economically, politically, educationally and otherwise deprived populations. In this sense the crisis cult would represent, as Firth points out, "an instance of incompatibility between wants and the means of satisfaction."[27] But may not the formula be too broad? Is not this incompatibility in some sense that to which every organism lies heir? Besides, in man, "invention is the mother of necessity." Needed for unhappiness are not only biological but also culturally induced wants—perhaps also the spectacle of cultural ways of gratifying them. This spectacle is afforded either in acculturational or in social-class contexts, which in effect often resemble one another. Aberle has borrowed Barber's (before him, Lasswell's and Nash's) insight, essentially the same as Firth's, and has refined it. Aberle believes that "relative deprivation" is present as a strain in all such movements (a view, again, that is curiously oedipal in its implicit assumptions). This relative deprivation is the "negative discrepancy between legitimate expectation and actuality," past versus present, present versus future, and one's own versus others'.

It is immediately apparent that "relative deprivation" would apply widely to cargo cults, and in all contacts of societies that have differing economic potential, to numerous African and Melanesian and other anti-colonial political movements, to most post-contact and acculturative movements, to the majority of internal class revolutions, and indeed to some international wars as well. Aberle vigorously denies that "pure existential unease or concern with spiritual discomfort dissociated from the social condition of participants forms a useful basis of explaining these movements."[28] Of course all cults must express a felt need, but the gravamen of Aberle's argument is to change a psychological explanation into an economic one, and all acculturation becomes a disguised Marxian class conflict.

Aberle is surely right that the mere presence of psychic stress is not enough to produce a crisis cult. On the one hand, suicide, war, crime, psychosomatic disease, psychosis, apathy and anomie are some alternative ways of responding to psychic stress. On the other hand, the hunter who fails to find game on one of four days may go hungry, but he sets up no cult (says Aberle) if such deprival is his standard expectation. Still, the millionaire reduced to his last town house and country home could suffer psychologically from the discrepancy between expectation and actuality, but would suffer no hardship biologically. Hence much hinges on the qualifier in the phrase *"legitimate* expectation," since we are notoriously latitudinarian when "legitimate" applies to ourselves.

The formula may be too narrow. At times, and for some people, mere naked wish qualifies psychologically as legitimation, and the mere frustration of wish may invite reaction of some sort. Who is to say that the frustrated hunter might not set up either private magic or a group cult to promote greater success in hunting? And might not the oil millionaire "relatively deprived" of his "legitimate expectation" to depletion allowances originate or join a nativistic Texan cult? A complete theory of crisis cults ought to explain those of the "haves" as well as of the "have-nots." Aberle's formula at the same time may be too broad. Does the hard-working Melanesian have the same "right" to cargo as idle members of the society that created it? Does the African once arduously Christianized now have a legitimate expectation of radios and motorbikes in default of the historic culture and technology producing them? Do autistic Hindus who refuse to eat beef have an earned right to the wheat grown by a "materialist" technology? How much does humanity have a right to American cargo? How much right has the remittance hipster to the clothing produced by a poor-white textile worker in a southern mill? And does the envious poor white have the same claim to a fine motor car as the professional man disciplined a lifetime to earn it? "Legitimate" is a judgmental word that is hard to handle, and it is questionable whether we need Aberle's note of class invidiousness in all cases, though his formula has great inclusiveness.

Burridge has an interesting psychological formulation, though modestly intended to apply only to Melanesian movements. Cargo ideology, he thinks, is expressed in a "myth-dream" which is "a series of themes, propositions, and problems which are found in myths, in dreams, in the half-light of conversation, and in the emotional responses to a variety of actions, and questions asked."[29] The myth-dream explains present reality and future hope alike; the charismatic leader embodies the "new man" who will transcend present limitations and lead the people to a new cultural dispensation; while cult ritual expresses the myth-dream behaviorally. Burridge's theory is an attractive one, with far wider application than the cargo cult alone. It derives ultimately from the "mystic communion" described by Durkheim, perhaps also from Malinowski's Appendix to Ogden and Richards' *The Meaning of Meaning*.[30]

The reaction of one reviewer to Burridge's provocative book is interesting and significant.

One is disturbed to find an anthropologist writing that the followers of cargo cults behave "in accordance with the dictates of their emotions rather than their intellects" (p. xviii) and that the Tangu live in a "dreamland beyond the confines of civilized men" where "are lodged those truths which white men tend to hide in asylums".[31]

Why not? It is indeed disturbing to have it hinted that part of culture can be irrational—and fairly enough so long as one does not confine this privilege to "prelogical" primitives, but extends the franchise to all men. It is precisely the need to rationalize all culture into terms acceptable to ourselves (itself a culturally homeostatic device) that blinds us to an understanding of the nature and function of culture and of cults.

We must protest the insistence on rationalizing the irrational. An arrant example of this rationalizing process is to be found in a recent article by Marvin Harris on the cultural ecology of India's sacred cattle.[32] Harris argues that a consequence (though surely not the intention?) of the taboo on eating beef is to provide marginal and depressed castes— through *breaking* the taboo!—with an occasional though critical source of protein. He further quite dubiously imputes to Mahatma Gandhi a full and conscious understanding (the author's own) of the ecological factors in his argument, although, since Mahatma Gandhi did not institute the taboo, the relevance of this point escapes the reader, unless this means that mystics are our best ecologists.

The argument, spelled out, is that no matter what the native rationale of a culture trait may be, the mere *existence* of the trait must demonstrate its ultimate rightness and objective adaptivity in some remotely arguable sense. (Does the *de facto* existence of a madman's belief make it valid? or by calling him mad do we remove him from the privilege of our rationalizing?) If the clear purpose of the taboo on cow-eating is thus rational, why did not the Indians formulate their alleged objective on "rational" grounds? Did orthodox Brahmans anciently have the future benefit to outcastes in mind when they set up this

totemic taboo—so that in *contravening the taboo* and at the price of
social outcasting and other crippling disadvantages, outcaste Hindus
might eat beef or beef carrion? The outcaste has adaptively substituted
social punishment for ecological deprivation? Is the price, on the whole,
worth the benefit? If so, and if misbehavior is thus adaptive, why do not
more Hindu castes adopt it? If to be un-Brahman in behavior benefits
the non-Brahman, how does the taboo benefit the Brahman who instituted it? Cannot Brahman motives be Brahman motives, despite the
offense to our cognitive categories! Dr. Harris, most ingeniously, but
against his intention, has merely demonstrated that *anti*-cultural behavior has been adaptive (this much must be conceded)—and his argument is in obvious defense against a troubling awareness that huge
populations, for long centuries, under cultural impetus, *can act irrationally*. They can. No emic-etic re-rationalization can change this fact.

To argue ingeniously that the benefit to outcastes is an unintended
outcome of the taboo is one matter—but only if we admit that cultural
speciation is random, irrational and blind, just as biological mutations
are. To undertake to defend all traditions of all men in this fashion
takes a truly talmudic tortuousness and industry. There is no rationality
to be defended here, and certainly the explicit meaning of the taboo in
Hinduism ("The cow is our Mother!") does not explain the "ecology" of
the matter. If grass-eating cattle do not compete with man in any
ecological niche, what is to prevent his eating them? How then is fore-
swearing beef beneficial? Cannot culture traits, on occasion, be dysfunc-
tional! If biological analogy is to be used, at least use it tough-mindedly
and correctly! Even if culture is man's biologically adaptive technique, in
a more precise and accurate sense, is all biological (and hence cultural)
innovation necessarily adaptive? Obviously it is not, or we would have
no fossils of extinct species and no human history. This insistence on forever translating native *emic* meanings into our own *etic* ones not only
masks what is happening in native culture, but also what is happening
in our super-added own. An anemic argument has been transformed into
an emetic one.

Sir James Frazer, in his forgotten little book on *Psyche's Task*,[33] long
ago produced a number of similarly naïve re-rationalizations of native
practices—but Sir James is out of date with social anthropologists, who
insist on knowing only the present, which they can explain functionally
quite without reference to the past. If man's rationality be insisted on,
must not each generation of anthropologists, as our culture changes, re-
re-rationalize the alien—and the past?—for even the cognitive categories
of our science change in historic time! Let us say hastily now that not

eating beef reduces cholesterol deposits in artery walls—but, alas, this pretty theory is already a decade out of date! What *did* the ancients know that we do not yet know! Must the "functional" explanations of social anthropologists descend to such jesuitry? Is it Psyche's task merely to be clever?

It is of course a generous and worthy impulse of Burridge's reviewer to protect primitives from the imputation of *always* embodying a "prelogical mentality" invidiously from our own, if such has been his motive. But this need to flay a dead Lévy-Bruhl is intellectually out of date too (the a-historical social anthropologists are ɔo obsessed with up-to-dateness!), and the price is evidently sometimes to embody prelogicality ourselves in the process. Meanwhile, when we examine what the unwittingly homeostatic function of such rationalization is to ourselves it appears less respectable intellectually. The wholesale transmogrification of motives and contexts is not only bad ethnography, whatever it may be as ecology, but also bad anthropology, because it stultifies our understanding of culture at large. Because cultures are valued we need not look on them as therefore valuable and viable and valid, but merely as sets of human hypotheses in the process of being tested biologically. Since we lack precognition of the results, we need in the process neither arrogant ethnocentrism nor condescending re-rationalization of the primitive.

Burridge, in fine, should be commended and not condemned for facing the possibility that Melanesian *mambu* may be in fact quite irrational, both in meaning and consequence. Our culture does not empower us to know. The ultimate adaptive consequences of "rational" and "irrational" culture alike may lie beyond our ken, however we busy ourselves in cross-cultural judgment—inevitably and understandably, the homeostatic function of culture being what it is. But in avoiding one crassly ethnocentric judgment (the "prelogical mentality of primitives") we fall into another more subtle and arrogant ethnocentrism (that all rationales must be rationalized into our own). Burridge may be right, whatever the immediate emotional and ultimately epistemological distress that this may cause us. Worse, Burridge may be right not only about *mambu* but also about man at large.

The most sophisticated thinking on crisis cults that we know of is Fokke Sierksma's, in his important work, *Een nieuwe hemel en een nieuwe aarde*,[34] termed by Werblowsky "a brilliant, exasperating, and at times infuriating book." It is regrettable to know the Dutch work only fragmentarily and at secondhand, through Zwi Werblowsky's review-summary. It is a gratification, however, to sense convergence in our thinking, developed in complete independence. For Sierksma evidently understands that psychiatry, if not human biology, must be called upon, far more largely than heretofore, for any understanding of crisis cults. Sierksma is manifestly sensitive to the culture-and-personality approach also, since he defends Williams' pioneering work on the Vailala Madness against Worsley's objection to such psychological, and indeed highly un-Marxist, concepts as Williams' on Papuan personality as a factor in the cargo cult. Sierksma dissects this to a degree that enables him to discriminate between certain traits in the Papuan "cargo cult" and the Plains "ghost dance"—a welcome skill indeed. Most stimulating indeed is a single statement in Werblowsky that "Sierksma's way of putting the matter can be summarized thus: Acculturation produces socially disintegrating and individually neuroticizing effects."[35] It is plain that Sierksma trends toward the holism of dynamic understanding that crisis cults demand.

A few other theories are worthy of note. Firth[36] proposed a theory of cargo cults based on his work in Tikopia; but Berndt[37] thought the Elcho Island movement had no "cargo" significance unless the wish for goods is so generalized as to become meaningless. In his stimulating and important writings, Worsley[38] saw cargo cults as nascent Melanesian nationalism, just as Edmonson, wryly, wrote that "In its nativistic aspect anthropology is nascent internationalism."[39] It is interesting that "cargo" ideology has occurred quite independently other than in Oceania. The Zurvanite notion was that the seven planets, spawned by Ahriman, "intercept all the goods bestowed by the constellations and divert them to the use of the demons."[40] This view is pre-Marxian.

G. S. Parsonson[41] has the curious theory that Polynesian thievery, and the custom of loosing moorings to cause shipwreck for plunder which Captain Cook encountered at almost every island he touched, may be the true origin of cargo cults. Stifled in Polynesia by the rapid victory there of Christianity with its teaching of respect for private property, cargo ideology was significant only in Melanesia, where the influence of Christianity was slower to come and less wide. In effect, their *not* being Christian-acculturated explains the Melanesian cargo cult! The details are a matter for Melanesianists to settle, and yet it is to be hoped that any theory adequate for one area would serve to understand all crisis cults everywhere.

Enough has been argued now to make it reasonably clear that no particularist explanation—whether political, military, economic, psychological, or cultural—can exclusively and exhaustively "save the data" of any single crisis cult. This conviction comes not from any willingness to forego the doubtless exhilarating process of whittling out one more causal explanation, and still another typology, but rather from a growing apprehension of what as scientists we are really doing in the process. Unless we also understand the meaning of culture in human biology, we will have quite missed the point.

Finding native beliefs unbelievable, some "realists" insist on *simpliste* "natural law" politico-economic explanations. Thus Rosberg and Nottingham tend to be short with anthropologists and their cultural-background "myth of mau mau"[42] and to set anthropologists straight with the true explanation provided by their own specialty, political science. Nativistic, spectacular, complex and murderous, *maumau* is really only Kenyan nationalism! It may be that. But the explanation impoverishes the phenomenon. At least the anthropologist Jomo Kenyatta was somehow part of it too, and also ancient Kikuyu religious forms.

This example implies no animus toward political scientists, but only to the tunnel vision that they and others would enforce upon us. An example could just as easily be taken from economics—that cargo cults are purely economic phenomena, both fomented by and explainable by Marxism alone. Each of these employs only one disciplinary "language" to describe a holistic human phenomenon. Another language might describe the complex event equally well, and equally poorly. Indeed, much can be translated into another explanatory system, since the military is the arm of the political, but the motive of each may be economic, hence psychological, at the same time that all the behaviors may be seen culturally. Instead of abusing German for not being English, or claiming that French is a better language to describe crisis cults than either, it may be more edifying to be polylingual, or at least to be able to listen to, if one cannot speak fluently, these many languages. Since crisis cults are, after all, human behavior, it may be that all the behavioral sciences are needed —including human biology, since other primates appear to lack crisis cults.

In the study of crisis cults, evidently the word "and" serves better than the contumelious and contentious word "only." For example: the White Mountain Apache prophet of 1920 reincarnated the native Slayer-of-Monsters *and* he held his dances on the Christian Sunday; *and* he was anti-witchcraft, yet got his shamanistic songs in power revelations; *and* he was in some ways anti-nativistic, yet his cultists danced with live snakes (Hopi acculturation?) from which he got his power; *and* they knew of the historically earlier Cibecue Apache *darodira* cult of 1903–6 in which dancing would lift the faithful to the sky while a flood purged the earth, yet they claimed that neither the Prophet Dance nor the Ghost Dance had ever reached them; *and* the Cibecue prophet claimed to bring back the dead, yet lost his life in a battle with government troops; *and* they fought the whites, yet a major figure in their song cycle was "Black Coat" representing a Catholic priest; *and* they were miserably poor compared to the Pueblo Indians and the whites; *and* Geronimo had been defeated in battle; *and* . . .[43] We need to know all these things, and more, if we want to understand how it felt to be a White Mountain Apache in 1920. And we must avoid doctrinaire disciplinary reductionism even though we can use only one language in one breath. The Taiping Rebellion was truly a politico-economic war of partly non-Chinese poor farmers against the Manchus; but this does not alter the fact that its originator Hung Hsiu-ch'üan did suffer a psychotic break when he again failed the government examinations. Many human vectors are components of the final N-dimensioned poly-parallelogram of force in social movements. And many factors influence human beings. Crisis cults are complexly caused; in Freud's sense they are intricately "over-determined."

The emotional and intellectual base of every people's life is an accepted model of the world. And, if they reach this sophistication, some self-made model of themselves. Of these outward and inward landscapes communication alone makes this social animal human. However—since symbols are what they are, adaptive man-made artifacts—the human predicament forever is that, in every case, each system is only an ideology or a language of reference. So long as one's fellows believe in this ideology and use this language, the paradigm is our biological substitute for the universe. On that faith our fate depends.

But in every age, sensitive, aberrant, creative individuals, in their personal anguish with life and defrauded of the comforts expected from old truths, indeed seemingly promised in childish experience of parents, now disenchanted by maturity come close to awareness of the dire contingency of all symbols and imagine their own, which, in being nearer to contemporary need, may spread like an intellectual epidemic, while the old belief-world vanishes into myth. Cognitive innovation is the individual's temerarious mutation, as culture is the speciation of the society. In this animal, the Other is always in part the creature of our need, and truth an experience of alienation. If any men could understand this, it should be we, for we have been living in such an epistemological crisis for some time. In fully apprehending our existentialist predicament, belief itself becomes obsolescent. Perhaps we should settle for repeated loneliness and scientific systematic doubt.

NOTES

(IX Culture and Acculturation)

1. Leon Festinger, *A Theory of Cognitive Dissonance* (Evanston: Row, Peterson & Co., 1957).

2. L. Festinger, H. W. Riecken and S. Schachter, *When Prophecy Fails* (Minneapolis: University of Minnesota Press, 1956).

3. John Lofland, *Doomsday Cult: A Study of Conversion, Proselytization, and Maintenance of Faith* (Englewood Cliffs: Prentice-Hall Paperback, 1966). See also B. Bernardi, *The Mugwe, A Failing Prophet: A Study of a Religious and Public Dignitary of the Meru of Kenya* (London: Oxford University Press, 1959).

4. C. S. Belshaw, review of Guariglia in *Current Anthropology*, 6 (1965) 448. B. Thomson, "The Kalou-Vu (ancestor-gods) of the Fijians," *Journal of the Anthropological Institute of Great Britain and Ireland*, 24 (1895) 340–59. James W. Fernandez, *Symbolic Consensus*, pp. 902–29. On pre-white spread in New Guinea highlands, Worsley, *Millenarian Movements*, p. 21.

5. Andersson, *op. cit.*, p. 57. Fuller discussions of these movements will be found in La Barre, *Crisis Cults*.

6. Williams, *Vailala Madness*, p. 2.

7. Edwin W. Smith and A. M. Dale, *The Ila-Speaking Peoples of Northern Rhodesia* (London: Macmillan, 2 vols., 1920, II:197–212). Audrey Richards. "A Modern Movement of Witch-finders," *Africa*, 8 (1935) 448–61. H. Debrunner, *Witchcraft in Ghana, A Study on the Belief in Destructive Witches and its Effect on the Akan Tribe* (Accra: Presbyterian Book Depot, 2nd ed., 1961). M. G. Marwick, "Another Modern Anti-Witchcraft Movement in East Central Africa," *Africa*, 20 (1950) 100–12.

8. Shepperson, *Nyasaland*, p. 157.

9. F. G. Speck, "Catawba Religious Beliefs, Mortuary Customs, and Dances," *Primitive Man*, 12 (1939) 21–57.

10. Shepperson, *Nyasaland*, p. 148.

11. John Useem, "Report on Yap, Palau, and the Lesser Islands of the Western Carolines" (Honolulu: U. S. Commercial Company Economic Survey, October 1946, pp. 130–33).

12. H. G. Barnett, *Indian Shakers, A Messianic Cult of the Pacific Northwest* (Carbondale: University of Southern Illinois Press, 1957). On this cult, see also J. Collins, "The Indian Shaker Church: A Study of Continuity and Change in Religion," *Southwestern Journal of Anthropology*, 6 (1950) 399–411; and Erna Gunther, in Marian W. Smith, *op. cit.*, pp. 37–76.

13. As to reverse acculturation, it is difficult to credit that the University of Chicago anthropologist J. S. Slotkin actually became a convert to peyotist ideology, but he nevertheless considered himself a member of the Native American Church (*Peyote Religion, passim*).

14. Bronislaw Malinowski, *Magic, Science and Religion*, pp. 30–31; the original formulation of this idea is in his article "Culture" in *Encyclopedia of the Social Sciences*, 4:621–46, p. 636. Thoughtful critiques of his position: Michael M. Ames, "Reaction to Stress: A Comparative Study of Nativism," *Davidson Journal of Anthropology*, 3 (1957) 1 [mimeographed]; and George C. Homans, "Anxiety and

Ritual: The Theories of Malinowski and Radcliffe-Browne," *American Anthropologist*, 43 (1941) 164–72.

15. W. A. Lessa, "The Social Effects of Typhoon Ophelia (1960) on Ulithi," *Micronesia*, 1 (1964) 1–47. See also A. F. C. Wallace, "A Study of the Literature and Suggestions for Further Research, Human Behavior in Extreme Situations," *Disaster Study No. 1, 1956* (Washington: National Academy of Sciences-National Research Council, Publication 390, Committee on Disaster Studies); *idem*, "An Exploratory Study of Individual and Community Behavior in an Extreme Situation, Tornado in Worcester," *ibid.*, Publication 392, *Disaster Study No. 3, 1956;* and *idem, Patterns of Group Behavior in Disaster* (Washington, D.C.: Walter Reed Army Institute of Research, Publication No. 584, 1958).

16. Hans Selye, *The Stress of Life* (New York: McGraw-Hill, 1956).

17. George Devereux first saw Selye's concept of decompensatory stress-physiology in psychological terms, in "Catastrophic Reactions in Normals," *American Imago*, 7 (1951) 2–9.

18. The germ of my insight comes from a letter of Freud to Ferenczi (1 January 1910) in a chance remark about religion on which he wrote "Its ultimate basis is the infantile helplessness of mankind"—to which he added, "But I don't intend to elaborate it [*Ausführung schenke ich mir aber*]," in Ernest Jones, *Life and Work of Sigmund Freud*, II:350.

19. "Regression in the service of the ego" is a precise formulation owed to E. Kris, *Psychoanalytic Explorations in Art* (New York: International Universities Press, 1952, pp. 56–63; also Schocken Books, 1964). On regression as an ego-defense, see Otto Fenichel, *The Psychoanalytic Theory of Neurosis* (New York: Norton, 1945, p. 160), who notes however that the part played by the ego in regression is different from that in all other defense mechanisms, since regression *happens to* the ego, decompensating under stress in peculiar conditions of passive weakness. See also H. Hartmann, *Ego Psychology and the Problem of Adaptation* (New York: International Universities Press, 1958). All these concepts derive ultimately from Freud, *The Problem of Anxiety* (New York: Norton, 1936).

20. With respect to technology and the *evolution of [material] culture*, it seems to me that anthropologists must agree with Leslie White, especially in the chapter "Energy and the Evolution of Culture" in *The Science of Culture* (New York: Evergreen Books, 1949, pp. 363–93). But non-material sacred culture is a different, and however much he deplores it, *psychological* phenomenon. Kroeber introduced the terms "reality culture" and "value culture" in *The Nature of Culture* (Chicago: University of Chicago Press, 1952, pp. 152–66); see also his "History of Anthropological Thought," in W. L. Thomas (ed.), *Yearbook of Anthropology* (Chicago: University of Chicago Press, 1955, pp. 293–311, p. 301)—with the useful distinction that some non-technological aspects of science also belong to "value culture." Like mine, Kroeber's concept derives of course from the sacred-secular dichotomy of traditional French sociology. A recent statement in this tradition is Roger Caillois, *Man and the Sacred* (New York: Free Press, 1960).

21. "Changes in Bodily Form of Descendants of Immigrants," in Franz Boas, *Race, Language and Culture* (New York: Macmillan, 1940, pp. 60–75). Since he cast his inductive net only thus far, Kinsey studied not *Sexual Behavior in the Human Male* (Philadelphia: W. B. Saunders & Co., 1948) but only in contemporary white males of the United States, and hence discovered only present-day folk myth, that males are oversexed—from which the anthropologist could correctly predict the folklore to be discovered in the second volume, that females have almost no interest in sexuality at all. Psychologists, but not sociologists, have already discovered the fallacy of metrical objectivism; see Sigmund Koch, "Epilogue" to *Psychology: A Study of a Science* (New York: McGraw-Hill, 7 vols., 1959–63, 3:730–83).

22. T. S. Kuhn, *The Structure of Scientific Revolutions* (Chicago: University of Chicago Press, Phoenix Books, 1962).

23. B. L. Whorf, *Language, Thought and Reality* (Cambridge: Technology Press of the Massachusetts Institute of Technology, 1956)—the linguistic portion of a larger Wittgensteinian revolution (L. Wittgenstein, *Tractatus Logico-Philosophicus,* New York: Humanities Press, 1961). Vasco Ronchi, *Storia della Luce* (Bologna: Nicola Zanichelli, 1939, 2nd. ed. 1952).

24. George Devereux, *From Anxiety to Method.*

25. J. von Uexkull, *Theoretical Biology* (New York: Harcourt, Brace & Co., 1926).

26. Festinger *et al., op. cit.* The difficulty of locating Sanandra on *Clarion* is that this hitherto unreported planet must be beyond the orbit of the farthest one known, Pluto. To converse with Sanandra and get an answer back would take two times the light years that Clarion is distant from the earth for each response, which must make colloquy something of a bore. At this rate, *Clarion* could not be, as it sounds, a *daily* newspaper; still, "Clarion" has an odd clang with "Marian"—but this leaves in some doubt yet the identity of Sanandra, though he or she evidently speaks good middle-western American English.

27. Raymond Firth, *Elements of Social Organization,* p. 113.

28. David Aberle, "A Note on Relative Deprivation Theory as Applied to Millenarian and Other Cult Movements," in Thrupp, *op. cit.,* pp. 209–14, p. 209. Barber, Lasswell, and Nash are cited in D. M. Aberle, *The Peyote Religion Among the Navaho* (Chicago: Aldine Publishing Company, 1966, p. 315n.). See L. Spier, W. Suttles, and M. J. Herskovits, "Comments on Aberle's Theory of Deprivation," *Southwestern Journal of Anthropology,* 15, (1959) 84–88. Ironically, the effectiveness and applicability of Aberle's formula is *owing to* its oedipal tone, a "universality" of explanation he consciously so impugns (Aberle, *A Note,* p. 213); again, such autistic dream movements may be a normal pan-human phenomenon, hence the universally human must be explained in terms of a human universal. By contrast, Clyde Kluckhohn accepted psychological generalization in nativistic movements ("Universal Categories in Culture," in A. L. Kroeber [ed.], *Anthropology Today* Chicago: University of Chicago Press, 1953, pp. 507–23, page 514).

29. K. O. L. Burridge, *Mambu,* p. 148. As a Dallas psychiatrist, Dr. A. W. Long, has pointed out in discussing a lecture of mine, ritual curiously tends to "validate" belief, i.e. as a *sensory experience* accompanied by stimulation of sight, hearing, smell, taste, touch, kinaesthesias, etc. To this I would add, ritual as performed in a wide-awake state is therefore *more convincing* than the dream (since the REM state is accompanied by a marked *cut-off* from myokinetic activity, sensory input, etc.) and since ritual is also a belief-supporting *social* experience. Liturgy therefore tends to "prove" dogma, at least as an emotional experience.

30. Malinowski, in C. K. Ogden and I. A. Richards, *The Meaning of Meaning* (New York: Harcourt, Brace & Co., 2nd rev. ed., 1927, pp. 296–336).

31. Burridge, *op. cit.,* p. 251. Burridge's reviewer is C. A. Valentine, quoted from the *American Anthropologist,* 63 (1961) 1114–15, page 1115.

32. Marvin Harris, "The Cultural Ecology of India's Sacred Cattle," *Current Anthropology,* 7 (1966) 51–59.

33. J. G. Frazer, *Psyche's Task* (London: Macmillan, 2nd ed. rev., 1913).

34. Fokke Sierksma, *Een nieuwe hemel en een nieuwe aarde: Messianistische en eschatologische bewegingen en voorstellingen bij primitieve volken* ('s-Gravenhage: Mouton, 1961).

35. R. J. Zwi Werblowsky, *op. cit.,* pp. 164, 166, 170.

36. R. Firth, "The Theory of Cargo Cults: A Note on Tikopia," *Man,* 55, #142 (1955) 130–32. Others: Judy Inglis, "Cargo Cults: The Problem of Explanation,"

Oceania, 27 (1957) 249–63; W. E. H. Stanner, "On the Interpretation of Cargo Cults," *Oceania,* 29 (1958) 1–25; and I. C. Jarvie, "Theories of Cargo Cults: A Critical Analysis," *Oceania,* 34 (1963) 1–31.

37. R. Berndt, *An Adjustment Movement in Arnhem Land, Northern Territory of Australia* (The Hague: Mouton, 1962, p. 85).

38. Worsley, *The Trumpet Shall Sound,* p. 193.

39. Edmonson, *op. cit.,* p. 200.

40. David Winston, "The Iranian Component in the Bible, Apocrypha, and Qumran: A Review of the Evidence," *History of Religions,* 5 (1966) 183–216, p. 193.

41. G. S. Parsonson, Review of The Journals of Captain Cook, *American Anthropologist,* 65 (1963) 959–61, p. 960. Some more general theories of explanation are those by B. R. Wilson, "Millennialism in Comparative Perspective," *Comparative Studies in Society and History,* 6 (1963) 93–114; Howard Kaminsky, "The Problem of Explanation," in Thrupp, *op. cit.,* pp. 215–17; and Marian W. Smith, "Towards a classification of cult movements," *Man,* 59 (1959) №2:8–12 and №27, p. 28.

42. C. G. Rosberg, Jr. and John Nottingham, *The Myth of "Mau Mau," Nationalism in Kenya* (New York: Praeger, 1966).

43. Grenville Goodwin, "White Mountain Apache Religion," *American Anthropologist,* 40 (1938) 24–37; see also G. Goodwin and C. Kaut, "A Native Religious Movement among the White Mountain and Cibecue Apache," *Southwestern Journal of Anthropology,* 10 (1954) 385–404.

X

Shamans and Societies

CRISIS cults show two salient traits. Culturally the times are out of joint; and historically some individual seems born to set them right. The society faces some unwonted crisis, and some unwonted individual appears as a new leader. Abnormality, in some sense then, seems characteristic of both in these crises. Functionally, culture hero and culture change are closely related. But who is "abnormal" in these crises, individual or society or both? And abnormal in terms of what criteria? Indeed, in what sense can a majority of individuals in a society ever be abnormal—all the more since the "ghost dance" state seems typical for all mankind in certain definable situations.

Certainly a disturbance of equilibrium is manifest, often through an irruption from outside. But, though historically common, acculturative contact of native with European societies is by no means indispensable; the commonness is perhaps more a matter of the expansive geographic imperialism of European culture than of any intrinsic content. A curious ambivalence toward culture, both native and alien, is also apparent in these crises. There is a quite varied willingness to give up the native or to borrow the alien, to refind the old or embrace the new. Indeed, the feckless classification of these gradations and combinations has been the obsession of the taxonomists of crisis cults, who tell us nothing but the amount of mixture. But until the nature and function of culture itself is faced, the essential dynamism will of course be missed.

Loyalty to the cultural past primarily is found in the revival of *huaca* worship in Peru; in the Burkhan theology and ritual; in the Baigona snake cult, the *sevese,* and the *harisu* cults of the dead in Melanesia; and in those Shaker traits taken from the old winter ceremonies, etc. But with revivalism may also come reform: the Shawnee rejection of shamans and their jugglery; the casting away of medicine bundles by Känakûk, peyotists, and others; the auto-da-fé of Chugal's household idols, the Altai burning of drums, and other anti-shamanistic acts; the African abandonment of fetishes; the destruction of New Guinea masks and rituals, etc. The Reformation too was a rejection of the worldly accretions of the Roman Anti-Christ upon the body of pure Biblical and primitive belief. Just as commonly, crisis cults reject alien elements too: for example, Handsome Lake's proscription of fiddles, liquor, and card-playing; Smohalla's anathema on the new agriculture; the killing of cats and abjuration of tobacco among the Altai Turks, and the like.

Anti-white elements are as common as European imperialism: in the religion of the Delaware Prophet; in Tävibo's white-destroying earthquake or flood; in the Xosa revival and other African cults; and in the fantasy of ships coming filled with rifles in the early Vailala Madness and other movements. Some crisis cults have clear politico-military intent to drive out invaders: the Pueblo Revolt, the Maya revolutionaries of the "Talking Cross," Tupac Amaru and Juan Santos Atahuallpa in Peru, the Guaraní revolts, the Conspiracy of Pontiac, Tecumseh's Shawnee War, the Nez Percé War, the Creek War, the Sioux Ghost Dance Uprising under Sitting Bull—all these in America alone. The same clear anti-white elements also enter into Mau Mau, the Altai Oirot Federation and, perhaps, the "Papua for the Papuans" movement. But reformism is not always a consequence only of European-primitive conflict. There is reformism in Ikhnaton's anti-sacerdotal monotheism in ancient Egypt; in Judaism throughout, in Moses and the Israelites, the Old Testament Prophets and their times, the Maccabean revolt against Rome, and the promised Jewish Messiah; in India, the rise of Sikhism and Buddhism as revolts against Brahmanism; in Islam, the rise of Mohammed and the revolt of the Sudanese Mahdi; in China, the Taiping, "Red Eyebrow" and Boxer Rebellions; in Europe, Hitlerism and the Germanic nativistic Ghost Dance, De Gaullism and its persistent xenophobia, and many others.

At the same time that whites and their ways are rejected, there is often also a simultaneous and naïve copying of white culture traits: for example, symbolism and songs in the "Salvation Army" cults of Africa; stick airplanes in the cargo cult; even, commonly enough, the divine culture hero of the Europeans himself. Culture heroes are often "Modernist" too. The Delaware Prophet had his Bible sticks and "writing." Smohalla's bells and candles were borrowings from Catholicism, as were White Mountain Apache "Black Coat" songs, and the angel garb of the Head-he-go-round Heaven. The Shawnee "shaking hands with the prophet" using a string of power-laden *Sophora secundiflora* beads forcibly recalls the rosary, despite the entrenched nativism of the narcotic bean itself. Slo-cum's Shaker Church had so many Christian traits, in fact, that in time it was amalgamated with Presbyterianism, which embraced Shakerism as the Catawba embraced Mormonism. Wovoka of the second Ghost Dance got many Christian elements from his protector, David Wilson; and al-though basically native in its form, Sioux and Ute peyotism incorporated many Christian elements. The Pandava Korra Mallayyam drill with bamboo "guns" recalls some features of the African "Salvation Army" cults. Smohalla's copying of military ritual is also paralleled in the New Guinea imitation of the "fall in" of police lines. Indeed, the use of flags in both cults reminds us that even alien tribal fetishes can be borrowed.

Occasionally some borrowings seem pathetic or outrageous, ludicrous or even blasphemous to the white culture donors: the San Poil Michel's boat-building in imitation of Noah; the notion that the Biblical revelations of yore could come to a poor Shawnee Indian; the garbled theology and the misunderstanding of radio antennae, dinner table and office rituals in Melanesia; the preposterously literal imitation of Christ by many mes-siahs; and the foolish mistaking of Chinnery, David Thompson, and Dr. Moszkowski for ghosts or gods. Perhaps white influences are present in other supernatural dispensations: New Guinea ghosts were sometimes white; the White Oirot came on a white horse; African Negroes would sit in white garments and white skins on good seats in a white heaven; and both the man and woman guides of the Delaware prophet were dressed dazzlingly in white costumes. And the New Hanover "Johnson Cult" even sought to buy a white President for their leader. He could not be sold.

Every cultist ingroup is incipiently an autonomous entity, a closed society, a political unit, and therefore every Church a potential State. Overemphasized in explaining crisis cults, the political has been curiously neglected in most studies of shamanism. Both North American and Siberian shamans, we have seen, were often leaders as well as protectors of their groups; and South American shaman-messiahs commonly com-bined political and magical power over men and cosmos alike. Paul Roux has studied the power equally over the elements and political events among the shamans of Genghis Khan[1]; and René de Nebesky-Wojkowitz has shown that the state oracle or ceremonial divination in Tibet is a prophetic trance of distinctly shamanistic character.[2] The ancient Chinese *wu* were political shamans too. Clearly the Asiatic and American shaman has the same traditional roots, and his intrinsic political aspect re-appears strikingly in the messianic ghost dance prophets of North America and in the god-kings and shaman-chiefs of South America, Amazonian and Andean alike.

The same politico-magic complex is traceable in ancient Europe. The original Indoeuropean bards were politically powerful magicians: Orpheus's cosmic and Apollo's political shamanism were originally one. The great political power of the ecstatic oracles of Apollo in Greece, and of the shamaness-Sibylls in Rome, needs only to be alluded to in order to be recalled; and in the classic world, religion was largely state ritual, as Fustel de Coulanges and others have shown.[3] Both Odhin and Zeus were trickster shamans before they became merely kings of the cosmos. The political influence of shaman-bards seems to have been particularly powerful among the Celts.[4] Himself Pontifex Maximus, Caesar well understood he must drive out the Druids before he could conquer Gaul.[5] And, having taken refuge in Britain and become entrenched, the Celtic bards of Wales had their political power broken by the English only very late, and those of Ireland only in 1689 in the Battle of the Boyne. Welsh bards were formidable because they combined the functions of historian, musician, magician and ambassador in their sacrosanct persons. Giraldus Cambrensis[6] wrote that in twelfth-century Ireland, despite Strongbow's military successes, such a prophet-bard predicted that the English would be weakened and an unknown king would come to drive most of them out of Ireland. Perhaps the power of the bard is not yet quite dead among Celts; political figures in Ireland still have the charismatic quality that literary intellectuals have in modern France and poets in Wales.

But the political power of magician-priests among Indoeuropeans is not unique to the Celts. Among ancient Aryans, the Brahmans were authentic tyrants over society who ascribed to themselves the status of gods, for all that it was the warrior Kshatriyas who tended ultimately to become the kings. The connection of the bard not only with magic but with the intellectual and other arts is also deep-laid among Indoeuropeans. The sun god and hunter God Apollo led the Greek Muses. The head of state as ritual patron of the arts in ducal Florence and Venice and in princely Germany is far earlier than the Sun King of France. Most of Persia's great art was connected with the exaltation of the deified kings. The first artist of Europe, at Lascaux and Trois Frères, portrayed himself, the dancing shaman, magic owner and artificer of animals. Almost startling, however, is the statuette of an *antlered monarch* of the Sasanian[7] dynasty who revived Persian art in the third century A.D. If in France the antlered shaman of Trois Frères became Cernunnus, an antlered Gaulish god of the underworld, in Iran the horned potentate became the divine king—both scions of the Eurasiatic antler-crowned shaman.

But this is not an end to the matter. Divine rain kings are apparently indigenous to Africa. But there are ancient Caucasoids in the Sahara and north Africa some of whose shamanic traits, Coon thinks, are as early as the Capsian expansion of the Mesolithic.[8] As though they were the relicts of a conquered people—they have a secret language, now dying out, of which Fuchs recorded a small vocabulary—the Saharan shaman-smiths occupy a low social level, even below that of slaves, and yet they are free to come and go as they please, like their fellows in Arabia and like the ancient European bard-ambassadors. Despite their caste position, these smith-artificers have immense power and play a vital political role in the Sahara. Each chief and wealthy man has his own, but held to him only by voluntary association, and the magician-artificer acts as the counsellor, companion, courier and secret intelligence agent for the chief or wealthy magnate. He also practices magic and medicine, beats the drum (which he made) at dances and, like the West African court musician, sings songs flattering to those whom he wishes to influence, and announces news in a loud and stately voice. This arbitrary combination of attributes in a region of ancient Caucasoids can only be compared with those of the archaic European shaman-ambassador-magician-bard.

The political significance of the north African shaman-magician and the European magician-bard rests, we believe, on actual culture-historical grounds, just as do similarities in Sibero-American shamans. If the north African type is Capsian in date, once again the shaman is traceable to Mesolithic antiquity and beyond. Yet even if one reject a very ancient culture-historical link in common, the descriptive similarities still need to be accounted for. Perhaps every political leader is in some sense a charisma-laden savior (but where else than from an historic shaman-protector comes the incredible charisma of European kings, of Asiatic and African divine kings? whence the divine right of kings than from divinity? and are pinnacled crowns only the shaman's horned headdress of antiquity?) Perhaps charisma comes merely from awe before a leader's functional fatherhood? Moses was a messiah to the Hebrews long before and above any other—for all that he may have borrowed his monotheistic god from the tradition of Ikhnaton; behaved like an Egyptian prophet on the Mount, like an African snake-shaman with Aaron before the Pharaoh, and a Pharaoh-like African rain king in the Wilderness; and like a Pharaoh wrote his edicts on stone, and was prophet to a shaman's and smith's god of fire—for like a sheikh-patriarch he did lead his chosen people out of bondage to the borders of a Promised Land.

In a crisis-cult context, the Babylonian captivity was indeed an alien enslavement of urban political, religious and economic leaders in Jerusalem; and the Maccabean state did struggle against the politico-economic power of an alien imperial Rome. The culture-symbolic language of traditional shamanism, however irrational, may be genuinely age-old. But the same secular fact remains. Recurrently, one society does attempt to exercise a father's arbitrary authority over another, and with the best of good will to impose its own cultural truth. And yet men within each society inveterately and willingly seek a charismatic leader to submit to. Men want both a savior and freedom from dominance by one another. They want both a man's independence and a child's dependency, and in seeking both they can ultimately have neither purely. Imitative apes, they want both family and society. Men make tremendous sacrifice, even of life, for the *pater* of their patriotism—if the conceptual brotherhood lie within the mystique of the family and the culturally familiar. The lines of social definition fluctuate constantly, as do those of culture geography, but the earnest human sacrifice of war seems built into our biology. How can we have loyalty to truth without loyalty to Truth? Men cling to old familiar culture, but in the stress of historic crisis they often encounter a more powerful or satisfying new one. The ghost dance is a bewildered seeking of a proper model for one's humanity, for a place to put one's filial loyalty and faith, hence the mixed chaos of borrowing the new and clinging to the old. It is the crisis of identity of a society. It is the same in each individual, a question of how can I become what kind of man. What is the best model to imitate?

Consequently, crisis cults often tend to be associated with the economic-ecological pressure of an overwhelming alien group, since a differing cultural potential is nowhere more effectively exerted or felt than in the area of better-adaptive technological superiority as an evident fact. But it is often hard for the neophyte to identify and discriminate the sources of that superiority. The whites had Christianity; and under the whites' guns came the loss of the buffalo and the Great Depression of the Sioux. Which was it more critical to borrow, Christianity, agriculture, or guns? Armed Russian imperialism similarly pressed politically on the central Asiatic Turks quite as the Orthodox religion invaded their shamanistic Buddhism ideologically. The Altai themselves were keenly aware of the economic aspects of their plight in land loss and the new trade economy, but ideologically they could take only irrational revenge against cats and tobacco.

Did Indians in their ghost dance do rationally better under American acculturation than the Altai under the Russian? An irrelevant question, since rationality is no part of either side. Was colonialism in America gentler than the Russian in Asia? Is there any reason to suppose that the conflicts of human speciation should be less painful and biologically costly than the blind genetic mutations of other animals? Is cultural imperialism in Vietnam more witting, astute, humane than in South Africa? The fact is South Africa Xosa, like the Kikuyu of the recent *mau mau* in Kenya, are being submerged economically in their own lands just as surely as the Indians were in colonial America and the Altai Turks in central Siberia. The cultural saviors in all cases are sure that each is bearing a better way of life. Perhaps. Who knows? But it must be admitted that in all these cases the economic stands that natives took were often grievously autistic, as autistic and disastrous as the racism of their masters. Again, indentured labor for the whites broke up ceremonialized Melanesian economics at the same time it destroyed native village social life. But the Melanesians learned the wrong economic myths, a mere pseudo-technology of trade and communications, and irrelevant religious and social protocol.

In the crisis cults of European class-defined *Plebejereligionen,* certainly from classic and Christian times onward, sheer culture-deprivation, the lack of class-indigenous cultural know-how, passed down in family and class lines, is very conspicuous in the proletariat. "Hard-core" poverty itself, to an important degree, is a literal lack of middleclass cultural know-how. What strikes the observer of nativistic cults is this same helpless autism in (cultural) reality-deprived people under stress—deprived, that is, both of their own traditional explanatory myths and also of appropriate information about the cultural workings of the new economic myths. Stress, trauma, and wounded narcissism invariably thrust both individuals and societies back onto autistic preoccupation with the old and intimate. Autism is a state of preoccupation with subjective thoughts or fantasies, and ranges from brief indulgent revery in healthy persons to completely self-referrent ideas and magic ritual behavior without reference to any immediate outside reality.[9] Ultimately, autism is limited to one's limited cultural subject matter. Autism in the crisis cult is precisely that of the culture hero's dream. But to be successful he must dream in the cultural tongue and wish the wish of the society. "All men dream: but not equally," wrote T. E. Lawrence.[10] "Those who dream by night in the dusty recesses of their minds wake in the day to find that it was vanity: but the dreamers of the day are dangerous men, for they may act their dream with open eyes, to make it possible."

Culturally, one can operate only with what he knows, or thinks he knows. When the Allies bombed his Japanese-occupied village in Dutch

New Guinea, the young Papuan Stephanus noted that many Japanese were killed but no Papuans. Not recognizing a miracle of precision bombing, he decided the Papuans were a chosen people and the Japanese would perish. Then he remembered the teaching of old Angganita, the leper prophetess, about the redeemer Manawar. The missionaries had deceived them and had torn out the first pages of the Bible indicating that Jesus was a Papuan. So they killed missionaries and burned churches, but nevertheless gave their villages holy names like Jerusalem, Bethlehem, and Galilee. The legendary Manawar had been born of an immaculate conception; and when he returned, food would fall like manna from heaven, and the free Papuans would no longer need to work. But a famine threatened the followers of Stephanus who over-consumed their food in ritual feasts, so they successfully raided villages whose inhabitants would not join his cult. However, when they attacked Japanese corvettes with only wooden rifles, hundreds were killed, including Stephanus.[11]

Tokerua, the Massim prophet, got up one morning with his face transfigured "like a man whose wits had left him" after an interview with a spirit the night before.[12] During the next moon, thunder and rain would come in a gale of incredible fury, an earthquake would lift up a new island in Milne Bay, and a tidal wave would drown the coast for two or three months. Annihilation would come to all who refused to obey the behests of Tokerua, notably to give up matchboxes, knives and any other useful treasures from the *dimdim* or white men. As instructed by the prophet, the faithful villagers of Gabugabula abandoned their village and moved inland. Tokerua promised that when the catastrophe was over, the wind would veer to the southeast and waft ashore a huge ship crowded with spirits of the dead, and the balmy air would cover the land with gardens of yams and taro, and trees with delicious fruit. So they ate all their food, and ordinary gardening ceased; they even killed and ate three or four hundred of their beloved pigs. No cataclysm came, but many natives almost starved.

In 1902, after headhunting had been suppressed among the Toradja of Celebes, there was intense anxiety lest the ancestral spirits, no longer fed with a "harvest" of enemy heads, would perforce eat the villagers themselves. In central Sulawesi, a woman named Liombee then began a *mejapi* or religious retreat to the woods, and dressed in the evening like a male warrior, at which time the ancestral spirits spoke through her. Her prophecies did not come true, but this did not lessen her influence. It would be unnecessary now to plant the fields or care for livestock, and soon all people would go to the upperworld without dying. Cultists built a long wooden structure on stilts to be rowed into the air, after the old idea that the *tadu* or shaman flew to the sky on a boat rowed by other spirits. A later leader, Makusi, had no cultivated fields at all by his *mejapi* village, since food would be brought by a special ship from heaven; and no one should use curse words or the ship would capsize. But no ship of souls reached heaven, no ship of food came from it, and people died in still greater numbers.[13]

Such autistic fantasies about food seem especially common in crisis cults. To be sure there is the ecological fact of insufficient food among some primitive groups, whether famine is chronic, seasonal, or sporadic. And ever since Adam, labor to produce food has been arduous and unwelcome. And yet the arrant autism of some prophecies about food makes one wonder if they do not borrow their tone from the familiar autism of schizophrenics about food—that is, an authentic schizoid component in the prophet or the temporary schizophrenia of his dream speaks to passive fantasy in his faithful communicants. There are numerous examples of this. One Congo prophet prohibited all work, and no food crops were to be planted since people would now subsist on weeds.[14] Kimbangu's followers could not plant peanuts (rich in protein for a protein-poor people) otherwise women and domestic animals would become sterile[15]; also, blankets against the cold would be too heavy to wear at the Resurrection to the skies and must be sold for white clothing (and on these transactions some "Salvation Army" teachers became rich). In Alor, on the day the Good Beings were to arrive, people must kill all their pigs, cook rice, and then throw the food into a ravine—for no kin were supposed to eat at a death feast, even now that the dead were to arise and immortality for the living was to be accomplished by peeling off their skins. An earthquake would turn the world upside down, and there would then be plentiful food, said the prophet Malekala.[16] Autistic food fantasies of the Xosa prophets, the Shawnee Prophet and others with respect to crops are not uncommon elsewhere. In North Borneo, the Murut messiah Garing, who controlled 7700 spirit beings, would merely point to the ground and say "I grow food" for a crop ready to harvest to appear. The old would become young, the sick well, no one would die, and everyone would become *anbabangum* or divine. The Murut believed that Garing himself was invulnerable.[17]

The paranoid fantasy of invulnerability is found many places in the world, and is especially interesting psychiatrically. For example, in June 1898, Teungku Tapa, a Garo tribesman of Atjeh in northern Sumatra, gave out that he was invulnerable and could render impotent the weapons of unbelievers. Although the Achenese thereupon recognized him as Malém Diwa returned to life, Teungku Tapa and his followers were promptly defeated by Dutch troops. In 1899, however, this time with a band of followers from the Gayo country, he renewed his revolt; but in 1900 the god was slain near Piadak.[18] In 1930, in the hitherto only revolt of this century against British rule in Burma, Saya San raised an army of men in the Tharrawaddy district, tattooed them with *galons* or mythical eagles and also gave out charms of invulnerability to gunfire. But before the rebellion was suppressed, two thousand of his tattooed impregnables were shot dead, Saya San was captured in the Shan States, and in March 1931 executed in Tharrawaddy jail.[19]

In South Africa, Enoch Mgijima's "Israelites" fearlessly charged the guns of the civil authorities at Bulhoek Common, but 163 were killed and 129 wounded. In Nyasaland, in the coming American Negro invasion, bombs from planes would selectively kill only white people.[20] In America, Tävibo, Cheeztahpaezh, Sitting Bull, and Yellow Bird were all invulnerable; in fact, visionaries were quite commonly regarded as bulletproof in the warlike Plains.[21] In Middle America, in Quintana Roo, the "Talking Cross" was sent by God to protect the Maya against the firearms of the Djules (Spanish and Creoles of the ruling class).[22] In South America, Canella cultists all had invulnerability, a trait common enough to shamans there in any case. In Siberia, Chot Chelpan's Burkhan preserved him from Russian bullets.[23] In the Philippines, the Mindanao messiah claimed that bullets could not hurt him, but after five sect members were killed in Dukidnon Province others learned to use peasant women and children as shields against the provincial police. In the New Hebrides, despite promises, the "Naked" cultists of Tsek were by no means immune to shelling by HMS *Sydney,* though in prison Ronovoro died fearlessly in still unshaken belief in his invulnerability.[24]

The identical belief is common in Africa. Witch doctors in the *Kiluawa,* one of the "Kartelite" cults active early in 1961 in Kasongo, were believed to obtain invulnerability and immortality through human sacrifice.[25] When government troops occupied Kamaniola in the Congo in mid-June of 1964, they seized an old Bafulero woman, said to be the chief witch in the Kivu rebellion under Gaston Soumialot; Bafulero sorceresses made anti-bullet pills that turned enemy fire into water; and some soldiers also had straw "anti-dawas" tied around their rifle barrels.[26] On 3 February 1964, more than a hundred natives, armed only with bows, hatchets and *panga*-knives, were shot down by machine guns in an attack on the government garrison at Gungu in Kwili Province in the Congo. Their leader, Pierre Mulele, had fired blank cartridges against his chest to convince them that they would be invulnerable; they were said also to have been drugged with hashish.[27]

While it is highly possible that all the above Congo cases of "invulnerability" are simple cultural diffusion from earlier African crisis cults, the world-ranging concept itself rests upon universal body-image symbolisms of *impotentia penetrandi* and micturition.[28]

Sometimes indeed a magic liquid confers impregnability. In China, the Dowager Empress Tzu Hsi declared (though on advice she later denied) that the Boxers had an elixir which rendered them invulnerable.[29] In Biak, in Dutch New Guinea, millenarists attacked a Japanese warship, their only weapons being "blind" wooden rifles, their only armor a holy-water drink of invulnerability; but the Manseren cultists were mowed down in scores.[30] The *ngunzist* Kimbangu was deported to Katanga in 1921 and one day was to be shot, but according to legend "only water came from the soldiers' rifles."[31] In Indonesia, in the Radja Damai or "Prince of Peace" movement during the war occupation, Japanese bullets would turn to water when they struck the native drinker of the holy water of invulnerability.[32] The Majimaji Rebellion of 1905–6 in Tanganyika, East Africa, and also cultists in many well-known Islamic uprisings, had similar illusions (*maji* means "water" in Kiswahili). The Nuer prophet Gwek, in the Sudan, had invulnerability of the *majimaji* type, but this interesting symptom may have been complicated by his custom of sitting on a magic cattle-stake up his anus.[33]

Psychoanalysts say that the fantasy of invulnerability is a symbolic defense against an unconscious and forbidden sexual wish.[34] There are other means of obtaining invulnerability. In a Siamese cult, when the *Chao* or "demon lord" is obliged by conjurations to descend into the body of the *khon song,* a man dressed like the demon lord, the man is invulnerable as long as the god is in him, and cannot be touched by any sort of weapon.[35] In Siberia also, the shaman is invulnerable while the spirit possesses him; in the Southern Appalachians, snake-handling cultists are immune to snakebite, so long as the spirit of the Lord is within them.[36] Interesting fantasies exist in Europe. Angiolillo, bandit chief of the Neapolitan Revolution of 1799, was reputed to have a magic ring that warded off bullets. The Czech robber Nikola Shuhaj (*fl.* 1918–1920) was invulnerable—theories interestingly differ—either because he had a live green twig to wave aside bullets, or because a witch had given him a potion to resist them, hence ultimately he had to be killed with an ax. The legendary eighteenth-century Carpathian bandit-hero Oleksa Dovbush, "could only be killed with a silver bullet that had been kept one year in a dish of spring wheat, blessed by a priest on the day of the twelve great saints and over which twelve priests had read twelve masses."[37] He seems nevertheless to have died a violent death, but a number of desperadoes in the days of the wild West also claimed they could be killed only by a silver bullet.

Nudity in battle is another way to gain invulnerability.[38] The Gaulish Gaesatae or "spearmen" went to war entirely naked, carrying only a spear, an archaic Celtic custom that gradually died out as each tribe came under civilized influence, but attested to in the Pergamene sculptures, on Roman and Celtic coins, and alluded to in Old Irish texts. This was not from sheer bravado, as the Romans thought, but was rather an invocation for magic protection, a practice that in fact had also been widespread in Greece and Italy in earlier times. In the Great Plains, Blackfoot warriors commonly rode into battle entirely nude, except perhaps for warpaint. Nakedness to frighten off demons is of course very common in various contexts in folk Europe. The classic psychiatric paper on "Nakedness as a Means of Inspiring Terror" is Ferenczi's, in which he correctly surmises merely from case material that "one is not dealing here with an idea peculiar to individuals."[39] As for the various body-images naïvely behind theories of invulnerability, one has only to study the data themselves closely, though the Freud-Ferenczi understanding of clinical paranoia may perhaps give deeper insight.

Quite as common as the belief in invulnerability is the psychodynamically related fantasy of world catastrophe. A fundamental theme in Guaraní culture, overshadowing all others, is belief in the imminence of a world-shattering cataclysm, along with a myth of the Earthly Paradise or Land-Without-Evil that promises salvation. Schaden tends to support Nimuendajú's thesis that the cataclysmology of the Guaraní comes from a recension of Jesuit teachings. It would be difficult to find a better authority on the Guaraní than Nimuendajú, and yet a deep sympathy with his adoptive tribesmen may have led him to attempt exonerating them from having held these disturbing ideas aboriginally. For it may be remarked that most of the Indian tribes of the North American west coast have apparently aboriginal fantasies of world disaster or body destruction in one symbolic form or another, e.g., the Modoc burning of the sky in the *aurora borealis,* and the Athapaskan prophecies of world-end. And chiliastic theories of earth-cataclysm were extremely common not only in both Ghost Dances but also in many pre-Ghost Dance crisis cults of the Eastern Woodlands besides. The Shawnee prophet for example saw the world's end coming, the Cherokee expected apocalypse, and even Pontiac could cause an earthquake. Hence an eschatology of catastrophism may be pan-American. In any case, many Guaraní groups, having lost their protective priests, have been seeking the legendary Land-Without-Evil ever since 1820, all over middle South America from the Atlantic to the Andes, and some migrations were continuing as late as 1954 or after.[40]

The aboriginality of the belief can scarcely be proven, since the prevalence of cataclysm-ideology almost matches the prevalence of missionaries. But even though the world-destruction theme is thus far flung, we may still harbor some doubt of its exclusively Christian origin. In contrast to the clustering of *arbitrary attributes* of shamans in Asia and America, and in Europe and north Africa (which lead us to suspect a common historical origin, however ancient), the variety and *lack of specific content* of cataclysmologies lead us not to an ethnological but a psychological conclusion. Floods, tidal waves, earthquakes, volcanoes and typhoons occur widely over the earth, in no discernible relation to culture areas or known vectors of historic influence, and native world-destruction fears have a variety similar to the natural destructive means. The Maori and the Xosa cults, with no possible connection with the Amazonian Guaraní, nevertheless expected cosmic catastrophe, hence a psychological theory seems preferable to an acculturational one. Fear of catastrophe owes more to psychic disturbances of body image and fantasies of body destruction than to any universal culture trait.

The Central Highlands of New Guinea have been open, in fact, only since the 1930s, and yet the people there seem capable of chiliasms and catastrophes quite unrelated to Christianity. Again, the catastrophism of the Batak headhunters in the jungled highlands of Sumatra came specifically among the hostile anti-Christian factions that systematically rejected missionary influence. In 1862, Ludwig Nommensen and the Rhenische Mission began decisive Christianization among the Batak, who soon split irreconcilably into mission converts and the followers of Ompu Pulo Batu, tenth and last Si Singa Mangaradja. After the 1876 rebellion there were savage reprisals, and in some districts all the huts were burned. Rebellion flared again in 1883, this time with the aid of the fanatically Moslem Achenese. In 1907, the legendary priest-king was killed in a skirmish with the Dutch, but hundreds rallied around his cause and formed several sects, including the still existing *pormalim*. When a *guru* prophesies nowadays, he is believed to be seized by the spirit of Si Singa Mangaradja, who prescribes work and animal sacrifices, the skins of which are kept in the temple and the eating of which makes one an *orang pangulima* or "invincible man."[41]

In 1915–17, the Parhudamdam movement began among the die-hard opponents of the hated Dutch *herendiensten* or adult male labor tax. This offshoot of the earlier Mangaradja disturbances began in Tapanuli but soon spread to nearly all the Batak country, amid fevered rituals and much collective excitement. One legend was that Mangaradja had sunk into the sea and there met God, who took pity on him and sent him upward to the land again, there to teach rituals to save his believers from a rain of stones that was imminent. Reforming their earlier nude bathing, the Batak should now cover themselves and after bathing gather round the *guru,* who, with *taba* chants and special *mudra*-like gestures, taught them *ngeratip* or invincibility. Seated and swaying more and more rapidly, in old Indonesian dance style, some would jump up and in a kind of glossolalia announce themselves as one or another legendary figure. Pigs, frogs, and cucumbers were prohibited as food. Soon would come the end of the world, but Mangaradja would protect his followers during the apocalypse. If each one carried rice, salt, scrapings of his house and utensils, and a hair or feather of domestic animals and fowl, personal property would be multiply restored from these afterward. The *guru* gave each man a magic four-inch knife with seven notches; the enemy would see a knife of enormous length, or the knife would otherwise change the owner's appearance in the eyes of the enemy. It is difficult to detect specifically Christian elements in these ethnographic details! Some nativistic Batak have never been Christianized, and these irredentists, in fact, are still conspicuous in the civil riots against the central government of the new state of Indonesia in Java.

The world overturn of the Alorese and many other apocalypses do not seem especially Christian either. In short, apocalypse may be as truly native as messianism. The fantasied destruction of the world should be seen as a *paradigm of the felt state of people in the society;* and world-rebirth, a symbol of the hoped-for social reform. Threatened societies feel their whole world threatened, yet the tribal society is somehow immortal. To some degree, perhaps, invulnerability also is an analogue of cultural impregnability by the enemy, or impermeability by alien ways, a social integrity based on a model of body integrity. More immediately, however, invulnerability is an autistic fantasy tailored to the fact of the greater potency of European weapons. Moreover, magic drinks to confer invulnerability to weapons, enjoined nudity, or nudity-reform coupled with tumescent knives, internalized cattle-stakes and the like, more compellingly suggest psychic states and body-image symbols of the prophet than of the body politic. Such symptoms are clinically familiar to the psychiatrist.

With inside and outside, self and not-self poorly discriminated, the narcissist feels the whole world threatened, literally, to the degree that he *is* the world. To the narcissistic paranoid his mind, and to the schizoid with feeble ego-boundaries his body, is the world. World destruction, then, can be seen as a projection of fears of body-disintegration, and *fear for oneself* the pattern of fears for the world.[42] Indeed, it could hardly be otherwise, since experience indicates it is the human self that dies, not the universe, however much we might wish to purloin this attribute of the universe for ourselves. I. M. Kogan has written of the characteristic world-destruction experiences and rebirth fantasies of a schizophrenic patient, Hans Graber of reality testing and world-destruction phobias, and Freud of an auto-biographical account of a case of paranoia. There is no reason to suppose that primitive persons under stress cannot be paranoid or schizophrenic too, simply because many other people in the society join in their beliefs—and even enthusiastically, since for the same psychologically defensive reasons. There is no belief a psychotic is susceptible to that a society is not, since all societies are made up of individuals. In a mob state, people can as easily abdicate their intelligence as their morality. And diffusion in cult and culture is identical.

Faced with the massive irrationality of religions, primitive and their own, both theologians of the nineteenth century and scientists of the twentieth have taken interesting positions. Curiously, the theologians concerned themselves with the cultural, the revelation, and the anthropologists with the messiah, the shaman. Anthropologists, in their tradition of easy tolerance and unconcern with the truth of the folklore they examine— and also because they unconsciously regard the object of study as "objective" and consider all culture as rational, equally "good" or necessarily somehow adaptive because it *exists* and because the *function* of culture is to be adaptive, or because all tribalists resolutely and unreflectively believe it is, or because anthropologists professionally uninterested in judgment and epistemology regard the content of belief in a culture hero, a cult or a culture as irrelevant or crossculturally sacrosanct or beyond rational assessment or not needing it—have entered into a bootless argument concerning the sanity of the shaman, to which, in a moment, we will return.

Theologians, by contrast in a tradition of intolerance and burning epistemological concern with belief, reached their conclusions about sacred culture somewhat earlier. Whether the individual anthropologist knows it or not (whence the value of knowing one's own culture historically and critically), his stand is the product of Romantic period theology which long since side-stepped the issue. Roundly defeated by the rationalists of the Enlightenment, religionists of the Romantic period declared a truce by stating that religious belief need not depend on any rational grounds, thereby gaining victory by retreat. Religionists of Catholic

Europe, quietly abandoning the long Augustinian and Thomist tradition of attempted intellectual rationalization of belief, finally agreed that religious truths are not a product of the intellect, and forever withdrew from the rationalist field of battle. Chateaubriand, Joseph de Maistre, and Lammenais rested the case on traditionalism or categorical acceptance of revelation or the "legitimacy" of the reign of ideas. Protestant theology in turn, to assure religion against attacks in the intellectual sphere, took refuge in the subjective feelings of the individual—Lessing and Fichte relegating religion to a separate and unassailable sphere of morality, and Herder, Schelling and Schleiermacher to personal feeling, thus proving that literary theologians are often better logicians than philosophers are. And Kant, magisterial philosopher of them all, proclaimed a final dichotomy in his critiques of pure and practical reason.

We are all heirs, often unaware, of the peace of Königsberg. But the terms of the protocol have often since been misinterpreted, by Christian "Scientists" holding that reality is not real, by Mormons and other Modernists that tradition can be invented ready-made, by the Baha'ists that despite logical conflict all traditional irrationalities are simultaneously true and, in a more modernist but still oligophrenic form, the lay cliché that "true" religion and science really say the same thing. A more legitimate heir of Kant, *enfant terrible* Freud, who did not forget Kant's lesson about the irrationality of man, asked "Why then must I believe just this irrational belief and not another?" and ended by becoming our Moses in the wilderness of the irrational.

It is interesting to see how Romantic theology influenced early anthropology. Catholic anthropologists took refuge in a legitimatizing ethnology and discovered a "high god" everywhere among primitives, though on the way they invented some monstrous "historical" fossil-ethnography to prove it. In a Judaic tradition, Lévy-Bruhl, Durkheim and Lévi-Strauss found that the reality of religion lay in no messiah but in the traditionalist group and its structures of kin and clan. And Protestants, given the epistemological predicaments consequent to their earlier option, understandably became psychologists of religion and began worrying about the legitimacy of individual revelation. For when every man is priest then no man is, and cut off from the patent of legitimated monopolists of sacred culture, psychologists of belief can only explore a free market of competitive shamans. If historic culture can be guaranteed as a trademarked commodity, obtainable only at the exclusive stores of certified dealers, the Catholic need not question the manufacturer or the advertising concern; but if traditional culture is to be questioned and brands compared by shoppers, then the Protestant consumer must have a look also at the inventor of the new and improved product, the prophet. It pays to know the people you deal with.

It is quite striking, however, how gingerly anthropologists approach assessment of the purveyors of gods, as if the old Horatian phrase had been revised to *de deis et de moribus non est disputandum,* as if the morality did not matter so long as one had morals, and as if the most important human adaptive techniques, culture and morality, whatever their source, were not to be critically examined and judged. Surely, however, in naïve commonsense terms, crisis cults have often enough had prophets showing evidence of mental instability, or of abnormality even in their specific culture-context, for the question of their mental status to be raised. Apart from their mere dreams, which all men have, what empiric evidence have we that some prophets were psychotic, chronically or in some crisis? First, the stolid American Indians.

Handsome Lake, for one, had an apparent persecution mania, and delusions of reference which ultimately hampered his mission. Smohalla had trance states beyond the norm of cultural expectancy. Skolaskin and Suipuken showed odd sexual behavior that was at least criticized by their contemporaries. The Athapaskan prophetess was transvestite, with apparent sexual inversion, an anomaly even among people with the usual male transvestites, however "normal" we assess these. Short Bull, who advocated naked male and female dancing, must be thought voyeur to the degree that he offended proper customary Plains behavior in mixed dances. And Albert Hopkins, the visiting imposter of the Sioux Ghost Dance, would seem to be a paranoid personality in both white and Indian terms.

We must be careful to put aside those cases that seem culture-patterned. The symbolic bisexuality of Toradja shamans in Indonesia[43] is not only a cultural expectation there but also an attribute of Asiatic, especially Siberian, shamanism at large, and indeed, to a degree, of American. Thus the Yurok *wegern* or male transvestite shaman, who voluntarily did women's work, may be let ride as a kind of "standard deviant" until Posinsky,[44] a psychiatrically qualified observer, specifically states that these male shamans were individually more deviant than women shamans, for all that the latter also showed good symbolic evidence of atypical masculine protest. Similarly, the shift from male transvestite shamans among the Araucanian Mapuche of Chile to females (discussed by Métraux, Cooper, Titiev, and Faron)[45] does seem to involve some order of psychopathy beyond the customary cultural norm.

Quite apart from discoverable old native culture-sources of *bizarreries,* in the millenarian cults of Melanesia there would appear also to be distinct individual psychopathies as part-sources of these movements. Several prophets clearly show the "erotomania" of paranoia. Ndugumoi of the Ndengei-snake Tuka Cult, for example, certainly had paranoid delusions of grandeur, and his harem of young girls in the Yalewa Ranandi suggests paranoid erotomania. The Baigona Cult leader had *jipari* fits and hallucinations of body-destruction (though these were partly cultural styles for Melanesian magicians), but he was also possessed by a divine spirit-snake to a grandiose degree approaching paranoia. Buninia of the Taro fertility cult had men's tools placed against his body to infuse them with his immense spiritual potency. Evara of the Head-he-go-round Men spread a stylized epilepsy in his group, apparently genuine in him originally. Some evidence must be used cautiously as being perhaps marginal. The so-named "Vailala Madness" had an autonomic snake-pole, and the vulva-attacking snakes of the white "spirits" from the great bird belly would also appear to be phallic, striking the secular mind as a distortion of the true situation in contact with white men—but some of these fantasies had quasi-cultural roots.

On the other hand, the atypically unmarried Mambu, with his pursuit of nuns and public washing of the genitals of his cultists, evidently suffered some sexual pathology beyond the expectancies of either white or native culture. The Mansren snake myth embodies a perhaps universal wish for eternal youth and potency and resurrection never vouchsafed men; nevertheless, there can be no doubt of the prophet Manamakeri's megalomania and claim to omnipotence. Again, the public coitus and sexual communism of the "Naked Cult" together with the advocacy of lineage-incest suggest some transgression of preferred norms that indicates sexual pathology in the prophet. Perhaps John Frum's mixed-sex dormitories had remote Oceanic if not local cultural antecedents; perhaps, too, traditional patterns may appear in Ronovoro's mutilation and part-cannibalism of a white man. Nevertheless, in all of these, aberrant sexual motifs are apparent.

Elsewhere in the world, the Murut messiah Garing was frankly hallucinatory and megalomaniac. The Alorese prophet Malekala was at least a borderline case of marked neurosis. Gwek of the naked Nuer had culturally atypical ways of seating himself. One Congo prophet visioned a moon-halo that suggests the epileptic aura; St. Paul, Mohammed, and perhaps Moses should be added in this list. Shabbathai Zevi, a famous seventeenth-century messiah of international consequence about whom we know a great deal, is a classical textbook case of fully clinical paranoia. And we must reject the suggestion that Hitler could not have been paranoiac simply because he seduced a sick nation to his psychosis.

Magnitude of social impact is not an accepted psychiatric criterion for psychosis, and in any newspaper one may read of mass murderers easily adjudged insane who kill far fewer victims.

Of the modern American messiahs in Braden's well-documented series, certainly everyone would agree that some were "ambulatory" clinical cases. The late "Father Divine" was at least a borderline case of well-preserved paranoia. Beauregard Barefoot, of the snake-handling cult of the southeast, was clinically a psychopathic character, and a number of his clientele were bona fide trance-hysterics. The Korean messiah Chang of the "Doomsday Cult" not only conferred magical invulnerability but also had elaborate bathroom-purification rituals and was otherwise classically paranoiac.[46] The Karen messiah was preparing himself to be the universal monarch at the time of his death; the Pau Chin Hau visionary, after a protracted illness, from 1900 onward had a long series of apocalyptic trances or dreams. The author of the Book of Revelation writes like a paranoid schizophrenic. The reincarnated Christ of the Skoptzi, Selivanov, despite the archaic cultural roots of his cult and the considerable size of his following, was manifestly psychotic. And the leader of the Taiping Rebellion, Hung Hsiu-ch'üan, was explicitly described as mentally ill by an internationally known Chinese psychiatrist, Dr. P. M. Yap.[47]

Despite voluminous evidence of this kind, some students nevertheless insist that the prophet-shaman cannot be abnormal or insane.[48] A. P. Elkin argues for the non-pathological character of the Australian shaman; Hans Findeisen considers the *Schamanenkrankheit* as merely the trappings of an initiation rite. Erwin Ackerknecht is at pains to argue that the shaman can not be psychically abnormal. It must be confessed, however, that the qualification of some anthropologists to make psychiatric assessments is open to question. One anthropologist, for example, wrote an article to prove that in Japan the snake is not a phallic symbol—and then went on to recount the superstition that a peasant girl imprudently taking a nap in the fields should beware of a snake there that would crawl into her genitals! Another averred, "It seems to me almost impossible that the informant could move in and out of 'psychotic episodes' without a well-trained ethnologist being aware that he was dealing with a poorly integrated personality."[49]

Evidently it is possible. For Devereux took this same man's field work and noted in it that the son of a Ute shaman seeking medicine power developed hysterical blindness, that the "rational and poised" shaman had the psychotic fantasy of an internal evil-eating homunculus, the paranoid fear his power would turn against him, and the dissociated fantasy that the shaman has no control over the evil potentialities of his power and may plead in vain against it, etc. Nevertheless, Honigmann, in a review, applauded this anthropologist for "refuting Devereux's unwarranted generalization, based on Mohave data, that the shaman is a neurotic who uses socially sanctioned defenses"![50]

It would seem that Devereux, who is both an analytic therapist and an experienced ethnographer, has much the better part of the argument. Some of his opponents appear to feel that a psychiatric diagnosis is a slanderous *argumentum ad hominem,* instead of a descriptive statement, and give the impression they are bravely defending their natives against some monstrous charge. Some of them demonstrate repeatedly they cannot discern evidence right in front of them and could not recognize a psychotic unless he were the legal inmate of a certified mental hospital with a notarized label to that effect hanging around his neck. Many anthropologists also have the usual amateur notion of the categorical black-or-white nature of mental illness and believe that, without modulation, an individual totally "is" or is not insane. They lack the experienced clinician's awareness of the continuous gradation, the uniquely individual combination, the dynamic fluidity and individual range of symptoms alternatively used. Further, however fleetingly, all of us share the identical defense mechanisms of the most dilapidated patient; the total psyche is not displayed at any one instant, nor is it the same at every instant over time; and the major proof of mental soundness is the ability to discern and criticize one's own temporary symptoms. Nor need a patient be "climbing the walls" or state in a loud clear voice that he is psychotic for this to be the case.

Kitigawa writes that among the Ainu of Japan, a woman *must have* "a slight mental disease" called *imu* if she is to become a shamaness. This disease is attributed to her having been possessed in childhood by a serpent, and later (one must be hysteroid to be hysteric) the mere mention of a serpent will cause her to show "manifest emotion disturbance" and the symptons of her *imu.*[51] Czaplicka, Jochelson, Shirokogoroff, and especially Ohlmarks, regard true shamanism in Siberia to be a psychopathological phenomenon related to arctic hysteria. Yakut shamans get *menerik,* "which is something like epilepsy."[52] In Malaysia, shamans are typically epileptic; but if they actually are not, they must imitate the manifestations of epilepsy as best they can if they wish to be accepted as genuine. This phenomenon suggests the explanation both of alleged impostery in shamanism and of the "shaman's sickness" as stylized into an initiation ceremony. The authentic bizarrerie of psychosis must be witnessed by the people, that is, for them to be impressed with it as an extraordinary, odd, supernatural or sacred state. Hence initally or basically, the shaman is one who suffered an authentic nervous ailment or mental illness, but his symptomatic manifestations later become routinized by the ungifted, desirous of entering into the profession. As an attenuated comparison, perhaps one could consider the range of emotional authenticity in stories of being "called" into the ministry.

Some of the disputation over the shaman's mental state comes from diagnostic ineptitude, some from an undiscriminating and monolithic thinking about *the* shaman. Institutionally, shamanism is merely an identifiable social role. But as individuals, prophets and shamans run the full gamut from self-convinced and sincere psychotics to epileptics and suggestible hysterics, and from calculating psychopaths (more rare than commonly believed) to plodding naïfs only following the cultural ropes. Intellectually too, they may range from *Propfschizophrenie* in the feebleminded to individuals of real intellectual distinction, like some Indoeuropean bards, Biblical poet-prophets, and Navaho shamans who perform incredible feats of memory in days-long rituals.

They vary in integrity too. The Winnebago Crashing Thunder was a man of monumental unself-deceived probity, who all his life longed for a shamanistic experience. In the Medicine Dance as a youth he was given a gray squirrel skin for a medicine pouch and was told he could make it cry out; he had always envied the ability of others to do this. In the medicine "shooting" he was shown how to fall down and lie quivering on the ground and how to appear dead. Crashing Thunder was much disappointed, because he had had a much more exalted concept of the shooting, and thought the old men had deceived him only to make money. He honestly knew he never had a real visionary experience until he ate peyote.[53] By contrast, Lone Bear or Empty Wagon of the Kiowa was so clumsy a shaman that the ethnographer could see him fumble red clay from his pouch and chew it in his mouth, later to be spit out as his own "blood."[54] Such events explain why shamanism sometimes has to be *taught*. Shamanistic "tricks" point to another role of the shaman, that of self-impresario and entertainer. The stage magician is still another scion of the magician-shaman-showman; and even a modern medicine man must have a bedside manner.

Although he well knew better, Simon Kimbangu allowed cultists to believe that the "S" on the collar of Salvation Army uniforms denoted his own first name, a Savior whom God had miraculously restored to them. Diamond Jenness presented his theory of Copper Eskimo shamanism as an indissoluble mixture of intense emotional excitement, self-hypnosis and showmanship. The shaman's insertion of teeth of the animal familiar and wearing of its fur become the make-up and stage scenery serving to heighten the illusion, and make-believe is encouraged by a willing audience.

The shaman is not conscious of acting a part; he becomes in his own mind the animal or the shade of the dead man who is deemed to possess him. To the audience, too, this strange figure, with its wild and frenzied appearance, its ventriloquistic cries and its unearthly falsetto gabble, with only a broken word here and there of intelligible speech, is no longer a human being, but the thing it personifies. Their minds become receptive of the wildest imaginings, and they see the strangest and most fantastic happenings.[55]

The resemblance to stage illusion is striking, and every enthusiastic playgoer has experienced being lost in an absorbing drama. Jenness believes that even if a shaman begins by consciously deceiving his audience, repetition of the drama, belief that others have done what he is pretending to do, as well as the auto-suggestion and self-hypnosis of entering into the part, together lead him into deceiving himself; and enthralled audiences magnify the tales as they pass them from mouth to mouth. But this elegant ethnographer ends on a sober note: "I may remark that nothing that I actually saw with my own eyes appeared to suggest the operation of any spiritual or mental forces with which we ourselves are not perfectly familiar." How does the shaman make the séance tent shake? By the same naturalistic means the séance medium makes the table tip.

Knud Rasmussen adds notes for the same Copper Eskimo. He thought the shaman's activities very naïve. One shaman, possessed, ejaculated weird words and wild howls, the meaning of which was gradually pieced together by an old woman expert in shamanistic séances. One clever girl, urged to become a shaman, was encouraged with these words: "Once you start lying and the people are listening, you can almost always hit upon something." How could one fail, with such a co-operative audience? When she refused, everyone around laughed, and the shamans the most heartily, "for they knew that people were so enthralled by all that is incomprehensible between earth and sky that nothing could shake the faith of their audience when a real séance was going on, no matter what was said." The shamans themselves regard their various tricks as techniques to get in touch with the spirits. "The relationship between the natural and the supernatural is in itself so problematic that it is of no consequence if there is some 'cheating' in the ritual during an invocation."[56]

As traditional societies age, and spirits grow into gods, so the shaman, by constant imitation, fades into the priest. Shamanic feeling is institutionalized into ritual, and finally into mere drama; solemn Greek tragedy began in wild Dionysiac dance. But the shamanic type is perennial. As his illness progresses, the individual paranoiac prophet often becomes the god himself. So one need not be shocked at Zuñis and god-impersonation in general. But theirs is an institutionalized, deliberate, "straightforward" fakery. Every adult Zuñi knows that the rain-dancers are only men dressed up as gods, for he has learned the secret at his initiation. But like a compulsive neurotic he remains entranced by his belief, for beliefs are learned. A little Hopi boy may try to beat a drum as kachinas do, copy the steps of the masked dancers and practice bits of songs. He is told that people when they die become kachinas and if the little boy has a favorite one, he will say, "When I die, I'm going to be such-and-such a kachina.[57] Thus far can imitation go. And how many of the faithful remember they are ritual cannibals when they eat the wafer and drink the wine?

NOTES

(X Shamans and Societies)

1. Paul Roux, "Le chaman gengis-khanide," *Anthropos*, 54 (1959) 401–32.

2. René de Nebesky-Wojkowitz, "Das tibetanische Staatsorakel," *Archiv für Völkerkunde*, 3 (1948) 136–55.

3. N. D. Fustel de Coulanges, *The Ancient City* (Garden City: Doubleday Anchor Books, 1956).

4. In their early youth Irish bards memorized 100 chief stories and 175 secondary ones by the end of the sixth year of bardic schooling; by the seventh, they could compose poetry in some of the more complex metric forms, and then went on to etymology and learning by heart legends of the Irish kings; and after fifteen years (now magicians, prophets, and clairvoyants) they could raise storms and winds like any other Eurasiatic shaman (Ann Moray, "The Celtic Heritage in Ireland," *Horizon*, 7, ♯2 [Spring 1965] 33–39, p. 34).

5. Caesar wrote (*De Bello Gallico*, Bk. IV) that the Druids of Gaul sent their most brilliant youth to study in Ireland. A tradition? — for later, in Dark Age Christianity, Ireland sent missionaries even to Rome.

6. Giraldus Cambrensis quoted in F. P. Barnard, *Strongbow's Conquest of Ireland* (London: D. Nutt, 1888, p. 125).

7. The antlered Sasanian king is pictured in Terrence O'Donnell, "Twenty-Five Centuries of Persia," *Horizon*, 5, ♯3 (January 1963) 40–72, p. 57. For another shamanic connection with rulership, cf. Rudd, *op. cit.*, p. 10, on the Chinese ruler, whose behavior affects the whole animal world; and Walter Krebs, "Zur kultischen Kohabitation mit Tieren in Alten Orient," *Deutsche Akademie der Wissenschaften, Forschungen und Fortschritte*, 37 (1963).

8. On the shamans of the ancient Saharan Caucasoids, known since the time of Herodotus, see Carleton Coon, in a review of Peter Fuchs, *Die Völkern der Südost Sahara* (Vienna: Wilhelm Braumüller Universitäts-Verlagsbuchhandlung, 1961 = *Veröffentlichen zum Archiv für Völkerkunde, Museum für Völkerkunde in Wein*, Band 6), in *American Anthropologist*, 65 (1963) 476–78, p. 478.

9. Definition of autism modified from *Psychopathological Disorders in Childhood* (New York: Group for the Advancement of Psychiatry, VI, Report No. 62, p. 330).

10. T. E. Lawrence, Suppressed Introductory Chapter for *The Seven Pillars of Wisdom*, quoted in A. W. Lawrence (ed.), *Oriental Assembly* (London: Williams & Northgate, 1939, p. 143).

11. Pos, *op. cit.*, pp. 561–64; see also J. V. De Bryn, "The Manseren Cult of Biak," *South Pacific*, 5 (1949) 1–10.

12. Chinnery and Haddon, *op. cit.*, pp. 448–63—the first report of a "prophet" movement from Papua (Stanner, *op. cit.*, p. 61).

13. Van der Kroef, *Messianic Movements*, p. 88; cf. D. A. ten Haaft, *Manserenbeweging*.

14. Andersson, *Messianic Popular Movements*, p. 88.

15. Andersson, *loc. cit.*, p. 133.

16. Cora Du Bois, *The People of Alor* (Minneapolis: University of Minnesota Press; 1944; Cambridge: Harvard University Press 1960; and Torchbooks, 2 vols., pp. 292–343).

17. Thomas Rhys Williams, "The Form of a North Borneo Nativistic Behavior," *American Anthropologist,* 65 (1963) 543–51.

18. Notes by the translator, A. W. S. O'Sullivan, of C. Snouck Hurgronje, *The Achehnese* (Leyden: E. J. Brill. 2 vols., 1906, II:128).

19. J. L. Christian, *Modern Burma* (Berkeley: University of California Press, 1942, p. 239).

20. Shepperson, *Nyasaland,* pp. 152–53.

21. Mooney, *op. cit.,* pp. 701, 706, 849, and 868–69; on the invulnerability of Plains visionaries, Ruth Benedict, *Guardian Spirit,* p. 23.

22. Zimmerman, *op. cit.,* p. 52.

23. Krader, *op. cit.,* p. 285.

24. Worsley, *Trumpet,* p. 141.

25. Associated Press dispatch, 20 March 1961.

26. J. Anthony Lucas, "Congolese Soldiers Seize a Rebel 'Witch Doctor,' " New York *Times,* 16 June 1964.

27. "Drugged Terrorists Slaughtered in Congo," New York *Herald Tribune,* UP-International dispatch, 4 February 1964.

28. Karl Abraham, "Ejaculatio Praecox," in *Selected Papers,* 280–98, expecially pp. 281–82, in the aggressor (projected *impotentia* and *praecox*); and in the recipient on paranoid defensive fantasies of body-impenetrability, S. Freud, "Psychoanalytic Notes upon an Autobiographical Account of a Case of Paranoia (Dementia Paranoides)," *Collected Papers,* 3:387–470, Std. Ed., vol. 12.

29. M. Collis, *The Land of the Great Image* (London: Faber and Faber, 1943, p. 244).

30. Pos, *op. cit.,* p. 563; cf. Worsley, *Millenarian Movements,* p. 21.

31. Andersson, *op. cit.,* pp. 68–69.

32. Worsley, *Trumpet Shall Sound,* p. 141.

33. P. Coriat, "Gwek the Witch-doctor and the Pyramid of Dengkur," *Sudan Notes and Records,* 22, #2 (1939) 221–38; cf. E. E. Evans-Pritchard, *Nuer Religion* (Oxford: Clarendon Press, 1956, p. 305).

34. Classic papers on the dynamics of paranoia: S. Freud, *Psycho-analytic Notes,* in his *Collected Papers* (London: Hogarth Press, 4 vols., 1925 III:390–470); Sandor Ferenczi, "On the Part Played by Homosexuality in the Pathogenesis of Paranoia," *Contributions to Psycho-Analysis* (Boston: R. G. Badger, 1916, pp. 154–84) and "Some Clinical Observations on Paranoia and Paraphrenia" (*loc. cit.,* pp. 282–95); Viktor Tausk, "On the Origin of the Influencing Machine in Schizophrenia," *Psychoanalytic Quarterly,* 2 (1933) 519–56; and the specific papers by E. Bibring, Helene Deutsch, Feigenbaum, Jelgersma, Landauer, van Ophuijsen, Annie Reich, Sauvage-Nolting, Schilder, Melitta Schmideberg, Shackley, and Staercke cited in Fenichel, *op. cit.,* p. 427.

35. P. W. A. Bastian, *Völker des Oestlichen Asiens,* (Leipzig: O. Wigand, 6 vols., 1866–71, III:282, 353), quoted by Dodds, *op. cit.,* p. 280 fn. 33.

36. Czaplicka, *Aboriginal Siberia,* p. 176; W. La Barre, *They Shall Take Up Serpents,* pp. 8, 19–21, 41–42, and 98.

37. On Angiolillo, Shuhaj, and Dovbush, see Hobsbawm, *op. cit.,* p. 15.

38. Nudity: Gaesatae, T. G. E. Powell, *The Celts* (New York: Frederick A. Praeger, 1958, p. 108); Blackfoot, the late Clark Wissler, in conversation.

39. Sandor Ferenczi, "Nakedness as a Means of Inspiring Terror," *Further Contributions to the Theory and Technique of Psycho-Analysis* (London: Hogarth Press, 1926, pp. 329–32). "Going naked as a sign" was a Quaker practice in the seventeenth century; Fox spoke in favor of it at times. Cf. the Doukhobors of Saskatchewan. And compare some disestablishment hippies, *Hair,* Woodstock, Lennon.

40. Egon Schaden, *Aspectos Fundamentais da Cultura Guaraní*. p. 382; cf., for Apapocuva Guaraní, R. H. Lowie, *Tropical Forest*, p. 42.

41. On the Batak Mangaradja cults, *pormalim* and *parhudamdam*, see Van der Kroef, *Messianic Movements*, pp. 98–106.

42. On world-destruction fantasies in psychotics, see Freud, *Psychoanalytic Note*, pp. 390–470; Fenichel, *op. cit.*, pp. 417–18; I. M. Kogan, "Weltuntergangserlebnis und Wiedergeburtsphantasie bei einem Schizophrenen," *International Zeitschrift für Psychoanalyse*, 18 (1932) 86–104; G. H. Graber, "Realitätsflucht und Weltuntergangsphobie," *Zeitschrift für Psychoanalytische Paedagogik*, 3 (1929) 213–21; and W. A. Spring, "Observations on World Destruction Fantasies," *Psychoanalytic Quarterly*, 8 (1939) 48–56. The unwitting concurrence of Eliade is found in his *Sacred and Profane*, pp. 172–75. A great many curious "mass insanities" are discussed in A. Hirsch, *Handbook of Geographical and Historical Pathology* (London: The New Sydenham Society, 1883–86, 3 vols., especially III:524–26), to which should be added the readily accessible sources on tarantism, witchcraft manias, etc. For a contemporary example, see Alan C. Kerckhoff and Kurt W. Back, *The June Bug, A Study of Hysterical Contagion* (New York: Appleton-Century-Crofts, 1968).

43. J. van der Kroef, *Indonesia in the Modern World* (Bandung: M. Baru, 2 vols., 1954–1956, chapter VI, "Transvestitism and the Religious Hermaphrodite," 2:182–97; this chapter appears as an article in the *Journal of East Asiatic Studies* [Manila], 3 [1954] 257–65). The theme of sexual ambiguity in the vatic is ubiquitous: in ancient Sumer there were two dialects, one standard Sumerian, the other used by women and priests (E. I. Gordon, *Sumerian Proverbs: Glimpses of Everyday Life in Ancient Mesopotamia*, Philadelphia: University of Pennsylvania Press, 1959).

44. S. Posinsky, "Yurok Shamanism," *Psychiatric Quarterly*, 39 (1965) 227–43.

45. M. Titiev, "Araucanian Culture in Transition," *Occasional Contributions of the Museum of Anthropology of the University of Michigan*, no. 15, 1951, p. 117. Métraux and Cooper in L. C. Faron, "Shamanism and Sorcery among the Mapuche (Araucanians) of Chile," in R. A. Manners (ed.), *op. cit.*, pp. 123–46.

46. Lofland, *op. cit.*, p. 230, on the Korean messiah Chang's invulnerability and bathroom rituals; T. Stern, "Ariya and the Golden Book: A Millenarian Buddhist Sect among the Karen," *Journal of Asian Studies*, 27 ＃2 (Feb. 1968) 297–328, on the Karen messiah. On Pau Chin Hau, see *Census of India 1931*, vol. XI, Burma, Pt. I, Report, Rangoon, 1933, pp. 217–18.

47. P. M. Yap, *op. cit.* Dr. Yap is a London-trained (Maudsley) psychiatrist (University of London), the Medical Officer-in-Charge in the government mental hospital in Hong Kong. Although psychiatrically sophisticated, as a Chinese he is still a competent within-the-society-judge.

48. "The dividing line between common insanity and prophetic madness is the fact hard to draw" (Dodds, *op. cit.*, p. 68). It is indeed, in purely descriptive terms, hence we must seek a dynamic-functional context. But there is perhaps a special difficulty in our tradition: Dodds thinks "the association of prophecy and madness belongs to the Indo-European stock of ideas" (p. 70); cf. A. C. Pearson, "Possession (Greek and Roman)" in *Hastings Encyclopedia*, 10:127–30, possession in India, etc. If even the Greeks were irrational, why not others? As to Baha'ist total ecumenism, there is still the problem of the three Christs of Ypsilanti.

For the "shamanic disease," see Eliade, *Recent Works*, p. 158, and *Le chamanisme*, pp. 45–47. H. Findeisen, *Schamentum*, pp. 50–60, 209–13, and "Die 'Schamanenkrankheit' als Initiation," *Abhandlungen und Aufsätze aus dem Institut für Menschen- und Menschheitskunde* [Augsberg], No. 45, 1957; given his position on the *Bessessenheitspriester*, Findeisen necessarily, though untypically, regards the shaman as an initiated priest.

49. A. P. Elkin, *Aboriginal Men of High Degree* (Sydney: Australian Publishing

Co., 1946). Respect for aboriginals is one matter; but some persons have the air of defending shamans against gross charges in being called mentally unstable or neurotic, an excess of cross-cultural courtesy that recognizes neither what neurosis is nor its prevalence. But to the degree he is a "culture" innovator the shaman *must* have an atypical "personality." Erwin H. Ackerknecht, "Psychopathology, Primitive Medicine and Primitive Culture," *Bulletin of the History of Medicine,* 14 (1943) 30–67. M. E. Opler, "Japanese Folk Belief concerning the Snake," *Southwestern Journal of Anthropology,* 1 (1945) 249–59; see La Barre, *Human Animal,* pp. 352–53 (paperback edition, pp. 365–66). Quotation from M. K. Opler, "On Devereux's Discussion of Ute Shamanism" *American Anthropologist,* 63 (1961) 1091–93, p. 1092.

50. M. K. Opler, "Dream Analysis in Ute Indian Therapy," in M. K. Opler (ed.), *Culture and Mental Health* (New York: Macmillan, 1959, pp. 97–117, especially pages 101–3); J. J. Honigmann, review of Opler. *op. cit.,* in *American Anthropologist,* 62 (1960) 920–23—on the one side. On the other—A. L. Kroeber," Psychotic Factors in Shamanism," *Character and Personality,* 8 (1940) 204–15, also "Psychosis or Social Sanction," in *The Nature of Culture,* pp. 310–19; G. Devereux, *Dream Learning,* pp. 1036–45, "The Function of Alcohol in Mohave Society," *Quarterly Journal of Studies on Alcohol,* 9 (1948) 207–21, "The Origin of Shamanistic Powers as reflected in a Neurosis," *Revue Internationale d'Ethnopsychologie Normale et Pathologique,* 1 (1945) 19–28, and *Normal and Abnormal,* pp. 3–32. See also Lommel, *op. cit.,* pp. 8–9; Yuji Sasaki, "Psvchiatric Study of the Shaman in Japan," *Transcultural Psychiatric Research,* 4 (1967) 15–17; J. Silverman, "Shamans and Acute Schizophrenia," *American Anthropologist,* 69 (1967) 21–31; and Robert J. Beck, "Some Proto-Psychotherapeutic Elements in the Practice of the Shaman," *History of Religions,* 6 (1967) 303–27. The position of the psvchiatrist L. B. Boyer ("Remarks on the Personality of Shamans: With Special Reference to the Apache of the Mescalero Indian Reservation," in W. Muensterberger and S. Axelrad, *op cit.,* II:233–54) appears to me uncertain and ambiguous; but see L. B. Boyer, B. Klopfer, Florence B. Brower, and Yayao Kawaii, "Comparisons of the Shamans and Pseudoshamans of the Apaches of the Mescalero Indian Reservation: A Rorschach Study," *Journal of Projective Techniques and Personality Assessment,* 28 (1964) 173–80—although it seems to me that natives should decide who their shamans are, and not the categorizings of social scientists. G. A. Welken, "Het Shamanisme bij de Volken van der Nederlandsch Archipel." *Bijdragen tot de Taal-, Land en Volkenkunde van Nederlandsch Indie,* (1887), thought that shamanism began among mentally sick people, and only later were well but susceptible people brought into the profession; cf. E. M. Loeb, "Shaman and Seer," *American Anthropologist,* 31 (1929) 60–84. MacCulloch considers that "on the whole, the shaman is abnormal, neurotic, and epileptic; his functions are based on his abnormal qualities and aggravate these in turn" (A. MacCulloch, "Shamanism," *Hastings Encyclopedia.* 11:441–46, p. 441). Because he was a man of God, a few critics have considered that my diagnosis of Beauregard Barefoot as a psychopathic character was a blasphemous defamation of character (*They Shall Take Up Serpents,* pp. 113–75, contains the evidence that anyone who will may see). However, since the publication of Ari Kiev (ed.), *Magic, Faith, and Healing* (New York: Free Press, 1964), anthropologists will be forced to take a more sophisticated position on the mental status of the shaman.

51. J. M. Kitigawa, *Ainu Bear Festival,* p. 120.

52. On Yakut *menerik,* Levin and Potapov, *op. cit.,* p. 269.

53. Paul Radin, *Crashing Thunder: The Autobiography of a Winnebago Indian* (New York: D. Appleton & Co., 1925, p. 125).

54. The Kiowa shaman Lone Bear was also called "Empty Wagon," because as

an *ωde* or institutionalized "favorite child," a wagon-load of goods had been given away in his honor; information is from my fellow fieldworker among the Kiowa in 1935, Dr. William Bascom, who observed Lone Bear in action.

55. Diamond Jenness, *The Life of the Copper Eskimo* (Ottawa: Report of the Canadian Arctic Expedition, XII, 1923, pp. 216–17).

56. Knud Rasmussen, *Intellectual Culture of the Copper Eskimo*, pp. 27–30.

57. Wayne Dennis, *The Hopi Child* (New York: D. Appleton Century, 1940, p. 113).

XI

Culture and Culture Heroes

T HE stoutest defense of the shaman's normality is by Siefgried Nadel, who writes categorically: "No shaman is, in everyday life, an abnormal individual, a neurotic or a paranoiac; if he were, he would be classed as a lunatic, not respected as a priest. Nor finally can shamanism be correlated with incipient or latent abnormality; I recorded no case of a shaman whose professional hysteria deteriorated into serious mental disorder."[1] Nadel's statement contends that the shaman is in every way a normal citizen, run-of-the-mill, a mere journeyman. In most cases, if indeed not all, this is simply not accurate ethnographically, even discounting the psychiatric discernment of many ethnographers. In fact, most societies, Siberian certainly, do not *expect* normality as the prime requisite of the shaman. And if he purveys only the natural, why do all societies regard the shaman as *par excellence* the messenger of the supernatural? If the shaman is only a secular hack, whence his professional preoccupation with the sacred? Further, the visionary shaman is an ecstatic and, to a degree, the innovator of his cult, not the Apollonian priest of a static ecclesia. The shaman in fact characteristically leaves workaday time and space; his very *métier* is dealing with the non-usual, the abnormal, the problematic, and the supernatural that sometimes he alone knows.

"In everyday life"?—an escape clause; but is not the real social significance of the shaman just his sometime vision? Does the shaman never raise cultural question with the supernatural? How can revelation present only the banal, the routine, the known, the totally accepted, the hundred-percent expectation of all—and still be revelation? Does revelation contain no innovation? Is it open to all, with no personal coloring whatever? Whence the prophet's exciting charisma if he states only simple and sometimes unwelcome secular truth? Is his tone merely declarative, or seductively optative? And how did "professional hysteria" ever get into his performance, if the shaman is merely president of the local Chamber of Commerce? The prophet is without personal problems? And speaks to a serene society? The shaman is not even "incipiently" troubled or even "latently" irrational, such are manifestly normal people like, and so perfectly can psychological science predict?

It is plain that anxiety over the "abnormal," psychiatric and cultural, has distorted judgment and illustrates the very point we would make about culture and personality as defenses. Logically also, Nadel has boxed himself into a familiar philosophical corner. He defines the cultural norm as the universal individual norm, and so rigidly that neither culture change nor personality is possible. In biological terms, it is as if the existence of organic pattern allowed of no possible mutation. The meta-physical necessities of actual existence permit of no *process,* lest this impugn categorical *being.* In terms of physics, this is the old Parmenides-Heraclitus impasse. For Parmenides, only Being can be, Not-Being cannot be, therefore all Being is a packed Plenum whose total density of being allows of no motion or change. Absurd, Heraclitus replies, for Change is manifestly king everywhere. No man can step into the same river twice, hence the only reality is change. (But then there is no existent to which change can occur. The only solution, of course, is that of the Atomists Leucippus, Democritus and Lucretius, who postulate both Atoms and the Void to account for Permanence and Change; and modern physics still needs space-time and energy-mass to make sense of the physical universe.)

Platonized absolutes always collide. The only saving grace of Nadel's ukase is that he implies that *society* is the judge of whether a man is a shaman or a psychotic (which is true). And if it be further admitted that a society of men could be mistaken, then for the first time shamans and sacred culture and culture change become possible (not to say personality, and human culture at large). Absolute Rationality is as much a metaphysical stumbling block in all behavioral science as the assumption of Absolute Being is for physics. It is time to accept the *irrational* as a component of human affairs, to recognize that men adapt both to an outer, rational, secular world and to an inner, irrational, sacred world whose locus they have misplaced as being outside. And it is time to give up Culture and Personality as platonic absolutes as well, and look again at the animal that prates of them.

Classic rationalists believed that fear was the root of all religion. Lucretius quoted the famous phrase of Statius that *Primus in orbe deos fecit timor,* "Fear first made gods in the world." The rationalist Hobbes also thought that "The feare of things invisible is the naturall seed of Religion."[2] And—since any theological proposition concerning the Unknown is a statement about the oedipal self—Melville too could write of "terrors unborrowed from anything that visibly exists."[3] But why only *fear* of the supernatural (unless of course we project only hostility, in a murderously Melvillean quarrel with God)? In full round, the unresolved oedipal attitude toward the father is really one of ambivalence. Fear and hatred of the repressed unknown are only part of the totality. There are also trust and love that one may feel.

As Sabatier correctly notes, "In itself alone, fear is not religious; it paralyzes, stupefies, and crushes. In order that fear become religiously productive, there must be mixed in it, from the beginning, a spark of hope; man must, a prey to fear, conceive the possibility in one manner or another of surmounting it, that is to say, he finds outside above him an aid, a help to conjure the dangers that menace him."[4] The frightened person therefore projectively finds a personality to succor him. The pattern of this projection lies deep in human biology and real childhood experience: the god one expects is the parent he knew, which is why gods differ from person to person. Not only fear but also dependency cry out in oedipal ambivalence and crisis. In times of helplessness and crisis the childhood father lives again. The ghost of a real father lies behind the mystic father, the shaman. This father-surrogate, in human flesh, is the culture hero.

When old "cultural" means fail to provide social equilibrium (in times of tribal clash, acculturation, or failure of culture to defend peace of mind), we seem invariably to witness the rise of these new vatic "personalities" to compose the difficulties. But this appearance of a miraculous coming and of a separate duality in culture and personality comes only from our technique of analysis. It is not inherent in the data of reverberant human reactions themselves. "Culture" and "personality" are merely two ways of viewing the same phenomenon, human behavior. This is not to say we do not get recognizably different piles of data as a result of the differing ways of *arranging* the data; we do insist, however, that before this arranging we did not have two different *kinds* of data. Culture and personality are two ways of conceptualizing and talking about the same thing, interpersonal cognitive and phatic communication in human beings. Problems of culture *versus* personality are bogus ones, and when properly understood, mere artifacts of our own conceptualizations.

In a brilliant essay, Spiro has shown that "culture" and "personality" are a spurious dichotomy.[5] "Culture" is in fact a mere abstraction, used to describe the *regularities of behavior* in members of a socially contiguous and an historically continuous group of persons. At the same time, "personality" is no less an abstraction too. Personality is the *integration of regular behaviors* in one individual—all of which he has learned from experience of himself and of other individuals, all members of the "society" bearing a common "culture." Culture exists only because human individuals influence one another. Personality exists only because the human individual has been formatively influenced by others. *Culture and personality have no other existence than in these observable facts of human biology.*

In the innovator or culture hero, the new culture-stuff seems to come from nowhere, from "out of the blue" so far as the native society is concerned. That is to say, it comes from the "supernatural," from the "other world." A false problem. Naturalistically we are quite able to see that the culture hero speaks from the "supernatural" of his own unconscious mind. Naturalistically, too, his mystical "charisma" is but a measure of the group-acceptability of his teachings, viz. his current personality. Nevertheless, our own mystique of *personality* encounters quite as grave difficulties as the native concept of the *supernatural* does. And why? Because the supernatural and personality (as we have tended to define it) are the same thing.

Analytic psychology has convinced us that human personality is a realm of orderly naturalistic conditionings. Personality is a world as lawful in its causality as is the physical universe.[6] It is not argued here that we know all about personality, or know all there is to know about a personality, but only that personality is knowable. But sacred awe easily overtakes the oedipal animal here too, if he sacralizes his ignorance. When we speak of the "mystery of genius" in the culture innovator, we are insisting that, after all our causal analysis has been made, there remains a residue that is inexplicable. Not only is this residue inexplicable, we say in wonder, it is also beyond the realm of secular causality entirely. The innovator's creative "genius" is a spark of the divine within him. And we find this divinity plausible, because we suppose that there is within each one of us the same residue of the totally unconditioned, or even unconditionable, the sacred and imperishable individual "free will" or soul.

All this is fallacy. Subjectively, the illusion of free will depends on two facts. First, the psychic system is by no means necessarily aware in detail of its own causalities. Indeed, psychiatry constantly shows us why the system (given its homeostatic rationalizing function) *does not want to know* about the sources of its actions, even supposing that these can be made available to the person. Thus an unwillingness to know makes suspect the protest of unknowability. More insidiously still, and more impregnably to logic, is the fact that our subjective conviction of "free will" is a cherished and unsurrenderable fragment of our childhood fantasies of omnipotence. Hard experience of the world has repeatedly taught us its stubborn necessities quite beyond the reach of our own "free will." Physical reality never cheats; it encompasses us; and it is uncheatable. And, further, we are readily willing to admit that, superficially, as psychic systems, we are also often plainly subject to historic conditionings by other psychic systems, human beings, viz. in our "culture." Cultural truth, like the world, we imagine sovereign—and yet, surely, we cry, there remains some central core of manifest free choice, the Person, the Unconditioned, the Soul? God (the world, physical and moral) is omnipotent—reverently we submit—and yet, despite what this does logically to God's omnipotence, we imagine we also have each one crumb of omnipotence, our soul's "free will." Hear species-specific oedipal man philosophizing!

Both "personality" and "culture" are fully determined systems. It is not so much that Leslie White's culturology is mistaken in recognizing the determinateness of culture as that he platonizes Culture into one divine hypostatized omnipotent Determiner, and will not see that ontogenetically determined individual personality and human biology are also part of the larger determinate system. If, however, culture and personality are not seen as absolutes but only as hypothetical manners of speaking, then anthropology and all the other relevant sciences consistently agree. The neuro-anatomist Sherrington, for example, considers free will "scientifically unthinkable" if it means a series of brain events in which the succeeding are not conditioned by the preceding.[7]

Again, the psychologist Boring points out that when one believes free will to be operating, it always resides in an area of ignorance, for with known laws there is no freedom.[8] It is highly significant that indeterminacy and freedom always lie in this area of our ignorance, and that when we do know, new determinacies become understood. In fact, knowing as a process cannot operate upon the unique or the wholly antic, because knowing is in essence an experience of recognized regularities and categories. *Quid deus sit, nescimus,* Aquinas wrote; What god be, we do not know. Of course. "God" is this identical ignorance of ourselves, projected; and all his "attributes" (illegitimately postulated, logically), invariably our own. The two ignorances—of God and of oneself—are the same.

Further, the biologist Conklin writes that "Animals which learn little from experience have little freedom and the more they learn the freer they become. Freedom is the more or less limited capacity of the highest organisms to inhibit instinctive and non-rational acts by intellectual and rational stimuli and to regulate behavior in the light of past experience. Such freedom is not uncaused activity, but freedom from the mechanical responses to external or instinctual stimuli, through the intervention of internal stimuli due to experience and intelligence."[9] Thus past-determined culture and personality, in increasing the complexity and improbability of the total system, increases its unpredictability, i.e. freedom. Consequently, the man who knows most about the cultural past, and most about his own psychological past, is the most free of all.

A communications theorist might point out that as unpredictable "improbabilities" there are differing *levels* of freedom, depending on the amount of information that can be fed into a system. That is, the freedom of a system is related to its competence, viz. to what it can do. Therefore the most sophisticated of modern computers give an uncanny impression of almost human "personality" (i.e., freedom, but equally illusory perhaps in either case). Kant included freedom and determinism among his "antinomies," fundamental contradictions indicating limitations of human understanding, to be used as alternative models as it suits thought. But these are not so much "antinomies" as they are reciprocals, mutually, of our knowledge versus our ignorance—the only problem being that we never know certainly what we know, and hence can certainly not discern either the locus or the magnitude of our ignorance. Our cognitive mutations are not all of them adaptations, but (so far as we know) only random mutations, because *sapiens* as an organism (cultural, personal) always introduces a new (unknown) complexity into the total system.

The logical incompatibility of free will and omnipotence, and the fact that determinism in the human psyche is *both inside and outside* the system—old learning versus new adaptation, both only supposititiously "known"—would further suggest an oedipal paradigm to the analytically-oriented cultural anthropologist. The problem is, in fact, highly significant in the sophisticated metapsychology of modern ego analysis. Ernst Lewy has profoundly discussed responsibility, free will, and ego psychology.[10] And George Wilbur has shown the entire consistency of Freud's difficult concept of Thanatos in analytic metapsychology with the Second Law of Thermodynamics in physics.[11] As to both ego psychology and Thanatos, the difficulties in understanding are not only owing to the complexity of the concepts and the amount of psychiatric experience required to understand the issues but, even more importantly perhaps, to our inveterate psychological infantilisms.

In recent decades, the Heisenberg "principle of indeterminacy" has been seized upon by this desperate infantilism of man (theology always distorts the facts) as purporting to prove that the prestigious physical world itself behaves in ways that we would like to believe true also of ourselves. What is astounding is our duplicitous distortion and stubborn misapprehension of the evidence itself—always in the direction of our desire! The empirical facts are such as these. In a speck of radium, for example, we are unable to determine beforehand *which* of the atoms will disintegrate at the expected time. All we can ascertain is that, statistically, atoms will disintegrate at a given rate in time within the radium. This never varies. Now, instead of reasonably inferring from this that the atoms must obviously exert some determining equilibrium-effect upon one another in the system, even though we cannot for technical reasons ascertain this, we now suppose instead that each atom is endowed with unconditioned free will as to when it will disintegrate— even though we can observe that this is specifically not the case! All that Heisenberg shows is that we cannot "determine" (ascertain beforehand, know before the observation) which atom will be involved, because our very means of observation must affect what we see.

Now this is a very sophisticated scientific notion, the implications of which reverberate throughout the rest of science from mathematics to linguistics, indeed to all cultural studies, and certainly to psychiatry. But the believer in free will rejoices, "See, even atoms have free will!" What he will not see is that "indeterminacy" does not mean this. Indeterminability (human) is by no means the same as indeterminatedness (physical). Unascertainability and unpredictability on the individual atomic level is not the proved absence of all causality on the molar psychic ("soul") level! Meanwhile, whatever the indiscernibility and unpredictability of the single-atom phenomenon, nevertheless the radium atoms still disintegrate lawfully at statistically determinable, invariable, and predictable rates.

Indeed, if all atoms did not behave thus lawfully, then there could not be such lawfulness as we are able constantly to observe in more complex, even in psychic systems! If atoms too have free will, then we have built our atom-constituted bodies and brains on the shifting sands of chaos. How can we have free-will command over what has an animistic free will of its own beyond our command? Witness the narcissism of a big-brained oedipal ape at work! What the animistic thinker is doing is plain. He is imputing his own wished-for free will to the atom, despite logical havoc to him as an organism, in order to support his ancient cherished fantasy. He is certainly not discovering proof upon which to erect his (O psychologically undetermined!) theory of free will after the fact.

We can now see the ratiocination. The native imputes the culture innovation naïvely and directly to the outside "supernatural" while the modern animist imputes it to the super-natural element in another's soul or "personality," the genius which is within him.[12] In the one case it is outside, in the other inside man. But it is the same supernatural. O where do omnipotence and godhood lie, in the self or in the Self, in the child or in the father?

Or does finite, limited causality operate both in the cosmos and in all men who are within it? And can a lawful relatedness of events— economic, political, psychological and the like—operate even in such complex systems as the culture of a society? We shall assume this, if only because, if we do not so assume, both psychological and cultural science are impossible. Besides, regularities *are* in fact observable. The crisis cult is knowable. The impact of cultures (persons) is the more easily seen, perhaps, the greater the magnitude of differences between the "civilized" and the relatively "primitive" persons (cultures) we have observed. But all compulsive tribalisms invariably change only under a kind of "individual acculturation" or "culture trauma." That is, both individuals and societies behave in lawful terms within their total respective environments. A culture is no regnant transcendental godlike monad, as Culturologists allege, causally unresponsive (since omnipotent) to the nature of human nature psychologically. And, psychologically, the individual is no atom, supposedly disposing culturally of unconditioned pure free will.

Neither culture nor personality can be reduced platonically to the smile on a Cheshire cat by removing the cat, man. There are only Cheshire cats, smiling. "Culture" is an abstraction which exists only in *people,* "personality" is an abstraction that exists only in *persons.* To suppose that, additionally, there resides in each individual some wholly unconditioned quiddity that "chooses" is to suppose a "soul" disposing of free will, a chaos-creating concept under which no psychological science (indeed no psychic system) can operate. *The illusion of free will rises from the duality of id and superego in human biology and psychology.* Man is an organism (id) that speciates morally (superego); but man is a lawfully causal system, even to his works.

In his hereditary human-biological nature, the individual is exhaustively the product of a chain of blind, reality-probing, evolutionary events which reach back to his remotest organic ancestors. This structured "id" —that is, the *kind* of organism that is doing the reacting—is certainly a necessary part of the interacting process of culture. The organic id has a monumentally stubborn, but hardly a "free" will. Id is organic pattern that *will* realize itself, because it has learned to be so constituted that it *can*. But the organism is itself the product, even to its organic "wishes," of a strict causality so far as we can observe it. If gratified *adaptation* to the outside world, through the ego's mediation, constitutes the twice-imprisoned id's "free will," then this is a pathetically arrogant and self-deceiving illusion, since the organism is bound both by its own nature and the nature of the outside world. The organic id is the slave of biological history, and "wishes" only what it must. Staying alive is the successful accomplishment of its unfree willing.

Similarly, in his social human nature, the individual is likewise the result of the impingement of human individuals upon one another (culture) and upon him (personality). But being, on occasion, not *totally* influenced by other non-omnipotent individuals does not mean that the individual has at that point made an omnipotent unconditioned choice; it merely demonstrates that Culture is not omnipotent. He is not the slave but only the child of human history. The biological chain is causally binding enough: our would-be adaptive culture is also a reality-probing process. *Both* biology (blindly achieved) and culture (blindly proposed solutions) are contingent determinants of individuals. But to attend only to this second or social chain of causality is to commit the error of the "culturologists" and to make the Marxian deification of the iron god History. For the culturologists[13] maintain we should ignore the biological and psychological human being as irrelevant to the study of his Culture. Culture, they say, should be studied as if human beings had never existed! Theologians remove the Cheshire cat and think they have left a smile, the soul. Culturologists subtract the cat and think they have left: Culture.

This is of course absurd. We can agree that individual men lack free will (viz., some precious sacred area of limited fractional omnipotence, totally unconditioned causally)—and indeed every time this omnipotence turns up, it looks suspiciously like God-baby, however much it pretends its omnipotence is only a small scrap of Omnipotence, that the fraction is equal to the Whole, and the Whole is not diminished by its fractionation. (Whatever would happen if all these billions of omnipotences should collide!) We can also agree that any culture is a tyrannical system, though fortunately no one is ever completely enculturated. Culture is not an autocratic God-father; it is behavioral patterns diversely particulated into many unique personalities. Biology and culture, however, are both cause-and-effect systems; indeed, culture (personality) may be only another, species-specific, mode of blind mutation, differentially adaptive and hence ultimately biological too.

The curious mathematical phenomenon already noted may rescue us from the determinist doldrums, nevertheless. The more complex a system becomes—and even the individual human is biochemically and neurologically complex far beyond most men's imagining—the more it becomes "improbable" in the strict mathematical sense. The richness of new alternatives, of unpredictability, even comes to resemble "choice," so delicately equilibrated is the future. (Since our more complex electronic computer systems sometimes behave with the improbability of "personality," if many computers could communicate, hitched up sufficiently reticulated, would we get an electronic "culture"?) When we fully understand how culture, in fact, potentially makes billions of individual human systems into a gigantic meta-organism,[14] the order of improbability staggers thought, and makes of unpredictability a moral burden. Even if one thinks he knows himself, who knows what comes next in history? Let us then unleash adaptive intelligence and human wish upon the chaos of contemporary (eons-long) history! That should keep us intellectually interested and morally busy enough for the foreseeable future, a very God's task. But mankind's complexity is not free will. It is only improbability.

In the strict sense, personality is the culture of one individual.[15] Personality is his peculiar ordering of culture elements, and his affective tones toward behaviors that have arisen in his life-experience of other individuals, that is his "socialization" or "enculturation." Indeed, to the degree that the schizophrenic is *not* socialized to an outer world of things and of other people, he is the *more* imprisoned, maladaptively and exclusively, in his organic id. He possesses only hereditary biological adaptations that have, moreover, been traumatized; he is, psychologically, humanity-deprived. He has perforce accepted his biological heritage and has grown physically. But he has not been able to accept his historical heritage or to grow socially, i.e. culturally, psychologically, and his personality (culture) tends to be a relatively closed self-system. That a single personality—relatively closed or relatively open—does not exhaust the possibility of other such "cultures" is not to prove that personality is not a socio-cultural artifact. For where do the "cultures" of "societies" reside except in identifiable individuals? And is this precipitate of influence not each individual's personality?

If we reify "Personality" in the individual, we then have some mystic and unreal locus of unconditioned free will or "soul"—in the general region of Descartes' pineal gland?—when, actually, all we have is a (culture-) conditioned (biologically-) given organism. It is well to be tidy about these basic things and to remain clear about where they are located. Again, if we reify "Culture" then we have no place to put it except in some equally ghostly "Group Mind" or perhaps, part of it anyway, in a mystic Jungian "Group Unconscious" wherever that lives. Thus we have on the one hand the platonizing theologian, an unsound psychologist, anxious to preserve the unreal basis of his sacred culture (the God-Soul); on the other, the platonizing "culturologist," an unsound anthropologist because he ignores the existence of his subject matter, man. Culturologists easily perceive the fallacy of the psychological individual when presented as a free-willed "soul" vis-à-vis Culture; but they fail to see that, in parallel, they themselves have platonized Culture. Theologians seem equally blind to what a culture, their own included, is, and to what, actually, personality is. Both perishable products! What is permanent is matter (mass-energy), not the larger improbable permutating patterns of it.

Every item of *culture* is a learning from other individual persons. Every *person* is a construct of his learnings and experiences of himself and other individuals. Now, since we have two more terms, we are accustomed (as if they were different processes) to call "enculturation" the influence of the mass of persons in one society upon one individual, while "acculturation" is the massive effect of one society of individuals upon the individuals of another society. But let us not reify Society! Both acculturation and enculturation are mediated only by, and occur only in, individuals. It is only the alien versus the tribal locus of the culture-stuff that enables us to distinguish between "acculturation" and "enculturation" (socialization). Similarly, it is only the mass and locus of the behavior-stuff that enable us to distinguish between a culture and a personality. All culture is thus in a sense the product of *acculturation* —the constant, sometimes unwilling, accommodation of an individual's "private" culture-stuff to new alien consignments from without, viz. that of other individuals. Or, since all his sources are always and equally human beings, he undergoes a constant process of *enculturation,* but now, suddenly, in the crisis cult from new sources.

Seen in this way, the culture hero's predicament becomes crystal clear. There is in strict reality no "mixing" of Cultures in some transcendental pot from which the individual sups. The *process* in enculturation and in acculturation is the same. Only the source of the materials is different. If alien to the person's customary society it is called "acculturation." If taken from his own, then it is "enculturation." (Hence, in a mild way, even marriage can bring "culture shock," since some wives outlandishly use horse radish with beef, whereas some husbands know it should be used only with pork.) Both processes, acculturation and enculturation, can be a painful imposition of other persons' wishes and attitudes upon his own. The conflict for the culture hero arises in this way: shall the models for my behavior be the old ambivalently loved persons of my tribe?—or the new ambivalently hated persons of a more powerful alien tribe?

The predicament of the culture hero is precisely that of the neurotic: shall I operate with the defense mechanisms devised in my childhood (to which I am bound because they are compulsive, absolute, inviolable, and mostly unconscious in any case)? Shall I operate with the sacred defense mechanisms of my *society's* past (to which, with complete loyalty!, I have painfully, sometimes unwillingly, become enculturated, and which, all too often, actually conflict with the secular experiences of my personality)? Or shall I attempt new adaptations, heretic to both the native and alien tribal pasts I have learned (and what supernatural can aid me now except my own dream-improvising self, my wishful unconscious mind)? The culture hero has been "let down" by his past tribal culture in a new social situation, quite as painfully as the neurotic has been let down by his past personality in a new psycho-sexual situation (social and psycho-sexual, in man, are here identical). Aliens assail the individual everywhere. Should I learn from the alien white man? Should I learn from the hateful psychiatrist? Should I trust the scientist? For all these individuals assail the sacredly cherished defense mechanisms with which the individual has hitherto sought to operate, and which now somehow seem to fail him.

In borrowing, the culture hero has a double guilt of disloyalty, both to his individual and to his tribal part. Conflict is naturally to be expected in either case. Actually, a neurotic can be as conflictual about the culture of his father and that of his mother (their personalities) as any culture hero can, faced with cultures of diverse historical origins. Except in amount of difference, these two predicaments are the same; in fact, in the child of an occidental-oriental marriage, the predicament is identical. To a minor degree, in the family, every adolescent is a culture hero willy-nilly, "choosing" his cultures (viz. integrating his personality). If we were realistic in tracing down each ultimate sub-culture, we would end, inevitably, with the individual and his personality. In this sense, private culture is always somewhat in conflict with another private culture, and personality an endless integration of a self with the selves it loves.

Isolated primitive tribes resemble separate animal species: genes and culture traits remain within these isolated entities. But, with writing, a civilized society, whose members move about much geographically, both accumulates more completely the *past of its own society* and incorporates more massively the *pasts of other societies.* (Technically the most civilized, then, is the man who has received cognitive and phatic communications from the largest number of cultures and personalities in space and time. The primitive man, like the primitive personality in our society, is the individual who has not had enough news about mankind. And the scientist is the man who has been intellectually forced, by the technical conditions of acculturation present in a civilization, to a better knowledge-technique than tribal tradition.)

In its nature and complexity, a civilization resembles the biology of *Homo sapiens.* Unlike most inbreeding wild animal species, the human species is "polytypical." That is, *Homo sapiens* comprises many genetically different races that are interfertile with one another within one single species. Similarly, a civilization has achieved the same kind of polytypical incorporation of many social heredities. Hence a civilization has a complex of sub-cultures within it, functionally analogous to races within the species *Homo sapiens.* Put in another way, the more civilized a society becomes, the more specialized *different kinds of men* (sub-cultures, personalities) exist within the whole, and the more complex must communications among them become.

Again in terms of communication, an isolated primitive group is analogous to a wild animal species. Culture traits so to speak "breed true" in an undisturbed primitive society, as in a wild animal species. But in the historical conditions of acculturation that give rise to a civilization, there is an immense and continuing social hybridization. Genes that become isolated into different non-interbreeding wild animal species are no longer isolated in polytypical man; so too, culture traits are no longer isolated in civilized man. Logically, if it is constant intertribal warfare (in competitive head-hunting for soul-stuff) that helps keep both Burman Nagas and Amazonian Indians socially isolated and primitive, then a total civilization of mankind would abolish war. For war is a breakdown in cultural communication in a species that already has genetic communication. Civilizations should hunt brains, not heads; and minds, not souls. Which is to be preferred, tribal peace of mind that is adaptively less secure, or civilized insecurity of mind that may be adaptively better?

But this incipient love, beyond patriotism, for people in other societies may be only rationalized moral yearning for a larger Other—an intellectual hope for the still more improbable, since fragmentary civilizations have been as yet only partly, and precariously, achieved. Evolution occurs, though, only through what organisms become and do. Still, the situation biologically may be other than we can wish into political reality. For this kind of animal has deep wells of irrational hostility, unacknowledged (the nice Germans!) and unconscious (the patriotic Americans!), filled in each childhood from biological springs, as well as from enforced humanization. Can a species with this ontogenetic pattern achieve such a phylogenetic goal? Is man (oedipally, patriotically defined) a viable possibility for the future, given his present self-environed predicaments?

As in animal biology, when the reptile constitutes a superior organic adaptation and becomes ecologically the amphibian's most formidable competitor, and in turn the mammal becomes the dominator of reptiles, so also it may be in our curious and unexplored human biology. Can this organism invent new (social or organic) reality? Or—just as all kinds of plants and animals are competitive for life space, and form part of one another's total ecological environment—must human societies also compete through their cultural speciations, and form part of one another's total, indifferent or hostile, ecological environment? Among competitive societies, it would be the one which has the best *contemporary cultural adaptations* that would survive historically—though likely never in so cleancut a fashion, but more huggermugger even than in competing animal ecologies, since human societies confusingly borrow one another's social genes. Such complexity contains many alternative improbabilities! Evidently a literate civilization's political and cultural imperialism over primitive societies is a demonstration of this crude and cruel competitive power. However, this is not the kernel of our interest—the historic accident that white men have come to the possession of this cultural power, and hence are the almost ubiquitous element in latterday Ghost Dance phenomena. Rather, we are interested in these historic events primarily to descry in them the generalizations that will help us understand the crisis cult itself as the origin of the "sacred"—for sacred culture may be another curious kind of speciation.

Every culture is the adaptive mechanisms of a society. And much of its material culture must surely serve the survival needs of the society, (1) since material culture is man's new alloplastic-prosthetic adaptation which reshapes the environment to which he must adapt; (2) since material culture manifestly does accumulate and evolve as adaptive techniques; and (3) since the quality of material culture appears to be the prime tool or weapon influencing selection among competing societies. But all culture is not material. And just as all biological mutations are not necessarily adaptive, so all cultural speciation also is not necessarily adaptive. Nor is all culture necessarily "adaptive" only to the outer physical world. Some culture is at best adaptive to man's own inner psychic world, and to his sometimes unreal anxieties. Consequently, there are two realms of culture, the secular and the sacred. In fact, the sacred and the secular are even commonly, though not always, discriminated in the thinking of primitive people themselves—though, if so, not always accurately, the one being sometimes confused with the other.

What is the nature of these two realms of culture? In each society, the secular is the realm of technical control and ego-adaptation. It deals with the natural and the known. The sacred is the realm of the "supernatural" Unknown. Since man fatuously assumes he knows himself, this Unknown is thought to be primarily outside of man, and he behaves toward it as if it were outside of him. And yet, since the Unknown is not known, he necessarily deals with it projectively by means of his own unexamined nature. Hence the structuring of this as-if-outside Unknown is done with that which is within him, his categoric id demands and struggling superego countermands.

Culture, then, is man's ways of handling his total life needs in this enlarged sense. Some of these needs are simply "biological." But these life needs include "psychological" ones as well—problems of how men can live together, how animals with diverse equipment and biological interests can live together in the family, and how animal wish can be disciplined to social demands, etc. Therefore every culture must have means of handling the anxiety arising from id wishes unmet by the known, and from the ego's and the historic superego's uncertain and fallible means of ministering to these psychological needs. We can rationally fear the known, but can only be anxious about the unknown. Culture is thus necessarily in part a defense against irrational anxiety—"irrational" since it is not a real fear of the known but of the unconscious or the repressed, and "anxiety" because it is from the Unknown within us.

Personality is, in part, defenses against the id self. And so of course is culture. Therefore, when the various events of acculturation threaten these old cultural defenses, in the competition with a more powerful society, and when belief in the adequacy of the "sacred" culture mechanisms wears thin, then the society suffers, so to speak, a collective trauma. Of course no "society" can actually undergo a "collective trauma" to its "group mind." This way of phrasing the matter is useful, however, because it is *not only a single individual's trauma.* It is a shorthand way of saying that when the individual's defense mechanisms wear thin, he is threatened by an overwhelming anxiety—but the anxiety is the greater when he also loses the phatic support of his fellows, suffering simultaneously the same vicissitudes. He may suffer a "nervous breakdown" from the conflict; the society, a "Ghost Dance." For sacred culture is a way men have of sharing one another's emotional burdens and perplexities.

Culture is at once the *system of defense mechanisms* (either technical-secular or autistic-sacred) and *the mode of speciation* of men in societies as well—*as* individuals and *as* societies—except that the "genes" of this speciation are communications (personality, culture), not chromosomes. But cultures historically are not "equal" in adaptive potential. Indeed, conquest by Europeans and others is ultimately if dimly perceived by natives themselves as owing to possession of a better, since more powerful, culture. And this spectacle motivates native change, much as a boy emulates his father. However, with a critically significant difference: natives are not children, but men. They are already deeply bound unconsciously within to loyalties arising from their earlier taking-on or "introjection" of tribal values. The psychological ground is already occupied, but now powerful competing beliefs appear, the ideal conflict-neurosis situation, affecting the whole "society" because it affects all the individuals in it. (There remains only to note, for those who cannot find a human psychological truth true until it has been demonstrated in laboratory animals, that neuroses have been created experimentally by conflictual conditioning now in dogs, pigs, and sheep; and over-crowded rats can become suspiciously like neurotic humans.)

In the conflictual reaction to "acculturation"—conflicting enculturation—when the culture hero seeks to strike a new balance or individual psychic homeostasis, there is inevitably a mixture of the old and the new. The culture hero is the "uncanny" mouthpiece of the summarized unconscious wishes of the other individuals in his society. His selectivity and ambivalence toward old and new are plain—no person has ever been socialized entirely willingly to any culture—for side by side with *revival* of old culture elements, and side by side with a *rejection* both of old native and new alien evil ways, there is also half-conscious *borrowing* of another culture (from differently enculturated personalities). Every prophet is at once revivalist and modernist. The culture hero is the creative artist in cultures. His crisis *is,* in the large sense, the transcultural problem—of father and son, of society and society.

Every movement finds its culture hero or prophet. His genius is communication. In one sense he is an exponent of the standard psychic state of his contemporaries, spokesman for his generation. In another sense, his creative fantasy, if apt, becomes by psychic contagion and irrational phatic communciation a *folie à deux* raised to a geometric power equal to the number of his communicants. A "folie à deux" is the diffusion, usually in a mental hospital but by no means only there, of attitudes and symbolisms (culture) from one individual we choose to call a "psychotic" to another, usually of the same or similar antecedent "personality." This diffusion of culture is primarily through *phatic* communication. That is, although the *folie* pretends, especially in its paranoid forms, to be formal and systematic description of the universe, the communication is really a recognition and mutual acceptance of the same affective stance *within* two or more individuals. Phatic communication, in man as in apes, is merely the establishment of similar subjective states in a group of animals—which is why the shaman's message need not be notably rational cognitively, and very often is not. For two psychotics, via communication, can create a bona fide culture in a society of two persons. The idea is repellant to those who think that psychotics cannot create authentic culture, and to those who suppose all culture is necessarily rational. Actually, it is less repellant than a whole nation of Nazis. Or of Americans in Vietnam.

Each most catholicly established church was once a sect, each sect a cult. And in every revealed religion, the cult had its beginning in one person's revelation. The number of communcants at any time, then or now, guarantees nothing; it demonstrates only a human ability to be awed by numbers, to join crowds, and to abdicate independent judgment of the truth-value of propositions. The distinction between a *cult* and a folie à deux is nonexistent. Once we have left the individual and his private psychosis, once we have attitudinal and symbolized stuff held in common, then undeniably we have culture. Truth is not a function of the number of believers but a culture is. Socially, the critical change of phase is the line between the private psychosis and the folie à deux, not between a cult and culture. Once phatic or cognitive communication has been established, the only difference between folie and culture is quantitative—two persons or two million.

Thus, when two or three have been gathered together in the name of a communicated set of symbolized stances, there abides culture. Note that we do not "equate culture with a psychosis" as some critics have alleged —for this is to miss the point entirely. We maintain simply that a cult is in every respect culture. Hence it behooves every individual to keep his reality testing alert. The proper referent for any objective statement is the object itself; but to use the minds of one's fellows, rather than the object, to establish a truth, is precisely to use the phatic technique of sacred belief, not cognitive proof in a secular fashion. This might be called "the Socratic fallacy" and produces only an ethnographic statement of consensus, not verification. A statement of belief is only a statement of belief.

Furthermore, the diffusion of the symbolic and ideational content of a folie is identical with the diffusion of a culture. Both rest largely on the similarities in personality (-culture) encountered. The "truth" in either case rests on other operational criteria than diffusion, such as reality-fit, not in the phatic consistency of personalities with one another, and not in the equal success of phatic communication in folie and in cult. It must follow, then, that any society's discrimination between its "psychotics" and its "culture heroes" rests in the society's appetite for their respective products. This difference is a psychological one. The narcissistic psychotic arouses other persons' anxieties and alienates the olonist from them. The culture hero allays anxieties and becomes their shaman-teacher.

Not experiencing this differential in the proper cultural key, the outsider must often regard the culture hero and the psychotic as the same. That is to say, the outsider has difficulty in discriminating between the olonist and the shaman. After all, it is not his psyche that is being frightened or solaced, it is not his culture-and-personality that is being modulated! Rather, in this, the ethnographer is himself making an implicit cross-cultural reality-judgment which is irrelevant, except to objective truth; he is unconsciously allowing *his* anxieties to be manipulated. Inappropriately to appeal to truth is to miss the ethnographic fact. To the outsider, the old cultural behavior and the new personality's behavior are both equally inapposite to the world he himself sees—but not to the prepared personalities of the culture hero's communicants! To call the personality of the shaman "sane" is to display ethnographic unawareness of the cultural process, to mistake a priest for a shaman, and to be insensitive to culture and personality differences.

Another example may help make the point. In ancient Japan, in 644 A.D., when impoverished peasants were writhing under early feudalism, a prophet arose who persuaded his neighbors to worship a green caterpillar with black spots as the "God of the Eternal World" and their "God of Gods." Wealth would come to the caterpillar god's devotees, who were to throw away all their property onto the highroads in order to accomplish the miracle. The caterpillar cult spread astonishingly—so widely and so rapidly, in fact, that the authorities intervened, executed the prophet, and rigidly suppressed his new religion.[16] Since we do not know the cultural antecedents and symbolic meanings of caterpillars in seventh-century Japan, we are likely to see the movement as totally bizarre from start to finish. However, our implicit decision to worship or not to worship a green caterpillar with black spots is really not very relevant. More relevant is that we do not know enough properly to weight idiosyncratic personality versus peasant sub-culture.

What we can judge, though, is that the prophet's cult matched prior culture well enough to obtain a hearing and increasing belief among the peasants. At the same time, the cult must also have been unconventional enough and threatening enough to the mainstream of the Great Culture of the time for it to be so rigorously destroyed. Perhaps we might surmise so far as to class this a ghost dance *Plebejereligion* of a sub-culture in an unsuccessful civil uprising. It is also possible that what the authorities seem to have judged "criminal" we might call "psychotic"—but for this we would welcome more clinical details. Of course there are non-content, processual phenomena that make an individual psychotic in whatever culture. And since the human body is crossculturally very similar, one might entertain the clinical hunch that the body-image symbolism of this Japanese peasant-prophet resembles that of paranoid schizophrenia.

All religions, we believe, once had their origin in a crisis cult.[17] The great ecumenical world religions, however, have a special problem. In civilized societies that have writing, there is a greater half-remembered continuity with the past than in simpler non-literate societies. In fact, this continuity with the past constitutes a civilization's main hope for therapy—to recapture awareness of old forgotten premises and symbolisms, so that we may reassess the situation with new eyes, test out new solutions if these are possible, and recognize the inexorable when we encounter it. The only rub is that sacred culture, like a neurosis, permits no such scrutiny and jealously guards from question its mysteries from the past. Old wounds must not be reopened. God did not die.

At the same time, a literate civilization is potentially faced with a greater unwelcome insight into the meanings of the past; and vatic personalities must constantly reinterpret the revelation from the sacred past in order to maintain a current homeostasis.[18] It is inevitable then that as ideology sacred culture should appear characteristically so shoddy cognitively and so shopworn, if it is intrinsically and systematically out-of-date ethnography from the sacred past. Establishment foments no ghost dance (until, of course, it is disestablished), and the contemporary ecstatic shaman is the least of its needs, and even a dangerous nuisance.[19] An Establishment needs a priest, a modernist to update eternal revelation, to deny history and yet to cope with secular change, and to transform past ethnography into present plausibility. Not a shamanistic visionary but a priestly theologian is now the man of the hour: he must, in fact, be the "sanest" of rationalizers available, a high-church member of all the best men's scientizing societies.

Vatic fatherhood has its own non-bodily apostolic succession. Each successively discovered error must be hastily reclothed in new symbolic language lest the naked fallacy offend new culture; each vatic personality must reaffirm the omniscience and infallibility of his predecessors in the cult he serves; the priest's is an even more parasitic manhood than the shaman's. Remembered revelation makes the priest struggle desperately against new culture change; the shaman is not thus burdened with history. Fettered to the past like a compulsive neurotic, a priestly culture cannot change though it constantly must. But the priest has the same vatic personality, if anything intensified through the very establishment of his god. *Nemo venit ad patrem nisi per me.*

The selfless service of the vatic is vanity disguised, an arrogant humility that is boundless, the smug condescension of the god-wielder. Morris Opler met an *ojha* in India who "whenever his interpretation was questioned, silenced the incredulous by a withering glance and the words, 'The goddess has spoken.' "[20] And Kosambi, describing "living prehistory in India" among the Pardhi, an archaic hunting people, tells of a transvestite priest who stated even more categorically, "I *am* the goddess."[21] Is this not the voice of paranoia? Chang, the Korean messiah of the Doomsday Cult, generously shared his megalomania with his cultists. "There was no generation in the past whose task was related to the whole cosmos," he said. "We are cosmic persons who are responsible for the restoration of the entire cosmos. This is why we have the highest privilege in all history."[22]

The more literate and learned a cult of the book, the more religious mechanisms verge toward the compulsive. But the unlettered and the primitive, not so bound, can naïvely avail themselves of a newer hysteria or paranoia, no patched hand-me-down but a new system custom-made to fit the times. Although all religion begins in revelation, the literate society is bound so long as it professes exclusive loyalty to *the* revelation in its sacred past; whereas, without written memory, contemporary revelations may change with unselfconscious ease in the rise of each new shaman, whose ignorance of the past is a positive advantage. The violence evoked throughout the history of each book-religion, when any individual has questioned explicit sacred tenets, is a measure of the compulsiveness with which these tenets are litigiously maintained. Literacy burdens a society with compulsive religious defense of fossil culture.

For this reason, in primitive societies, the "choice of neurosis"[23] in ghost dance crisis cults can range on a wider psychiatric gamut than compulsiveness, and the style of the defense mechanisms will vary precisely with differing culture-and-personality factors. For example, a society may use the chief defense mechanism of hysteria, simple denial. Thus painting bones red with life-fire-blood ochre may represent simple denial of death in Old Stone Age burials, and magic rebirth. Again, when individual messiahs are illiterate in their own cultural past, the same naïve hysteric mechanisms re-emerge and cultists institutionalize the hysteria of the founder, in her bland denial of evil and sickness and death as mere illusions.

The great variety of autistic projections in crisis cults is no problem to explain, once it is understood that birds of a feather self-selectively flock together, *folie-á-N*-wise, to the cult of an *individual*—who will have called on any defense mechanisms that, psychiatrically, he needs. If explosive rage or projected hostility threatens body-disintegration, the cult projects schizophrenic fantasies of world destruction. Or mutilation-threat from oedipal guilt means that men must soon die. One may regress, in varying degrees, even to infantile omnipotence and magic manipulation of reality: the psychokinetic, tent-shaking shaman is Master of Animals and paranoid sovereign over life and death, the magic god-baby. Or paranoia may be a half-literate's half-Biblical religion, as in Joseph Smith, with angelic voices, mysterious visitations and secret languages, erotomania, and grandiose pseudo-systems of history and anthropology.

Withdrawal from a troubled or vexing world is found repeatedly, in cult self-segregation, in Buddhist, Islamic, Hindu and Christian monasticism, in Siberian olonism, Indonesian *mejapi* and the Kwakiutl initiation-flight into the woods, in the vision quest and the psychedelic drop-out alike. Psychopaths can thread their exploitative way through the worst of culture-chaos; the snake-handling cult is an instance of this kind. There are phobias we can call on, when we see, as if outside us, the threats and demons that are within, as in any bellicose nationalism, German, Russian, American or whatever: but war is acting-out, not therapy. Many ghost dances, too, reject the alien and are paranoid. Some cargo cults show self-contempt and masochistic destruction of the old culture, identify with the aggressor, and are depressive.

Primitive or civilized, societies use the same psychic defenses. Many primitive religions are largely simple phallic fetishisms; and for the naïve, there are the Buddha's tooth or toenail, saints' bones, holy medals and talismans, fragments of the true fetish, and holy water. Some religions are oedipal totemisms, like that of Australian Bushmen who eat the magic father-foodstuff; but instead of wallabies and witchety grubs, one may have the Eleusinian grain-wafer and Dionysian wine-blood of pre-

Greek cults of god-eating. In conversion hysteria we can autoplastically deform and mutilate and punish the sinful self, as in Hindu and other asceticisms, or in our own Dark Ages. We may shout hysterical denial that the bullets will affect us, or take refuge in a paranoid impregnability to foreign bodies. Or we can, in manic rage, undisciplined, destroy the past, like Red Guards in China. All these psychiatric mechanisms can be found in one crisis cult or another.

There can be no question of the validity of clinical terms to describe individuals. Methodologically, in studies of societies, the only problem is to discriminate *which individuals* in what sub-cultures, how many, and to what degree the terms individually apply—sometimes difficult, but not forbidden by theory, nor are the clinical syndromes absent in the data. Many mixtures of symptom and defense in crisis cults are to be expected in the kind of animal that experiences varied states of anxiety and degrees of omnipotence in his experience of a mother, a father, and himself. In many cults the symptoms are in fact mixed. We may burn our medicine bundles, shamanistic drums and ego-masks; we may even burn a few shamans as false messiahs from the past—and still give up tobacco, cats, and Russian handshakes. We may wallow in the wasteland of the present, in self-pity and neurasthenia—and still, sometimes, flee schizoid into the womb of some Golden Age of the sacred past.

The historically *echt* messiah need not display symptoms less mixed than a run-of-the-mill clinical case: Hitler, to all appearance, was a choice mixture of hysterical phobias, conversion symptoms, and classic paranoia. Nor need a society have fewer than the humanly available: Stalinist Russia, in retrospect, looks like a mixture of cut-throat psychopathy and air-tight religious paranoia, not really dissimilar to modern Red China. Indeed, the ideally ecumenical cult would supply all the identifications a father, a mother, a daughter, a son needs and a complete drugstore of defense-medicines to exhaust psychiatric possibility. In this it must be like a modern American political party, ideally or at least apparently all things to all men.

All advance in secular culture has meant a brave assessment of the situation, an accessibility to new information, and a stolidly naturalistic new way of dealing with the crisis, rejecting the charisma of each comforting savior for an undeceived view directed toward the relentless reality of that which is. But sacred culture defends its comforting dogmas at all cost, as long as it can refuse to countenance the new, whether data or theory; and when finally forced to, after cultural change, then through the busy work of modernism it pretends that this was what it said in the first place. Dogma is sacred, like an untouchable neurotic system. And sacred culture is the neurotic side of history.

That neurotic and even psychotic ways of dealing with our problems have been rife in the past, no close student of our culture history will deny. And neither time nor many cultists can make false . solutions valid, based on whatever forgotten premises. Western religion, and much of its philosophy from Plato to Kant, is the historic detritus of the Ghost Dance of three great cultures, the Hebrew, the Greek, and the Roman. The magnificent prophetic and progressive strain in old Hebrew culture came to disaster in Pharasaism and its fossil, Talmudic culture, and in otherworldly Essene cults, at the destruction of the earthly Kingdom of the Jews. In the Hellenistic era, at the wrecking of Alexander's empire, anthropomorphic Olympian nature gods, non-experimental humanistic rationalism, and the tight Greek city-state together failed to hold back a flood of Asiatic gods and fantasies of decayed despotisms.

Only contact with another culture, alien to their own, makes men aware that they *have* a culture. But man-based Greek rationalism, the dialectic technique of knowledge of the Greek-ethnographer Socrates, and the deification of Greek categories by the shaman-philologist Plato were not adequate ways of dealing with cultural alternatives of belief, since these epistemic methods all depend on ethnic consensus. Ionian nature-philosophers and the Atomists are the fathers of modern science. But Plato is the father of the Greek ghost dance and the father of the Great Tradition of speculative philosophy, and as such is still loved and worshiped. Borrowing from both the Greek and Jew it defeated, the Ghost Dance of defeated imperial Rome is embodied in the platonic-christian Church of Rome. The great heresies and the Crusades were incidents in later ghost dances of the Church, and so too were the Inquisition, the Reformation, and the Counter-Reformation.

The peculiar *Weltschmerz* of the Ghost Dance is always and everywhere characteristic of threatened or disintegrating societies. Man is stripped of his protective cultural garments, and for a while he is exposed to the heartless winds that sweep the universe. When he discovers the existentialist fact of History, and his species-aloneness before the fact of evolution, and when he learns that culture is his own creation, and an imperfect ungodlike one at that, then he experiences again an aching helplessness, in a world which is not his childhood home. Has one the right to expect of society more than he expects of himself? Is human society more than human? Is Society the savior? Is the Church? There are no messiahs anywhere, only men!

But these Ghost Dances are not mere dead events. They are contempo-

rary. Red China is the violently confused heir of the warlords following
the fall of the Manchu Empire. Ghost Dances race through post-colonial
Africa and Oceania, not able to achieve even the cult of the Nation
(but not without the intervention, it would seem sometimes, of an international communism that seeks its chance in fomenting chaos). In the
eastern Mediterranean an Islamic tribalism was aided into power by the
same democratic Atlantic states that secured Iberian fascism in the
western Mediterranean. In South Africa arises an archaic racism as
vicious as any German one. In France, terrified of any political power
in their leaders since the Napoleon-swindled Revolution, where will the
people find their next charisma-drenched messiah to revive pre-Revolu-
tionary *gloire?* In England, colonial glories past, new Toynbees still seek
to persuade tired men back into the womb of History or to creep into
the protection of the dim lights of some Anglican cathedral. And once-
Revolutionary America, the last best hope of man, now with incantations
of hired Madison Avenue shamans zealously intervenes, a new Rome,
to maintain each hopeless vicious status quo, and makes massive messianic
visitations to ensure genocide for the people's own good.

Tribalism, corporate-capitalist or Christian or whatever, is in time of
necessity deeply anti-democratic in its ghost dance attempts to preserve
a sacred status quo. It is now also anti-human, whether the bomb be
used to make the world safe for capitalists, communists, or Chinese.
In this our own Age of Anxiety there threatens an apocalyptic end
to the whole world. The young hero is dead. And what say our lesser
culture heroes? In America, where once Melville's Ahab battled his
Leviathan, Tennessee Williams can write only of the impossibility of
love, and others dramatize only the essential absurdity of life. Psyche-
delists drop out from society to some ineffable inner world, mixing LSD
with studiously irrational Zen and a tireless cult of extra-procedural
pure protest. And Rhine seeks God with dice and cards.

The world grown dire, man retreats into himself. For in crisis cults,
subjective narcissism is the other side of the coin of objective unrealism. That is, the less loyalty to the acerb secular Reality Principle
in any adaptation, the more there is an indulgence and conditioning
by the Pleasure Principle of sacred subjective wish. Which reality, inner
or outer, is to prevail? It is no cosmic sin for an organism to wish,
since an organism is the sum of past successful wishes. But many crisis
cult heroes make an egregiously false analysis of the situation and of
what it might take to resolve their predicaments. Some culture heroes,
we have seen, under stress seem to react to old inner and irrelevant
anxieties, not to realistic new outward fears. The new predicament is

seen not as due to the discrete outer fact of alien powers, new ecological situations, and the problems that changed environment may pose; it is, mistakenly, seen as the result of something *we* have done in terms of our limited inner moral world. Our straits are owing to an old offended god, for we have sinned, we must confess, reform. Like neurotic narcissism, tribal narcissism supposes that everything in the world arises from our own magic-omnipotent acts; there is vague or insufficient acknowledgement of equivalent personal or other tribal powers. (How can absolute America strike a balance between enormous *hubris* and enormous *aretē?*) Hence, like Ghost Dance plainsmen, we imagine each new crisis is all our doing.

Superego anxieties arise from old acculturation and the unconscious, not from realistic ego-assessment and new conscious adaptation to external realities. Hence, like unquestioned "omnipotence," *unrealism* is the hallmark of all sacred cults. New autoplastic chastening and distortions of the self are called for in autistic cults, not reasonable alloplastic revisions of the environment. The sacred can never be assailed (i.e. the id denied). But true technological adaptations need no justification or moral defense beyond their own animal success. They represent a slow but continuously increasing technical command of the environment, a cumulative ecological adaptation. Under great stress, in societies as in individuals, there is often not only over-reaction to re-establish an old equilibrium, but sometimes also reaction in precisely the wrong direction. Thus in the dirigible *Shenandoah* disaster in New Jersey many years ago, frightfully burned people in their delirium ran directly back into the holocaust they had just escaped, instead of running farther away from it. Social examples, of unequal innocence, include Goldwaterism of the vanished frontier, KKK nostalgia for the Old South, the Nazi quest for a Germanic Holy Roman Empire, and the latest political crusade. Mind and society, under stress, like the body, "decompensate."

There are many ways to express psychic conflict—among these as an intellectual, a criminal, an artist, a psychotic, or a shaman—and each one of these can be confused with any other[24] Each, in his way, is a lightning-rod for social stresses, a man who in his person does psychic work for the rest of us. Like the bad dream of each childhood, the nightmare of history must be told; it is unfinished dream-work. As the poet is the daydreamer for his society,[25] so the shaman is neurotic in the service of his society. He is the "deputy lunatic" for his people. Recovered from his visionary spirit-sickness, the shaman invites others to join his medicine society. The shaman, like every messiah, is sick for the sake of all of us, the scapegoat of our sins, and inevitable martyr.

The inarticulate mass of men must express themselves through the new-styled man most capable of assuming his and their responsibility before history. Sometimes society does not recognize itself in the man it creates, much as the painter's model may be shocked by his portrait. But the gods that get invented are only images of the shaman's self. Reciprocally, he is compassion: the shaman differs from the idiot-monad psychotic because of the shaman's pseudo-fatherly social concern for people in some therapeutic, political, or economic way; he is identified by stress-infantilized personalities with a child's-eye view of the omnipotent father.

Nevertheless, the shaman is himself basically a child with whom childlike communicants identify. Devereux has brilliantly shown that, institutionally, from the child's-eye view of a disturbed youngster, shamanism broadly considered is a socially offered and culturally prepared bromide for his psychic headache. Culturally, it is the type-solution for his conflicts, insofar as these are also typical of his society. Psychologically, the shamanistic pattern is a socially tendered defense against internal tension. With Linton and Kroeber, Devereux considers that "the shaman is a fundamentally neurotic person who is fortunate enough to be able to cope with his problems by means of socially sanctioned symptomatic defenses, instead of having to improvise his own socially penalized symptoms and defenses, like the psychotic."[26]

The aura in crisis of unresolved problems and of unfinished history makes the resemblance to adolescence not adventitious.[27] If the culture hero creates his culture as the shaman-artist creates his cult and his god, the resemblance to the creativity of adolescence is no accident either— for what, dynamically, is the adolescent but a personality in process? If the cultural ecclesia seems settled and secure, it has merely forgotten its cultist youth: adults are priests of themselves who have forgotten the shamanistic anguish of adolescence. The shamanistic and the initiation ordeal of adolescence, in fact, often coincide. The psychosexual symbolism of death and rebirth is apposite too: the child must die to become the man. The creation of personality is the creation of culture. Essential shamanism is thus at once the oldest and newest of religions, because it is the *de facto* source of all religion.

NOTES

(XI Culture and Culture Heroes)

1. S. F. Nadel, *A Study of Shamanism,* p. 36. Cf. Albert Schweitzer, *The Psychiatric Study of Jesus* (Boston: Beacon Press, 1948), who makes a sophisticated exception of Christ as a religious paranoiac by proving that the Biblical texts suggesting this conclusion are "for the most part unhistorical," but he accepts evidence for megalomania and, perhaps, hallucinations at the baptism (*op. cit.,* p. 75). Contrast George de Loosten, M.D. (pseudonym of Dr. Georg Lormer), *Jesus Christus vom Standpunkt der Psychiaters* (Bamberg: Handels-Druckerei und Verlagshandlung 1905); William Hirsch, M.D., *Religion and Civilization: The Conclusions of a Psychiatrist* (New York: Truth Seeker Company, 1912); Charles Binet-Sanglé, *La Folie de Jésus* (Paris: A. Maloine, 4 vols., 1908–1915); and Emil Rasmussen, *Jesus, eine vergleichende psychopathologische Studie* (Leipzig: J. Zeitler, 1905).

2. Thomas Hobbes, *Leviathan, or The Matter, Forme, & Power of a Common-Wealth Ecclesiasticall and Civill* (London: Andrew Crooke, 1651, p. 51 [Reprinted from the Edition of 1651, Oxford: At the Clarendon Press, 1909, p. 81; cf. pp. 44, 83]).

3. Herman Melville, *Moby Dick or the Whale* (New York: Random House, 1930, p. 261; cf. p. 447).

4. Quotation translated from Auguste Sabatier, *Esquisse d'une Philosophie de la Religion* (Paris: Fischbacher, 1897, p. 13).

5. M. E. Spiro, "Culture and Personality, The Natural History of a False Dichotomy," *Psychiatry,* 14 (1951) 19–46. By contrast, Honigmann's "putting man back into culture," "personality *in* culture" and "socialization from within" seem to me thoroughly confused and confusing (J. J. Honigmann, *Personality in Culture,* New York: Harper and Row, 1967).

6. On determinism in the physical operation of the mind, A. C. Crombie, "Helmholtz," *Scientific American,* 198 (1958) 94ff., p. 95. Regarding determinism in culture, Edward B. Tylor wrote that "the history of mankind is part and parcel of the history of Nature, [and] that our thoughts, wills and actions accord with laws as definite as those which govern the motion of the waves" (quoted in Ernest Jones, *Life and Work of Sigmund Freud,* I:366). On psychic determinism, Sigmund Freud, "Determinism, Chance, and Superstitious Beliefs," Ch. XII in *Psychopathology of Everyday Life,* in *The Basic Writings of Sigmund Freud* (New York: Modern Library, 1938, pp. 150–78).

7. C. S. Sherrington, in Boring.

8. Edwin G. Boring, *When is Human Behavior Predetermined?,* pp. 190, 192.

9. Edwin Grant Conklin, *Heredity and Environment* (New York: Johnson Reprint Corporation, 6th revised edition, 1965, p. 237).

10. Ernst Lewy, "Responsibility, Free Will, and Ego Psychology," *International Journal of Psycho-Analysis,* 42 (1961) 260–70.

11. George B. Wilbur, "Some Problems Presented by Freud's Life-Death Instinct Theory," *American Imago,* 2 (1941) 134–96 and 208–65.

12. Freud expressed his thoughts on genius most fully in *Leonardo da Vinci, A Psycho-Sexual Study of an Infantile Reminiscence* (London: Kegan Paul, 1922). Freud himself was not above awe at the charisma of artists of genius. "He seemed to take the romantic view of them as mysterious beings with a superhuman, almost

divine afflatus" (E. Jones, *Life and Works*. II:344). This is an oedipal fallibility in Freud.

13. The *fons et origo* of "culturology" is Leslie A. White, *The Science of Culture*.

14. The concept of the species *H. sapiens* as a metaorganism derives ultimately from J. von Uexkull, *Theoretical Biology*, p. 243.

15. Edward Sapir wrote that "The concept of culture, as it is handled by the cultural anthropologist, is necessarily something of a statistical fiction . . ." It is not the concept of culture which is subtly misleading but the metaphysical locus to which culture is generally assigned ("Cultural Anthropology and Psychiatry," in D. G. Mandelbaum [ed.], *Selected Writings of Edward Sapir*, Berkeley: University of California Press, 1949, pp. 509–21, p. 516). Again, "The more fully one tries to understand a culture, the more it seems to take on the characteristics of a personality organization" ("The Emergence of the Concept of Personality in a Study of Cultures," *loc. cit.*, pp. 590–97, p. 594). The more standardized an individual, the more statements about his personality are equivalent to "culture"; the more finely delimited the subculture, the more nearly a statement made of it is of "personality."

16. W. G. Aston, "Fetishism," *Hastings Encyclopedia*. 5:894–98.

17. The origin of all organized religions in crisis cults was, I believe, first suggested by Anthony Wallace in *Revitalization Movements*, p. 268.

18. The usefulness of ambiguity (or symbol "over-determination") to bridge past and present in "modernist" reinterpretation is found also on the primitive level; see J. W. Fernandez, "Unbelievably Subtle Words: Representation and Integration in the Sermons of an African Reformation Cult," *History of Religions*, 6 (1966) 43–69.

19. The contrast between the *zar* (shaman) and the *ulema* (priest) among the Diga [=Azande] is especially well shown by Brenda Z. Seligman, "The Part of the Unconscious in Social Heritage," in E. E. Evans-Pritchard, *et al.* (eds.), *Essays Presented to C. G. Seligman*, pp. 307–17. Mrs. Seligman writes of "an elaborate system of myth and ritual, which is familiar and on which behaviour during dissociation [in the shaman's possession-trance] is based. There is thus a reservoir of material upon which the disordered self can draw, and to which it constantly adds. The social significance given in this way to unconscious material becomes a very powerful factor in culture" (p. 315). Bastide believes that old myths disappear in urbanization, hence the unconscious is no longer modeled on a folk tradition but dictated by individual libido, thus the gods that are invented (e.g., Cabocle, Plume Verte, Pierre Noir, Michel Shango, etc.) are only images of the possessed ecstatic's own self (Roger Bastide, *Les Religions Africaines au Brésil: Vers une Sociologie des Interpénétrations de Civilisations*, Paris: Presses Universitaires, 1960). See also M. E. Opler, "The Creative Role of Shamanism in Mescalero Apache Mythology," *Journal of American Folklore*, 59 (1946) 268–81.

20. M. E. Opler, "The Human Being in Culture Theory," *American Anthropologist*, 66 (1964) 507–28, p. 620.

21. D. D. Kosambi, "Living Prehistory in India," *Scientific American*, 216 #2 (February 1967) 105–12, 114, p. 114.

22. Lofland, *op. cit.*, pp. 235–36; on "arrogant humility" see Lofland, p. 242, fn 30; Eric Hoffer, *The True Believer* (New York: New American Library, 1958, p. 23), and *The Passionate State of Mind* (New York: Harper and Row, 1954, p. 128). Howitt maintained that "arrogance and atrocity are prominent and imperishable features in the priestly character" (William Howitt, *Popular History of Priestcraft in All Ages and Nations*, London: E. Wilson, 1833). But the characteristic arrogance of the vatic personality can also be shared by a cultic

or tribal ingroup as well. The Ranters (a sect contemporary with the early Quakers) made "their 'oneness with God' absolute, and confused the possibility of Divine Guidance with the assertion of personal infallibility" (Rufus M. Jones, *Studies in Mystic Religion,* New York: Macmillan, 1923, p. 465). Jones says knowing is a social process, and on this ground explains the success of Quakers and the failure of the Ranters.

23. On religion as a "neurosis of mankind," see S. Freud, *Moses and Monotheism* (London: Hogarth Press, 1939, p. 91; cf. pp. 94, 129). The parallel was introduced earlier in *Totem and Taboo, passim.*

24. The interchangeability of intellectual, criminal, artist, psychotic, and shaman, in the eyes of some, is plentifully documented. Camus, for example, lists examples of the criminality of art in the view of many revolutionary reformers (Albert Camus, *The Rebel: An Essay on Man in Revolt,* New York: Vintage Books, 1956, pp. 222–23). The intellectual also is clearly a suspicious character in the *Report of the Reece Committee to the House of Representatives,* which darkly warns that "The trustees of the tax-exempt foundations should . . . be very chary of promoting ideas, concepts, and opinion-forming material which run contrary to what the public currently *wishes, approves,* and *likes*" (quoted by Senator J. William Fulbright, in his Editorial, *Saturday Review,* 38, ₦7 [12 February 1955], p. 22). If sacred culture *eo ipso* must be market-researched, surely not aesthetic and intellectual culture too?

25. S. Freud, "The Relation of the Poet to Day-Dreaming" (Hogarth Press ed., 4:173–183; Collier Books, BS 193V, pp. 34–43).

26. The concept of "deputy lunatic" is from George Devereux, *Origin of Shamanistic Powers.* Quotation from G. Devereux, *Dream Learning,* p. 1044; see also his "Shamans as Neurotics," *American Anthropologist,* 63 (1961) 1088–90. A. L. Kroeber, *The Nature of Culture.* Ralph Linton, *Culture and Mental Disorders* (Springfield, Illinois: Charles C. Thomas, 1956); other supporters of this opinion are W. D. Hambly, *Origins of Education among Primitive Peoples* (London: Macmillan, 1926, pp. 217–22, 258), and Derek Freeman, "Anthropology, Psychiatry and the Doctrine of Cultural Relativism," *Man,* 65 (1965) 65–77.

27. My views on adolescence owe much to colleagues of the Committee on Adolescence of the Group for the Advancement of Psychiatry, to which I have been Consultant since 1959 (*Normal Adolescence: Its Dynamics and Impact,* GAP Report 68, 1968, also New York: Charles Scribner's Sons, 1968, hardback and paperback). Editions have also appeared in Swedish, Italian, and Portuguese.

XII

Charisma and Mana

W E HAVE pointed earlier to the rootedness of magic and religion in human biology. The biologically infantilized human learns his humanity from infancy onward. This humanity arises in the psychological experiences of his peculiar animal milieu. The emotional reality of magic and religion lies precisely in these experiences. Indeed, without further psychic growth, magico-religious convictions rest unshakable—and even so, in crises, frightened men return to the mystique of earlier archaic securities.

The adult-infant contrast shapes belief in power. Only the *location* of arrogantly unbounded will distinguishes shaman and priest. The magician-shaman embodies mana; the priest serves the mana of some awful god. But the feeling of mana and godhood both originate in a child's experience of his father, as based on earlier experience of the mother. Mothers make magicians; fathers, gods. The magician retains the imperiousness of the womb-born and the suckling; the religionist preserves the vatic priesthood of his father's omnipotence. For the understanding of crisis cults, it remains to explore further the dynamic operation of these principles in institutional and ethnological reality.

To any encounter with the unknown, people primarily bring themselves. It is not only that new experiences are inevitably colored and conditioned by old ones, but also that the *modality* of an earlier adaptation shapes the later encounter. Thus one common way to cope with the sacred or the unknown may be in the archaic terms of simple oral adaptation[1]: magic coercion through the spoken word or formula; or naïve oral incorporation may be the way to take in divinity or immorality, through a simple eating of the god; or, in the attempt to please the gods or to give them life, food will be the sacrifice; or giving up food by rigorous fasting may be the self-punitive discipline or supernatural bargain to earn divine favor. Again, the giving up of possessions, self-direction, or even sexuality may seem a suitable childlike sacrifice to the spirits.[2] However, since the physical environment does not really care whether an organism eats or destroys food or breeds or does none of these, magico-religious ritual borrows plausibility only from the style of the human animal's significant dealings with his parents.

Often persons and societies still use, as their prime means of adaptation to the sacred, one of these archaic modes of coping with the not-self. But the efficacy of oral magic, for example, will remain confined to its effects on a world of *persons;* the magic word coerces only other human beings. New ways must be found to deal with *things.* The child's experience of things is of their built-in consistency and inexorability, and so his maturing ego finds an emotionless and secular control of things in further ego adaptation. But in ignorance or indiscrimination or frustration, he may again treat things angrily as if they had separate obdurate wills like people. Experience of persons is of contingencies: sometimes they behave, and sometimes they do not, in terms of his unconditional wish. In further growth from such experiences there emerges the moral superego, as an adaptation to this new world of persons and their demands; and on this later kind of adaptation may be built his "sacred" world, as well as his ethical response to persons.

Frustration and reward teach him the reality of an outer world of persons, apparently like himself in having wills, but nevertheless wills distinct from his own, that urge him into bodily and social disciplines, not always willingly. Epistemologically, he is now an "animist"—and may falsely impute will and consciousness to mere things. But his cries no longer move events in the same old magic "manaist" way. He must hammer out a new separate self on the resistant anvil of other selves. He may still obtain his needs—for only final gratification can induce the organism to accept the ego's learned cautionary devices—but his wishes now encounter the price of "goodness" of behavior in the arbitrary system of his parents' society. In the process of exemplifying, teaching, and mediating tribal ways, parents can induce frustrations, give and withhold satisfactions and love, and in their omnipotence and infinite righteousness they can punish. Here again, so potent is this training that some persons can never criticize (or even become aware of) their tribalism. The painted tribal stage scenery is mistaken for the rock wall of a real world by fundamentalist authoritarian personalities. They can never see the world for the crowd of people talking around them.

With these mixed and confused conditionings, specific to his kind, the human being meets the dry uncaring final world. In physical growth, he has greatly multiplied his size and powers. But this outer world is still far immenser than he, and its potencies overshadow his. Is it any wonder then that he sometimes continues to respond to the universe as to his father? Or in times of powerlessness and stress, to seek to emulate or to call upon him? Given his strange animal experience, the human is always the child of this world in some sense, and in every man the child lives on. Awe, mixed of fear and love, is the child's feeling toward his all powerful parents, and sometimes reverence or trembling apprehension at their unpredictable commands. Thus too he approaches the universe.

The human family is the fountainhead of the divine in all its guises. The first *mana* a child knows is in his creators. The first "supernaturals" that command his world, the first *animas* that shape his conscience, are the child's own parents. Awe is a suitable response to the great power of his creators over him. The unregenerate child who would still command the mana-laden spirits becomes a shaman; the one who would domesticate God, manage, cajole or placate Him, the priest; and the one who would identify with the artificer-creator, the "maker" *poiētēs*, the "shaper" scope,[3] becomes the culture hero. In the presence of all these men, all communicants must feel awe. For each one, in his way, possesses divinity.

This praeternatural and awe-inspiring quality in a man is his *charisma*.[4] Max Weber borrowed the term from theological literature, to designate the supposed spiritual gift, grace, genius, merit, or personality-power in an individual, allegedly from a supernatural source. Like Wach,[5] and other sociologists of religion, Weber emphasized only the descriptive fact of the followers' belief in this gift, but did not consider the objective existence of the gift in supernatural terms. And rightly so, for charisma has identifiable and grossly secular origins. The subjective claim on which spiritual authority is based, derives ultimately from the self-consciousness and self-designation of the holy man; while in social and historical terms, he may be accepted at either more or less than his own claims. Thus his historical stature, in the last analysis, is a matter of his social acceptance by other people—a phenomenon examined earlier in ethnographic data on the olonists of Siberia, and again in psychological terms in the cult as an expanded folie à deux. Charisma is only the reification and the rationalizer of the event or process. To sense charisma is to re-experience another's mana and to be again coerced.

Weber emphasized the seemingly "supernatural" charisma of the messiah or culture hero. This person achieves his status through no ordinary secular means such as formal election or appointment, but rather through the uncanny fascination in the culture hero's personality, which seemingly lifts him far above all other mortals. Psychiatrically, this fascination is initially the hero's narcissistic fascination with himself,[6] a mother-given mana and mission as Freud observed.[7] Analysts are well aware of the uncanny identification that others may have with such narcissistic personalities, whether actors, movie stars and other publicity-created personalities, political Führers or messiahs. Such narcissists embody what others only dream of being; a somebody is nourished by and absorbs the identities of many nobodies. The "gift of personality" is really only the naïve luck or passive fate of confidently being a contemporary social cynosure,[8] a process in which, wryly, character is destiny. And in religious leaders, the "supernatural" gift is no more than the messiah's phatic prescience of the people's needs. His communication is not new information on the structure of the world, but only of new inner emotional structuring in people's culture-personality. The supernatural is the subconscious.

Charisma is a leader-people process in another way as well. Freud has shown, in *Group Psychology and the Ego,* that in "crowd" situations of stress,[9] persons abdicate their individual consciences or superegos, and for these they substitute the more-desired superego of the leader. They become the suggestible passive instrument of his will, sometimes in a kind of half-hypnotic state, quite like the suggestibility of clinical hysteria. Thus, in mob actions and with psychopathic leaders, savageries are possible which the individual superego in a normal state would categorically forbid. The repressed hostility and ambivalence to rules in each mob-individual is released and reverberates throughout the whole social group, in an impressive kind of "instant enculturation" and magnified folie. It will therefore seem that a compelling mesmeric power streams from outside the individual psyche, from the supernaturally ordained leader whose superego they have adopted, and who has merely released their own unconscious feelings from repression. He is the "liberator." But worship of another man's charisma, when paranoia speaks to paranoia, is also an abdication of the individual ego. Hence hard-won reality judgment can be lost, as well as individual conscience, and anti-adaptive acts then typically ensue in the ghost dance behaviors of whole groups. If no one in the group insists on individual reality-testing, then, necessarily, the whole group lacks it.

In stress situations, there is massive individual regression to an earlier psychosexual stage of growth. In the mob situation, with the once-introjected taboo now forcibly rejected, and rejected with social support at that, the individual can now gullibly succumb to the charm of his own unconscious wish, expressed with such fascination by the leader. He may even parade the "morality" of his true-believer loyalty to the leader's "cause"—though this is transparently devotion to himself and his own repressed wishes. Id and ego can now join forces to reject the old tyrant superego. It is in just this state of flux and psychic revolution that the person is accessible to new introjection of id-appetizing and ego-syntonic suggestion. The phatic fascination of a *Führer* is, then, the welcomeness of his message to his communicants, and for this they exalt and love him. He has freed them from the chains of the old stress-inadequate tribal superego. He takes the place of the old gods, the fathers, quite literally. In one sense, the shaman is the revolting son and social olonist who must be punished and martyred; but, in another sense, the shaman is a new god himself. His charisma is his phatic skill.

There is still another aspect of charisma. Max Weber explicitly identified the *charisma* of European theologians with *mana* and similar concepts of primitive peoples. "[For] these extraordinary powers that have been designated by such special terms as 'mana,' 'orenda,' and the Iranian 'maga' . . . we shall henceforth employ the term 'charisma' "[10]—and Weber went on specifically to designate the sacred chiefs in Polynesia as "charismatic princes."[11] Ephraim Fischoff, Weber's translator, adds that "Such uncommon qualification is the basis of the influence exerted by those individuals who come to be regarded as exemplary, superhuman and divinely conditioned, and hence are accepted as leaders in the capacity of rulers, party chiefs, prophets, founders of religion, etc."[12]

Both in the guise of a divine quiddity that enters into and empowers the messiah, and as an animal-magnetic influence that emanates from him into his followers, charisma is ambiguously outside-inside—quite as, before reification, an interpersonal influence properly should be, and, before introjection, a moral influence necessarily is. But primitive platonists reify an interindividual emotive process into a quasi-thing, with an expected position in space. Mana is immaterial—and yet movable and possessable. The locus-ambiguity of mana-power, personality-force, moral or physical virtue or strength, is in fact intrinsic to it. Mana even seems like an animal-aura, his but outside him, in the sense of Hall's "proxemics."[13] Great men have an invisible space-envelope. Auden only half-playfully warned that "Some thirty inches from my nose/The frontier of my Person goes."[14] Still more potent, the "taboo of majesty" forbade a son even to approach his father armed, Reinach wrote,[15] with the oedipal result that in Ireland boys were brought up in strange families or by Druids, a custom of which he thinks British boarding schools may be a survival.

The impersonality of mana, though embodied in persons, must be insisted on. Gilbert Murray, a justly famed classicist, felt that the only serious error later students found in the work of the distinguished Semitist, W. Robertson Smith, was Smith's too deliberate notion of sacrifice among ancient Semites as affording communion with the tribal god. "There was no god there, only the raw material out of which gods are made. You devoured the holy animal to get its mana, its swiftness, its strength, its great endurance, just as the savage now will eat his enemy's brain or heart or hands to get some particular quality residing there."[16] Communicants devour the mana of messiahs to become immortal or divine; cultists of a personality worship his charisma and seek to share it or bask in its radiance. Like the supernatural, then, charisma-mana is ambiguously outside-inside, both collective and divisible. In a sense "spirits" are the ghosts of persons, and mana the food of spirits.

Mana is thus a curiously impersonal "outer" personality-stuff or force that the individual can incorporate or embody in his "inner" self. Mana evokes the same awe as supernatural charisma, the same awe once felt toward the father. The recurrently oedipal, intrinsically male nature of mana is especially visible in its Indoeuropean version. The "virtue" of anything is its effective purpose or purposeful efficacy, but, literally, Latin *vir-tus* is the latent morality and realizable strength of a *vir* or adult male, the sap, *vis* or essence of honorable virility. Linton defined Oceanic *mana* very similarly as abstract "power for accomplishment" whether in man or fish-hook or enemy-killing spear; as such, *mana* is identical with the Greek *aretē*.[17] This curious, almost untranslatable word means the inner virtue or essence, effective purpose or excellence of any thing. In a man it connotes virility and manliness, wholeness, integrity, purpose, moral clarity, decision and self-responsibility—in a word "spunk." In things, *aretē* is their effectiveness with reference to their intrinsic function. With proper hesitancy and reservation, the classicist Cornford[18] adopted the suggestion of Hubert and Mauss, that the Ionian image of *physis* was in some ways like *mana*, the living substrate of the nature of things, the life-force that every sentient being feels as a driving power within it; but surely the later development of *physis* is far from this daemonic view, which is really more animistic than manaist or physical. Closer to the generic Indoeuropean view of "mana" is the Iranian *maga*, which implies intellectual power, magnitude, magic wisdom and wizardry—quite as if a mage were a Siberian shaman with secret magic or cosmic medicine-power. The Latin *magnus* as a person is a "magnate" and the Indic equivalent is close to this too. The Tantrik concept of *shakti* is the "emanation" or sexualized objectified magic efficacy of a male god; Nölle, in fact, saw true shamanism in shaktism; and Rahmann even viewed aboriginal Munda shamanism as a reinforcing pre-Indoeuropean influence on shaktism in middle and northern India.[19]

Although the concept of mana is very old, there is no reason to suppose a common root other than simple humanity in most cases; at least the generic idea configurates with some differences in widely scattered cultures despite a persistent basic human similarity. Nevertheless, the Sibero-American concepts (perhaps also the Oceanic and primordial Indoeuropean ones) at least may have a common Mesolithic-old historic base. The numinous *kuoyka* of the Siberian Ngansan, for example, is as close to the Bolivian Aymara *huaka* as one could well imagine. Again, Lowie reports that Indians of the Guaporé believe in an invisible "fluid" that shamans, for good or evil, can put into food or human bodies; it is an impersonal, non-sentient power prominent in prescriptions and taboos incident to birth and other critical events that shapes individual fate. It is not unlike the Jivaro *kakarma,* "personally acquired impersonal power" that surges into a man who has acquired *arutam* from successful head-hunting; kakarma also increases intelligence and physical prowess, and makes it difficult for a man to lie or act dishonestly. Variants of the mana concept are evidently pan-American, reappearing in North America as the Algonkian *manitou,* the Siouan *wakanda,* and the *orenda* of the Iroquois. Although these groups belong to apparently different linguistic stocks, the concept is of a same vast reservoir of "medicine power" a young man taps in the vision quest, and we must believe them all related, as they are all surely related to similar concepts in Siberia.[20] In psychiatric terms, the vision quest is adolescent introjection of the father's masculinity and male power and identification with him. It is the coming of that potency and power that each man needs to become a man; and if the process goes awry, he remains the not-man *berdache,* frozen in a frightened pre-masculine childhood. This power is the "medicine" of each man, most especially of the shaman; and in Amazonia this power raises shamans to the status of living gods. The power concept is a native rationale of the "facts of life," of puberty, male potency and procreativity.

Creativity is also intrinsic to the Oceanic concepts of mana.[21] The Polynesian sacred chief had intense taboo- or mana-placing power primarily because, as the first-born of many first-born lineages, he embodied as a living god all the procreative power of the god ancestors, and for this reason no commoner could stand higher than the high chief's sacred head, the site of his mana. But the same creative power was also possessed by the *tuhunas* or priest-craftsmen of Polynesia.[22] The making of a canoe was not merely a manufacturing, it was a sexually creative act, a building of something new into the structure of the universe and mediated by the magic ritual songs through which the tuhuna infused his power into his creation. The very gods had sung the universe into its present being by such songs.

In Australia, the Ungarinyin *ya-yari* is vital energy, the substance of a man's psycho-physical existence that makes him feel, think and experience; it is also his sexual potency and derives from *yari,* meaning dream, dream experience, visionary state, and also dream totem. Above all, ya-yari enables a man to reach sexual excitement, the dream state and the trance, that "yari" so important to cultic life since it is also a term for the period of the cult-heroes, the spirit world and the great cultic feasts. Jensen wrote, "Therefore, we might view *ya-yari* as an internal bond between individual men, primal times, its heroes, and its creative events . . . Primal time thus becomes eternal time and a magnitude divorced alike from past, present and future." *Ya-yari* is cultic male logos, as widely shared, and as eternal as tribal culture. For this timeless holy state Elkin coined the term "Eternal Dream-time." The Arunta "alchuringa time" is this same sacred timeless state—of the dream, of the culture-creators, of recurrent cult ritual. The *churingas* or bull-roarers are the men's secrets. The patrilineal spirits of ancestors enter the bodies of women from hidden churingas and make them pregnant; churingas are also used with penile blood-letting in fertility rituals to promote the increase of totemic plants and animals. Since the fieldwork of Róheim on the Bonaparte expedition to Australia, there can be no doubt that the bull-roarer is a phallic symbolism. Another *mana*-equivalent in Australia is *boylya,* but there are many other tribal names for virtually the same concept.[23]

In nearby New Guinea, the Gururumba consider the body's vital essence the *GwondEɉoJE,* present in one's reflection, breath, saliva, phlegm, semen, or blood from the arms and legs. But *GwondEɉoJE* is more than animating force, however. "It is identified in and with the prowess of a living body, the sexuality of men and women, and the self-assertiveness of the adult male . . . also the specific capacity to be strong and nurturant, capacities enabling one to participate effectively in human affairs as the Gururumba know them."[24] Elsewhere is Asia, mana is the *petara* of the Sea Dyak, and the Vietnamese *tinh*. Perhaps *yang* in classic China also had some of the features of male mana, with *yin* the female equivalent.

In Africa, the well-reported *tsav* of the Tiv is a non-animistic power that talented people or born leaders have, or those with any developed ability or skill. Beneficent and dangerous both, tsav may be increased by eating human flesh. Also connected with political power that, Tiv think, consumes others, tsav is a male oedipal phenomenon in plainly oral-incorporative terms. Concepts of mana are widespread and apparently old in Africa since they occur in ethnographically most disparate groups. The Hottentot *!nau* is dangerous, and especially active at puberty, childbirth, the death of a spouse, remarriage, in certain diseases, and at the slaying of an enemy or big game animal. The Masai of northeast Africa have *ngai,* prominent at puberty and other states of transition like death, but also connected with the procreative principle. The Malagasy of Madagascar have *andriamanitra* and *arungquiltha,* and the Bantu a similar *mulungu.* Even the primitive Pygmy have *oudah.*[25] Each of these sampled groups in Africa belong to different culture-areas or cultural horizons.

In classic European concepts of the "holy" the ambiguity of the unknown power is much emphasized, depending on whether it is domesticated to men's uses and benevolent or dangerous. The Latin *sacer* (French *sacré*) means both "cursed" and "holy"—poorly translated by our "sacred" since it means, rather, something imbued with mysterious mana, a power dangerous or beneficent, "loaded." The Greek τo $\H{a}\gamma o\varsigma$ means both "the holy" and "the impure" or supernaturally dangerous, and the derived adjective $\H{a}\gamma \iota o\varsigma$ has the same ambiguity, while $\dot{\epsilon}\nu\alpha\gamma\acute{\eta}\varsigma$ means "accursed" or "sinful" as of a tainted and taboo-breaking criminal. In its specific uses, even the power of the Greek gods had the same ambiguity. The divine fire of Zeus from sun and sky created life— the same fire that Prometheus stole from heaven, for which the eagle (Zeus) consumed him—and yet with his thunderbolt the All Father blasted his sons, the guilty Titans.

Like the Greek τo $\H{a}\gamma o\varsigma$, the Hebrew קדש could mean at once "unclean" or "holy" depending on its negative or positive action. Thus the pig, an old totem animal of the Semites, was both unclean and holy, tabooed and sacred; and the "uncleanness" of women, dangerous to men, was also close to the sublime mystery of procreation. The Power resident in the Ark of the Covenant was clearly much like mana, automatically punishing contact with the tabooed. It struck down the well-meaning Uzzah (II Samuel 6:6–7) who merely sought to save the Ark from falling off an ox cart. The killing of Uzzah was not the act of a moral Person, able to discern simple good will and to appreciate näive concern—but rather a mechanical, abstract, categorical and magic power that was impersonal and morally blind. All these concepts of mana derive from the same universal familial source—the child's fear and awe toward the father, symbolized as his maleness, generalized, reified, and projected into the supernatural unknown, but representing a very archaic stage of ego differentiation.

This human experience is the taproot of religion. The very stuff of religious feeling—as it is of all revelation, and hence of all revealed religion—is a human experience of the "holy" or numinous, supernatural, sacred or divine. The religious psychologist Rudolf Otto considered the numinous[26] (Latin *numen,* "supernatural presence") to include anything that is uncanny, weird, eerie, awful, fascinating, majestic, sublime or ecstatic. Many religionists have subsequently seized upon his implicit argument: that for the numinous experience to occur, there must exist an objective something to cause the experience, a *mysterium tremendum et fascinosum,* the divine object or the objectively divine. The will to believe is manifest in the epistemological naïveté of the reasoning, for it is possible to take a Kantian position that the potential for the experience may lie in the mind of the believer. Another objectivist, Mircea Eliade,[27] an historian of comparative religion, has even proposed the term *hierophany* to designate "the *act of manifestation* of the sacred"—as if hallucination actively chose when to occasion its appearance.

No one would deny the psychological fact of this subjective experience, any more than he would deny the ethnographic fact of revealed religion. What is so astonishingly naïve, however, is to identify *present inner experience* as being wholly caused by some entity presently outside, and to mislocate the inner as being outside. The ability to have a "numinous" experience is really the *having experienced* this feeling in relation to earlier objects! The mana-vehicle of this *mysterium* is no mystery. Mana or supernatural power is the main trait of the gods. But the possession of mana was precisely the main trait of parents in one's childhood! An unusually magnificent or morally majestic man can still cause in any of us a quick thrill of admiration, just as the femininity in any woman will inspire a reverent tenderness and feeling of protectiveness. But such epiphany of feeling, strictly speaking, is in part a transference of affect from the childhood experience we have of parents: we bring to the experience a capacity to respond.

Even love is in part an epiphany of the subjective, of the emotionally learned. The present love is *déjà vu* in childhood. Again, the subjective component in aesthetic experience is very plain indeed. The truly sublime quality in some passages of Mozart or Bach must be brought to the experience by the hearer, since the same objective combination of sounds leaves another listener cold, or even uncomfortable. To one man God is another man's oedipus. Similarly, any "hierophany" or appearance of the sacred or supernatural is merely uncritical hallucination of the visionary dream-figure as being here-and-now present; or there is some experience of the mundane to which the person brings his own *frisson*. To accept the numinous as *really* supernaturally outside *now* is for the psychologist to turn theologian, as has Otto, or for the observer to betray the believer, as has Eliade.

The crass subjectivity of epiphanies of feeling is all the more evident because the same stimulus *object* can evoke quite different apperceptive responses in different persons. To one man, a volcanic eruption demonstrates the irrational dread mana of a sacred mountain; to another, it is a god exploding in wrath at the sins of his guilty children; while a third man will think of the Wegener hypothesis of continental drift on earth-core magma, fault lines in the earth's crust, and the like. In each case the perception is a function of maturity of ego in object discrimination—not differences in rock composition, temperature, viscosity, flow rate, and such-like objectivities. The very concepts of *mana* and *anima* themselves give indication of their subjective psychic origin and anthropomorphic nature. Narcissism sees its own face in the mirror of an opaque universe.

Mana or abstract power is incorporated from outside, quite as men incorporate the power and energy of animals by eating their meat (or the baby, infallible power, wins his imperious organic wish by imbibing the magic fluid). At its simplest, mana is the stuff and essence of the power and potency of *things,* man himself included. But to the baby, as to every narcissist, the "object" is at first *only an extension of its own activity,*[28] hence force in the self and force in the world are not differentiated before self and world are discriminated. Mana is, as it were, a subjective experience before there is really a subjective person. The impersonality of relation to the father does not disturb the original impersonality of mana, despite later oedipal increments, if the essentially oral-incorporative nature of mana remains the core of the concept. Therefore, despite its origin as a notion projected from within us, mana remains fundamentally impersonal "force." Mana, in fact, for all that force is ultimately male fundamentally, retains other intimations of its origin *in relation to* dimly maternal, tergiversating Fate. For mana is also luck ("Lady Luck"),[29] nurturantly biased happenstance, wish reified into happy fate—not quite grimly unalterable and inalternative "things as they are" but a contingent benevolence. An emergently personal maternal presence haunts, the ghost of omnipotent wish lingers in, this tailored-to-self infantile gambler's universe. The oral optimist knows that things are really on his favored side.

In this, once again, mana betrays its human origin; and in this again mana differs from authentically impersonal, coldly scientific exterior causality. Mana is a kind of supernatural grace accorded to lucky persons or things. Mana is a reification of the mystery that "eventuates events," now sometimes in this way, now sometimes that, but always in ways beyond our comprehension. Indeed, mana is a mystery we *can not* understand, unless we codify our ignorance and make it a principle of explanation. For in impersonal mana is also the father as first dimly discerned. Mana is a projection of our awe at the spectacle of the "holy," the uncannily numinous, the *mysterium tremendum et alienum,* the unreachable other. Subjectively experienced, the numinous is taken for an external epiphany of mana. For mana is intrinsically unknown, except as a mysterious and unpredictable quasi-physical force, or awesome energy presumed to be manifest in things, living or dead.

Religion in the strict sense requires a less inchoate ego for its rationale than does magic. Thinking, here, must have discovered personality, one's own and that of others. But self-consciousness of one's person, and accordance of personality to others, requires a more discrete sense of particulated powers than collective undifferentiated mana. By contrast with mana, *anima* is the principle of discrete animal animation (to put it awkwardly but accurately), i.e. the "soul" of living things, whether animal or human. In itself discrete, anima may also be discrete, at times, from any embodiment. Whereas mana is sometimes quasi-material and "objective," anima is intrinsically "spiritual," subjective. Mana is personally ownable, but it is owned in notably variable amounts. That is, individuals differ greatly in "personality force," and the amount of mana in a person from some indefinitely large, impersonal collective reservoir may fluctuate greatly from time to time. By contrast, an anima is specifically a quantum of particulated and individual soul-stuff. Each anima is the soul of a living thing. Sometimes, mistakenly, anima is imputed to objects supposed to be "animate" because they seem to show volition (the sky, the "weather"), or move and are warm (fire), or move like living beings (clouds, planets, streams), but the anima is always individuated and even quasi-personified.

Mana rationalizes differences in personality. But anima is a reification of life itself, the algebraic difference between a living animal and a dead one, the mysterious X that leaves a living body at its death. It is a personification of the living process, in particular of consciousness, animation and will. Anima is an identity, the separable soul of a person that travels far off in dreams, often of the long ago, and reappears in dreams and memories of dead persons—the memory of a dead man *is* his anima standing present—but an anima is always an identity, living or dead, a "person." Subjectively, anima is what we already have inside, and impute to other persons, animals or things; mana, "objectively," the power we have *in parvo* inside but long for more of from outside. The oedipal nature of mana is again manifest in its very impersonality, and its invidiousness betokens social hierachy deep in the biology of man.[30]

These two primitive and archaic ideas of powers, personal and impersonal, inside and outside, are rooted in subjective anthropomorphisms, and specifically in the neoteny of human beings. In several senses, a lucky fate is, literally, kind parents, just as "Lady Luck" is a gentle mother, tendentiously concerned for her favored child. To put it biologically, lizards can have no idea of "luck" because they never experience it: they *lack mammalian nurture.* The notion of one's own "luck" would hardly arise except in an animal that had at some time *experienced* being favored by parental grace, an arbitrarily kindly moderation of the rules, or intentionally protective editing of the environment by another organism, and an effectively "omnipotent" one in the situation. The physical world, when studied, can always be seen as rigorously expectable. But luck is the specifically unpredictable, hence the real locus of luck can only be in the arbitrary grace of friends and others we love. Latin *gratia* as a preposition means "for the sake of." "Luck" is a conceptual artifact possible only for one who had a human childhood.

The same is true of the subjective soul or anima. To an animal its animation (if it thinks about it at all) must seem self-evident, inevitable and timeless—and that's the beginning and the end of the matter all in one. Even though they are mammals, cows can scarcely be metaphysical animists until they acquire vivid personalities about which to be self-conscious, until they can conceptually envisage their own death and think long narcissistic thoughts about it. Nor do they love one another enough as persons, irreparably to mourn as we do the death of individuals to whom for long years we were intensely committed emotionally. Only *human* children, and the adults they become, can have a poignant experience of another person's death. And perhaps it is only the aging man or woman, with some part-experience of individual decay, who can have any real emotional conviction about his own death. Awareness of death—perhaps even more than the phenomena of procreation, birth, life and individual consciousness—is the foundation of metaphysical animism.

In a long series of insults that began at birth, death is the final insult to narcissism. Yet for all our human consciousness of it, the animal inexorability of death is softened by other intensely human phenomena. We have an indefinitely continuous *consciousness* of a persona—which, surely, must be as endless as it seems? We still have a *timeless contact,* unwelcome or remote as it may be, with the child-person we were once long ago. We have *memory* of persons that persists even long after their death. We *are* still what our parents, dead and gone, have made us. Our bodies and germ plasm are both part of the *immortal stream* of our species' being. We belong to the body of that *society* that bears a culture, and we are aware that each innermost "personality" is intimately connected with that larger reach of our "culture." The essence of culture is its historicity. Man *is* history, and in a sense a man *is* eternal past biological, cultural and psychological time. If time is eternal, are we then to be finally defrauded of eternity? Or, if "spirit" is immortal—one's own, of course, in particular—then there is the problem of the immortal spirits of ancestors, and again the immortality of Society. We have dim intimations of all these immortalities, spirits and powers. But we do not know. We can only approach the Unknown awesomely as if it were a person.

That is, if we persist in preferring to see the impersonal as personal and are terrified at the discovery of an unpeopled inhumane universe. But theologians and their followers invariably opt for the wished-for and the irrational, since these are closer to the heart's desire and more manageable by unsurrendered "omnipotence" than is the objectionable objective world. Theirs is a basically tender-minded temperament, with the requisite narcissism to confer a greater reality on the subjective-preferred than the existentially experienced. Every man, theologizing, behaves in this way. Schweitzer, after demonstrating, with magnificent erudition and against his own preference, that the documents allow no view of a historical Jesus which would meet the ordinary canons of secular historical scholarship, nevertheless studiedly chose Christianity on intuitional grounds deep in his childhood, an intellectual choice of some ethical dignity, but with a chosen "reverence for life" surpassing any reverence for the non-living That Which Is.[31] Tillich, after a notably powerful précis of the existentialist tradition, nevertheless leaps against his own arguments to a "God above God."[32] Bultmann laudibly would "demythologize" traditional religion; but if rigorously pursued this tentative would leave religion without any supernatural base and leave him an ordinary secularist and man of no special distinction or cosmic worth.[33] The rare thinker about God who remains persistently naturalistic, Feuerbach, ends in discovering that all the supposed attributes of "God" are only the idealized traits of men. Feuerbach wrestles with angels, but his feet are on the ground. Barth calls him "the thorn in the flesh of modern theology" and concedes that subsequent supernaturalists cannot transcend, but only bypass Feuerbach. For with Feuerbach theology has become anthropology.[34]

Sacred-cultural responses to the Unknown are inevitably patterned on man's own experience of himself and of the human biological life-space that shaped him. It is a question of whether one is able in practice to discern himself in his defensive dishonesties. It is also in theory not a question of whether manaism or animism "came first" in any necessary or real or universal evolution of historic religious ideas. For the subjective psychological states behind both of these conceptualized experiences are present in every human being, and *these* on necessary and universally human biological grounds. Human origin of both mana and anima as concepts is clear—and sacred culture in fact evinces both, with easy alternativeness or untroubled simultaneity. They merely mirror two closely related states of narcissism in the ego-formation of the individual. The idea of mana is only more primitive than that of anima in *ontogenetic* time. But since both are present in all men, this argues nothing necessarily about priority in cultural or "phylogenetic" historical time. If any culture emphasizes one over the other, then this is only a matter of the ethos of the society at that time.

The "personality" of culture heroes and the "ethos" of the culture are very close indeed, dynamically. Their place in culture promulgation is also very clear. They are new mystic fathers. Whether shaman as god-innovator or priest as faithful servant of established tribal gods, both claim to "know" how to deal with the Unknown. Since in simple fact these persons can not do this, the vatic personality would seem necessarily paranoiac, if he believes in his omnipotence and in his delusions of reference, or necessarily a spurious mountebank and psychopath, if he merely knowingly exploits the people's fears to his own ends. However, it is easy to over-estimate the vatic personality's insight into himself, especially when under stress. Empirically, the vatic personality ranges from paranoiac to psychopath, with some a mixture of both, but with naïveté probably commoner than ill will, and the vatic the first deceived and the self-deceived. To accord the vatic personality a guiltless paranoia may be only a judge's equanimity at the possibility that men and societies can be mad. But to accuse him of psychopathy implies an insight into fundamentalist truth that perhaps ought to be demonstrated. In psychologico-cultural fact, either judgment may be incompetent; in historic fact, it may also be largely irrelevant. Both vatic types pretend false omniscience of the Unknown, false power over the omnipotent "supernatural." But it is the frightened people who have required this total power in their vatic fathers, who will mediate between the people and the supernatural, in their times of stress. Hence the difference between self-deceived paranoia and conscious psychopathy in the vatic is only an historically negligible $N \pm 1$, of psychological but not appreciable cultural relevance.

The shaman embodies omnipotence himself, the priest has found the omnipotent Person to submit himself to wholly. "Charismatically," neither is psychosexually a mere man, for he borrows transference-mana from our own real childhood fathers. And from his own: empirically, we even find gradations between the father-possessor and the father-possessed. When the shaman identifies himself as the First Doer and controls cosmic weather, he is very close to being God himself. When he merely manages an externalized "Master of Animals" or only speaks with the voice of the "Master of Life," then he is one stage demoted in the power hierarchy. The humble-grandiose messiah is normally only the executive officer of Omnipotence; and yet he too sometimes moves in the direction of identification with the commanding officer. And, ordinarily, the prophet-founder of a religion is only the communications officer of the Divine.

But the range of founders is also up and down the scale. Mohammed was at first repudiated by the people when he called on them to respect him as a messenger of God; but he was posthumously promoted to something like his only Prophet. Moses was at most only a shaman-sheikh, yet he spoke with the voice of the Most High, though to a sometimes unbelieving people. Jesus at first refused to admit his messiahship during the Galilean ministry, and yet it transpired later that he was the Son of God, or in some views God himself. Gautama Buddha the prince, and Confucius the scholar, both manifestly historical personages, were both promoted upward toward godhood after their deaths. But Alexander and the Caesars were gods even during their own lifetimes. The prophet-reformer ordinarily makes lesser claims, and yet with Calvin and Luther and other authoritarian personalities it is sometimes difficult to decide just where absolute power and righteousness reside. Saints and faqirs are a more masochistic lot, minor martyrized Sons, and they are placed at the right hand of deity mostly because of their sufferings at the hands of inscrutable providence. The priest is at the bottom of the sadomasochistic heap: he is the total servant of the Father. The vatic, then, continually vacillates between two poles, whether to be or to bow down to omnipotence. Never having found his father, he has never discovered his mere humanity. The vatic personality is imprisoned in psychosexual childhood; and this is why he speaks so powerfully to the regressively childlike in other men.

Either vatic state is a failure in growth, a failure in the exercise of the merely contingent powers of an adult, or a regression to one or another experienced states of infancy. The "supernatural" can be seen precisely in terms of ego boundaries, therefore, since one's view of it is a matter of ego growth and inside-outside locus. Mana is thus sometimes still outside the person, an impersonal power that may reside either in the outside or be incorporated into the inside world. Mana is power at a "pre-person" stage of ego growth, its location therefore remaining ambiguous. One's felt confidence is a measure of its possession and incorporation; but one's felt dependency and need are a measure of its still remaining partly outside. Only in one case does a person have total mana or possess all the mana available; only in the psychically deformed paranoiac is the person "really" omnipotent subjectively.

By contrast with mana, as we have seen, anima is the personalized essence of a person, his experienced vir-tus or power. Though it may come and go in bodies, it is always a spiritual entity, a *person*. Hence anima is a concept of a later stage of ego-identity. Anima transcends ego boundaries too, being equally present also in others, and present in the living but absent in the dead "person." Since anima rests ultimately on experience of the inner psyche, it is in essence an attribute of the person and in origin wholly "inside." But the religionist-animist distorts quite as much as does the magician-manaist. Only distorted human narcissism can maintain that the personality ("soul") can exist outside the person, i.e. an anima that persists after the person is no more.

Magic and religion differ then in two ways: in the degree of personalization of power, and in the question of who has the power. The magician has mana and personally controls the impersonal world in which he is really the only person. If he fails to do so, this is a slip merely in his use of the magic words, a tic in the nerve-strings that control the world-body so that the mischance only demonstrates his omnipotence over results once again, since *he* made the mistake after all, although sometimes it is the dim persona of another magician with competing mana, omnipotence divided, a frustrating malevolence. But mostly the magician never questions his possession of mana. By contrast, the religionist worries for his soul, feels his helplessness, and dependently implores an external Anima to use its power on his behalf.

However, since all practitioners of the sacred arts have a quite secular narcissism, it is natural that magic and religion should sometimes phase into one another. For example, the shaman is the man-god or magician, but even he has an animal "familiar" whose power he borrows or incorporates or (full cycle again) *is*. The priest claims a special entrée with a god-man, that is a power in the universe he has the presumption to suppose is both manlike and concerned for man. To the shaman, in self-love, microcosm and macrocosm are one. For the priest, microcosm and Macrocosm merely "love" one another.

There are no biological grounds for either belief. As an external entity to which *fatherly* attributes are imputed, the concept of Macrocosm has evidently confounded the moral environment with the physical environment, the "creator" of the individual with the whole Creation, and the father with the universe, since both profoundly influence the human child. Such a Macrocosm is an indiscrimination between the human and the non-human aspects of the not-self seen *en bloc*. It is true that, as son and father, human "microcosm" and "macrocosm" are similar to one another, and normally the son does "identify" with the father. But son and father are nevertheless biologically discrete, for all their genetic continuity. Psychologically too, despite oedipal longings, the son can never stand in his father's shoes, he can never *be* his father. In this sense, microcosm and macrocosm, son and father, must forever be oedipally separate. And since the oedipal situation is loaded with ambivalences, we should be alerted to the ultimate goal of this metaphysical gambit, viz. that the shaman can now "be" the god, or that the priest can now ambiguously "serve" the God. The one is paranoid, frozen in infancy, the other re-infantilized, neither of which is biologically adaptive or desirable.

There is another side to the confusion also. If the "microcosm" now means the self or the *organism,* and the "Macrocosm" the *environment,* then there is no biological ground either for believing that the microcosm and Macrocosm are one (shaman) or that they "love" one another (priest). Organisms and their environment are always perfectly distinct, and there is surely no evidence in paleontology that a changing environment ever "loved" extinct species that became fossils. If *H. sapiens* has a special dispensation, then this must be visible in species-specific human biology. It is visible: in the conditions of neoteny and dependency that give rise to these peculiar fantasies. Shamanistic practice and priestly theology alike are antic results of human biology, not correct statements of it.

As concepts, mana and anima, microcosm and macrocosm all show a confusion of self and not-self, son and father, father and universe, organism and environment, and the moral and physical environments. Since shaman and priest have shadowy ego boundaries, it is small wonder that these six paired categories constantly slide into one another. The real irony is the shocking impiety of shaman and priest: they invariably opt for the prepotent subjective wish, instead of achieving a genuinely chastened view of That Which Is. The magician lacks all humility; the "humility" of religionists is wholly, if subtly, spurious in that they will not subject wish to experience. They inveterately prefer tender-minded, narcissistic, subjective fantasy to tough-minded knowledge and assessment of man's nature and predicament. There is not only anthropomorphic distortion of the objective world, but also some dissociation within the self as well, with a confusion of ego, superego, and id among themselves, and with reality. Both shaman and priest lay claim to omnipotence or the manipulation of it, though there is really no such commodity lying around loose to be so used; there is only the vatic's grandiose "will to power." Behind shaman and priest is only an undiscerned and demanding human id. *This* is the "compelling" by the Supernatural. Hence, despite his pretensions, the vatic personality ends up being compelled both by his own unconscious (organism, id wish) and by his moral Father (superego, society), as well as by physical reality, just like the rest of us. He merely lacks self-discernment, and discrimination of which is which.

Stress situations—how to act before the unpredictable Unknown in father-person terms—are naturally complicated by our ambivalences toward the father. Small wonder, then, we see his mana also as ambiguous! His moral (cultural) edicts were introjected and made one's own only, in the last analysis, through his *force majeur*. The revolution against conscience is constantly brewing. For behind the mask of God is the face of the father. No tribal conscience that he mediates is ever wholly replicated in an individual, and never without some ambivalence toward the father and the tribe. The masked gods, we must always somehow suspect, are our fellow-tribesmen.

Ambivalence is the hallmark of all religion and morality. The "unco guid" profession of infinite obedience to the father is always rightly suspect of hypocrisy, and of being in need of this paraded overprotest, to deny the smoldering rebelliousness within (any who cannot acknowledge this smoldering is a stranger to his own dreams). Moral goodness is not given us with our genes! In consciousness, we still hear the quarreling voices of the Promethean will and the superego "god within us." God is indeed ambiguously inside-outside. In mania this inner tyrant-god is dethroned, and fled from like the Hound of Heaven. In depression, he reigns cruelly and autocratically over us, accusing us of infinite sin and worthlessness. In schizophrenia I am the only God. In paranoia the accusing conscience speaks as if with outside voices, or praises us to a conviction of our very godhood.

The organic person and the social person in us are never quite at one. For this reason of imperfect introjection from outside, the inner god is still a little bit alien, a compulsion possessing us against the conscious will and self. The god comes and goes and is variously inside-outside. To seek God is to seek moral truce with the divine Other—who is within us! But to obey him categorically sometimes seems to unman us, a masochistic mutilation and submission of the "real" organic self. But this moral god once came to us from the outside tribe and through the father. Hence the fatuous and unbelieved solemn protest that all "altruism" and obedience to the tribe is "good" but all "egoism" and loyalty to the self is "bad." Hence the adolescent crisis—and hence the crisis of the culture hero at conflicting acculturation.

Manaist and animist mistakenly project and personify these psychic forces into gods or powers that are outside. But they oversimplify: all these psychic forces are within the same complex human personality. Their dissociation is always in some way a sign of mental "disintegration" literally. The integrated person is a delicate balance of them all, a federated state with several separate democratic voices and divided powers. To seek God is a politic and endless diplomatic quest to find a worldly peace of id and superego, between self and tribe. But when the "culture" ambient itself changes, then both self and tribe are disequilibrated at once, each individual balance is shaken as well as inter-individual supports against these forces, and anomie and anxiety reign.

Anxiety and stress situations, personal or cultural, may be considered in terms of Cannon's concept of *homeostasis*.[35] Homeostasis is a physiological principle based on the body's "inner environment,"[36] as conceived by Bernard. Each living organism seeks constantly to maintain a host of physico-chemical inner "steady states," the totality of which is organic life itself. When physiological activities or outer environing forces disturb a steady state (e.g. raise the CO_2 level of the blood), then the body begins immediately to correct the disequilibrium toward the organically desired direction. The whole *purpose* of an organism is to maintain its homeostasis as a matrix for its life economies. But sometimes it "decompensates."

Decompensation as a process is perhaps most clearly seen in cardiac decompensation. With exercise, and a consequent decrease in oxygen and increase of CO_2 in the blood, the heart beats more massively and more rapidly until organic equilibrium is regained. With chronic exercise, the heart of an athlete "compensates" for the larger load by becoming larger.

"Cardiac decompensation" is some form of actual breakdown, for example the bursting under further strain 'of stress-weakened heart-nourishing coronary arteries. Psychic stress is not an "analogy" to this process, for the psychic often comes to the *identical somatic end,* e.g. hypertension or duodenal ulcer. The psychiatric, psychosomatic and other disease crises of visionaries are also *the same phenomenon,* not analogies. Nor is crisis cult and neurosis mere analogy either, but only phenomena of different magnitude and locus.

The same seeking for homeostasis is true in the psychic economy. Freud has shown, and unmistakably, that the purpose of the mind is not so much to secrete truths about the outside universe (our senses are geared to know changes in the environment, not its nature) as it is to respond to changes and to maintain an inner psychic homeostasis. Ferenczi's brilliant concept of "perigenesis" has also taught us to see in organic evolution ever more complex somatic structures designed to preserve the homeostatic inner environing sea of the immemorial single cell.[37] And Róheim has still further shown that the culture of a society is one more outpost of these organic defense mechanisms.[38] No organism ever has "total" loyalty to each environing status quo, for if it did, then there would be no inside or outside, and the organism would be inorganic. The whole purpose and meaning of an organism is stubborn loyalty to inner necessities too. *Human thought and culture are still organic acts, the activities of meta-organisms or societies.* For society, too, is an organic invention to enhance the survival-chances of the individual. Since inner-outer mediation is the nature and function of somatic evolution, of thought, and of cultural speciation, then obviously not all culture is rational (secular, outer-adaptive); some of it is homeostasis-making (sacred, inner-adapted).

Selye's work has shown us that some *stress reactions* are anti-adaptive physiologically, and give rise to decompensation of the homeostatic functions.[39] That is, some disease processes (perhaps cancer is one of them) are not merely signs of equilibrium-establishing reactions (like fever) but signs of the homeostatic mechanisms of the body itself having "gone wild"—responsive less to the magnitude and the nature of the stressor than to the body's own built-in reaction-systems' excessive activity (e.g., the orderly replacement of burned or tar-insulted cells in a smoker's lip decompensates and grows wildly in a cancer). In psychiatry, these same "wild" anti-adaptive decompensations can be seen in the "symptons" present in neurosis and psychosis. And, finally, it is here contended that the same principle applies to the defense mechanisms that constitute a society's culture (e.g., the destruction of food for symbolic supernatural ends becomes anti-adaptive: up to a point, sacrifice may aid psychological homeostasis, but beyond that point it is biologically dangerous). Such ghost dance extravagances are the "symptoms" of a disequilibrated society suffering dangerously decompensated stress reactions. The individually neurotic has *by simple cultural diffusion* become the socially neurotic. A ghost dance is the neurosis of society.

In the stress situation of acculturation, the interpersonal matrix (society and culture) may suffer traumatic disruption and hence "decompensation" of the intrinsically homeostatic functions of culture and society. Here, too, it is not so much a responding to the nature and magnitude of outside forces, as it is a responding overmuch in terms of human beings' archaic built-in defense mechanisms, individual and cultural. Ghost-dance responses overly assert the sacred reality of the superego (sacred culture), and assault id need (destroy or reject effective old or new secular culture), and respond too little in ego-adaptive terms to the actual realities environing the society. They project the structures of the inner world (Pleasure Principle) rather than learn anew the structures of the changed outer world (Reality Principle).[40] To depend overmuch on past adaptations is to shirk making new ones.

In neurosis and psychosis, the attempts at restitution of an earlier psychic equilibrium are not true adaptations to some new vicissitude (e.g., an hysteric's adaptations to her father are not wholly useful in adapting to her husband). Symptoms indicate a decompensation of ego-functioning. Instead of learning currently from the new situation, the neurotic or the psychotic regresses to more archaic oral-dependent or oedipal-religious techniques of adaptation to new figures in the social drama, using techniques now inapposite. In the ghost dance, there is the same decompensation and regression of society to more archaic ego-adaptive techniques, either infantile-magic or oedipal-religious. Ghost dances are cultural defense reactions (Róheim) undergoing decompensation under stress (Selye).

Since cultures are defense mechanisms, the homeostasis they provide may be threatened by new cultural vicissitude. Each Hellenistic "failure of nerve" is a loss of confidence in our cultural (personal) ability to achieve satisfactions, biological or social or emotional. Need for food and love, for the distancing of pain and disease and death, still remain. If one's fellows also suffer the same privations, then the source of strength they ordinarily constitute for us, is gone from us also, and neuroses merge into a folie. The *typicality* (culture) of the reaction (personality) is a measure of its social massiveness, and this factor alone distinguishes a neurosis from a ghost dance (olonism from mass arctic hysteria). In private unhappiness we often need only copy our more happy fellows and learn from them. But their concurrent unhappiness is our private catastrophe as well. In these straits, to seek in *ethos* what only *physis* can provide, and to learn their illness, is to be doubly lost.

The danger of crisis cults and tribal cultures is that men use other men to support their beliefs, when at best they should only support their courage, since truth is not a function of group wish but of external fact. Thus an *ethos* is made to support epistemological burdens that only *physis* can bear. Societies are as much built on common fears as on common accomplishments. In subgroups, too, men of like belief join to preserve preferred emotional states and tend to consort only with those who will not disclose or criticize their peculiar mechanisms of defense, the "authority" of their culture hero the solace echoing the needed wish.

At every point, the new vicissitude probes at our ambivalence, scrutinizes our real loyalty to the cultural faith, heightens unresolved socialization-hostilities, and threatens us from within. A compulsive but despairing nativism is one possible response: let us flee back into the sacred past for our refuge! But doubt is the father of fanaticism, the root of faith; and doubt is raised by the spectacle of an alternative faith (another culture). Reactionary "faith" then becomes obsessive-compulsive: Freud and Reik note that a religious dogma is the social counterpart of an obessional neurosis; a sacred ritual, the social counterpart of the individual compulsive act.[41]

All sacred culture once began as an attempt to outmaster something that could not be mastered (for example, most typically and universally, death). But the new and constant teaching of experience threatens to rediscover the unbearable fact or unresolved problem and to reactivate the traumatic experience, hence the religion must erect newer and ever newer defenses of the faith—not to accommodate new hypotheses to new facts but to defend old dogma (there is no death) from recurrent doubt, since the sacred obsessional (defensive) postulate *may not* be changed. To deny and mask the trauma, the original "mystery" must never be examined. At each secular change, the society must devise new "modernist" symbolisms and new rituals to defend the psychic status quo and to scab the unhealed wound, as in the individual compulsion neurosis.

Thus in nativistic cults, communicants protest a fulsome worship of the past in an attempt at restitution. The revelation is divine and unchanging (= some old fantasy or wish of our childhood = some unexaminable cultural postulate from an earlier crisis cult). But ambivalence peeps through at every point in the threadbare cultural fabric. The process of taking on any culture makes for some frustration, hostility, and inevitable ambivalence in every human child. Thus hate and love, fear and trust are invariably part of all religion. Each world view is a protrait of the psychosexual maturity of the self—essentially magic, if this is the phatic way the individual *feels* toward the not-self, or oedipal-religious—and *because* it is based categorically on feeling, no rational argument can shake either view, since a post-oedipal world view is based in turn on still another level of feeling and adaptation. Metaphysical position rests on the ego-tonus of the self involved, in any dealings with the not-self as still Unknown. Each stage is a successive surrendering of narcissism, a phase-growth of the ego.

Ambivalence toward past culture is the same that was felt toward the parents, the socializers of the individual to the culture. Similarly, an attitude toward his parents may be reproduced in an individual's attitude toward his society, which also rewards and punishes, and also becomes a foil for his wishes—and he uses the same characterological containers, compulsive magic faith, unending oedipal revolt, or ethnographic realism. That individuals should show similar feelings toward parents and society is plain enough. Less obvious is that, by the same transference, the individual brings the identical characterological defenses to the encounter with new culture and powerful new acculturators.

Man creates God, therefore, not precisely in his own image, but in "anaclitic" or need-assuaging counter-images of the Other which symbolize his conflicts in the realm of the Unknown (himself as well as universe!) and his persistent efforts to resolve them. Magic and religion are narcissistic, impatient, intolerant of anxiety and ambiguity; the answers must come *now,* even if they must be manufactured out of the unconscious and its irrational pressures on the ego. Often, therefore, in crisis cults, the unconscious of the visionary reaffirms an archaic infantile total-mana that moves the world by magic, like the god-shaman in South America when he turns culture hero. If such are his culture-personality premises, in revelatory conversations with himself he discovers he is god, whose universe he moves at will. But if regression under stress is only to the oedipal stance, then he invents vaguely nurturing and protective parental figures like the Great Spirit, the Great Ancestor, or such culture heroes as Manibozho or Coyote or Candir. Or even more specifically, he may bring back the ghosts of persons, of the ancestors and chiefs and heroes—or of the father himself, as did Evara of the Vailala Madness. All minister to his dependency and his need for an external authority for his acts and rituals. He finds a Person, whose mere prophet he consents to be, and puts forth his rules as if they were the god's. But his ambivalences remain obvious. His destructive hostility is the Apocalypse and the World Death; guilt finds expression in new moral fiats, often naïvely relevant to himself; and his regression to a Golden Age of dependency is a passively enjoyed Utopia (literally "no place" because it was never in this born world), a World-Without-Evil or some new effortless era, the biological roots of which are ontogenetically archaic indeed.

No one dare be cavalier about human nature. After enculturation, part of what a man fears is himself, his own repressed id impulses. Some of the unconscious is made up of these repressions; but some of it the ego never knows, since no man fully knows himself. Even what we pretentiously denominate "Reality" is only knowable to the conscious ego through wish-contaminated eyes and senses, via hidden cultural hypotheses, and through symbol-tools that man has made himself. And the superego, finally, is replete with judgments made on forgotten premises and ancestral false solutions to often bogus problems. Much of the content of the tribe-inherited conscience is consequently quite irrational. And, many times in the past, not knowing what to do in ego terms, like us, our ancestors could only try to please or placate nature by superego means.

Every human, daily, has conflict of wish, conscience, and world-view. Additionally, both individuals and groups of individuals may experience "strains of inconsistency" in the conflicting world views they encounter in acculturation—since all human idea-systems, of whatever tribal origins, are secondary defensive artifacts, not direct animal adaptations to ecological states-of-affairs, i.e., cognitive communication achieves human meta-organisms, but in the process adds adaptive fictions to the blindness of animal genetic contact with nature. Such ideational conflict on the level of "personality" is neurosis; conflict on the level of "culture" or "society" is the ghost dance phenomenon.

But even psychotics do not promulgate entirely "crazy" (wholly unconditioned) systems, with no relation to their experience or to their culture. Psychotic systems have understandable meanings and discernible purposes; in fact, psychotic systems of persons in our own society are a bit more easily learned than a foreign language or an alien culture, both of which they resemble. Like dream work, psychoses deny unpleasant or unmanageable realities, symbolize conflicts, and assert preferred solutions to sometimes unsolvable problems; and each psychosis is a kind of chronic and uncritical dream. When the visionary or revelation experience is not in fact a literal dream, it is very like a dream in these respects, a temporary psychosis. For it denies the common sense or the morality of contemporary culture, it wrestles with a conflict, and states a poorly disguised wish. In the supernatural dream–encounter the prophet encounters himself.

The revelation is the reified dream, the unconscious wish projected into reality. As a projective structure, the revelation has the identical homeo-static function as the dream; and it states the tensions of the inner known, the unconscious self, not the nature of the outer unknown, the world. In fact, as we know from sensory deprivation and dream studies, visionary revelation bears the signs of a relative inattention to the outer world as sorely present. In the cult of the caterpillar god, for one, so omnipotent is the wish, that, in order to obtain future riches, a naïve talion bargain is made by sacrificing vitally needed present goods—hardly a transaction that an astutely aware and reality-bitten ego would let pass uncriticized. Such revelation *denies* the unbearable reality and its power, and sub-stitutes the inner wish instead.

Art and religion alike arise from unsatisfied desire. In the revelation, the visionary withdraws his trust and love from the Reality Principle, and offers them passionately to the Pleasure Principle. That a stubbornly unreasoning "will to believe" is at work is shown in the prophet's desper-ate hatred of the unbeliever and promise of dire punishments upon him. Such a critical unbeliever represents the ego functioning of the society. He is the vatic's worst enemy. The Apocalypse must overwhelm him for the sin of disbelief. The spectacle of unbelief (disobedience to the prophet's overwhelming wishes) is unbearable, an affront to his categori-cal and godlike id. The skeptic is to be as much hated as the reality, and for the same reason: wish frustration.

Unbelief is no neutral matter, approachable by dispassionate secular means of proof. A ghost-dance theology is the more compulsive when doubt-riddled or unsupported by manifest reality. The eternal church in each divinely right fanatic would burn the unbeliever at the stake. His own inner compulsions make the visionary compel belief in his com-municants. The Altai supernaturals returned in thunder to convince un-believers in Chugal's first vision. Tävibo of the first Ghost Dance was forced, like Moses, to a second revelation from the outraged super-natural. The Shawnee Prophet had to make an eclipse, his brother had to stamp the ground and make an earthquake, to compel the people to believe. The religionist cannot forgive the heretic who will not share his fears and compulsions. The neurotic hates the psychiatrist whom he can-not convince, who will not join his cult. No *odium theologicum* is bitterer than in the patient whose neurosis is unbelievingly scorned.

NOTES

(XII Charisma and Mana)

1. "The First Pregenital Stage of the Libido," (pp. 248–79), and "The Influence of Oral Erotism on Character Formation," (pp. 393–406), in Karl Abraham, *op. cit.*

2. R. Money-Kyrle, *The Meaning of Sacrifice* (New York: Johnson Reprint Corporation, 1965).

3. The arrogance of claim in shaman and priest is plainly evident; that of the poet-bard often less so. The figure of culture hero-creator is very striking in Stephen Dedalus: "I go to encounter for the millionth time the reality of experience and to forge in the smithy of my soul the uncreated conscience of my race . . . Old father, old artificer, stand me now and ever in good stead"—the concluding lines of James Joyce, *A Portrait of the Artist as a Young Man* (London: The Egoist Ltd., 1916, p. 299). The Person in "epiphanies of Himself" is plain: it is the artist himself.

4. The *locus classicus* of the use of the old theological term "charisma" in the sociology of religion is Max Weber, *Theory of Social and Economic Organization,* (Glencoe: Free Press, 1964, pp. 358–92 [=Ch. IV]), translated from *Wirtschaft und Gesellschaft,* Part I=Vol. III of *Grundriss der Sozialoekonomik.*

5. That supernatural authority is always based on subjective claim is pointed out by Wach, *op. cit.,* p. 338.

6. On the fascinating effect of the narcissistic personality, C. Olden, *op. cit.*

7. Freud, in Jones, *Life and Works,* I:5.

8. W. La Barre, "Social Cynosure and Social Structure," *Journal of Personality,* 14 (1946) 169–83; also in D. G. Haring (ed.), *Personal Character and Cultural Milieu,* (Syracuse: University of Syracuse Press, 1956, pp. 535–45); and "Cynosures (points de mire) et structures sociales," *Revue de Psychologie des Peuples,* 8 (1953) 362–77.

9. Crowd psychology has been well known descriptively since Gustav Le Bon, *Psychologie des Foules* (Paris: Alcan, 1895), but dynamically only since Freud's *Group Psychology and the Analysis of the Ego* (London: Hogarth Press, 1922).

10. Max Weber's assimilation of charisma with *mana* and *orenda, The Sociology of Religion* (Boston: Beacon Press, 1963, p. 2).

11. Weber, *Sociology of Religion,* p. 38.

12. Fischoff, in Henry P. Fairchild (ed.), *A Dictionary of Sociology* (New York: Philosophical Library, p. 38).

13. The pioneer in proxemics is Edward T. Hall, *The Silent Language* (Garden City: Doubleday & Co., 1959); *The Hidden Dimension* (New York: Doubleday & Co., 1966); "Proxemics: The Study of Man's Spatial Relations," in Iago Galdston (ed.), *Man's Image in Medicine and Anthropology* (New York: International Universities Press, 1963, pp. 422–45); "Adumbration in Intercultural Communication," *American Anthropologist,* Special Issue, The Ethnography of Communication, 66, no. 6, pt. II (1966) 154–63; and "Proxemics," *Current Anthropology,* 9 (1968) 83–95. See also W. La Barre, "Paralinguistics, Kinesics, and Cultural Anthropology," in T. B. Sebeok, A. S. Hayes, and Mary Catherine Bateson (eds.), *Approaches to Semiotics* (The Hague: Mouton & Co., 1964, pp. 191–220), reprinted in F. Matson and Ashley Montagu (eds.), *The Human Di-*

alogue (New York: Free Press, 1967, pp. 456–89); also E. T. Hall, "Silent Assumptions in Social Communications," *loc. cit.*, pp. 490–505.

14. W. H. Auden, *About the House* (New York: Random House, 1965, p. 4).

15. Salomon Reinach, *Orpheus*, p. 116.

16. Murray, *op. cit.*, pp. 20–21.

17. Ralph Linton on *mana, The Tree of Culture* (New York: Knopf, 1955, p. 189); W. La Barre on *aretē, Human Animal*, p. 325.

18. On *mana* as *physis*, F. M. Cornford, *op. cit.*, pp. 12–13.

19. W. Nölle, "Schamanistische Vorstellungen in Shaktismus," *Jahrbuch des Museum für Völkerkunde zu Leipzig*, 11 (1952); R. Rahmann, *Shamanistic and Related Phenomena*, pp. 681–760.

20. Levin and Potapov, *op. cit.*, p. 578; W. La Barre, *Aymara Indians*, pp. 165–67; Lowie, in Steward, *op. cit.*, 3:52. M. J. Harner, *Jivaro Souls*, p. 260, on *kakarma;* soul-stealing involves drinking large quantities of an infusion of the "death vine," *natemA (Banisteriopsis* sp.), a violently hallucinogenic drug —in good Amerindian shamanic fashion (pp. 262–63).

21. A classic source on mana is R. R. Marett, *Threshold of Religion*, pp. 118–21; Marett's celebrated critique of Tylor, pp. 102–21. But Marett's very title is still culture-evolutionist.

22. E. S. C. Handy, *Native Cultures of the Marquesas* (Honolulu: Bishop Museum, Bulletin 9, 1923); and Ralph Linton, "Marquesan Culture," in A. Kardiner, *The Individual and His Society* (New York: Columbia University Press, 1939, pp. 137–96, page 146). The differential-*personal* aspect of mana is plain: a tabooed object (e.g., a fruit tree) is one onto which a powerful person has put his mana, endangering anyone who infringes this supernaturally sanctioned property right. A person with greater mana could infringe with impunity, but not one with lesser. On the sacred as something not to be touched see S. Freud, *Moses and Monotheism*, p. 190; cf. Robertson Smith, *op. cit.*, pp. 161, 163, and Judges 17:2. R. Firth, "The Analysis of Mana: An Empirical Approach," *Journal of the Polynesian Society*, 49 (1940) 483–510.

23. *Ya-Yari*, A. E. Jensen, *op. cit.*, pp. 117–18, quoting H. Petri, *Sterbende Welt in Nordwest Australien* (Braunschweig: Limbach, 1954, pp. 97–98); W. B. Spencer and F. J. Gillen, *The Arunta* (London: Macmillan & Co., Ltd., 2 vols., 1927); G. Róheim, *Social Anthropology* (New York: Boni and Liveright, 1925).

24. Gururumba *GwondEfoJE*, P. L. Newman, "Religious Belief and Ritual in a New Guinea Society," in J. B. Watson (ed.), *New Guinea, The Central Highlands*, Special Publication, *American Anthropologist*, 66, no. 4, pt. 2, 1964, pp. 257–72, page 258. S. A. Cook on *oudah, petara*, etc., in Robertson Smith, *op. cit.*, pp. 550, 554; Vietnamese [Annamese] *tinh, Hastings Encyclopedia*, 8:677.

25. P. Bohannan, "Extra-Processual Events in Tiv Political Institutions," *American Anthropologist*, 60 (1958) 1–12; A. W. Hoernlé, "Certain Rites of Transition and the Conception of *!nau* among the Hottentots." *Harvard African Studies*, 2 (1918) 65–82.

26. Rudolf Otto, *Idea of the Holy;* for Otto's conservative religionist view, see J. W. Harvey, "Translator's Preface," *op. cit.*, ix–xix. *Numen* as *mana*, H. J. Rose, *Religion in Greece and Rome* (New York: Harper Torchbooks, 1959, pp. 165, 168).

27. M. Eliade, *The Sacred and the Profane* (New York: Harcourt, Brace & Co., 1959, p. 11); also *Patterns in Comparative Religion* (New York: Sheed & Ward, 1958, 7ff).

28. Object as extension of infant's activity, H. Hartmann, "Contribution to the Metapsychology of Schizophrenia," in *The Psychoanalytic Study of the Child* (New York: International Universities Press, 1953, 8:177–98, p. 181); cf. J. Piaget, *Construction of Reality.*

29. "Lady Luck" in the psychopath and gambler, W. La Barre, *They Shall Take Up Serpents*, pp. 147–49, 156–58.

30. If apes with dominance-hierarchies could talk, would they discuss the relative *mana* of individuals in the group? For they have something like the social hierarchy giving rise to the concept in the human family and society; but without language could they have the concept?

31. Albert Schweitzer, *The Quest of the Historical Jesus* (London: A. and C. Black, 1910, and New York: Macmillan, 1956).

32. Paul Tillich, *The Courage to Be* (New Haven: Yale University Press, 1952).

33. Rudolf K. Bultmann, *Jesus Christ and Mythology* (New York: Scribner's, 1958). "In my opinion," wrote Bultmann, "we can sum up what can be known of the life and personality of Jesus as simply nothing" (quoted in M. I. Finley, *The World of Odysseus*, New York: Viking, 1954, p. 190).

34. Ludwig Feuerbach, *The Essence of Christianity* (New York: Harper Torchbook 11, 1957). Introductory Essay by Karl Barth, x-xxxii, p. xxi.

35. W. B. Cannon, *The Wisdom of the Body* (New York: W. W. Norton & Co., 1932).

36. Claude Bernard, *Introduction to the Study of Experimental Medicine* (New York: Macmillan, 1927).

37. Sandor Ferenczi, *Thalassa, A Theory of Genitality* (Albany: Psychoanalytic Quarterly, Inc., 1938, p. 46). Originally in *Psychoanalytic Quarterly*, 2 ⅜3–4 (1933) 361–403.

38. Géza Róheim, *Origin and Function of Culture*.

39. Hans Selye, *The Stress of Life*.

40. Sigmund Freud, *Beyond the Pleasure Principle;* art and religion, E. Jones, *Life and Works*, II:217.

41. Moore has shown that sometimes we encounter ways of behaving understandable only in terms of an hypothesis of group neurosis, something that inhibits a direct and simple approach to current problem-solving. A listing of instances shows the binding neurosis more active in those whose way of life is most committed to the church: an idea-structure made over-rigid by polemics; and fossilization intervenes between the individual and a basic commonsense approach to life-problems (Sebastian Moore, "A Catholic Neurosis?" *Clergy Review*, 46 [1961] 641–47). It is difficult not to regard current compulsive dogma about birth-control as anti-adaptive, both for the victimized faithful and in the long run for the revolt-weakened institution.

XIII

The Dancing Sorcerer

IN ASTRONOMY, which deals with the unreachable, we assume that matter and energy remote in space-time behave in the same gravitational and electromagnetic ways that they do here and now; and upon observation of stellar phenomena, in accord with this abstract principle, we can now produce nuclear fission and fusion here on earth. Indeed, on the same simple assumption of *universe,* the chemical element helium was first observed spectroscopically in the sun before it was discovered on the earth. Geology deals largely with the far past of the earth, inaccessible in time—and yet, assuming a simple uniformitarianism, geologists can "see" strata laid down in accord with the same ways that sediments are deposited observably now in a river delta, or recognize an ancient lava flow, or a Rift Valley fault athwart Africa produced by an unimaginably monstrous earthquake long before the time of man. Paleontology, too, depends on assumed biological-geological uniformitarianism—an assumption so practical in fact that, knowing the climates that present species adaptively need, we can reconstruct past climates and environments in reverse on the basis of mere plant and animal remains in the rocks, e.g. polar bear and hairy mammoth bones in paleolithic France imply a cold Pleistocene climate; but bones of hippopotamuses and tropical rhinoceros species, a warm climate; horse bones imply dry grasslands, not forests; and birch-pollen a cool climate.

The study of man should also be able to avail itself of the same scientific assumption of uniformitarianism. The difficulty is that we have not discerned the legitimate entities of that uniformity, which are biological—man's species-specific nature—but instead have tried to use such *observably non-uniform* evolving entities as cultures! Thus culture-oriented, and hence inevitably culture-bound, we have not only the motivated finding of a High God, unimportantly present at times among "primitives," but also the careless assumption that gods were "known" even to men of the Old Stone Age. Now it is true that any culture has an astonishing continuity backward into time and that, contrary to Functionalist dogma, the essence of culture is its historicity. But this is true only contingently, for what our study has taught us also is that cultures do nevertheless change. Consequently we should not project cultural meanings beyond reasonable inference based on demonstrable continuity and rate of change—and always with close respect to consistencies in geography and time.

On these grounds, despite the immense expanses of space and time involved, one has no hesitation whatever is believing with Narr and Maringer that the paleolithic bear cult, archeologically best manifest in Drachenloch, Petershöhle and Salzofen cave I, is related to such remote Eurasiatic relics as the "bear songs" of the Finnish epic *Kalevala* and to the present-day bear cult of the Ainu and other Paleosiberians, or that "bear ceremonialism" in upper North America is historically and ideologically related to that of East Asia. The whole enormous area of bear ceremonialism in Asia and America has been patiently pieced together by Hallowell on sure grounds of diffusion and minute ethnographic resemblances in a vast circumboreal "culture area." To extend this in time we need only datable and authentically archeological data; and, already given confidence in great age from the huge area of Hallowell's ethnographic complex, we make no unwarranted inference in connecting Alpine cave cults of the bear with later bear ceremonialism, all the more since arbitrary details persist and other kinds of evidence consist with it.[1]

On the other hand, given even such datable data as the "Dancing Sorcerer" of Trois Frères cave, it is wholly illegitimate to infer from this that Old Stone Age man worshiped a "high god" somehow epiphanied in a monstrous hippogryph of mixed animals never seen on land or sea. On the contrary, if we can abjure the wish for confirmation of our own theological beliefs, it is far simpler, given the ubiquity and antiquity of shamanism, to see this manlike dancer naturalistically as a dancing shaman—especially since all the adjunctive evidence in the same caves shows a concern for hunting magic and for the fertility of the hunted species. Since men can be seen but not gods, it is evident that the Trois Frères figure is not the epiphany of any supernatural "Master of Animals" but only a man dressed up in animal skins. One must also have a reasonable sense of context. Even a hunting people, routinely covering a considerable expanse of territory, can have only a limited conceptual geographic world; and if a shaman claims competence in such a space-bound small terrain, he is not to be compared for arrogance and absurdity to a vatic stand-in for the Creator of the Universe of later and larger cosmic and political proportions. There is no post-Hellenistic Emperor of the Universe in this cave, only a prehistoric shaman, a functionary like those of most historic hunting peoples. God, too, is a creature of history in ethnographic fact.

Ideally, of course, one would prefer to base inference about past man only on the "legitimate entities of uniformity," that is, on our animal similarities with past man himself as known archeologically and paleontologically—his sexual dimorphism and human division of labor, his neoteny and comparative longevity, his ecologic adaptations in a manifestly hunting culture, the evidence he gives of the animals he hunted, the social organization this implies for him, etc. Meanwhile, for the study of his religion, a Stone Age painting is more useful even than present-day theological truth. Admittedly, in a universe as huge and as complex as it now seems to be, a high god would be more comfortable to believe in than a mere shaman, of which we still have a plenty; for gods must be as big as man's world and man's needs. But it is precisely of contemporary culture and its limiting preconceptions that we should attempt to be emancipated when seeking to understand Old Stone Age religion. And we now know enough about man as an animal to discern the nature of his religion. Anthropology cannot remain a branch of theology, despite the charisma of some of anthropology's current prophets, but, like psychology earlier, must free itself from the last vestige of ties to Moral Science and strike out on its own.

Not the masses of later metaphysics but a sure clinical knowledge of the metaphysician, oneself, actually puts one closer psychically to the religion of prehistoric man; a sense of basic human biology vis-à-vis genuinely old archeological remains; an assiduous sense of culture, not a preoccupation with any fixed content of culture but an abstract understanding of what culture is about. To the anxious objectivist, this dive into the subject may smack of mysticism. It is not. Religion, like culture, is inside and among people, and there is little to be gained by pretending that anthropology is not about people too. Why should not candor confess what can not be concealed? Religion is a subjective stance that any discussant is bound to discuss subjectively. But in this lies strength and potential insight—if the motive is not mystical. When subject is object, the hazards of discriminating oneself from the subject matter are very complex indeed, and would seem to call upon horrendous structures of protective "methodology." The question is, how much method does one need to keep from lying?

Any method is good enough that keeps one from doing this; and no contrived methodology is adequate if it enables one to persist in lying. What computer can protect one from the most sophisticated computer of them all, the human mind? Undoubtedly, sophistication about the purposes of thought and a constant scrutiny of one's own thinking can serve us better in humanistic study than prosthetic crutches like computers that here allow us to lie only more elaborately. The "method" of the present chapter is that of an anthropologist, which is one kind of naturalist, in this case a humanist without punch cards who loves art, sufficiently endowed with a sense of others' alienness, who went into Altamira and Lascaux and other caves to learn everything possible about them and the men who created this astonishing art.[2] Since religion is close to art, and both are of man, no apology for such humanistic method need be made: it is only a man studying men. Meanwhile, the findings are no more precarious than those of any other anthropological field work in alien places in which, admittedly, method is the man. Fortunately the evidence is of many kinds.

Climate repeatedly has played a massive role in human biology. As noted earlier, the drying up of Miocene east Africa and the replacement of jungles by scattered groves of trees and grasslands originally changed arboreal apes into terrestrial, protohuman australopithecines. Savannas are relatively poor in fruit and plant foods that anthropoids can eat, but they are rich in grass-eating animal life. Australopithecines likely stayed gatherers as well, but when hominids became hunters of game, man began to become human, anatomically, psychologically and culturally. Later, in Europe, in the Pleistocene, four Ice Ages brought a virtual disappearance of suitable plant foods and enforced hunting even more rigorously upon early man. Man the hunter managed to survive in Europe even during the height of the last great glaciation.

During and between the four Pleistocene ice ages, and during the hesitant retreat of the last glaciation, climates fluctuated greatly in different eras, and consequently men hunted different animals. All this is faithfully reflected in the art and religion of the different epochs, and indeed also in recoverable ethnology. As we have seen, bear ceremonialism dates back to the ice age times of the terrifying and formidable cave bear, *Ursus spelaeus,* whose ritually disposed bones are most plentifully found in caves of the Alps and the Alpine foothills—and with whom, like the cave lion, early man had to compete for shelter. The spearing of bears and lions is found depicted in caves as late as Montespan, and the bear at Combarelles shows over thirty javelin thrusts. Neanderthal man, with an early paleolithic Mousterian culture, lived in caves and hunted such behemoths as the hairy mammoth (we have an engraving of one made by a human hand on a piece of mammoth ivory) using only long spears in this blood-curdling encounter—and the range of this big-game hunting now appears to have spread over arctic Asia even into the central regions of North America.

In the tundra period, Stone Age caves show numerous pictures of reindeer, often in sexual contexts with humans, and many artifacts of reindeer horn; the late Aurignacian and early Magdalenian is the period of "reindeer shamanism." In the milder steppe climate, Solutreans who came later hunted herds of wild horses on the grassy plains that then stretched across middle Europe eastward into Asia. Paintings of horse-hunts indicate that Solutreans used the bow, which came into Europe in the preceding Aurignacian period, possibly from Africa, and the spear-thrower, also available from an earlier period. Either because horses are less dangerous to hunt than other animals and mainly require stalking skill and longer-range weapons, or because Solutreans camped mostly in the open, the art of Solutrean horse-hunters is less plentiful than in either the preceding Aurignacian or the following Magdalenian periods of cave art. But the thousand-foot corridor of Les Combarelles contains about four hundred engravings, mostly of horses, though there are animals of other climatic eras to indicate that this cleft was a sacred place during millennia; and the commonest animal at Aurignacian-Perigordian-Magdalenian Lascaux is also the horse. As a once staple food, the ancient *Equus hemionus* retreated with the grasslands on which it flourished back into central Asia, on the steppes of which the last representatives of the ancient wild horses, *Equus przewalski,* still survive in the Gobi region and are known in zoos.[3]

In the moister climate of the Magdalenian culture period, much of Europe was covered with great forests, and new varieties of large food animals were adapted to the more temperate climate. Far the most important of these was the aurochs or ancient wild cattle, *Bos primigenius*[4]— so splendidly shown at Altamira, Font de Gaume, Les Combarelles, La Mouthe, Pech Merle, Le Portel, Teyjat and elsewhere, but most impressively at Lascaux because of the great size and prominence of the wall paintings there. One bull at Lascaux is a life-size eighteen feet long! The aurochs was an animal of tremendous bulk, often six feet and more high at the shoulder, quick and powerful in movement, and imposingly long-horned, one extant horn measuring an incredible forty-two inches in length and seven inches in diameter near the base.[5] The aurochs ranged not only in southern Europe and northern Africa but also eastward into Asia, which may have been its place of origin. Assyrian kings hunted it

in Mesopotamia; it is the mysterious *rëem* of the Old Testament portrayed
on the Ishtar Gate, and it appears in the legends of the Jews.[6] Herds of
these giant wild cattle still existed in the Hercynian forest of Germania
in classic times. Caesar wrote, not too inaccurately, that they were "a
little below the elephant in size, of the appearance, color and shape of a
bull, of extraordinary strength and speed, and spare neither man nor
beast they espy."[7] In Roman imperial times the wild bull, Latin *urus,*
was a favorite animal imported for the great slaughter-spectacles in the
Roman circuses. This magnificent animal was choice game for the
Gauls, but in Clovis' time (A.D. 488) became so rare only the king
could hunt it, and disappeared from the Vosges and Pyrenees in the
twelfth and from the Black Forest in the sixteenth centuries. A small herd
of aurochs survived last in the wild forests near Sochaczew in Poland,
where it became extinct in 1627.[8]

Wild cattle were herding animals, a number of cows and immature
animals being dominated by a single fierce bull. Consequently any who
would hunt the aurochs must first account for this paramount bull, that
bore cruel horns able fatally to rip a man with a single toss of the head.
These combative bulls did not easily lie down and die to appease men's
hunger. They had to be fearfully hunted, battled with and killed. Prehistoric aurochs hunts must have been savage and bloody events, in
which men were killed nearly as often as the wild bull. The religious awe
in which late Paleolithic hunters held this great beast carried over with
little diminution into later times. Egyptians, Helladic peoples and early
Semites all knew and some still hunted the aurochs. The rain bull became
the chief deity of Neolithic farming peoples from Asia Minor into northwestern Europe, and from early Egypt to prehistoric south India. The
peoples around the eastern Mediterranean were virtually obsessed for
millennia with the bull as a fertility deity and symbol of kings. The bull-
gods of Semites and pre-Greek Dionysian mysteries alike have left their
mark on contemporary symbol and ritual so deeply that of all animals
that shaped European religious belief from beginning to end, the bull of
the eucharistic feast was by far the chief one.

Comfortable city men have forgotten how dangerous their staple food
animals were when hunted on foot as larger wild animals, and with only
flint-tipped weapons to hack them to death. Virtually forgotten also is
the razor-tushed wild boar,[9] once prevalent in the great forests of de-
ciduous trees after the ice age, on the plentiful oak mast of which droves
of these wild beasts once fed. The Calydonian wild boar hunt of the
heroes, the pre-Hellenic Pelasgian sow as the mother-earth goddess, the
totemic wild boar that slew Adonis and other such "dying god" consorts of

the Great Mother in Asia, the totemic pig god of ancient Semites—all these are only a small fraction of the uninvestigated rich symbolism of this animal in European and Near Eastern religion. The hairy mammoth[10] and the giant cave bear became figures in a forgotten nightmare. Hunting them on foot with only spears had been frightful beyond imagination. But so also killing and mutilation by the savage-horned wild bulls and keen-tushed wild boars men later hunted, were greatly to be dreaded. Both these ferocious animals were the chief game of later Stone Age men, and the very staple of life must quite often have brought bloody death to the hunters. The first totemic "gods" of protohistoric religion were the great bull and boar of Neolithic peoples, and both have left deep and ineradicable marks on the religious thought of western man.

Although plants and other objects are pictured in paleolithic art, the predominant figures are those of the wild animals killed for food with barely adequate weapons in successive climatic periods. Hunting large animals that have their own formidable defenses entailed constant danger, but other than hunting and gathering early men had no technological means of getting food. They also had no technical way of controlling the availability or the production of new food. Though domestic cattle and swine became the main meat staples later in the Neolithic, Paleolithic man had neither agriculture nor domesticated animals, and all human life depended on success in finding and killing wild animals, and gathering wild plants.

We suppose, fatuously and a little proudly, that only our civilized time can be an "Age of Anxiety." But anxiety, from inner psychic and outer environing sources alike, is always and everywhere the lot of men. We fear, not mammoths, but some political behemoth beyond the horizon, with unthinkable weapons to erase human life. And, appropriate to the Space Age, some even begin to fear monsters from the other planets we prepare to invade. We do indeed know anxiety. But endowed as we are with many technical means of mastering old problems of survival, it is difficult for us to imagine the dangers and anxieties of Old Stone Age life simply in obtaining enough food to stay alive. We can only seek analogies. The Eskimo hunter sometimes endures almost unbelievable hardships in a struggle against starvation in a hostile Ice Age-like climate; but the Eskimo have a notable technology and material culture for hunting. For the element of wild danger, perhaps the lion-hunting spearsmen of east Africa might make a contemporary analogue; but these tall Nilotics have cattle, and their serfs are farmers. A better case might be the Pygmies of central Africa, who in small groups still attack elephants afoot with their tiny bows and spears.

Old Stone Age religion, as seen in cave art, was related precisely to the specific anxieties of these hunting peoples. Cave art turned upon the two main uncontrolled elements in their lives: luck in hunting, and magic increase and replacement of the animals they killed and consumed. Nearly all cave art is one or the other: hunting magic, or fertility magic. The first specimen of Stone Age art to be discovered—an engraving of two hinds on the cannon bone of a reindeer—was found in the cave of Chaffaud (Vienne), but no one then recognized its enormous antiquity. Cave painting was first seen in modern times in 1879 by a little girl, in the much-told story of four-year-old María, daughter of Don Marcelino de Sautuola, who looked up restlessly from play as her father archeologized on the floor of a cave near Santander in northern Spain—crying "Papa, toros!" as she saw the great aurochs bulls portrayed on the ceiling of Altamira.

But conservative opinion long remained skeptical that the hand of man could have painted an extinct animal. The first unarguable proof that this could be the case was Lartet's finding in 1864 at La Madeleine the outline of a mammoth scratched on a piece of the fossil ivory of the mammoth itself—a contemporaneity of man and mammoth since amply confirmed by a Pindal Cave crude mammoth outline with an "X-ray" seen heart for target, an early Aurignacian wall outline in red of an elephant-like animal in Castillo cavern (Santander), a later Aurignacian woolly mammoth wall-engraving at Les Combarelles, a Magdalenian IV mural at Font de Gaume, and a superimposed mammoth-reindeer-bison-horse palimpsest of various Magdalenian periods there also—not to mention a human head, that of a young girl, and the torso of a more mature female, both in ivory, and both from the Grotte du Pape at Brassempouy.

At the cave of La Mouthe, on 12 August 1902, a party of scientists first officially recognized cave art there as paleolithic in age. Salomon Reinach,[11] then curator of the Musée des Antiquités Nationales at Saint-Germain-en-Laye near Paris—that same one housing the first-recognized but long-scouted stone age flints from Abbeville of Boucher de Perthes—first proposed the "magic theory" of cave art, in an article in L'Anthropologie in 1903. Unaccountably, a German tradition of interpretation for some time argued "art for art's sake"[12] in Old Stone Age man as if his sometimes dangerous labors were mainly aesthetic in motive—unaccountably, because the same spot is often painted and repainted again, obviously not for show but as though this had proved a lucky place. But modern authorities largely agree with Reinach's theory of magic art, though Leroi-Gourhan argues that fertility magic is even more prominent than hunting magic in some places, notably at Le Portel where a projecting stalactite forms the enormous phallus of a human figure (there is another one in Ariège at Bedeilhac).

Breuil thinks that the prints of human hands, both positive and negative, and often with missing finger joints (a mourning sacrifice among many modern natives all over the world) are the earliest of all.[13] If so, these hand-prints would embody the most naïve and direct magic mastery conceivable, the laying on of hands, and are not mere identity-mementos as of romantic tourism, however poignant because of their age. Snakes and snakelike "spaghetti" lines, apparently made by fingers trailed along wet clay, especially at La Pileta (Malaga) and Baume Latrone (Hérault), Breuil thinks, were made at the very dawn of the Aurignacian. Curiously, there are other indications of similar magic preceding pictorial art in some places. In the so-called Hall of the little Bison at Font de Gaume, so narrow a cleft that two people can hardly stand there at the same time, the wall was smeared over with red ochre before any paintings were done; and in a side recess at Altamira, and another at Gargas, the walls remain rubbed all over with red ochre only. Since this pigment was often painted on the bones of the dead and seems to have symbolized life, blood or fire (the paleolithic ochre burial at Sungir in Russia had even had a layer of live coals laid beneath it), the painting of cave recesses with red ochre would appear to mean the magic making of life deep in the earth, as though in the menstruous womb of a woman.

The most remarkable and significant feature of cave art is that it is not found in shallow caves used as living quarters, where it might be seen daily if intended to be for secular enjoyment. Instead, the art is placed deep under the ground and is reached only after hazardous crevasses, low seams, and slippery tunnels have been traversed, with feeble lights battling the unknown eternal darkness. Forces greater than fear must have driven the Magdalenian and other magic artists far inside the earth, where one can easily be lost in tortuous labyrinths or be killed by accidental slipping into time-forgotten depths. Old Stone Age art is not passively aesthetic. The concept of aggressive magic creation by the artist is almost enforced upon us.[14] Minute configurations of the rock walls have been seized upon by the imagination of the artist and ingeniously drawn into a picture of some animal, and in many cases the same irregularities were conceptualized again into a quite different animal.[15] The patent virtuosity of the artist suggests a literal creator or transformer, the *deus artifex* and *deus pictor* who creates life in a whole new world.[16] The shaman as fertility daemon and Master of Animals inseminated the earth with animal life; he was the magic consort of the Mother Earth. Painting was literally a creative act. Very old legends all over the world conceive of animals as being born from caves in the earth, and the cave was the first adytum of protohistoric religion in the whole Mediterranean region. The cave is the first nave of spiritual (animistic) religion. The land of the spirits is beneath the earth, as it is also in the skies.

The caves best known to travelers, Altamira and Lascaux, are scarcely typical. And the caves do vary.[17] There is the gigantic maw of the Mas d'Azil—whole landscapes of forests and fields may be seen atop it—a cave so named because the huge tunnel was a fortified refuge for armies in the Middle Ages. What is now only an elevated ledge above the tiny village of Les Eyzies, center of the cave country around Montignac, was a fortified place from prehistoric down into feudal times; and French peasants lived in the shallows of Cro Magnon, not a painted cave, until the last century. Altamira of the bulls, in the Spanish Pyrenees above the village of Santillana del Mar near Santander, is relatively easy of approach. And so is the modern antrum cut from an adjacent cave into recently reclosed Lascaux, the original entry to which was a narrow nineteen-foot shaft or an unknown one lost in the well at a far arm near the scene of the bird shaman. What is characteristic, however, of most of the painted caves of southern Europe, is the almost extravagant *inaccessibility* of the art.[18]

To look on cave painting, like prehistoric men we must grope our way through twisting, often very tight, and always slippery corridors, cling uncertainly to wet curtains of glistening stalagmite and stalactite, climb down into treacherous abysses, jump through cold waterfalls and creep through narrow chimneys, in order to arrive at a flesh-creeping immensity of darkness as at Niaux. Niaux is a huge cavern formed by water and an ancient subterranean glacier, some 4500 feet deep, the gigantic size of which tiny lamps could never have revealed all at once to Stone Age man, and the art of which appears only after one has ventured 1500 feet into the bowels of the earth. At La Bastide we must descend a vertical pit that opens, a hundred feet down, into another gulf with only a narrow ledge to walk on before attaining to huge halls under the ground. At the Cabrerets labyrinth one must clamber about precariously everywhere to view the many paintings and engravings. La Pasiega has a manhole with a subterranean river below, dashing itself against precipices above whose most dangerous climbs are painted animals and mysterious symbols. It takes three hours at Montespan to overcome barriers before reaching the natural stairway rising to a tiny sanctuary with molded clay figures on the floor covered with the ruins of reliefs. Young Casteret first reached innermost Montespan only by putting his light into a bathing cap and then diving foolhardily through a siphon, formed where a black underground river seems to flood out from the living rock! As at Montespan, a sunken river guards the fearsome Tuc d' Audoubert, two hundred long underground feet of which one breasts or boats upon before the first land; then comes a precarious thirty-foot steep shaft up ladders placed there and slippery pegs; and next a crawl through claustrophobic low passages, to reach the startling footprints of ancient dancers in bare feet and the models of copulating bisons, in clay on the floor beyond. In the Font de Gaume crevice, the first murals occur nearly halfway to its end. At Les Combarelles, engravings cover both sides of a sluice averaging only about a yard wide, and in some caves an awkward sprawl is needed to see any pictures at all. Ancient Pindal cave opens at a completely remote point on a coastal rock high above the Atlantic. The adytum of the cave at Clotilde in Spain must be crawled to, reverently or ridiculously, on hands and knees. And only after slithering through a culvert-like tunnel and inching up a rock chimney, a foot on each side above the abyss, can one make the hour's walk through devious corridors to view, finally, the famous "Dancing Sorcerer" at Trois Frères.

The extreme difficulties in placing paintings, sculptures and engravings in these remote and perilous sites can only have been overcome by determined motivation. To make magic art demanded overcoming anxiety not much less than the anxiety of the hunt itself. By such desperate bargains with fate do men achieve peace of mind. Coming out into the sunlight, after such dangers underground, seems like a rebirth. This is not idle metaphor. For magic art in caves is clearly a supernatural, quasisexual, creative act of the shaman-artist to promote the increase of animals in the womb of the earth. Some art at least is also intended to procure human fertility: the famous "Cogul Dance" at Roca del Moros is a painting of a nude ithyphallic figure around which a group of women dance.

Though the first such discovered (1909), Cogul is not an isolated find. In 1923, the Cave of David (so named for its discoverer, a fourteen-year-old boy) was found in Lot, with its engraved figures of ithyphallic men followed by women with pendant breasts, a scene dated to the Aurignacian or Magdalenian; in the Mas d'Azil, an engraving on bone of a dancing ithyphallic man, perhaps with an animal head, was found; and in Lascaux, the so-called "Dead Man" or Bird Shaman is ithyphallic too. Hornos de la Peña has an engraving of an ithyphallic man; and Peña de Candamo also. The Dancing Sorcerer of Trois Frères is genitally nude though not ithyphallic. But in the Gorge d'Enfer, a baton of reindeer horn was found, carved in the form of a double human phallus; in Les Roches (Blanchard), a phallus carved from bison horn, of Aurignacian date; and another at Teyjat engraved on reindeer horn, of upper Magdalenian date. Vulvae in Aurignacian mobile art have been found at Laussel, Cassares, La Ferrassie, Croze à Gontran, Lorthet, Montespan, Les Roches and perhaps at Pair-non-Pair.

That fertility magic is intended seems clear not only from the ithyphallic figures themselves but also from the fact that representations of human phalloi and vulvae[19] are found in the same caves that show animal-human coitus (e.g. Pech Merle), and that the "femme au renne" engraving from Laugerie Basse implies human female and reindeer coitus. That the concern was ritual is clear in that the copulating bisons at Montespan are surrounded by the heel prints of human dancers (and for human footprints, compare Niaux and the Grotte d'Aldène at Hérault). Again, the phallic stalactite at Le Portel attached to a human figure also leaves little doubt in interpretation; further evidence from the figures of "sorcerers" will be adduced later. Nevertheless, we are not to suppose that these straightforward representations of animal and human sexuality are deep in the caves for any reason of prurience or cultural repression. On the contrary, every indication is that sexuality was approached reverently as the central mystery of life; and any salacity is contributed by latter-day viewers, influenced by a religion long in rivalry and conflict with the old religion.[20] The scenes are deep in the caves only to symbolize mysteries deep in the body of the earth, and the only complexity comes from the symbolic implication of coitus with the hunt and from the assimilation of human and animal sexuality.[21]

The concern of paleolithic art with sexuality is no mere inference of a later psychiatrically sophisticated age; the data admit of no alternative interpretation. The clay floor relief of a female bison in the Tuc d'Audoubert is closely followed by a male bison about to mount; and near the entrance to this chamber, 770 meters from the cave mouth, numerous small clay models of human phalloi were found, with the impression on the floor of five rows of youthful human heels turned toward the phalloi, a circumstance Breuil thought evidence of a puberty rite.[22] Near one of the Magdalenian-date female figures at Angles-sur-l'Anglin is a female bison in heat, possibly indicating a similar girls' puberty ceremonial.[23] At Teyjat an aurochs bull closely follows a cow; one of the masked shamans at Trois Frères, blowing a flute, follows two chamois or reindeer does, one of which has turned her head to him, Wendt thinks seemingly adopting a posture for copulation.[24]

The range of the old fertility religion is impressive. To the west of the classic stone age French caves, the Cogul scene of the ithyphallic male surrounded by dancing females at Roca del Moros (Lerida, Spain) was repainted repeatedly, evidently to renew its potency. Here, too, females touch the sides of bulls; a male figure touches the horns of a bull with a typical shamanistic trident; and on a nearby wall are votive inscriptions in old Iberian and archaic Latin (fourth or fifth century B.C.), indicating that this rock shelter was a sacred place for two or three hundred generations.[25] To the south, Iberian rock paintings affiliate both in style and in period with those of north Africa: animal-human association is common around Oran, and Tassili shows numerous people with animal heads and frequent coital scenes.[26] To the north of classic caves like Tuc d'Audoubert, we have depicted animal couplings such as the elks of the Kløtefoss (Buskerud, Norway) rock-engraving of the Bronze Age[27]; in Denmark, an early ithyphallic figure in wood from Broddenbjerg is matched by a female one from another North Jutland bog, both perhaps associated with the later fertility gods Njord, Frey, Freja, and Nerthus.[28] Contemporary with those of late Old Stone Age France are figurines from Lake Baikal in southern Siberia, a cult that reappears perhaps in the earliest ceramic periods of the New World: paleolithic pecked-rock art on the walls of the deep Solsem cave in Siberia shows twenty human figures, two in coition, the males usually with phallic emphasis.[29] In western Europe, in fact, phallic cults persisted into historic times.[30]

Further significant proofs of the interest in fertility, of course, are the numerous upper-paleolithic figurines or "Venuses" with their exaggerated secondary sexual characteristics, some fifty of which are now known.[31] The most famous and the most striking artistically are the Venuses of Brassempouy, Mentone, Willendorf, Laussel and Lespugue. Brassempouy (Landes) yielded three such headless torsos in mammoth ivory; Barma Grande, one of the Grimaldi or Baoussée-Roussée series of caves near Mentone (Liguria), five nearly complete statuettes of crystalline talc or steatite, one very wide-hipped, another grotesquely steatopygous like a modern Bushman or Hottentot woman. Willendorf, near Krems in Austria, produced a limestone statuette with traces of red painting on its surface, from an Aurignacian loess-bed settlement; the Willendorf Venus has heavily pendulous breasts and very adipose torso and legs. Laussel in Dordogne has the celebrated bas relief of a woman with very fat hips and large breasts, holding a bison horn in her right hand; this figure alone would confirm our belief that the horns and antlers of animals (perhaps also the ivory tusks of elephants) embodied a fertility symbolism for paleolithic peoples, from this "horn of plenty" through Mesolithic and Neolithic times, down to the proto-historic symbolisms of Indoeuropeans so abundantly described by Gertrude Levy. Lespugue (Grotte des Rideaux in Haute-Garonne) contained an almost complete but excessively stylized mammoth ivory statuette that Boule considered "of such beauty as to

establish it as a queen amongst the Aurignacian 'Venuses.'" Not everyone shares this opinion; it is certainly the most extremely grotesque and
unreal of them all.

What is so very extraordinary about these Aurignacian mother-goddesses
—facts long noticed by archeologists but never explained by them—is
that, almost invariably, they have featureless heads and have no feet.
Although Brassempouy also produced the thin-necked head of a young
girl, all three of the splendidly mature maternity figures found there lack
heads and feet. Perhaps in the case of these, it may be the result of breakage; but MacCurdy considered one of them "so much like the figurines
from Lespugue, Willendorf, and Grimaldi, that one is justified in assuming
for it a head without features, diminutive arms (or perhaps none at
all), and feetless legs tapering to a point."[32] The head of the Willendorf
statuette, which is present, has only seven parallel rows of stylized short
ringlets, and seems simply to lack feet. The head of the Laussel Venus
is only a geometrically stylized volute. The grossly steatopygous Venus
from one of the Grimaldi caves has a conical head, and the legs taper off
without feet. The Barma Grande Venus from Mentone has an entirely
featureless egg-shaped head, and she also lacks feet. The Lespugue figure
has the head reduced to a volute like a sprouting fern or a fiddle-head,
featureless except for parallel vertical grooves perhaps indicating hair;
in this specimen the feet are intentionally lacking and have not been
broken off. Curiously, too, the Isturitz (Basses-Pyrénées) bone engraving of a nude woman lacks a head, though the head is present in the male
figure slightly below her with his hands upraised as in prayer; the Magdalenian engraving of the "Venus of Couze" lacks head and feet, in this
case not possibly from breakage since it was drawn thus. Because these
mother-figures so consistently lack heads (or if they have heads, they
lack features), Max Kohen has suggested that they represent literally the
faceless woman of the oedipal nightmare, mother-images in every respect.[33]
It might be added, also, that the lack of feet suggests an erotism of female
feet still present among Paleosiberian and Eskimo tribes, and also a
symbolism or metaphor prominent in both Semitic and Indoeuropean
languages.

Quite as unmistakable as the evidences for fertility magic are those for
hunting magic. Throughout the upper paleolithic, animals of varied climatic species are depicted with a barbed spear engraved or painted on
the body.[34] Sometimes, in reverse, a bison or ibex is carved on a spear-
thrower—as though these horn-weaponed creatures in particular, from
their habit of goring or butting, would give magic propulsion to projectiles.
Many man-made effigies of animals give evidence of having been phys-

ically attacked in magic rituals. For example, the clay horse of the Grotte de Gantier (Haute-Garonne) shows plainly more than two dozen deep spear thrusts. The lions and bears at Montespan were speared, possibly also a bear at Combarelles. One effigy of a headless bear had fragments of a cave bear skull fallen between the front paws of the floor sculpture, from which it has been inferred that it was once covered perhaps by a bearskin with the head still attached; this effigy also shows spear thrusts. And in Lascaux a disemboweled bison attacks a man who is falling over backwards; weapons lie on the ground in the scene.

Apparently only animals difficult or dangerous to hunt were shown, for ancient man did not paint frequently all the animals he knew, or hunted judging from their bones. For example, hares were abundant and much eaten in Iberia, and yet only one depiction is known, that at Le Gabillou[35]; evidently men needed neither hunting nor fertility magic for hares. The puzzling "tectiform" drawings in caves, somewhat resembling a skin tent or a hut roof, have most usually been interpreted as deadfalls or traps for animals, and Pericot thinks that the spider is prominent in Spanish art (e.g. the friezes at Ares) because of the spider's skill in netting its prey. Lattices at Lascaux, usually in front of an animal but sometimes on its body, suggest nets too.[36] As human figures become more numerous in later art, especially in the Epipaleolithic of Spain, we see many actual hunting scenes with both men and animals.

One of the most fascinating finds is a broken bone pendant from the Raymonden cave at Chancelade, showing the engraved heads and upper torsos of seven men flanking a bison carcass. Scale is ignored in the beautifully drawn forelegs and head of the bison in order to give it greater prominence; by contrast, the human figures are mere profiles or silhouettes. The best-drawn man, at the lower right, has a curious trifurcated object coming from his upper chest—a name- or attribute-indicating symbol? a representation of speech?—and he faces, not the bison, but two bows and two arrows standing on their ends, as if giving grace to them at meal. Fifteen-some notches near the pierced end of the pendant suggest that it was a hunter's tally. The backbone of the bison is exposed and schematically represented, showing that the scene was a hunters' feast.[37]

Although human figures are occasionally present, upper-paleolithic cave painting is overwhelmingly animal art.[38] This preoccupation is shown not only in the obvious subject matter but also in the very technique of painting, which surely indicates no abstract and disinterested aesthetic tendency. Obsessed with animals, the artist saw them everywhere with a Rorschach eye. The actual surface of the rock suggests animal forms to him.[39] A small hole in the wall becomes for him an eye, and a whole animal is drawn around it. At Lascaux, each of the forelegs of a horse is perceptively and even playfully used to outline the head of another horse, and the head of one small deer is entirely formed from natural rock-spalls. The genius of the artists is especially evident at Lascaux, for when a flashlight is played about, shapes that seemed flat in a fixed light now suddenly emerge meaningful in moving lights and shadows. Indeed, the beautiful relief of a reclining woman on the wall of La Madeleine in Tarn, an accessible site well-explored by Lartet and Christy in 1863–64 and visited by thousands since, was discovered only in 1952. The very skill in modeling contours with polychrome, as at Altamira, may lead us to neglect the artist's apperception of natural modeling in the rock. The exploitation of these natural accidents of configuration suggests that the painter merely urged into existence what was already half there, awaiting only human wish to bring it into being. The shaman was only a demi-urge or transformer, not a Creator from nothing.

At the beginning of the 1960s, some 32 sites could be counted with human figures in the mural art.[40] The depicted human form as such is now known in both mobile and mural art, often in several specimens, from upward of 65 stations in Europe—at least 32 in France, 24 in Spain, 3 in Czechoslovakia, and one each in Austria (Willendorf), Belgium (Magrite), Germany (Mainz), Italy (Barma Grande), and Russia (Mezine—there are others in Asiatic Russia, notably at Malta, near Krasnoyarsk in Siberia). But the connoisseur and humanist will wish to go beyond mere counting to more discerning insights. Curiously, in style, the masked human figure at Font de Gaume, the Bird Shaman at Lascaux, the human figures at Les Combarelles, the man of Peña de Candamo, the Sorcerer of Pech Merle, the masked man at Roc de Sers, and the human silhouettes at Altamira and Le Portel—all of them from the high periods of Franco-Cantabrian art—are notably crude compared to the usually superb portrayal of animals. For example, the single engraved line depicting a bear at Teyjat has so Picasso-like a precision of line that its exact species, Ursus arctos, can be unmistakably discerned; and the horses at Chaffaud and Lascaux are certainly tarpans of přzewalski type.

Trois Frères has over four hundred engravings of more than a dozen species of animals, but only the lion and the sorcerer are outlined in black, raising the question of a different style or period for these two. But the sorcerer (like the small bison-masked shaman there) is skillfully drawn in precisely the same high style of the classic upper-paleolithic period. The contrast in depiction of man and animal is nowhere more striking than at Lascaux. Though by no means the most splendid specimen of animal art at Lascaux, the wounded bison near the well is in high Magdalenian style

—but the falling man at his horns is by comparison only an absurd picto-
graph. The contrast is so striking, one is tempted to invoke two different
art-periods, and yet bison and man are logically and unmistakably parts
of the same hunting scene.

It is as though upper-paleolithic artists could draw animals superbly,
but men only indifferently. Les Combarelles shows a recognizably human
thigh among numerous crude anthropomorphs, Les Espélunges a human
leg, La Madeleine an arm, Marcamps a head in reindeer horn and Brassempouy an inferior head in ivory, but the reliefs on limestone from
Terme Pialet, the humans engraved on bone from La Colombière, Les
Eyzies, Mas d'Azil, Raymonden and Rivière-de-Tulle, the figures from
Gourdan, and the mural figures at Les Eglises, Marsoulas and Le Portel—
all are sorry sketches of human beings. Elegance and realism are reserved
for the animals themselves, as though they were the true psychological
focus, not man. Only the so-called Archer in low relief at Laussel is done
in anything like a finished style in stone, and he by no means approaches
in execution the headless "Three Graces" at the Roc aux Sorciers in
Vienne, or even the new mural Venus of La Madeleine. The different
treatment of the sexes in paleolithic art may also be remarked upon. With
late exceptions to be counted on the fingers of one hand, in the whole of
Old Stone Age art no human being is ever presented sensually or aestheti-
cally, as a sexually desirable *person*. The interest is purely functional. The
males are merely schematic, as though they served only an abstraction like
sexual potency, shamanistic power, or skill in hunting. The faceless females are only heavily symbolic of fertility.

There are many delightful aspects to Stone Age art, but these occur
mostly in animal art—the truly beautiful and majestic animals of Altamira
and Lascaux; the impressionistic treatment of a herd of reindeer, engraved
on the wingbone of an eagle from La Mairie (Dordogne), only the first
three and last of which are drawn complete, the rest merely a forest of
antlers; an equally impressionistic herd of horses, on a stone engraving
from Chaffaud (Vienne), the leader with replicated head to show its vigorous motion in galloping; the replicated neck of a crane, to show its sinu-
osity, on a pebble from Monastruc (Tarn-et-Garonne), like the "strobo-
scopic" chain on the *Moving Dog on Leash* by Giacomo Balla or the
cubist *Nude Descending a Staircase;* the impressive dart-thrower in reindeer horn, also from Monastruc, carved as a rampant mammoth, feet
gathered to charge, whose out-stretched trunk is the handle and curled
tail the nock-hook (*that* should give heft to any spear!); the curious
stateliness and ethnic quiddity of style in the color-modeled bisons at Altamira; the veritably Africanesque liveliness in the hunting and other

scenes of post-Capsian Iberian art onward to the Epipaleolithic—all are captivating and engrossing. But as if to drive home the consistent functionality of the art in both the contrastive animal and human styles, the famous "twisted perspective" in the paintings of animals always shows a maxium profile of body, and so too do horns and feet, though a head is sometimes turned back and drawn upon the animal's shoulder; the Gourdan moose engraved on reindeer horn is in fact the only animal one recalls seen head-on. The animals are presented in profile as they would be ideally as targets for the hunt; or as points of primary concern, since twisted perspective in horns persists, as at Lascaux, long after it is gone in the feet. Old Stone Age art has a highly practical and non-abstract interest in animals!

Beyond an interest in hunting magic and animal fertility, what can we safely infer about Old Stone Age religious concepts? Surely there was some further concern about man himself? There does indeed exist such evidence, gruesome though it is. First of all, there seems to have been a very ancient concept of *mana,* apparently resident especially in the head, and obtained through eating the brains of other men. Sergio Sergi carefully studied the Monte Circeo I skull of a Neanderthal, which had a deliberate breaking away of the bone at the base of the skull around the foramen magnum. Vallois suggested a similarity to cannibalistic practices in recent African tribes, and Blanc[41] adduced a skull from the d'Entrecasteaux Islands with mutilation almost identical with that of the Monte Circeo skull. From his exhaustive study of the Ehringsdorf skull Weidenreich[42] concluded that the individual was killed by a stone weapon striking the frontal region and that the absence of a cranial base indicated the skull was then intentionally opened to extract the brain. Berckhemer[43] confirmed the conclusions of Sergi and Weidenreich through his work on the Steinheim skull, discovered in 1932. Von Koenigswald pointed out the similarity of mutilation in the eleven skulls that he and Ter Haar discovered at Ngandong in 1931 to those made on skulls by recent Borneo headhunters in that region; again, the arrangement of the Ngandong skulls was like that of the late-paleolithic skulls at Ofnet. At Grosse Ofnet (Bavaria)—a cave with an unbroken sequence from the lower Aurignacian through both Iron Ages into historic medieval times— there were discovered, in 1908, in the Azilean-Tardenoisean layer, two nests containing respectively six and twenty-seven human skulls, concentrically arranged three feet apart with all the faces turned to the west, some with upper vertebrae still attached but with marks of forcible decapitation; another such nest was found in the Höhlenstein cave near Württemberg in 1937, both male and female showing skull fracture

as from a heavy blow and marks of decapitation on the cervical vertebrae. Breuil and Lantier[44] found the skull cult throughout the entire
Upper Paleolithic.

Blanc concluded that the mutilation of the base of the skull in the
Monte Circeo, Ehringsdorf, and Steinheim skulls showed the practice
of brain-eating both by early and late Neanderthals for about 250,000
years, and pointed out that body-cannibalism is well known from the
Mousterian period (Krapina is the classic European site). Bergounioux,[45] with the concurrence of Carl Sauer, recently suggested that
Neanderthaloid headhunting was for this purpose. As to the possible
range of this originally Neanderthaloid trait, it might be pointed out that
over forty individuals at Choukoutien[46] were represented by their skulls
and skull fragments but by very few limb bones, a circumstance which
Blanc believes strongly points to headhunting in ancient China. Burials
of skulls[47] in Upper Paleolithic and Mesolithic sites in Europe (Arcy-
sur-Curé, Placard, Ofnet, etc.) point to similar practices; Blanc adds
pictorial evidence of ritual slaughter from engravings in the Upper
Paleolithic cave of Addaura (Palermo).[48] The Ertebølle people, from
indications at the Dyrholmen site in East Jutland,[49] after scalping a
decapitated human head, seem also to have eaten the brains.

Headhunting for this purpose survived in late European prehistory into
the Bronze Age, as evidenced in the "Bell Beaker" skull from Wansleben
(Saxony), the base of which Gerhardt proved had been intentionally
mutilated; another similar one is known from the immediately following
"Frühaunjetitser" culture in Saxony.[50] Headhunting survived in Great
Britain until protohistoric times, to judge from evidence both in archeology and in the Cú Chulainn epics.[51] The Gundestrup Cauldron from
Jutland, made in the Celtic Iron Age, pictures human sacrifice in association with a reindeer-antlered Master of Animals. Powell[52] believes
that headhunting among the protohistoric Celts (known from the
Roqueperteuse finds as well as a late first-century Roman arch at Orange
in the Vaucluse) was connected with a fertility cult. A pre-Iron Age
cult of the skull has actually survived in fragments among the Slavs[53]
until the second decade of the present century.

Maringer tends to argue against brain-cannibalism *because* of the
absence of other post-cranial bones that would indicate flesh-eating, although he discusses the skulls of Monte Circeo, Ehringsdorf, Krapina,
Great Ofnet and Höhlenstein. But brain-eating does not depend for
proof on evidences of body-cannibalism, which may or may not occur in
connection with it. In fact, there is voluminous evidence from the later
Paleolithic and Mesolithic into historic times that because of its association

with the brain and its spirit-potency, the upper skull or brain case was afterward used for ritual drinking. Maringer himself notes human skulls converted into drinking cups, from Swiss Lake Dwellings and Neolithic sites in France, as well as Solutrean and Magdalenian finds at Placard that Breuil and Obermaier thought were skull-cups. These are found widely in Europe from the Upper Paleolithic of Castillo (Spain) to Unter-Wisternitz (Moravia) archeologically[54] and, ethnologically, among historic and protohistoric peoples eastward into Tibet.[55]

Herodotus wrote that the "Issedones" (?Tibetans) drank from the gold-mounted skulls of their ancestors, and the thirteenth-century missionary William of Ruysbrook wrote the same of Tibetans; James Rennel saw finely lacquered human skull cups in Bengal. Plutarch wrote that ancient Teutons drank from the skulls of their bravest enemies to imbibe their courage; so too did the Scythians. Even medieval Christians made cups of skulls of slain foes; for example, in 88 A.D. the Bulgarian prince Krum had a cup made of the skull of the Byzantine Emperor Nicephorus II. In 1875, a skull was found at Pompeii, mounted in precious metals and with the inscription in Greek, "Drink and you shall live for many years"[56]—as if longevity could be increased by imbibing life-stuff. In fact, there is much evidence that the *contents* of the "cup," the brain *muellos* or skull "marrow" was the life source and seed itself—a notion traceable from Bronze Age Indoeuropean times[57] at least down to Renaissance Leonardo[58] and Shakespeare.[59]

Beyond the philological evidences, there are indications in vocabulary itself for cup-skull connections in thought. Italian *coppa* is also "cup," but the cognate Provençal *cobs* is "skull." It might also be pointed out that the Greek κεφαλή and Anglo-Saxon *hafala* agree with the Sanskrit *kapāla,* which means both cup and skull; that in the Germanic languages *Kopf* and cup are cognates; that the Scandinavian *skoal* means drinking bowl, like the Scottish *skull,* a bowl or goblet for liquor; and that even the French *tête* from late Latin slang means a pottery bowl. Such consistency in Indoeuropean languages suggests more than poetic metaphor. Apparently the "genius" of a man could be obtained by eating or drinking it.

It seems reasonable to infer from the finds that ancient Europeans, from Neanderthal onward, had some sense of the individual "spirit" too, if indeed not an "afterlife" of this spirit. So we would infer from the intentional burial of humans with their useful or valuable possessions, which would seem unreasonable to throw away in this fashion unless there were some spirit still to possess and use them and to enjoy later, especially since much labor was often expended in making them. At Cro Magnon, for example, several burials contained pierced sea-shell necklaces. At the Grotte des Enfants, an old woman and a young man of Aurignacian period were buried side by side, she with shell bracelets and he with a beaded headdress, and nearby were the skeletons of two children, each with belts containing over a thousand perforated shells of *Nassa neritea,* the bones deeply colored with red ochre. The belief in Europe, Asia and elsewhere in an afterlife scarcely needs documentation, certainly from the Neolithic onward, and it seems possible from the above considerations that the belief goes back at least to the Middle Paleolithic as well.

Again, the use of red ochre in burials from the Old Stone Age onward points also to a belief in, or at least a wish to procure, an afterlife for the person buried. Red ochre seems to have symbolized then, as it did later, blood or warmth magically to endow the corpse with life again. In France, the classic Cro Magnon male skull and femur were colored all over with hematite. The bones of Chancelade Man were colored brick red from a layer of iron peroxide, and the Combe-Capelle skeleton is red also. Flint tools, an engraved reindeer-horn baton, and a red-deer tooth with a hole drilled in it were present with the proto-Magdalenian ochred bones at Les Hoteaux. Above the Neolithic sepulture in Duruthy cave at Sordes, the earth was extremely red. In Germany, the Aurignacian Brünn man was saturated with ochre, as was the Solutrean Klause (Bavaria) skeleton. At Obercassel, near Bonn, were found the red-colored skeletons of a man and a woman accompanied by pieces of engraved animal bones of Magdalenian style; the Giesslingtal (Austria) Aurignacian finds included an ochre burial. The Neolithic burials so plentiful around Worms (Hinkelstein, Rheindurkheim, Alsey, Rheingewann, etc.) still contain ochre. In Italy, the triple burial of Barma Grande at Grimaldi contained a large quantity of iron pigment; and the head of the skeleton found there by Julien had a thick coating like a skullcap. The skeleton at Baousso da Torre was covered with ochre; and the Aurignacian man of the Grotte du Cavillon was thoroughly sprinkled, as indeed was everything buried with him, and in addition a mass of powdered hematite filled a furrow in front of the skull. Around the heads and around the skeleton of the young male of the Grimaldi "Negroids" was much red ochre, but around the skeleton of the old woman no trace; for this among other reasons, the Aurignacian "Red Lady" at Paviland (Wales) has been thought a male skeleton. But in Italy as late as the Sgurgola entombment, the face had had red ochre smeared on it.[60] Bridget Allchin, in fact, connects the practice of ancient Stone Age hunters with the custom of living stone-age hunters in the Old World of burying their dead with red ochre.[61]

Much of the above is carefully pieced together inference. But all of it appears to be confirmed in the recent spectacular find by Otto Bader[62] and Mikhail Gerasimov in 1964 at Sungir, near Vladimir some 130 miles east-northeast of Moscow. Below the permafrost line, are two burials which are probably the earliest yet known, with a radiocarbon date determined in Moscow and Stockholm to be between 33,000 and 40,000 years ago. The first burial is a skull associated with red ochre; the second is of a male about fifty-five, of classic Cro Magnon type around five feet eight inches tall. His grave, a narrow oval basin, was first strewn with unextinguished coals, next a layer of red ochre, after which the corpse, lying on its back with the hands together at the waist, was interred, then heavily covered with red ochre which subsequently stained it. He wore two dozen bracelets made of thin plates of mammoth ivory, and there were many rows of ivory beads sewn on his clothing. He was dressed in tailored trousers and pullover shirt, both of fur, and wore strands of Arctic fox teeth. A flint knife, a massive scraper, and a pierced stone pendant were also in the grave. This man lived when the region was a cold steppe with patches of birch and pine. He and his comrades killed reindeer, bison, moose, horse, hare, Arctic fox, and the hairy mammoth.

The religion of the Stone Age hunting peoples now appears to be the simple animism that is fundamental to all other subsequent religion in the world wherever found—Tylor's classic "belief in spiritual beings." We must be careful, however, not to make inference beyond the concrete evidence, nor to press too far the definition of "spiritual beings." We really have no evidence for Stone Age men's worship of gods. Neither their social nor cosmic horizons press this assumption upon us; nor have we reason to suppose paleolithic hunters early had more complex ideas than any later hunting people has. Besides, god-worship implies a degree of superordination-subordination we have no reason to assume in Stone Age hunting society, since hunting societies everywhere else are notably non-autocratic and open, and the most we find is invidious amounts of luck, mana or skill of much the same kind. All that is archeologically and logically there is the belief in a life-entity, a spirit (anima) or a substance (mana) that is in living bodies and leaves at death. Indeed, far too much has been made of later conceptualizations that tend to dichotomize or differentiate mana and anima, for these are merely percepts characteristic of two clearly related stages of ego growth in all human beings. And they are often quite clearly implicated with one another. A chief has mana because he *is* a chief, and he is a chief because he *has* mana; thus a Polynesian first-born sacred chief has merely inherited, through spiritual primogeniture, the accumulated mana of many great ancestors. So much mana from ancestors makes one great-souled, literally magnanimous. The eldest closest to the father is closest to being the father. But the sacred chief is still only a man.

We see in the caves not gods, but only animals and men. Anima is in both animals and men—the Pindal artist apparently thought it centered in the mammoth's heart, but other hunters thought it resided in the head, at least of men—and whichever man or animal has the greater mana kills the other. (In cave art we often see men killing animals, and only rarely animals killing men; magic, being wish, keeps the proportions appropriate!) This life-entity in animals and men can be magically fomented and controlled by the means evident in cave art: hunting magic and fertility magic, through the magic of art itself on the walls and cave floors. In the ritual burial of persons with their possessions we can discern no more than a belief or hope in the persistence of anima (the simple staying-together of an individuated amount of spirit-stuff); in head-hunting and red ochre, no more than the idea that anima can be nourished with mana, or life fed by energy (as food feeds the body).

To be sure, the belief in gods can very well develop out of such purely humanistic archaic animism—especially when the social conditions of man and man become widely divergent in later non-hunting societies—and in many religions it evidently has, even in some that began frankly with human beings, such as Buddhism. For such a result, all that is needed is the historic persistence of a great or magnanimous spirit (*maha-atma*) in memory to achieve the social magnitude of a distinct or remembered spiritual being; that is, the supposed spiritual part of some one's being becomes a distinct and separate "spiritual being." This is not to argue that every god must once have been a human ghost— as if *real* gods were only large masses of *real* spirit-stuff—but only that some great object in nature (e.g. the moody, idiosyncratic, and arbitrary sky) has *imputed* to it man's psychological consciousness of his own spirit, the same conceptually but magnified. Not all gods were once ghosts; but all religions are made of the stuff of man's "spirit." Since we have no empirical evidence of gods or spirits, the possibility arises that there are none; but this inference imposes the burden of explaining how the non-existent came to be believed in.

With Occam's razor of minimal inference, we now approach the central figure of Old Stone Age religion, the Dancing Sorcerer of Trois Frères and other caves.[63] German anthropologists and others influenced by Pater Schmidt have tried to see the sempiternal High God in this dressed-up dancer. He is actually not even a supernatural Master of Animals, but only the original "master of animals," the dancing shaman himself! He is only a man; but a mana-laden one, because (as a person) he possesses the spirits of animals, or (as a body) he is possessed by them. The same humanity is implied in all other shamanistic claims. All men have a mysterious potency to create life. The shaman merely has more of it, and extending to the animals of whom he dreams. Hunters have power to dominate in the hunt; shamans only claim more of the same mana. And within these narrow horizons, a rain maker is not a cosmic colossus, but only a man with a special magic. The Rainmaker, mighty Zeus himself, once arose from the mere earth, a babe born in the Dictyean cave, and he grew in magnitude only with men's views of the cosmos.

The actual extreme diffusion of certain core traits, Kluckhohn thought, would indicate that "all known cultures derive eventually from a generalized Paleolithic culture."[64] Certainly the evidence for shamanism, both from the caves and in world cultures, lends support to this stand—not to mention other archeological, cultural and linguistic "universals." Actually, with respect to religion, the relation is perhaps even closer culture-historically. The religion of Stone Age hunting peoples seems to be the same simple shamanism still found in subarctic regions—regions similar to and contiguous with late Pleistocene climatic regions in Europe and Asia—as well as the basic shamanism found among recent hunting peoples elsewhere all over the earth. Similarities in European Paleolithic and Asiatic Paleosiberian shamanism, indeed, are present even down to arbitrary details. For example, the Old Stone Age had both bird and reindeer shamans quite like those of recent Paleosiberian tribes described earlier. The reindeer shaman has been known from Trois Frères since 1914, but the bird shaman at Lascaux only since 1940. The reindeer shaman shows an extraordinary continuity in Europe down to protohistoric and modern ethnic times; the bird shaman can be traced from Magdalenian to modern Siberian times.

The celebrated "Dancing Sorcerer" or "Reindeer Shaman" of Trois Frères wears the antlers of a stag, an owl mask, wolf ears, bear paws and a horse-tail, but is otherwise a nude human male dancing, perhaps wearing streaks of body paint. A man masked and dressed like animals plainly has some special relationship to them. Through his ritual identification, he must have some sympathetic magic power over them. If we emphasize mana, these appurtenances represent his "animal familiars" whose power he borrows or possesses by dressing up like them. If we emphasize anima, then the shaman embodies or is "possessed" by the spirits of the animals he controls, changes into or magically is. The difference is only in degree of individuation. In either case, we have a man pretending to possess needed powers, a man who controls the most important aleatic element in his environment, the animals around him. He is the perfect fusion of wish and capability.

The Trois Frères shaman is a generalized or composite "master of animals." There also exist dancers who are "masters" of only one animal species. At Trois Frères too, and in similarly elegant style, there is a dancing man wearing a bison head; his human arms end in bison hooves, and a long tail is tipped with a tuft of hair. That he is human seems insisted on by the more lightly drawn-in picture of a bearded man on the torso, an identity of man in animal and animal in man here *replicated*. He carries a bow, which some see as a hunter's, but others as a shaman's musical bow because of its position close to the mask; others see it as a shaman's drum, but this interpretation is improbable since foreshortening is absent in cave art. Another, somewhat later example from the Gasulla gorge in Spain also plainly insists on the dancer's humanity—a bull-tailed man with a bull mask slightly *above* his head, who carries what is apparently a spear. A staghorn baton from Teyjat has no fewer than three crudely engraved figures wearing chamois heads and pelts, a circumstance that has led some to suggest hunters masked for stalking. Such an interpretation seems unlikely in this case, because two of the figures are vigorously dancing with bent knees, which is no way to stalk chamois. Moreover, the figures show a marked pelvic thrust that suggests the fertility motif, the more plausibly since both the Lascaux bird and the Trois Frères bison shamans, and many others, are ithyphallic, a state not appropriate for hunters, but plausible in shamanic dreams.

Ithyphallic also is the dancing man engraved on a shoulder blade from the Mas d'Azil. Though he is otherwise fully human, his head is so markedly snouted as to suggest an animal head, an interpretation supported by the peripheral body hatching, which in both the reindeer and reindeer-wife and other engravings indicates animal fur. The freakish heads[65] of the Marsoulas hominids are so ugly and monstrous likewise as to seem animal, not human. At Albarracin, La Viega and Las Aguas de Novales, quite ordinary men hunt animals, though at Alpera one man among them carrying a bow and arrows has an animal head (an animal-familiar source of power in the hunt?). But despite their odd heads, the figures at Altamira, Les Combarelles and Cro Magnon are all human and, although stylized, the figures at Velez Blanco and Předmost are manlike too. The dancers at Aurensan, Gourdan, Le Portel and Hornos de la Peña are all plainly human—even though the last, despite human hands, feet and face, wears a tail. What remains of the so-called "Archer" of Laussel—more probably a dancer—is completely human, but the head is critically missing. In any case, in all these, it is not gods but men who dance.

Reinach,[66] joined by Hamy and others, early suggested that these hybrids were totemic ancestors, an opinion given little credence now. The ithyphallic bird-headed man with the bird-tipped staff, discovered later at Lascaux, would perhaps seem to support the thesis of Reinach. But the context here appears to be hunting-, not fertility-magic. For another matter, though mythic animal-human sexuality is well documented in the drawings, Laming points out the darts and wounds on the bodies of the same animal species, which therefore were hunted and killed, hardly supports a totemic hypothesis. Nor is the masked-stalker hypothesis much better, for why should a technologically effective disguise be needed in cave magic? The specifically *ritual* activity of shamanistic figures in drawings, like the humanity of the shamans, is shown in the fact of their *dancing,* an activity confirmed not only in many drawings themselves but also by the footprints, not made by gods, at Montespan and elsewhere. If full-fledged gods like Shiva and Dionysus danced, it is because shamans before them danced, not because dancing is intrinsic to godhood: *dancing is magical.*

Any discussion of the matter should include consideration of effigies as well as drawings, e.g. the curious Pech Merle find of bears' skulls covered with earth to represent what seem to be human torsos, i.e. bear-mana directly infused into humans. Breuil ingeniously suggested that "tectiforms" resemble the overall grass mask-skirts of various Negroid sorcerers, and Laming concurs in this; but this does not explain all tectiform drawings, which seem, rather, to be associated with hunting. On the whole, late drawings serve only to reinforce the interpretation of anthropomorphic hybrids as masked shamans; e.g. the (probably) epipaleolithic silhouette with phallus and long horns from Cueva de los Letreros in Spain, and the Bronze Age rock engraving at Cape Bessov-Noss (Lake Onega, Russia) showing a ?wolf-masked man carrying large ritual objects and closely following an elk doe—both of which heads irresistibly suggest the animal-headed men engraved on slate palettes from early Egypt, there probable forerunners of animal-headed nome-deities or gods.

Upper Paleolithic deer shamanism continues into the immediately following Mesolithic period in western Europe, notably at Star Carr.[67] Star Carr, five miles south of Scarborough in Yorkshire, yielded flints of Maglemosian culture type, from the boreal post-glacial period, with a Carbon$_{14}$ date of 7538±350 years ago. The Maglemosian type site is in

Denmark, but *crannogs* or bog dwellings in Ireland, Scotland and England show that this culture extended westward to a Britain once geologically continuous with Europe (until about 5000 years ago). Amber at Star Carr indicates Baltic contact; also, a multi-barbed Maglemosian harpoon, found in a piece of peat, was fished up from the North Sea 25 miles off the Norfolk coast. Remains of 60 red deer and 66 roe deer show they were mostly deer hunters; but bones representing 18 aurochsen and 10 wild boar show they hunted these animals too, probably with bow and arrows, though apparently they did not hunt the abundant wild horses then in the area (later evidence seems to suggest that in England the horse was a ritual animal, perhaps tabooed for eating). The lake shore site and the barbed harpoons of deer antler suggest winter ice-fishing, and other Maglemosians are known to have had skin boats. Only a tenth as large as typical early Neolithic sites, the settlement was built on a birchwood-mattress platform, roughly 230 square yards in area, on which perhaps four families with three children each had camped in the reed swamps looking southward over a post-glacial lake. Deer antlers, the main material of their tools and weapons, formed the greater part of the animal remains and were concentrated in roughly two fifths of the total site. Star Carr men made fire with flint and iron pyrites, using the dried bracket fungus *Fomes fomentarius* as tinder.

The most remarkable Star Carr finds, however, are the twenty-five deer frontlets, specially worked from parts of the skull bone with antlers still attached. These were scarcely trophies, to be put on stakes, for all were selected from stags mature enough to have well-formed antlers, yet young enough for them to be lighter than the antlers used for ordinary manufactures. Further, they were reduced by a third or quarter of their weight by carefully hollowing and scraping the tines to give the largest profile for the weight; also, the rims and inner surface of the bone had roughnesses and protuberances smoothed away. Straps were evidently laced through the supraorbital foramen in front and holes bored in the parietals at the side, of which both were present in eleven specimens even in their present damaged state. Without doubt, the Star Carr deer frontlets were worn on the head in some fashion.

Their surprising number suggests that they may have been used in stalking deer, as Boas noted the Boothia Peninsula hunters do, in order to attract stags within shooting range. The fierce rutting fights of red deer and the predominance of stags in the remains both suggest this (and curiously, as Laming points out in another connection, all the cervids at Lascaux are stags with magnificent antlers, but no hinds, and all the ibexes are males too—as if the mystery of male fertility and power were the significant point at issue). As an alternative to the use of frontlets in stalk-hunting, the prominence of other deerhorn manufactures at Star Carr allows the possibility that there may have been a factory for shamanistic paraphernalia here too. Further, the antlers on the classic Ariège "sorcerer" are similarly attenuated; and of course Tungusic reindeer shamans still wear antlers in their rituals.

More than a technological use of frontlets with horns in hunting seems implied, for paleolithic batons or shamans' scepters were also made of staghorn and often had animals and even shamans carved on them (e.g. three chamois shamans from the Maglemosian V of L'Abri Mège), and horns are a fertility symbol in later European thought. Clark himself, the excavator of Star Carr, thought the frontlets were worn in some sort of dance ritual to help the hunter's luck and to increase the fertility of deer or natural increase in general.[68] The yearly growth of stag antlers and the obvious connection with the sexual cycle suggest fertility and reproductive potency; the autumnal shedding and spring regrowth further imply seasonal rebirth and immortality in nature.[69] That horns symbolize life force is unmistakable from the heaps of red deer antlers piled on Tardenoisean graves on the islands of Hoëdic and Téviec near Quiberan (Morbihan).[70] Some of the dead in the Téviec rockbuilt tombs wore antler headdresses, and the custom of piling antlers on tombs persisted into the Bronze Age in Britain, e.g. at Three Hills, Mildenhall (Suffolk), where eighteen fine red deer antlers were heaped over a primary burial. That the Three Hills burial was of a woman and burial D at Téviec of a woman and child both strongly suggest the motifs of life force, rebirth and immortality, since women and children are not deer hunters—an interpretation moreover consistent with the widespread use of red ochre in graves and in several cave grottoes. In fact, the fertility motif is still found in the yearly Horn Dance of country folk at Abbots Bromley in Staffordshire, where staghorns are ritually carried in a seasonal ceremony.

In western Europe, the reindeer shaman persisted in the Celtic or La Tène Iron Age, and even later as a god into protohistoric times. In 1891, while digging for peat near Gundestrup in northern Jutland, a farm laborer found the celebrated silver and gold Gundestrup Cauldron, nearly three feet in diameter, and now in the Danish National Museum in Copenhagen. One of the large oblong inner plates displays a seated cross-legged man wearing staghorns, holding in his left hand a snake with a ram's head, an exclusively Celtic motif, and in his right hand a penannular torque of familiar Bronze Age type. He wears belted knee shorts of north Gallic style (Strabo), known also from Neolithic Iberian sites—e.g., the "zaragüelles" at Secans (Mazaleon) and the Cova Remigia (Ares) still worn in rural Levantine Aragón[71]—and a jerkin with arm-length sleeves in northern Eurasiatic style. Flanking the reindeer-horned man are a stag and a wolf who gaze at the god, also a lion, two other felines, and a boy astride a dolphin, the latter suggesting Celtic acquaintance with pre-Roman Etruscan motifs in north Italy. Other decorations on the Cauldron associate the reindeer-man with human sacrifice, thunder and lightning, and war.

The deer-horned figure is undoubtedly the old Celtic god Cernunnus,[72] the Master of Animals and a Pluto-like god of fertility and wealth, and like Dis connected with spirits and the underworld. The reindeer shaman of the deep caves is now a god of the underworld, still controlling fertility, spirits, and wealth. Nor is the Gundestrup Cernunnus unique in Gallic iconography. Three stone sculptures of a seated and cross-legged Cernunnus come from Entremont near Aix-en-Provence, a headless example from Roqueperteuse near Velaux, and another from Russan, all in Provence. The Cernunnus in the Musée de Beaunes is a standing, staghorned, nude male god associated with a bullheaded god in the same sculpture, quite as if the two masked shamans of the Trois Frères cave had not yet been forgotten. The Vendoeuvres Altar, now in the Musée de Chateauroux, bears a cross-legged horned god with a moneybag in his lap, and is flanked by two gods, each standing on a serpent. The "divinité aux serpents" of Sommerécourt, now in the Musée d'Epinal, is a male god with stag's horns, seated with characteristically crossed legs.

Even more startlingly, Cernunnus has been found in two of the greatest religious centers of France. The Reims Cernunnus, now in the museum there, is a stone carving in deep relief of a bearded staghorned man, seated cross-legged, below him a bull and a stag, and above his head a rat symbolic of his connection with the underworld. He wears a penannular button-ended neck torque, and from a bag on his lap he pours coins down between the bull and the stag, an act symbolic at once of wealth and of fertility. This Cernunnus is of Gallo-Roman date, as is shown by the Roman gods chosen to flank him, Apollo the wolf-god and hunter and lord of fertility, and Mercury, serpent-staved and winged, emissary between spirits and men—as a totality a superb symbolic syncretism of shaman-deities.

The site of another find is most striking, in the old section of Paris that has been settled since prehistoric times. In 1711, a four-sided altar was discovered deep under the choir of the cathedral of Notre Dame de Paris. On one side, carved in deep relief, was the now-familiar horned god, with a garland of plenty on each horn—thus evidence of the late worship of Cernunnus by the Celtic Parisii in their very stronghold, the Ile de la Cité itself. This altar is now in the nearby left bank Musée de Cluny, but its original site beneath Notre Dame de Paris is not without symbolic archeological significance, since the Master of Animals was an ancestor, by several routes, of the god worshiped above. (For example, early Christian iconography sometimes shows Christ as an Orpheus-like master of animals too.)

There is also a horned god inscribed CERNVNNOS on the restored "Monument des Hautes" in Paris. Perhaps to be associated with Cernunnus is the headless, seated, cross-legged god with a bag in his lap on the back of the Autel des Saintes; the "Divinité Gauloise" from Nerés (Allier) which has a bag in its lap—and, though less probably, the statue of the "Dieu forestier" bearing a bow from Mont St. Jean (Sarthe), also the two Gallic hunter-gods, one ornamented with torques, in the Musée d'Autun, and two others in the Musée d'Epinal. Copies of those in this last list are in the museum of Saint Germain-en-Laye just outside Paris. Standing forms of Cernunnus also come from Ablainseville (Pas-de-Calais, across the present Channel from Star Carr), from Blain (Loire-Inferieure), and from Val Camonica in northern Italy.

The location of all these finds is surely not accidental. The Roqueperteuse, Velaux and Russan statues of the staghorned Cernunnus came from southern France not far from the reindeer shaman of Trois Frères. The Val Camonica Cernunnus came from Celtic north Italy, a region which also influenced the Gundestrup Cauldron iconography; and the Gundestrup Cauldron itself, though made in northern Gaul, was found in the same Danish marshes as the mesolithic Maglemose finds—and these in turn were culturally related to Maglemosian Star Carr of the deer frontlets, the latter again not far from the several Tardenoisean, Bronze Age and modern ritual use of deerhorns in symbolisms of rebirth and fertility! The shamanic significance of deerhorns cannot now be doubted; and the late Paleolithic and early Mesolithic deer shaman of western Europe turned gradually into the Celtic Cernunnus. In this well-documented sequence, the man-god became in time an authentic "god."

In their preoccupation with the impressive big-game animals that served as food, prehistorians have perhaps neglected the considerable paleolithic finds pertaining to birds.[73] These are by no means negligible. In mural art there are the Aurignacian snow owls and their young at Trois Frères and the two-legged wading bird at Gargas; the wild goose of La Bastide, the penguins and ?vulture of El Pendo in Cantabria, the goose and crane of the Minateda frescos, the bird panels of Monte Arabi in Murcia, and the stylized birds of El Tajo de las Figuras in

Cadiz; while the Romanelli cave (Otranto) has many engravings of birds and one of a horse. In portable art there are birds on objects from Arudy (Grotte d'Espélungues), Bruniquel, Fontarnaud, Gourdan, Isturitz, L'Espelunge (Lourdes), Mas d'Azil, Raymonden, Soucy, and Teyjat. Because of the persistent sober practicality of Old Stone Age art, we are forced to take all of these seriously, certainly not as exercises in abstract design or lessons in early ornithology, and not so much perhaps as game birds but as potential sources of magic power. The owl, for example, has a nearly world-wide connection with spirits of the dead. And vultures eat the dead, but are not themselves very edible. The materials on which the birds are carved, deerhorn and ivory, may have some magic significance too.

The little crane from Monastruc has already been described. Fontarnaud, interestingly, yielded heads of deer and birds engraved on the same bone. The Magdalenian dart-thrower of reindeer horn from the Mas d'Azil is a ptarmigan or grouse cock, the tail of which is the nock-point, both birds of impressively projectile flight. Teyjat has a shaman's baton of reindeer horn engraved with swans. The carving of birds on reindeer antler is matched by the carving of reindeer on bird bone, for instance the herd of reindeer on the wingbone of an eagle, of upper Magdalenian date, from La Mairie (Dordogne); Teyjat has a contemporaneous carving of horses on a bird bone also. The Dharvent collection has a paleolithic carved stone bird head; and the base of a staghorn from Andernach in Germany is carved into a bird. An ivory bird comes from the upper Aurignacian or Magdalenian of Mezine in Russia; and in Siberia there are numerous Solutrean-Magdalenian figurines of birds in mammoth ivory. The persistent reciprocal association can hardly be accidental.

The suggestion that birds may be connected with shamanistic power no longer remains mere inference since the discovery of the "Bird Shaman" of Lascaux,[74] in the well to the right of the Chamber of Engravings before the Nave. This shows a backward-falling man at the horns of a charging, disemboweled bison; he has a bird head, and near him is a staff topped with another bird. This remarkable scene has been subjected to a number of interpretations. Pericot,[75] following Reinach, thinks the figure indicates totemism. But a man may belong to a bird totem without having a bird head and carrying a bird staff into the hunt. Danthine[76] considered it a totemistic initiation scene, showing the ritual "death" of the candidate. But one is *born* to totem membership and need be ritually *initiated* into a fictitious "blood brotherhood" only when in fact blood kinship does not exist; furthermore, why should the patron deity at whose action the bird-man "dies" be a bison and not a bird? Maringer[77] considers it the representation of a death-memorial (*Totenge-dächtnisbild*), for which reason the falling shaman is sometimes called "The Dead Man." None of these interpretations is really acceptable.

Eliade[78] points out that the motif of a bird perched on a post is found on the tombs of Yakut shamans. However, a *dead* shaman need not be implied, for the Hungarian shaman or *táltos*[79] had a post before his hut on which perched a bird, an emissary he sent wherever he would have it go—recalling Odin's raven and the bird familiars of other gods. Nor are deep caves usual burial places for dead shamans or others. Furthermore, the Bird Shaman is represented as falling, not lying horizontally on the ground, and whatever it means the bison is certainly part of the action; besides, the fact that the shaman is ithyphallic does not suggest death but rather fertility—a motif far more in context with cave art than death is. Pfeiffer[80] relates a frankly "science fiction" story told him by Bordes: a bird-totem hunter was killed by a bison, and a man of the rhinoceros totem painted this picture of revenge, disembowelment by a rhinoceros. This is ingenious, but farfetched. Allowing for errors in the retelling, one might still point out that too many events successive in time are pictured simultaneously, the "dead man" is not dead, we have no indication of "totemism" or of the artist's being of the rhinoceros totem and, further, the rhinoceros to the left of the scene appears to be quite unassociated with it, in position, art-style, or logic.

Hugo Kirschner[81] thinks the scene of the falling bird-man represents a shamanistic trance, with the shaman collapsing in ecstasy. The ithyphallic state is not inconsistent with epileptic "trance" nor with visionary dream, shamanic or other; yet it allies him rather with the dancing bison shaman of Trois Frères, and similar others, in a context not of death but of shamanistic influence over animal fertility. A dream animal as incubus or succubus is in fact a sexual phenomenon, but totemism in essence forbids sexuality within the totemic group. Furthermore, if he is a bird shaman as his mask and staff indicate, why does he collapse at the instance of a bison as a "power" animal? And why should he kill his power source, indicated by the weapons on the ground, and why should the shamanic power source be disemboweled and dying too? Totemic interpretations do not logically fit. The larger context of such figures, most of them similarly masked and ithyphallic and dancing, well enough implies shamanism, but not totemism. Logically, too, the individual animal familiar or guardian spirit precedes in time the totemic clan ancestor; and totemism is a sophisticated system of social organization, evidence for which is lacking among these Stone Age men, whereas we do have plentiful evidence of shamanistic animal-man relations.

To avoid improvising paleo-ethnography, the "native" context must be carefully scrutinized and assiduously used to criticize each theory offered. By this criterion we have got no farther than the reassurance that the bird man is a shaman. But there is one more striking circumstance to be noted: at the Roc de Sers there is another similar scene of a musk ox charging a man with a stick over his shoulder and associated with a bird. This fact suggests that bird shamanism may be commoner than we have suspected, for it is reasonable to expect more reindeer- and other animal-shamans underground than bird-shamans, whose realm is the sky; and all that this juxtaposition need imply is that the artists were culturally familiar with both kinds of shamans. That there are *two* somewhat similar pictures of animals charging a bird shaman suggests still another alternative explanation: the existence of a diffused myth of a shaman's death before a charging animal, which is all both pictures seem to tell us, a bison in one variant of the story, a musk ox in the other. If so, we would then have the motif of a shamanistic "trickster" who bites off more than he can chew and comes to grief (bird "power" has no power over a charging bison or musk ox), a story perhaps of "shamanistic rivalry" illustrating the inappropriateness and powerlessness of an Orphic bird shaman in the underground world of the reindeer shaman—a tendentious story to be sure, but in that very fact not inappropriately pictured in the realm of the reindeer shaman. This reasoned conjecture is consistent at all points, unlike some others, but is of course consistent only with a shamanistic interpretation. The falling bird-man is being killed by an animal he tried to kill, perhaps magically; or he is a bird-man in shamanistic rivalry with the animal.

Thus, however variously interpreted, the majority of students would agree that the bird-headed man with the bird staff is a bird shaman, perhaps like the bird-headed men at the Roc de Sers[82] cognate with the bison-masked shamans, the chamois shamans, the dancing shaman of Trois Frères, etc. Not only ancient context but also contemporary ethnology support this view. According to the recent Levin-Potapov anthology on Siberia, the Altai and Kachin shaman's garb symbolizes a bird, and birds are associated with shamanic spirit travels. The Ngansan shaman's accouterments especially included bird and animal skins. The Sel'kup raised tame nutcrackers and cuckoos, the latter especially being considered a sacred shamanistic bird, often pictured on the shaman's costume.[83] Eliade[84] even states that the shaman's costume constitutes in itself a "hierophany," providing the shaman with a new magic animal or bird body, as well as symbolizing a religious cosmography, thus revealing not only a sacred presence but also symbols of the cosmos and metapsychic itineraries. Wensinck, it is true, finds the bird, like the tree, a widespread cosmological symbol in western Asia, but these are obviously aspects of a later and more developed shamanism, though they develop logically enough from bird shamanism.[85]

That animals and birds are the most conspicuous categories of "animated" objects in his environment, and moreover warm-blooded like himself, would seem to make the two kinds of animate power source well-nigh inevitable to man. But we have much evidence that the dichotomy was in fact the case. That the distinction of the bird shaman from other shamans must be extremely ancient is shown in the fact that, of several categories of Kurnai medicinemen, the *bira-ark* (bard, singer, and seer) alone can ascend upward with his spirits, can undergo trance, and is the "real shaman" according to Stiglmayr.[86] And if one but give thought to it the realization emerges that in America feathers are invariably and specifically associated with power, whether in the shaman's medicine paraphernalia or in the brave's war bonnet. The association of shamanism and bird feathers with spirit power in South America (Lowie citing Nimuendajú)[87] is "well illustrated at *Palicur* festivals, where each decorative feather on a dancer's headgear is the seat of a supernatural guardian, and the feathered staffs bounding the ceremonial square warn the protectors against the advent of demons, who bump against the cord connecting the posts. Moreover, the pole erected as a path to heaven is topped with a dance rattle bearing two of the spirit feathers guarded by half a dozen feathered staffs at its foot." The association of birds and spirits also seems indicated in the fact that Toba and Mbaya men wishing to produce abundant sperm drink broths made of various birds.[88] But of course the "soul-bird" is an ancient intercontinental belief also.[89]

The association of birds with shamanistic powers is well documented for Europe. For example, Étaín, the Celtic Aphrodite, changes into a raven or crow to induce panic and weakness among contending warriors in the Cu Chulainn legends[90]; and the Irish had bird-headed shamanistic figures.[91] In Denmark a late Bronze Age urn burial (of a shaman?) contained four pairs of bird wings, three of jackdaws and one of a rook or crow; a popular present-day Danish funeral hymn still associates bird wings with the dead spirit.[92] Shaman-bird connections persist in the form of familiars or "attributes" of deities even into classic times. The Greek Aphrodite, like her Near-Eastern cognate goddesses, had the peaceful dove as her familiar; her sometime consort, the war god Mars, had his own bird, the woodpecker. Zeus the eagle was a swan to Leda (but of course a bull to Europa and many other creatures to other loves). Athena's wizard owl was oracular, and Aphrodite's dove gave omens; geese foretold an attack on early Rome. Greeks and Romans alike practiced divination through observing the flight of birds—and why not since birds were the spirit familiars of shamans! Recently, in the Comitium area of the Forum, were found the bones of a vulture—sacred to Mars and preferred above all for taking omens—sacrificed in the sixth–seventh century B.C.[93]; Romulus himself founded Rome when he saw the flight of twelve vultures.

It is tempting to see in the underground reindeer shaman and in the bird shamans that range the air the beginnings of the "departmental" nature-deities of later classic religion, Olympian Zeus and chthonic Dis. For not even the Greek gods were quite pure anthropomorphic deities of nature-realms, but carried with them the old shamanistic attributes of animal and bird. Animal-headed men *became* the gods in Egypt; animals and birds became the "attributes" of Greek manlike gods; and in India animals and birds became the *vahanas* or "vehicles" of the Hindu gods, Saraswati's peacock, Durga's lion or tiger, Vishnu's *garuda*-bird, elephant-headed Ganesha's rat, and the like.

If the reindeer shaman of the underworld controls the fertility of animals, magic success in the hunt and by derivation wealth and plenty, it is the bird-shaman who is associated with the weather and the spirits of the sky. There is another feature inextricably entwined with shamanism, viz. music and magic songs. For to become like animals and birds, one must not only dress in their skins and masks but also imitate their behaviors. In addition to birds' mastery of the air, which shamans achieve in trance and in their flying dreams, the major attribute of birds is their song. Nadel[94] advanced a theory that men used singing because they wanted a special language other than ordinary speech, in which to address their gods. More simply than that, bird shamans borrowed song from their sources of power.

Yakut shamans, for example, are remarkable for their imitation of birdcalls that come in the shaman's reverberant conical tent sometimes from above and sometimes from below, sometimes in front of and sometimes behind the shaman. Shierozewski reported remarkable imitations of calls of the lapwing, falcon, woodcock, eagle, and especially the cuckoo, the shamans' special bird familiar. Castagne wrote that the *bacqa* of the Kirghiz imitate the songs of birds with great fidelity, and the various sounds of their wings. And Lehtisalo noted that many words in the shaman's séance, especially meaningless vocables, originated in the cries of birds or animals; and the shaman's falsetto indicates that not he but a supernatural spirit voice or bird speaks through him. Indeed, the Germanic term for magic formula, *galdr,* is related to the verb *galan,* "to sing," applied more especially to bird song[95]—which is reasonable enough whether one is speaking in this way to a bird familiar, or the supernatural were speaking thus through the shaman's mouth.

Eliade[96] thinks that many epic subjects, motifs, and clichés in the *Odyssey,* the Finnish epic *Kalevala,* etc., are of ecstatic origin, that is, they are borrowed from the narratives of shamans telling about their journeys and adventures in the spirit world. Certainly the *Kalevala* is full of shamans and spells, and the Finns are traditionally notorious as wizards. And Odysseus in his journeys more than once encountered sorcery, even that capable of metamorphosing men into animals, and siren songs with magic compulsion in them (indeed, in Greek iconography, sirens and harpies were women-bird monsters, like Scylla). Even a modern bard must invoke his Muse, be inspired by his dream love, or consult his "genius." But then the bard is only another facet of the old shaman, who enlightens, solaces, and entertains with his story-songs. Orpheus and Homer and Euripides are in origin one.

It is also significant that all early musical instruments—drum, musical bow, rasp, rattle or harp—were originally shaman's magic paraphernalia specifically and still are among primitive Siberian and American Indian tribes.[97] In fact, Indian music in some cases is hard to collect, because singers refuse to perform songs outside their appropriate magic context. We are familiar enough with the inveterate association of music and religious ritual in Europe, but it is interesting that as late as Sumer, music still was never used for anything except religious purposes. Also, music remained closely related to cosmic magic in early China and India, and even in Pythagorean Greece. Every magic "enchantment" means to *incantare,* and every charm is a *carmina.*

Shamans anciently were rain kings, magic protectors, chiefs, artisans and ambassadors, and they are the forebears both of priests and of modern men of medicine. But shamans, the men who dream beyond the workaday world, are also culture heroes of all the European arts—the magic artists of the caves, the shamans behind the dance-drama of the goat-god that grew into Greek tragedy and comedy, the juggler-magicians of secular entertainment, the historian-bards and Homers of epic poetry, the Orpheus-shamans of questing Argonauts—and indeed shamans are the very ancestors of the gods. But the harp-singing shaman Apollo—lord of animals, hunt-master, oracle and fertility daemon of the oxen of the sun—was leader of the Muses above all because of his secret magic, music.

NOTES

(XIII The Dancing Sorcerer)

1. Drachenhöhle held the bones of 30,000–50,000 cave bears, killed over 10,000 years; Drachenloch is the richest in ritual finds; Petershöhle (Franconia) contains "tremendous collections of cave-bear bones, and skulls tucked away in almost ever niche" (Maringer, *op. cit.*, p. 31). Zotz found still another, Hellmichhöhle (Silesia), in 1936. W. Koppers first connected ethnographic (Gilyak, Ainu) with prehistoric cults in "Der Bärenkult in ethnologischer und prähistorischer Beleuchtung," *Paleobiologica*, (1933) 47–64, following old accounts in P. F. von Siebold (1835) and L. von Schrenck (1881); cf. K. J. Narr, "Bärenzeremoniell und Schamanismus in der Älteren Steinzeit Europas," *Saeculum*, 10 (1959) 233–72; Hans Findeisen, "Zur Geschichte der Bärenzeremonie," *Archiv für Religionswissenschaft*, 37 (1941) 196–200; L. F. Zotz, "Altsteinzeitlicher Bärenkult in den Sudeten," *Altschlesische Blätter*, 1937, pp. 4–7; and Eliade, *Recent Works*, pp. 183–84. C. C. Clemens, Bolke von Richthofen, Leonard Franz, Georg Kraft and others concur in connecting paleolithic finds with modern bear ceremonialism (Maringer, *op. cit.*, pp. 26–42). Cf. reference footnote 35 to Chapter IV, p. 158.

2. H. Breuil and H. Obermaier, *The Cave of Altamira* (Madrid: Hispanic Society of America, 1935); F. Windels, *The Lascaux Cave Paintings* (London: Faber & Faber, 1949); and P. Graziosi, *Palaeolithic Art* (New York: McGraw-Hill, 1960).

3. Photograph of living specimens, G. G. MacCurdy, *Human Origins* (New York: Johnson Reprint Corporation, 2 vols., 1965, Fig. 87, I:175). The wild horses of Strabo survived in Europe until the fifteenth century; all modern horses are *Equus caballus*, a cult of which is known in prehistoric England and northern Europe in the Neolithic and Bronze Ages, coming with Indoeuropeans into Greece with the horse-god Poseidon. This "Thunderer" or earthquake god was originally an inland one.

4. F. E. Zeuner, *A History of Domesticated Animals* (London: Hutchinson, 1963, pp. 215–36); and Wolf Herre, "The Science and History of Domestic Animals," in D. Brothwell and E. Higgs (eds.), *Science in Archaeology* (New York: Basic Books, 1963, 235–49, pp. 241–48).

5. The "Great Drinking Horn," mounted in gold and silver, British Museum.

6. Ginsberg, *op. cit.*, pp. 16, 543.

7. G. Julius Caesar, *op. cit.*, Bk. VI, xviii, p. 125.

8. A painting from life of an aurochs bull was found in an Augsburg antique shop in 1827 (Annette Laming, *Lascaux, Paintings and Engravings*, Baltimore: Penguin Books, 1959, facing p. 105; see also pp. 133–37).

9. Zeuner, *op. cit.*, pp. 258–64. The boar was sacred to the Iron Age Celts, among others, and was the emblem of the famous XXth Roman legion; its iconography and cult presence is much neglected for prehistoric times, but see F. C. Sillar and R. M. Meyler, *The Symbolic Pig* (Edinburgh and London: Oliver and Boyd, 1961 for historic times. On Semitic boar totemism, Michael H. Day, *Guide to Fossil Man* (New York: World, 1965).

10. Prehistoric drawings pictured in S. Reinach, *Répertoire de l'Art Quaternaire* (Paris: Leroux, 1913, pp. 27, 54, 58, 70, 71, 72, 81, 100, 164, 165, and 174); M..cCurdy, *op. cit.*, I:193, 218, 219, 224 and 231; Laming, *op. cit.*, pp. 36, 37; T. G. E. Powell, *Prehistoric Art* (New York: Praeger paperback, 1966, Figs. 16, 18, 19); and John E. Pfeiffer, *The Search for Early Man* (New York: Harper &

Row, 1963, pp. 96–97). In Siberia the mammoth became extinct only in protohistoric times; several specimens have been found in the eighteenth and nineteenth centuries frozen in the permafrost, and mammoth ivory is still an occasional article of trade in inner Asia.

11. S. Reinach, "L'art et la magie," in his *Cultes, mythes et religions* (Paris: Leroux, 5 vols., 2nd ed., 1908–12, I:97, 126ff, earlier an article in *L'Anthropologie* in 1903, pp. 125–36). In 1933, Frederica De Laguna found Kodiak shamans still making pictures before the hunt for good luck—as Kühn notes many circumboreal peoples still do, especially the Lapps, to this day (Maringer, *op cit.*, p. 137). Cf. G. Hallstrom who in 1910 saw Lapps make offerings to a prehistoric rock picture on the Kola Peninsula (Maringer, *op. cit.*, p. 138)—a nice example of the transition from magic to religion.

12. M. Boule persists in the discredited German theory of *ars gratia artis* (*Fossil Man*, New York: Dryden Press, 1957, p. 271 n. 5); cf. G.-H. Luquet, *The Art and Religion of Fossil Man* (New Haven: Yale University Press, 1930, p. 97).

13. H. Breuil, *Four Hundred Centuries of Cave Art* (Montignac: Centre d'Etudes et de Documentation Préhistoriques, 1952, pp. 38, 256, and 363 on hand prints; pp. 81–82 on ochred caves). Serpentine lines drawn in soft clay by human fingers have been thought to be still earlier than hand prints; the recently discovered "Dome of Serpents" at Rouffignac is an especially fine example with hundreds of intertwining lines scored in the soft clay surface of the ceiling sometimes in three or four parallel groups as if by the fingers of one hand.

14. André Leroi-Gourhan, *Préhistoire*, emphasizes the specifically sexual in "magic creation." P. J. Ucko and A. Rosenfeld, *Paleolithic Cave Art* (New York: McGraw-Hill, 1967) is largely a rejoinder to Leroi-Gourhan. It seems to me that Leroi-Gourhan has somewhat the better of the argument. That there should be sexual motifs in the anxious visionary dream now seems enforced upon us by new knowledge of the REM state; and that oedipal superego anxiety should be mixed with secular ego-anxiety in the dream is equally to be expected (the "faceless woman of the nightmare," full "totemic" displacement onto the shamanic animal consort, spirit wife, succubus *familiar*). When prehistoric artists *themselves* painted and carved the evidence (animal consorts, fertility motifs, phalloi, "Venuses") it is hard to shirk plain insights, though easy to understand why authoritative denial might be welcome to many people. What motive lies in denying erotic dreams to early man can only be surmised, unless it be a defense against insight into themselves in contemporary men. What *would* be surprising would be that, given a human familial-social predicament in social groups, primitive early man were somehow uniquely "pre-sexual" in his dreams.

15. MacCurdy, *op. cit.*, I:208–9, Fig. 142, p. 243; Luquet, *op. cit.*, p. 145; Laming, *op. cit.*, pp. 28–29, 62, 66, 78, 188; Pfeiffer, *op. cit.*, p. 90; and Powell, *Prehistoric Art*, Fig. 31, p. 47.

16. God as an artist, *deus artifex*, and the artist as god-man, *deus pictor*, were ancient metaphors still current in the Middle Ages (K. R. Eissler, "Psychoanalytic Notes," in Morris Philipson [ed.], *Leonardo da Vinci, Aspects of the Renaissance Genius*, New York: George Braziller, 1966, pp. 284–339, page 318); cf. E. Kris, *Psychoanalytic Explorations in Art*, pp. 79, 150. On the God complex of the artist, the art critic, and the id, see Daniel E. Schneider, *The Psychoanalyst and the Artist* (New York: Mentor Books, 1962, pp. 55–56).

17. Figure 156, I:257 in MacCurdy is a convenient map of the Dordogne caves around Les Eyzies; for sites in western Europe, map on pp. 258–59, with keys pp. 259–61, in Powell, *Prehistoric Art*; see also Figs. 3 and 4 in G. Rachael Levy, *Religious Conceptions of the Stone Age* (New York: Harper Torchbooks, 1963, pp. 11–12=*The Gate of Horn*, London: Faber & Faber, 1948); and Maringer, *op. cit.*,

pp. 204–5. Reinach's *Répertoire* is still valuable for its systematic line drawings of important pictures cave by cave; more up-to-date, but still incomplete, the best "Repertory of Paleolithic Art" is MacCurdy's (II:419–57) arranged by country and alphabetically cave by cave. Breuil's *Four Hundred Centuries of Cave Art*, lavishly illustrated, indifferently written, amateurishly translated sometimes into a kind of pidgin English, is quite unworthy of the greatest authority on cave art; it should have been, but is not, the classic source. Herbert Kühn counted 71 decorated caves in France (mostly in Dordogne, Ariège and Lot) and 34 in Spain (especially in the north), plus 29 painted rock shelters in the Spanish Levant (Maringer, *op. cit.*, p. 82). Photographs of general views of caves: MacCurdy, *op. cit.*, Les Eyzies (Fig. 4, I:21), Castillo (Fig. 5, I:22), Drachenberg (Fig. 18, I:78), Pindal (Fig. 182, I:289), Tuc d'Audoubert (Figs. 145, 146, I:246–47), Font de Gaume (Figs. 153–54, I:254–55, and Fig. 171, I:272), Laugerie Basse (Fig. 155, I:256), Hornos de la Pena (Fig. 174, I:275), and Mas d'Azil (Fig. 255, II:4). Maringer, *op. cit.*, shows photographs of the Maz d'Azil (Pl. I), Pech Merle (Pl. 2), Lascaux (Pl. 11), and a plan of Niaux (Fig. 15, p. 74). Pfeiffer, *op. cit.*, shows Les Eyzies (pp. 27, 87), La Mouthe and Laugerie Basse (p. 57), Le Moustier (p. 63), L'Abri Pataud (pp. 114, 120–21), and Mas d'Azil (pp. 136–37); and Laming, *op. cit.*, the (now closed) entrance to Lascaux (p. 45) and a view of the "Main Gallery" (p. 21).

18. Levy, *op. cit.*, pp. 11–12; Laming, *op. cit.*, pp. 157–58; Maringer, *op. cit.*, pp. 75–77, 85–87, and 93; and Pfeiffer, *op. cit.*, pp. 93, 108.

19. On ithyphallic figures and phalloi, see the *op. cit.* of MacCurdy (I:265–67), Breuil (pp. 355, 386), Maringer (p. 99), and Reinach, *Répertoire* (pp. 5, 7, 31, 56, 57, 82, 83, 99, and 171). See also Graziosi, Pl. 96 and p. 250. On representations of the vulva, Breuil (pp. 257, 279, 307, 319, 334, and 391), and Maringer (p. 228).

20. The "Old Religion" of the phallic Cogul Dance seems to have survived in early Dionysian rites and satyr plays, legends of the promiscuous Zeus, Apollo and his Muses, Orpheus pursued by maidens, etc. The late-paleolithic fertility religion was not only old but widespread. The neolithic Mohenjodaran bull god is cognate with the South Indian Krishna-consort of the cow-maidens, the Vaishnavite communicants of the Lover, and ancestral to the bull-attended phallic Shiva and later Shaivite Tantric erotic cults—all sacred fertility-dramas of animal-deities in origin. Ancient Chinese religion was not only shamanic, but had animal-human ritual coitus (Krebs, *op. cit.*). Spirit-human sexuality so prominent among Paleosiberians survived until recently in Japan, where coitus between an apprentice shamaness and her spirit-familiar (impersonated by a priest of the shrine) was part of the initiation (Matthias Eder, *op. cit.*, p. 374)—and similar "temple prostitution" was also known not only in historic India but also in early Asia Minor. *The common theme throughout from the paleolithic onward is god-shaman-animal coitus with humans.* Dr. Margaret Murray considers that *The God of the Witches* (Garden City: Doubleday Anchor Books, 1960) is direct folk-tradition from the shamanic "horned god" to the Devil of surviving English witch "covens."

21. On animal-human sexuality, see the characteristic Old Stone Age "drawing at Les Combarelles [that] represents animal courtship and must have been used in fertility rites: a man disguised as an animal, and with a prominent phallus, bends over and pursues a woman also in animal disguise" (Maringer, *op. cit.*, p. 104). Cf. the pregnant woman lying beneath a reindeer from Laugerie Basse (Reinach, *Répertoire*, p. 98); and cf. this "Reindeer Wife" with the modern Mountain Lapp "Mistress of the Reindeer" who looks like a woman except that she is covered with hair, and who sends the reindeer to be killed by the hunters (G. Róheim, *Hungarian and Vogul Mythology*. p. 15). Compare also the "Bear Mother" of Northwest Coast legend, etc.

22. Herbert Wendt, *The Sex Life of the Animals* (New York: Simon & Schuster, 1965, p. 40).

23. Maringer, *op. cit.*, p. 100.

24. Wendt, *op. cit.*, p. 41.

25. Luis Pericot, "The Social Life of Spanish Paleolithic Hunters as shown by Levantine Art," in S. L. Washburn (ed.), *Social Life of Early Man* (Chicago: Aldine Publishing Co., 1961, pp. 194–213, page 209=Viking Fund Publications in Anthropology, 31).

26. Henri Lhote, "Faits concernant la chronologie relative et absolue des gravures et peintures pariétales du sud oranais et du Sahara," in L. Pericot Garcia and E. R. Perello (eds.), *Prehistoric Art of the Western Mediterranean* (Chicago: Aldine Publishing Co., 1964, 191–214, p. 213=VFPA, 39); see also P. Bosch-Gimpera, "The Chronology of the Rock-Paintings of the Spanish Levant," in Garcia and Perello, *loc. cit.*, pp. 125–29, esp. p. 128, Fig. 3; and F. Mori, "Some Aspects of the Rock Art of the Acacus (Fezzan Sahara) and data regarding it," in Garcia and Perello, *loc. cit.*, pp. 225–31.

27. Maringer, *op. cit.*, Pl. 51, between pp. 158–59.

28. Ole Klindt-Jensen, *Denmark Before the Vikings* (London: Thames and Hudson, 1957, p. 80; cf. p. 90).

29. Maringer, *op. cit.*, p. 135.

30. E.g. the enormous white marble phallus encircled with garlands from a site near the ancient baths at Aix in Provence, and the colossal phallus from the site of a Roman town, Le Chatillet (Champagne); the cult flourished especially at Nemausus (modern Nîmes) where many "fanciful or even playful" phallisms are almost obsessively and in multiple ways associated with *birds* (R. P. Knight and T. Wright, *Sexual Symbolism, A History of Phallic Worship*, New York: Julian Press, 1957, p. 10). See also R. A. S. Macalister, *Ancient Ireland* (London: Methuen, 1935, pp. 112–14), and *A Text-book of European Archaeology* (Cambridge: At the University Press, 1921), p. 474 for prehistoric examples from Brassempouy, Laugerie Basse, and Grotte du Placard; H. M. Westropp, *Ancient Symbol Worship* (New York: J. W. Bouton, 1875); J. G. Bourke, *Scatalogic Rites of All Nations* (Washington: Lowdermilk, 1891, pp. 431–33); G. R. Scott, *Phallic Worship* (Westport [Conn.]: Association Booksellers, 1958); and G. B. Stettin, "Uber den Ursprung des Phalloskultus und seinen weiteren Ausbau," *Baessler-Archiv*, 14 (1930–31) 149ff.

31. The Venuses of Brassempouy, Lespugue, Willendorf, and Laussel are often pictured; less commonly reproduced are those from Grimaldi and Barma Grande (MacCurdy, *op. cit.*, I:259–62); Vibraye from Laugerie Basse, the Lalanne and Berlin specimens from Laussel, and Le Portel (Reinach, *Répertoire*, pp. 99, 120, 172); the Gagarino Venuses, the Lalanne engraving from Laussel now in Bordeaux, and Woolley's figurine from northern Syria (Levy, *op. cit.*, Plates 6d, 6e, 7c–d, 8a–b); the three Mentone Venuses, Sireuil, the new La Madeleine mural Venus, the schematic female figurines from Mezine (Ukraine), and the Neolithic Znojmo (Czechoslovakia) and Saint-Sernin in Aveyron (Maringer, *op. cit.*, Figs. 29–32, 35, 55–56). Pfeiffer shows the Sireuil Venus in profile in color, and the elegant little one from L'Abri Pataud (*op. cit.*, pp. 118, 135); and Powell, the Dolní Věstonice (Moravia) pottery Venus, Savignano, Ostrava-Petřkovice, and late examples from Cucuteni, Karanovo and Střelice, the Neolithic chalk figure from Grimes Graves (Norfolk), and late figurines from Senorbi, Sardinia, and the cycladic Amorgos Island (*Prehistoric Art*, Figs. 1, 4, 7, 87–88, 91 and 97–100).

32. MacCurdy, *op. cit.*, I:260, description under Fig. 161.

33. Max Kohen, "The Venus of Willendorf," *American Imago*, 3–4 (1946) 49–60. Powell (*Prehistoric Art*, p. 16) finds the Venuses faceless since "where but downward does a mother look when nursing her child?"—but not a single paleo-

lithic Venus figurine, engraving or painting is shown holding a child, much less nursing it. The real emphasis, in fact exaggerated, is on fecundity features; indeed, one of the Laussel reliefs (Levy, *op. cit.,* Pl. 7d) and perhaps the Syrian Venus (Pl. 8a) appear to be *giving birth.* Furthermore, the Magdalenian *line engraving* of the "Venus of Couze" is also arbitrarily footless and headless (D. de Sonneville-Bordes, "Upper Paleolithic Cultures in Western Europe," in J. R. Caldwell, *op. cit.,* 127–48, p. 148). Powell (p. 17) argues further that facelessness is a matter of scale—but the Willendorf Venus has carefully delineated rows of curls, other Venuses have similar small-scale details, and scale is ignored in many cases on matters of interest (e.g. the Chancelade "bison hunt"). I see no slightest suggestion of any self-conscious "aesthetic" preoccupation in the (here if ever) intensely practical orientation of paleolithic art, beautiful though much of it is. The elongated pyramidal and volute heads are extravagant *avoidance* of facial features, I believe for quite unconscious reasons, as Kohen would submit. Further, penile erection in REM sleep (with detumnescence as non-REM sleep ensues) should be recalled: the shaman's succubus-dream of the animal-wife is a "totemic" *displacement,* for oedipal reasons.

34. Maringer, *op. cit.,* pp. 91–94, 97, and Figs. 14, 16, 17, 19, as well as Plates 23–25, make hunting magic quite unmistakable; cf. Breuil, *op. cit.,* pp. 24, 236–38; MacCurdy, *op. cit.,* II:437, etc. See also, besides the many animals with weapons drawn on them, the trapped mammoth in the "tectiform" (Fig. 23, p. 97, in Maringer) there interpreted as a pitfall.

35. *Opera cit.* of Breuil (p. 310), Pericot (p. 196), and Laming (p. 23).

36. On the spider, see Pericot, *op. cit.,* p. 203; R. B. Onians shows that the Indo-Europeans were much preoccupied with the metaphor of the entangling net and hunting noose (*The Origins of European Thought,* Cambridge: At the University Press, 1954, pp. 332–35, 362–440, *et passim*). Tectiforms as masks, Breuil, *op. cit.,* 146–47; cf. Laming, *op. cit.,* p. 84; see also Maringer, *op. cit.,* p. 106.

37. Pictured in MacCurdy, *op. cit.,* I:238; Maringer, *op. cit.,* Fig. 11, p. 64; Reinach, *Répertoire,* p. 54, etc.

38. MacCurdy (*op. cit.,* I:272–85) has convenient lists by country and by cave of the representations in paleolithic art of mammals, birds, fish, invertebrates, and plants.

39. Laming, *op. cit.,* pp. 62n and 188; "twisted perspective" is Breuil's discovery, well-discussed in Laming, pp. 44, 46, 62n and 78.

40. Human depictions: MacCurdy, *op. cit.,* I:265–67; Reinach, *Répertoire,* pp. 1–8, 24–26, 28–29, 54, 56–57, 62, 68–69, 81–83, 98, 100, 120–21, 145, 147, 168, 171–73, 181, 187 and 189. On their crudeness, Laming, *op. cit.,* p. 25.

41. Alberto C. Blanc, "Some Evidences for the Ideologies of Early Man," in S. L. Washburn, *Social Life of Early Man,* pp. 123–32.

42. F. Wiegers, F. Weidenreich and E. Schuster, *Der Schädelfund von Weimar-Ehringsdorf* (Jena: G. Fischer, 1928).

43. F. Berckhemer, "Der Steinheimer Urmensch und die Tierwelt seines Lebensgebietes," *Naturwissenschaftliche Monatschrift der Deutschen Naturkundeverein* [Stuttgart], 47 (1934) 4.

44. H. Breuil and R. Lantier, *Les hommes de la pierre ancienne* (Paris: Payot, 1951, pp. 289ff). See also A. Glory and R. Robert, "Le culte des crânes humains aux époques préhistoriques," *Bulletin de la Société d'Anthropologie de Paris,* (1948) 114–33; P. Wernert, "L'anthropophagie rituelle de la chasse aux têtes aux époques actuelle et Paléolithique," *L'Anthropologie,* (1936) 33–43, and "Culte des crânes: Représentation des esprits des défunts et des ancêtres," in M. Gorce and R. Mortier (eds.) *L'histoire générale des religions* (Paris: A. Quillet, 1948, pp. 50–102); and

G. Pinza, "La conservazione delle teste e i costumi con i quali si connette," *Memorie della Società geografica italiana*, 7, no. 2.

45. F. M. Bergounioux, " 'Spiritualité' de l'Homme Neanderthal," in G. H. R. von Koenigswald, *Hundert Jahre Neanderthaler*, pp. 151–66, especially pp. 151, 153.

46. André Senet, *Man in Search of his Ancestors* (New York: McGraw-Hill, 1956, pp. 113–14).

47. MacCurdy, *op. cit.*, I:403–4.

48. The Remigia cave scenes, of five individuals in one case, ten in another, raising their bows, as another individual at some distance falls pierced with arrows, was recognized by Obermaier as ritual human sacrifice. Compare the later Gallic "Hanged Man" killed in a suspended wicker cage, the Celtic human sacrifice by drowning on the Gundestrup Cauldron, and the Tolund Hanged Man of Denmark (Palle Lauring, *Land of the Tollund Man*, London: Lutterworth Press, 1957). Is the St. Sebastien legend a distant echo of the arrow-riddled human sacrifice?

49. Blanc, *op. cit.*, p. 123; Klindt-Jensen, *op. cit.*, pp. 36–37.

50. K. Gerhardt, "Künstliche Veränderungen am Hinterhauptloch vorgeschichtlicher Schädel," *Germania*, 29 (1951) 3–4.

51. On Catuvellauni head-hunting in Hertfordshire and among other tribes elsewhere in Britain, see I. A. Richmond, *Roman Britain* (Baltimore: Penguin Books, 1960, pp. 11–13); in Gaul cf. pp. 192–93.

52. Powell, *Celts*, pp. 108, 110, and 266–67 (Plates 50–51); Celtic Iron Age headhunting lasted in France until historic times (Stuart Piggott, *Ancient Europe, from the Beginnings of Agriculture to Classical Antiquity*, Chicago: Aldine Publishing Co., 1965. Pl. XXXVIII, p. 219; also pp. 223, 230, and 259).

53. Evel Gasparini, "Studies in Old Slavic Religion: *Ubrus*," *History of Religions*, 2 (1962) 112–39.

54. Maringer, *op. cit.*, 20–24, 54–55, 130, 178; compare K. Krenn, "Schädelbecher," *Sudeta*, (1929) 73–122.

55. On other Eurasiatic relicts of the ancient skull cult, see A. Gahs, *Kopf-, Schädel- und Langbeinopfer*, pp. 231–68; W. W. Rockhill, "On the Use of Skulls in Lamaist Ceremonies," *Proceedings of the American Orientalist Society*, 40 (1888 [published 1890]) 24–31; Berthold Laufer, "Use of Skulls and Bones in Tibet," *Field Museum of Natural History, Department of Anthropology*, Publication 10, 1923. It is interesting that, traditionally, the pre-Buddhist Tibetan Bon religion was founded by a shaman; some Tibetans link the office of shamanism with the exercise of rulership; and some shamans appease "earth owners," have shamanistic rivalries, control the elements, are connected with human sacrifice, etc. (R. B. Ekvall, *Religious Observances in Tibet: Patterns and Function*, Chicago: University of Chicago Press, 1964, pp. 20–21, 32, 38–39).

56. Maringer, *op. cit.*, pp. 55–56. Here, to drink life is literally to prolong it. Consequently it is natural for all Indoeuropeans to invoke "long life" for one who drinks from the life-container, or "skoal."

57. Onians, *op. cit.*, pp. 110–30.

58. Leonardo did twelve coition studies, several of which show ducts from the spinal canal to the male genitalia that do not exist (e.g. drawing No. 19097v. Windsor Castle Royal Library, *Quaderni d'Anatomia*, III, 3v, pictured in Philipson, *op. cit.*, p. 283, Fig. 70; cf. pp. 245, 289); see also Edward McCurdy (ed.), *The Notebooks of Leonardo da Vinci* (New York: Braziller, 1954, p. 24).

59. Shakespeare: "manly marrow" (*All's Well*, ii, 3, 298), "minds and marrows of our youth" (*Timon*, iv, 1, 26; cf. iv, 3, 193; and v, 4, 9); also *3 Henry VI*, iii, 2, 125, and *Hamlet*, i, 4, 22. Cognate or identical with "marrow" is "tallow," e.g., "piss my tallow" (*Merry Wives*, v, 5, 16); cf. *Comedy of Errors*, iii, 2, 100; *1 Henry IV*, ii, 4, 252; and *Romeo and Juliet*, iii, 5, 158.

60. MacCurdy, *op. cit.*, II:503; Luquet, *op. cit.*, pp. 162–64; Onians, *op. cit.*, pp. 535–36; and David Trump, *Central and Southern Italy Before Rome* (New York: Praeger, 1965, p. 75). Greek, Roman and Etruscan burials and sarcophagi bore traces of red paint in their interiors; Homer and other classic authors that the dead were wrapped in red shrouds, a custom still followed for fifteenth-century Florentine noblemen—and indeed a dead pope is still enveloped in a red shroud (Blanc, *op. cit.*, p. 123).

61. Bridget Allchin, *The Stone-Tipped Arrow: Late Stone-Age Hunters of the Tropical Old World* (New York: Barnes & Noble, 1967).

62. Otto Bader, "The Oldest Burial?" *Illustrated London News*, 7 November 1964, p. 731. Bader is a senior scientific worker of the Archaeological Institute of the USSR Academy of Sciences; see also "Paleolithic Burial," *Scientific American*, 212 #2 (February 1965) 53–54. At Spy, fires were burned over the dead (Maringer, *op. cit.*, p. 19).

63. Cited works of Breuil (pp. 164, 331, 391), MacCurdy (I:265–67), Laming (pp. 25, 27–28, 160), Blanc (pp. 121, 123). Luquet (p. 194) states that in view of the abundant evidence it would be "prudence exaggerated to the point of timidity to refuse . . . the most reasonable interpretation without possible contradiction that [the Trois Frères masked dancer] represents a sorcerer in the performance of his functions." A "reindeer shaman" lesser known than that of Trois Frères, cruder but still convincing, is the bearded and bald-headed man wearing deer antlers and a horse's tail, engraved on a slab of slate from Lourdes (Maringer, Fig. 27, p. 103). Both share these two animal appurtenances.

64. Clyde Kluckhohn, "Recurrent Themes in Myths and Mythmaking," in Alan Dundes (ed.), *The Study of Folklore* (Englewood Cliffs: Prentice-Hall, 1965, 158–68, p. 161)—an article originating in *Daedalus*, 88 (1959) 268–79. However, Kluckhohn wisely qualifies his quasi-Jungian thesis with a proper Freudian empiricism: "But, again, [certain cultural items'] persistence cannot be understood except on the hypothesis that these images have a special congeniality for the human mind as a consequence of the relations of children to their parents and other childhood experiences which are universal rather than culture-bound" (p. 161).

65. Notable at Altamira, Baoussé-Roussé, Cogul, Combarelles, Cro Magnon, Les Eyzies, Font de Gaume, Laugerie-Basse, Laussel, Marsoulas, Mas d'Azil, Placard, Le Portel, Předmost, Teyjat and Willendorf (all pictured in Reinach, *Répertoire*, pp. 7–8, 25, 56, 57, 62, 68, 69, 98, 100, 120, 145, 147, 168, 171–73, 181, and 187).

66. Laming, *op. cit.*, pp. 162–63. Some fifty-five portrayals are known in Ice Age art of human beings dressed in skins, often in a dancing posture (Maringer, *op. cit.*, pp. 102–6). The wolf-masked man following an elk, engraved on a rock at Cape Bessev-Noss, Lake Onega, U.S.S.R. (Maringer, *op. cit.*, Pl. 54, between pp. 158–59) cannot possibly be a "stalker" (a "wolf" would frighten an elk away) or a "god" or anything other than a shaman or man with wolf-power for hunting elk. Tectiforms as masks: Breuil, *op. cit.*, pp. 146–47; Laming, *op. cit.*, p. 84.

67. J. G. D. Clark, *Excavations at Star Carr, An Early Mesolithic Site at Seamer near Scarborough, Yorkshire* (Cambridge: At the University Press, 1954).

68. For deer antlers and fertility, Clark, *op. cit.*, pp. 170–72; fertility and horns in general, Levy, *op. cit.*, pp. 59, 66–67, 100–1, *et passim*. The British Museum has a Shang-Yin period antler with a *genealogy* engraved on it; and of the same date, a deer mask above a human one on a bronze finial. In ancient Nara, first permanent capital of Japan, the Shinto ceremony of removing the antlers of the sacred deer in the temple park is performed every year by *seko* or veteran deer-catchers. Accompanied by elaborate ritual, all the severed antlers are offered at the

Kasuga Shrine to acknowledge the relation between the "patron" animal and the shrine (Konosuke Muramatsu, "The Antlers of Nara," *Natural History*, 66 ≠2 (February 1967) 30–33. The Paleosiberian affiliations of Shintoism are well known, as of course are also the far eastern use of various powdered horns as potency-restorers.

69. The sexual behavior of stags—relevant to any explanation of the use of Star Carr frontlets—is described in F. Fraser Darling, *A Herd of Red Deer: A Study in Animal Behaviour* (Oxford: Oxford University Press, 1937=New York: Anchor Natural History Library paperback). For modern ethnographic parallels, see Bengt Anell, "Animal Hunting Disguises among the North American Indians," *Studia Ethnographica Upsaliensia*, 21 (1964) 1–34. That all the Lascaux cervids are stags with full antlers, and all the ibexes male too, is pointed out (though without further comment) by Laming, *op. cit.*, pp. 141, 143. All these data are consistent with the belief that antlers have a "magic" attraction (i.e., are behavior-releasers or ethological stimuli) for stags, whether in stalk-hunting or in cave magic.

70. M. & S.-J. Péquart, M. Boule, and H. V. Valois, *Téviec, station nécropole mésolithique du Morbihan* (Paris: Masson et Cie., 1937). M. and S.-J. Péquart, "Le nécropole mésolithique de Téviec," *L'Anthropologie*, 39 (1929) 373–400; *idem*, *Hoëdic, deuxième station-nécropole du mésolithique côtier Armorican* (Anvers: De Sikkel, 1954).

71. Pericot, *op. cit.*, pp. 204–5. For pictures of the Cauldron: MacCurdy, *op. cit.*, II:260, Fig. 384, and II:261, Fig. 385; also Ole Klindt-Jensen, *Gundestrupkedelen* (København: Nationalmuseet, 1961, Figs. 4–5, pp. 8–9, showing the horned Cernunnus wearing short breeches; cf. also figures on pp. 13, 33, 41). I have to thank Dr. Howard E. Jensen for his kindness in translating the Danish of Klindt-Jensen for me.

72. Klindt-Jensen assimilates the Gundestrup Cernunnus with that of the Musée de Saint Rémy (Fig. 7, p. 11); cf. Robert Payne, *Ancient Rome* (New York: American Heritage Publishing Co., 1966, p. 286; and Luigi Pareti, *History of Mankind* (New York: Harper and Row, 1965, II: Plate 72b, facing p. 723). The tail-capped *shaman* (Klindt-Jensen, Figs. 10–11, pp. 14–15)—surely not a "god" sacrificing to himself—about to drown a human sacrifice head-down in a cauldron, also wears *zaragüelles*, as do the warriors before whom he performs. The largest collection of statues and casts of Cernunnus is in the museum of St. Germain-en-Laye, e.g. those of the Monument des Hauts, Reims, Vendoeuvres, Roqueperteuse, Autel des Saintes, Nerès, and Notre Dame; also a seated three-headed Gallic god flanked by a nude male deer-horned god and, in the tympanum above, a bust of a man with bullhorns, as well as the Mont St. Jean "Dieu forestier" with a bow, the Autun museum "Gaulois en costume de chasse avec du torque" (Item 8278, also a similar 8279; cf. Musée d'Epinal 20332, 20333).

73. Birds in parietal art: Breuil, *op. cit.*, pp. 44, 151, 159, 352, and 428; in portable art, MacCurdy, *op. cit.*, I:193, 208, 232, 280, 286, and II:442; and in the Siberian Paleolithic, A. P. Okladnikov, "Ancient Population of Siberia and its Culture," in Levin and Potapov, *op. cit.*, 13–98, p. 21. See also Elliott W. Dawson, "Bird Remains in Archaeology," in Brothwell and Higgs, *op. cit.*, pp. 279–93; note also Wensinck, *op. cit.*, on the bird as a "cosmological symbol" in western Asia. Graziosi, *op. cit.*, Pl. 75 and Pl. 78a, p. 247, also pictures birds at La Bastide; and a Magdalenian V bird and bison engraved on sandstone from Puy-de-Lucan Corrège.

74. Bird Shaman of Lascaux: cited works of Breuil (Fig. 115, p. 151), who thought the dead hunter's grave lies beneath the wall scene, though no one has yet excavated to see (Maringer, p. 58); Breuil also thought the rhinoceros part of the scene and the cause of the bison's disembowelment (Maringer, p. 59), but Laming

(Plate 35) shows the whole scene and properly notes that the rhinoceros is done in a quite different style from that of the man, bird, and bison (the whole scene is also in Maringer, Pl. 14, between pp. 158–59, and in Powell, *Prehistoric Art,* p. 63).

75. Pericot, *op. cit.,* p. 196.

76. H. Danthine, "Essai d'interpretation de la 'scène du puits' de la Grotte de Lascaux," *Sédimentation et Quaternaire,* (1949) 203–20.

77. J. Maringer, *Vorgeschichtliche Religion* (Einseideln: Benziger, 1956, pp. 128–30=German original of *Gods of Prehistoric Men*) advances the *Totengedächtnisbild* theory.

78. Eliade, *Recent Works,* pp. 183–84.

79. G. Róheim, "Hungarian Shamanism," in Róheim (ed.), *Psychoanalysis and the Social Sciences,* 3 (1951) 131–69, p. 138: also, *Hungarian and Vogul Mythology,* pp. 49–50.

80. Pfeiffer, *op. cit.,* p. 90.

81. Hugo Kirschner, *Urgeschichte des Schamanismus,* pp. 271–73; cf. Narr, *Bärenzeremoniell,* pp. 257–59.

82. The Lascaux Bird Shaman is not the only bird-headed man in paleolithic art; there are several dancing shamans, one ithyphallic, with bird heads at Altamira (pictured in Reinach, *Répertoire,* p. 7), and Breuil mentions (p. 352) another drawing of a musk ox charging a man with a stick over his shoulder associated with a bird. Cf. note 90, below.

83. Levin and Potapov, *op. cit.,* Altai (p. 325), Kachin (p. 358) shaman's garb symbolizing a bird; the bird and the shaman's travels (p. 601); Ngansan shaman's bird skins (p. 578); Sel'kup shamanic birds (p. 591); cf. the Shor, Khant, and Nansi belief in "spirits of ancestors in form of people with wings" like the shamanistic spirits drawn on the shaman's tambourine (p. 442). Compare Smohalla's promise to restore the earlier wings of ancestors.

84. Eliade, *Sacred and Profane,* p. 11.

85. The Eurasiatic-American sky bird associated with lightning and water is found also in Africa, there also associated with the male principle-fire-sky-bull-rain-spirits of dead (T. O. Beidelman, "Swazi Royal Ritual," *Africa,* 36 [1966] 373–405; cf. B. A. Marwick, *The Swazi,* Cambridge: At the University Press, 1940, p. 243).

86. E. Stiglmayr, "Schamanismus in Australien," *Wiener Völkerkundliche Mitteilungen,* 5, no. 2 (1957) 161–90.

87. R. H. Lowie, in Steward, *op. cit.,* 3:48, citing Nimuendajú.

88. A. Métraux, in Steward, *op. cit.,* I:197–370, p. 317.

89. The soul-bird is not merely European, but also Malayan, etc. Egyptian papyri show the belief that souls of the dead, changed into birds, could leave their tombs to sit in the sun and peck in the fields; the belief is Mediterranean and western European also. C. Schuchhardt so interpreted the famous painted sarcophagus of Hagia Triada with birds perched on obelisks (Maringer, *op. cit.,* p. 166).

90. Powell, *Celts,* p. 123.

91. Nora K. Chadwick, *Celtic Britain* (New York: Praeger, 1963, Plates 31 and 47, pp. 225 and 228).

92. Klindt-Jensen, *Denmark,* p. 72.

93. A. C. and G. A. Blanc, cited by Dawson, in Brothwell and Higgs, *op. cit.,* p. 286.

94. S. F. Nadel, "The Origins of Music," *Musical Quarterly,* 16 (1950) 538–42.

95. Shierozewski, Castagne, Lehtisalo, and the *galdr-galan* etymology, cited from M. Eliade, *Yearning for Paradise,* pp. 257–58. Nanay [Goldi] epics could be performed only by men, since women were forbidden to sing at all (Levin and Potapov, *op. cit.,* p. 710; cf. p. 720). To "report" historical facts and ideas accumulated

for generations, to "shamanize" and to perform "story-singing" are meaning-related words found in all Tungusic languages (Negidal, Evenk, Oroch, Ulch, Nanay and Udege) except Manchu (Vasilevich, in Michael [ed.], *op. cit.,* p. 46).

96. Eliade, *Recent Works,* pp. 185–86.

97. A. P. Merriam, "The Importance of Song in the Flathead Indian Vision Quest," *Ethnomusicology,* 9 (1965) 91–99. The Sel'kup shaman's "tambourine was a reindeer on which the shaman went to the sky and to the underground world" (Levin and Potapov, *op. cit.,* p. 601); and the sign for "rattle" in the Plains sign language is the basis for derived signs referring to the sacred and the supernatural. Greek gods were associated with particular musical instruments, e.g. Apollo-lyre, Athena-flute, etc.; so also were Hindu gods, e.g. Shiva-doubleheaded drum, Saraswati-*vina,* Krishna-flute, Vishnu-conch, etc. As is well known, Pythagoras considered music to have planetary-cosmic significance, a notion that is also Sumerian, Babylonian, Gnostic, Hindu, and Chinese. The new Chinese emperor, on his accession, carefully sought the *huang chung* or "Golden Bell" absolute pitch so that his reign would be auspiciously "on pitch" or in tune with the cosmos. Hindu *ragas* were associated with particular gods, time of day, etc.; cf. the Chinese *lü* or musical modes. All these circumstances suggest a magic-shamanic connection of music with the physical world.

XIV

The Deathless Gods

GREEK civilization arose from the uneasy and ultimately unstable mixture of two diverse traditions, one an old eastern Mediterranean culture of probable Semitic affiliations, the other the north European or northern Eurasiatic culture of invading Indoeuropean tribes, Dorian, Phrygian and others. The aboriginal "Pelasgian" culture related backward in time to those of Egypt and Asia Minor, and was found also in Crete, Cyprus, Malta and southern Italy, and perhaps also in part among the Etruscans.[1] The pre-Hellenic culture of the Cyclades Islands is sometimes called "Cycladic" and sometimes "Minoan" from the title of the sea kings of Crete; that on the mainland of Hellas, "Helladic," or "Mycenaean" from its chief city-state, Bronze Age Mycenae. The Indoeuropean[2] culture-tradition is the "Achaean," from the fair-haired people who brought it from the north, and the heroes whom the bard Homer celebrated.

An old tradition of humanistic scholarship has been to ally the religion of "chthonic" earth-gods of the indigenes with Dionysus, the arcane "mystery" religions, and the folk-irrational. By contrast, the Indoeuropean "Olympians" are the sky gods of clarity and rationality, allied with the sun god Apollo, prince of the intellectual arts, under another and supreme sky god, the All-Father and god of justice, Olympian Zeus.[3] This earth-sky division of deities,[4] however oversimplified, has been useful from classic to contemporary times. It may even have a base in the departmental shamanisms of underworld and sky in the Paleolithic, still discernible in Paleosiberian shamanism.

Although the Apollo-Dionysus dichotomy of deities is neater than the facts (the name of Apollo may come from Asia Minor, the etymology of Dionysus is Indoeuropean, and some of the Olympians themselves betray Pelasgian "chthonic" origins) nevertheless two religious traditions on mainland Greece are evident archeologically from the "Shaft Grave" period onward. The Mycenaeans managed to combine after a fashion the old "Aegean" fertility cult of a mother-goddess with their own masculine Indoeuropean "departmental" deities of nature from the north. This "marriage" of earth and sky gods is symbolized in various Greek myths as the marriage of Indoeuropean Zeus with the great earth-mother goddess of the Aegeans—though in the final analysis it must be admitted that we have a surplus of sky gods (Zeus, Apollo, Phoebus, Dionysus), considerable duplication of earth mothers (Ge, Rhea, Demeter), and a Zeus who married or made love with many goddesses indeed. The gradual rise to dominance of the Olympians in myth seems to express the gradual political dominance of the Indoeuropeans over the native Aegean peoples.[5]

But the old beliefs never disappeared. They remained strong, especially among country people and peasants; the fact that literate "Apollonian" city folk were those who left us the records may also distort our sense of proportion. In general the Indoeuropean gods took their place in a public state cult of the Twelve Olympians; the native chthonic gods later re-emerged in the individual-salvation cults of the Hellenistic Mysteries. But this formula oversimplifies too. Among the Olympians themselves, Hermes, Demeter, Artemis and Athena retained many ancient Aegean attributes; and Dionysus, like Demeter closely associated with the Mysteries, displaced Hestia, the old Indoeuropean goddess of the hearth, from among the Twelve. Archeology attests to acculturation also. Several sites can claim unbroken survival from the Bronze Age to the classical Greek era. As theologically it should, the little Mycenaean megaron at Eleusis lies directly under the Telesterion where the Mysteries of Demeter ("Earth-Mother") and Persephone ("Destroyer of Death") were celebrated centuries later. Another ancient holy place was Delos, inhabited since the Early Cycladic period—but it was the classic sanctuary of Apollo!

To complicate the matter, the two renowned tombs of the Hyperborean Maidens at Delos date from the sixteenth- and fifteenth-century period of influence from Crete, but by legend the Maidens were brought from beyond the north wind when the hunting deities Artemis and Apollo first came to Delos—as though shamans, in the process of coming south, became shamanesses (Teiresias, now one sex, now another, is not an example of this but seems rather to echo the standard Paleosiberian shaman's magic change of sex). One must suspect in these legends some tendentious syncretism. As at Delphi, the oracular Apollo seems to have superseded female deities[6]; but as we shall see, the sun god himself retained numerous shamanistic features as well. Hesiod, a near-contemporary of Homer, tried to make sense of the two quite different traditions in his *Theogony*, or treatise on the genesis of the gods. In this difficult task, Hesiod was the first theologian; for a complacent tribal cult needs no apologist or rationalization—only problem-posing mixtures of conflicting irrationalities do. In Hesiod's twistings and turnings we can see the first dim Ghost Dance of the earliest Greek acculturation.

Nor are the Olympians quite pure "departmental deities" of nature. They are thoroughly anthropomorphic, and they behave with unselfconscious similitude to human beings, their only difference from men consisting in their greater mana and immortality—which they nourish by taking magic substances, nectar and odorous ambrosia, quite as shamans might take mead and mushrooms.[7] The Olympian gods carry with them sometimes quite arbitrary animal "attributes," many of them meaningless with respect to their special realm of nature—the sea lord Poseidon, for example, is an old horse god from the northern interior plains, and his trident is an ancient shamanic symbol, like the *trisula* of Shiva—but these are entirely plausible as the animal "familiars" and paraphernalia of shamans. In fact, the eagle of the sky god Zeus who controls lightning, thunder and rain and is in general king of the weather, is the direct cognate of the shamanic sky bird of the whole northern hemisphere; he is also the sky bull of the Levant, a golden rain to Danäe, a swan to Leda, etc.

Other god-animal associations are plentiful.[8] Athena has the snake and the owl; Apollo, oxen, the wolf, and at Clazomenae the swan; Artemis, the stag, in Ionia; Aphrodite, the turtle at Aegina, but more usually the dove elsewhere; Demeter, the sow; Hermes, the goat, at Aenus in Thrace, etc. That such association is Indoeuropean (even if it is Aegean too) would seem indicated by the *vahanas* or "vehicles" of Hindu deities, the lion of Durga, the peacock of Saraswati, the *garuda*-bird of Vishnu, and the like, though the Indoeuropean sky god Varuna obviously acquired his elephant in India, Shiva's bull is Mohenjodaran, and the seated elephant-headed Ganesha[9] is an old god of wealth and good luck like Pluto and Cernunnus but only in part Indoeuropean. Even human Greek heroes are sometimes associated with animals. Theseus, who had a spider-helper in Ariadne and so escaped sacrifice to a bullheaded Minotaur, introduced a crane dance at Delos; and the lion-pelted Heracles rendered Ajax like a lion, which to Marie Delcourt[10] suggests male initiation, but may indicate only shamanic transmission of power. Atlas is "a being of mischievous spirit who knows all the sea chasms" (*Odyssey* 1:52), a curiously shamanic power for one of the underworld Giants (Gigantes) literally "born of Earth." The tenth book of the *Iliad* seems oddly shamanistic too: Dolon wears a wolfskin and a cap of marten skin—and why, as scouts among the enemy, should Agamemnon and Diomede go out under a lion pelt and Menelaus in a panther skin, unless these gave magic power,[11] for the enemy would as soon shoot these animals as they would men, if they saw them.

There are also many shamanistic echoes of association with birds. Athena made Teiresias—he who changed sex—into a prophet by cleansing his ears with the tongue of her serpent Erichthonios, so that he could understand the language of birds. But then, as Koronis the crow, Athena was mother to the snake-man Asklepios.[12] Her crow or raven[13] was long-lived[14] and an oracular bird,[15] the harbinger of rain and occasionally propitiated to bring it.[16] Athena, the owl and raven, was also other birds, notably the vulture,[17] also a bird of Zeus, and the sea crow or sea gull, soul of those drowned at sea as well as a weatherbird predicting storms.[18] Like so many shamans credited with the invention of a musical instrument, Athena invented the flute, to imitate the cries of the other Gorgons when the Medusa was killed.[19] In the classic period Aristophanes, in *The Birds,* made a number of god-bird equations as though these were still perfectly familiar to his audience, Aphrodite-coot, Poseidon-duck, Herakles-cormorant, and Apollo-swan, as well as Zeus-eagle—and seems to be ridiculing the shamanic pretensions of some philosophers to be able to fly to an ideal bird heaven.[20]

In Neolithic and Bronze Age Greece, these animal and bird familiars of men must be regarded as relics of an earlier shamanistic age of hunters. The hero Heracles indeed still may have hunted a rare aurochs bull and a great wild sow on the soil of Hellas.[21] But the "Nemean" lion that, after the glaciers, once lived wild in the Balkans and Asia Minor, had probably disappeared from Greece by Homeric times, and already survived only as a heraldic beast attending the Great Mother at Mycenae (the Eurasiatic lion, still hunted in Mesopotamia and Iran in historic times, is now found wild only in Gir, a small game preserve in Kathiawar, India, between the Ranns of Cutch and Cambay).[22] But the cult of *arktos,* the bear, surely survives from the earlier time of the ancient Great Mother. Indeed, the bear dance belongs to the cycle of Artemis. In a unique instance, two little girls dressed as she-bears in saffron-colored clothes danced in the city of Brauron to the Mistress of Animals, in a relict of the magico-religious propitiatory ritual associated with the bear hunt of prehistoric times—and as such is connected with the bear cremonialism of the northern hemisphere of demonstrably immense antiquity.

We have already noted that the shamanistic trickster Atlas was "earthborn"—an attribute that suggests further chthonic Aegean contributions to later Greek myth. Jane Harrison[23] saw in the Titans the white-clay-smeared figures of an old initiation ritual which still included the use of a bullroarer; and in the Titans' eating of Zeus-Zagreus, a totemic feast on the slaughtered bull, god-patron and enfraternizing sacrifice consumed in communion. That Titans are under the earth, whether by tradition or (as later represented) by fate, also strongly suggests earth-shamans with rituals underground, that is, animal shamans of caves as opposed to bird shamans of the sky. Originally Giants and Titans (discrete in theogonies though earthborn both, but not always discriminated in usage) seem to be earth powers in the usual shamanistic rivalry with sky beings, since the groups of both realms once appeared near-equals in power. The finally defeated earth powers seem better to have retained their original human lineaments, but the triumphant sky beings were promoted to become gods. As is common in myth, we have here the henotheistic demotion of earlier powers to earth daemons, in parallel to the political conquest of Aegeans by Indoeuropeans. The Titans and Giants consequently often appear as rebels against Olympian Zeus, and in late legends they are twelve against the gods. There were giants in the earth in those days.

Titans and Giants are close to the early generations in Hesiod's theology. The giants were born of the seed of Ouranos that fell to earth when Kronos unmanned his father, as Zeus did his; and being earth creatures, they have a scaly snake-tail, like Pelops and Erichthonius, instead of legs. Thus they are older than Zeus, son of Kronos. In Greek legend the Titan-Giants keep the characteristics of trickster, culture hero, and hero in revolt against greater powers.[24] Philoctetes, Palamedes and Ajax have long been recognized as ancient shaman-*daemones,* but in their insertion into the Homeric epics they are preserved as merely human heroes of distant times past. Nevertheless Philoctetes, incurably wounded as only a human can be, had (or had invented) the magic bow and infallible arrows on which the conquest of Troy depended. Palamedes is even more clearly a Promethean culture hero. He invented letters, gaming with dice, and signaling with fire; he clairvoyantly discovered the way to the precinct, the order of watches, and organized the distribution of food; and he led to Troy the sisters Oenotropes who magically changed all they touched into wine, oil and grain. (Interestingly, all the inventions credited to Palamedes are Minoan in origin, which argues antiquity in the Greek world.) His Titanism is even demonstrated in his death, when he was stoned or cast into a well by Odysseus and Diomede. Shamanistic also seems his prescience of the ruse of

Odysseus, who shammed madness to escape going to Troy (an olonism that by contagion accidentally passed into his entourage). And the name of Palamedes' brother, Oeax, in the absence of any other detail, would seem to designate him as the inventor of the ship-rudder.

The greatest culture hero of all, of course, was Prometheus—one etymology of whose name suggests he could predict the future, but another makes his name cognate with the Sanskrit *pramantha,* "firestick" —who in myth stole fire from heaven and for this was punished by Zeus. His brother Epimetheus, "Hind-Sight," a lesser doublet, had more of the awkwardness that lets every trickster be outwitted sometimes. The sons of Iapetus, in fact, are all ultimately punished by exile: Prometheus chained to his lonely rock in the frozen northeast, Atlas to hold up the sky at the westernmost limit of the world, and Menoetius to Erebus to attend the flocks of Hades. In the end, at the word of an oracle, Ajax was buried under a load of clay by the people of Troy, and despite his shaking it like an earthquake into two mounds, he died like Palamedes, like Kaneus and the crushed Giants. As Lapiths, the Giants became heroes, like Ajax; these others too rose to become enemies of the Olympians.[25] In late days, "titanic" implied presumption and rebelliousness, describing Phaethon who would drive the chariot of the Sun, and Bellerophon who would climb the heavens, one to a fate like that of Icarus the birdman who aspired too high toward the sun.

Like his three enemies—Palamedes, Philoctetes, and Ajax—Odysseus is *polymētis,* which in this competitive context surely must mean more than "fertile in ruses" for he was successful also against the witch Circe, the Cyclops, Scylla, the Sirens and others. But Odysseus is fully and unquestionably human in spite of his magic powers and tricks. Like Orpheus, Odysseus also went down like a shaman to the dread underground place of spirits and returned alive. Other heroes were shamanic too. Prometheus had tried unsuccessfully to prevent Zeus from flinging souls into Hades; Asklepios, the snake shaman, was lightning-blasted by Zeus for bringing back father-defying Hippolytus to life. Heracles did succeed in bringing Alcestis back, but this was before she had gone down to the realm of Dis; and after his descent to Hades, Heracles killed his own sons, as if Hell claimed a ransom. All this traffic in souls smacks of a greater shaman, Hermes; but he was a god. Power over spirits, whether those of men or their ghosts, is the prerogative of the Greek immortals, who alone eternally possess their own life. The comparison is bold, but one might say that at one extreme of its spread, shamanistic power became somewhat democratized in the Americas and accessible, in varying degrees, to all self-reliant men among hunters;

in the social context of Neolithic and Bronze Age Greece, however, the Olympian gods absorbed a monopoly of magic power.

E. O. James argued that "the excessive humanization of the Olympians led to their loss of transcendental status and religious significance."[26] This is a typical error of the insistently theistic approach to religion, as though gods were there first, and are there now. On the contrary, the Greek nature-gods are manlike because they began as men. However lofty they had become, all the Olympians plainly began as human beings, mere shamans with special mastery given by their familiars or some departmental power over nature as animal-shamans over earth spirits and fertility, or bird-shamans over the sky and the weather. And they could never be "transcendental" until it was believed that the *surviving* spirits of dead shamans (now gods) really did have power over nature, that is, continuing to wield magic power as before but now as categorically indestructable spirits. For if there is anything that Greek religion from Homer onward insists upon and reiterates, it is that the difference of gods from men is only in their mana and immortality. The Olympian gods were never anthropomorphisms *discovered* in nature.[27] If they lack edifying ethical dignity, that is because they were no more than human, or at most picaresque Tricksters. And they began in shamanistic magic, not lofty religion; *in control of,* not "worship" of nature. Only on the basis of an earlier belief, that shamans controlled nature, was it possible to believe that manlike beings controlled nature, i.e. the gods. Gods arise quite simply from the premises of animism, should some separable souls manage to persist intact, perhaps those with more mana[28] in the first place. It should not be surprising if these persisting souls, immortal gods, kept the specific traits of the shamanic souls that they were and, it was believed, still remained. The Olympians grew in majesty only as political and world-horizons grew. It was the secularizing Ionian nature-philosophers, in fact, abjuring animism in their search for a material substrate of nature, who finally made the world too big and too impersonal for anthropomorphic gods to live in. Even mighty Zeus himself, as will be seen, started out his career merely as a shamanic fertility-*daemon* and trickster, and only much later was he god of justice in a greater political cosmos.

We suggested earlier that the Olympians absorbed into themselves a monopoly of shamanic or supernatural magic power (for all that the oracles associated with Apollo and Zeus remained human god-inspired soothsayers). This may be in general true, but there are additional traces of the earlier pre-theistic shamanism of Greeks. Careful reading of Apollonius is enough to establish Orpheus as the somewhat androgynous war shaman of the Argonauts.[29] Again, the famed "intervention" of the gods on both sides in the Trojan War considerably resembles *shamanistic rivalry* (including Hera's trick to outwit Zeus)—especially in Books XIV and XV of the *Iliad*—which goes beyond mere human fighting with the aid of war shamans on each side.[30] Both Empedocles and Pythagoras seem curiously shamanlike to the anthropologist. True, Empedocles does not ride an arrow like Abaris or appear as a raven like Aristeas (two other shaman-journeyers); he is never in two places at the same time and does not descend to the underworld like Orpheus and Pythagoras. But Empedocles could use drugs against sickness and old age, quell and raise wind, abate and bring rain, and bring back the dead; and he claimed to be a god, having been in earlier incarnations of another sex, a plant, a fish, and a bird—all of which sufficiently suggest shamanism. So also can one read Empedocles' curious injunction, "Abstain wholly from laurel leaves," in one of his surviving Fragments.[31]

That Greek religion began in shamanism is an idea entertained by Hellenists for almost half a century now. Implicit in Jane Ellen Harrison's *Prolegomena* and *Themis,* the insight into Greek shamanism seems to have found its first complete statement by Gilbert Murray. The shaman who wears an animal's skin and its head as a mask, he thought, is the first θεός (god) or θεσός (incarnate mana, medicine power, or magic spell) that his society knows.[32] Erwin Rohde, in his *Psyche,* also perceived the manipulation of soul-spirits as shamanistic.[33] Karl Meuli, in a now-classic article,[34] gave great impetus to this interpretation in his comparison of Greek ecstatics like Abaris the Hyperborean, Aristeas of Proconneus, Epimenides of Crete, and Hermotimus of Clazomenae with then-contemporary Scythian and modern Turco-Mongolian shamans, and he was followed in this view by Diels and Nilsson, as well as E. D. Phillips. W. K. C. Guthrie[35] clearly discerned Orpheus as a shaman, and F. M. Cornford has a chapter on Greek shamanism in his *Principium Sapientiae.*[36]

The most important recent authority is E. R. Dodds, Regius Professor of Greek in Oxford, who noted the shamanistic nature of Theoclymenus in the *Odyssey,* the Apollonian Pythia-oracle, the priestesses of Zeus at Dodona, and Cassandra, in his already classic work on *The Greeks and the Irrational.*[37] He has also well perceived the special connection of shamanism with fire.[38] He noted too that Aeacus, an old and perhaps Minoan sacral figure that Epimenides claimed to reincarnate, was in life a magic rain maker, and after death doorkeeper of hell and judge of the dead.[39] More recently, Marie Delcourt is especially sensitive to the "trickster" and culture-hero aspects of Greek demi-gods, and to the shaman as artificer.⁴⁰ Burkert, Robertson Smith and others have also made contributions.⁴¹

The magico-religious origins of Greek drama also manifest clear shamanistic elements. Whether τραγῳδοί, "tragedians," were satyrs dressed in goat-skins for some antique religious reason (Euripides),⁴² or bards competing for a goat-prize (Horace)⁴³ or lamenters of the ritual sufferings and death of the goat "god" or scapegoat (Dionysus himself, in a prehistoric animal-cult Mystery)⁴⁴—the fact remains that even in the time of Aeschylus, Sophocles and Euripides, tragedies were presented, usually in threes, as *competitions among bards,* as in ritualized shamanistic rivalry, and a prize formally awarded. The dramatic shaman contest dates from the earliest Greek times as we learn from Hesiod⁴⁵; and although nonhistorical and of mixed date and origin, *The Contest of Homer and Hesiod* is itself an imaginary example of this kind. In fact, Aristophanes' *Frogs* had as its plot just such a contest. The newcomer Euripides would sit in the Chair of Tragedy heretofore occupied by Aeschylus, whose right to it even Sophocles would not dispute; only if Euripides dethroned Aeschylus would Sophocles enter the contest; and, appropriately, Dionysus, god of the theater, would be the judge. The frequent references in their plays to other dramatists, and the critical to raucous tone of these references, also make sense if we keep in mind that Greek dramas were *bard-contests.*

The Greeks were competitive and male-centered; always a "public" people, they were shame-sanctioned, not guilt-sanctioned,⁴⁶ in Dodds' view; that is, they were coerced by external public opinion, not "Protestant-ethic"-like conscience or a rigorously internalized superego. It is worth looking again at their character, and its religious projections, in a specific social context; for Dodds has shrewdly pointed out that, sturdy as they were, the early Greeks seemed always to feel manipulated by forces from outside. Homeric heroes were mundane men; magic power for warriors lay outside themselves, and was vaguely possessed only by a few like quasi-shamanic Odysseus and other Mycenaean squires or petty "kings." Religious projections can have their origin only in the secular situation, and nowhere else. If Titans smolder against gods as Greek myth develops, we may discern submerged Aegeans and their culture under conquering Achaeans. And if gods had absorbed powers once potentially available to all men, we must expect to find some trend of revolt against petty kings, archons, and a conquest aristocracy of powerful eupatrid families.

In any case this power-conflict was in fact the steady tendency of Greek history from the Mycenaeans to the time of Thucydides. And the archaizing nativistic outburst in the time of Plato, following the defeat of Athens as a democratic city-state, was precisely an attempt to re-establish a much earlier political status quo ante; and with the destruction of the rational state matching the debâcle of Apollonian religion (and here the oracle of Apollo was late as much on the wrong side as was Plato), there ensued a typical Ghost Dance revival of religious and philosophic archaisms. And whether we approach this history from a study of individual personality or of institutionalized culture, the result will be the same. We will seek in a moment to understand the historic changes in Greek character as best we can. Meanwhile, since the rise of the *polis* is central to the Greek experience and ethos, the history of Greek religion is also the history of the secular state.

The family, and other basic social structures, shape character and outlook too. Matrist[47] deities of the settled agricultural Aegeans imply different structures from those of the patrist gods of nomadic and horsed pastoral Indoeuropeans; similarly, Mycenaean religion should differ from the classic pre-Socratic nature philosophy that gradually replaced it, quite as squirearchy differs from intellectual and political democracy. In the old deities of the Mother Earth, and her son or daughter, there was later to be refound a promise of new and everlasting life, as planted seeds are reborn—an immortality quite lacking for men in the theology of the implacable masculine sky gods. In Apollonian religion sons and fathers, gods and men, are immeasurably removed from one another; in the Dionysian Mysteries and revived Magna Mater cults, god and man, father and son, are magically identical. If, in classic times, the dark chthonic gods seemed driven underground, nevertheless in the Hellenistic Mysteries, when that male-made structure, the rational and civilized state, was shaken, the old Mothers re-emerged, with salvation for the individual at least, if not in this world then in some rewon utopian Nowhere.

The masculinity of the Homeric heroes is emphatic, almost a caricature of unmodified patrist masculinity as in brawling and belligerent boys, in a wholly male world with sons always at their fathers' sides and strenuously emulating them from youthful days. The Achaean character embodied an inexpugnable self-respect and rock-solid *aretē*. As he is presented in the *Iliad* we have a stubborn bulldog Ajax, whose virtue is not so intricate a thing as courage, but only a simple unself-questioning assertion of his stand in any situation. The greatest hero of them all, Achilles, sulks in his tent when his honor is not fed. And there is the high-spirited Diomede,[48] with all the fire and boldness of a young man. Indeed, Homer puts a literal fire upon his helmet crest when Diomede is in battle. The youngest of the heroes after Achilles, Diomede is bold before his elders in the scene of the Night Council. He fluently and impetuously criticizes even Agamemnon, and asks the king of kings to make reparation to Achilles, one even more youthful than himself, and whose affronted youthful dignity he understands.

But on the battlefield, with that categorical internalized sense of hierarchy that only males can understand, Diomede submits to military discipline, accepting even the most unjust reproaches of his commander-in-chief. He respectfully brings old Nestor on to fight great Hector—and Zeus, who wishes Hector's victory, has to drive them off with thunderbolts! Even so, Diomede does not tremble before God. The other heroes do not battle with the Immortals, who are naïvely intermingled with them on both sides of this mortal combat. But Diomede, in one grandly dramatic passage, dares even to pursue and to confront not only Aphrodite and Apollo but the very war god Ares himself, whom he wounds in the groin! (Ares complains to Zeus that men should not be allowed to do such things; Zeus treats him with contempt.) Nevertheless, Diomede has no arrogance and makes no impious boasts; he burns only with an inner fire that dares any physical audacity. How could such an ethos end in anything but democracy among Greek men? It is an ethos that disciplines self-boundaries, that demands clarity of thought and argument to persuade the minds of other men, and creates a necessary political machinery for the solution of differences among men in a free society with one another.

Not that they ever falsely muted masculine aggressiveness! Masculinity, unfettered, is always by nature invidiously combative, comparative and competitive. Greeks keenly enjoyed competition of all kinds, from drama-contests to athletic games, and rewarded victors with high public honor. Both drama and games were religious in formal origin. But Greek humanism turned drama from rural religious rites into urbane aesthetic form with high ethical ends—the great Greek tragedians, not the philosophers, were the leaders in moral perceptiveness—and turned formal athletic rituals into games. The Greeks were the first historic people to *play*. And they played in a great variety of ways—with torch races, boat races and horse races, singing contests and dramatic competitions, dancing on greased skins to display a nice balance of body, games of leaping in and out of racing chariots, discus throwing, wrestling, and many other sports.

The brutal gory Roman spectacles, in which one gladiator killed another, or in which wild animals were pitted against men in mutual slaughter, were not games in the Greek sense at all. In Greek games, men strove specifically with other men in a display of human skill and strength, for the abstract glory of winning within the rules. In the Greek Olympic games many people played; in their circuses, the Romans watched others play—if "play" can include bloody no-quarter strife and any trickery that ends in death for one contestant. The drama of dominance to death better fitted Roman tastes; Greek games were to assert life, not to produce death. It was a Roman who wrote that it is sweet and fitting to die for one's country. Fitting perhaps, a Greek might agree, but not sweet. Greeks died, and died bravely, at Marathon and at Salamis for great civic causes. But they never had the sentimentality to call death sweet. The gallantry of Homeric heroes was all the greater because they knew only a dim Hades awaited those who left the sunny upper world in death. The nobility of the Greek mind lies not alone in its expectation of facing facts; to the classic Greek it seems never to have occurred that he should want to escape facts. And this included the most dread fact of all, death. The tragedian wrote, "We must endure our going hence even as our coming hither." And the naturalist Lucretius[49] still in late times expressed a superb Stoic realism about death which good sense must always endorse.

The earliest Greeks knew their gods as manlike. And then, having done so, they found the greatest men to be godlike. Hesiod, it is true, wrote of "a god-like race of hero-men who are called demi-gods," but there are no demi-gods in the *Iliad* or the *Odyssey*.[50] Homer never blurs the sharp line between the mortals and the immortals. Great kings were honored, but they were never worshiped as in Egypt or in the absolutist Orient. And even though some heroes were reputed to be descended quite actually from the gods, it was not ichor that flowed in their veins but mortal blood. Heroes were men, and all men died. But though all men were mortal, they might at least be manly in this life.

And so Homeric Greeks were. There is no word for "god-fearing" in the *Iliad;* nor does the "love of god" enter Greek philosophy until the *philotheos* of Aristotle in post-classic time. The Homeric and classic Greek did not grovel before monstrous idols, half-animal and half-human demons, or shapeless ghosts of his own imagining. He was a man, and his gods were like men. To see the gods as essentially manlike is in itself the consequence of an audacious pride in one's own humanity. The value of being human is simply assumed without any question, and this view of the gods expresses at once self-confidence and a naïvely projected consciousness of self. There is no reverential *fear* of the gods in Homer. They are all-powerful forces of nature. A man must make his peace with them, and that's the end of it. In Dodds' ringing words, Homeric princes bestrode their world boldly, and men feared the gods only as they would their own mighty princes and heroes. The men of the *Iliad* sought help from the gods much as they relied on the support of their fellow men, and on the institutions and customs by which they lived.

There is undoubtedly a relationship between Greek character, humanistic religion, and Greek democratic institutions. And there is a psychiatric soundness and sweetness in a straightforward and unquestioning acceptance of the father, immutably like oneself if here still a little larger than life. For what father, however human he may come to seem, can ever be less than the creator of one's being and the shaper of one's character? Differing only in degree, gods, men and heroes were similar in kind in Homeric Greece, the heroes sometimes greatly noble, *isotheos* or "godlike" —and the gods in turn themselves sometimes reprehensibly human, in the brawling and wenching of a masculine world. In morals and behavior, gods and men are much alike. It was the *deathlessness* of the gods that made their difference from men. Such unassailability of the gods, the fathers who cannot be destroyed, is a sound oedipal paradigm and a healthy one in Homer, to be contrasted with Hesiod's bloody chronicles of father-mutilation by the gods. Though the Greek is always mindful of his own humanity, the human paradigm-god does not die. The *Logos,* pattern of one's ethnic and ethical being, is immortal, thought the Greek.

One may understand, even briefly believe in, the larger-than-life enhancement of the Other, who made us culturally and characterologically what we are. But his deathlessness is an oedipal defense and a fallacy. All fathers die too. And so do all biological paradigms, and all ethnographic eternities. Pattern, which Plato still thought immortal, is not eternal.

Theologically, the difference between gods and men is immutable in Homer. Heroes like Heracles were *theioi,* never *theoi*—much as the Roman Augustus was *divus,* but not *deus.* Pindar, representing all that was conservative in classic Greece, is full of admonitions that mere men should not aspire to the condition of gods. "Seek thou not to become a god," he writes in the *Olympian Odes.*[51] And "Desire not, thou soul of mine, life of the immortals" is his constant theme. For what but this *hubris* or insolent pride would more swiftly bring death to a man from the anger of the gods? "The gods are jealous gods," says Jane Harrison,[52] "there is θφόνος; the gods begrudge a man the glory that may pale their own splendor."

The matter is at the core of Greek manhood: the delicate balance between *aretē* and *hubris,* between the self-assertion of inner manly strength and the knowledge of a greater outside world of Fate or

Ananke that is above even Zeus. The classicist Onians is struck by
the fact that Homeric heroes, for all their superb vitality, feel themselves
not free agents but at every turn victims or passive agents of outside
forces.[53] It was not only that they lived dangerously and held life and
fortune as precarious possessions; but more than that, a man felt he could
not help his own actions. An idea, a feeling came to him, he acted im-
pulsively, and then rejoiced or lamented later; some god had led or
blinded him. His affairs flourished, then he was poor, perhaps enslaved
too in some suddenly lost battle. He was healthy, torn with disease,
and died, all in helpless and irrational sequence, divinely ordained
(θέσφατον), his lot (αἶσα, μοῖρα), fated from long before. An oracle or
soothsayer might foresee his fate in advance, and one might then seek, like
Oedipus, to avoid it. But always—sometimes in infinite irony—Fate wins.

Dodds observes the same phenomenon, that of the outer coercion
felt by the Greek consciousness, and explained by them as the work
of outside gods and daemons.[54] Dodds thinks the reason for this haunted
feeling is that the Greeks had no psychology of the irrational. Hence
they were ultimately defeated by the irrational in themselves they thought
was outside. Dodds' view is illuminating. For, historically, it was precisely
the forces of unreason and blind feeling that ultimately overwhelmed
Greek reason. For one matter, no humanistic Greek rationalism can
hope to cope with the final absurdity of the universe. But more importantly for Dr. Dodd's point, no Apollonian clarity or reason understands the dark Dionysian forces deep within the self, if one is not aware of
and does not acknowledge their existence. We must understand the inner
irrationality, the organism's arbitrary id, just as much as we must seek
to understand the outer irrationality, inhuman and impersonal *Ananke.*
And we must expect neither to be like the clear and conscious self.

We would go further. The Greeks were mistaken to impute conscious
human rationality to the outside world. They made the world similar to
this portion of themselves and were then baffled by it (shamans never
really had omnipotence, nor when their human ghosts climbed into the
sky did this really explain nature). The world, in fact, was neither like
themselves, nor did they know all of themselves. Classic Greeks, male-
centered and narcissistic, took themselves far too much for granted.
Likewise, the Greeks theologically externalized the potency of men—
exalted, magnified and personified it—and then felt themselves helpless
before these divinities. To the puzzled Greek consciousness of the opposition of wish and event, Plato gave a seductive answer. In this
philosophy, the only ultimate reality was the Logos, the soul-like, inseminating, and incorporeal male principle, ideal Form, the conceptual

creator of all imperfect things. These philosophers had turned their faces away from hateful, feared and contemned matter. Fortunately, an alternative Ionian naturalism was in time to discover a godless world, neither for us nor against us, neither mother nor father, neither father nor son, neither godlike nor human. The cool, clear minds of Xenophanes and Leucippus, Democritus and Lucretius, were ancestral to modern atomic physicists.

The Homeric Greek was at home in his body. Still, for all his love of life, he did not shirk the fact of death. "Don't try to explain away death to me!" cried Achilles to Odysseus in Hades.[55] If life itself is the supreme blessing, then the undisputed fact of death only adds poignancy to human life. Life lasts only for a time, and death comes inevitably to everyone. For the Indoeuropeans, life was a quasi-material thing: Greek *thymos,* Latin *fumus* ("smoke"), Sanskrit *dhumas,* Old Slavonic *dymu,* and the like.[56] In violent death blood leaves the wound, and life leaves the body like a material thing. In Homer, *thymos* is a vapor literally collected in the *phrenes*—the midriff, heart and lungs—seat of feeling, speech and mind. In Xenophanes, who first named it *pneuma,* the life-substance still appears to be a warm "breath." Thus if breath rejoins the ocean of invisible and moving wind at death, it is clear why to Anaximenes the boundless substrate of all being was the air (though to Thales this substrate was water, to Heraclitus fire, and to Anaximander a material *physis*); and it is also clear why to Greeks at large the great Father of all was the open heaven, Zeus, "the shining one." Thus to the Ionian nature philosophers, individual life was part of a great cycle in which men (their bodies and life-stuff) circulated in and out of a universal material One which alone Xenophanes was willing to call God.

But these nature philosophers were proto-scientists, all of them later subtler and urban minds. The early warrior Greeks in Europe were simple animists: gods were spirits, and men had spirits. Among spirits, the mighty ones, gods, were eternal, and they could materalize in manlike form at will—*or as animals,* and indeed the fifteen books of Ovid's *Metamorphoses* are a long compendium of just such acts.[57] But the spirits of men were of uncertain and brief duration, once having left the human body at death. Only duration and magnitude of spirit divide them; nevertheless this gulf between gods and men is insurpassable in Homer. The only "sin" in Greek theology was the hubris of attempting to bridge this gulf.[58]

Apollo flayed Marsyas alive for daring to rival him in making magical music; what was once a shamanistic contest is now an uncompromising separation of men from the gods. Each sin is a direct affront to a specific god. Ixion, condemned to his wheel, had assaulted Hera, wife of Zeus. Tityos had outraged Leto, mother of Apollo and Artemis. Sisyphus disclosed a secret sexual intrigue of Zeus. And Tantalus, unforgivably, made himself immortal by stealing the divine nectar and ambrosia of the gods. Each sin is oedipal *lèse majesté* in god-man terms. Extension of life among these wretches was only in order to prolong their punishments.

Prometheus stole sacred fire from the Sky, the shamanistic secret of Zeus, his lightning, and was chained to a rock, his liver eaten by an eagle, or a vulture, both doublets of Zeus. This is the dilemma of all culture heroes also, to discriminate *hubris* and *aretē,* to know the limits of their strength and not to presume to godhood. The ambiguity of such Titanic contests with gods is possible for two reasons: originally these were only shamanistic rivalries among near-equals, gods and titans; and also the Greeks lacked any priestly hierarchy to punish intellectual heresy—Socrates was condemned by civil authorities for treason against the state—a dispensation that may also have fostered the growth of Greek science. Prometheus taught men to build houses, to count and write, to construct the farmer's calendar, to domesticate animals, cure disease with herbs, practice divination, build ships, and work in metals— indeed, Aeschylus wrote in *Prometheus Bound* that "Prometheus founded all the arts of men."[59] This tragedy follows the Aristotelian "unities" that Aeschylus never heard of, but it is the greatest drama of Aeschylus and the one that speaks best to the modern free mind. Those who love God first will soon find an autocratic Father and found a theocracy; those who love men first will find brothers. In his magnificently defiant colloquy with Oceanus, and again with Hermes, the proud thief of fire is an anti-Job, and no two literary works better mark the difference between the Greek ethos and the Hebrew than *Prometheus Bound* and the *Book of Job*.

Guilt, such as that of Oedipus or Orestes, involved other powers more mana-like than god-like. Greek guilt was not an agonizing consciousness of sin and not necessarily earned by conscious moral choice after a wrangle with conscience, but rather a quasi-material contamination as the result of sometimes innocently blind acts as in the case of Oedipus. Guilt was put upon a man by a Fate beyond the gods, and as such was inexorable in its working. No pity or prayers could move Fate, which gave no grace. Neither lack of knowledge of transgression, nor individual worth, nor good intentions could modify the iron workings of the moral law. For the Greeks, this gave a tragic inevitability of doom to their dramas, which for superficial modern readers, forgetting how sins of fathers are visited psychically on sons, seems emotionally alien and merely arbitrary injustice. Still, if character is fate, is it not equally arbitrary in giver and receiver? How blame the father, who was once a son?

In the vague Homeric hell all souls, good or bad, seemed to dwell, at least for a time after death, as pale and gibbering ghosts. But the only tortured ones there had all been offenders against the gods, raised to edifying significance and a longer duration of suffering by the magnitude and nature of their crimes. For the others, death itself was sufficient punishment for being human. The dim afterworld was in no wise a desirable place to be. This life above on the sunlit earth was a precious thing precisely because it did not last forever. It is this poignant humanity and tragic vulnerability of Homeric heroes that makes them morally attractive above all others who are promised the reward of immortality, a shabby business, for their bravery. Would war end if men honestly knew themselves mortal?

The famous admonition that Apollo wrote in large letters above the entrance to his sanctuary, GNOTHI SEAUTON, "Know thyself," meant to the classic Greek something like "Beware here of your mere humanity" or "Know thyself to be mortal" in this place of the god-oracle, that is, "Remember here thy mortality" much as Egyptians brought a skeleton to their feasts for the same purpose. Apollo's injunction was merely a bit of ethical advertising or shamanistic "bedside business" to put consultants into a proper state of awe, and to convince them the fee had bought their money's worth. It emphatically did not mean the fatuous self-analysis that Socrates adjured upon his listeners, which, misinterpreting the god "as his manner was" (Zimmern dryly comments), Socrates "made the basis of his philosophical thinking."[60] The deliberate misinterpretation by Socrates, in point of fact, was not Apollonian but specifically Dionysian. Falsely, in those decadent times, Socrates cleverly twisted it to mean that men should know themselves from the memory of many pasts to be immortal! A neo-Orphic, Socrates evidently thought he was immortal, as Pythagoras thought himself earlier, and the shaman Empedocles. Hence Socrates, knowing full well he was guilty of the political crime of betraying Athens to the Spartans, drank the hemlock calmly—because he believed in the Pythagorean transmigration of indestructible souls in a kind of animistic Law of the Conservation of Soul-stuff. In his fellow-traveler sentimentalizing of the event as the pious martyrdom of an intellectual, Plato makes the death of Socrates noble, whereas it was only misguided. The motivating guilt for Socrates' suicide was direct and real, the bravery cheap because inauthentic, and the belief itself illusory. Like the Old Testament Hebrews, the classic Greeks are an exhilarating people, because both dealt with moral realities. But Socrates and the Hellenistic Paul, fathers of a new cult, were merely pusillanimous in their lack of self-knowledge concerning the fact of mortality.

The relationship of mortal men to the gods was a straightforward one of *do ut des*. To obtain the favor of the mighty ones, men sacrificed animals, in particular (on the most solemn occasions in old Indoeuropean times) the highly valued horse, in ritual performed for the common tribal good. The automatic efficacy of the sacrifice seems to have been little questioned, for in the cognate Brahman cult of India the ritual prayers of the Vedic books became *mantras* or outright magic formulas. The smoke of the fat of slaughtered animals, rising upward to the skies, was a feast for the immortal spirits, summoned to the sacrifice by name and indeed, in India, such sacrifice nourished their immortality; sometimes the communicants could tidily eat the roast meat themselves, the spirits having been fed on the rich odors. The man-like spirits had powers over nature. Quite as men had earlier approached their shamans, they therefore sought relationships to these gods, using logical and reasonable human inducements. The food offerings were *bargains* or payments for services rendered or about to be rendered; a straightforward commercial *quid pro quo,* not emotional beseechments. Significantly, the word *religio* originally means "binding," and if the early Indoeuropean cult was naturism in kind, it tended to be magical in means. The "binding" was a supernatural *contract* or covenant between gods and men, as between shamans and their communicants or clients.

In Greece, the Indoeuropean religion became the official state cult as in Rome, a settled affair with solemn public ritual of low emotional potential, the orderly and serene Apollonian religion, gravely and naïvely masculine in a man-centered world. Its ethic emphasized the solid satisfactions of this sunny and material upper world. "Nothing in excess" was the Apollonian ideal, and it produced the calm and measured beauty of the Parthenon, the stately and noble prose of Pericles' Funeral Oration, the static balanced beauty of the sculptures of classic Greece that even in motion are poised and controlled. With these characteristics, nothing could be imaginably more foreign to Apollonian religion than the later Dionysian Mysteries—dark and chthonic, feminine, of the underworld and night, wailing, emotional, ecstatic, irrational and frenzied, not openly for the state comity but secret and shamanistic, and only for individual salvation from the common lot.

The classic Greeks had a magnificent materiality, saneness and clarity of mind. The love of this life and of the physical body is Greek to the core. Who can despise men who so loved their humanity? This love was naïve and complete: the Greeks had no horror of the naked body. As early as 720 B.C. the athlete Orsippus discarded the usual brief loincloth, ran completely nude, and won the event. Thereafter his practice was universally adopted, first in the games for Zeus at Olympia, and then in public festivals, gymnasia and other public places, whether indoors or out, throughout ancient Greece. In Sparta,[61] where athletic contests were encouraged by the state for girls and young married women as well as for men, the custom of female nudity was easily adopted also. Organized athletics as a way of worship given to God, the body perfectly trained as a noble thing dedicated to the Father, is a new and startling concept in the history of man. But it was entirely consistent with Greek humanism.

The central attribute of Zeus was that of All Father, and creativity was his essence to a degree that was even disturbing to the later Greeks. Though other gods shared it to varying degrees, Zeus possessed *par excellence* lordship over fertility, the essential and ancient daemonic trait of shaman and master of animals. Greeks saw creative power not only as the prime force on which men and indeed all life depended, but as the very *mysterium tremendum* of godhood itself. Zeus was the greatest spirit, and pure spirit was the abstract essence of life itself. In Anaxagoras this principle was the base of a whole metaphysical system, *Nous* as mind and the creativity immanent in Creation, a humanistic similitude of microcosm and Macrocosm. More than this, a host of terms like "genius" and "generation" indicated the sameness to the Greeks of consciousness, intellectual creativity, and sexual procreativity. Genius was genital, so that the springing of Athena directly from her sire's brain, though an unusual, was still a completely plausible birth.

This was for Greeks no metaphor but a literality to the point of their supposing that the *muellos* in brain and spinal marrow was not so much the source of *but the same substance as* semen. The growth of beard and head hair (and its later loss), as well as of pubic hair, were all explained on the ground of the closeness of these parts to the vital substance of mind-male productivity. Even as studious an anatomist as Leonardo in the high Renaissance was still drawing a supposed, but nonexistent, canal between the lower spine and the male genital, as a result of this erroneous theory. In Hellenistic and Christian times "continence" meant literally the *saving of life* as the careful retention of a stuff finite in amount, since every sexual act was a little death. Still millennia later, "loss of mind" was fearfully equated with "loss of man-hood."[62]

The Greeks approached each evidence of the creative *mana* of Zeus with holy awe. It was direct reverence for the genital power that had peopled the earth, provided the abundance and variety of living creatures, and created the gods.[63] The pagan Cerinthus replied to an early Father's horror of the phallic by stating simply that man should not be ashamed of what God had not been ashamed to create. Hence Greeks carried in the most solemn religious ceremonies simulacra of what Creativity had chosen to create, with innocent respect and jubilation, and they named αἰδοῖον "that which inspires reverent awe" what later men called *pudenda* "those things of which one must be ashamed." It is difficult for us, after centuries of Christian body-hating and dismay at the material world, to recapture the simplicity and directness of their attitude, in which there was no suggestion of prurient salaciousness but only thankful delight. Since the generation of life was the prime manifestation of divine power, it was only proper that the organs of generation should be reverenced as divine symbols of deity. And un-Greek as he was in so many other ways, Plato is still Greek in his exaltation of the metaphysical *Logos,* the conceptual Model, the demiurgic Idea creative of all things.

The nature gods of the Achaean Greeks were of a simple pantheistic kind. When men directly observe movement, growth and life in Nature, it is easy to see in such natural objects the same consciousness, volition and mind that man finds in himself. Grains and fruits grow, and the eating of them gives life. Even more obviously, animals have a life plainly close in kind to that of men. But many other things in Nature also move and change, and hence they must have life too. The weather from the sky is like the moods of a powerful and unpredictable father, variously angry and benign. Winds teach early man that things not seen can yet have force; and shadows, that things seen may yet lack substance. Water comes and goes in rain and rivers, and water may change its form through heat and fire as vapor, dew and rain. The sun and moon, the planets and the stars all move, so by easy inference they must have life also. If man is "animated," then so is Nature. And man surely is, for do not dreams show something in himself that can visit past and future times and far-off places? Are not sleep, death and memory all aspects of manifest life or soul? The animist need only think the outside world is like himself; the pantheist, to find such souls in the whole of Nature.

Zeus, Father of gods and men, kept throughout the chief clue to his Indoeuropean origin. He is "the shining one," the sky itself, light, day.

Hence when the moving forces of the sky and the changing aspects of weather are explained as the work of a person, an *anima* or soul, it is a man-like Zeus who gathers the clouds, sends down the fructifying rain, shines warmly and benignly, or hurls his angry thunderbolts, as once did a living weather-shaman. Perhaps also, if in a new way, Max Müller was right to see Indoeuropean grammar creating gods. For later Romans it was still not simply a "raining occur" (as in Navaho) but an *"it* rains" as in English: the subject-and-predicate habit of Indoeuropean speech still had a Latin "Jupiter Pluvius" transitively *raining* the rain. Gods are a figment, too, of compulsive grammar. With such a grammar, there must be a Subject *causing* the event. But such a naming of the parts of Nature as *causes* contains within itself the seed of its own decay and destruction. Such *numina* or mana presences were seen by later men for what they are, mere *nomina* or names for nature seen animistically, pantheistically and anthropomorphized. Once, a person controlled the weather; now, a Person does. But the Subject as Cause evaporates from nature if only events eventuate events, if god-persons are banished from reality to leave only abstract manas or "forces" in operation.

Not only do the gods fall down grammatically, but in time morally as well, if they are merely man-like. For all his inveterate conservatism, it is plain that Pindar, like Aeschylus, felt strongly that orthodox theology held much of what was inconsistent with a "worthy" concept of the gods. He would have sympathized with the Xenophanes who criticized both Homer and Hesiod, "who have attributed to the gods all things that are a shame and reproach among men." A revisionist, Pindar wrote: "Meet it is that a man should speak noble things of the gods: the blame is less."[64] It is unfortunate the first tales about gods were really about men, shamanic tricksters. And gods are doomed if men achieve historically a morality higher than that of old gods; human sacrifice to gods, one wryly notes, lasted longer than cannibalism in Europe, since gods' tastes are evidently conservative. And even self-perpetuating holy-human institutions lag and give no special moral light (Pius in the Nazi holocaust of Jews) when they become only fossils of past culture. As for Pindar's squeamish Modernism, it is really the fault of ethnographic history that gods began as they did, in shaman-tricksters.

Curiously, the Cretan Zeus was born in a cave, a deity of the earth as a shamanic bull-god might be expected to be. But these are syncretistic contaminations of Zeus Pater as an Indoeuropean god, better seen in his Latin form of Jupiter. Like many sky gods elsewhere, Jupiter was worshiped on hills, on the Alban Hills south of Rome as Jupiter Latiaris (who "lies hidden" popular etymology has it). His oldest temple on the

Capitoline Hill, under the Tarquin kings, was Etruscan in style. His sacred oak there grew next to a still older shrine of Jupiter Feretrius, a feretory of the god himself, in which the chief cult object was a *lapis silex*,[65] probably an Old Stone Age flint celt but believed to be a thunder-bolt, a sacred object on which oaths were taken and treaties concluded; almost until our day such "thunder-stones" were thought to be actual "lightning-bolts." The equation may very well be for the reason that the spunk or spark lies latent in a flint, until struck onto a punk—since Mesolithic times a dried fungus, the mushroom too being thought to be created by lightning strikes.

The Indoeuropean word root **diw-* that appears in *Ze*us Pater (Latin *Ju*piter, Sanskrit *Dy*aus Pitar), in *Di*ana, *Di*one, *Di*onysus and in *theos-deus-divus* and "divine" originally meant light, fire or soul, that is, the divine source of life, the male principle, the unseen mystery of life. In the nineteenth century it was much argued just *what* Zeus *was,* the day, the sun, or the heavens, but it seems clear enough now that the term is an allusive one, meaning simply "the Shiner," or "the shining one" or "that which shines" and as such was freely seen in various guises by the ancients themselves.[66] Thus as light and fire, Zeus is the hidden divine source, mysterious and unseen, of all life and spirit in the universe; as late as Heraclitus the ground of being was fire. Zeus is the male counterpart of the ancient earth goddess Ge, Gaia or De-Meter who is the substance, as he is the soul, of plants and animals—the earth to which all return, in a relation as simple and physical as that of a mother and her child, of death and burial, and as visible and concrete as the male spirit-component is invisible, mysterious and unknown. The shaman who is master of fire, who juggles and swallows coals of fire, is in simple literalness Master of Life.[67] Shiva holds a flame of fire in one divine hand, Zeus hurls fire; Prometheus is a late-comer shaman and creative culture hero in the midst of already emergent deism, a Marsyas to Zeus' Apollo.

Like ithyphallic cave shamans and sorcerers, the function of Zeus is to foment fertility in animals and men through all his shocking appearances and his divine bestialities.[68] There is no suggestion in the *Iliad* that Zeus is concerned with abstract Justice[69]—a late Hellenistic idea, shaped by the Egyptian *ma'at*[70] and the Heraclitean concept of cosmic Justice as a quasi-physical process (like Newton's "action and reaction" or Hegel's "thesis and antithesis"). In his exhaustive monograph on Zeus the northern oak-god, Cook shows how even the Homeric Zeus has undergone some expurgation. To be sure the amorous intrigues with females, human, animal and divine, still remain—as is appropriate to the All Father, whose very tree bears the many-times-reduplicated *glans* or acorn, whence comes the notable fat-*muellos* and fertility of pigs that live on the *mast*-virility or seed of the oak. In his earliest forms, and even in his later, Zeus had many wiles, much like the crooked wizard Odin in whose stories a real human being[71] quite naïvely still may be seen (though the weather shaman's thunder was inherited by another Norse sky-god, Thor-Donner, who flung flint hammers from the sky as lightning). Such was the origin of Zeus too, as a human,[72] though conflicting stories of his birth and place of birth are found fused in his myths.

The nobly bearded Counsellor and Cloud-Compeller of classic Athens, symbolized in Phidias' great statue of a gravely majestic and benign mature man, was once (so Gilbert Murray has well pointed out) the shaman and rain maker of Eurasia, the divine king or rain shaman of Africa, the man-god or magician of more ancient times, a ghost worshiped to supreme divinity. The assimilation of Zeus to other gods was done through epithets: Zeus Lykaios in Arcadia was once involved with human sacrifice (like Othin,[73] like the Celtic reindeer-crowned god and thunder god of the Gundestrup Cauldron), while Zeus Meilichios in Attica was once a serpent, a chthonic god of souls in the underworld. Jane Harrison attests overwhelmingly to the snake as the male principle, symbol of life, fertility and soul in the old chthonic religion: a snake disappearing into a cleft in the earth was the consort of the Mother; Hermes, Meilichios, Asklepios, Crecrops, Erichtheus and many others were snakes in body form or "attribute"; even Athena the Maiden was attended by a chthonic snake; and when a man died, a snake glided forth from his loins, to remain, as is the wont of snakes, immortal. As if Zeus Meilichios as chthonic snake were not enough, Zeus also reappears, somewhat startlingly for an All Father, both as a sacred babe and as a youth or *kouros,* in spring dances and initiation rites which came from earlier Helladic cults. He is also again the bull (the Europa myth, and the Minotaur in Crete) and Zeus-Zagreus of the Titan initiation feast, the Sabazius cult, and the Dionysian Mysteries. In all these forms, Zeus is a fertility daemon; and quite as often as not, the Shaman appears in the animal form of one of his countless familiars.

The earth as the Great Mother emerged in Greek myth in a plurality of forms also, simultaneously worshiped under separate names as independent personalities. She was Demeter, Athena, Rhea, Aphrodite, Artemis, and Hera. Hera, a Cretan-Argive form of the chthonic mother goddess, was wife to Zeus—though they never got along very well together because of Zeus' Olympian unfaithfulness. As official wife, she is usually presented as a jealous termagant. Perhaps her bossiness and more than touch of bad temper are also to be expected in one who was formerly the chief deity herself, though her name Hera means "clear sky." In the Olympian pantheon, Hera is an unsympathetic and curiously bloodless figure, with none of the awesomely overwhelming power of Aphrodite, the everpresent protectiveness of Athena, the inaccessible purity of Artemis, or the ample humanity and passionate motherhood of Demeter. Of the many roles of women, Hera's is only that of Wife.

Although there were four earth mothers on Olympus, in these latter days three brothers, the sons of Kronos, shared the rule of the universe: Zeus of the sky, Poseidon of the sea, and Dis of the underworld. Poseidon the Earth-Shaker was originally an inland god, later fused with a god of the sea-going Cretans; and Dis was an obscure primitive deity who ruled the underworld of souls in Hades, whose name means "riches" and whose realm may mean "the Unseen, Unknown." The Earth-Shaker kept his shaman's trident[74]; and Dis, like his Latin cognate Pluto, is an ancient underground shaman-god of wealth, a master of fertility and spirits much like the antler-crowned Cernunnus. At least Dis did not displace any of the earth mothers on Olympus, for he was not one of the Twelve—Zeus, Hera, Athena, Apollo, Artemis, Hermes, Ares, Aphrodite, Hephaestus, Hestia, Poseidon and Demeter.

In Greek mythology, Apollo is a complex figure, the product evidently of many syncretisms—of which the sole syncretic base and single uniting similarity is that of the shaman. In sculpture Apollo is usually shown as a handsome youth, unclothed or lightly draped, his "attributes" the bow and arrows, the laurel, the lyre, the oracular tripod, the snake, and the dolphin. The Delphinian Apollo of the dolphin, the sprightly and companionable porpoise, was the protector of sailors, navigation and marine life, a realm that might seem somewhat outside of his orbit; but in keeping with his shamanic origin Apollo was generally a powerful apotropaic protector from evil, all-seeing and prophetic. His main centers were Delos, one of the smaller Cyclades or Aegean islands, and Delphi, an old Bronze Age town on Mt. Parnassus in Phocis, on the mainland of Greece.

Apollo was a fusion of the northern Phoebus ("radiant" or "shining") with an old Aegean hunter god, wolf god, and protector of flocks, in which latter guise he was an iconographic forerunner of Orpheus-Christ. As a sun god, Apollo's attributes in some ways duplicate those of the sky god Zeus, though Apollo is a youth and Zeus a mature man. Appropriately, in classic myth Apollo was called the son of Zeus by Leto, "Darkness," for he was also connected with fertility, cattle, and the increase of wild animals. In Homer and Hesiod there is no indication of Apollo as a sun god. But after his identification with Phoebus, Apollo in later times was easily identified with the Sun proper, Helios.

Born in Delos, Apollo slew the Python, which had been the attendant serpent of an oracle of Ge-Themis, the old earth goddess at Delphi. For this crime he was made to visit the Vale of Tempe to obtain the purifying laurel, and afterward the oracle of the now "Pythian Apollo" was the center of a cult to give purification from great crimes, especially that of murder. Hrozný believes that as sender and healer of the plague, Apollo is the Hittite Apulunas.[75] Not all recent scholars agree, but Dodds thinks Apollo an Asiatic of some sort, from the evidence in the *Iliad*. The Greeks, probably in error, etymologized his name to mean "Destroyer"[76] but he was in fact a light- and life-giver—and indeed he bestowed his powers as medicine man on his son the snake god Asklepios. Catharsis and purification was originally a function of chthonic deities, though here taken over by Apollo. But it remained nevertheless a *priestess* who chewed the narcotic(?) laurel leaf and was the voice of the Pythian Apollo. No wonder Apollo was famed as a misogynist!

For all his "Apollonian" serenity as successor to Themis, goddess of law and order, Apollo also inherited from Ge-Themis of the Python certain distinct traits as an ecstatic shaman. The Pythia made contact with the god via his sacred tree the laurel—either by holding a branch of it as Themis does in a fifth-century vase painting, or as Plutarch says by censing herself in its burned leaves, or as Lucian stated by chewing laurel leaves.[77] The notion of intoxication by earth vapors, in a seer seated on a shamanic tripod, would be attractive in a prophet or prophetess of chthonic origin and inspiration. But as Wilamowitz seems to have been the first to point out, the vapor-intoxication theory was of later Hellenistic origin. Plutarch, with reason to know the facts, raised questions about the vapor theory and finally rejected it entirely. But like the Stoic philosophers who first promulgated it, nineteenth-century rationalizers of myth[78] accepted with alacrity a good concrete materialistic reason. However, French diggings at the Delphic adytos discover no vapors now and no chasm from which noxious vapors could have come. With considerable plausibility, Dodds thinks that the idea of a chasm or cave under the temple of an earth oracle is older than the notion of psychedelic vapors and may have suggested it.

As Apollo Citharoedus, lord of the lyre, with which like Orpheus he enchanted the animals and charmed all nature, as seer and oracle, as hunter god, as provider of catharsis and protector from evil spirits, and as associated with a ritual narcotic, Apollo has multiple links with the shaman-bard of the north. As Apollo Sauroctonos or dragon slayer, he also seems allied to an old northern hero (St. George is still a favorite saint in modern Greece). As Apollo Hegemon ("leader") and Apollo Ktistes ("founder") he was the patron of colonies. As Apollo Kouros he was the idealized youth and athlete, and the chief figure in Greek art from the archaic period to classic times. He was also patron of the intellectual arts through his half-sisters, the Nine Muses, daughters of Zeus by Mnemosyne ("Memory").[79] Apollo is the most quintessentially Greek of all Greek gods. If Zeus the Father was the most revered and respected, Apollo the son was surely the most loved.

As the son, and in some ways the doublet of Zeus, Apollo was the appointed mediator between gods and men through his oracle at Delphi, "the navel of the earth." But there is nothing in the legend, and no economic or other material circumstance in the environment of Delphi, to account for the spectacular rise of the Oracle to become for several generations the greatest religious force in Greece. It is, rather, that the classic Greek was an intensely civic and political animal, and these were dangerous times for the Greek city-state menaced by the colossal and all-conquering Empire of Persia. Further, the old Indoeuropean shaman-bard from the beginning had many political traits, being emissary and advisor to the ruler, and at times he was even the sacred king himself. But though church and state were close, the Greeks clearly separated them, and unlike the situation in contemporary theocracies in Egypt and Asia Minor, the civil power was unquestionably pre-eminent in Greece. The nearest approach to a priestly system transcending the single city-state in Greece were the *exegetai pythochrestoi* who expounded Apollonian sacral law at Athens and, Nilsson thinks, elsewhere also. So long as they served a significant civil purpose, the oracles of the Delphinian Apollo were a powerful political force in Greece.[80]

They were, that is, until the "cringing priests at Delphi" (Zimmern), perhaps bribed, appeared to be tendentiously favoring Sparta over Athens in the Peloponnesian War. But the secularizing trend had already begun in the Persian wars, and in particular after the victory at Salamis. Gods had been on both sides in the legendary Trojan War, but they stood on the sidelines in the far more threatening Persian Wars at home. The Greeks beat the Persians by no godly miracle. They beat them four or five times, in Greece, Asia and Sicily, in battles on land and on sea. It was not gods but men who won at Marathon and Salamis. And not only Greeks changed their attitude toward themselves after Salamis, but to Egyptians and others who had formerly thought them rough brawlers and crude tribal hill people the Greeks were now respectable and respected.

In their greatest national crisis, tergiversating when a shaman most owes reassurance and protection to his people, the Olympians were aloof and disgracefully neutral. Apollo tried hard to re-edit and explain his oracles after the event, but to hardbitten men this was a deathblow to his national prestige, and for some generations afterward oracular religion went unheeded in Greece. It was the city patroness Athena who was thanked in the Parthenon, and Periclean Greece put more faith in the powers of men than of gods.

Artemis, the sister of Apollo, was associated with an old Aegean bear-goddess, as he was with a wolf. Like Apollo, she is a hunter. Like Apollo she is also a patron and protector of wild animals, "mistress of the animals" and "mother of the wild" resembling the northern "owners" of animals that shamans called upon, embodied or controlled. As Apollo was the sun, so Artemis was the moon, later somewhat mechanically assimilated to Diana the virgin huntress. Twin sister to Apollo, she, as he, punished evil with her arrows and pestilence, and protected mortals from danger and sickness. As a deity of light, her identification as Moon belonged rather to Selene ("brightness") hence also called Phoebe to parallel Phoebus. But as Hecate[81] ("far-working" like "far shooting" Apollo) she remained the goddess of witchcraft deep into the Middle Ages; and much like the island sorceress Circe who turned men into swine, Diana, surprised in bathing, turned Actæon into a stag. She also drove men mad; as Luna, she made them "lunatic," in her Roman form. Misandrous as Apollo was misogynist, she was, as in most of her attributes, a mere copy-cat and feminine doublet of her brother; but in Asia Artemis was fertility itself as an earth mother and many-papped "Diana of the Ephesians." As the Bœotian Artemis she is close to the Mycenaean and Cretan snake-holding mother and mistress of animals. She may also be associated with initiation rituals, as in the bear dance of girls to honor the Brauronian Artemis, in the magic flogging of youths before Artemis Orthis, and perhaps also in the olive branch fetish of Artemis Korythalia.

A goddess somewhat like her may have come with the warriors from the north, but the name of Athena is not Indoeuropean. Local goddess of Attica and patroness of Athens, with which city she was more than etymologically connected, Athena has the owl of clairvoyant wisdom (perhaps also the shaman-bird of dead spirits) and the snake which betrays her chthonic origin. It was she who sprang directly from the brain-source of Zeus' virility and creativity, without following the usual spinal marrow path of procreation. Athena personifies the clear upper air, mental clarity and acuteness, and embodies the spirit of truth and divine wisdom. She is clothed in the aegis, a sort of goatskin mantle fringed with serpents, symbolizing the dark storm cloud and its lightnings, and she is also armed with the irresistible spear of lightning. This aegis of Zeus was lent both to Apollo and to Athena, but gradually it became her attribute. As the clear upper air, Athena is a doublet both of Zeus, the shining sky, of Hera the clear sky, and perhaps also of "shining" Phoebe— not to say Ouranos, ancestor of them all, and Urania the Muse or "heavenly one" who was half-sister of Apollo the sun god. As wielder of lightning in the dark sky, Athena is at one with Zeus and Apollo. The Greek pantheon is an untidy collection of duplicate impersonations or names that reiterate and confirm origins, but in their conflicting and inconsistent attributes the gods should not be rationalized but seen only as syncretisms from diverse origins. Bright sky or dark sky, with her bird Athena is simply a weather shamaness, a sky power associated with spirits: and a wielder of lightning.

To Athena as godly wisdom to aid statesmen and rulers there clings also a firm connection with artisans,[82] which except as another shamanism is otherwise inexplicable. Carpenters and masons owe their T-square to Athena. She protected the metallurgical arts that used fire. She was especially the patroness of the host of potters that gave their name to the large suburb of Athens, the Cerameicus. Athena as culture hero invented the potter's lathe, and she herself made the first vases in terra cotta. She was on hand to prevent accidents in laying on colors, and also in the firing of pots, driving off the demons Syntrips, Sabaktes, and Smaragus who lurked in the oven or the clay and broke the pots or cracked the varnish. All branches of the ceramic craft invoked Athena, and so did all other artisans. And in the contest with Poseidon to become patron deity of the city, Poseidon produced the horse but Athena created the olive and won.[83] As protectoress and tutelary deity of the city, Athena has a shield—there is an old connection of shamanism and war in the Indoeuropean north—and at her feet is Erichthonios, an old snake god attending the earth mother and chthonic place deity of the Acropolis from immemorial times. Never was a part-alien deity more naturalized citizen than Athena! But Athena was goddess only of righteous wars and became a homebody. When Alcibiades invaded overseas Syracuse in a most un-Athenian, unwise and undemocratic adventure, his luck and the goddess clearly remained at home.

Hephaestus as artisan, like Athena as potter, seems an odd denizen of aristocratic Olympus.[84] But if it appear strange that a mere smith should be a god, we need only remember that, anciently, both in north Africa and Paleosiberian tribes (not to say trickster Loki[85] of the Indoeuropean north and Daedalus of Crete), artisans were commonly shamans. There is no Greek logic either for the husbandhood of a lowly artisan Hephaestus with the great goddess of love, dread Aphrodite—only the antique association of the shaman with the fertility goddess of the earth. Here, as so often is the case, contemporary religion is explainable not in terms of reason but only of the irrational past. That Hephaestus was a worker with fire is still another shamanic attribute.

Hephaestus was the Olympian smith and artificer, his name being of great antiquity and belonging to some non-Indoeuropean language spoken before ever the Achaeans came to Greece. He was a culture hero and magic artificer, and with Athena he taught men the arts of life. Perhaps originally, as some think, his name meant simply "fire," for he can be heard toiling with his men at a workshop-forge inside the volcano: Vulcan is his Latin cognate. Certainly, like Prometheus, he is closely associated with fire. He too escaped or was cast out from heaven (and fell like Icarus, son of Daedalus) onto the isle of Lemnos to become the god of the early metal workers, and as a consequence he was permanently maimed, like Oedipus and Philoctetes, in the foot. Since in some versions it was he who made the aegis, and since he is fire fallen from heaven, Hephaestus seems at least a fragment of the sky-fire-lightning god. But in myth he is merely the son of Zeus and Hera.

His wife Aphrodite was born directly of the fire of Ouranos which fell to earth when Kronos mutilated his father the Sky, but in a traditional and probably erroneous etymology she was "foam" born of the sea, and like the Phoenician Astarte was herself the germinal power in nature. For love is a goddess. To the Greeks even love, and especially love, arises not from one's inner nature or wish; it is the great and dread Aphrodite, wracking us to display her power. But the fickle Aphrodite, never an original Olympian anyway, herself fell in love with Ares, war. Hephaestus should have married Hestia, the modest hearth goddess, who goes back as far as anything we know of the Greeks,[86] and in the *Odyssey* Homer uses "hearth" to mean "family." For Hephaestus and Hestia were both earthly fires for human use. But in time this humble keeper of the fire was forgotten on Olympus, and Hestia was replaced among the Twelve by the boisterous and rowdy wine-god Dionysus.

Not that Aphrodite escaped her enamorment with fire; for the bird of Ares, the Great Black Woodpecker, was the bird of fire.[87] This woodpecker, the *Picus Martius* of Linnaeus, had prophetic power. It was also too potent magically for any sorcerer's nail or *defixio* to remain driven into a tree in which it nested. The bird's connection with the god of fertility and war, Onians thinks, comes from the virility "fire" on its head; this woodpecker is wholly black, except for its head of flaming scarlet. In any case, the Latin Mars seems to be maleness itself, for Varro gives the ancient explanation of his name as *mas,* "male" in the oblique form *mar-is;* and Onians gives much illumination in his etymology (*Maspiter=Marspiter,* and *Mavors=Mas=Mars,* or *Ma+vers* as in *verres,* since the *ver sacrum* was usually his) if the god of fertility and war indeed be the god of virility, manifest in fervor and fierceness—and, one might add, like the fire above Diomede's head in battle.

In Greek the name Ares is associated with the word *aretē* meaning *vir*-tue, the basic essence or worth or purpose of anything, and in men virility, power, strength and manhood. Some ally his name to *eris,* strife, discord, personified as Eris, his sister and companion, who excites to war; but the folk etymology is artificial, and quite without his sister Ares was insolent enough himself in his arrogance of power. Ares was an alien Thracian in Greek myth to the end. In Homer, Ares is only half-accepted by the Olympians, who regard him as a ruffian and swashbuckling boor; and like Aphrodite he escaped to his original home away from Olympus, when he was released from the iron net of the clever smith and wronged husband Hephaestus. Not greatly admired by the Greeks—though they admired basic creative sexual virility sufficiently in Zeus and Hermes and Apollo—Ares was an outsider. Jane Harrison thinks we may detect the Homeric attitude to Ares in art. Ares to be sure is among the archaic seated gods on the frieze of the Treasury of Cnidos discovered at Delphi, but he is seated at the end by himself. Even on the east frieze of the Parthenon, "where all is softened down to a decent theological harmony, there is just a lingering, semi-conscious touch of the same prejudice." Ares is there, but not quite comfortable among the easy aristocratic Olympians. "Grouped with no one, he leans his arm on no one's shoulder" and his pose is too self-consciously stiff to seem really assured."[88] Even after a resoundingly successful defensive war, the Athenians did not honor War. War never really belonged among the urbane gods of light and reason, and he always remained a crude Thracian boor.

Hermes was born in Arcadia the son of Maia and Zeus. He is one of the most interesting of Greek gods, and most typical in his confused syncretism and sharing of attributes with other deities half his duplicates, being a god of souls and the underworld like Dis, and a fertility daemon like Zeus and Apollo, among other attributes.[89] His basic Indoeuropean nature can be established through Sanskrit cognates. Hermes' name in the dual, Sanskrit *sāramaya,* refers to two dogs, spotted (*kerberos*) like the three-headed Cerberus who guarded the way to the place of the dead; they were messengers of Yama—*Sarama,* an emissary of Indra the sky god, plus *-eya,* suffix of relation or descent, the "sārameya" being therefore the canine "Hermeids." (Yama, the "twin" and son of the Sun, was the first mortal and Adam of the human race, and so the first to go to the world of spirits, where he became king and judge of those that followed him; Zeus's brother, underworld Dis is still a "shining" god.)

In Greek mythology, Hermes was variously the herald and messenger of the gods; the protector of herdsmen; the tutelary deity of highways and boundaries whose *herm* or torso on a post stood at street corners, gymnasia and other public places as well as in fields as a boundary post; and the culture hero or god of science, commerce and invention, later identified with the Roman Mercury, a much more sordid character concerned with trade (*merx, merc-is*) and patron of merchants and travelers, and as god of darkness patron of tricksters and thieves. But every one of his miscellaneous traits is consistent with his original shamanism. Hermes carried the *caduceus,* a herald's or bardic ambassador's staff, originally a plain rod entwined with fillets of wool for safe passage, an ensign of peace, authority, quality and office—but Hermes' caduceus was soon easily confused with the twin-snake-entwined shaman's staff,[90] an old emblem of medicine-men such as the snake-demigod Asklepios and cognate healers in Mesopotamia and Semitic snake shamans (Moses, Aaron). In late forms the caduceus is even winged, as if the symbolism needed any further reinforcement. The *petasus,* a low-crowned and broad-brimmed felt hat worn by Hermes as traveler, became a winged cap as worn by Mercury. The *talaria,* bird-winged sandals of Hermes, are also seen in the iconography of Iris, Eos, Eros, the Furies and the Harpies to signify speed, but all of them are evidently derived from the appurtenances of the old bird-shaman. The shamanistic aspect of Hermes, however, is sufficiently attested to in other ways: he gave the fabulous herb *moly,* black-rooted and white-flowered, to Odysseus to counteract the metamorphicizing sorcery of Circe (though Dioscorides, the later plant-medicine compiler, de-romanticized *moly* to the wild garlic, *Allium subhirsutum*). And when "thrice-greatest" *Hermes Trismegistus* was identified with only "twice-greatest" Thoth in Hellenistic times, he was still firmly a magician, with forty-two books of arcane lore attributed to him by Clement of Alexandria.

Like Zeus and Apollo, Artemis and Aphrodite, Hermes is connected with fertility and procreation—which indeed seems to be the divine essence of all the gods. But Hermes, like the phallic Shiva, is as much a god of death, in a sense, as of life. More exactly, Hermes is the god of souls, or the individual lives of plants, animals and men. As such, there is really little inconsistency, since souls are souls whether incarnate or not. Again, much like "familiars," each Hellenistic god still has his sympathetic representative in the plant or animal world which is, or embodies, a *symbola* of its divine cause, and is in harmony with it. Thus, in late Greco-Egyptian magic, Hermes is invoked by his plant and his tree, the moon-goddess is summoned by reciting a list of animals, etc.[91] Even the planets, as gods, are seated on their zodiacal signs, Venus on the Bull, Mars on the Ram, Sol on the Lion, and so on. The doctrine of "signatures" in Hellenistic plant medicine is allied to this sympathy also, so that we know bloodroot is good for the blood, heartsease for the heart, and hepatica for the liver.

Closeness to disembodied souls is especially characteristic of Hermes. For example, on the third day of the Anthesteria festival in February, a pot of seeds of all possible kinds was boiled and offered to the spirits of the dead, which were roaming freely though the city on these three days. The *panspermia* or pot of seeds was given to Hermes, at once phallic deity and fertility daemon, as well as a chthonic god and guide of the dead in the underworld. This festival of all souls was a time of fear among the common folk; the Athenians wisely chewed buckthorn, performed apotropaic rites of protection and purification, and daubed their doors with pitch to keep off evil spirits. Again, in the Thargelia ritual (*thargelos,* a pot of grain), in midsummer just before the harvest, people brought all the first fruits—not to be eaten by the worshipers in communion with the god, but rather as a sacrifice to the spirits and in placation of them. At this same time, the *pharmakos* or scapegoat ceremony occurred. Two men, usually criminals, were loaded with all the accumulated sins and evils of the year and were beaten and driven from the city, never to return. In these chthonic rites men wanted to keep away from spirits, or at least to keep them away from men!

Originally, it seems, Hermes was simply the phallus, an upright stone carved with the usual Pelasgian symbol of sexuality and procreation. As phallus he is messenger of the procreative gods par excellence. Erected over a tomb, he is the power that generates new life; or more correctly, in the ancient view, he brings back souls to be born again. This was not especially a belief in the immortality of imperishable souls as individual conscious identities. It was, rather, the naïve concept of a fertility cult, the belief in a life-stuff immanent in the universe, which in cyclic course entered into and left the material bodies of plants and animals, mana become anima for a while. Greek fertility rites were therefore merely the symbolic or magical statement of what, in their simplicity, they thought were the manifest facts of life.

As a grave-figure, the phallic Hermes was *Psychopompos,* "guide of souls" and male conduit for their return to life in the body of a new mother. Thus Hellenistic Gnostics would explain his double attribute as god of life and death: coital "knowledge" is a part-death of the individual psyche, but in this act Hermes brings back to life a new soul. He was therefore set above the grave to guide the soul-stuff or spirit to another life. Hermes is often portrayed at tombs or burial urns with his serpent-twisted wand summoning out the soul, which appeared as a serpent—quite naïvely like a primitive shaman bringing a deathly sick man back to life or raising the dead. Logically enough, on these premises, as "Hermes Trismegistus" he was the thaumaturgic god all over again of shaman-mages, in the preposterous Gnostic cults of the Hellenistic period when superstition, grown old, put on ever more and more meretricious finery.

As the guide or leader of souls, Hermes was thus literally like a shaman go-between, the "messenger" between two worlds, the world of souls in bodies among living men on this earth, and the world of chthonic snakes and god-creators who are the reservoirs of disembodied life, divinity, spirit-stuff or souls. Originally, as Jane Harrison has shown, the snake gods of the Pelasgians were quite plainly only *disembodied* souls. That is, they were the snakes that emerge from human bodies when they die. The soul-stuff, the snake, is immortal. The immortals, then, are merely snake-presences that never enter into a body but retain their pure essence as the *psyche*-snake. Thus, when later Greek gods make physical appearances, it is as easily into an animal as into a human body that they enter, or into those parts of nature we think "inanimate." Since Hermes was the intermediary between the two worlds of men and of spirits, anyone who had a message for the dead had simply to speak this to the Herm at the grave. Similarly Zeus could send Hermes as his messenger to other spirits, gods, and also to men. Here, naturally, he would "enter" their minds. Throughout, Hermes is the shaman-intermediary between the two "worlds" of men; and that the Gnostic Hermes was also an interpreter of dreams comes as no surprise.

Hermes was guardian and watcher as well as herald, and as well as symbol of life and resurrection. As Priapus or god of boundaries, the phallus was in fact the guardian of morality in property, and so he was set about as boundary posts on land. Gilbert Murray, in fact, thinks that his use as Terminus may have aided the idea of Hermes as herald: for the boundary stone is your representative, the deliverer of a message to a neighbor or alien; if you wish to parley with him, you advance to your boundary stone; if as a herald you go peacefully into his country, the Herm is your witness and you place yourself under the protection of this last sign of your own safe land; and if you are killed or wronged, the immovable Watcher will avenge you.[92] The argument is ingenious, but this seems a static life for so mercurial a spirit, and Hermes the messenger needs no further demonstration as herald if only he keep this old function of herald from his shamanic past. Still, a Herm as boundary stone seems a fit symbol or place for a man's territory-claiming mana to dwell, and acorn-topped posts still adorn New England fences.

As for the function of Hermes as herald or ambassador, that simply harks back again to the Indoeuropean shaman-bard. For these magic singers of the old Indoeuropeans were also ambassadors and political go-betweens. In their Celtic form of Druids, priests of the oak tree, Caesar actually had to drive them out of Gaul into Britain in order to consolidate his conquests as Roman Pontifex Maximus. In Britain, Irish bards were troublemakers until the Battle of the Boyne, when they were stripped of their political power; and when patriotic *eisteddfod* assemblies were revived in the eighteenth century, Welsh bards kept only their magic power as poets, though they were still shamanistic rivals in song.

The progressive enoblement of the phallic Hermes into the high moral figure of paternal justice itself parallels somewhat the history of the greater Counsellor, Zeus. For, like the All Father, Hermes was in earlier tales sometimes unreliable and even something of a trickster. This is not to imply for a moment that the classic peoples felt any itchy salaciousness over a candidly phallic figure; such a horrified and sniggering attitude about sexuality is post-classic and Christian. It is merely to emphasize that, once again, Greek gods sometimes bear the faint lineaments of the northern trickster-gods and shamans in whom they began their careers as nature deities. From snake-spirit of prehistoric times to mage-god of the Hellenistic era,[93] as phallic fertility-daemon and magic shaman, Hermes retained his identity the best of all. The double phallic baton of the Gorge d'Enfer, it would seem, is the first magic twin-snaked wand of the shaman Hermes.

NOTES

(XIV The Deathless Gods)

1. Indoeuropeans now seem earlier in the Levant than was once thought (John Chadwick, *The Decipherment of Linear B, The Key to the Ancient Language and Culture of Crete and Mycenae*, New York: Modern Library Paperbacks, 1958); but the script may have been used to write several languages (Saul Levin, *The Linear B Decipherment Controversy Re-Examined*, Albany: State University of New York, 1964). A current view is of early Semitic sea peoples bearing the mutual influence of Mediterranean islands and the Palestine coast (Page, in Emily Vermeule, *Greece in the Bronze Age*, Chicago: University of Chicago Press, 1964, p. 347 n 11); another, of Mycenaean-Phoenician colony- and trade-rivalry, with Aegean Crete bringing Minoan culture to the Phoenician coast (Donald Harden, *The Phoenicians*, London: Thames & Hudson, 1962, pp. 61–63, 115); and still another, of common Greek-Hebrew origins in a cosmopolitan Crete-centered culture of the second millennium B.C., begun by refugee Nile delta Egyptians of the 12th Dynasty (Cyrus H. Gordon, *Before the Bible: The Common Background of Greek and Hebrew Civilization*, New York: Harper & Row, 1962; and "The Greeks and the Hebrews" *Scientific American*, 212 #2 [Feb. 1965] 102–6, 109–11); compare Geoffrey S. Kirk, "Hesiod and Gilgamesh: A Preliminary Study in Function," [Yale University] *Ventures*, 7 #1 (Spring 1967 23–29, p. 24–25). Etruscans, I think, were basically Villanovans, but with distinct Levantine Semitic accretions.

2. Indoeuropean separation from other stocks was Mesolithic, sub-stocks forming in the early fifth millennium B.C. Neolithic; by the Bronze Age many groups are localizable and identifiable (Marija Gimbutas, "The Indo-Europeans: Archeological Problems," *American Anthropologist*, 65 [1963] 815–36, pp. 815–17). But the argument against a European homeland is not acceptable; on ecological grounds of common fauna-flora names it was in the Poland-Lithuania-Ukraine area (H. H. Bender, *The Home of the Indo-Europeans*, Princeton: Princeton University Press, 1922, p. 50), or in the Oder or Elbe river valleys (Paul Thieme, "The Indoeuropean Language," *Scientific American*, 199, #4 [October 1958] 63–74). Moreover, before the Wasun-Hunnic migrations, the whole population of the Eurasian steppes west of central Siberia was Europoid in physical type and Indoeuropean (Iranian) in speech (G. F. Debets, "The Origin of the Kirgiz People in the Light of Physical Anthropological Findings," in H. N. Michael [ed.], *Studies in Siberian Ethnogenesis*, Toronto: University of Toronto Press, 1963, pp. 129–43; compare L. P. Potapov, "The Origin of the Altayans," *loc. cit.,* 168–96, p. 170, and M. G. Levin, "Ethnic Origins," *loc. cit.,* p. 27). In the Early Han, Indoeuropean-speaking *Yüeh Chih* (Tocharians) were even in western Kansu (Latourette, *Chinese*, I:109).

3. Useful summaries of recent scholarship are H. J. Rose, *Religion in Greece and Rome* (New York: Harper Torch Books, 1959), W. K. C. Guthrie, *The Greeks and Their Gods* (Boston: Beacon Press, 1956), and Charles Seltman, *The Twelve Olympians and Their Guests* (London: M. Parrish, 1956). Still valuable in its field is M. P. Nilsson, *The Minoan-Mycenaean Religion and Its Survival in Greek Religion* (Lund: C. W. K. Gleerup, 1950).

4. Emily Vermeule, *Greece in the Bronze Age*, Chicago: University of Chicago Press, 1964, pp. 280–81, 287; see also E. O. James, *Sky-God*, p. 20, a dichotomy used by Nietzsche, Spengler, Ruth Benedict, etc. The real precedence in Greece of

maternal before paternal deities (A. Zimmern, *The Greek Commonwealth,* Oxford Paperbacks, 1961, 75 n 1) perhaps inspired the culture-evolutionist overextensions of Bachofen and Briffault that this was everywhere uniformly an "earlier stage."

5. Use of iron, horses, and spoke-wheeled chariots accounts for the conquests by Indoeuropean Hellenes, Hittites in Anatolia, and Aryans in India (V. G. Childe, "Wheeled Vehicles," in Singer, *op. cit.,* I:716–29, pp. 725–26). Achaeans were largely masters of mainland Greece by c. 1750 B.C.; the last or Dorian invaders were rough warriors, but they had iron, a metal nearly as rare as gold or silver among their predecessors (A. Bonnard, *Greek Civilization,* I:21). Iron-making came through Greece and Macedonia to Noricum (eastern Alps of Austria) in the Hallstatt period, 600 B.C. Greece had many early bloomeries, of local importance only; most prehistoric iron in Europe came from Noricum and, except for slightly later La Tène iron, no other European iron deposits had more than local importance until about 300 B.C. (Jacquetta Hawkes and L. Woolley, *Prehistory and the Beginnings of Civilization,* New York: Harper & Row, 1963, I:598); see also G. Sarton, *A History of Science, Ancient Science through the Golden Age of Greece* (Cambridge: Harvard University Press, pp. 61, 105, 136).

6. E. O. James, *The Cult of the Mother Goddess* (New York: Thames & Hudson, 1958); more controversial, O. G. S. Crawford, *The Eye Goddess* (New York: Macmillan, 1957) suggests a westward wave of diffusion from Syria c. 3000 B.C. to s.e. Spain (and thence to the Canaries, Brittany, Ireland, England and Denmark) of a syncretized fertility deity and goddess of death and resurrection, whose stylized eye identifies her iconographically.

7. The Wassons suggest the use of hallucinogenic mushrooms in Greek shamanism, as in Siberian (Valentina P. and R. G. Wasson, *Mushrooms, Russia, and History,* I, pp. 117, 190–91). R. G. Wasson, somewhat less plausibly I think, argues that the Eleusinian Mysteries involved "theotropic" mushrooms. But since grain was used to make Eleusinian ritual cakes, was perhaps the ancient grain *Triticum Spelta* subject to some fungus infection like the LSD-containing smut on rye *Claviceps purpurea?* But Wasson's ambrosia=mushroom is most impressive in its evidence: many northern Eurasiatics thought mushrooms (Porphyrius' "nurslings of the gods" *apud* Giambattista della Porta, *Villa,* Frankfurt, 1592, p. 764) were engendered by Jupiter Fulminans, since mushrooms appear after rain, are phallic for many peoples (like Zeus' oak *glans*), and are assimilated in symbolism to fire-containing flint "thunderstones" and the punk-spunk-sponge-hongos-σπογγιά-fungus group of words; most significantly, Greeks called mushrooms *brōma theon* or "food of the gods"—as though these delicately odorous plants were ambrosia, almost invariably described as richly perfumed and meaning "immortality [food or drink]" (R. G. Wasson, *Hallucinogenic Fungi of Mexico,* pp. 149–51, 158). The Sanskrit cognate of ambrosia, *amrita,* is the spume from the primeval churning of the ocean, symbolically cognate enough. "Toad-stools" are probably so called because both toad skins (bufotenin) and some mushrooms (fly agaric and *teonanacatl*) contain powerful hallucinogens. On paleo-ethnological grounds I consider the use of narcotic mushrooms at least Mesolithic in antiquity. See R. Gordon Wasson, *Soma, Divine Mushroom of Immortality* (New York: Harcourt, Brace & World, The Hague: Mouton & Co., 1968); and my review, *American Anthropologist,* 72 (1970) in press.

8. The standard coins of Athens had an owl on one side, the goddess on the other. But birds and animals were common on the coins of city-states: Aegina (turtle of Aphrodite, standard currency in the whole Peloponnese until Athens defeated Aegina), Clazomenae (swan of Apollo), Ephesus (bee), Chairimenes (stag of Artemis), Phocaes (seal), Himera (cock), Agrigentum (eagle and crab), Messana (dolphin), Segesta (dog), Aenus (goat of Hermes), Mende (crow riding an ass of ?Dionysus); and Metapontum, a Greek colony in Italy, had coins with the grass-

hopper, ant, lizard, praying mantis, bird, crayfish, cicada, owl, and mouse (Joan Fagerlie, "Monies of Antiquity," *Natural History*, 73 [January 1964] 20–25). The seventeen districts of Siena are still known by their traditional symbols: Giraffe, She-Wolf, Owl, Unicorn, Eagle, Wave, Panther, Caterpillar, Porcupine, Goose, Sea Shell, Ram, Tower, Snail, Wood, Tortoise, and Dragon; and in the horse race three times around the Piazza del Campo, the horse of each district is named for its symbol. The coins of modern Eire are elegant for their many animals; the ancient symbol for Ireland was the sow, as Joyce has reminded us.

9. Edmund R. Leach has ingeniously shown that Ganesha, god of "luck," is a psychopompic shaman, as well as a full-blown oedipal figure ("Pulleyar and the Lord Buddha: An Aspect of Religious Syncretism in Ceylon," *Psychoanalysis and the Psychoanalytic Review*, 49 [1962] 80–102, pp. 82, 88–89).

10. Marie Delcourt, "The Last Giants," *History of Religions*, 4 (1965) 209–42; sees many links among the Greek trickster, culture hero, and the hero in revolt. Shamanistic elements are numerous and implicit; perhaps in no theogony are oedipal motifs more explicit than in the Greek.

11. On primitive shamanistic rivalry, often in the form of animal familiars, see the references to Friedrich, Schmidt and Diószegi in Eliade, *Recent Works*, pp. 162–63.

12. Pindar, *Pythian Odes* iii. 8; Pausanias *Descriptio Græciæ* ii. 26. 5.

13. Pausanias, ii. 11–12; iv. 34. 6; Harrison, *Themis*, p. 113; Ovid, *Metamorphoses* ii, 536–632.

14. Lucretius, *De rerum natura*, v, 1083; Horace, *Odes* iv. 13, 25.

15. Pausanias, ix. 38. 3; Aristophanes, *Clouds*, 133; Callimachus, *Hymns* ii. 66.

16. Artemidorus, *Oneirocritica*, ii. 20; Horace, *Carmen* iii. 17. 12.

17. *Odyssey*, iii, 371–72.

18. Pausanias, i. 5. 3; i. 41, 6; Pliny, *Natural History*, notes a number of shamanic birds.

19. Pindar, *Pythian Odes*, xii, 6ff.

20. Aristophanes, *The Birds*, lines 565–67 and 769–72.

21. Hunting, except of hares, was rare in historic Greece (Zimmern, *op. cit.*, p. 237 n 1). I infer that the aurochs was rare because of the lack of oak forests except in Arcadia (*op. cit.*, pp. 45–47).

22. Momolina Marconi, "Can the Cosmogony of the Greeks be Reconstructed?," *History of Religions*, 1 (1962) 274–80. The distribution of the Asiatic lion has decreased dramatically since just 1800, when it was still found in parts of the Middle East, Pakistan, and Iran (though gone in Greece in pre-classic times); see the distribution map in Norman D. Newell, *op. cit.*, p. 86.

23. Harrison, *Prolegomena*, pp. 480–92.

24. Delcourt, *Last Giants*, pp. 211, 215, 219, 235–36, and 242, on culture heroes.

25. The Giants were ordinary warriors on vases and the sixth-century B.C. frieze of the Siphnian Treasury at Delphi; but four centuries later on the frieze of Pergamos (now mostly in East Berlin) they are serpent- and bird-like monsters (Delcourt, *Last Giants*, p. 212 n 3). This seems an archaizing henotheism.

26. E. O. James, *Sky God*, p. 127; cf. the "humanization of the gods" in M. I. Finley, *The World of Odysseus* (New York: Viking, 1954, pp. 146–47).

27. Bonnard (*op. cit.*, I:142) notes the minutely described humanity of the gods: the hair of Zeus and Poseidon is so black as to seem blue; Hera's jewels are as big as mulberries, her shining hair hangs down on both sides of her head, and her perfume fills heaven and earth; Athena's eyes glitter, Aphrodite's shine like polished marble; Hephaestus sweats and mops his face, his chest is hairy and he limps. Can such humanity be *acquired* by the heavens, sea, and fire? Rather, these traits are

possessed by human shamans; cf. Robertson Smith, *op. cit.*, p. 83. To believe in the powers of manlike gods is little more than to believe in shamanic magic.

28. Cornford early perceived the Greek equivalent of *mana* (*Unwritten Philosophy*, pp. 12–13), as did Dodds (*op. cit.*, pp. 8–10, 13–14, 16–17, and especially 23 n 65, and 42). The Greek *moira* as "portion" or "fate" is impersonalized *mana* as "luck" in the same era when *daemon* is personalized—both of them "outside" psychological projections and defensive disclaimers in a shame-sanctioned as opposed to a guilt-culture.

29. Apollonius of Rhodes, *The Voyage of Argo* (Baltimore: Penguin Books, 1959).

30. William H. Desmonde advances the provocative argument that the Sophists derived from the archaic shaman, whose function was to exhibit his great knowledge, and like a visiting athlete to challenge local talent and defeat his rivals in a public verbal *agon* ("The Ritual Origin of Plato's Dialogues: A Study of Argumentation and Conversation among Intellectuals," *American Imago*, 17 [1960] 389–406, p. 395).

31. Empedocles' Fragments 111–13 and 117 (for his claims) and Fr. 140 (for his injunction) in John Burnet, *Early Greek Philosophy* (New York: Macmillan, 4th ed., 1930, also Meridian Books, 1957, pp. 221–23, 226). Again, Empedocles' religious poem "Purifications" (*Katharmoi*) owes much to the Orphics and Pythagoras for whom he has great admiration (*Fragment* 129D). But contrast C. D. Kahn, "Religion and Natural Philosophy in Empedocles' Doctrine of the Soul," *Archiv für Geschichte der Philosophie*, 42 (1960) 3–35, pp. 30–35.

32. Gilbert Murray, *Five Stages of Greek Religion*, pp. 22–25; but first stated in his lecture in R. R. Marett (ed.), *Anthropology and the Classics* (Oxford: Clarendon Press, 1908, pp. 77–78).

33. Erwin Rohde, *Psyche, The Cult of Souls and Belief in Immortality among the Greeks* (New York: Harcourt, Brace & Co., 1925), especially pp. 299ff. and 327ff.

34. Karl Meuli, "Scythia," *Hermes*, 70 (1935) 121–76. E. D. Phillips, *op. cit.*, pp. 176–77.

35. W. K. C. Guthrie, *Orpheus and Greek Religion: A Study in the Orphic Movement* (London: Methuen & Co., 2nd ed. revised, 1952, p. 28 *et passim*).

36. F. M. Cornford, *Principium Sapientiae* (Cambridge: At the University Press, 1952).

37. E. R. Dodds, *op. cit.*, pp. 66, 70, 72, 74, 88, 140–45, 161 n 32, 162 n 37, and 292–93.

38. Dodds, *op. cit.*, pp. 272, 310.

39. Dodds, *op. cit.*, pp. 144, 165 n 59, citing Plato and others.

40. Marie Delcourt, *Last Giants*, pp. 209–42; and *Héphaistos ou la légende du magicien* (Paris: Société d'édition "Les Belles Lettres," 1957).

41. Walter Burkert, "ΓΟΗΣ, Zum griechischen 'Schamanismus,'" *Rhenisches Museum für Philologie* [Frankfurt a. M.], (1962) 36–55. Robertson Smith, *op. cit.*, p. 83. See also Ernst Topitsch, "World Interpretation and Self-Interpretation: Some Basic Patterns," *Diogenes*, 88 (1959) 312–25, p. 325 n 4.

42. Euripides, *Cyclops*, 80–81.

43. Horace, *Ars Poetica*, 220.

44. The much-disputed etymology of the word "tragedy" has still other aspects. Although Jane Harrison was concerned with spelt not for pharmacological reasons (note 7, above), and long before the contemporary interest in psychotropic drugs, her interpretation would give a new turn to the matter. "Tragedy I believe to be not the 'goat-song' but the 'harvest-song' of the cereal τράγος, a form of spelt known as 'the goat' [from its being bearded]. When the god of the cereal, Bromios-Braites-

Sabazios, became the god of the vine, the fusion and confusion of τραγῳδία, the spelt-song, with τρυγῳδία, the song of the wine-lees, was easy and inevitable. The τραγῳδοί, the 'beanfeast-singers,' became τρυγῳδοί or 'must-singers'" (Harrison, *Prolegomena*, p. 420). *It is enough to suspect psychotropic spelt-smut of causing hallucinatory ecstasy in the Mysteries.* If the *bean* be implicated, the question becomes still more complex: it was a totemic Indoeuropean plant (A. C. Andrews, "The Bean and Indo-European Totemism," *American Anthropologist*, 51 [1949] 274–92), the eating of which by some persons caused psychotomimetic consequences (G. Sansone, A. M. Piga, and G. Segni, *Il Favismo*, Torino: Edizioni Minerva Medica, 1958), perhaps genetic at base and favoring patrilineal kinship (E. Giles, "Favism, Sex-Linkage, and the Indo-European Kinship System," *Southwestern Journal of Anthropology*, 18 [1962] 289–90), as well as totemic food-taboos (J. L. Fischer, Ann Fischer, and Frank Mahoney, "Totemism and Allergy," *International Journal of Social Psychiatry*, 5 [1959] 33–40)—altogether a formidable argument for a holistic approach to human behavior!

45. Hesiod, *Works and Days*, lines 654–57.

46. Dodds, *op. cit.*, pp. 28–63. Shame sanction is consistent with the "externality" they felt in the forces moving them. In analytic terms, the superego was in fact incompletely internalized; hence, with no psychology of the irrational id and only a phallic-stage internalization of the superego, to the Greek both impulse and conscience would necessarily seem to remain daemonically "outside." This is consistent also with Greek democracy and Greek rationalism (and the fallibility of both): political truth and philosophical truth are in the minds of [other] men, available for the asking (voting; the Socratic method). The phallic stage of maturation is psychiatrically consistent also with Greek *paiderastia*.

47. "Matrist" and "patrist" depend on mother-identification and father-identification and the related political, sexual and intellectual attitudes; these are psychiatric concepts and have nothing to do with the ideas of Maine, Bachofen, Morgan and others (Rattray Taylor, *Sex in History*, New York: Thames & Hudson, 1954, pp. 76–84). Heterosexual love among the Greeks seems to have been low-keyed and unromanticized (Finley, *op. cit.*, pp. 136–37). But the battle of Hipparchus and Aristogiton over the handsome Harmodius had political bearing and ended in the death of both Hipparchus and Harmodius (see the sixth book of Thucydides' *Peloponnesian War*). Thus important too was Achilles' love of Patroclus; the girl Briseis is barely named. For a typical *apologia* of Greek homosexuality see Burn, *op. cit.*, pp. 124–33.

48. Bonnard, *op. cit.*, I:38–39; by contrast with Homeric Diomede, the Idas of Apollonius (*op. cit.*, pp. 18, 48) is a braggart who, in his cups, boasts that as a fighter he is *better* than the gods. And when Ajax boasted he had escaped drowning in spite of the gods, the angry Poseidon split the rock on which he sat, and Ajax drowned (*Odyssey* iv, 502ff; *Iliad* v, 380, 403, 406–15; cf. 434–42).

49. Lucretius, *De rerum natura*, iii, 830–1094.

50. Finley, *op. cit.*, pp. 146, 150–51.

51. Pindar, *Olympian Odes*, v, 58; *Pythian Odes*, iii, 59.

52. Harrison, *Epilegomena*, p. 30.

53. Onians, *op. cit.*, p. 303.

54. Dodds, *op. cit.*, pp. 8–17, 29, and 58 n 76.

55. Rohde, *op. cit.*, p. 14. Compare B. C. Dietrich, *Death, Fate and the Gods: The Development of a Religious Idea in Greek Popular Belief and in Homer* (London: Athlone Press, 1965=University of London Classical Studies III).

56. Theodor Gomperz, *Greek Thinking, A History of Ancient Philosophy* (London: J. Murray, 4 volumes, 1901–1912, III:10).

57. Ovid, *Metamorphoses* (New York: G. P. Putnam's Sons, 2 vols., 1926).

58. On Greek "sin" as *lèse majesté* alone, see Harrison, *Prolegomena,* p. 606; and Seltman, *op. cit.,* pp. 12, 27–28. It remains to remark that this status is phallic-oedipal. Note also the *categorical* punishment of Oedipus, who was not even consciously an offender against his father.

59. Aeschylus, *Prometheus Bound,* in David Grene and Richard Lattimore, *The Complete Greek Tragedies* (Chicago: University of Chicago Press, 4 vols., 1959, I:311–51). Prometheus as culture hero, Cornford, *Unwritten Philosophy,* p. 124; on his sin, Hesiod, *Theogony* IX, 507–616. N. O. Brown, *Hesiod's Theogony* (New York: Liberal Arts Press, 1953, p. 67) makes his sin similar to Job's in not recognizing the incommensurability of god and man.

60. For Socrates' clever distortion of Apollo's GNOTHI SEAUTON, Zimmern, *op. cit.,* p. 122. Olmstead considers that Socrates' influence on science was "catastrophic" (A. T. Olmstead, *History of the Persian Empire,* Chicago: Phoenix Books, 1959, p. 446).

61. Plutarch, *Life of Cimon,* §7, in *The Rise and Fall of Athens: Nine Greek Lives* (Baltimore: Penguin Classics, tr. I. Scott-Kilvert, 1960, p. 152). Such easy public nudity may have had Indoeuropean roots. Nordic nude bathing was known anciently and is known in Denmark and Germany. In Ulster, in Queen Elizabeth's time, the O'Cane himself, who spoke Latin fluently, "welcomed a Bohemian nobleman to the Hall of his Great House in which The O'Cane and all his sixteen ladies sat down naked, inviting the embarrassed and unwilling foreigner to undress and be comfortable." (Seltman, *op. cit.,* p. 46, citing Fynes Moryson [1617]).

62. The ancient fantasy of cerebrospinal origin of sperm (e.g. Alcmaeon's experiment, Gomperz, *op. cit.,* I:148) persisted from prehistoric to modern times (see notes 57–59, Ch. XII, above). For two of many modern references, see Georg Groddeck, *Book of the It* (New York: Vintage Books, 1961, Letters V, XXV, pp. 43, 187). The view lends countenance to the argument of some historians of philosophy that pre-Socratic *physis* was not the later concept of lifeless *materia* but rather a kind of Zeus-*Nous* or world-marrow, i.e. the male rather than the female principle.

63. Intrinsically generative power, Zeus even produced puberty; he appointed Apollo, with the aid of the male Rivers and the nymphs, to "bring young boys to manhood" (Hesiod, *Theogony,* 63).

64. Pindar, Aeschylus and Euripides on godly misbehavior, A. W. Mair, "Pindar" *Hastings Encyclopedia.* 10:35–36, p. 36. But sexuality is to be *expected* from the All-Father fertility daemon, and the protest makes little sense except as the attitude of later uncomprehending "modernist" gentility. Xenophanes' attitude was, by contrast, a free-thinker's rejection of anthropomorphic nonsense. As to shamanic *origin* of gods, it is the very *function* of tricksters humorously, even obscenely, to contravene the social rules.

65. James, *Sky God,* p. 133, on Jupiter Feretrius; p. 114, etymology. Lightning does occasionally fuse quartz; but the result is not the cause.

66. A. B. Cook, *Zeus: A Study in Ancient Religion* (Cambridge: At the University Press, 3 vols., 1914–40).

67. Fire *is* the "spirit" the shaman manipulates. See Dodds, *op. cit.,* pp. 298–99 for Greco-Egypto-Chaldean examples; cf. p. 310 n 118. See also Carl-Martin Edsman, *Ignis divinus: le feu comme moyen de rajeunissement et d'immortalité: contes, legends, mythes et rites* (Lund: Skrifter utgivna av Vetenskap-Societeten i Lund, 34, 1949); and Gaston Bachelard, *Le psychanalyse du feu* (Paris: Gallimard, 1935).

68. A characteristic shamanic-animal story: Nemesis "when pursued by Zeus, assumed the form of an animal, transforming herself into beings of the earth, sea,

and air, and, finally, into the form of a wild goose, had forced union with the god" (Furio Jesi, "The Thracian Herakles," *History of Religions,* 3 [1964] 261–77).

69. On Zeus as a non-ethical god in the *Iliad,* Dodds, *op. cit.,* p. 32. Bonnard (*op. cit.,* I:144) suggests the gods in the *Iliad* care little about justice since it would limit their sovereign power, but this is mere intellectualizing rationalization of a later philosophical view of the gods.

70. *Ma'at* as cosmic order and justice, John A. Wilson, *The Culture of Ancient Egypt* (Chicago: Phoenix Books, 1951, p. 48), *ma'at* and the Good Shepherd (p. 133), Akh-en-Aton and the "feeder on *ma'at*" (p. 218), and immortal *ma'at* and Change (p. 318). *Ma'at* is quite similar to Anaximander's physical principle of cosmic Justice.

71. Odin is pictured in sagas as a chief with shamanic powers who could change at will into a bear (berserker means "bear-shirted"), a wolf or a bird, and all the early Viking kings claimed literal descent from him; but later he became the chief Nordic god (F. R. Donovan, *The Vikings,* New York: Harper & Row, 1964, p. 19). Cognate Nodens was a healer, finder of lost property, and one of the many hunting gods in Britain—Callirius, Toutates, Alator, Camulos, Nuada, Cocidius, Maponus and Vernostonus—variously identified with Silvanus, Mercury, and Mars (Richmond, *op. cit.,* pp. 139–44, 187, 194).

72. The shaman-king survived unchanged farther north. In Germanic society even after the fall of the Roman Empire, kings openly practiced magic, and so people of high rank at least did in Frankish circles; in Scandinavia all magic came from one single family and its three specific forebears; in Sweden, king Erick "of the windy hat" (a weather shaman?) had great repute as a magician; and Loki, certainly no one to talk, accused both Odin and Freja of witchcraft (J. C. Baroja, *The World of the Witches,* London: Weidenfeld & Nicolson, 1964, pp. 47–48). The psychiatrist John W. Perry has traced in myth the Father as King and bond between man and nature and the gods (*Lord of the Four Quarters,* New York: Book Find Club, 1966). In imperial Augustan Roman times, Tacitus mentions transvestite shamans among the Nahanarvali, an eastern Germanic tribe bordering on the Sarmatians (*Germania,* §43, in Sir Willliam Peterson and Maurice Hutton [trs. and eds.], *Dialogus, Agricola, Germania,* New York: G. P. Putnam's Sons, p. 325 and end map). On shamanistic elements in Germanic religions: Horst Kirschner, *op. cit.,* pp. 277–86; A. Sicht, "Die Religionen der Germanen in ethnologischer Licht," *Christus und die Religionen der Erde* [Wien], 2 (1952) 286ff.; and a "Referat" in the *Jahrbuch für Volkskunde,* 2 (1956) 231–32, to W. Muster's dissertation, "Der Schamanismus in der Saga, im deutschen Brauch, Märchen und Glauben," at the University of Gratz.

73. Othin, the great magician of the Teutonic warrior aristocracy, may have had a Celtic origin, and human sacrifice to him is known (Powell, *Celts,* pp. 154–55). When the Viking raider Ragnar Lodbrok (Hairy Breeches) sailed up the Seine to Paris in 845, he hanged 100 prisoners there as sacrifice to Odin, until Charlemagne's heir, Charles the Bald, bought him off with 7000 pounds of silver (Eric Oxenstierna, "The Vikings," *Scientific American,* 216 ⅙5 [May 1967] 66–78, p. 72). According to Powell, Celtic "gods" were more strictly supernatural magicians (p. 127). The Celts themselves were overtly shamanistic into historic times; e.g. at the choosing of a new king at Tara, the eating by the ecstatic *fáith* of the bull-sacrifice, at which, after wrapping in the bull hide as incantations are recited over him, the shaman falls into a *tarbfeis* or "bull-dream" and prognosticates the circumstances of the rightful claimant's approach to Tara (Powell, *op. cit.,* 156–57). In Wales, Merlin of the King Arthur legends seems to have kept many wizardly traits.

74. Despite innumerable texts, Buddhism left no positive statement about the origin and meaning of the *trisula,* though, as is Hindu wont, a fantastic web of symbolism has been woven about it (Eugène Goblet d'Alviella, *The Migration*

of Symbols, London: A. Constable & Co., 1894, pp. 240–44). The *trisula* is simply the Eurasiatic shaman's trident, here probably from Indoeuropean sources.

75. Dodds, *op. cit.,* pp. 69 and 86 n 32. But the position of Hrozný is not general.

76. Apollo as Apollyon, a name given the Destroyer, and only in Revelation 9, 11, was the Angel of the Bottomless pit corresponding to Hebrew Abaddon, and wholly alien to the other attributes of Apollo. But the godly father creator-destroyer is not unknown (e.g. Shiva). The problem, of course, can be resolved only on philological grounds, not by "attributes." If the Greek etymology is not in error, this would mean that Apollo, still another sun god, was also still another underground god of spirits in this attribution.

77. Psychedelic drugs and classic ecstatics, Dodds, *op. cit.,* pp. 296–97; the laurel and supposed vapors of the Pythia, p. 73. To obtain an oracle dream, the dreambooks recommend sleeping with a branch of laurel under your pillow (p. 110), but this is only magical and derivative, if indeed laurel leaves are psychotropic. Professor Oesterreich, an authority on ecstatic possession, once chewed a large quantity of laurel leaves experimentally but was disappointed to find himself no more inspired than usual.

78. Max Müller was the foremost nineteenth-century "rationalizer" of myths in trying to reduce them to commonsensical terms; but Andrew Lang kept up for decades a constant ironic barrage against the naturalistic explanation of myths. The ultimate irony is that myths probably do take off reasonably from unreasonable premises, but that our "explanations" are new etiological myths. See W. La Barre, "Professor Widjojo Goes to a Koktel Parti," *New York Times Magazine,* 9 December 1956, p. 17 *et seqq.;* also in Lester Markel (ed.), *Background and Foreground* (Great Neck: Channel Press, 1960, pp. 256–61); in A. C. Spectorsky (ed.), *The College Years* (New York: Hawthorne Books, 1958, pp. 396–98); and in R. W. Hoffman and R. Plutchik (eds.), *Controversy* (New York: G. P. Putnam's Sons, 1959, pp. 129–32).

79. A fertility-shaman's association with women inevitably recalls Cogul: the statue of the Delian Apollo held a bow in one hand and figures of the Three Graces in the other—in whom it is tempting to see cognates of the ancient Celtic Three Mothers. Iconography of these figures, even to details of pose, is persistent for some millennia; *vide sub* "Three Graces" in Sir Kenneth Clark, *The Nude* (Harmondsworth: Penguin Books, 1960, p. 407). Though Hermes stole his cattle by making them walk backwards, killed and ate them, and then lied about it, Apollo was enchanted by the lyre music of the baby Hermes, and let him study divination with his sisters *Thriae* (Hesiod, *Hymn to Hermes*); Hecate was three-headed, etc.

80. Zimmern, *op. cit.,* pp. 123, 181–82; and Dodds, *op. cit.,* p. 93 n 73.

81. Medea, who had cosmic powers, and Circe, with her metamorphicizing magic, were both daughters of three-headed Hecate (cf. three-headed Cerberus), queen of spirits of the dead; she had a mysterious bird-familiar Jynx and was invoked by a bull-roarer—all archaic motifs. Much worshiped in Boeotia, Hecate was a favorite goddess of Hesiod; she was the giver of prosperity, the first and proper goal of man being wealth according to Hesiod, and like Hermes she makes farm animals multiply (*Theogony,* VII, 404–52; see also T. A. Sinclair, *A History of Classical Greek Literature from Homer to Aristotle,* New York: Collier Books, 1962, pp. 69, 75). Classical-period "witches" are well-discussed in Baroja, *op. cit.,* pp. 17–36, who gives copious Greek and Latin sources.

82. Athena as artisan-patroness, Bonnard, *op. cit.,* I:145–46. In iconography, Athena as goddess of wisdom is usually shown attended by a serpent, whose

"wisdom" is understandable if he *is* the psyche, more especially of Zeus. Behind the vast reputation of Athena for reason, technical science and wisdom lies a semi-magical background of shamanism, prophecy and arcane knowledge; the evidence is summarized in R. Luyster, "Symbolic Elements in the Cult of Athena," *History of Religions*, 5 (1965) 133–63, pp. 145–48.

83. Kendrew's map of the distribution of Athena's olive tree corresponds almost exactly to the limits of Greek civilization, but not of Roman (T. W. Freeman, *A Hundred Years of Geography*, Chicago: Aldine Publishing Co., 1961, p. 74).

84. Hephaestus is also plausible among the Twelve if we see Olympus simply as an early Greek village. Among the ancient Doric magistrates is one called *dēmiourgos* or "public worker"—"the same name that early Greeks applied to their craftsmen, the smith who kept the village in horseshoes and the potter who kept them in water-jugs" (Zimmern, *op. cit.*, p. 105). Hephaestus is the shaman-artisan still not quite deified.

85. Loki is variously a god of death and darkness, an enemy of the Asa gods; a fire demon or water spirit; a culture hero, trickster, and ancestor of demons; originally the spider-trickster (Anna Birgitta Rooth, *Loki in Scandinavian Mythology*, Lund: C. W. K. Gleerup, 1961). As inventor of the hunting net, Loki would be part of a very old Indoeuropean tradition (Onians, *op. cit.*, pp. 362–440). On the net of Hephaestus to catch Ares and Aphrodite, *Odyssey*, viii, 265.

86. Zimmern, *op. cit.*, p. 72. n 1.

87. Onians, *op. cit.*, pp. 470–71.

88. Harrison, *Prolegomena*, p. 376.

89. As there is a plethora of sky gods, so there are many duplicates of "infernal deities" and heroes connected with the shamanic underworld—Dis, Hermes, Hades, Persephone, Orpheus, Heracles, Perseus, etc. Recent scholarship on heroes as earth daemons is summarized in Furio Jesi, *op. cit.*; cf. C. Kerényi, *Hermes der Seelenführer: Das Mythologem von männlichen Lebensursprung* (Zurich: Eranos-Jahrbuch 1942, 1943).

90. The caduceus or herald's wand originated from Hermes' function as ambassador or nunciator or neutral messenger, an old north-European shamanic office. One etiological myth is that Hermes once separated two serpents in mortal combat and thenceforth carried messages between enemies; another myth is that one snake is male and the other female, since Hermes presides over coitus. The serpent staff of the medicine-man is also very old and is found from paleolithic Europe to Paleosiberians, in Africa (in Egypt the snake-hieroglyph symbolizes deity), and perhaps even into Mesolithic America. But all are shamanic associations.

91. On the *symbola* of gods, Dodds, *op. cit.*, pp. 292–93; on carry-overs in later iconography, Panofsky, *op. cit.*, p. 464; and J. Seznec, *The Survival of the Pagan Gods* (New York: Harper Torchbooks, 1961).

92. Murray, *op. cit.*, p. 53.

93. The continuity of Hermes as mage from Bronze Age to late Hellenistic times is quite remarkable. Even the literal "tricks" of primitive shamans as sideshow self-impresarios persisted, in actual juggling with knives, wine glasses, eggs, etc.; the identification of "juggler" with "Magus" was quite current in the Hellenistic world, and the term juggler was used, often pejoratively, to denote a magician (Jacob Neusner, "Rabbi and Magus in Third-Century Sasanian Babylonia," *History of Religions*, 6 [1966] 169–78, p. 169). The French *jongleur* (German *Gaukler*, English *juggler*) is derived from the debased late Roman *joculatores*, popular entertainers and conjurers. Thus, today, circus juggler, stage "magician" and folk-song *jongleur* are all remote descendants of the age-old shaman-musician and showman.

To the anthropological eye, the considerable survival of shamanistic elements in the *Odyssey* is remarkable. Not only is Athena (virgin, mother) repeatedly at the side of Odysseus as a supernatural helper (rivalrous with Poseidon) but there are also many other shamanic motifs such as many-formed Proteus, soothsayer and master of seals (*Odyssey,* 1:400–459, 4:381–86, 401–13, 455–59), magic potions (4:220–21), weather magic (7:15–16), spirit-loved bards (8:479–81), prophecy (8:79, etc.), enchanted animals (9:212–15), animal-transformation (9:233–43), clairvoyance in magic-singing monsters (12:189–91), magic-induced madness (14: 178–79), and metamorphoses (17:485–86, etc.). If, as Dodds has shown, the *Iliad* is full of shamanic *animal* motifs, the *Odyssey* is curiously full of shamanic *birds*. Athena somewhat disingenuously informs Telemachus she is "no prophet, nor do I know the ways of birds clearly" (Richard Lattimore, *The Odyssey of Homer, A Modern Translation,* New York: Harper Torchbooks, 1968, 1:202), but then "departed like a bird soaring high in the air" (1:319–20). At his prayer to Zeus, the god of justice sent two eagles which ominously tore at each other—as would Odysseus and the suitors, in the interpretation of Halitherses who was "far beyond the men of his generation in understanding the meaning of birds and reading their portents (2:58–59), though Eurymachos interpreted bird omens differently (2:180–82). After Nestor's telling about Agamemnon and Menelaus, the disguised guest Athena "went away in the likeness of a vulture" (3:371–72), and came in a dream to Penelope (4:795–807). Hermes flew over the sea to Calypso's isle like a shearwater (5:51); as Odysseus escaped on a raft, Leukothea in the shape of a gannet took pity on him and gave him a magic cloth (5:336–38, 351–53). In Hades, Odysseus saw Herakles and "all around him was a clamor of the dead as of birds scattering scared in every direction" (11:605–6). Zeus is Master of Birds (12:262–65).

At the court of Menelaus, Helen herself reads the portent of the eagle with a goose in its talons (15:160–78); as Telemachus returned to Ithaka, Theoklymenos read the omen of the falcon tearing apart a pigeon (15:525–34). When Telemachus and Odysseus embraced, "they cried shrill in a pulsing voice, even more than the outcry of birds, ospreys or vultures with hooked claws" (16:216–17), for Theoklymenos' interpretation of the bird signs (17:160–61) was soon to be prophecy come true. Odysseus himself translated the dream of Penelope about the great eagle killing the twenty geese (19:531–78) as, meanwhile, the suitor Amphinomos interpreted the flight of an eagle carrying a pigeon (20:242–47). The bowstring of Odysseus sang like a swallow (21:411); indeed, at the final confrontation, Athena, "likening herself to a swallow in their sight, shot up high aloft, and perched on a beam of the smoky palace" (22:238–40) as Odysseus and his men came "like hook-clawed, beak-bent vultures descending from the mountains to pounce upon the lesser birds" (23:302–3). Laertes learned that "the bird signs were good at his going" when Odysseus left for home (24:312–13); and indeed Odysseus finally swooped "like a high flown eagle" (24:537) upon the suitors, until eagle-thunderbird Zeus himself hurled a bolt to stop the slaughter (24:539–40).

XV

The Death of the Gods

GREEK religion was a compost of shamanistic nature gods of people from the north and the old fertility rituals of the native country folk.[1] Despite the differences, however, the two were rooted in the same animistic world view, with no intrinsic factor impeding a tolerable amalgamation. But the fusion was never quite successful because, to a degree, the two traditions ran side by side on different social levels.[2] On one, that of Ionian philosophy, the nature gods were subjected to increasingly refined and rationalized statements of the nature of reality, and the manlike was gradually driven out of nature—an intellectual movement toward science imperfect only in certain limitations of method that were in essence socio-political. On the other level, folk religion continued to dramatize, by analogy and symbol, recurrent seasonal events in nature that, misconstrued as "immortality" when applied to man, came into violent contradiction with the other tradition. The Ghost Dance catastrophe of this unstable acculturation was in the end as much socio-political as it was philosophico-religious, for there existed also in Greece two diverse political traditions.

Achaean and Aegean acculturation took two distinct directions regionally in Greece, the Athenian and the Spartan. In Attica, of which Athens was the capital, there was a considerable fusion of invading Hellenes with the native peoples of Greece. Out of the clash and stimulus of the two cultures arose the first example of what one might technically call a "civilization"[3] as opposed to mere tribal culture—the civilization of the classical Athenian Greeks. The mixture of blood and of culture, as of the pantheons of two sets of gods, was sufficiently complete by the time of the historian Thucydides[4] for there to be no memory of invasion from the distant Indoeuropean north, and no disposition to look for Achaean origins beyond the borders of Thessaly.

The Athenians became a highly articulate, urbane and intellectually questing people; indeed, the dogmatic mind of Paul criticized the Athenians, even in their decline, for their restless search for new ideas. Founded first by conquest, the city-state of Athens was cosmopolitanized by trade, and Athens remained a maritime and outward-looking state until the end, in the brutal and exhausting Peloponnesian civil war—an end heralded in fact by a stupid arrogance of power in the calamitous Athenian overseas adventure in the conscienceless invasion of Syracuse in Sicily.

Athens first grew great on trade and only secondarily became a political power, sometimes by dubious means in the Athenian League, in consequence of her trade-based maritime strength. The spare land of Greece found compact and easily exportable agricultural products in olive oil and wine. The various Greek potteries supplied not only home need for containers, but also exported widely and especially to the west. In the beginning, Corinth, astride her isthmus, dominated this trade. But gradually Athens became the chief ceramic center in the Mediterranean, a position she kept until about 400 B.C., and Athenian vases of the sixth and fifth centuries B.C. were the acme of Greek pottery,[5] both technically and artistically. Since exports through Athens were carried largely in her own ships and financed by her own bankers, and since this trade ranged from the Black Sea to Spain, Athens became a great naval power.[6] Quite early Achaeans in fact besieged Asiatic Troy—probably not to repossess an errant Helen but rather to secure free passage through the straits for trade into the Black Sea—and with their navy, Athenians defeated in Europe that great land power, the empire of the invading Persians, whom Alexander the Great subdued ultimately in their own land.

The amalgamation of cultures went furthest in seacoast Athens, and classical Athenians had an outspoken pride in their cosmopolitanism. Isocrates,[7] champion of unity among Greek city-states, said "Our city has caused the name of Greece to appear no longer a sign of blood but of mind; it is those who share our culture who are called Greeks, rather than those who share our blood." The impartiality of the well-traveled Herodotus surprised and vexed the later Plutarch, who scornfully called Herodotus a "barbarian-lover" ($\phi\iota\lambda o\beta\acute{\alpha}\rho\beta\alpha\rho o\varsigma$)[8] and begrudged his objective tribute to the bravery at Plataea of the Persians, bitter enemies of the Greeks. And it was the late Athenians, not the fiercely tribalistic Jews, who were responsible for the idea of all men under one great god of the universe—a concept following upon Alexander (taught by the Athenian Aristotle), who first dreamed of one world, though he sought it falsely, like the Romans, through military conquest.

Greek tolerance of alien ways and peoples, and especially among the sea-oriented Athenians, was a new phenomenon; and comparison is the very food of intellectual growth. The fact is that lack of ethnocentrism was by no means characteristic of Indoeuropean peoples. On the contrary, widespread military conquest if anything only reinforced initial Indoeuropean chauvinism. In Aryan India, for example, invading Indoeuropeans founded the tight caste system of *varna* ("color") in which the arrogant racism of the priestly Brahmans kept pace with the militarism of the Kshatriyas, with Vaisyas and Sudras and despised outcastes at the base of their rigid and closed society.

The Spartans were closer in spirit to the Aryans of India than to their neighbors the Athenians. The Lacedaemonians, so-called from their provincial capital, were a fierce and proud people noted for their fortitude, bravery, endurance—and above all their taciturnity, the famous "Laconic" inarticulateness. The Spartans were a conquering nobility, but they remained an ignorant and hidebound rural gentry, ultraconservative, bucolic, and suspicious of anything alien or unfamiliar. In Sparta arose the garrison state, so admired by that most un-Athenian of Athenians, Plato. Here the conquering invaders placed themselves as a ruling caste above the helots,[9] the conquered local folk with whom they little mixed their blood. The militarism of the invading pastoralists was increased and perpetuated in the process, and the necessity remained of keeping the conquered natives of the land under control.[10] The helots remained submerged agricultural serfs—or worse, for young Spartan bucks sometimes organized parties to hunt down helots like wild animals. The Spartan state was "racist" and terrorist, violent, explosive and absolute.[11]

The Athenians meanwhile got rid of their archaic and almost legendary kings, and substituted elective archons taken from the noble eupatrid families. The harsh Draconian laws were an early attempt to preserve aristocratic privilege, but the milder laws of the reformer Solon introduced basic economic reforms, as Cleisthenes likewise brought political reforms. By the time of Themistocles and the exultant defeat of the Persians, the Athenians had already established a democracy, the most remarkable political invention in history. Grown men were now politically brothers, not some of them the arbitrary mystic fathers of others.

The openness of Greek thought and society was contributed to by another fact. Greek religion was in our sense curiously untheological.[12] Hesiod struggled with the mixed heritage of gods, but in the lack of any critical-historical method he was less a systematist than mere compiler, and he had no immediate successors. The Greeks had no seminaries to educate priests, who learned the rite of a god simply by serving him; also, as in republican Rome, aristocrats and men of affairs were often the sometime priests, and had no permanent preoccupation with or profound theologic questioning of received public rites. The Greeks therefore never had a priestly clergy like those of India, Persia, or Gaul. The nearest thing to this was the mystical confraternity of Pythagoras in Greek southern Italy, but its orientation was individual, and its influence was religio-philosophical; moreover, Pythagorism was never the exclusive philosophy or the established state cult in Greece. As for the oracular shaman-priests at Delphi, although they were often embroiled in attempts to influence pan-Greek affairs politically, they never sought (for example) to exalt Apollo theologically above Zeus. Democratic, the classic Greeks were also cheerfully polytheistic.

Greek religion was embodied in a literature, the universally known epics of Homer; and beyond an expected acceptance and respect for their power and immortality there was no litigious notion of heresy, for the gods were too familiarly human. Though some conservatives might be disturbed, Anaxagoras[13] could state flatly that the sun and moon were merely material bodies and not in themselves divine; and it should be remembered that even in the most troubled later times Socrates, like the early Christians, was punished for political not theological crimes.[14] Besides, Greeks were too enthusiastically rational not to appreciate a neat logical point. Xenophanes scornfully bade the worshipers of the dying god Adonis in Ionia to take their choice: either mourn such beings as mortal men, or worship them as immortal gods, for they could not be both! Moreover, Aeschylus and Euripides, in publicly performed plays, continually criticized the Homeric concept of the gods. Euripides wrote that "If the gods do evil, then they are not gods!"[15] Aeschylus cared little for the vatic personality. "Indeed, whatever good have priests yet brought to men? Wordy craft, your message speaks only through evil; seers bring terror but to keep men afraid." Even the arch-conservative Pindar, chief protagonist of Delphi, wrote "Hateful is the poet's [Homer's] lore that speaks slander of the gods."

Easygoing Herodotus was as little taken in by Greek gods as he was by the foreign gods he learned about on his travels. Some have called "the first sight-seer in the world" a gullible man; but unjustly, for he considered the gods part literary creations. He stated quite explicitly: "Whence the gods come, whether they always existed, and what they looked like, was unknown until just yesterday so to speak. Homer and

Hesiod lived no more than four hundred years ago, and it was they who taught Greeks the gods' descent and gave them their names and features. . . . For myself, my duty is to report all that is said, but I am not obliged to believe it all."[16] The habitually calm and critical mind of Thucydides[17] sometimes rose to a cool repudiation of god-miracles about which he felt skeptical; besides, he belonged to a circle of thoughtful men among whom disbelief was taken for granted, needing no special comment or defense.[18] And if the inherited conglomerate of local peasant legends, old traditions, half-remembered and half-understood rites witnessed in childhood, hymns of praise to particular gods, epigrams, old wives' tales and explanatory interpretations were all so ludicrously inconsistent and contradictory, then this was occasion only for urbane speculation or quiet amusement to the Greeks.

The literary trend against anthropomorphic gods lasted throughout formal Greek philosophy as well. Heraclitus had early condemned Homer. Theagenes broke down Homeric myths into allegories: Poseidon personifies the sea, Apollo fire, Leto oblivion, etc. Protagoras and Xenophanes were thoroughly agnostic. Prodicus explained religion as arising from human needs; Critias attributed political origins to religion. But Plato was the most important critic. He roundly condemned Homeric myth as immoral and unfit for exposure to children; and Plato left no room for personal gods in his philosophy. Aristotle attributed to natural forces all the benefits formerly thought to be divine gifts, and completed the secularizing process. His Prime Mover is a physical force far removed from anthropomorphism.[19]

Greek gods began quite simply as men. But as moral models for men, much less explanatory principles of nature, the gods could not keep pace with changing morality or increasing intellectual insight, so long as the old tales about them were believed. Already in Hesiod the archaisms accumulated and preserved by a literate culture were burdened with inconsistencies. Again, in the Greek system, the non-human nature of Nature could only end in being re-encountered—for above the gods is *Ananke,* impersonal Fate and the nature of things. What good then are the gods in explaining Nature? They are only men, plus immortality. The ultimate world is still non-human. Greek theology was therefore entirely lost motion intellectually. As a consequence, by the time of Plato, the Greek gods were dead as the objects of an informed man's worship.

Quite paralleling the freedom of political discussion, the absence of any *odium theologicum* in Greek intellectual life made possible free attention to the study of *physis,* the material world. Though gods were presumably behind nature, Greeks could still speculate about nature.

Lacking the notion of heresy, pre-Socratic nature philosophers[20] could argue as they would on the nature of the basic substance of divine reality. Indeed, Strato of Lampsacus declared that he "did not make use of the gods to explain the origin of the world."[21] Thus, inadequate as their method was, the nature philosophers founded secular science. A millennium of Greek science began when Thales of Miletus correctly predicted the eclipse of the sun in 585 B.C.—and ended in 529 A.D. when the Christian Emperor Justinian closed the schools of Athens.

Thales found animal seed and the source of all life in the rain, and for him therefore *Water* was the fundamental stuff in his universe. The conception is not really distant from the older animistic one of Zeus and his rain. But the important difference in Ionian science was the conclusion based on empirical observation, however crude, of silting in rivers, the freezing of ice, and the evaporation of water into the air upon boiling it with fire, thus accounting for the different phases of matter. Consequently, viewing the same changes, though somewhat differently, Anaximander thought warmth and cold, densities and their distributions, explained the visible. Again, though rather more animistically, Anaximenes thought the base stuff in the world was all-pervasive *Air*, and he himself compared the breath of divine life with the winds of heaven.

The bitter "weeping philosopher" Heraclitus, by right city-king of Ephesus (in his time beneath a foreign yoke), saw Change the chief reality in *Fire,* the vital heat rising and falling, unceasingly transmuted by Strife and Eros. No man can step into the same river twice, for everything flows. Nothing ever *is,* since everything is Becoming. The one wisdom in the Macrocosm is Fire; in the microcosm only fire (life, anima) is conscious, and all else in man, earth and water, is worthless. The dream is a fire burning alone, out of contact with the world fire common to all. And at the end of the Great Year (10,800 or 18,000 solar years) would come pure Change, the world conflagration in fire, and the great cycle anew.

But abstract Change must have some substance for change to *happen to.* Heraclitus had warned, quite like a modern symbolic logician, that "Eyes and ears are bad witnesses to men if they have souls that understand not their language." By pure reasoning, Parmenides reached a conclusion counter to those of both Anaximander and Heraclitus. All Being *is.* Not-Being, logically, cannot be. Therefore the necessary status of Substance, whatever it be, was one packed and monolithic Whole, the *Plenum* or "the Full." The logic seems impeccable. However, Zeno showed that a Plenum allowed of no motion, and hence no change was possible. Greek rationalism was at an impasse: irresistible Change had now met immovable Plenum. Both static Being and pure Happening were logically impossible.

To account for change, which also manifestly *is,* Democritus therefore boldly invented Space. The Full (or substance) is divided by the Empty (thus allowing for change). Since we do perceive change, the Full must be divided into imperceptibly small particles or "atoms" and the motion of atoms must be possible in space, the Empty. Heraclitus had said that "Neither God nor man made the Universe,"[22] but Democritus was further convinced that the universe could not die either, in a Heraclitean apocalypse. Both the absolute creation and the absolute annihilation of the eternal and imperishable world were impossibilities. The universe is the true "immortal" for existence simply *is*—a reasoning which stands in the most modern times as the refined Einsteinian "Law of the Conservation of Energy-Mass." The atoms of Democritus still have the same eternity of being as Parmenides' whole Plenum. But there is an infinity of infinitesimal "plena"—packed, indivisible atoms. They neither come into being nor do they pass away. But, unlike the one Plenum of Parmenides, many infinitesimal atoms can change their position and configurations in space.[23]

All qualities of the visible world rest on the varying configurations in space of imperishable and indivisible atoms. On the elegant reasoning of the Greek Atomists rests the whole edifice of present-day physics and chemistry. It is true we have refined the Greek concept of Substance, and now know well that Mass can change into Energy. But a later attempt to make the Atomists' Void into a Parmenidean thing failed totally when the Michelson-Morley experiment showed that a pervasive Ether for the propagation of energy waves does not exist. Space is still stubbornly No-Thing, and $E=Mc^2$ remains our best understanding of the affair. Democritus thought all four *kinds* of elements exist, the pure fire (of round, smooth, small atoms alone) and the mixed elements of earth and air and water. He was wrong of course, but also right, and made modern chemistry possible; for one step behind the atoms of many differing elements stand the same protons and electrons. There seems to be no escaping his logic. Democritus even had a crude evolutionary theory of the cosmos and all the life in it, and an anthropology with much to commend in it. In his cosmos of moving sun, moon and stars, and living organisms whose life and death surround us in changing vortices, Necessity is god. Through Necessity, so he thought, man learned to combine with his fellows in common defense against wild animals. Need of understanding in such societies created language. And by a gradual development of technology (for which animals, he says, provided many models) and the use of fire, man eventually raised himself above the animals and created civilizations. Life is a determinate adaptation (so it would seem Democritus is saying) to a universe of lawful and necessary causality.

Because they are so directly our intellectual ancestors, we could wish we knew more about the Greek atomists. It is little enough. Behind Democritus was Leucippus, whose work on *The Great World Order* is lost, except for a single short extract. There are those who would exchange for this one work a baker's dozen of other manuscripts that have come down to us. But Democritus, who overshadowed him, incorporated his doctrine so fully that as early as Aristotle, Leucippus and Democritus were invariably quoted together. Our chief source for both is the long poem *On the Nature of Things* by Lucretius, who received the tradition via Epicurus.[24] Like Thales and Xenophanes, Democritus traveled widely. After leaving his native Abdera (seat of the Atomist school and not far from Stageiros, the birthplace later of Aristotle), Democritus traveled over much of the then known world, visiting Egypt, Babylonia and Persia, and settled finally in Athens, then beginning to be the center of the Greek intellectual world. Like Aristotle, who was especially interested in him, Democritus had a universal mind. He was interested alike in mathematics, music, ethics, physics, and technology—a materialist who spent his whole life in research and counted it greater to discover one new causal connection than to wear the crown of Persia. Democritus was called "the laughing philosopher."

Xenophanes of Kolophon had a secular mind of typical Ionian clarity. When driven from his home by the Persians as a young man of twenty-five he began a life of travel and observation, and he was still writing at the age of ninety-two. He denied the anthropomorphism of gods completely, saying caustically that if horses and cows had hands to draw, they would paint their gods like cows and horses; indeed, "Ethiopians make their gods black and flat-nosed, and the Thracians say theirs have blue eyes and red hair." Xenophanes was also critical of what he thought nonsense in Hesiod and Homer. Aristotle tells a story of the people of Elea asking Xenophanes, in the days of new superstitions, whether they should sacrifice to the dead Leucothea. "If you think she is a goddess," he said, "do not mourn her; if you do not think so, do not sacrifice to her." He also remarked somewhat acidly that a winning wrestler, or a chariot racer who got great acclaim, was not so valuable to the city as a thinker like himself, and that a winning boxer or runner neither helped the city to be governed better nor increased the wealth in its storehouses. Theophrastus said Xenophanes found impressions of shells on inland hills, of fish and seaweed in the quarries of Syracuse, of a bayleaf inside a stone at Paros, and of marine animals at Malta, and argued for their being fossils.[25]

Pythagoras of Samos was part of the religious revivalism that swept over Ionia when the Greek cities were conquered by Persia. The revival had connections with the then far north of the Hyperboreans, people thought of as living on the Danube, whence "holy things wrapped in straw" were passed until they reached the ancient shrine of Apollo at Delos. The connection of Pythagoras with Delos is of course well known. The half-mythical Abaris the Hyperborean and the visionary shaman Aristeas seem to have brought concepts of the soul new to the Greek world.[26] To the north also, in Thrace, the orgiastic worship of Dionysus was associated with the name of Orpheus,[27] a shadowy figure said to have accompanied the Argonauts of Jason on their wild adventure into the Black Sea to the Danube.

Although Plato regarded Orpheus as an authentic ancient poet, like Homer, there is grave doubt whether he ever existed at all.[28] The quest for a historical Orpheus is in all probability illusory. Orpheus is the very type of the shaman, however—a psychopomp, *berdache,* misogynist, an underworld shaman connected with Zeus Chthonios and the ancient bull-roarer, and an ascetic. His "documents" obviously have been tendentiously redacted at a much later date.[29] Orphism, rather, was a sixth-century ghost dance or revival among the common people, associated with the names of Epimenides of Crete (c. 600 B.C.) and Onomacritus of Athens (c. 510 B.C.), the "oracle-monger" who was exiled by Hippias. These writers revived a much older Zeus-Zagreus cult, and tried to ascribe the myth to an Orpheus older than Homer.[30] Certainly the cult is far older than any orphic *literature* that we have. Moreover, the intent and effect of this proselytizing literature on the Dionysian Mysteries were similar to those of the *Hymn to Demeter* for the Eleusinian Mysteries.

The whole context of Orpheus is mythological. Dodds points out that by his magic music Orpheus summons birds and beasts, visits the underworld to recover a lost soul, and is a characteristically shamanistic poet, magician, religious figure and oracle giver—even his singing head reappears in Norse and Irish myth—and Dodds concludes that "Orpheus is a Thracian figure of much the same kind as Zalmoxis, a mystical shaman or prototype of shamans."[31] His function for the Argonauts was exactly that of a war shaman, in one instance to protect them from the Sirens with his lyre music in a magic power contest; and we can compare Orpheus in this function directly to the sorceress Medea who sang spells to stop the bronze giant Talos from harming the same Argonauts far away in Crete.[32]

In art, Orpheus is usually presented lounging in an effeminate pose. Emily Vermeule, recalling that the Muses crippled Orpheus' companion Thamyris for arrogantly challenging them to a contest,[33] suggests of the womanishly dressed poet on the well-known grave relief from Pylos that "Perhaps this [crippling and loss of magic power to play the lyre] explains the apathetic posture of the Pylos poet—Thamyris looking wistfully at a bird for inspiration, with limp hands."[34] But on a tomb such a figure would be perhaps more likely Orpheus himself; in any case, the Homeric story of Orpheus and the Muses, like the Apollo-Marsyas one, implies Mycenaean singing contests between shamans. Diogenes Laertius and Pausanias both say Orpheus was slain by a bolt from Zeus (as a power rival?); but Plato says it was for cowardice. Other stories say the Maenads tore him apart because of his misogyny.

The idea that a singing head (or skull) could shamanize as an oracle long after its owner's death, as both Virgil and Ovid asseverate,[35] suggests the immense antiquity of the old Stone Age skull cult. Philostratus wrote that Orpheus' "head came to Lesbos and took up its dwelling in a cave and delivered oracles from the earth," and even Persian Cyrus the Great came to the famous oracle.[36] Macchioro notes that the salient characteristic of Orphism was its indifference to the state religion, accepting neither its gods nor its myths, though it had neither a rich pantheon nor any considerable mythology of its own. "Far from being a constructive element in the history of Greek religion, Orphism appears to have been thoroughly alien to it."[37] Perhaps Orphism was alien to Greek state religion because it came down from the long bygone days of hunting-band and war-party shamanism?

Another trait of Orphism was its intense conservatism. The Zagreus myth of fifth-century Athenian archaizers was the same as that of Bronze Age Thracian tribes; and the gold tablets of Thurii buried as late as the third century B.C. contain doctrines taught two centuries earlier by Pythagoreans. Macchioro believes that "The Orphic-Eleusinian mysteries were performed without interruption from at least the eighth century B.C. down to 396 A.D., when the sanctuary of Eleusis was destroyed by monks in the train of Alaric."[38] Indeed Macchioro argues the continuity of deeply entrenched Orphism with Pauline Christianity.[39] Linforth finds Dionysus in fact, the god Orpheus served, a striking five-fold syncretism of an antique god of the vine, a Cretan and an Egyptian god, archaic Zagreus, and a still more ancient snake deity.[40]

In contrast with Olympian state religion and the strict Homeric separation of gods and mortal men, the ancient Orphic-Pythagorean folk cult held a strange and as it were almost blasphemous theology. In *ecstasis* or "stepping out" of the body, the soul revealed itself, not as a feeble Homeric ghost of uncertain viability, but as a fallen god that must be restored to a former high estate by *katharmoi* ("purifications") and *orgia* ("sacraments"). Orphic rites taught by Pythagoras were to release souls from the "wheel of birth" and reincarnation in plants and animals.[41]

Xenophanes, fellow Ionian and contemporary of Pythagoras, had only contempt for this idea. He told the story that Pythagoras once heard a dog howling and begged its master to leave off beating it, because he recognized in the dog's howling the voice of a departed friend.[42] In later times, Plato was profoundly interested in Pythagorism, but he was always strangely reserved[43] about Pythagoras himself, mentioning his name only once in all his writings, in the *Republic,* and then only to say that Pythagoras won the affection of his followers to an unusual degree by teaching them a "way of life" (a concept copied in the Platonic "philosophia") still called Pythagorism. Even the Pythagoreans Plato mentions only once, again in the *Republic,* where Socrates is made to say they regard music and astronomy as sister sciences.

This reserve is all the more strange since Plato's students Echecrates and Philolaus were Pythagoreans—we know this from other sources but could only broadly surmise it from their role in the dialogues—and we are not even told that Timaeus, who voices an unmistakably Pythagorean cosmology, was a Pythagorean, and we are left to infer it obliquely from the fact that Timaeus came from Italy, a country strongly Pythagorist in its southern (i. e. Greek colonial) regions. Aristoxenes was personally acquainted with the last generation of the Pythagorean Brotherhood at Phleious, but he was anxious to represent Pythagoras only as a man of science and to refute the known fact that Pythagoras was a religious teacher. Similarly, Dikaearchus, in retrospective falsification, tried to make out that Pythagoras had been merely a statesman and reformer. But already in Aristotle we are told dryly of the legendary golden[44] thigh of Pythagoras, how he was seen at Kroton and at Metapontion at the same time, and how when crossing the Kasas River, Pythagoras was spoken to by a voice from the sky. By the time of the Lives of Pythagoras by Iamblichus, Porphyry, and Diogenes Laertius,[45] we are back again to the miraculous fiction of a shamanistic wonder worker[46]—who visited Hades, called an eagle down from the sky, practiced divination and auguries, was the god Apollo come again from the far north, was welcomed aloud by the river Nessus, and set up many taboos including that on eating beans, not stirring a fire with a knife and so on.[47]

Some explanation for all this obliquity may lie in two quite un-Greek characteristics of Pythagorism, first, its origin in revelation (which the thin gold plates, discovered at Thurii and Petelia,[48] inscribed with Orphic verses make clear); and, second, the organization of Pythagorism into secret politico-religious brotherhoods. Plato's "Noble Lie" of his fascist state might aspire to the authority of revelation through terrorism and early childhood indoctrination, but at least never loses its indentification as pious flummery. More serious, in the politically very troubled times of the aristocratic Athenian conspiracy with Sparta and the Persians, would be the suggestion of a secret brotherhood, for Pythagorism was notorious for meddling with politics in southern Italy and Sicily; and while Plato got his notion of the perfect state from Pythagoras,[49] he would not wish to have it identified with Pythagorism. Hermippus said that when Pythagoras was killed by the Syracusans, thirty-five of his followers were burned at the stake in Tarentum for trying to set up a rival government.

This second curious trait of Pythagorism, its organization into conspiratorial communities based, not on city-state or real kin ties, but on secret initiation into fictive brotherhoods, is far closer in theory to a shamanistic "medicine society" than it is to the theory of the democratic city-state.[50] Philosophy might inveterately return to political concerns for the Greek *zoon politikon*. But Pythagorism was untypical among urbane Athenians in its mystic Orphism—so much so that Socrates, in presenting to Greeks the outrageous doctrine of an *immortal human* soul could appeal to the Orphics for support only in half-serious irony. That the Noble Lie, secret political conspiracy, and the blasphemous doctrine of human immortality all belonged to the circle of anti-democratic reactionaries and traitors would certainly do little to recommend them to democratic Athenians. "The initiated," said Aristotle puzzledly, "are not supposed to learn anything, but to be affected in a certain way and put into a certain frame of mind"—another reason why neo-Orphic Pythagorism would have little appeal to classic rationalism.[51]

There are other important sources in Ionia for the eclectic philosophy of Plato. Heraclitus,[52] mentioned earlier for his Substance-less physics, hated the democracy of the western Greeks as much as he did the foreign Persian tyranny in his native city of Ephesus. Moreover, he was so contemptuous of the acts and opinions of other men that he became a recluse in the shrine of Artemis. The office of sacrificial priest to the Great Mother was hereditary in his kingly family, but he employed his not inconsiderable talent for invective on the other Mysteries, the Dionysian orgies. His quality as displaced fellow-aristocrat may have been his initial appeal to Plato. But, more importantly, his concept of the fiery spirit-logos in nature (not inconsistent with his service to the great Mistress of Animals) was a source of the demiurgic Platonic Idea, as was also his downward-upward concept of the progressive contamination-purification of the fire-soul from material engrossment. The divine principle was cyclically imprisoned in and freed from an illusory substance he quite begrudged existence to, but would one day be emancipated in the holocaust of the universe. Heraclitus was an angry mystic in a disjointed world he hated.

But for every Pythagoras and Heraclitus who influenced the Athenians, Ionia sent a Xenophanes and an Anaxagoras. By contrast with Heraclitus, Anaxagoras was quite non-mystical and was consciously and deliberately the first pure contemplative thinker. He considered knowledge the business and goal of life and was certain of its ethical influence. Anaxagoras took Ionic naturalism to Athens, where Pericles, after the glorious defeat of the Persians at Salamis, had made this city-state the center of the Greek world. Like the Atomists and Xenophanes, Anaxagoras had a matter-of-fact mind. When a meteorite fell on Aegospotamae in 467–466 B.C., instead of thinking it some supernatural portent of pestilence and famine to come, he studied it carefully and decided this must be the nature of heavenly bodies. Although conservatives called him an atheist, he suggested the sun must therefore be a burning stone. Similarly, its phases show the moon to be a reflecting body, but non-burning like the earth. He solved the mystery of the Nile floods, long credited to deities, by pointing to the melting of snow on Ethiopian mountains. He considered divination nonsense and rejected the notion of miraculous interference by the gods in the everyday course of nature (if he was imprisoned, as some say, for this and other impieties, it is probable that he was quietly let out and sent away for a while by his pupil Pericles, for such things did happen in easygoing Athens). Man had mind, Anaxagoras said, because he first had hands.[53] The universe was lawful, reasonable, and ruled by Nous, "Mind." In this there was no dualist or idealist snobbism of mind; his sunny Apollonian Greek mind simply found Order basic in this beautiful real world.

But in the concept of Nous, of which Plato later made so much use or misuse, we begin to see a dangerous defect in Greek rationalism. For Nous—distorted beyond Anaxagoras' meaning of knowable order or intelligible scientific law—can become a humanistic projection, easily contaminated by tenderminded fantasies. Instead of being a toughminded objective Ananke (the Way Things Are), cosmic *Mind* then becomes only a refined animistic form of the shaman's venal *familiar* seen in Macrocosmic-microcosmic terms. This is doubly dangerous, for the easy

Greek anthropomorphism of nature is then coupled with the imprisonment of the Greek in his own rational mind. If man and nature are à priori alike, how then are we to discover the many ways in which external nature differs from one's own? To project too manlike a Nous into Nature is to risk discovering only the ethnographic contents of one's own mind.

This is a delicate anatomy to dissect, since the ethos making for democracy, Greek art and athleticism alike is the same humanism that is found in Greek naturism in philosophy and anthropomorphism in religion. Protagoras summed up the whole Greek ethos in his famous aphorism, "Man is the measure of all things."[54] Thus no abstract mystique of The State, no tyrant divine or otherwise, but the individual man is the measure of all things political. Greek democracy rests on an almost visceral and automatic feeling about individual manhood, above which no transcendent arbitrary authority of The Man can be. Greeks loved democracy as they loved themselves—"the very name of it is beautiful!" cried Herodotus.[55] If the Greek passionately loved his city-state, it was because he knew it to be *his* creation. In the famous *Anabasis,* when an overcocky military adventure to the orient collapsed, it collapsed *into* a democracy, with the civilian Xenophon as leader and the generals his underlings. In crisis, eloquence and reasoning took over again, even from formally ordained authority.[56]

This inveterate democracy is the root of Greek rhetoric and Greek rationalism alike. The art of persuading the free minds of other men puts a premium on eloquence and skill with words. Leadership *is* eloquence in the *Odyssey,* and eloquence *is* philosophy in the Platonic dialogues. Greeks were a verbal people, a public people[57] demanding substance in utterances, which accounts perhaps for the marvelous terseness of Greek literature. This is the reason public drama[58] was pushed to heights which music (abstract private art) never did reach in Greece. And this is the reason that rural and provincial Dionysian rites, actually of the same origin as drama, were contemned by city intellectuals as private rites, not open to the public eye, that took refuge in the night and depended not on frank and manly open argument but on irrational intoxication on wine, and were of the lower classes and slaves, ignorant country folk and home-bound women.

This "show me" attitude of Greek pride in manliness may make for touchiness, ever ready for a brawl, and the proud sulkiness of some Homeric heroes. But the assertion of aretē is possible only through recognition of the manhood of other men, which alone makes democracy possible. It was Alexander, heir to an archaic kinghood in wild primitive

Macedonia (and fathered, it was said, by a snake on a half-mad Dionysiac mother) who had the hubris to set himself above other men and become a god. Greeks brought to their intellectual life the same tough masculine spirit they brought to politics, athletic contests and their shapeless brawling individualistic wars.

To be Greek was to be critical, to take nothing on another man's say-so, to make up one's own mind and to demand cogent arguments from those who disagree. Just as Greeks took for granted no absolute political authority above individual men, so they found no external authority above their own minds. This rescued them from *guru*-ism and the absurd flatulence of endless apodictic nonsense in sacred books as in India—but it left them finally stranded in humanistic rationalism. For there *is,* we insist, an authority above and beyond the logic of the mind to justify the mind's beliefs: the Nous of Anaxagoras, to be found by testing each microcosmic thesis against the Order of the Macrocosm. Zeller has well shown the weakness of Greek rationalism, in that instead of appealing to the unpredictable and often surprising evidence of objective experiment, it appealed instead to some subjective, even aesthetic, sense of appropriateness.[59] This is true of—perhaps especially true of —Socrates and Plato. My assimilation above of political to epistemological authority is not, I think, far-fetched. The most "empirical" of the major Greek philosophers, Aristotle, states the Greek view on truth in ethics and science with quite shocking clarity. "It is absurd," he says emphatically, "to object that what all strive after is not therefore necessarily good. Of that which appears to all to be true we have a right to say that it *is* true. Those who would rob us of this guarantee for our opinions will hardly put a better one in its place."[60] Aristotle is being neither cynical nor facetious in these views, but only quintessentially Greek. Truth is thus left mere tribal consensus: truth is what *we* make it.

With respect to the physical world, Democritus and the Atomists had in a sense answered the question first raised by Thales, at least to the degree that pure rationalism might define the problem. But political and other events led to a distrustful feeling toward the world, drastically different from the confident rationalism of the nature philosophers. The achievement of the Atomists tends to be masked by the massive Platonic denigration of the physical world which reigned over the ensuing millennia; but the true significance of the Atomists may be assessed more fairly in view of what their recovered tradition has accomplished since the Renaissance, in particular in the last half century. Whatever its success in physics, however, Greek rationalism came to debacle in its study of man. At least there was only one physical world to argue about; but it was soon seen there were many worlds of man.

Toward the end of the pre-Socratic period, philosophers began to criticize the roots of human custom with the same ruthlessness they had used in attacking the older theological concepts of nature. These critics of custom formed two main schools, the Sophists and the Cynics. The travels of many Greeks from Thales and Xenophanes to Hecataeus, and later Herodotus, Pausanias and Plutarch (in legend still earlier in Jason, Heracles, Theseus and Ulysses) had made everyone aware of the diversity in human custom. Protagoras, who had studied under Democritus, was the first and greatest of the Sophists.[61] A citizen of Abdera, an Ionian outpost in barbarian Thrace, Protagoras knew intimately from personal experience the great difference in human cultures. In his hands, philosophy took a new direction of interest. The subject matter of the Sophists was not nature but man, as an individual and as a social being, together with his culture—his religion, language, art, ethics, poetry, and politics.

The Sophists asked a new and disturbing question. Do all the differences in institutions and beliefs—from the diverse worship of gods down to the differences between Greeks and barbarians, free men and slaves—rest on nature, and are hence inviolable, or do they rest merely on blind custom and tradition, and are hence subject to criticism and improvement? The question seems to us naïve, but for the Greeks it was a real one. Pindar[62] was as ready to believe all human traits innate as were the traits of horses; even later, Aristotle was still confident that slavery, for example, was a natural state. The matter is as much an ethical as it is a scientific one, and any obviousness to us of the answer is a measure of the completeness of the Sophist achievement. The result of the inquiry was inevitable: custom is man-made and man-propagated. "Man is the measure of all things," said Protagoras. He thus began two trends of interest that were to be characteristic of Sophism to the end, the proper education of the young,[63] and the art of rhetoric in influencing adults.

Pre-Socratic philosophers had had groups of students about them; indeed, Pythagoreans even formed a brotherhood for cult indoctrination. But it was the Sophists who gave the greatest impetus to the founding of open schools[64]—for the education of the aristocratic young at least —which flourished later in the Academy, the Lyceum, and the Stoa. As to the other Sophist tradition of persuading the adult, the Sophists were led into a variety of trends, to the development of rhetoric, and to what in modern times we might call "mass communications" and "the psychology of advertising." The implicit verbalism in Greek philosophy and formal rationalism came to full flower in the Sophists. But it was not linguistic skill that offended the Greeks; it was, rather, the Sophist professionalization of speech and their habit of taking money for the public commodity.[65] The term "sophist" originally implies only learning, and Sophists like Hippias and Gorgias were learned men.[66] The bad odor in which "sophistry" came to be held later, like the later term "jesuitry," rose quite naturally when rhetoric became motivated and venal casuistry. As in advertising and propaganda, it is the motive that counts in judging the moral uses of linguistic skill. And opprobrium attached to the activity was deserved by the Sophists, as also by Socrates and Plato, insofar as all pretended to "teach virtue."[67]

As with the Cynics in the sour distrust of men by the gross Diogenes,[68] a tradition of pessimism grew up around the Sophists, in particular Prodicus. Prodicus was from the island of Ceos, whose natives for some reason were notorious for their pessimistic views on life. The critics of Prodicus represented him as a neurotic invalid who complained about each of the ages of man, and who argued (an early Adlerian) that the most important professions and life itself were but the "echoes" of bodily infirmities. The theodicy of Euripides' *Suppliants* may have been directed against the pessimism of Prodicus. The Sophists also sometimes partook of the tone of Cynics, and if Socrates was well in the Sophist tradition, Plato was additionally in the Cynic, in his projected view of the untrustworthiness of men.

Hippias of Elia[69] was a man learned in many fields from mathematics, music and astronomy to grammar, rhetoric and literature. Like a true Sophist, and like Socrates later, Hippias felt the urgent need to give his learning to others, "even at the tables in the market place," according to Diogenes Laertius. Convention, Hippias believed, was often at odds with nature, *nomos* against *physis*. To Pindar, poet of conservatism, traditional usage was a legal ruler. But to Hippias, custom often was only a common tyrant. Human custom, he thought, must be corrected by natural law, which is the proper measure of custom, not Protagoras' man. Consequently, Hippias looked beyond tribalism to a larger world order of all rational men who might, if they would, base their common views on a mutually aided critique of custom by nature. In this internationalist stand, Hippias was one of the first proponents of world citizenship,[70] the lofty aspirations of which appear again in Aristotle and his pupil Alexander. As a rhetorician and student of literature, Hippias was also one of the first rationalizing "Symbolists" of religion and literature. In his reinterpretations of Homer, Odysseus became the symbol of unscrupulous craft, Achilles of manly boldness, Nestor of mature wisdom, etc. These didactic devices may be useful in education, though this may be questioned, but it is highly questionable that they were so intended by Homer. In later thinking about religion, Symbolism became a deplorable and wholly meretricious technique for the reinterpretation and the falsification of ethnography.

Still another non-Greek shaped Plato, Gorgias of Leontini.[71] The long life of Gorgias (483–375B.C.) spanned deeply significant times. He lived through the Persian wars and the Peloponnesian War until the mature years of Plato, who dedicated one of his major dialogues to Gorgias. Gorgias was a complex and passionately intellectual man whose successive philosophic states of mind mirror clearly the growing malaise of his times. He was first a student of Empedocles, that strange mixture of scientist and shaman,[72] and early devoted himself to natural science in the service of man, in particular to optics and astronomy. Later he came as ambassador on a diplomatic mission from Italian Magna Graecia, to ask the aid of Athens against Syracuse, name of disastrous omen. Gorgias also traveled in provincial Boeotia and Thessaly, gathering many pupils around him. At Olympia and Delphi, and especially at Athens, he argued eloquently for pan-Hellenism. In this period the young Gorgias is an attractive figure, both the thoughtful man of science and the *homme engagé* of practical political affairs.

But his basic earnestness of mind seems to have been deeply wounded and frustrated in his search for truth in physics and for rationality in politics. Gorgias became the prototype of Hellenistic man. His science turned into the deepest and most savage skepticism, his politics into something even more dubious. His later life shows the tragedy of a fine mind. Zeno's paradoxes about motion, based on the system of Being and Not-Being of Parmenides, led Gorgias to a categorically nihilistic epistemology—this last another paradox, since in a statement of the theory of knowledge it is logically self-contradictory.

His system can be stated in three theses: Nothing exists; if it did exist, it could not be known; and if it could be known, such knowledge would not be communicable. The very first proposition shows the provocative subtlety and the perverse ambiguity of his mind, for Nothing could as well connote pure Heraclitean Process which exists without substance or Being, as it could the postulated Void, no thing, of Democritus, which exists; or it could mean that the nonexistent (Nothing) *is,* or that the process or state of existing ("is") is not to be ("Nothing"). Or if we take his following propositions as contingent on the first, and we can not, Gorgias may merely mean (outrageously to a Greek mind) that Existence does not exist and only "Nothing is." A fitting influence on Plato.

But taken as a whole, the "epistemology" of Hippias may mean no more than a clever and cynical sophistry, reflecting his acute awareness of the arbitrary and contingent nature of language—however naïvely a less adroit mind later stolidly made language into a metaphysical absolute, ingenuously (or disingenuously) missing the insight of Hippias completely. It is possible to be mistaken in attributing a linguistic insight to Hippias; but Plato's whole metaphysic is proof that Plato did not have (or did not honor) that insight, since he absolutized the relative and the contingent. In any case, the "conclusions" of Hippias, with which nothing can be done—like Zeno perhaps he so intended—are the extreme of tentatives foreshadowed in the pre-Socratic nature philosophers. But one is tempted to think that Gorgias perceived the linguistic phenomenon: Parmenidean Being or *Plenum* (reality as Noun) clashes with Heraclitean Process or Becoming (reality as Verb). We know the two are the same, $E=mc^2$, if we may add an adverb: Becoming is the How-squared of Being. That is to say, Change is Thing times the squared Cosmic Constant. Process is Substance in space-time (the Void times the Mystery) squared.[73]

Small wonder that Heraclitus became so pessimistic about the possibility of communicating through words he knew were mere conventions, that he argued in the end all men could do was to point.[74] On reasonably fair grounds, Gorgias might be claimed as an ancestor of symbolic logic or of some of the insights of modern metalinguistics. In his curiously titled work *On Not Being or Nature,* Gorgias raised a basic question in epistemology, that of distinguishing between ideas to which a reality corresponds and those to which no reality corresponds. But when he notes that linguistic terms by no means correspond with these things, he seems to attempt a *reductio ad absurdum* of all Eleatic philosophy.

It can be done. And in a word or two: is a "seat" a chair, bench, barstool, or something in a car, trolley, train or plane, is it an elective office in the legislature, a country place, a capital, is it the bottom of one's trousers or a privilege one buys at a ball game for various prices depending, has free on the floor in front of the TV, or struggles to keep on a horse or tractor, but should not keep when a lady is present? And for that matter, is a "chair" a kind of formal public leadership, usually exercised standing up—(no, it is "bench" on the judiciary, *other* people stand up, and it begins when the man sits down)—what judges give murderers to their dismay, or a university professorship one avidly seeks and exercises mostly standing up, leaning on a podium, or sitting on the corner of a table? As for "table" (that favorite object of philos-ophers), well, that is a protean word too one probably should table here. Connotation is never identical with denotation in any language!

Gorgias gave up all hope of philosophy when he discovered the improbity of language and became thenceforth a rhetorician. But with no sound view of nature, how could a sophisticated man be a teacher of virtue, *aretē,* which must be based on nature? Gorgias therefore gave up also the old Sophist ambition and claim to teach virtue. But Gorgias could not help remaining an intelligent and honest if somewhat disenchanted man. He became at once the founder of "mass communi-cations," the "psychology of advertising," public relations, and classical aesthetics. He developed evocative suggestion, as a conscious and de-liberate art, into a powerful tool to sway men's minds, but one which he recognized could be used to good or bad ends. Suggestion, he found, was also the basis of art and illusion. The theologian Hesiod[75] and the lawyer Solon had not been able to distinguish art from lying, since both were falsehood. Gorgias then formulated the idea of justifiable deception, not only in art but also in ethics, and argued for the practical values of untruth.[76] In politics, contrived untruths were a practical necessity. In religion, known illusions were soundly therapeutic. And in aesthetics the created falsehood purges the emotions. The medico-thera-peutic metaphor implied by Gorgias is not a forced construction upon him, for he wrote of ideas as medicine or poison; and his comparison of purges on the body anticipates Aristotle's aesthetics on the purging of the emotions by tragedy. Indeed, the later Sophist Antiphon[77] of Athens undertook to free men of their sorrows by purely oral psychotherapy.

With respect to religion, Critias, who in his exile in Thessaly had been influenced by Gorgias, was even more explicit. Just as human laws were nothing but a means of taming the wild beast in men, so also some shrewd man had "invented" religion with its powerful and invisible beings who could see and punish crimes committed even in secret. It is true that later we find Plato, the cousin of Critias, consciously and deliberately using the "lie with a purpose" in religion, education, and politics. But as an explanation of the origin and nature of religion, or even of animism, the theory of Critias is quite inadequate. Animism may be a false theory, but as an explanatory principle it was put forth in all moral innocence.[78] The theory of Critias assumes, on the basis of a later age's insight into the untruth, that the culture hero who originated it also necessarily knew its untruth. But the culture hero in religion, because of his own peculiar problems is usually the first convert to his fantasy and may not always be accused of being a conscious illusionist, which, in fact, he cannot afford to be, in his own immediate self-therapy.

Parmenides and others had done their best to make language correct and logical. But Gorgias, satirizing Parmenides, made it exciting entertainment for the language-loving Athenians. The intent seriousness of the naturalists, the gravity of political orators and statesmen like Pericles and Themistocles, dignified by the public issues they shouldered, the spine-thrilling dramas of tragedians in searching moral issues—all had exploited noble language as a vehicle. But virtuosity of language as a thing in itself, and to serve any personal end, became in Isaeus such a suspect skill that to employ him for legal defense virtually implied guilt.[79] At an earlier time, free language served public ends. Now rhetors and philosophasters took money for teaching their tricks. Sophists became litigious hucksters of the word.

The sophistic Socrates, like Hippias, loitered in the gymnasia and marketplace, in idleness enjoined on him (so he said) by divine command, questioning citizens about their lives, teazing out meanings too loosely expressed, a gadfly (he says) goading people out of their dull complacency—but Aristophanes called Socrates "an idle and penniless chatterer, with wit for everything but earning an honest living."[80] The bland assumption in Plato's *Dialogues* also is that truth can be found simply through the public exploration of Greek words. The Greek, knowing only his own tongue, could hardly understand how one term does duty for many tacitly assumed connotations and denotations. Greek philosophy falsely assumed also that associations in thoughts reproduce connections in things —or, as we would say, that the (unexamined) structure of Greek grammar mirrors the structure of the world.[81] And yet at the same time Plato wrote, less glamorous but more empirical Greek writers were discovering the parts of speech and other linguistic phenomena,[82] the knowledge of which would have obviated his whole metaphysic!

Since most western languages are (like Greek) Indoeuropean, and contain the same syntactic structures, it is still easy to be seduced by the logic-soft semantics of literary Platonism. To seek built-in semantic consensus is to turn the search for truth into a mere political process. The "Socratic method" of questioning rational Greek minds, when it encounters some Gallup poll of intellectual agreement or assent, is a technique not of physics but of ethnography, and it discovers not science but folklore. The Platonic metaphysic is linguistic logodaedaly, undiscerned Greek grammar, not a discovered universe. Indeed, Schrödinger shows in his *Nature and the Greeks*[83] that these patterns built into our physics have persisted insidiously until modern times. To us, "Man is the measure of all things" is a sad sophistication, but to the Greeks it was a naïvely proud assertion.

That the Sophists—Protagoras, Gorgias, Hippias, and Prodicus—were all foreigners should in itself mean nothing at all. For most of the nature philosophers were foreigners too—Thales, Anaximander, Anaximenes, Pythagoras, Heraclitus, Parmenides, Zeno, Empedocles, Anaxagoras, Leucippus, Democritus, and Xenophanes, whose very name means "foreign-looking." On the one hand, since (as Aristotle said) fire burns the same in Athens and in Persia, perhaps the internationality of nature philosophy and the attempt to make statements shorn of local ethnicities and linguistic idiosyncrasies would foment science. On the other hand, perhaps the early Sophists, who took man for their subject matter, were thus alerted to the phenomena of culture differences by the very fact of their being foreigners.

Athenian tolerance for ethnic difference, however, was at last being strained, the more especially when in Plato and Socrates the ethnocentric inadequacy of Greek epistemology would finally lie openly exposed. Perhaps Greek narcissism, untutored by foreigners, could never have achieved this awareness of culture all alone. The honorable and significant fact is that the Athenians did listen to the alien Sophists. But culture difference was a predicament their epistemology could never transcend, inasmuch as that epistemology was only Socratic ethnography and un-witting Platonic linguistics. Thus, finally, even the Athenians suffered the trauma of acculturation. They began to discover the nature of culture.

Interestingly, however, it was not alienness itself that brought the break, for Greeks had from the Bronze Age onward shown an ability to assimilate new gods. It was, rather, that the theological doubts of some relativists were arousing anxiety to the point of intolerablity. In the days of recrudescent folk Orphism and its eternal godlike soul, Protagoras considered the soul to be nothing apart from the senses. Diogenes Laertius quotes him: " 'As to the gods, I have no means of knowing either that they exist or that they do not exist. For many are the obstacles that impede knowledge, both the obscurity of the question and the shortness of human life.' For this introduction to his book the Athenians expelled him; and they burnt his works in the market place, after sending round a herald to collect them from all who had copies in their possession."[84]

Book burning is an infallible sign of approaching authoritarianism, for books offer not merely dangerous alternative views but an escape from the tyranny of the contemporary. And it is but one step from a dawning awareness of relativism to the authoritarian personality's brutal fascistic insistence on *his* re-absolutized truth only. Plato was a would-be book burner. "Aristoxenus in his Historical Notes affirms that Plato wished to burn all the writings of Democritus that he could collect, but that Amyclas and Clinias the Pythagoreans prevented him, saying that there was no advantage in doing so, for already the books were widely circulated."[85] Laertius goes on to note that Plato, who alludes to nearly all of the early philosophers, never once mentions Democritus the Atomist, even when it would be necessary to controvert him, because he feared to match himself against "the prince of philosophers." But this may be unfair to Plato. He simply was not interested in the world of *physis,* indeed he was contemptuous of

In Critias and Antiphon of Athens, Sophism became domesticated. In Socrates and Plato, Sophism was universalized. It had been a long journey. In discovering the human nature of his gods, Greek man was faced with an even greater mystery, himself. He began dimly to discern that his culture was a product of himself, of human culture heroes and not of demigods, a product of his own unknown mind. There were many alternatives to his culture in the world. More grievous still, with the fall of Athens the Greek began to doubt that his society, even the city-state, could provide for him a sure means to the good life. The Greek critique of the gods had laid bare *physis,* but Greeks did not know how to make inquiry of her or how to cope with godless, heartless ananke. And now came the Greek critique of *nomos* or custom, and the frightening discovery of its contingent and merely human nature. Protagoras had embarked on the education of the young, and the art of persuading the adult. Dangerous enterprises both. In the hands of Plato, prophet of the Greek ghost dance, Greek culture and a first brave struggle toward humaneness were destroyed for millennia.

Platonism is not the summit of Greek philosophy but its final catastrophe, not an original and self-contained system but an eclectic mixture of intense nativisms. To understand this fact we must study further his revived Pythagorean and Orphic cultisms made metaphysical, and examine the many aspects of the Greek massive despair in the world around him. We must see the functioning of Platonism as a desperate historic crisis cult; and we must see Platonism in its context as only one of the attempts at reactionary defense of classic tradition.

At the dawn of Hellenism, in Homeric battles the gods intervened on both sides, almost like naïve spirit-familiars in shamanistic rivalry. But now, in late classic times, the nature philosophers had pressed nature gods almost out of nature, or at least had changed manlike gods into fatelike principles with no special concern for man. Insofar as they are human it would seem that all gods must die! Xenophanes had shown unmistakably that man makes gods; perhaps one last subtle form of this was the philosophy of Anaxagoras, who thought to find mindlike rationality in nature's Nous. But when cosmic Order is thus anthropomorphized, it too is false. Greek rationalism then becomes not a saving aretē but fatal hubris. Mere Greek categories became cosmic Universals.

With the Sophists, Cynics, Stoics, and Epicureans, Greek philosophy took on an increasingly disheartened tone; the very names display it. The same great cataclysmic change is visible in literature. The tragic poet Sophocles,[86] the great conservative who saw his world a shambles, cried "Never to be born is the best fate of all!" Aeschylus[87] wrote in hard-bitten fashion of

God, whose law it is that he who learns must suffer. And even in our sleep, pain that cannot forget falls drop by drop upon the heart. And in our own despite, against our will, comes wisdom to us by the awful grace of God.

What are we to think of Aristophanes' savage indictment of Euripides in *The Frogs,* where he complains this popular playwright had taught the Athenians "to think, see, understand, suspect and question everything"?[88] Why the witch hunting—had not Greek thinking and free inquiry been going on all along? And what had happened to the Greeks anyway, that such a thing however true be said of Euripides *as criticism!*

To the robustious and feisty Homeric Greek, life had the countenance of a Zeus shining, Apollo's gold light, and Hera's bright unclouded sky. Life was still glorious in the triumphant Athens of Pericles and the Parthenon. But between Homer and Herodotus, dark angry clouds seem to have gathered, and this world came to wear the gloom of the pale underworld of Dis. Perhaps, as Gomperz noted, one key may lie in the complaint of Herodotus, that in his time Greece had witnessed heavier afflictions than in twenty preceding generations. But History cannot explain history! Was it a failure of faith in religion, beyond repair? But if so, why? Was it a failure in epistemological technique, so that at the end of the Sophist tradition Plato would angrily try to establish truth by political fiat in the Noble Lie? But there was also the Ionian tradition, alternative to the Socratic needling of microcosmic *nous* and Platonic quest for truth embedded in *Logos,* the sacred Word. There were Xenophanes, Anaxagoras, Democritus, and many others too! Did failure, perhaps, lie in the lack of adequate scientific method? But Aristotle patiently observed and collected facts, and Alcmaeon of Croton, and others, performed experiments. What, then, can account for, in the celebrated phrase of Gilbert Murray, the Greek "failure of nerve"?[89]

Was it simply that Greeks had discovered the existential status of man, on his own like any other animal in the universe, and that the total adaptive techniques in Greek culture were inadequate to sustain the society? Perhaps we cannot finally explain, but only point to the many facets of the phenomenon—political, philosophical, religious, social, and moral—in the light of our understanding of many another crisis cult. As human defense systems, perhaps societies and cultures die too.

But new epistemological crisis is not the automatic death of old assumption. Any thesis, by appealing to common sense (that is, still intact contemporary folklore) can usually find quite serviceable secondary defenses. Greek theology primarily used three such defenses, Polyonymy, Symbolism, and Euhemerism. Polyonymy ("many naming") is the simple assumption that when two pantheons meet in acculturation, all we have are duplicate names for the same gods. Thus one can say that Diana is Artemis, Hera Juno, Minerva Athena, Apollo Sol, and Zeus Jupiter.[90] Difference is thus explained as being merely a language difference.[91] In the case of Zeus Pater and Jupiter, of course, the "two" gods are in fact the same Indoeuropean sky god in two dialectical forms: thus far the method is sounder than it knows. But "Hera" is *not* the etymological cognate of "Juno" in any combination of Grimm's, Verner's and Grassman's Laws. Small problem though, since a chief god has to have a wife, and if their legends and attributes are not too widely different, they may be assimilated to one another, especially if the two Indoeuropean pantheons start out fairly much alike. Early theologians were not pursuing etymons here anyway, but goddesses.

The game can be played indefinitely. With no shred of philological legitimacy, Latin Diana-Luna can be Greek Selene-Artemis-Hecate. The difficulty is that as attributes pile up so do inconsistencies. Luna and Selene can be the Moon all right, but Diana and Artemis are hunting goddesses, evidently on the earth. And what is Hecate, an underworld goddess, doing in the sky? Furthermore, who is to say that Artemis as Great Mother is not, rather, Ge-Gaia, Demeter, and Rhea? But these are fertility goddesses of the earth, which seems to impugn Diana's sky-goddess virginity. Polyonymy only accumulates contradictions! The alternative is the system, or rather lack of system, that Hesiod had of simply piling up gods seriatim or tandem. Who, after all, is the one-and-only, first and original sky god—Zeus, Ouranos, or Kronos? Who is "the shining one"—Zeus, Dis, Phoebus, Apollo or Helios, Diana, Luna, or Selene? And just who is in charge of fertility—Zeus, Apollo, or Hermes, Demeter, Artemis, or Aphrodite?

The difficulties of syncretism increase when on further acculturative contacts really alien gods must be assimilated. The Egyptian says "Osiris" but of course what he actually means is Zeus—or ought he have said "Serapion"? Still, one's faith in cows is hardly shaken when a Frenchman says *vache* though the German is surely closer to the truth when he says *Kuh*. But when Yahweh is assimilated to Zeus, that is plainly either the extreme of weakminded goodwill or crafty political conniving.[92] The system has limits of plausibility too. A single accidentally shared attribute does not make two or three gods one. Because Zeus and Yahweh and Shiva are all sky bulls even before they meet, does this mean they all can be rolled up into one? Well, hardly, because Zeus is an eagle, swan, oak, rain, flint, snake, and much else besides, whereas Shiva already has a preposterous baggage of "attributes"—fire, phallus, snake, crescent moon, a third eye, elephant and tiger hides, a trident, skulls, a river, and what not else.

On the level of science, the Greek nature gods gradually and quietly died, to leave behind only serenely immortal nature. On the level of religion, they lived on. Greek deism did not die in polyonymy, only logic. Indeed, if anything, re-encountering the "same" gods elsewhere by this method only reinforces belief. For deism is bound up with a far more fundamental fantasy that was born with but did not die with Neanderthal man, the animistic belief in spirits that survive death. The fantasy that defies our common metazoan fate is at the core of every religion. Indeed, gods are only one kind of instance of the basic belief in animism. Because men find the fantasy attractive, it survives the destruction of each successive rationale used to support it. If Greek physics will not, then foreign folklore may.

Like other Eurasians, Indoeuropeans began with shamans and their spirits; Brahmans are still living gods, priests to themselves. But Achaean Greeks found immortality in their shamanistic nature gods. Later Greeks gradually found that immortality to lie only in Nature or the Universe. Meanwhile the Immortal Idea of animistic spirits of the Achaeans encountered and fused with Aegean snake-immortals. The noble fantasy does not fit the facts of experience? Small matter! The Hypothesis is not discarded, it is only that new rationalizing must be found for it. The religionist of every period must be both Fundamentalist and Modernist, conservative in his beliefs and radical in his reasons for them. Religionists cannot really equate themselves prestigefully with scientists in this; for scientists *discard hypotheses*. When the sociologist of knowledge asks "What does the new theory *do for* the generation that holds it?" the answer for the religionist is always the same irony: "It lets people keep *old theory* inviolate and unchanged, it preserves Sacred Culture, the Wish whose rationalization is the whole motive of the system."

When Socrates passed onward the old Pythagorean-Heraclitean theory of the immortal soul, brought it was said by the "Hyperborean" Apollo, he wakened no one from his dogmatic slumbers. When Plato added Orphic-Dionysian theology to this, he enabled men to keep on dreaming a Stone Age dream. The function of dream-work in the individual is to allow him to continue sleeping; the function of up-to-the-moment theology is to let men continue dreaming. Let reason keep silence. If a Symbolist theologue of late Hellenistic times re-proves the reality of a god by saying in his manly modernist way that Apollo is really the Sun—is the sun then a python, a wolf, a huntsman, a cowherd, the plague, and thrower of lightning bolts besides? For Symbolism tells us loftily in any age that the ancients did not mean what they said but what we do, and then goes on to improvise *ad lib* what they really meant. In this way one can borrow the ancients' prestige without troubling to understand their ethnography. Thus Samson was not a strong man who had his hair cut off by a temptress (and thus *in ancient terms* lost his great strength), but "symbolizes" the Moon who lost her rays in an eclipse.[93] Thus also Hermes the phallic god is really the virgin Moon. These are actual examples of the luna-tic school of interpretation!—deep mysteries that only theologians can know about, and only Jungians explain. But any difficulties that Syncretism gets us into, Symbolism will get us out of.

The third theological defense of belief was euhemerism. Euhemeros ("[having a] happy day," that is, "cheerful") was a Greek philosopher who wrote his *Hiera Anagraphē* about 280 B.C., setting forth the view that the gods arose from the deification of dead heroes. Written in the spirit of the political utopias of his time, the book is a tale of a mystical Aristeas-like journey to the Happy Isles, somewhere between the Red Sea and the Indian Ocean. At "Panchaia" he saw a temple on the gold pillars of which Zeus had inscribed the Hesiodic stories of Ouranos, Kronos and himself. That is, King Zeus had simply written down the history of his own family. If this history was as bloody as that of the tragedians' cursed family of Atreus, the euhemerist fable at least rescued the majesty of nature from the objectionable humanities of the Olympians that all late Greek philosophers and literary men had complained about. The whole effect was to reduce Zeus to human size, of a king deified after his death.

The Romans took over euhemerism quite seriously, for that was exactly what they were doing in deifying still-living emperors. Christians later used euhemerism as an apologetic weapon against the heathen, accounting for pagan gods in euhemeristic terms, but neglecting to note however that this was exactly what they were doing to their own Christ. In the rationalizing eighteenth century, euhemerism became the favorite "key" to all mythologies.[94] In the nineteenth, a subtle form of euhemerism dissolved religion into the earthy and appealing humanism of Feuerbach that Marx and Engels so bitterly attacked. (He thought all the attributes of God were the idealized virtues of men; they thought all the gods were contrived weapons in the class struggle and religions part of history-by-plot). The twentieth-century reaction to euhemerism is to wonder how on earth it explains anything, since it merely substitutes the unproven for the absurd. To a classic Greek, also, euhemerism would seem at first an impious attack on all the gods. But a moment's thought would show that, in terms of assumptions then still living among the Greeks, euhemerism was matter-of-fact to the point of banality. Indeed, the late classic world seized upon euhemerism with delight as though it were a truism.

If it fails to impress us because we quite miss the point, then this means only that theology goes out of date as the content of "common sense" changes. But it is important to see the high plausibility of euhemerism in terms of the whole Hellenic-Hellenistic tradition of thought if we are to understand its usefulness for theology. Archaic Greeks believed in literal, immortal snake-souls that crawled out of the spinal *muellos* when a man died, the life-stuff of his conscious thinking and his provable procreativity, and surely akin to the divine creativity visible in nature they called gods.[95] Classic Greeks remained animistic—whether the divine soul-essence were Thalean rain-seed, Heraclitean fire, or Anaxagorean *Nous*. Still animists, late Greeks could still easily believe that the actual souls of "magnanimous" heroes persisted in objective fact as great souls or gods. Again, the proponents of the neo-Mystery cults, Pythagoras and Empedocles, both modestly claimed to reincarnate such god-souls; and the founders Orpheus and Musaeus were considered in Plato's time to have been real, albeit shadowy, historic figures.

Of course for latter-day heirs of monotheistic religion, the *scale* of one grandiose high god behind the universe is so magnified that euhemerism is quite staggeringly blasphemous to the degree that we still believe in such a once-human god. But worlds differ in size and number of spirits.[96] For polytheistic Greeks euhemerism was neither a rationalizing defense of belief nor free-thinking cynicism but a good "scientific" explanation of the true (animistic) facts. Real gods were the real immortality of once real men. In animistic terms, euhemerism is a marvelously "rational" way to account for the origin of all gods in heroes, except of course of one's own true god (charisma *is!*). Better yet, euhemerism is available for the uses of the new true religion: if gods are immortal souls, then what about one's own?

Another point to note, if we would understand ancients in their ethnographic terms and not ours, is the enormous social differences then to be encountered in the Hellenistic world.[97] Earlier Homeric gods were in projective scale with real Mycenaean princes. The tone taken toward kings and heroes and gods was naïvely similar. Diomede was not wounding Jehovah in the groin but only Ares, and he was talking back manfully only to Agamemnon. But the social distance between Alexander the Great and a helot conscript was great enough for the world emperor to seem godlike, and the gods to be commensurate with such a hero.[98] With enormous accumulations of capital and military might in one man's hands, the psychological distance between Caesar or *divus* Augustus and a peasant foot soldier was of similar magnitude.[99] What is meant by gods, he would say, if these men are not godlike? In fact the social humbleness of one man *creates* the heroic in another—a fabulously wealthy Drake, a Frobisher, a Gloriana, to a poor London navvy after the miraculous defeat of the Great Armada.[100] Mana, charisma, is not a metaphysical but a socio-psychological phenomenon. (Surely that man Mozart was hardly human; certainly no man can chant with words like Shakespeare, Melville, Joyce since Orpheus!) To a child a father can be god, more real than any that he later knows, and more intensely loved.

It is difficult to recapture a close sense of the mighty fertility daemons of our race's childhood. The Titans of Greek prehistory preserve majesties already ancient in the time of man. In the Zeus-Zagreus rite of the Titans, Jane Harrison has taught us to see an initiation ceremony into manhood, with the primeval Stone Age bull-roarer and the old totemistic meal of blood brothers eating the strength of the sacrifical god-animal. To the Titanic rite still clings the shadow of the under-earth rite of dancing shamans, and behind the Zeus-Zagreus animal stand the mighty aurochs, the cave-bear, and the mammoth. In Neolithic religion the fertility of flocks and fields still comes from the great bellowing rain bull of the sky— Zeus, Yahweh or Shiva. And still, above some, sits the Father of the Universe.

NOTES

(XV The Death of the Gods)

1. After Homer and Hesiod, our main sources on Greek religion are much later: Apollodorus, *Bibliotheca;* Plutarch, *Quæstiones Grææcæ;* Strabo, *Geography;* and Pausanias, *Descriptio Græciæ*. Though polemicists against paganism, early Church Fathers like Clement of Alexandria were converted pagans and at least knowledgeable; see also Arnobius, Eusebius, Augustine and Athenagoras. For the Romans we have Ovid, *Metamorphoses;* Aulus Gellius, *Noctes Atticae;* Cicero, *De Natura Deorum,* etc.

2. Gomperz, *op. cit.,* I:80, 130, 135–36; Vermeule, *op. cit.,* pp. 280–81; Sir William Ridgeway is the ultimate source of our discernment of two main ethnic strata of gods in Greece.

3. Technically, a civilization is a group of co-existing and markedly different *subcultures* or specialized *kinds* of men in the same society, as opposed to tribal societies having mostly only specialization of labor by sex. Primitive-civilized in this quantitative sense is therefore a gamut, not a dichotomy.

4. E. E. Sikes, *The Anthropology of the Greeks* (London: David Nutt, 1914, p. 94). But Thucydides first stated the principle that elements of primitive culture survive in later civilizations (p. 10).

5. Gisela M. A. Richter, "Ceramics, From c. 700 B.C. to the Fall of the Roman Empire," in Singer *et al., op. cit.,* 2:259–83, pp. 259–60, 267; cf. Sir Lindsay Scott, "Pottery," *loc. cit.,* 1:376–412, p. 409; Zimmern, *op. cit.,* p. 382.

6. Both the Trojan and Syracusan war raids might be called piracy—a condition endemic in the Mediterranean from Jason's trading-raiding adventure in the *Argo* until Thomas Jefferson's Tripoli. Policing of piracy by the dominant trading power is difficult to distinguish from the Athenian attacks on Melos and Syracuse; cf. the Atlantic from Elizabeth to the War of 1812—and the American "police action" in Korea and Vietnam. The Greek dilemma lay between the defensive navy of Themistocles at Salamis and that of the Second Athenian Confederacy. In 355 B.C. an Attic orator cried, "I am convinced both that we shall govern our city better and that we will ourselves be better off and prosper in every direction, if we give up striving after a maritime empire, for this is the cause of our troubles" (Isocrates, *On the Peace,* §28). See also A. T. Mahan, *The Influence of Sea Power upon History* (Boston: Little, Brown and Company, 1944, pp. 14–21).

7. Isocrates, *Panathenaicus and Panegyricus* (New York: G. P. Putnam's Sons, 3 vols., 1928–45, 2:259–83, Panegyricus, §50); cf. Thucydides, *The Peloponnesian War* (Baltimore: Penguin Books, 1961, i, 3); and Zimmern, *op. cit.,* p. 81 n 1.

8. Plutarch, *De Herodoti malignitate,* in *Moralia,* I:119–129, 854E (tr. F. C. Babbitt, New York: G. P. Putnam's Sons, 14 vols., 1927); cf. Herodotus, viii, 238.

9. On helot status, Zimmern, *op. cit.,* pp. 77, 85–86, 114, 353. The Spartans once had helots choose from among themselves 2000 men they considered had done most for Sparta on the battlefield during the Peloponnesian War. These were given garlands and paraded around the temple as though they were to be free— but no one ever knew exactly how each one of these potential leaders was done away with by the Spartan secret police (Thucydides, iv, 16, p. 276).

10. J. R. Newman calls Sparta "a harsh, barbarous city petrified in an attitude

of morose distrust . . . the ideal of a barrack-room sargeant-major" (in a review, *Scientific American*, 197 ✕5 [Nov. 1957], p. 165).

11. George Devereux has shown how helotism grossly warped the character both of helots *and of Spartans,* a situation he assimilates to racism in the United States ("Psychanalyse et Histoire: Une Application à l'Histoire de Sparte," *Annales: Economies, Sociétés, Civilisations,* 1 [1965] 18–44)—a kind of latent psychosis that "is one of the least known facts of history" (p. 43).

12. Reinach, *Orpheus,* p. 91; cf. A. G. Keller, *Homeric Society, A Sociological Study of the Iliad and Odyssey* (London: Longmans, Green & Co., 1902, p. 144). On the open state cult, Fustel de Coulanges, *op. cit.,* pp. 142–73; a good critique of Fustel de Coulanges is in Zimmern, *op. cit.,* p. 82.

13. Burnet, *op. cit.,* pp. 256, 269; but the moon as reflecting sunlight may be Parmenidean (Fragments 14, 15, *op. cit.,* p. 177 n 1).

14. S. A. Cook, F. E. Adcock, and H. N. Baynes (eds.), *Cambridge Ancient History* (Cambridge: At the University Press, 12 vols., 1923–39, 12:517); cf. S. S. Seltman, *op. cit.,* p. 26. A chief concern of Caesar and Augustus was to prevent the creation of new sodalities and to destroy old ones as potential centers of opposition, a reason Christianity at Rome for a long time seemed a kind of burial society whose earliest sanctuaries were the tombs of martyrs (Zimmern, *op. cit.,* p. 150 n 1, citing Renan). The Church also tries to monopolize all the social activities of its communicants; for when a cult becomes an ecclesia and the religion a state (or the State becomes a religion) no rival can be tolerated.

15. The leading argument of Euripides is that the evil in myth and religion comes from men imputing their own evil nature to the gods (*Iphigenia in Tauris,* l. 391); but he also disliked prophets, and distrusted Delphi. Aeschylus, *Agamemnon,* lines 1132–33.

16. Herodotus, II, 53 and VII, 152.

17. Gomperz, *op. cit.,* I:509; cf. Antisthenes, in II:165. On cultivated Greeks in general, Seltman, *op. cit.,* p. 27.

18. The Greek intellectuals' critique itself gave rise to a later traditional view that the gods had been somehow gradually "humanized" (e.g. L. R. Farnell, "Greece, Greek Religion," *Hastings Encyclopedia of Religion and Ethics,* 6:392–495; cf. L. B. Patton, "Baal, Beel, Bel," *loc. cit.,* 2:283–98, p. 285). On the contrary, nature philosophy was gradually de-anthropomorphized.

19. Heraclitus, Fragment 42. Plato, *Phaedrus,* 246B; *Republic,* II, 377E; *Euthyphro,* 6B, 7B; *Laws,* XII, 941B, etc. Aristotle, *Physics,* II, 8, 198b, 18; *Divinatio per somnum,* 2, 463b, 12, etc. For a summary of this trend, see V. D. Macchioro, *From Orpheus to Paul, A History of Orphism* (New York: Henry Holt & Co., 1930, pp. 209–10).

20. The best brief account in English of the pre-Socratics is that of Burnet, who also includes the known fragments of Thales (pp. 40–50), Anaximander (pp. 50–71), and Anaximenes (pp. 72–79). The classic is Hermann Diels, *Die Fragmente des Vorsokratiker* (edited by Walter Krantz, 2 vols., Dublin, Zurich: Weidman, 1966), translated into English by Kathleen Freeman, *The Pre-Socratic Philosophers* (Oxford: Basil Blackwell, 1948); see also G. S. Kirk and J. E. Raven, *The Presocratic Philosophers* (Cambridge: At the University Press, 1957). For Greek philosophy in general, Gomperz's four-volume *Greek Thinkers* is for specialists; a good one-volume summary is Eduard Zeller, *Outlines of the History of Greek Philosophy* (New York: Meridian Books, 13th ed., 1955).

21. For Strato who "had no need of that hypothesis" (La Place), Gomperz, *op. cit.,* IV:50.

22. Heraclitus, Fragment 20, in Burnet, *op. cit.,* p. 134.

23. Michael Balint thinks temperaments are divided into those who unconsciously

theorize in terms of matter and place, and others in terms of space and process, energy and motion between points. If so, Democritus was remarkable in being able to encompass both Parmenidean and Heraclitean types. Again, if Parmenides' reality is noun-like, and Heraclitus' verb-like, then Einstein is remarkable in encompassing both. But we have not escaped the predicament: is E in E=mc^2 a Heraclitean wave or a Parmenidean particle? In a sense, Hume discovered Causality to be the Indoeuropean transitive verb; animists and religionists project pronouns.

24. Lucretius' *De Rerum Natura* was called by Rémy de Gourmont "the most beautiful perhaps of the works of men." W. H. D. Rouse, in his edition of Lucretius (New York: G. P. Putnam's Sons, 1928, p. viii) calls the atomic theory "the most brilliant, and the most fruitful, of all scientific hypotheses."

25. Xenophanes on the gods, Fragments 15–16 of his *Satires* (Burnet, *op. cit.*, p. 119); on Homer, p. 114; on Leucothea, p. 115; on athletes and philosophers, *Elegies,* Fr. 2, p. 117. Hippolytus preserved Theophrastus' account crediting Xenophanes with the discovery of fossils, but Burnet (p. 124) thinks Anaximander may deserve the credit; cf. Gomperz, *op. cit.,* I:162, 551. "The One is god" of Xenophanes clearly implies the concept of universe (Aristotle, *Metaphysics,* 986. b 24); he was concerned to deny the gods in the sense that there is "No god but the world" (p. 114).

26. The reincarnation-fantasy is based on *déjà vu*—the overwhelming conviction one has occasionally that once before he has lived this moment in identical detail and circumstance. Psychoanalytic theory considers that some minimal present cue reawakens a whole unconscious set of associations, really experienced before in a forgotten dream (S. Ferenczi, "Hebbel's Explanation of 'Déjà Vu,'" in *Further Contributions,* pp. 422–23; cf. Dodds, *op. cit.,* p. 173 n 107). One might paraphrase Heraclitus: the waking world is the common Fire-consciousness (secular-scientific world), sleeping the private individual fire (source of the sacred, sometimes transduced into others). A. Brelich notes that Greek culture was unfriendly to and unimpressed by the dream as an individual not a social concern; and oneiromancy was not important in early times compared with haruspicy, etc., until about the fifth century B.C. when dream dictionaries began to be much consulted, as it were in *ad hoc* Jungian fashion ("The Place of Dreams in the Religious World Concept of the Greeks," in G. E. von Grunebaum and Roger Caillois [eds.], *The Dream in Human Societies,* Berkeley: University of California Press, 1966, pp. 293–301). Curiously, the *Iliad* reports male dreams only, the *Odyssey* female ones only.

27. The best general sources on Orphism: W. K. C. Guthrie, *Orpheus and Greek Religion;* Ivan M. Linforth, *The Arts of Orpheus* (Berkeley: University of California Press, 1941); Vittorio Macchioro, *From Orpheus to Paul;* and Karl Kerényi, *Pythagoras und Orpheus* (Zurich: Rhein-Verlag, 2nd ed., 1950).

28. Sinclair, *op. cit.,* pp. 170–71; cf. pp. 12–13. It is not that a *type* of living men, shamans, could not have given rise to the figure of Orpheus; it is rather that the received Orpheus cannot be an authentic historic individual, but rather a compost of widespread mythological motifs. Nonetheless, all the legends, from that of Jason's journey to that of the Hyperboreans and Delos, uniformly agree on an alien northern shamanistic source on the Danube of the "Orphic" revival of Thracian folk-religion in Greece. Hyperboreans (Pindar, *Olympic Odes,* iii, 14–16); Abaris (Herodotus, iv, 36), Aristeas (iv, 13–16). Plato, *Apology,* 41a.

29. On the syncretic shamanistic character of Orpheus and the inauthenticity of his documents, see Guthrie, *op. cit.,* pp. 28, 31–33, 61–62, 67, 112–15, 195–96, 206, 255.

30. Aristophanes, *The Frogs,* line 1032.

31. Dodds, *op. cit.*, p. 147; cf. 170 n 88.

32. Apollonius, bk. iv (*op. cit.*, p. 192).

33. *Iliad*, ii, 599.

34. Vermeule, *op. cit.*, p. 308.

35. Virgil, *Georgics*, iv, 523; Ovid, *Metamorphoses*, xi, 50.

36. Linforth, *op. cit.*, p. 129.

37. Macchioro, *op. cit.*, pp. 205–7; cf. pp. 212–13. The term "mysteries" comes from the verb μύειν, "to close [the eyes and lips]"—an attitude toward belief in itself preposterously un-Greek.

38. It should be noted that early Christianity was very like the Pythagorean brotherhoods of south Italy, and the main dogma in each was immortality. The eleven-century span Macchioro notes for Orphism is indeed only part of its lifetime. Mid-European soul-beliefs long antedated it; and if Orphism was a recrudescent mid-European shamanism in Greece and Italy, and Pauline Christianity descended from Orphism, the central rite of each being god-eating, then this religion reaches from the upper Old Stone Age to the present day. The immortality-cult is itself immortal. Supernaturalists, naturally, are concerned to argue the uniqueness of Christianity and to eschew recognition of its authentic ethnographic historicity and continuity, both of which are obvious to the secular anthropologist.

39. Cf. Guthrie, *op. cit.*, pp. 193, 195, 207, 268; Orpheus as "the Good Shepherd," pp. 264–67, etc.

40. Linforth, *op cit.*, on Dionysus as a syncretism of a vine-god (pp. 214, 357), a Cretan (p. 215), Egyptian (pp. 207, 217, 243), Zeus-Zagreus (p. 311), and an old snake-deity (pp. 207, 220, 226, 244).

41. Guthrie suggests real similarities between Orphic teachings and the Buddhist doctrine of *karma* (*op. cit.*, pp. 164, 195, 208). But the Gallic Druids also taught the transmigration of souls (Caesar, *Gallic War*, vi, 14, 5), hence the idea may have come directly with Orphism from the north (see Burnet, *op. cit.*, 82 n 2). Still, Heraclitus' concept of the immortal Fire-soul is like the Iranian in being tinged with invidious dualism; and Heraclitus had historic Persian contacts (cf. A. J. Carney, "Zoroastrianism," *Hastings Encyclopedia*, 12:862–88, p. 866). The very ubiquity of the belief makes tracing elements difficult; on the whole it seems to me simply meridional Asiatic shamanism, with at best Celtic-Iranian colorings of a basic Indoeuropean idea. This is not to argue against a still older and wider related head-cult, which is a motif in Orphism but intercontinental.

42. Diogenes Laertius, *Lives of Eminent Philosophers* (New York: G. P. Putnam's Sons, 2 vols., 1925, 2:353=Laertius VIII, i, 36).

43. Burnet, *op. cit.*, pp. 85–87—a deviousness all the more strange since the *Phaedo* was dedicated, so to speak, to Pythagoras (pp. 82–83), and his influence on Plato is profound and unmistakable (pp. 276–309). Was subversive and meddling Pythagorean politicism too inflammatory to mention when urging what so much resembled it, Plato's ideal fascist state? Why was he motivated not to mention his main source?

44. Gold was an important Orphic symbol for the soul because of its chemical "incorruptibility" or immortality, its almost infinite extensibility as gold leaf (hence its assimilation to the infinitely extensible fire-soul and the Logos as a kind of spirit Master-of-Animals or soul of the species), its connection with kings, the sun, etc. Significantly, Orpheus (on Cheiron's advice to Jason) went with the Argonauts *seeking* the Golden Fleece, a long time before even the Trojan War; Danubian natives flowed gold-bearing sands over sheep-hides, to the lanolin of which gold dust clung, after which the fleece was burned to recover the gold (Strabo, *Geography*, I, 2, 39 and XI, 2, 19, in Apollonius, *op. cit.*, p. 21 n). Another Orphic symbol of immortality was the sacred spring or fountain, because of its ever-flowing water. In the sixteenth century Ponce de Leon was still seeking both gold and the Fountain

of Youth (Ethel King, *The Fountain of Youth and Ponce de Leon,* Brooklyn: Theodore Gaus' Sons, Inc., 1963)!

45. Diogenes Laertius, *op. cit.,* 2:321–67. On the eagle of Pythagoras, Plutarch, *Life of Numa,* 8; he also tamed another northern shamanistic animal, the bear (Iamblichus, *Life of Pythagoras,* 60). Animal familiars?

46. An unremarked echo of shamanism: the relation of Pythagorean music-magic with the animistic planet-powers of the sky. The sky shaman's music has power over nature through anthropomorphic spirit-familiars. The magic connection remains in astrology, but reversed: stars move men now, not men the stars—another index of failure of nerve? A comment on the changing Greek ethos: Greeks had long earlier had contacts with Asia Minor, but in all Greek literature astrology is first mentioned in Plato (*Timaeus,* 40 c 9). The Pythagorean notion that *things are Number* remained fundamentally magico-shamanistic in Hellenistic Gnosticism and the Kabbala. Devereux (*Normal and Abnormal,* p. 29) agrees with Dodds that Pythagoras was essentially a shaman—for the reason that he *uses* numbers for mystic, not scientific ends. Dodds (*op. cit.,* p. 175 n 119) thinks the Pythagorean use of the "language of spirits" derives from the shamanistic tradition (note also that in his madness Ajax talks a sinister language no man taught him but a demon—Sophocles, *Ajax,* lines 243f).

47. The injunctions of Pythagoras sound more like magical taboos than ethical prescriptions: Don't poke the fire with a knife, Don't step over the beam of a scales, Don't sit on your quart-measure, Don't eat the heart, Don't help a man unload a burden but help him on with it, Always roll up your bed, Don't put the image of a god on the circle of your ring, Don't leave the imprint of a pan on the ashes, Don't clean up a mess with a torch, Don't make a nuisance toward the sun, Don't walk the highway, Don't shake hands too enthusiastically, Don't have swallows under the eaves, Don't keep birds with hooked talons, Don't urinate or stand on your nail- and hair-trimmings, Turn the sharp blade away, and When you travel abroad, don't look back at the frontier (Diogenes Laertius, *op. cit.,* 2:335–37). Of course Laertius heavy-handedly "symbolizes" them (VIII, i, 18).

48. Harrison, *Prolegomena,* Appendix, within which Gilbert Murray translates and discusses the Orphic texts.

49. The Spartan Xenophon had one too in his *Cyropaedia* (New York: Macmillan, 2 vols., 1914). Pythagoras founded his Order at Croton in south Italy, one of the Achaean cities in which Pythagorism had grown to supreme power, but the people revolted against the Brotherhood. Despite such facts, Burnet firmly insists Pythagorism was only a religious fraternity, not a political league (as argued by Krische, based on Dikaearchus, in a tradition presenting Pythagoras as a practical man), whereas Aristoxenus would have the Brotherhood a scientific society (Burnet, *op. cit.,* p. 89). The combination of cult, polity, and lore sounds more like a medicine society than a classic city-state. Still another tendentious notion is that Pythagorism expressed the "Dorian aristocratic ideal." But as to his racist fascism, Pythagoras was an Ionian (like aristocratic Heraclitus), and the Order was orginally confined to Achaean city-states.

50. The story that Pythagoras was killed with forty followers rather than cross a beanfield when pursued by angry Crotonians (Laertius, *op. cit.,* 2:355–57) would suggest a totemistic taboo: beans were tabooed because they contain the breath of life and would disturb dreams (2:341), are like the genitals or the gates of Hades (2:349), like the head of one's father, etc. Andrews (*op. cit.,* pp. 274–92) elaborates the complex symbology, noting that "no plant or animal known to the Indo-Europeans produced a more luxuriant growth of beliefs" than the *fava* bean (cf. Boyd, also Giles, *op. cit.,* and Ch. XIV, note 44, above). P. Davies ("Favism," [Harvard] *Postgraduate Medical Journal,* 37 [1961] 477–80) showed that this

disease occurs in 5 per 1000 individuals among some Mediterranean populations. Giles showed elegantly, in genetic terms, how in a matrilineage the disease would appear in a maternal uncle and nephew, but would disappear in a patrilineage, except for chance reintroduction of the deficiency gene by marriage. On Pythagorean sexual abstinence, Burnet, *op. cit.*, p. 84.

51. Socrates and the Orphics, Plato, *Phaedo,* 69 a 3. Aristotle, Fragment 45 (1483 a 19) in Burnet, *op. cit.*, p. 84 n 4. Aristotle is critical of the Orphism of Plato and Pythagoras because (as he says in his careful way) they assume a soul is attached to or enclosed in a body but without determining how this happens or what the condition of the body is; yet an explanation is needed, if the one acts upon and moves, and the other is acted upon and moved; and in two things taken at random no such mutual relations exist; hence to speak of the soul and have nothing to say about the body is absurd (*De Anima,* I, 3, 407b). But of course Aristotle was a biologist, and Plato was not. The soul-concept developed in a recognizably continuous sequence: simple animism (soul of individual person or object, consciousness), master of animals (shaman), Master of Animals (Father- or species-soul), Heraclitus (world-fire Soul and fragmentary souls), Anaxagoras (*Nous* or World-Soul), Pythagoras (immortal soul-stuff reincarnating in men and animals), Orphism (immortal head-psyche soul, related to the ancient *muellos-* snake-soul, Plato (creative demiurgic Idea-souls for each species of particulars, whether organisms or things), and then subsequently the Stoics (*logoi spermatikoi*). It is interesting that the shaman's old specialty, fire (Change, becoming) substituted for *physis* in Heraclitus. This animistic tradition, throughout, sought the sacred formative male principle; the Ionian tradition from Thales to Atomists directed attention to the nature of the female principle, mundane materia.

52. Standard sources: Burnet, *op. cit.*, pp. 130–68; Zeller, *op. cit.*, pp. 60–64; consult also Gomperz, *op. cit.*, index. As usual, Diogenes Laertius (*op. cit.*, 2:408–25) should be used with caution.

53. The meteorite made a deep impression at the time (468–67 B.C.) and was still shown to travelers in the days of Pliny (*Natural History,* ii, 149) and Plutarch (*Life of Lysander,* §12); cf. Diogenes Laertius, 2:139. On the Nile floods, Fragment 5 (Burnet, *op. cit.*, p. 276); on the mind and hands, Aristotle, *De partibus animalium,* Δ, 10. 687 a 7). Mystical revelation requires us to accept the proposition of absolute knowledge imparted by unreasonable and unknowable processes, and moreover non-learned from secular empiricism—notions naturally abhorrent to the rational and secular minds of Anaxagoras and Aristotle.

54. Diogenes Laertius, *op. cit.*, 2:462–65.

55. Herodotus quoted by Edith Hamilton, *The Greek Way* (New York: W. W. Norton, 1942, Mentor Books, 1948, p. 124).

56. *Anabasis* in Xenophon, *Hellenica, Anabasis, Apology and Symposium* (New York: G. P. Putnam's Sons, 3 vols., 1928, II–III). On oratory and leadership, Keller, *op. cit.*, p. 264. Hesiod makes even the power of Zeus depend on his *metis,* cunning, craft, wisdom in counsel (*Theogony,* in Brown, *op. cit.*, pp. 20, 55).

57. Classic Greek men were seldom at home except to eat or to sleep; all their institutions took place in the open and in public; on this quality of Greek life, Zimmern, *op. cit.*, p. 60.

58. Athenian drama was so much a public affair that the state paid the entrance fees of those too poor to pay. Philosophers, especially Epicureans, were the first to withdraw into the privacy of their gardens, a fact in itself diagnostic of a change in Greek ethos; earlier, the agora, the stoa were characteristic places for philosophers. Modern Greeks do not value privacy, and expect long-continued discussion of issues (Ernestine Friedl, "The Role of Kinship in the Transmission of National Culture

to Rural Villages in Mainland Greece," *American Anthropologist*, 61 [1959] 30–38, pp. 33–34).

59. Cf. Murray, *op. cit.*, p. 124.

60. Aristotle quoted in Gomperz, *op. cit.*, IV:308.

61. Diogenes Laertius, *op. cit.*, 2:463–69.

62. Pindar's belief in aristocracy, as such belief usually is, was bolstered with notions of heredity (*Pythian Odes*, X, 71–72). But he had the grace to say (Sinclair, *op. cit.*, p. 139) that although great wealth is a good, in allowing the subsidy of public sport and song, it may lead to *kóros*—a word for which our only translation would be "fatcat" since it implies both a surfeit of wealth and the smug self-approval it induces, breeding lawless and insolent *hubris,* and inviting heaven-sent *ate* or disaster.

63. *Paideia,* inculcation of culture, the Greek theory of child-raising, is best delineated in Werner Jaeger's *Paideia, The Ideals of Greek Culture* (New York: Oxford University Press, 3 vols., 1945), though not everyone will share Professor Jaeger's standardized adulation of Socrates and Plato. On other aspects of *paideia,* see Gomperz, *op. cit.*, IV:284; Gomperz was well aware that Plato was a reactionary (II:250–51, 262; III:69, 248, 255–56, 261–62).

64. The term *scholē* means leisure, an idea that seems to have been lost with respect to modern schools.

65. Protagoras and Prodicus had public readings for which they charged a fee, even up to a hundred minae (Diogenes Laertius, *op cit.*, 2:463 and 465), but Prodicus also wrote of *Forensic Speech for a Fee, Two Books of Opposing Arguments,* as though the new practice of teachers' taking money were highly controversial (Diogenes Laertius, *op. cit.*, 2:467). Until recently, when learning has become a bourgeois commodity, the compromise seems to have been to keep the matter as close to *gratis* as possible. The same principle, of course, applies to scholarly books.

66. Zeller, *op. cit.*, pp. 92–111 on the Sophists.

67. The teaching of *aretē* here means teaching expertise in a subject, not necessarily "goodness" in the moral sense.

68. The Cynic Diogenes, like some of his modern equivalents, appears to have been intentionally offensive; see Laertius, *op. cit.*, 2:23–25.

69. Zeller, *op. cit.*, pp. 102–4.

70. Thales is said to have urged a federated Ionian state with its capital at Teos (Burnet, *op. cit.*, p. 46).

71. Zeller, *op. cit.*, pp. 104–7.

72. Empedocles was a flamboyant personality, if we are to believe the stories told about him, an ancient Faust intent not on questioning but mastering nature, half mage and miracle worker. He was a doctor and an orator, but was convicted of stealing the discourses of Pythagoras and, like Plato, was excluded from his school. Despite his Pythagorism, he was a great democratic leader at Akragos—yet at Olympia he demanded excessive deference. He thought light took an infinitesimal time to travel, and stated clearly that hair, feathers, scales (and leaves) were cognate—but Satyros said Gorgias saw his teacher performing magic. To his student Pausanias he imparted his nature lore as if it were higher revelation demanding faith; Pausanias was present when he raised a woman back to life. Empedocles claimed to have been incarnated several times before, and had reached the highest circle of rebirth where the next step was but to rejoin the gods. He was a medicine man, he could raise and abate winds and rains—and he founded a medical school. Laertius said that never was anyone more talked about in gatherings of his friends than Empedocles (*op. cit.* 2:367–91).

73. Linguists, to my mind, have never adequately met the issue of the Sapir-Whorf

hypothesis, despite a symposium ostensibly devoted to it: H. Hoijer (ed.), *Language in Culture,* Memoirs of the American Anthropological Association, 79, 1955; but see the articles by Fearing, Hoijer, and Hockett, the remarks by McQuown (p. 208) and by Kaplan (p. 209). The mystery, time, is viewed differently by different philosophers and in different cultures. On Parmenidean and Heraclitean time, J. T. Fraser (ed.), *The Voices of Time* (New York: Braziller, 1966, pp. 14, 56–57). Greek time was cyclic, with the *logos*-return (species); Hebrew time was linear and finite, with God's-world's life finite like man's (individual). Medieval time was finite and uniquely occurring (J. L. Russell, "Time in Christian Thought," in Fraser, *op. cit.,* pp. 59–76, esp. pp. 66–70). Heller observes that the Greek consciousness lacked a historical sense and revolved about the Pure Present, rejected the Egyptian time-obsession, and "found it appropriate to burn their dead rather than mummify them for all time to come" (*op. cit.,* p. 163).

74. Speechless pointing as a concept was also imputed to Cratylus (Aristotle, *Metaphysics,* 5, 1010 a 12).

75. Hesiod, *Theogony,* 27, 97–98.

76. A distinguished psychologist asks, "is it ever good for man to believe a superstition? Probably yes . . . Patriotism [for example] . . . these kinds of behavior are examples of good false beliefs—that is to say, false in their manifest content, yet good to have because of the psychological effect of having them" (Boring, *op. cit.,* p. 193)—a shocking position, I think, both anti-rational and anti-scientific. Error can never be *in general* good, and *if ever* "good" then only adventitiously and in terms of some *ad hoc* casuistry. To cite "patriotism" is to make exactly the reverse point; if this be a superstition, then it may inhibit a larger and more useful concept of human relations. The question should always be asked, too, *for whose benefit* is a falsehood "good"?

77. Zeller, *op. cit.,* p. 108.

78. On animism as a "scientific" explanation of many phenomena, see La Barre, *Human Animal,* pp. 267–302.

79. Sinclair, *op. cit.,* p. 346.

80. Aristophanes on Socrates, Fragment 352 (Kock) in Sinclair, *op. cit.,* pp. 273–74; Socrates as gadfly, Plato, *Apology,* 30e. Socrates is generally credited with the "define your terms" tradition in philosophy. But this was commonplace among antecedent Sophists: Antisthenes said that "The examination of terms is the beginning of education" (Epictetus, *Diss.* i, 17. 12); Plato himself records that Prodicus said "a right use of terms is the beginning of knowledge" (*Euthydemus* 277E; cf. *Cratylus,* 184; *Protagoras,* 337; and *Theaetetus,* 201E). It is therefore difficult to discern just what *was* Socrates' contribution to philosophy, unless he thought definition was not for *clarity* but for *knowledge.*

81. Cornford, *Unwritten Philosophy,* p. 43.

82. Despite Laertius' ridicule of grammarians (*op. cit.,* 2:29), Protagoras, for example, had distinguished the tenses of verbs (*op. cit.,* 2:465). Unfortunately, the treatise of Antisthenes *On Words,* which would have given us a more exact measure of accomplishments, is lost.

83. Cited in S. E. Hyman, "The Ritual View of Myth and the Mythic," in Sebeok (ed.), *op. cit.,* 84–94, p. 94.

84. Diels, Fragment 4, in Laertius, *op. cit.,* 2:463–69, p. 465. The strikingly un-Greek prosecution of intellectuals began about 432 B.C. with a law aimed at Anaxagoras, making disbelief in the supernatural and the teaching of astronomy indictable offenses. In the next thirty years many liberal thinkers in Athens were successfully prosecuted, and Euripides unsuccessfully (Dodds, *op. cit.,* p. 189; cf. Sinclair, *op. cit.,* p. 175).

85. Laertius, *op. cit.*, 2:449, 451. In any case, whereas all the works of Plato (alone of Greek philosophers) are known in their entirety (Gomperz, *op. cit.*, II:276), no book of Democritus has survived. Only his atomic theory, from fragments.

86. *Oedipus at Colonus*, lines 1224–1225.

87. *Agamemnon*, lines 176–183. All learning is an experience of alienation.

88. Aristophanes, *The Frogs*. On Euripides as a social thinker, see Gomperz, II:13–15. The best *vademecum* is H. D. F. Kitto, *Greek Tragedy* (Garden City: Doubleday Anchor Books, 1954).

89. Murray, *op. cit.*, pp. 119–65; cf. Dodds, *op. cit.*, pp. 44–45, 76, 193–94, 244–46; Gomperz, *op. cit.*, II:10; Rohde, *op. cit.*, p. 536; and Zimmern, *op. cit.*, pp. 158–59 n 2, 352, 431–32. An early expression of the concept: George Norlin, "Ethnology and the Golden Age," *Classical Philology*, 12 (1917) 351–64, p. 355 n 1. The earliest use of the phrase may be by J. B. Bury (see F. W. Walbank, *The Decline of the Roman Empire in the West* (London: Corbett Press, 1946, p. 58).

90. Syncretism or theocrasia was especially rife after Alexander's conquests. Herodotus made some wild syncretisms of Greek with wild Scythian gods: Hestia-Tabiti, Ge-Apia, Apollo-Goetosyros, Aphrodite-Argimpasa, and Poseidon-Thamimasadas. Under the Seleucids the gods of Asia Minor were cavalierly assimilated to Graeco-Roman ones, Nabu with Hermes-Mercury, Nergal with Ares-Mars, Ninib with Chronos-Saturn, Ishtar with Aphrodite-Venus—but each time creating grave problems for future Hesiods. Roman writers identified Wodan, god of wind and air, with Mercury, Donar (oak and thunder god) earlier with Hercules (because his club=hammer, thunderbolt) but later with Jupiter (because both were thunderers, though Donar was not the chief god but Wodan), and Ziu-Tyr with Mars (though philologically Zeus-Jupiter would be better). Scholars are still trying to disentangle the historic origins of the many goddesses Lucian so easily assimilated into one in *De Dea Syria*.

91. Reinach (*Orpheus*, p. 89) is in the Max Müller tradition of myth as a "disease of language" when he states that adjectives separated from the divine name they qualify become independent gods themselves (Phaethon, "the brilliant," becoming in myth the "son" of Apollo). The reverse may be true: part-syncretism of originally independent or cognate deities.

92. Varro, in James, *Sky God*, p. 136; but Zeus=Papaeus (Herodotus), Bel-Marduk =Zeus-Jupiter (Seleucids).

93. Thus the German "Comparative Mythologists." But for the same reason of lost rays, Samson was also a sun god (Gomperz, *op. cit.*, I:35). See Richard Dorson, "Theories of Myth and the Folklorist," *Diogenes*, 8 (1959) 280–90, pp. 282–83.

94. Authenticated nineteenth century "cases" of euhemerism include the worship of the bandits Gandak and Salhas of Bihar, Gauraia or Goraiya of Sharpur, Bhukhiya, etc. (Hermann Jacobi, "Heroes and Hero-Gods (Indian)," *Hastings Encyclopedia*, 6:658–61, p. 659 n 1); Bhadu, a princess of Pachet (*loc. cit.*, 2:328), Hardaur Lal, a young Rajput prince (*loc. cit.*, 3:313), and a Russian major named Yefim Pavlovich Sedykh, whose ghost cured epizootic cattle disease (Demetrius Klements, "Buriats," *loc. cit.*, 3:1–17, p. 7). But of course Indians even deified Mrs. Moore, in *A Passage to India*! Zeller suggests (pp. 132–33) Euhemerus may have had Egyptian inspiration for his theory, reasonably enough in view of the living god Pharaoh.

95. Pythagoras taught that "Sperm is a clot of brain enclosing hot breath within it" (Laertius, *op. cit.*, 2:344). Alcmaeon of Croton disproved this by direct animal experiment (Gomperz, *op. cit.*, I:148). Parmenides had written cryptically, "On the right boys, on the left girls" (Fragment 19, Burnet, *op. cit.*, p. 178); Laertius, (*op. cit.*, 1:139), attributes this to Anaxagoras however), but Aristotle disproved this experimentally by tying off spermatic ducts in turn. Pythagorean asceticism comes

from feared soul-loss; asked when a man should consort with a woman he answered, "When you want to lose what strength you have" (Laertius, *op. cit.*, 2:329). Dodds considers this "Puritan psychology" inherent in the shamanistic tradition (*op. cit.*, pp. 149, 154–55); doubtless correctly, considering mutual selectivity of shamanism as an institution and the paranoid vatic personality. But is the *Nous* of Anaxagoras, and the Platonic transformation of it, merely the ancient *muellos* brain-sperm idea stated philosophically?

96. Modern men think blasphemous or cynical the classic "deification" of real men in their lifetime; but anciently it was matter-of-fact and plausible, considering the original identity of political and magic power in the shaman, the then-accepted belief in animistic souls and hence the near-identity of spirits (souls) and gods—a mere matter of locus and magnitude of the anima. The Byzantine scholar Tzetzes wrote that "Zeuses the ancients used to call their kings," repeating this six times in extant texts; but this sounds more like Hellenistic euhemerizing than authentic ancient tradition. But Miss Harrison shrewdly points out (*Epilegomena,* pp. 18–19) the story in Virgil of how "the mad and blasphemous Salmoneus King of Thessaly was blasted because he dared to counterfeit the thunder and lightning. But it occurred to no one that in the eyes of the people he *was* Zeus and *had* to make the weather . . . The personality of the king and god alike develop out of the head medicine-man, and the business of the head medicine-man as we have seen is to be food-producer and rain-maker." The distance between Zeus the rain-maker and Prometheus the fire-wielder was originally small, and grew only with the majesty of the god. At one time it was plausible enough for Marsyas to challenge Apollo (disastrously to be sure) in rivalrous magic music-making; indeed Orpheus was early enough to resemble Apollo as a shaman and to get by with it; the boy Hermes shamanistically rivalled Apollo also, but by that time both were gods. Cf. Zimmern (*op. cit.,* p. 71 n 1) on the "Medicine King, whose memory survived in Greece in many curious forms." Christianity itself is *dogmatically* euhemeristic.

97. Dodds (p. 242) thinks Hellenistic ruler-worship was *always* insincere. But it is surprizing what distance and time can do: does Peter's mystic scion not in fact speak for heaven, through an ascetic Essene who became God? Self-deified Pythagoras and Empedocles (Laertius, *op. cit.*, 2:323 and 357; 2:383 and 385) were hardly more than arrogant in the ideology of their day in southern Italy. Plutarch (in his *Life of Lysander,* §18) made bland remark that Lysander "was the first Greek, so Duris tells us, in whose honour Greek cities erected altars and offered sacrifices."

98. Thomas Buckle acutely noted that "The tendency of Asiatic civilization was to widen the distance between men and their deities; the tendency of Greek civilization was to diminish it" (*History of Civilization in England,* New York: D. Appleton & Co., 2 vols., 2nd ed., 1929, I:102)—a principle that applies exactly to political relations also, and indeed derives from them. (But both derive ultimately from ethnographically diverse oedipal styles in the family.)

99. In post-Alexandrian Caesarism, people had long been familiar with the established cults of god-kings in Asia and Egypt. Augustus used his cult as an instrument of policy. His successors recognized its worth as such, though Vespasian on his death-bed cried facetiously, "Dear me! I think I am becoming a god!" Tiberius, and Claudius—first emperor to organize a province without needing Senate consent (Richmond, *op. cit.,* p. 187)—both cautiously underplayed to suit occasion the assumption of superhuman role at least at Rome, where republicanism was not yet dead. Gaius and Nero, however, exploited it to suit their personal megalomania. Gaius was ready to outrage the Jews by promising to set up his statue as Jupiter in the Temple itself; but at their reaction he relented, saying characteristically they must be fools rather than knaves, to miss such an opportunity. Domitian liked to be addressed as

"Our Lord and God" (*Dominus et Deus Noster*), and Diocletian was the first consciously to model his public style on that of Oriental rulers, dressing in robes of silk and gold, wearing a diadem of pearls, and demanding prostration in the Imperial Presence. With Diocletian began the historic Caesaropapism inherited by the Church (Gough, *op. cit.*, pp. 37–38, 51). What is preposterous? To whom? And when?

100. Julius Caesar "borrowed" $450,000 in gold for his conquest of Gaul, and sold Egypt for $7,500,000; and Queen Elizabeth had a regular non-parliamentary yearly income of £200,000 at a time when the official stipend of the Lord Admiral of England was £2000. Two hundred *tons* of gold and 18,600 of silver poured into the vaults of the kings of Spain in a century and a half. What kinds of personality and folk charisma shape these phenomena? Perhaps physical facts impress one most: the ruins of Hadrian's immense villa at Tivoli and his stupendous tomb at Rome; 2000-room Whitehall, and Hampton Court near London, not to mention Versailles.

XVI

The Greek Ghost Dance

MEN must have self-reliance, if only because they have nothing but themselves to rely upon. In ecologic adaptation, every animal is biologically on its own. No power in the environment appears to exist that will rescue any species from the false starts and blind alleys into which its adaptations may have led it. Environments have no problems; only organisms do. When the environment changed, no god rescued the dinosaurs; the saber-toothed tiger did not find salvation, nor the giant-antlered elk.[1] No Master of the animal species preserved any one of them. In fact, the human belief in such protectors is a projection only of the unique *psychological* ecology of the human family. The acerb fact: if adaptations are inadequate to meet new vicissitudes, the species then in time becomes extinct.

Human speciation, we have argued, is chiefly cultural. This proposition must be true biologically, since man's special and universal adaptations —hands, brains, society, family, and symbolizing—are all directed to the end of culture-making. Therefore, if the culture of a society can no longer serve to adapt the group to its new historic predicaments, then that society—not necessarily as a group of organisms but rather as the bearer of a specific culture—becomes extinct. This is not to say that all traits of a surviving society at any point in time are therefore adaptive, nor that the survival of a culture trait proves it adaptive; it means only that man too is an animal species and in his own way is subject to animal necessities. There is no false analogy here between species and their traits, and societies and their cultures, because society is the major fact of man's ecology, and because cultures are the specifically human adaptation.

Since society and family are critical facts of human biology, we must expect that cultural institutions will in various ways express and support these basic speciations. In human ecology, hominid mothers did in fact nurture each child during its long and earliest culture-imbibing infancy. And fathers did in fact obtain food for and protect the primitive hunting group. But no fathers have omnipotence in these functional tasks. Human vulnerability, though, may be defended in two ways—through cult and culture hero. The *de facto* reliance of man on man can be ritualized and proliferated in such *de jure* institutions as the state, and cemented in a cult morality that binds men together. The myth binding men together for common ends is thus far biological in its adaptive relevance, no matter how irrational the mystique that effects this social animal solidarity. The new adaptive rub however is *to what common ends* affecting the whole group is the solidarity wielded? Human association is biological, and evidently adaptive. What a society *does* is the critical point at the new level of cultural adaptivity.

The cult is basically an initiation into brotherhood. The gods wear masks; the gods are unmasked as men.[2] To share the secret of morale and morality is to be brothers, a mystic state often further sealed in a common ritual meal and a common tribal sign on the body. Since the cult celebrates the change from boy to man, it is not uncommon that the tribal mark is genital or symbolically such. The communion meal quite commonly asserts the symbolic ingestion both of the shared maternal milk that accompanies uterine siblinghood, and even more commonly (since it asserts a less obvious biological tie more in need of statement), of the *mana* and strength of a common manhood from the same father or ancestor—nectar and ambrosia, milk and meat, wafer and wine, double sign of mystic brotherhood. Sometimes, further, a new group exogamy is enjoined that again signalizes the magic making of a new cult family. The cult may then both celebrate blood ties backward in time beyond the present nuclear family and also magically forge them outward in space to embrace new tribal "brothers."

Herein the cult society mystically extends the family. But behind the cult is the great ancestor who makes the members brothers. The creator of culthood is thus ultimately fatherhood. As shaman, this "father" preserves morale only, since he only magically protects the group against the supernatural danger of spirits and the real danger of enemies, and only magically makes fertility in animals and procures success in the hunt. Nevertheless, to the degree that his magic does support the morale and hence the success of hunters, then effectively the shaman supports the role of fathers if only at second hand; it is not the myth but its effect in action that adjudicates a group's survival. By contrast with the shaman, the culture hero is symbolic father *at first hand* when he invents some new technique to enhance real group survival. But since the environment selects, and not wish-vitiated minds, a group cannot usually discriminate its culture heroes from its shamans, and only the survival of the culture bearing group can even tend to show it finally. Meanwhile, both Church and State will be associated, inevitably, intrinsically and in multiple ways, since they are sacred and secular means to similar ends of social control.

As group power-wielding techniques, political systems invariably symbolize one or another of the paradigms predominantly of male relationships in the family,[3] or the compromise and mixture of the two in varying proportions (e.g., the king can reign but not rule, brothers can "elect" fathers, fathers delegate to sons, etc.) One reason Greeks and Hebrews will always fascinate students of man is that each, more fully than other societies, has explored one of the extreme possibilities, the brotherhood of man and the fatherhood of God. Each tradition has institutionalized "truths" that exist in the biology of man. Among the Greeks, nature shamans, grown to nature deities, were resecularized to human stature, and the gods euhemerized to mere heroes; from *kouros* to Pericles, Greek humanism focused on man as son and brother. Among the Hebrews, partriarchal sheikhs and shamans were sacralized into a God-intoxicated cultural theocracy unique in ethnology. The history of Europe is that of the dynamic tension of Greek and Jew, the counterpoint of Hellenic and Hebraic cultures. The Greek expressed himself naïvely as a political animal, but without moral gods. By contrast, each political disaster the Hebrews experienced led them deeper into the mystery of the moral animal before God. The Greek adventure is unfinished; the Israelite still lives.

The Greek emphasized society as State; the Hebrew, culture as Church. In seeking brotherhood, the Greek destroyed the fatherhood of gods and shamans, to find men brothers alone in the universe with Ananke, and to discover the state was wholly men's own creation and responsiblity. The Athenian had almost a religious infatuation with his *polis,* or city-state. It is impossible to understand a Greek of any period without reference to politics and the current condition of his beloved state. Aristotle was never so much a Greek and a biologist as when he proclaimed that "He who is unable to live in society must be either a beast or a god; he is no part of the state"—expressly assuming that man is a *zoön politikon,* a political animal. Even the cosmopolitan Antisthenes felt that a man could be "burnt" by too close a contact with the political, but one who kept too far away would surely be "frozen." After all, Pheidippides asked in

Aristophanes' *Clouds,* how do we differ from cocks except that we have votes?[4] Most dreaded by an Athenian was simple banishment from the City. So real was the feeling that sometimes ostracism was used purely as a political weapon, as when the Athenians banished Themistocles about 472 B.C. "They made use of the ostracism to humble his great reputation and his authority, as indeed was their habit with any man whose power they regarded as oppressive, or who had risen to an eminence which they considered out of keeping with the equality of democracy," wrote Plutarch,[5] in naked statement of the lengths to which Athenians would go, even with their greatest leader in the successful war against Persia.

Soon after the Persian War and the surprisingly swift economic recovery from it, Athens under Pericles became the wealthiest and most powerful city-state in the Greek world. The gradually collected Athenian League was in origin the expression of protective political power extended to smaller city-states. But in her growth, in blind hubris, Athens became aggressively imperial, and in so doing destroyed both herself and Greek democracy. The brilliant but unprincipled Alcibiades,[6] pathic darling of the group around Socrates, persuaded the Athenians to send an overseas expedition to conquer Syracuse, one of the great colony-cities of Magna Graecia in Sicily. The navy that had routed Persian despotism at Salamis was to be subverted to such ends! The self-disciplined Athenians, who had listened to Themistocles and built a defensive navy with private citizens' self-levied funds, now listened to an undisciplined adventurer intent on Persian-like hegemony in distant places!

In a confusion of hawk and dove factions and feckless political ambivalence, Alcibiades was recalled as leader soon after the fleet reached Sicily. But rather than face his bitter enemies in Athens, Alcibiades defected to Sparta, that police state of Aryan arrogance which had been the historic and unrelenting enemy of Athens. Thucydides, the most majestic of all historians, has told the tragedy from beginning to nearly the end in his *Peloponnesian War.*[7] Thucydides clearly understood the moral issues at stake, and he wrote in chagrin and cold despair. In the sea fight near Syracuse under petty and inadequate leaders, the great fleet of the Athenians was outmaneuvered, and the ships were beached and abandoned. The army, now retreating by land, had no food and no provisions of any kind. After days of starved marching, the van lost touch with the rear, and the Syracusans overwhelmed first the one and then the other. The last scene of the battle found the Athenians crazed with thirst rushing down to a river, not seeing and not caring that the enemy was upon them. The river flowed with blood as the men fought to

reach it, and as they drank they died. All surviving prisoners were enslaved, the bulk of them to labor in the stone quarries of Syracuse in the
torturing heat. "There never has been," wrote Edith Hamilton, "there
never could be a more complete defeat. To inflict on the enemy what
the Athenians suffered in Sicily is still the brightest hope that can animate
a nation going to war."[8]

But the greater calamity recorded in Thucydides' history was the
disintegration of a great people and the decay of democracy at home in
Athens. Several minor events show the tragic decline of the democratic
spirit. One of these concerned an island tributary to Athens, which took
this opportunity to seek its own independence. The furious Athenians
voted to send a fleet which would kill every able-bodied male and
enslave all the women and children. The demagogue of the moment
warned the people not to fall prey to the three foes of empire: pity,
free discussion, and fair dealing. But the Athenians, their fleet launched
and on its way, later came to their senses and sent a ship racing to over-
take it, the rowers straining at their oars to outspeed injustice. Another
event concerned the little island of Melos, which wanted only to be
neutral. The brilliant colloquy between the Athenian envoys and the men
of Melos is in gist in Thucydides, the Athenians standing arrogantly on
the rights of might, the Melians arguing for the greater principle of justice.
The Athenians fought and won the battle with little effort, putting the men
to death and enslaving the women and children. The easy victory was a defeat, for in accomplishing it Athens put herself to death and enslaved her
own democracy to immoral force.

After the catastrophe at Aegospotami, a small clique of extreme conservatives called "The Thirty Tyrants" seized power in Athens, with the
aid of the despised Spartan army, and ruled for eight months. At one
point, to secure their hazardous position, the Thirty took the unprecedented step in retaliation of putting to death 15,000 citizens, men of
democratic enthusiasm and leadership who had resisted the dictatorship.
Critias, a cousin of Plato's mother, was one of the Thirty, a champion
of the aristocracy who shrank from no extremity of violence. Critias,
whom the young Plato loved and admired, became one of the most hated
characters in Greek history. Plato's uncle Charmides, also on the side of
despotism, was killed in these civil wars, which may have contributed
further to the youthful Plato's estrangement from Athenian democracy.[9]

An absolutist fanatic, Plato made violent and repeated attacks on the
candid but frightening relativism of the Sophists. Nevertheless, Plato continued the same Sophist interest in education, *nomos,* and political technique. The epistemological death of Greek man occurred when the touch-

stone of truth, "man the measure," in the Sophist trend from Protagoras to Hippias, was discovered to be in fact quite invalid. Neither Socrates' market research in truth nor Plato's syntactic dialectic ever really repaired the intellectual damage. Greek society was traumatized by the discovery that both its view of the gods and its view of nature were only rational humanistic artifacts. This was one of the great turning points of intellectual history. For instead of taking here a new adaptive turn (enhanced experimental science might have been a new epistemological technique for them), the Greeks made a sacral nativistic assertion of old anthropomorphisms already shown to be inadequate. The reaction to stress became anti-adaptive. Plato's Closed Society was to replace Athenian democracy and free intellectual inquiry. Plato's crisis cult was the historic decompensation of Greek culture as an adaptive mechanism.

After the Sophists, the cultural relativity of *nomos* was plain for all to see. But instead of a coping with the new discovery, Platonism promoted a nativistic reactionism. Since morals are discovered to be man-made, let us promote the status quo ante through blind force and by sacralizing nomos, and let us consciously contrive new fictions as it suits our political advantage. There is no evidence that Plato understood what he was doing *metaphysically,* i.e., sacralizing the noun as holy name into a kind of creative Idea or Nous-father of each species of particulars, or in organisms creating a Heraclitean Fire-father in the Macrocosm for each microcosmic fire-soul. But *politically,* Plato's shamanism was quite conscious jiggery pokery, and deceptive jugglery or sleight of hand.

The "Noble Lie" of Plato, that gold and silver men and political helotism were statuses inherent in nature, became the foundation of his *Republic.*[10] But the Noble Lie contravened Greek man's awareness of his nature as he had learned it from the great tragedians, and especially from Euripides, who had written that only Fortune separates eupatrid and slave. Therefore the Noble Lie must be actively propagandized, inculcated, and rigorously enforced. Political belief must become religion. The best rhetoric, advertisement, and sophistic public relations must cozen adults to assent in the fascistic myth; all information and education must be controlled, a youth movement formed and guided; and any leftover dissenters must be extinguished or terrorized into silence by a Spartan helot-vigilante or state legion, holy Inquisition, Gestapo secret police, or politicized Bureau of Information. Political religion, youth-indoctrination, thought-control, and terrorism form the rationale of all absolutisms, Hellenistic, medieval or modern—from Plato and his Church to Stalin and Hitler. Monolithic public consensus however achieved must replace the democratic processing of differences. The conscious Big Lie of Hitler is the same contrived Noble Lie of Plato, just more audaciously barefaced.

The stylized admiration of Plato is inevitable among absolutists and comes from many sources, among tender-minded philosophers from Plato's metaphysicizing Macrocosmic *Nous* out of infantile "omnipotence of thought" in the microcosm into God, and from Plato's making the categorizing function of the mind into Creator; and among more tough-minded authoritarian personalities, from the historic fact that each European absolutism has been the heir of Platonism. Plato fathered the Great Tradition of western philosophy, through a Hellenized Paul the historic Church, and through Machiavelli *Realpolitik*. To pretend that in Plato and the Great Tradition Europe was the heir of classic Greek culture, is to falsify ethnographic fact completely. On the contrary, at every major point—from the stance toward *physis,* the locus of immortality, and political theory alike—Plato is at direct odds with the classic Greek ethos. Historically, Europe first suffered the long Greek Ghost Dance in Plato. Only very much later did the secular side of Hellenic naturalism and politics revive in the scientific tradition and in the rise of modern democracy. In the Great Tradition, in fact, the sacred side of decadent Hellenistic culture survived in the institutions and forms of our own sacred culture—and at every point, historically, the sacred cult has fought our quest for secular sanity.[11]

Unexamined attitudinizing toward Plato comes from an indisposition to scrutinize our sacred culture and its historic psychological origins. To treat Plato as the high point of Greek thinking is to misunderstand the Greek ethos and Greek history entirely. The hubris of rationalism destroyed both Greek religion and Greek science; the hubris of Platonism destroyed Greek democracy, and with it any better hope for man. Like his masters Heraclitus and Pythagoras, Plato was among the most un-Greek of Greek philosophers. The authentic Greek thinkers were the pre-Socratics. Save for Aristotle, perhaps Socrates was the last truly Greek philosopher—though our chief sources, Plato, who idolized him, Xenophon, incapable of understanding him, and Aristophanes, who ridiculed him, together may have falsified Socrates as much as Paul did the historic Jesus. In any case, Plato was not the savior of Greek thought but its unmitigated disaster.

The dates of his life, 470–399 B.C., show Socrates[12] to have been essentially a man of the Periclean era. He was of humble origin, by trade a stonecutter, but a man of great integrity and nobility of character, kindly, cultured, with great social charm, witty, of unfailing good humor and an imperturbable serenity. Socrates was born ten years after Salamis, was a young child when the Persians were defeated at Eurymedon, and a young man of twenty-two at the peace between Athens and Persia in 448 B.C. He matured in the splendid Golden Age of Athens when this city-state, well aware that she had saved the cause of Greek liberty in the defeat of Persian despotism, went on with Anaxagoras and Aeschylus and Phidias to become the center of a free artistic and intellectual life that has never been surpassed. Socrates surely would have seen the first performances of *Antigone* and *Hippolytus;* he must have witnessed and, as stonecutter, even participated in the building of the great Parthenon, noblest building ever made by man. He was already nearly forty in the first year of the Peloponnesian War, fifty-seven when Alcibiades disastrously invaded Sicily, and drank the hemlock five years after the surrender of Athens when the Long Walls were pulled down and a Spartan garrison had occupied the Acropolis.

Plato, by contrast,[13] was not born until after the death of Pericles, when great hopes had perished in disappointment. Plato was born in the fifth year of the twenty-eight-year Peloponnesian War, during the fourth invasion of Attica. His youth was spent in a time of mounting disaster, culminating in the fall of Athens when he was twenty-three. He was a young man of twenty-eight, already traumatized by the death of several admired older male relatives, when his master Socrates died. The death of Socrates has been heavily sentimentalized in a dialogue of his disciple Plato, surely the suavest sophist public relations job ever to cozen later times, in which Socrates is made to seem a martyr to intellectual liberty for his traitorous subversion of Athenian democracy.[14]

Actually, even in the Platonic dialogues themselves, Socrates is presented as no friend of democracy, for democracy did not harmonize with his doctrine of the supremacy of the intellect. Socrates had been married already to Xantippe, represented as a shrew who would force any man to become a philosopher, because of her repeatedly stated displeasure at the stonecutter's habit of busybodying about the agora and buttonholing citizens, away from his work. Socrates later remarried into a proud patrician family, with which his sympathies evidently lay. When the democratic group in Athens regained control, Socrates was naturally arraigned as a traitor himself and as a leader of the traitorous group that had betrayed Athens to Sparta and Persian sympathizers. In conformity with long-established custom, the democratic party originally wanted merely to have him exiled. But Socrates refused exile, refused to defend himself, and, although a prisoner, even refused any compromise on the issue. As an alternative, he arrogantly and preposterously proposed that he be entertained in the Prytaneum free of charge for life. This was too much for the jurors to countenance, and in exasperation they pronounced Socrates guilty, which he undoubtedly was. Thirty days of the Delian festival followed, during which the drinking of the hemlock was to be stayed, and during all this time the stubborn old man refused any of the usual opportunities offered to escape into exile. The death of Socrates was thus literally a suicide, possibly of a defeated and disheartened old man, but represented in Plato as resting on a trustful anticipation of future life, which may be as un-Socratic as it is un-Greek.

Socrates was seventy at his death, and Plato then twenty-eight. Plato's bitterness against democracy in Athens, reinforced still further by these events, never left him for the rest of his life. Unlike the plebeian Socrates, Plato had been born a member of several aristocratic families which had kept their lands and privileges throughout the strife. Judging that Athens was now no place for the openly anti-democratic like himself, Plato took to travel with one of his hot-headed, blue-blooded friends, who actually may have been under more of a threat than Plato. For some years he was in southern Italy where he learned the Pythagorean mysticism and political autocratism; stories are told of his difficulties with plagiarizing Pythagorism[15] there, and later he sent a hundred minas to buy three unique copies of Pythagorean books that Philolaus had brought out. He traveled also in Sicily and in Egypt.[16] In Syracuse, Plato became involved as a foreigner in an effort to revise the city government, being kidnaped for his pains and sold into slavery, from which he was ransomed by a friend.

From the beginning of his flight in the spring of 399 B.C., Plato spent some dozen years abroad. Characteristically, Plato especially admired Egypt, as is still evident in the *Timaeus,* one of his last works. As Gomperz writes,[17] "The continuity of tradition, lasting for thousands of years; the immovable solidity of the priestly regulations governing all intellectual life; the fixity of style, crystallized long ago, and now apparently unchangeable, in music and the plastic arts, the 'hoary science' —all this was for him an imposing spectacle." Plato stayed a long time at Heliopolis, the original source of Egyptian religion and priestly lore; at about the beginning of the Christian era, the geographer Strabo was shown the rooms formerly occupied by Plato in Heliopolis. At last Plato returned safely to Athens and founded the Academy in the gymnasium of Academus, where, as Smith has said,[18] "he began to elaborate 'philosophy' into an overwhelming antidemocratic argument, by taking the argument from earth to heaven."

His aristocratic birth, his youthful admirations among teachers and relatives, his associates and his travels, seen in the history of his times, make quite understandable the tendencies in all the later thought of Plato. That he was a thoroughgoing reactionary, no clear-eyed reader of the *Republic* can fail to see. His solution for the troubles of his time was to freeze all privileges and occupations into a caste state. The inspiration was Spartan, Pythagorean and Egyptian; but his "gold," "silver," "copper" and "iron" men recall not a little the Hindu castes[19] with Brahmans, Kshatriyas, Vaisyas and Sudras respectively the head, arms, body and feet of the social organism. The gold rulers, philosopher-priests, were to have as "helpers" a *Schutzstaffel* or military caste of silver men, Jesuits or Janizaries to control the husbandmen and artisans.

Plato desperately feared the arts, even music, in his totalitarian state, for these alternative mythologizings might be the source of subversive social change. In the tenth book of the *Laws,* Plato decrees three kinds of heresy[20]: disbelief in the existence of the gods, disbelief in their providential care, and disbelief in their incorruptibility (by which he means to condemn the wickedness of the belief that the indulgence and favor of the gods could be won by good works). This grotesque stand concerning heresy seems almost ludicrously archaizing in Athens, a city that had been determinedly rationalist and hardheaded through its long history, that had known Anaxagoras and the nature philosophers, the Sophists and the Cynics—even the questing Socrates! Plato used all his considerable eloquence, and made threat of the severest punishments, to force the diffusion and to protect the type of religion he favored. His fanaticism was a measure of the real dubiousness of his propositions. His express declarations leave no room for question that he considered the institutions recommended in his *Laws* were in their essence final and incapable of improvement. In the *Laws,* which he wrote on until he was nearly eighty, Plato states that, supposing the whole arsenal of argument should fail, it would still be the duty of the statesmen to promulgate the Noble Lie for the good of the people. Perhaps one could not make all grown men and citizens believe it. But one could make their children believe it, and their children's children, and all who came thereafter. To an alarming degree he was right; his Reich stood for a thousand years and more.

But it is an outrageous and inhuman stand, this shamanist meretriciousness and fascist fatherhood. It is entirely un-Greek, not only in its hatred of humanistic democracy, but also in its deep distrust of reality. His metaphysic is unearthly too. Particulars are *unreal,* only Paradigm is permanent and holy. In Plato a puritanical hatred of the body parallels a fundamentalist fear of the mind. In all areas of his thought, Plato is an inhumanist, a perverse Greek.[21] Plato's politics are wholly rotten at the core: the truth as then understood was not good enough for the foundation of his state. In his Noble Lie Plato has the effrontery to suppose that deliberate chicanery either could or should prevail over the relativist truths of democracy, and that arbitrary force ought to be used to defy democracy! Even Gomperz,[22] usually the apologist of Plato, quails at these horrifying passages in the dialogues, "the bloodthirsty sentences passed upon irreclaimable freethinkers, upon proposers of political innovations, who are by no means necessarily apostles of subversion, even upon contentious advocates who make, or appear to make, a perverse use of their art—in close neighbourhood to all [of which] we meet with a contempt for individuality, an indifference to every form of personal initiative, a disposition, as we may even say, to enslave men's souls which is absolutely astonishing." What is even more horrifying is that this is not a peripheral part of Platonism but its hard core.

Gomperz is referring to the last book in the *Laws*, where military discipline is held up as the model for civic life. No one should ever do anything alone or for himself; everyone should always and everywhere look upward to some superior; every act from great to small should be done in obedience to an order, just as a soldier in barracks stands and walks, washes, feeds, wakes, and goes to bed, all at a word of command. The wish to keep man—the *zoön politikon!*—in such a lifelong straitjacket is the same Platonic temper that would imprison the freethinker in a reformatory (*sophronistérion*), there to rot deprived of all but spiritual consolation and indoctrination until he recants. If the "nocturnal council" fails in its work, then he is to be delivered to the ax of the executioner. Gomperz wrote before Buchenwald, and before brainwashing by sleep-deprivation, or his horror would have been greater still. In espousing the "deeper wisdom" of deliberate untruth, and in exalting the social utility of falsehood, Plato goes beyond Sophist rhetors and becomes a priest of a reactionary political cult, not a philosopher or disinterested "lover of wisdom."

Athens-loving Thucydides, with a longer perspective and a greater moral intelligence than Plato, could be quietly aghast at what the beloved city had done and suffered in the Syracusan adventure, a hideously reversed Hiroshima, Dachau and Vietnam. Thucydides' history is a longer and more heartbreaking Greek tragedy, not of a man but of a whole society. No man can read Thucydides without anguish, or without admiration for his unflinching and undeceived moral clarity of vision. Thucydides' work appeared a year or two after the death of Socrates, when Plato was abroad traveling. Plato learned nothing from it, indeed if he ever read it. Plato instead became the prophet of reaction. Conservative belief, threatened, in him turns into fanaticism. The fanatic knows, as Plato did, that the regime he advocates does not rest serenely on the nature of things as now apprehended by most people, and this state of affairs necessitates contrived "faith." But in the revivalistic assertion of the archaic, evidently faith is not enough either, and both conscious lies and overt force must soon be called upon. He who cannot himself believe, or enforce belief in threadbare fantasy upon others, ultimately can only kill. As the desperate advocate of totalitarianism, replete with security police, the concept of heresy, corrective torture and inquisition, brainwashing, the Big Lie, regimentation, and complete thought control, it is absurd to call Plato in any of these ways Greek. In the *Republic,* Plato rejected the basic political forms of his society, its laws of property and marriage, the contemporary state religion, and even the arts that were a second religion to the Greeks. In his fear of freedom and his contempt for democracy, in his hatred of free rationality and of the arts, Plato is the direct father of fascism in Europe. If we add to this the un-Greek dogma of godlike immortality for everyone, then Plato is also the first Father of the Church.

Antipathetic discontinuity with the past is as much a trait of the ghost dance as is selective nativistic reaction. Enough has been sketched of the politico-military history of Athens in Plato's time to suggest his place within its context. But the political is not the whole of life, even for a Greek and no one-man cause can explain the whole of any historic event. Besides, there were also the internationalist liberal Isocrates and clear-headed men like Thucydides to choose from, in Plato's own time. Only an accumulation of disasters and multiple causalities can make plausible the violent change of direction in Greek life. One factor was even climatic. The seasonal Etesian winds, which were the reason the Coryraeans had not been able to join the Athenian fleet at the naval battle of Salamis—the same winds that were the beginning of Odysseus' long woes—completely failed in the summer of 430 B.C., the second year of the Peloponnesian War, and the blazing heat turned Greece for a time into a tropical country.

All Attica and her allies lay crowded into Piraeus and between the Long Walls up to Athens, when Apollo struck terrifyingly with the Great Plague. Thucydides, who lived through it, could scarcely describe its horrors.[23] One citizen out of four died. The bodies of dying men lay one upon another, untended. Not only food but also water was lacking; the sacred places were full of corpses lying where they died; burials and funeral rites, the most sacred rites in Greek life, were performed as best they could be, or omitted. The disaster passed all bounds. Even Pericles, whose Funeral Oration the year before—perhaps the noblest speech ever made by any man—lay gravely ill. Athens never really recovered from the effects of the Great Plague. The impoverishment was spiritual as well as material. The City was the Liberator at the time of the Funeral Oration, but by the time of the Sicilian expedition Athens was a self-confessed Robber Empire.

But Athens had survived disaster before. When the Persians had invaded Greece, they laid waste all Attica, burned the City and razed the Acropolis; but the Athenians came back from their island fortress of Salamis to rebuild the high city and create the dazzling Age of Pericles. Why not now another Anaxagoras and why would there not be more Alcmaeons? The nature philosophers had taken the first step on the long path of science; the Greeks still had their superb sense of reality. And why was democracy not intensified, now that men had more need of one another than before? The Athenians, however, had taken too many crippling blows to their morale. Rationality faded with political hope and self-respect. Science and society are related; for science is finally a moral temper, and the state of society is a source of its morale. Science implies a democracy of free thinkers, and democracy is the morale of men who are emotionally brothers.

But Athenian democracy was an equality of men that did not embrace all men. It rested on a base of slavery. The conventional enthusiasts of Hellenism—those who look on classic Greece as a long Olympiad of suntanned athletes playing games in the morning, and lounging clean and anointed in the shady grove of Academe thinking profound thoughts in the afternoon, daytime Apollonians viewing Dionysian tragedies by day, and drinking Dionysian wine the festive night, with a rowdy and invigorating war raid from time to time to Magna Graecia or the Black Sea—these enthusiasts must not shirk the ugly fact of slavery. The primitive invading Greek tribes apparently had had no slaves under the original pastoral nomadic conditions. But bondsmen begin to appear in Homer with the settled agricultural life that made slavery economically worthwhile. The gradual rise of hand industry in Athens and the growth of trade only intensified the trend. Zimmern calculates adult slaves at 80,000 (over three fourths of the whole) and adult outlanders at 45,000 to a total of 125,000 non-citizens—not far short of equaling the number of adult native Athenians—at the time of the outbreak of the Peloponnesian War.[24]

In Sparta, helots, mostly agricultural, were ferociously treated because they were constantly feared, and only a permanent reign of terror would keep them obedient. Helots were forbidden, for example, under pain of death, to leave their huts after sunset; and the man-hunt or ambush of these coarse beasts was regarded as excellent training for war.[25] For Plato the slave was merely a kind of domestic animal, who should not rebel against the nature of things, and to treat a slave well was "more in our interest than in his." How easy, from a later vantage, to be horrified at past human inhumanities; how difficult the moral imagination to discern our constant massacre of human self-esteem and dignity, at home and abroad *now*, as casual and unconscious as that of the Greeks.

In most Greek cities, a slave was exposed to the violence of any free man, and any citizen could strike him with impunity in the street. Plato approved of this; other aristocrats were furious that, in Athens, they could not thrash their own slaves without rhyme or reason. In the end slavery was the cancer that killed classic society and culture, not only economically—for this factor came into full force only with militant Rome and massive slave-capturing in imperial wars—but most especially in the very center of Greek culture, its intellectual life. All intelligence draws its strength from and is flawed by defects in feeling. And no humanism can succeed when sustained by inhumanism. In a sense Greek theology and morality precluded the full development of science among them,[26] and it was slavery above all that made for the delay of the machine age.[27] For under the Greek system all contact with the technical reality of physical things was in the hands of untutored slaves, for whom effective innovation brought no immediate or personal reward. At the same time, intellectual life and the leisure (*scholē*) for learning and speculation were a monopoly of aristocrats, socially above labor and the disciplining of thought by things.[28]

Rationalistic philosophy and slavery were also related in Greece. Humanistic Greek rationalism was all too easily complacent in the belief that truth could be found in the free logic of the mind alone, and too little disposed to refer hypotheses to menial experiment. Thus the mind of the intellectual, divorced from hands, and playing only with language, was destined to remain imprisoned in linguistic forms, the metaphysical nouns of Plato, and the predicated qualities (predicate adjectives) attached to Pure Being by Aristotle (the subject of a sentence, qualityless until "is" adds predicated qualities to Existence, waiting meanwhile breathless in limbo without any qualities whatever).

In every industry slaves were used, the "instruments that work by themselves" of Aristotle, the "animated tool." Apart from its callousness, this language is significant. Why should *power machinery,* based for example on the principle of Hero's toy steam turbine, occur to men who already had slaves? Cosmologies and economies are both part of the same moral ethos. The Greeks well understood the principle of the lever, the wheel, the pulley, and all the other devices basic to machinery; but all these devices were connected only with animal and human sources of power. Made "tools" of others' wills, made specifically inhuman by the social definition of free men, slaves were then animals, and despised as inhuman. Slaves were technically then no more than treadmill *tools,* extensions of the animal body. The true *machine,* based on a non-human and non-animal source of power and with a built-in autonomy of working, was "uncanny" to the Greeks, accustomed as they were to thinking kinaesthetically always in the humanistic terms of their own bodies. Such inhuman projections as machines repelled them; they could use slaves as such "machines" only because, after all, slaves *are* human despite their social definition.

For a long time Greeks failed to perceive the mechanistic universe precisely because they viewed natural forces as manlike gods. Anaximenes had had a glimpse of an impersonal and mechanistic universe of pure causality. "We are wont [he wrote] to apply the term Fortune to the element of life *which is incalculable to man;* for, if we always went right in our judgments, the name of Fortune would never have been heard of."[29] Thus chance and accident are only names for our ignorance of the true causes that operate in the mechanistic universe. But, given Greek theology, how could man dare the hubris of creating for himself such impersonal part-universes? Machines would have an uncanny autonomous life and immortality forbidden to men. Prometheus was punished merely for stealing necessary fire from heaven!

Greek science and a Greek machine age were therefore impossible with Greek theology and Greek slavery. Men dare not seek to be gods and shamanistically to control impersonal things—indeed impersonal nature itself must be humanized with shamanlike gods controlling awe-filled natural events, lest man panic at the heartless impersonality of the universe —but only gods are vouchsafed such powers and only gods are immortal. Slaves must not revolt because their slavery is in the nature of things; all conservatives think *nomos* is *physis.* The paradigm is plain—slaves : men :: men : gods—and each must keep his place lest the heavens fall. Greek humanism took man the measure of all things as its model, put gods into nature and made them like men, thus falsifying nature in what it might teach them; and in the gods and Socratism alike the Greeks re-encountered only themselves. The hidden logic of man-made language sustained them no better either, and Plato could only end in pretending this *nomos* was *physis* too.

The animistic fallacy is evident in the confusion also. "All things are full of gods," wrote the nature-philosopher Thales,[30] and "the magnet is proved to have a soul since it can move iron." Such animistic naturism meant it was hubris ever to dream of controlling these sacred superior forces or divine supernatural beings. In becoming gods, shamans had absorbed entirely unto themselves all mysterious shamanistic (culture hero's) power over things, leaving none to men. To the classic Greeks the great gulf was between mortal men and the immortal gods, then, *in mana as well as in anima.* The prerogatives of gods were unassailable. But a slave was only another mortal, so what matter a man's treatment of another man he owned? By the crudest of naïve masculine measures— that some males are physically stronger than others—master and slave must be in the nature of things, like conqueror and vanquished, males and females, fathers and sons, gods and men. By the same reasoning, a Promethean posture before god-mana-infused nature was an impiety inviting the prompt rage and revenge of the gods—as though gods had the same arbitrary and unquestioned power over men and things as free men had over slaves.[31]

The final philosophy of antiquity, Neoplatonism, still espoused this stultifying animism of godlike powers in things. The poet's "water-nymphs moving the axle of the water-wheel" were still half real and not mere metaphor. Indeed, as a prime mover for industry, the water wheel was not used until many centuries later, for the Greeks had women and slaves that made machinery unnecessary, and the manlike machine that was not a man was somehow weirdly uncomfortable. Even the approach to such studies was socially déclassé. The first to apply themselves to mechanics were Eudoxus and Archytas[32] (little celebrated compared to theorists like Pythagoras and Archimedes) who solved certain problems not then understandable on theoretical grounds, through sensible experiment and the use of instruments. But Plato raged against them in real ire, for Eudoxus and Archytas had debased and corrupted the perfection of pure geometry by making it descend from the incorporeal and intellectual to sensible and corporeal things. Such experiment requires the use of matter, which involves labor and is the object of the servile trades. As a result, mechanics was separated from geometry, was despised and repudiated by philosophers and, neglected, sank to the position as a military art it still had in Leonardo's time,[33] or as an adjunct to showmanship in entertainment spectacles.

In classic drama, mechanical contrivances were frequently used to produce immortals miraculously on the stage, a literal *deus ex machina.* At the very end of Hellenic culture when the worship of Dionysus went to Rome in 186 B.C., the vulgar miracle of translation of a mortal to immortality in the Mysteries was also performed by machines. Contraptions were made onto which were tied those whose disappearance was to be accomplished, and they were then translated *in abditos specus,* and the miracle was announced, *raptos a dis homines istos,* according to Livy.[34] Homeric belief in the appearance of gods was as firm as Hellenistic belief in the translation of mortals to immortality; the latter was the same flim-flam, only with the machine in reverse. Machines were thus associated with the uncanny and miraculous, not the mundane and secular. In Latin *machina* always retained the aura of a crowd-gulling contraption as for tent-shaking in the shamanic spectacle, but from first to last wholly appropriate both to Dionysiac drama and Dionysian cult. In Latin, "machina" meant the fabricated device, stratagem or trick ("machination" as devious complot is from the past participle of the deponent verb *machinari,* "to contrive"); and in calling the Trojan Horse a "machine" Dryden was a sensitive classicist.

Slavery meant that everything manual was menial, even the art performance—"Aren't you ashamed," cried a king[35] to his son, "to play the lyre so well?"—so that the manual as opposed to the verbal approach to *physis,* nature, was contemned. Thus philosophic humanism was more easily able to countenance slavery than animistic theism was able to allow the exploitation of nature in machinery. Human slaves might be exploited, but not godlike Nature. This attitude, directly consequent on Greek body-image "humanism" projected onto the Macrocosm, with only the gods legitimately owning the powers of nature, in any case delayed the industrial use of machines in Europe for the next millennium and a half. Aristotle thought slavery the corollary of the existence of free men, much as Victorians argued the prostitute prerequisite to the lady, and some modern moralists that racism is the only root of self-respect. It is doubtless true that the fully humane life requires the control of far more power than any one man possesses in his body, and material culture would seem actually to progress in ratio to per capita command of power.[36] But the use of slaves as the source for this supply of power was a grave logical and ultimately fatal moral inconsistency in Greek humanism. And to locate "humanity" in Nature but not in slaves was doubly fallacious. (At the same time, "relative deprivation" in any society, become too marked, is one cause of cargo cults and other inevitable ghost dance phenomena.)

Of all the Greeks only Euripides, the last and in the judgment of some the greatest of the Greek tragedians, had the compassion and the moral perception to denounce slavery. He held there was no difference, save in name, between the kinless bastard and the true-born man of noble family, no difference in nature but only in custom between the slave and the free man. In one of his tragedies a character of Euripides says poignantly, "One is no less a man for being a slave than you are, my master; we are made of the same flesh and bones; no one is a slave by nature, it is fate that makes the bondsman."[37] Euripides was doubtless unique, and much misunderstood in his time, but his moral vision nevertheless prevailed and grew. Of the hundreds of tragedies performed in Athens in the fifth century B.C. only thirty-two have survived, the work of only three playwrights, and nineteen of these tragedies are those of Euripides. More than that, his plays were often revived after his death, and citations from Euripides in later writers outnumber those of Aeschylus and Sophocles put together. It was Euripides, more than any later teacher, who initiated the lingering death of slavery, just as it was his good friend Anaxagoras who first perceived Cosmos and prepared the way for one universal god of all men.

We praise the Greek invention of democracy, flawed though it was by slavery. But Greek democracy did not include more than the male half of society either. All public life in Greece, political, social or intellectual, was with few exceptions wholly and exclusively masculine. Perhaps humanistic man-centeredness, become narcissistic male-centeredness, was itself the defect, the self-love of Greek *paiderastia* or boy-love. How can behaviors which to ancient Hebrews were supernatural abominations, and to modern men the most desperate cripplings in ego growth, have been accepted and even praised by the Greeks in open institutionalized forms? Was this an ailment only of aristocrats, or mainly of the decadent society around Plato? This is one of the most difficult psychiatric-anthropological puzzles concerning ancient times, and perhaps we can never fully understand it. But we do know that Platonic love was no superficial matter, for it affected not only Greek political and social and military life, but also art and morals, character and education, and science and philosophy as well.[38]

The flaw in Greek humanism is no fault in humanism itself, but only its logical incompleteness in not including slaves and women and even all foreigners. With such limited humanistic imagination, the Greeks were capable of shuddering atrocities. On the morning of Salamis itself—the great naval battle in which, "holding on to liberty" as Herodotus has it, the Athenians saved Greek independence—Themistocles, a noble spirit and their commander, performed human sacrifice to Dionysus, "Eater of Raw Flesh." Three young prisoners had been brought before Themistocles as he was making libation at an altar beside the admiral's trireme. At a sneeze-omen, Euphrantides grasped Themistocles by the right hand and demanded the sacrifice, promising victory to the Athenians if this were done. Themistocles was appalled at this monstrous command from the prophet and attempted demurral. "But the people, as so often happens at moments of crisis," wrote Plutarch,[39] "were ready to find salvation in the miraculous rather than in a rational course of action." Shouting the name of Dionysus, they dragged to the altar the victims, three superlatively handsome young men, bedecked with gold and jewels, the nephews of the Great King himself—perhaps even in his sight, for at daybreak Xerxes sat on his gold throne on a high hill to watch the coming battle. Themistocles was compelled to slaughter the young men with his own hand, beside the flagship of his command, in the presence of the whole fleet. It was not an act of vindictive spite or petty reprisal on his part. It was an act of solemn consecration and of piety to the god Dionysus. So, in a wild earlier era, the half-mythical Agamemnon had slaughtered his own daughter Iphigenia at Aulis, before embarkation on the grandiose Trojan War. But these were civilized historic times!

The obscure primitive cult of Dionysus, which had had an earlier resurgence in the sixth century B.C., had been making new headway in these later anxious days. It is important to note that the private and secret cult of Dionysus was in complete contrast with the open state cult of Apollo. The deities and cults of ruling clans and eupatrid families had been merged in time with the *theos polieus* in most of the city-states of Greece and colonial Magna Graecia. The cult of the prehistoric snake-deity Erechtheus, place-daemon of the Acropolis, and to a degree the associated cult of Athena herself as tutelary deity of the City, exemplify this public religion. Founder cult, hero cult, and ancestor cult were all loosely included in the state religion. Public ceremonies attended the admission of a youth into full citizenship in his *polis* or city-state at about the age of sixteen or eighteen, a natural development from the very old Titanic initiatory rite by underearth shamans. "On that day [wrote Fustel de Coulanges] in the presence of the altar, and before the smoking flesh of a victim, he pronounces an oath, by which he binds himself, among other things, always to respect the religion of the city. From that day he is initiated into the public worship and becomes a citizen."[40] The Apollonian religion therefore symbolizes a binding (*re-ligare*) to the civic cult. The nature gods, in turn, are "etiological myths" which serve to explain the world to man as he found it.

Furthermore, the Dionysian doctrine of *human* immortality was utter blasphemy in Apollonian terms. The Mysteries were therefore not only "reinterpreted" distortions of old rural fertility rites, but also a ghost-dance *direct contravention* of earlier religion. That gods were immortal and man mortal, was a fundamental tenet of Homeric and classic religion alike. "Take comfort, child," when life brings pain, "no man is immortal," ran a phrase common among the people; it was inscribed by many on the graves of their dead, and even on early Christian graves.

"Once I was not, then I was, and now I am no more: what further is there to be said?"—so speaks the dead man from more than one tombstone. "Live!" he cries to the living, "for there is nothing sweeter granted to us mortals than this life in the sunlight." A man lived valiantly, joyously, and gloriously in the world; and then life left him. Death was death in classic Greece.[41]

The Homeric hero was magnificently self-sufficient; he called on gods as heroic allies, and the gods responded as they were embroiled in their own personal feuds, and sometimes as a hero were a god's son; otherwise the Olympians were not solicitous of the fate of self-reliant men. The nature gods go their own way, serenely oblivious to man and his emotional needs. The classic Greek was proudly self-sufficient intellectually in his rationalism; "the chill remoteness of the Olympians" grew as he no longer needed them to explain the natural world. As to immortality, how could he miss what he explicitly had never expected? What need had he of savior gods? Savior from what? From life? As to the soul, is it not life itself? But Plato, both in the early dialogue *Gorgias* and in *Cratylus* a late one, through a false etymology or Pythagorean pun, called the body (*soma*) the tomb (*sema*) of the soul. The classic dramatists never tired of hooting at this Orphic absurdity. The *psyche* was life itself, the material source both of sexual delight and knowledge too!

The Platonic theology is classic neither on the *psyche* nor its "immortality." The theory of the transmigration of souls, in the *Timaeus,* came directly from Pythagorean doctrine Plato had learned in southern Italy. At the end of the *Gorgias* there is an account of how the dead are judged, recalling not only Egyptian notions, but also the Triptolemus legend of the Eleusinian Mysteries, with both of which Plato was acquainted. The Orphics, not unlike the Hindus in their *karma* concept, held that the soul in its imprisonment in a living body was undergoing punishment for the "sin" of Eros in contaminating pure male spirit with earthly *materia* in sexual intercourse. Only in successive reincarnations could the soul be gradually purged of dross, much as the Heraclitean fire flies upward to rejoin the Empyrean. Life could be preserved only by hastening to unlive it again, and sexuality saved only by not using it. Salvation lay in not-living and not-loving. To the Athenians this was outrageous nonsense; not only was glorious life called a *punishment,* but sexuality was *sinful* and created not life but death! If not Persian armies and navies, then Persian dualism had at last conquered Greece.

Europe has so long mouthed this sacred nonsense as to have forgotten how preposterous Platonism was to classic Greeks. The sexual act of creating a new life is the basic wickedness of man! Posh. And yet, in

Plato, the defense of homosexuality, the theory of Ideas, and Orphic doctrines of the sinful soul are all most intricately intertwined and made logically dependent on one another. *Eros Pandemos,* popular love, was the wickedness engendering the *evil of life,* incarnation; only *Uranian* love of pure male spirit, the logos, is metaphysically admissible. Platonism skirts psychopathic[42] obscenity. And yet the central unnatural dualism of the Orphics and the Pythagorean Brotherhood had a perpetual fascination for Plato. Life is divided sharply and impossibly in two, the *sine qua non* necessity for life, the body, is made into an encumbrance to life, the source of evil, of which life must be purified—this crazy dogma permeates the *Phaedo* as does also much of the language Plato had "plagiarized" from Pythagorism. Plato's sickened hatred of reality is so pathological a world view, it is difficult not to see it as individually pathic as well, ghost dance and neurosis joined. In fact, the whole metaphysic of Platonic "Ideas" is derived from an absurd biology and embryology.[43] The best life, for the Orphics, consists in "practice for death"—in Greek terms this stress-induced dogma could only be pronounced insane.

What a far cry from the lusty Homeric Greeks, for whom all things of the body were dear and to be cherished! How basically different, too, from the pre-Socratic philosophers, who saw the life principle as immanent and inseparable from life—for them the divine *physis* is not so much the Ground for Being, physis *is* reality. Consequently the Athenians were moved to uproarious laughter at the ridiculous ideas emanating from the Socratic-Platonic circle. In *The Clouds,* the absurd old gaffer Strepsiades comes to the "Thinking Shop" of Socrates to learn how he can escape his creditors through these newfangled sophistries, and Aristophanes' foolery about Socrates in a basket between heaven and earth is a direct parody of the new rigamaroles, indeed of Orphic-shamanic flight.[44] There is no reason to imagine that in *The Birds* Aristophanes invented whole cloth the notions he ridicules, since we can recognize in them standard shamanistic motifs.[45] Aristophanes has only to state these for the audience to break into laughter. Two shady characters, Peithetaerus (Catch-Pal) and Euelpides (Full of Hope), also trying to escape their creditors, bought two crows in the agora to lead them to the mythic Tereus, now changed into a hoopoe and become master of the birds. After humorously rejecting all refuges from their problems that he suggests, they plot a city midway between sky and earth, where they can intercept communications between gods and men, especially the burnt offerings—like true shamans. With the nightingale flute the king summons the chorus of birds who, at first distrustful of their enemy man, are gulled by Peithetetus' proof that the Birds are older than the gods and men, the eagle older than Zeus, the owl than Athena, and the Birds the only true gods. The chorus is still unbelieving, but Peithetaerus points out that Hermes, Eros, Victory and Iris all fly on wings (for Athenians, delicious sophistry) and then comes a wild parody of Hesiodic and Orphic cosmogony, bird-divination enhancing their claims, and the two rogues reappear, each laughing at the other's feathered hierophany. The whole rodomontade assumes a wide acquaintance with bird-oracles and shamans' claims, and the whole tone is that of a knowing lampoon of medicine-man shows. It is possible, too, that Aristophanes knew of bird-batons like those found on Cyprus, Tiryrns, etc.; the birds "ruled with so strong a rule that any king in the cities of the Hellenes, Agamemnon or Menelaus, had a bird sitting on top of his sceptre, who shared in all the gifts."[46] The preservation of these multiple motifs into late classic times is really astonishing; the Greeks were not so far from the primitive as we may have thought.

Instead of fearing the blast of Zeus for the Orphic blasphemy of preaching mortal immortality, the Athenians responded with hilarity at so preposterous a *prêchiprêcha*. They laughed at Pythagorean vegetarianism. Demosthenes taunted Aeschines for his Orphism. The virile hero Theseus in Euripides' *Hippolytus* is contemptuous of the priggishness of the half-incestuous Hippolytus: "You are the veritable holy man! You walked with Gods in chastity immaculate! I'll not believe your boasts of God's companionship; the Gods are not so simple nor so ignorant. Go, boast that you eat no meat, that you have Orpheus for your king. Read until you are demented your great thick books whose substance is as smoke. For I have found you out. I tell you all, avoid such men as he. They hunt their prey with holy-seeming words, but their designs are black and ugly."[47] So worldly a man as Plutarch was generous toward Orphism, but even he cried out in exasperation, "These are the things that make men atheists—the incantations, the wavings and enchantments and magic, runnings around and tabourings, unclean purifications, filthy cleansings, barbarous and outrageous penances in sanctuaries, and besmirings." Once again, in writing of a superstitious man who ascribed his afflictions to punishment for sin, Plutarch says "It is useless to speak to him, to try and help him. He sits girt about with foul rags, and many a time he strips himself and rolls about naked in the mud; he accuses himself of sins of omission and commission, he has eaten or drunk something or walked in some road the divinity forbade him. When he is at his best and has only a slight attack of superstition on him he will sit at home, becensed and bespattered, with a parcel of old women round him, hanging on all sorts of odds and ends on him as though, as Bion says, he were a peg."

As Jane Harrison wrote, "That a mummery so absurd, with all its lei-surely House-that-Jack-built hocus-pocus, should be regularly carried on in the center of civilized Athens was enough to make the most careless and the most conventional reflect on the nature and strength of religious con-servatism."[48] Nevertheless, it is plain from the *Dialogues* that Plato regarded the old Orphic theology with a respect akin to reverence, and thought his philosophy of Ideas merely supplemented Orphic religion. On Aristotle's evidence, it is clear that Plato did not derive this system from Socrates. It is equally manifest that Plato developed the theme pro-gressively through his major dialogues, the *Symposium,* the *Phaedrus,* the *Phaedo* and the *Republic.* In the *Symposium,* Plato's famed argument for the spiritual superiority of Uranian or heavenly homosexual love over the pandemic earthly love of ordinary people, the doctrine of heavenly Ideas is only summarily used. In the *Phaedrus* it is already involved with psychology, the theory of knowledge, and ethics. In the *Phaedo,* the doctrine completely dominates his thought; here, too, the term ἰδέας, by which these supernatural entities are henceforth to be known, is first used. Even the generous Gomperz[49] felt that most readers of the *Phaedo* would regard the "proofs" there of immortality unconvincing, and find Plato's ascetic aloofness from life repelling; the three proofs, as Hermann Bonitz has exhaustively shown, are all based on the doctrine of Ideas. But since no philosopher, and not even theologian, ever takes these argu-ments seriously now, they need detain our attention not at all.

It is essential to note the *uses* to which the induced belief in im-mortality is to be put. *It is to swindle other men politically.* The social force of theism is increased when joined with the belief in individual immortality, for now there is a permanent soul to be rewarded and punished eternally by the eternal god. Childhood and parenthood are now frozen forever. Of course such beliefs cannot be proven; they may even be false; but it is *politically expedient* to seduce and to force belief in the falsehood. God made men of different metals; if a man of iron tried to be a man of gold and to rule, then the oracle would proclaim his destruction. Social caste is frozen rigid too. Thus people would re-main forever subservient to the Guardians, though it might be necessary to revise the strategic lies a bit from time to time. To obtain this barefaced *political* end, Plato was willing to prostitute all truth and all philosophy!

Is the folklore on the gods threatened, are oligarchs threatened by democracy? Very well, then; he, Plato, philosopher, "lover of wisdom" would re-establish aristocratism even if he must turn religion and nature upside down. The creatures of the system could have their illusory god-hood, immortality, while eupatrids continued to rule; and Plato's *nomos* could be declared more real than *physis*. Did Plato really believe his own larger Noble Lie? Or do those who gladly lie to others end in self-deception too? Only consider what defensive psychological uses the system can be put to also! Prating always of the "ideal" male world of fantasy, subjective idealists constantly blame Materia for their frustrations, as though she were a bad mother. Obedient only to God, we then abolish the Maya that as a female illusion alone separates man from God. An adroit way to resolve the oedipal problem—by abolishing Mother! At the same time, son melds into father, and man becomes God: I/He, the only True Reality; I worship Me. The subjective Symbol is projected, idea becomes idol; the System, made by man himself, is divine. Nature exists only as the paranoid persecutor of perfection, the tender imprisoned soul; idealists, with no effort, invent a better world (one better tailored to organic wish), and then pretend that this is more real than the real world. Hence their theology: it is not life that is good but the hypostatization of life, the soul. Further, life in the body is not real, but death is life; and this not-life is more eternal than living, since it does not exist.

Psychiatrically, matter can be "evil" only because it does not obey, immediately and magically, the infantile wish. It is the ob-jective frustrating aspect of nature that makes it hateful, but also real; the delays and detours it poses to gratification show it, in any case, to be not-self and "outside." Narcissism finds it "hostile" (not always patterned to meet the need and wish of the organism). *Materia* is the "bad mother," the world is evil, the world is an illusion; first the paranoid, then the schizoid gambit. But, ultimately, the despised Object is the only source, in open systems like organisms, or at least the only real source of need-succorance; hence, at other times, we apperceive, with similarly one-sided narcissism, that Nature is therefore "loving," i.e. the "good mother." Reality is neither hostile nor loving; we are.

Empirical monist materialism is respectful of that-which-is, an Ananke neither feared nor worshiped, but used, not soul-inhabited like ourselves, but different, and equally admirable in its difference. Throughout millennia the soul-hypothesis has never generated a single demonstrable truth; it must be a sacred Truth then. The matter-hypothesis however has made man the most magnificently adapted mammal in the history of evolution. It is not so much the nature of nature that is at issue, for this we still do not and may never fully know. It is the *direction of attention* libidinally that matters. Plato's hubris re-anthropomorphizes nature with soul segments, Ideas. But it is man, a skinful of purposes, that makes categories! The ultimate impiety is to assert that the only reality is the self or the projected categories of the self, that the world is created by the categories, that the world does not exist except as the world is my Idea. Subjective idealism not only denies the reality of the world of experience but also asserts the "higher" reality of the System of apperceiving it! In projecting the category-content of one's godlike soul, one's System becomes the Soul of things, the Master of the Universe. Subjective idealism is then revealed for what it is, covert paranoid schizophrenia in discreet metaphysical dress. Aretē asserts the equal dignity of self and not-self, hubris discovers only the megalomaniacal self which has been projected. Essential masculinity is to dare and to endure, to protect and nurture one's dependent own, to know and not to fear reality, to look the world in the face and take it for what it is, to discipline the mind to be undeceived. Platonism is not only the death of Greek naturism and of Greek humanism; but politically, morally, epistemologically, it is the death of Greek manhood and the Greek ethos as well.

Most people dip into Plato with prepared reverence, as the most genteel opinion has advised, wondering at their incomprehension of what business he is about, and finally blaming themselves that this pure metaphysic means nothing at all, and has no relation whatever to their experience. But Platonism is not a secular world view, intellectually to be taken seriously. It is a ghost-dance religion born of troubled times. And its roots also are historically in religion, Pythagorean Orphism; and this is a mixture of very old paleolithic and neolithic cults. The oldest cult we know is that of hunters: animals are killed and human animals live upon their life, but their pattern and species remain. Humans are solicitous of the Pattern, spirit, or species-life of these animals, which they imagine to be embodied in a fertility father or Master of the Species. The earliest magic of which we have record seeks to foment fertility in animals and to procure success in hunting. Essentially the same concept persists into the neolithic, now applied to cultivated plants. Plants die, but when the plant's head (as in "head of grain") or seed is buried, there is resurrection of new life again; how this is intertwined with the paleolithic head-cult and brain-seed *muellos* concept is evident. Thus, in neolithic agriculture, the grain spirit seems to have the same cyclic eternal return as do animals in their seed and offspring. Spirit-god-pattern-logos-life-soul is the mystery that the Mysteries celebrate; the fertility-daemon of the neolithic is descended from the paleolithic "owner" of the animal-spirits. Both imply a manlike and a male-life master of fertility, in human embodiment the shaman.

In the folk cult of rural people in Greece, "Agricultural religion and the cult of the dead are so closely connected that it is difficult to treat them separately. The dead are called both *chthonioi,* earth-people, and *demetrioi,* Demeter's people. Likewise the serpent, with which the dead are associated, is both a fertility power and a symbol or embodiment of the dead."[50] The Mycenaean-Minoan cult points, through Crete, also to an Egyptian cult of the fertility sun-bull and a cult of the dead; but originally it was only the Pharaoh, eternally reincarnated sun and sky bull, who had immortality. Mycenaean "treasuries" show also a cult of the dead, of kings, heroes and ancestors, that may have had further inspiration from the north. However, Greek folk notions in late times were quite vague, confused, and inconsistent on these matters. On the one hand, tombs were the place of pious veneration and sacrifice to ancestral spirits; but on the other hand, shadows of the dead had already gone to gloomy Hades or deep Tartarus, and the tombs were therefore empty, though souls might revisit them, especially when summoned to sacrifices. But on the whole, from Homer onward, classic Greeks gave little thought to life beyond the grave, though ghosts were feared as bearers of disease and demon carriers of catastrophes of all kinds.

The folk worship centered around Demeter and Dionysus, much as city-state religion centered around Olympian Zeus and city-protectors like Athena. Dionysus was an old Thraco-Cretan god, a late-comer to Olympus, for the Olympians were dead or dying as objects of worship by the time of the rebirth of Dionysus as the Dying God. Demeter by contrast was an Olympian by right of prior presence in Greece, a form of the ancient Mediterranean earth goddess, as old in time perhaps as the fertility figurines of the Aurignacian-Magdalenian; Demeter is the Magna Mater or Great Mother of Asia, who had been worshiped also by Helladic-Cycladic peoples, and who entered Olympus under an Indoeuropean name. But in the process, her youthful male son-consort Tammuz of Asia became in Greece a daughter, named Persephone. Demeter and Persephone in their oldest forms were, like Astarte of Byblos, originally neolithic sow-goddesses,[51] totemic deities of Semitic peoples. Thus Demeter the sow, like Dionysus the bull, was the focus of an old agricultural fertility cult of the earlier peoples in Greece.

The most famous of these cults were the Eleusinian Mysteries, originally a local cult of Demeter, perhaps conducted by the old royal house at Eleusis, an Attic village near Athens. The Eleusinian Mysteries were harmlessly and piously adopted by Athens as early as the seventh century B.C.; and later, through this fame, they were celebrated by initiates (*mystes*) who came from all over the Hellenistic world. The Greater Mysteries held at Eleusis were originally a simple first-fruits harvest ceremony offered to the Great Mother, cornucopia of plenty. The Lesser Mysteries, held at Agrae in early spring, celebrated the return of Persephone to the earth from her winter captivity in the underworld of her husband Dis. Persephone was an ancient queen of the dead, here identified with Korē the Grain Maiden, the dramatization of whose rape by Dis formed the plot of the sacred ritual. In the first stage of the Mysteries came purification and apotropaic magic, armoring the communicants against harmful spirits; in the second stage, the revelation of the sacred mysteries. The eight- or nine-day purifications at Athens ended when everyone bathed in the sea, each carrying his *pharmakos* scapegoat or sacrificial pig given to the sow-mother. Later they went in procession fourteen miles to Eleusis, carrying "unnamed things" (phallic images) and a statue of Iacchos, the Eleusinian god of wine. In this are blended the very old rite to the Master or Mistress at the slaughter of an animal, the apotropaic substitute-sacrifice, god-intoxication on wine, and a fertility rite.

In the Greater Mysteries harvest festival, the first fruits of every kind were offered to the Earth Mother and to her daughter Korē, the grain maiden. It was the people who had rapt away the heads of grain from the Earth, as though she were an ancient shamanic Owner, and had robbed her of her daughter. Hence it was they who had to be purified from the consequences of the deed; and hence it was the Great Mother to whom all first fruits were offered, for it was she from whom all of them had been taken. But now the people pretend that Persephone had been stolen away by the King of the Dead. The hierophants, especially women, roam the hills by night with lighted torches, drunk on the blood of the wine god, frenziedly seeking the lost Maiden, scratching their faces and tearing their hair like mad women, dramatizing the grief of the Earth Mother who had lost her daughter. Like her they fast, and like her they break the fast with a ritual meal of barley and water.[52] (They have to *dramatize* this because it is not true; *they* are guilty, not Dis.)

In the Orphic mysteries, the eternal cycle of nature is made into a symbolic analogy of the cycle of man's life and afterlife. Macrocosm is assimilated to microcosm, and plants to animals, and the cyclic yearly fate of plants is compared to the supposed life-death-life fate of the man plant. Men have anthropomorphized nature and so are guilty of "murder" as though plants were like animals they murder in the hunt. These are the Eleusinian Mysteries: the harvests have been gathered and winter is coming. Reality fear is mixed with superego anxiety; the people are frightened, guilty, and in peril. For they have killed the Grain Maiden and stolen her from her mother, and to preserve their own eternal life

they must dramatize her own. The Earth Mother is treated as though
she were the Owner or Mistress of the Plants.

In essence the Eleusinian cult was a magic ritual to influence events in
nature and to protect the people from danger and demon-death. The
meaning is naïvely lucid. In summer the Earth Mother smiles under the
rain and warmth of the Sky Father, and she brings forth riches of fruit
and grain. But in winter Demeter's daughter, green vegetation, is lost;
and, a Mater Dolorosa, Demeter wanders shrieking like cold winds over
the earth, seeking her daughter. In vain; for the *korē* Persephone is imprisoned under the earth in the realm of Dis, as grain is stored in the
great underground cyst-granaries of the Greeks. Sometimes the Divine
Child is male, the Hyakinthos-nurseling of Artemis, the holy child Zeus-
Zagreus, the male *koros* who was the earliest "Apollo" or fertility god of
archaic Greek sculpture. Or perhaps Persephone is only the seed buried
underground in the winter for spring growth. (Or, in a more northerly
version, John Barleycorn is dead).[53]

But when the sun shines warm again in the spring, the *korē* mysteriously
is born again from her buried tomb, the earth is clothed again with
green, and all plants are resurrected again from the death of seeds. For
if it die not, how can the seed be reborn? The Church calendar still
preserves the seasonal character of these earliest mysteries—Christmas is
an old cult of the winter solstice (absorbing part of the cult of the rival
god to Christ, Iranian Mithra) when the sun begins again his cyclic
journey north; Easter was an Anglo-Saxon goddess of the spring Resurrection of life; and the spring god-sacrifice repeats the bloody gelding
rites of the son-consort Attis-Adonis to fertilize the Great Mother of Asia.
In their oldest forms the mysteries are direct agricultural and hunting
magic. Ceres mother or grain is Persephone, the dead *korē* is the new,
daughter is mother reborn of mother. Attis-Adonis, son-consort, is both
god the father and god the son, himself a sacrifice to himself. Sameness,
cyclic identity of pattern, reigns and lives.

Even older than the Eleusinian Mysteries are the Dionysian. The
Dionysian Mysteries preserve the god-slaughter and eating of the sacred
animal, whose strength is reborn in the life of men. Preserved also is the
rite to the Master of Animals assuring that the soul of the game will
come again clothed in a new animal for the hunter. The aura of everything archaic surrounds the figures of Orpheus and Pythagoras, the priests
of a revival of the Mysteries in the sixth century; but under obscure
shamanistic influences from the north they transformed the old mystery
religions entirely. The immortalities in nature, not alone of the seasonal
sun and earth, but also of spring-born plant and animal species, were

originally celebrated in the agricultural mysteries. *But now they become magic rites to confer immortality on men as individuals, as indestructible, reincarnated souls.*

Orphism bears all the signs of syncretism and reinterpretation characteristic of other ghost dances everywhere. Dionysus himself is a fused deity, a composite made up of the Cretan bull, the Zeus-Zagreus god-animal, the rural domesticated goat of Greece, and the blood of the vine the god brought from Asia. Drinking the blood intoxicates, the spirits of the wine invade the communicant, sure sign of the god's presence in the imbibed immortality. In the Orphic form of the Mysteries, the immortalities of species-patterns become transmuted into the individual immortalities of men. Once, in Olympian religion, only gods had immortality —which they preserved by taking nectar and ambrosia. Now, in the revived Mysteries, all men could be immortal—by eating the cereal-wafer, the seed-*korē* of Eleusis, and by drinking the wine, life-blood of the god, Zeus-Zagreus-Iacchos-Dionysus.

It is oversimplified to see, in the Earth Mother cult of Ceres-Persephone, the ritualized art of agriculture passed on in mother-daughter fashion from female food-gatherers, as it is to see in god-slaughter only a male initiation rite of hunters, though this much of the association does linger (and in the anthropologist Linton's Quaker family, father still served the meat, and mother the vegetables). It is certainly an oversimplification too to suppose that immortality was "invented" by one historic culture hero, the misogynist shaman Orpheus, a should-be Cogul figure whom the maddened Maenads tore apart. Orphic stories are far too various (for example, Orpheus was Musaeus' master, Musaeus taught Orpheus, etc.), and far too stylized mythically (the shaman-hero visits the underworld, is master of animals through music like Apollo's, is associated with eternal gold and the fountain of youth, his severed head immortally sang on,[54] etc., etc.) to allow us to discern in Orpheus a recoverable historic character. Orpheus is no god and he is admittedly human, a wonder-worker. But most modern students would agree with Dodds[55] that Toynbee's "historic Orphic church" is an illusion. Orphism is only the miscellaneous detritus of age-old shamanism. And if Orphism did become a historic Church, that was centuries later, long after Pythagoras the immortal and his brotherhood died in Italy.

Plato made Orphism into a metaphysical system.[56] Platonism is a typical ghost-dance eclectic mélange of the archaic, the reinterpreted, and the improvised. Heraclitus had proclaimed a world with no elemental permanents in it; his *physis* was Change itself, noumenal Fire. Plato borrowed from him this immateriality of reality; but the Heraclitean Ultimate

Reality, Change as the divine principle, Plato curiously transformed into non-change, or eternal reality, *viz.*, the inseminating godlike Idea that never changes, that is the only Permanence behind imperfect and illusory particulars. For Plato, God is Pattern, eternal and incorruptible—almost as though its material non-existence conferred invulnerable eternity upon it. Heraclitean Fire was one half of an old Iranian dualism to which Heraclitus had been exposed—and borrowed from the enemy—and it is possible that Plato borrowed his marked dualism in turn from some lost teaching of Heraclitus, or from some other Persian-influenced source. The Platonic Idea certainly owes to Anaxagorean *Nous* or Macrocosmic Mind as well. But once· again Plato has changed the concept. In Anaxagoras, *Nous* was the all-pervasive One. But Plato has polytheized the One into an indefinite number of noetic Ideas, each Idea being the pattern for the appropriate species of particulars. A divine conceptual Chair conceives each individual chair, as ideational Cow fathers each cow upon a cow-sized quantum of materia. Psychiatrically, Platonism is the infantile "omnipotence of thought" raised to a cosmogony!

The reasons for designating Platonism as a typical "ghost dance" are many and specific. Those Greeks who held an archaic world view suffered "culture shock" in the discovery of alternative, more plausible, or more effective newer world views, and Plato produced metaphysical reasons to support a shaken folklore. Politically, Platonism was a violently nativistic reaction intended to preserve, or to re-establish, the past power of his class, which had been gravely threatened by the alarming growth of democracy in Athens. The cult represented, for Athenians, an "identification with the enemy"—in this case both Sparta and Persia. Further, Platonism was a crisis cult of historically shattered times, and depended not on reason but an authoritarian faith in a new myth, the consciously fabricated Noble Lie; perhaps nothing is so surely diagnostic of a crisis cult as the technique of coercion and promises of punishment the prophet uses to compel belief in what to contemporary "common sense" is basically improbable. Plato sets up laws, religion, state, and education to accomplish his ends. Certain older beliefs are stood on their head in the new dogma; for example the non-immortality of men, previously taken for granted, is treated wishfully with the hysteria of simple denial. The confused syncretism of Plato's Orphism confounded the life of plants with that of animals, as if the burial of men were to have results similar to the planting of seeds. The magic rite itself, in body-image terms, was the regressive and ontogenetically archaic one of orally ingesting divinity and immortality. And his rationale was dereistic in leaving the concrete

Hellenic earth for a Hellenistic utopian Nowhere. Platonism is a *kairotic* or "timely" event only in a timeless ghost-dance tradition.

What remains to be made clear is the startling archaism of the Platonic philosophy: *Plato has made into a metaphysic the basic theory of shamanism.* Platonism is a mystic embryological theory of organisms, extended to account for the origin of all *things* as well. The Master of the Animals was simply the model of fatherhood originally, projected as the abstract creative principle behind each patterned animal species; the Idea in Plato is the noetic "Master of Particulars"—the soul, the life, the male mystery, the *recurrent pattern of each species* now of things. All *things* are fathered, exactly like particular specimens of each organic species. More than that, *the Idea, born directly of the brain, is identical with that muellos which is the male seed,* the "logoi spermatikoi" of later Stoics. Anaxagorean *Nous,* fragmentized, has created the whole world. Behind each species of particulars stands its "Master," its own zeus, its own demiurge. Malehood, the mystery, is divinity; paternity, godhood. The Idea, Pattern, Word is the Creator, the seminal male principle, god, fire, soul, the fertility *daemon* of each species.

"In the beginning was the Word, and the Word was with God, and the Word was God. The same was in the beginning with God. All things were made by him; and without him was not any thing made that was made. In him was life; and the life was the light of men . . . And the Word was made flesh." Platonism is not so much a philosophy as it is a religion; it is Orphic shamanism[57] reborn and again transfigured.[58] Plato's subjective idealism is the infantile omnipotence of thought made into God. Like every metaphysical system it is an unwitting statement of the misunderstood facts of life; it confounds the communication of organic pattern with the communication of patterns in speech. The essential absurdity of that metaphysic is shown in the fact that, in discovering the holy Name, Plato attempted an embryology of grammar.

NOTES

(XVI The Greek Ghost Dance)

1. Cultural conservatism has an analogy with the giant antlers of the extinct Irish elk, as though "orthogenetic" perseveration in a trait could become maladaptive; that paleontology indicates many species have in fact become extinct would seem finally to disprove the platonist notion that each species had an eternal shamanistic Master protecting it, certainly that this particular Irish elk Master was omnipotent. Biological pattern is *not* eternal.

2. If cults make men symbolic brothers, the nearly universal use of masks *in initiation ceremonies* suggests that symbolic fathers (shamans or initiators) *impersonate* symbolic fathers (gods) or real fathers (ancestors). The Kàgaba virtually say as much "in a Kàgaba text taken down by Preuss, in which we learn that the Dema-like primeval priests *took off their faces* at the end of their order-creating activities *so that mortal man might wear them as masks* and thus be able to carry out the ceremonies needed to preserve the order" (Preuss, in Jensen, *op. cit.,* p. 114).

3. Orphic rite is strictly like initiation into a shamanic medicine society, the cult "secret" of which is the magic technique of getting godhood (immortality) by eating the goddess (Eleusinian meal-cake) or the god (Dionysian meat and blood). The shaman shares with his clientele the secret of his cure from mortality, just as one joins the Bear Society when the bear-doctor cures a client of the disease the shaman has cured in himself, so all now share the same "medicine power" over the disease. For a stimulating psychiatric treatment: William H. Desmond, "The Eleusinian Mysteries," *Journal of the Hillside Hospital,* 1 (1952) 204–18. Platonism easily could be ritualized into a puberty ceremonial: initiate-Philosophers learn the mystery of malehood, the Facts of Life, *viz.,* Ideas father Particulars as mind-*muellos* fathers children, and the Noble Lie of the *churinga* (-baton) that gives categorical father-power to rule over all non-initiates. Plato's political disingenuousness is curiously identical with shamanistic trickery. Further, "Symbolists" and "Modernists" of religion are also absolutists in pretending that ancient shamans, knowing the absolute truth, taught the people each ethnographic Noble Lie "for their own good"—but this reinterpretation is plainly the spurious judging the genuine ("Culture, Genuine and Spurious," in D. G. Mandelbaum [ed.], *Selected Writings of Edward Sapir,* Berkeley: University of California Press, 1949, pp. 308–31).

4. Aristotle, *Politics,* I, ii, 14; Antisthenes (Sikes, *op. cit.,* p. 96); Pheidippides (p. 19).

5. Plutarch, *Themistocles,* §22; cf. *Aristides,* §7, and *Alcibiades,* §13, where much the same reasons are given again.

6. Plutarch's *Alcibiades:* his beauty and his lisp (§1), running away from home (§3), debauchery, effeminacy and inconsistency (§16), ridicule of Mysteries, mutilation of Hermae and chameleon-like character (§23), and the psychopathy revealed in his transvestite castration dreams (§39).

7. For the Syracusan expedition and its total defeat, Thucydides, vii, 7.

8. Hamilton, *op. cit.,* p. 143.

9. Plato's aristocratic connections and toryism, Gomperz, *op. cit.,* II:250–51, 262; III:69, 248; on Socrates' toryism, II:114; his remarriage, Zimmern, *op. cit.,* p. 340 n. Treason of the aristocrats, Thucydides, *op. cit.,* pp. 26, 66; Plutarch, *Aristides,* §13. Thucydides said Brasidas was not a bad speaker, for a Spartan (p. 278). Indeed, the

words of Brasidas have a curiously contemporary ring: "We Spartans are only justified in liberating people against their own will, because we are acting for the good of one and all alike. We have no imperialistic ambitions; our whole effort is to put an end to imperialism, and we should be doing wrong to the majority, if we were to put up with your opposition to the independence which we are offering to all, etc., etc." (p. 280).

10. The Noble Lie, Plato, *Republic*, 414bc.

11. The classic indictment, thoroughly documented: Andrew D. White, *A History of the Warfare of Science with Theology in Christendom* (New York: Braziller, 1955).

12. It is hard to separate Socratic teaching from Platonic, since Socrates left no works; Plato's Socrates is to be compared with the legendary Pauline Christ. The "Ideas" not Socratic (Gomperz, *op. cit.*, II:60); knowledge as recollection represented as Socratic in the *Meno* (Sinclair, *op. cit.*, p. 328) and judgment of the dead in the *Gorgias* are clearly Pythagorean and Orphic (Gomperz, II:340).

13. Actually, Socrates and Plato appear to be of quite different temperaments. The *therapeia psychēs* of Socrates implies respect for the individual mind; but the techniques of control in the *Laws* indicate quite the opposite in Plato. The view of men as puppets of the gods parallels Plato's view that men should be puppets of the Guardians. Jowett Christianizes Plato, which is less inaccurate than Plato's Socrates. Warner Fite was a thorough debunker of tradition (*The Platonic Legend*, New York: Scribner's, 1934). The fullest modern treatment is the crushing attack by Karl Popper, *The Open Society and Its Enemies* (London: Routledge and Kegan Paul, 2 vols., 1925, vol. I, "The Spell of Plato").

14. There were other defenses of Socrates, including the Spartanist Xenophon's; the charge was dangerousness to the state, and none of the other apologists gave Socrates' reasons for dying at all recognizably like Plato's version in the *Apology;* see Sinclair, *op. cit.*, p. 311.

15. Laertius, *op. cit.*, 2:355, 369–71; on the shaman-oracle origins of Pythagoras, 2:327–33, 339.

16. Heinrich Heine complains of the "plague trailing along from the valley of the Nile, the sickly beliefs of the Ancient Egyptians" (quoted in Freud, *Moses and Monotheism*, p. 50 n). Plato may well have learned the pattern of theocracy on his visit to Egypt, but his doctrine of immortality is distinctly Orphic-Pythagorean, not Egyptian. Most scholars now agree that Plato had contact with the Pythagoreans of West Greece when he visited Italy about 390 B.C. Dodds (*op. cit.*, pp. 209–10 *et passim*) recognizes marked parallels between shamanistic thought and Platonism.

17. Gomperz, *op. cit.*, II:255–56.

18. H. W. Smith, *op. cit.*, p. 153.

19. On the influence of Oriental thought on Plato, see Kerschensteiner, Pétremont, and Festugière, as well as Dodds himself (*op. cit.*, pp. 228–29 n 33); as far as direct Mazdean origin of Plato's dualism is concerned, the conclusions of the first three authors are negative. But Plato knew Heraclitean doctrine. On the possible Indian influence on Plato, see Urwick, in Zimmern, *op. cit.*, p. 446.

20. Gomperz, *op. cit.*, III:255–56; on the permanence of the Platonic institutions, III:248.

21. "Plato is on most matters excellent evidence for what the ordinary Athenian did not think" (A. R. Burn, *The World of Hesiod, A Study of the Greek Middle Ages c. 900–700 B.C.* (London: Kegan Paul, Trench, Trubner & Co., 1936, p. xii). That every work Plato ever wrote has come down to us complete indicates not so much the judgment of his contemporaries as that of his successors. Plato did not even represent the Athenian aristocracy (Zimmern, *op. cit.*, pp. 158–60 and footnotes), but was personally a disengaged political quietist (Cornford, *Unwritten Philosophy,*

p. 54). Whereas the contemporaries of Socrates regarded this busybody as a figure of fun in Athens—though Aristophanes' (*The Birds,* ll. 1281–82) calling the "Spartan-crazy" (ἐγακωνυμάνουν) long-hairs in Cloudcuckooland "Socratified" (ἐσωκρατουν) is surely barbed—the contemporaries of the rigid and austere Plato were often con-temptuous of him. Diogenes the Cynic called Plato's lectures a waste of time (Laertius, *op. cit.,* 2:27). Plato had already been accused of plagiarizing Pythagoras while in Italy, but how much he took from Socrates is unknown to us; perhaps Plato was being only discreet in presenting his *Dialogues* as those of Socrates so far as Athenians were concerned. Further, Aristoxenus stated that most of the *Republic* was to be found in a (now lost) work by Protagoras (Laertius, *op. cit.,* 1:311; cf. Zeller, *Plato,* p. 429 n 7). Incidentally, Aristophanes likened his onetime friend Socrates to a spirit-calling shaman (*The Birds,* lines 1553–58; cf. *The Clouds,* lines 177–79).

22. Gomperz, *op. cit.,* III:262. Plato's ideals in the *Laws,* 942 AB, have been largely realized by the Roman Church; he felt the authority of Delphi should be absolute in religious matters (*Republic,* 427 BC; *Laws,* 738 BC, 759C). The "Schutzstaffel" would be like the 120 "Hellenic Youths" of the Four Hundred "whom they made use of when they had any rough work to be done" (Thucydides, viii, 5).

23. On the Plague, Thucydides, ii, 52; iii, 87. 3; ii, 64. 1.

24. Zimmern, *op. cit.,* p. 381; on slavery in general, pp. 263–64, 382, 389, 394–95, 398, 401–2, 450. Zimmern thought economic inequalities arose gradually out of Greek agrarianism (pp. 115–16); in general he paints a more humane picture for Greek than Roman slavery, and for Greek slaves than modern laboring classes.

25. On helots, I. Scott-Kilvert in his translation of Plutarch, p. 159; Zimmern, *op. cit.,* pp. 110, 111 n 1.

26. The exact Greek meaning of *physis* is much disputed; perhaps Burnet (pp. 10–12, 363–64) and others project too much of the modern soul-less, mana-less idea of matter onto it. Thales' "All things are full of gods" is as much panpsychism as hylozoism; cf. the later Stoic view of *pneuma* (ultimately from Anaximenes), and Heraclitus' fire-soul; indeed, God is still the Prime Mover for Aristotle. If god-mana inhere in *physis,* then crippling awe is added to uncanniness; one does not *dominate* but *prays* to God. Hence oedipal stance shapes the ethos of science/religion again.

27. Hanns Sachs, "The Delay of the Machine Age," *Psychoanalytic Quarterly,* 2 (1933) 404–24.

28. Contempt for physical labor is not Homeric; even heroes and "kings" are rep-resented as working on their farms (Keller, *op. cit.,* p. 85). Hippias was a notable polymath, but more amazing to Greeks was his skill in many manual crafts. He once appeared at the Olympic games dressed head to foot in clothes he had made himself (Sinclair, *op. cit.,* p. 178).

29. Cf. Anaxagoras in Plutarch, *Pericles,* iv (*op. cit.,* p. 169).

30. Thales, quoted in Aristotle, *De Anima,* A, 411 a7; A, 2, 405 a19. If the cosmos were not assumed to be godlike (animated like us) in Aristotle's mechanics (Prime Mover), then it might have occurred edifyingly to men to inquire of *its* ego-alien nature. We must learn Job's ego–alien that–which–is.

31. "Like the characters in the actions the [Homeric] audience accepted without demur the divinity of the gods and their right to human worship together with complete liberty to act as they pleased . . . Their sudden inspirations, their inter-ventions in battle are not unfair; they are the kind of unforeseen thing that does happen and against which the human race is powerless" (Sinclair, *op. cit.,* pp. 26–27). On men as chattels of the gods, Plato, *Phaedo,* 62B. In somewhat similar Elizabethan socio-economic terms, cf. Shakespeare, "Like flies to wanton boys are we to the gods, they kill us for their sport."

32. Plutarch, *Marcellus,* quoted in Singer, *op. cit.,* 4:666. It is only fair to state,

however, that, despite Plato's enormous influence, science has arisen only among peoples influenced by the Greeks (Burnet, *op. cit.,* p. v.). On Greek accomplishment in science, see S. Sambursky, *The Physical World of the Greeks* (New York: Macmillan, 1956). And if early science was largely systematic refutation of Aristotle, at least he taught us empirical observation and is not to be blamed for medieval Scholasticism: absolutist Christianized *reinterpretation* of a great empiricist.

33. Leonardo's non-Platonism, quite uncharacteristic of Renaissance Florence, was related to his empiricism, and his view and practice of the arts (Eissler, in Philipson, *op. cit.,* p. 307). Following Eissler's interpretation, I would venture to suggest that Leonardo had a distinct hand-eye erotization (La Barre, *Human Animal,* pp. 87–88).

34. Livy, 39, 13, in Rohde, *op. cit.,* p. 567.

35. King Philip on lyre-playing, Plutarch, *Pericles,* i; ct. the elegant *Alcibiades* (§2) on lyre- versus flute-playing, fit only for Thebans. Since many gods made and played musical instruments, one might suppose aristocrats could play them. But skill was *hubris* if emulative; and as a manual craft music was left to slaves.

36. With respect to moral empathy and body image, much as Greeks loved horses and important as chariots were in war, antiquity lacked a proper way to harness horses, which cannot pull efficiently with pressure cutting off the windpipe. The padded neck collar open at the throat was invented only in Charlemagne's time, and before that the hauling of heavy loads cost eight times what it should have, hindering the concentration of raw material for industry and manufacture (H. A. L. Fisher, *A History of Europe,* London: Edward Arnold & Co., 1936, p. 94).

37. Sinclair, *op. cit.,* pp. 12, 248.

38. Hans Kelsen, "Platonic Love," *American Imago,* 3 (1942) 3–110; cf. Zimmern, *op. cit.,* p. 344 n; G. R. Taylor, *op. cit.,* pp. 95–96; H. Licht, *Sexual Life in Ancient Greece* (London; Routledge & Kegan Paul, 1950); Burn (*op. cit.,* pp. 125–32) is at pains to argue that Greek homosexuality is not Homeric-Hesiodic. Plato idealized homosexual love in the *Symposium.* Plutarch (*Solon,* §1, *op. cit.,* pp. 43–44) implies that *paiderastia* was honorable, and for free men only. For Aristotle it was devoid of any ideality or romance (Gomperz, *op. cit.,* IV:295). Athens and other cities had public male beauty contests, for which the winner's prize in Athens was a shield (Bonnard, *op. cit.,* I:23). On the position of women, Zimmern, *op. cit.,* pp. 209 n, 267 n, 274–75, 333–44; cf. Keller, *op cit.,* p. 243. On ordinary friendship and conjugal love, Finley, *op. cit.,* pp. 136–38.

39. Plutarch, *Themistocles,* §14, *op. cit.,* pp. 90–91. Agamemnon's sacrifice of his daughter set off the cycle of murders in the Oresteia trilogy of Aeschylus—a noble act before a noble war to avenge affronted male pride.

40. Fustel de Coulanges, *op. cit.,* pp. 128–29; cf. M. P. Nilsson, *A History of Greek Religion* (Oxford: Clarendon Press, 1925, ch. vii on "The Civic Religion"). Cicero's etymology for "religio" from *relegere,* "to go through or read over again" (*De Natura Deorum,* ii, 28, 72) is incorrect, also the same verb as "gather again, collect," as if religion were a collection of formulas. The derivation of Servius from *religare,* "to bind fast," is etymologically correct (cf. "obligation," "ligament," etc.).

41. Rohde, *op. cit.,* p. 544, and the many references in his footnotes 166–168. Diogenes scoffed at exclusive salvation on moral grounds (was Pataecion the thief to be saved just because he had been initiated into the Mysteries, while Agesileas and Epaminondas went to Hades?), Antisthenes on logical grounds (when an Orphic priest told of good things to come in Hades through the rites, he asked bluntly, "Why then don't you die?"). When solicited for an offering to Cybele, Antisthenes replied that he supposed "the gods will be able to take care of their own mother."

42. The Uranian sense of "superiority," for dynamic reasons, is of course the hallmark of all sociopaths, or psychopaths in the strict sense (La Barre, *They Shall Take Up Serpents,* pp. 137–39).

43. Eliade noted the frequency of embryological metaphors in stories of Australian Bushman culture heroes: "It is as if the entire grandiose cosmogenic drama were being interpreted in terms of procreation, pregnancy, embryonic existence, and obstetric operations" ("Australian Religions," *History of Religions,* 6 [1966] 108–34, p. 134). So too in metaphysics when we regress from the specific to the speculative we tend to talk in disguised terms of the "facts of life" (e.g. in Hegelian "History" male *thesis* "posits" female *antithesis*—Shiva's *shakti,* a rib from Adam's side—and together they procreate the savior *synthesis*); hence to find Plato's ideal "Masters-of-Particulars" a shamanistic embryology is not surprizing.

44. Aristophanes, *The Clouds* (lines 218–34).

45. The trickster's flight on the back of a bird, and his fall, are echoed in the flight of Socrates in *The Birds* (lines 114–22, 209–22, 571–75) to "Cloudcuckooland" (l. 818); the whole play is replete with references to bird-shamanism.

46. Kings' bird-scepters referred to by Aristophanes (line 508) have been found archeologically (Vermeule, *op. cit.,* p. 344 n 21).

47. Grene's translation of *Hippolytus* in Grene and Lattimore (*op. cit.,* 3:948–58).

48. Harrison, *Prolegomena,* p. 112; the source also of the translations of Plutarch quoted. She cites amusingly one of the Orphic "characters" of Theophrastus also.

49. Gomperz, *op. cit.,* III:30.

50. H. L. Friess and H. W. Schneider, *Religion in Various Cultures* (New York: Henry Holt & Co., 1932, also Johnson Reprint Corporation, 1965, pp. 222, 225.

51. Reinach, *Orpheus,* p. 86; cf. L. R. Farnell, *op. cit.*

52. Barley was the cult grain in Homeric and later Greek times (Keller, *op. cit.,* p. 40). Not originally present in Sumer (S. N. Kramer, *History Begins at Sumer,* New York: Doubleday Anchor Books, 1959, p. 227), barley may be of northern provenience. As recorded by impressions of cereal grains on pottery, barley was much more grown in Bronze Age Britain than wheat, which surpassed barley only temporarily in the Iron Age and fell steadily through Roman and Saxon times, barley again surpassing wheat in Roman times. Rye had a brief peak in the Roman era below both wheat and barley (Grahame Clarke, *Archaeology and Society,* London: Methuen, 3rd ed. revised, 1957, graph on p. 194). Preferential use in beers may be a possible reason.

53. The "death" of malt is revived in *spiritus frumenti.* On John Barleycorn, see R. Merkelbach, "Origin and Religious Meaning of Greek Tragedy and Comedy, according to the *Erigone* of Eratosthenes," *History of Religions,* 3 (1964) 175–90, p. 188. That the Holy Child is sometimes called Hyakinthos indicates a pre-Hellenic origin of the cult, since the *-inth* ending (Corinth, labyrinth) is pre-Indoeuropean.

54. Also Norse, Irish, Thracian (Guthrie, *Orpheus,* pp. 35–37), the oracular, severed, singing head of Orpheus may be pan-Indoeuropean; the tradition is also found among Siberian shamans (Eliade, *Recent Works,* p. 173). See also W. Déonna, "Orphée et l'oracle de la tête coupée," *Revue des études grecques,* 38 (1925) 44ff.; M. P. Nilsson, *Opuscula Selecta* (Lund: Gleerup, 1952, 2:463 n 55); and Onians, *op. cit.,* [2nd ed.], pp. 101ff.

55. Dodds, *op. cit.,* pp. 147, 155, 170.

56. "I would go so far as to name the Orphics at least one of the influences which went to form the most characteristic part of Platonism, the sharp separation of the lower world of *sensa* from the heavenly world of the Idea" (Guthrie, Orpheus, pp. 156–57).

57. N. S. Nyberg (*Die Religionen des Alten Iran,* Leipzig: Hinrichs Verlag, 1938, pp. 180ff), G. Widengren (Stand und Aufbau der Iranischen Religiongeschichte," *Numen,* 2 [1956] 86–90), W. Nölle ("Iranisch-nordasiatisch Beziehungen im Schmanismus," *Jahrbuch des Museum für Volkerkunde zu Leipzig,* 12 [1953] 86–90), and F. Hančar (Altai-Skythen und Schamanismus," *Actes du Congrès International des*

Sciences Anthropologiques et Ethnologiques, 3 [Vienna, 1957] 183ff.) all think that
Iranian religion begins in shamanism. If so, then religions in all major divisions of the
Indoeuropean stock from Scandinavia to Ceylon have now been ascertained to derive
from shamanism.

58. When Tashtego falls into the Sperm Whale's well and is "reborn" with the aid
of Queequeg, Melville asks, "How many, think ye, have likewise fallen into Plato's
honey head, and sweetly perished there?" The "sperm" whale is so called because of
the spermaceti fat-*muellos* in his skull; however, though the whale is a mammal,
spermaceti has nothing to do with sperm. It is a special fat to absorb blood nitrogen
accumulated from prolonged deep soundings and blown out the blowhole to keep
the whale from getting the "bends."

XVII
The Immortal People

THE Athenian Greeks who so resonantly shaped all occidental history were only some thousands of men. Their imperfectly democratic state endured a few centuries only, until it was overwhelmed by the Irano-Spartan and Macedonian-Roman absolutism of the rest of the ancient world. Nonetheless, circumstances of geography and history in Attica gave birth to an ethos there that would not die and was revived again in the Renaissance, when the Roman ghost dance faltered in hopeless corruption. But the Athenians were a superbly intellectual, urbane, and wide-horizoned people. Why then should that other immense moral legacy from the past have come to us from an obscure gaggle of superstitious wild desert tribesmen, ethnocentric to the degree of fanaticism, and unable to form a state for more than a few generations?

Part of the answer again lies in geography and economics. Egypt, which possessed rich copper mines in the Sinai region, began her historic dominance—which was to last through the Bronze Age down to the fourteenth or thirteenth century B.C.—already in the First Dynasty, as is evidenced by the remarkable hoard of bronze tools and weapons in the modernly excavated tomb of a First Dynasty king at Sakkarah. Egypt previously had been only a collection of derivative neolithic cultures, a line of African totemic-animal nomes strung along the narrow Nile Valley. During the Bronze Age, however, from first to last, the monopoly of the Sinai copper mines by the Pharaoh (a term which means "great house," presumably that of some ancient African rain king whose symbol was the serpent) was the secret of dynastic power in the Egyptian Empire.[1]

About the middle of the second millennium B.C., iron smelting was discovered by the Hittites of Anatolia, the technique spreading westward into Europe to Macedonia and beyond—the rude Dorians' conquest of Aegean peoples in Hellas was owing to the possession of iron tools and weapons—and eastward into Mesopotamia, where thenceforward Iron Age empires held dominance in the Near East. The transitional period[2] from the Bronze to the Iron Age was, quite understandably, a time of restless movement of many peoples. Sometime toward the end of the Bronze Age the patriarch Abraham, legendary ancestor of the Hebrews and Arabs,[3] set out from Ur of the Chaldees, one of the earliest of the ancient empires. At the end of the transition period both the Egyptian and the Hittite empires had been destroyed, Iron Age Assyria had begun her rise to imperial dominance, pastoral Israelites and agricultural Philistines were struggling for possession of the Land of Canaan, the Phoenician city-states were spreading their great mercantile influence throughout the Mediterranean, and the Mycenaean-Minoan Greeks could be first discerned in their historic homes.

The eastern shore of the Mediterranean was anthropologically a very old land, the main-traveled bridge that joins three continents. Here Neanderthal man and modern *Homo sapiens* had met and interbred at Mount Carmel; at Jericho began the very earliest agricultural village known to archeology; and near Mount Carmel again was found the first evidence of the ancient levantine totemism of the wild boar. During the Bronze–Iron Age transitional period in question, in the first half of the fourteenth century B.C., the princes of Ursalim (Jerusalem) complained to their lords, the Pharoahs Amenophis III and Ikhnaton IV, that the marauding Habiru (?Hebrews) were threatening their power. A fourteenth-century text from Boghazköi indicates that the term "Habiru" covered a number of nomadic brigand tribes. Some scholars deny any relation of Hebrew-Habiru save the etymological, (?) "cross-river-man."[4]

It is essential to understand the central significance of Jerusalem[5] throughout Jewish history, the focal point of their much-buffeted state, and in each exile the land of their fervent longing. No other city-state, not even Athens, was ever so much both the real and the sentimental home of any people. Jerusalem had been a Bronze Age fortress of the Amoritic Jebusites, seated above the old coastal trade route between Egypt and Syria, at the spring Gihon of prehistoric age, with the forbidding Syrian desert lying to the east. After the explusion of the horsed Hyksos invaders, who reigned in Egypt from 1800 to 1530 B.C., the reinvigorated Egyptians extended their empire to Palestine and Syria, partly to hold the trade route to Mesopotamia. From the fifteenth to the twelfth centuries, Egypt controlled Palestine from a number of strongholds including Jerusalem. But beginning in the twelfth century the old power of Egypt began to decline as that of the Iron Age cultures to the east began to grow. At the same time the Hittites of Syria were weakened by the spread of Assyrian power, so that foreign rule in Palestine came temporarily to an end. Only in this brief interim was the little city-state an independent one.

As at Jericho, whose walls full many times came tumbling down, there is a succession of superimposed cities on the strategic site of Jerusalem. During the interregnum of the great powers, marauding Bedouin-like nomads continued, and now with greater success, to raid and invade Palestine from the desert east. After a period of rule by the "Judges" or tribal sheikhs, the "seer" Samuel made the warrior Saul the first paramount sheikh or king of the hardy, jealous, brawling allied Semite tribes, in whom the piecemeal conquest and successful occupation of Palestine fostered an emergent sense of nationhood, centered around the god of Israel, "El (god) who does battle," as the mythic ancestor Jacob's name, "battler of El," was reinterpreted. But the fortress of the now independent and unaided Jebusites resisted these early Israelite invasions; it is specifically stated in the Book of Joshua that the Jebusites dwelt in the midst of the Children of Judah, who could not drive them out. About 1000 B.C., one David, a harp-singer and leader of a Hebrew robber band, further uniting the Israelitish tribes, finally took Jerusalem, establishing there his despotic rule, and his extensive harem.

The great rebuilder of Jerusalem was his successor Solomon. But already under this king the limited economic power of the little state was overextended. Nevertheless, Jersualem remained the seat of one of two Israelite kingdoms, now tributary to Egypt, now to empires in Mesopotamia until it was destroyed in 586 B.C. by the new empire of the Babylonians. But the site remained strategic, located as it was both on the north-south trade route[6] and near the great mercantile coastal city-states of earlier Semitic peoples. In 538 B.C. the Babylonian Captivity of the Jews ended when the now-dominant Persians allowed the return to Jerusalem of the Judean exiles. Compared with other empires, that of the Persians treated the little city-state with clemency; a great warrior-savior, Cyrus, had come to the aid of a beleaguered people.

Jerusalem was again a prosperous capital under the Herods and, as Athens and Carthage had been, remained an obstacle to Roman military and economic dominance of the whole Mediterranean. Inevitably, in the year A.D. 70, Jerusalem was conquered by the Roman general (later emperor) Titus, after a bitter struggle that left its mark on Judaism forever afterward. The Jewish city of Jerusalem was obliterated by the Roman city, Aelia Capitolina, which the emperor Hadrian built upon its ruins in the second century A.D.; the present-day walls around the Old

City are early Ottoman Turk, whose long dominance (1517–1917 A.D.) followed various Crusader and Seljuk conquests, with Jerusalem the millennia-long shuttlecock among alien powers. After three decades of British Mandate rule, the United Nations declared a new Israeli State in 1949—its capital, Jerusalem, only to be under attack now once again by various desert-country Semites, very loosely called Arabs. Each conquest of Jerusalem has had its distinct repercussion on religion. The Jews have remembered every fragment of their long history. Much of their present ritual is clearly a dramatized memory of that history. Indeed, in a basic sense, the Jews *are* history.

The archeological prehistory and the political history of literate recorded times, as summarized above, was preceded by a long oral-legendary period —in which already the father-oriented ethos of the Hebrews appears substantially to have been set. Because the control of herds of large domestic animals and their protection from other men and animals in open country requires strength, skill, combativeness and stamina, there is a recurrent functional relationship between pastoral economies and male-centered societies everywhere in the world. The pastoralists of the marginal dry lands of the Semites exemplify this principle as much as do the reindeer-herders in central Siberia, camel-herdsmen in Arabia and north Africa, and cowboys of the Great Plains and the Pampas. In early times the battle for grazing lands in poor seasons, and prey for booty in times of scarcity and famine, may also foment a predatory and masculine-belligerent trend among pastoralists. The need in herding for many young and vigorous hands under one dominant male may also favor a patriarchal, patrilineal organization of society. Herding is one ecology too that fosters a rural fundamentalism.

Into the legendary days of the three patriarchs Abraham, Isaac, and Jacob are condensed many generations of men and perhaps a millennium of time. But Father Abraham seems to stand as the symbol of some great prehistoric revolution in religion—the abjuring of human sacrifice for animal victims. Behind the legend of Abraham and Isaac lies the old Semitic practice of child-sacrifice,[7] surviving in Phoenician Moloch-worship into historic times.[8] During the Monarchy, Hebrews (and neighboring Moabites) still practiced occasional child-sacrifice[9] especially of firstborn sons, in accord with divine command that "every firstborn is mine." Jeremiah protests the old view: Ezekiel felt he must rationalize the conflicting commands of God over historic time. The massacre of the firstborn in Egypt refers to the same tradition; so too the horrid atrocities of King Manassas' reign.

The later interpretation that, through his conflicting commands, God was merely testing cruelly the faith of Abraham, even to the sacrifice of his cherished son, rescues God from the theological dilemma of inconstancy over the centuries, but hardly enhances God's moral dignity. Historically the supposed wishes of "God" did change; but psychologically, and with better eternal human consistency, the "inconstancy" of God on Mount Moriah is better seen as the *ambivalence* of Abraham in counter-oedipal conflict over his son, for fatherly love of sons is by no means unwavering. On the deepest level, the *Akedah* or "binding" of god and man, father and son in society, must rest on that initial *religio,* the oedipal bargain between father and son in the human incest taboo.[10] On Mount Moriah, Abraham became not merely the "Father of faith"—literally of Judaism, Christianity and Islam—but, symbolically, the father of all human society. "And he shall turn the heart of the father to the children, and the heart of the children to their fathers," says Malachi 4:6. The Father (Abraham himself projected) tells the father to kill his son; but, again, the Father tells him not to.[11] This is the birth of a peculiarly human morality in the family—we take our human nature far too much for granted—since many male mammals kill their offspring as simple rivals for the female, and no infra-human animal has the human incest taboo. The religious rationale of the Akedah is only the apperception of God in terms of man's own poor perception of himself, and of his human nature. To Abraham's seed God promised Canaan (Genesis 12:1–7)—a "seed as the dust of the earth" in numbers (Genesis 13:16). The Covenant of Abraham with the fertility daemon he had earlier unwittingly entertained as a stranger, and who now returned the favor with the supernatural miracle of fertility in the aged Sarah, was explicit: the institution of the rite of circumcision.[12]

Isaac was born to Abram and Sarai when his mother was ninety and seemingly past child-bearing; as their only son, the poignancy of his near-sacrifice was acute, since the fertility god of the now renamed Abraham had promised him numberless offspring and now asked the sacrifice of the only means of having them, the son of Sarah, mother of nations. Isaac, who displaced his half-brother Ishmael,[13] son of Hagar, escaped murder by his father. But Isaac did not escape the rivalry of his sons Jacob and Esau,[14] nor the duplicity of Jacob in mulcting Esau of his birthright inheritance and blessing. Isaac, who loved venison, favored his hunter son Esau. But Rebecca preferred her herdsman son Jacob, and together Rebecca and Jacob contrived the stratagem to cheat Isaac and Esau.

Laban tricked Jacob by giving him the elder sister Leah first, so that Jacob had to serve twice-seven years for his preferred wife Rachel, and six years more for a share of the father-in-law's animals. In turn Jacob tricked Laban over the multi-colored animals in the flocks that were to be his,[15] and when the two separated, Rachel stole her father's god-images.[16] But Rachel was barren, in this much-promised but oft-threatened lineage, and Jacob needed the help of the same[17] fertility-god who had aided his grandfather Abraham. After the safe passage of his goods and chattels, Jacob wrestled with a daemon-man at the Ford of Jabbok; in the desperate struggle, not under Queensbury rules, one grasped the genitals of his adversary and a blessing was forced.[18] This "angel" was in fact God, for henceforth Jacob was called *Israel*, the "wrestler with God." That this El was a fertility-daemon was shown again in the blessing and the promise—the Land of Canaan for his "seed as the sand of the sea" (Genesis 32:12) and again "seed as the dust of the earth" (Genesis 28:14), exactly the same words as those given to Abraham, who also had had a barren wife. At Peniel Jacob saw God face to face, and wrestled with him. In a metaphorical sense the descendants of Israel have wrestled with the stern patriarchal God forever afterward, for Jews invariably perceive their Fate as the punishment of God laid on his chosen people fo their sins. The "punishment" upon an eternally minority people, in a small interstitial buffer state which was constantly being conquered, was in part a consequence of the geographic location of Palestine. The Jerusalem-centered state repeatedly suffered affronts to national pride, which if anything grew only more intense with each successive débâcle, and repeated nativistic religious reactions were exactly related to political tides in the levant, then as now.

That Moses, in a situation of danger in the Wilderness, still needed the rite of circumcision on himself, suggests some discontinuity between the Abramic Semites of the east and the Mosaic Hebrews of the west. Also, the people of Moses had to reconquer the Land of Canaan, long since promised and given to the Abraham-Jacob line, and occupied by all of Jacob's sons except Joseph. Again, the covenant with the fertility daemon or El of Abraham and Jacob-Israel seems redundantly repeated in the Mosaic covenant with the volcano god Yahweh—allegedly *adopted* from the ironsmith Kenites or Midianites of Sinai. If the people of Moses already worshiped the El of Abraham and Jacob, why did they have to adopt him again from the Midianites? Yahweh and El therefore must not be the same god; but why then was each covenant with him identical in both cases, the rite of circumcision? For Moses and his men had to be circumcised in the Wilderness—which could hardly be the case if they were good Abramic Hebrews like all the other Semitic sons of Isaac and Ishmael!

The problem is complex, but several facets of it are clear. The western

Semites, for example the Canaanites, did not circumcise. Thus the Hebrews of the Egyptian Capitivity were evidently West Semites. But the Egyptians, like the eastern Semites, did circumcise, as male mummies testify.[19] Thus the western Semites of Moses learned circumcision from the Kenites of Sinai. But Moses is part of an Egyptian name, explainable enough by the myth of his origin. If Moses were brought up as an Egyptian, or if he were an Egyptian as Freud suggests, as such in either case would he not already have been circumcised? Or did Moses and the Hebrews, uncircumcised, belatedly undergo an acculturative "identification with the enemy" Egyptians? Again, was the Mosaic "monotheism" suggested by the Egyptian monotheism of Ikhnaton in the Amarnah period? But much evidence indicates that both in Egypt and in the Wilderness Moses and Aaron were snake-shamans; and the Egyptian hieroglyph for "diety" is the snake, as though this were their animal-familiar. Further, the group emblem of Joseph, chief Rachel-tribe, was a bull; the Levite Leah-tribe, a snake. The worship of the new fire-god Yahweh was marked already in the Wilderness by a backsliding into the earlier worship of both Golden Calf and serpent. Evidently the Hebrews of the Egyptian Captivity were of several groups; and Moses, the first messiah-like leader of the Hebrews, was compounded of several men and is reduplicated both in Aaron and Joshua. As a man of many gods and yet stern defender of Yahweh, "Moses" cannot have been just one man.

Like Abraham, Moses is still a legendary figure, of whom consistency may not be expected. The foundling-child of the waters is a widespread myth, and one moreover of clear if complex symbolism: in the alleged life-history of Moses are many motifs of the "myth of the birth of the hero" as well as the usual "family romance" of royal parents and adoption.[20] As history, the Red Sea episode is unknown not only to any Egyptian text but also to the earliest Hebrew prophets. At most perhaps thousands of shepherd folk were in the Exodus, surely not the six hundred thousand of the text; forty, for the years spent in the Wilderness, is an old Semitic ritual number. The supernatural vision and the promulgation of a new god at Sinai may be historic if it is seen as a crisis cult of the oppressed, and the cult of Yahweh the local Kenite god of the volcanic mount, not necessarily the god of Abraham of Ur, and certainly not the universal Hellenistic God. But which are the true Commandments, for they differ greatly, those of Exodus 20 or Exodus 34?

The Higher Criticism of Wellhausen and other scholars, based on the careful comparison of internal evidence in the texts themselves, has long argued that the Pentateuch or so-called Five Books of Moses have been clumsily revised by priests, in Jerusalem and at a much later date.

The "Mosaic theocracy" is a fabrication which nowhere fits the early circumstances. The prophets, even in their most idealized picture of what the Israelite state should be, have no trace of an idea of such a theocracy—a theocracy which does, however, exactly fit Judaism after the Babylonian Exile. The priestly theocracy was borrowed from Babylon, and it revised Mosaic tradition considerably in order to support its claims. The unity of Israel, on which logic rests the supposed theocratic relation of God and the Jews, is by no means evident in the loose rabble constantly revolting against Moses and for centuries afterward even in Palestine still worshiping many strange gods. The priestly Jehovah himself is an odd syncretism of fertility- and place-daemons, fire- and volcano-god, Mesopotamian sky god and neolithic rain bull, shaman-husband of the land, and many others besides before the fiercely tribal god-protector of the Chosen People became the universal God of prophetic Judaism and late Hellenistic philosophy.

The images of gods that Rachel stole from her father Laban were unmistakably material objects, quite like the later brazen *Nehushtan* of Moses or the Golden Calf of Aaron—and also material was whatever mana-laden Thing that lay in the Ark of the Covenant. Despite express prohibition in the Decalogue (Exodus 20:4; Deuteronomy 5:8), the making and worshiping of "graven images" survived into late monarchic times. The "brazen serpent" attributed to Moses became a part of the Jerusalem Temple and was not removed until the days of the pious Yahwist king Hezekiah (II Kings 18:4). The Cherubim (Exodus 25:18–22) were winged images of beaten gold; in the Second Temple they were shown in sexual embrace—long after the serpent, with unusual repetitiveness and vehemence in the ultimate texts, had been henotheistically degraded to the satanic Adversary of God. The Blessing of Jacob (Genesis 49) makes the associations Judah-lion, Issachar-ass, Dan-serpent, Naphtali-hind, Benjamin-wolf and Joseph "a fruitful bough." Swine, dogs and mice were *sacrificed* in post-exilic times, but apart from the worship of bull and serpent (later regarded as idolatrous), no direct evidence of "totemic" worship has survived in Scripture.[21] Aniconism was facilitated perhaps by a *baal*-power's separability from its object, as mana is, so that one revered the power but not the thing, its mere physical fetish-container; in time the more personalized religious *el* came to prevail over the more primitive magic *baal*. Aniconism also characterized early Buddhism and Islam but did not remain in either. Prohibition by the Hebrew prophets against worshiping Yahweh in any visible form (his very Name was ineffable) raised deity to a purer essence of spirituality in the literal sense; perhaps, in fact, the demate-rialization of God enabled the priests' nationalistic god to prevail over the many local deities, some of which had visible animal form,[22] i.e. with political change any diety must change in projective nature and in number of communicants or constituency.

This change in God was the later result of many vicissitudes in Pales-tine, cumulatively interpreted as the anger of the Yahwist God at his fickle idol-worshiping people. Freud noted that the religion which began with a prohibition against making any image of its God, developed over the centuries into a religion of instinctual renunciation as well. The thesis would seem confirmed in that Pharisaic and rabbinic Judaism remained repressive and aniconic, while by contrast Renaissance Catholicism was both grossly indulgent and richly iconic in its religious art—in addition, both in the Trinity and in the cult of saints, departing widely from a rigorous Hebraic monotheism. Again, the puritanical and aniconic Protestant ethic was once more repressive of the instinctual and the sensuous. Furthermore, Tantric Buddhism and late Indo-Iranian Islam, like Renaissance Catholicism, each similarly became both sensualized and profusely iconic. A visualized God, whether animal- or man-like, re-mains external; but an abstract moral principle may be internalized.[23] Thus the differing gods are perhaps also related to shame-sanctioned ex-ternal coercive force (Greek) as opposed to an internalized guilt-sanc-tioned ethic (Hebrew). Also monotheism, perhaps, helps to intensify and focus projective fantasy onto a single mighty oedipal Person, as opposed to a depersonalizing diffusion into the many Thrones and Powers of more magic-trending polytheism.

The "historic" Moses of the Exodus was by no means the aniconic, monotheistic priestly figure tendentiously propounded in the later deu-teronomic or priest-contrived "second law"—which was quite unable fully to falsify the original Moses. As the Higher Criticism[24] plentifully demon-strates, the whole Pentateuchal Law had quite clearly *not* been given to Israel before the tribes crossed the Jordan. Obviously, the Torah is later than the eighth- and seventh-century Prophets, who know only a simple form of Mosaic code; and in fact the later prophets make their successive protests against the routinized hieratic and conservative state cult by rea-son of its lack, in their view, of an adequately moral code, the proof of which they allege is the repeated punishments of Israel by a moral god. The counterpoint between ecstatic prophet-shaman and priest of the establishment, faqir and imam, is to be found throughout Semitic religion. Judaism is in essence compulsive ambivalence between rigid loyalty to the past and eternal reform, the claims of the fathers set against the claims of the sons.

The priestly redactor of the Pentateuch is easily distinguishable from the ancient prophet Moses, moreover, both to the textual critic and to the ethnologist. The so-called Mosaic, i.e. deuteronomic, Law emerges quite suddenly and much later certainly than the Saul-Solomon line of kings; that is, the priestly Law arises in the politically decadent period after the Babylonian Exile, and shows all the signs of a borrowing of Babylonian priestcraft under the later disrupted kingdom—a "retrospective falsification" of traditional history made in order to borrow the prestige of the ancient Moses for the new priestly religion.[25] The priestly recension of the Pentateuch is so inept as to be highly visible to any careful reader; the interruptions of the narrative by later interpolation and the restitchings are so gross that Biblical philologists can state certainly which verses or parts of verses are the Yahwist text of the Southern Kingdom and which the Ephraimitic Elohist text, or Priestly Code, and so forth.[26]

The ancient Moses was clearly not a state-priest but an archaic tribal sheikh-shaman, patriarchal leader of many tribelets and families, but able to exercise a shifting secular power—as paramount sheikh over a loose amphictyony of lineages—only by reason of his supernatural authority. Moses is not a priest supported by settled institutions but a visionary shaman, a charismatic leader in whom the god (imperious id of the vatic) repeatedly speaks. The awesome magic omnipotence of Moses comes directly from Yahweh. His rigid rod changes into a lissome snake, and back again, a healthy hand into that of a leper, and water into blood (Exodus 4:2–9). With magic words and gestures, the now god-taught Moses causes the Ten Plagues. The Amalekites are defeated by means of Yahweh's rod in the hand of Moses (Exodus 17:8–12). Water gushes from a rock when struck by the shamanic wand. (Indeed, three Jewish heroes all achieve victories through weather magic: Joseph the dream reader successfully predicts the weather, Moses in Egypt wins in a series of shamanistic contests which include rain-making, Elijah defeats the prophets of Baal in a rain-making contest[27]—and weather control is as much an attribute of African rain kings as it is of ancient Eurasiatic and American shamans).

Moses had further magic power over nature. In Egypt he turned rivers into blood; his magic wind blew away the locust plague; at Horeb, wind, lightning and earthquakes preceded his god. Moses had explicitly the snake-power of the Leah Levites. In one of the many recurrent mutinies against Moses, Yahweh sent fiery serpents (Numbers 21:5–6), which Moses took away from the people by setting up a brass snake-image for worship (Numbers 21:7–9); he had of course many times before used his snake rod in Egypt and in the Wilderness. Snake worship flourished still in later Judea (II Kings 18:4) when Hezekiah came to the throne and broke that same Nehushtan of Moses who had instituted snake worship. Moses in the Wilderness was distinctly not a liege of the priestly god of the later kindgom!

Revolts against Yahweh are revolts against his prophet Moses. To the people, the edicts, actions and emotions of Moses are identical with his God's; they fear his fire-shining face (surely that now of some other Moses) because the *mana* of the mountain god is within him; he must cover his face lest the terrified people be destroyed (Exodus 34:29–35). He is at once sheikh, shaman, father and god, against whom all the ambivalences of the people are directed, as to all paternal promulgators of the law. The identity of Moses-Yahweh is remarkable. In the first encounter, Yahweh wrote down the commandments; in the second, Moses himself made the tables. Yahweh confides in Moses all his plans and commands, which Moses then puts forth. Moses alone is not consumed by the daemonic power when he physically associates with Yahweh and enters into the midst of the cloud (Exodus 24:15–18). Psychologically, Moses and Yahweh are one. Again, Aaron spoke to Moses as if Moses were Yahweh in the Golden Calf story; Moses raged like the daemon and meted out punishment (Exodus 23:19–22, 27). "And the Lord said unto Moses, See, I have made thee a god to Pharaoh: and Aaron thy brother shall be thy prophet" (Exodus 7:1).

The edict is sufficiently odd, but especially as coming from the volcano god, since Moses served a snake god and Aaron a bull; the language is colored also by later concepts, for Moses is not God but only possessed by a shamanic daemon-familiar. In consequence of this id-ego relationship, Moses has a quite paranoid vehemence and violence. He shatters the stone tables of the Commandments; quoting the Lord, he would have every man slay his brother, every man his companion, and every man his neighbor (Exodus 32:27); he wipes out his nearest kin, and then relays, presumably letter-perfect, thirty-four long chapters of what the Lord spake unto him (Leviticus 1–7, 11–27) and ten more in the next book (Numbers 1–2, 4–6, 8–10, 13 and 15), with one more to Aaron (18) and another to both (19) for good measure—surely a record performance if made wholly from memory.

The wild fury of Moses sometimes arouses even the wrath of Jehovah. The father, the patriarch-sheikh, must in reality have been powerful, ruthless and arbitrary among the Hebrews of the Exodus in order to have provided such a vivid double projection in Moses and Yahweh, still clear after great later revision and culture change.[28] Moses thoroughly resists remolding into a deuteronomic priest; he is a culture hero, a shaman, a charismatic cult founder. That Moses was so extraordinary and well-remembered an instance of the type, to whom several other leaders were assimilated and fused, suggests a powerful vatic personality under personal duress in grave social crisis. The Mosaic god Yahweh, also, is innovative to a degree usual in traumatic crisis cults.

If not certainly a historic, then surely an ethnographic Moses is clear. Behind the Moses who with his shaman's staff bested Pharaoh's magicians —who brought the magic plagues; who parted the Red Sea waters with the same sorcerer's baton that brought forth water from the living rock and (despite his fatigue in long hours of holding it up) defeated the Amalekites; who set up the snake-image to protect the Israelites from fiery serpents in the wilderness; and whose Midianite wife Zipporah "began" the custom of circumcision to imitate the immortality of the serpent that sheds its skin—behind this Moses was an awefull Familiar indeed, an Old Stone Age numen and now the seraph or winged serpent that had been the fetish of the Leah Moses-Aaron "tribe" of Levites.

Many scholars, including Albright, consider monotheism the creation of Moses. But this view is both ethnographically and textually dubious and leaves one the willing victim of the whole tendentious thrust of the later Priestly rewriting of the Books of Moses. That the Egyptian Pharoah Ikhnaton earlier proposed monotheism is well documented, and more plausible both psychologically and politically. Out of many animal-headed nome deities in Egypt, that of the dominant ruling sib became the chief or even the exclusive one, just as out of many *mispaha* "totemic" deities at the Exodus that of the Yahwist Joseph tribe ended predominant. Both are the accompaniments of political centralizing into a larger state. Even as now re-edited, the Pentateuch overwhelmingly supports this view despite later priestly attempts to project Jerusalemic monotheism back into Mosaic polyfetishistic times. Freud's thesis that Moses borrowed monotheism from the Egyptian tradition of Ikhnaton must run the gauntlet both of historic possibility and ethnographic plausibility. It does not fit the Durkheimian principle that the sacred-conceptual is the projection of secular social structure. In fact, the quite obvious priestly attempt to establish Mosaic monotheism precisely fits in time and context the later struggle to establish the centralized secular state in Jerusalem; and the need to make this attempt argues religious as well as political innovation and the prior absence of monotheism, for until the post-Exilic period certainly other gods than Yahweh were acknowledged and evidently worshiped in Israel, even in Jerusalem. As has been repeatedly pointed out, the Mosaic language is "Thou shalt *have no* other gods *before* me." Furthermore, the pastoral father-god and god of the patriarch-fathers had also to struggle against the worship of the mother-goddess and her divine son and lover, earlier deeply established among the western Semites as indeed also in ancient Greece and much of the late-paleolithic Mediterranean.

Even after the entry into Palestine, there are traces in the books of the Early Prophets of a conflict between theism and shamanism. After Saul "had put away those that had familiar spirits, and the wizards, out of the land" (I Samuel 28:3), he came into battle with the Philistines, when such war-shamans were by custom necessary in order magically to protect and to prognosticate in battle. Neither dreams nor divinations with the Urim could help him; and finally, his former edict notwithstanding, Saul sought out a shamaness, "a woman that hath a familiar spirit," and who "saw gods ascending out of the earth" (I Samuel 28:7, 13)—the Witch of Endor. With her necromancy she summoned up the soul of the dead shaman Samuel. But the old soothsayer upbraided the king as he had done in life, saying that Saul and his sons would be with him in the earth before another sun had set. The whole context is that of simple shamanism, familiar to us and interesting only in that the wonder-worker of the Hebrews was male, but the local one in Canaan a shamaness.[29]

Indeed, tendentiously or not, it was later represented that the shadowy snake-shaman Moses was left behind in the Wilderness *because* he had "trespassed against Me among the children of Israel at the waters of Meribah-Kadesh, in the wilderness of Zin, because ye sanctified Me not in the midst of the children of Israel" (Deuteronomy 32:51). This accusation would be patently unfair were there not another Moses, ancient or interpolated, since one at least is given as having persistently defended the volcano God of Isarel[30] against all rivals, e.g. the Golden Calf of his "brother" Aaron and indeed even of his own snake god. In any case, the fetish that prevailed was that of the Joseph tribe that possessed the Ark of the Covenant in which the bull God of Battle resided, the Ark that supposedly became the Tabernacle in the Temple of Jerusalem. Thus it was not the Moses-Aaron priestly "Levites" but a man of the Joseph tribe, Jeho-shua or Joshua, the first certainly Jehovistic name, who led the Hebrews into the Promised Land.[31]

But in that place, historically, existed no trace of brothers in Abraham to welcome them. The mercantile Philistines and Teucrians were settled in the coastal plain of Palestine in small city-states, each with its Mycenaean-like *sarens* or tyrant. They also had theaters and megaron-like buildings. The Philistines had marked material advantages over the nomadic Hebrews, for they had both trade and agriculture, and both chariots and iron—a metal they did their best not to let the Hebrews learn how to forge (I Samuel 13:19–21). In the time of the Judges or Hebrew sheikhs, the Philistines thus had cultural superiority over the pastoral desert tribes. Syria-Palestine had been valuable to Egypt as a trade route, but the Phoenician port of Byblos was additionally a maritime shipping point for cedar, perhaps also Mediterranean copper and tin, silver and obsidian and lapis lazuli from Asia, and the wine and oil of the eastern Mediterranean. The Egyptian Old Kingdom, we know from inscriptions, had a merchant colony at Byblos large enough to have a temple and to receive gifts from the Pharaoh.[32] But datable and inscribed Egyptian objects at Byblos came to a sharp break under Pepi II at the end of the Sixth Dynasty, the temple at Byblos was completely burned, and both Egyptian trade and political power suffered a blow from the desert Josephs who knew not Pharaoh.

In the interval when no great power like Egypt or Babylonia or the Hittites held sway in Palestine, the desert tribes were increasingly successful in their forays into the land of the Philistines, Palestine or Canaan. In the time of the Judges many Hebrew robber bands plundered the cities of the plain and enriched themselves on the spoils of the trade caravans and the coastal cities. In one instance, the spirit of the Lord of Battles came upon Samson and he went down to Ashkelon, killing thirty men and taking spoils and clothing with which he repaid a debt (Judges 14:19). In these robust times, however, such men did not always seek the common enemy; there was Jephthah to whom "vain men were gathered, and went out with him" (Judges 11:3). About the time of Saul and David, the balance of power shifted from coastal Philistines to the Hebrews in the central hills around Jerusalem.

The historic problem of how the many Mosaic-period tribal fetishes became fused and changed into a zealously national god, and of how this new god of a notably exclusive and ethnocentric people somehow became the One God of all nations, is usually treated as though there were a progressive revelation of an objective reality—as it were an inevitable event, as man gradually came to know the Unknown. But such theological explanation rests on an assumed reality of the unproven, shirking both ethnography and psychology. Further, each such liberal-evolutionist god risks being, in the future, false and not Eternal at all; the cognitive obsolescence of the past, if not honestly faced, pits intransigent but honest fundamentalism against inevitable but meretricious reinterpretation. Secular ethnographic grounds for the change in "God" are meanwhile quite evident.[33] Success under the God of Battle brought syncretism of gods, or rather the emergence of a pre-eminent one—given tribal familiarity with the generic type—as the tribes coalesced into one people in Palestine. Under many patriarchs the early Hebrews had many fetishes; under one king they began to worship one God.

The reasons for the change in God, therefore, were socio-political and military. The power of petty sheikhs who "judged Israel" during the Time of the Judges extended, before the Kingdom, only over families and lineages. To be sure, lineages often joined in common causes, and even tribes did, especially for military purposes. In a richer land they could afford to remain more closely together; and to conquer more of the land it was expedient to be so. But there was at first no permanent centralized political or military power. In the excitement of conquest or defeat, a prophetess like Deborah simply summoned the tribes; and Barak came forth as a leader against the Canaanites who were assembled under Sisera and other kings by the brook of Kishon with nine hundred iron chariots. It was a famous victory. Saul, a gigantic Benjaminite of Gibeah, aroused by taunts and gibes, called the tribes into battle not by virtue of any office he held but rather through the contagious enthusiasm of his mighty impulses. He began as a herder of asses, and when he lost them he sought the help of the visionary Samuel, who told him where to find them, a usual shamanic skill. The two then summoned the tribes under magic compulsion, and after Samuel brought supernatural thunder and rain he made Saul king. Saul's protégé and rival was David, in retrospect a charisma-laden figure.

The charming and later-idealized picture of King David hardly fits the reality.[34] Davis began as the chief of a rebellious robber band, "And every one that was in distress, and every one that was in debt, and every one that was discontented, gathered themselves unto him; and he became a captain over them: and there were with him about four hundred men" (I Samuel 22:2). With the pattern of Saul's kingship before him, by means of violence, cunning, and some assistance from women, he became a brutal and selfish leader, killing friends and foes alike to establish his despotic rule. But under King David the last fortified cities in the plateau were finally conquered, including Jerusalem, as unusually well placed and almost impregnable site that controlled all the roads in Palestine from the south.[35] Enriched by booty and power over the foreign trade between Egypt and the north, David expanded his control and subjected the Bedouin tribes as far south as the Red Sea, and with the aid of tributary Phoenicians—for the Israelites did not know the arts of navigation—Solomon expanded Red Sea trade to Sheba, the Saba of southern Arabia, whence formerly goods came by the land route.

The long reign of David was the golden age of the Hebrews, for they now dominated the important trade routes of that era in western Asia Minor and for a time reached an intoxicating wealth and power. David's successor Solomon[36] built the great Temple in Jerusalem, but despite the inflated tales of the wisdom and glory of Solomon there were already signs of a military decline and political dependence on Egypt and Tyre. The united kingdom from Saul to Solomon (1020–922 B.C.) lasted less than a century. Jeroboam led a revolt during the lifetime of Solomon and after Solomon's death brought the northern tribes into the Kingdom of Israel, with the two tribes of Judah and Benjamin forming the weak Kingdom of Judah to the south, doomed to impotence and vassalage. In Israel, true to the precedent of Saul and David, bloody palace revolutions frequently led to a change of dynasties. Worse, a reawakened Assyrian empire reappeared in Syria to the north.

Assyrian expansion in Mesopotamia had begun with Tiglath-Pileser I (1115–1102 B.C.), and the first penetration of Syria proper came under Salmanassar II (859–825 B.C.). The Assyrians made a cuneiform report of Israel in 842 and of the tribute of King Jehu, the oldest historic representation of an Israelite individual that we have. After two hundred years of continuous war, the Syrian states were either totally destroyed, conquered, or made vassals. Israel's role in all this was varied, and not always admirable. At one time she joined other minor states to attack Damascus, already sore pressed by the Assyrians; again, sometimes under pressure, Israel joined Damascus against Assyria. Sometimes expedience ruled, and sometimes the most narrow self-interest. Worse yet, the two Hebrew states often attacked one another, and Judah was long Israel's vassal. In the short span of the Hebraic state, not enough had been learned of the value of larger coalitions, nor enough experience and perspective gained to assess long-range self-interest. Finally the protective bulwark of Damascus was destroyed, and neither tribute nor desperate revolts could now hold off Assyria. King Hoshea, relying on aid from Egypt that did not come, refused tribute to Assyria in 724 B.C. At this defiance, Shalmaneser V marched against Israel, defeated and imprisoned the king and besieged his capital Samaria, which yielded only after three years to Shalmaneser's successor, Sargon the Great, in 722 B.C. The Assyrians devised the strategy of removing the leaders, the ruling classes, the most distinguished and warlike and wealthy or otherwise motivated men, to remote places. According to Assyrian records 27,290 persons were carried off, and foreign bureaucrats put in their place. Judah had been shuttled meanwhile among Tyre, Israel and Egypt although it kept the same dynasty; and when Assyria conquered Israel, Judah became the staging area for Assyrian assaults against Egypt and Tyre, with Jewish soldiers sometimes joining as the mercenary troops of a tributary state. Without an occupying army or a foreign bureaucracy, local rebellions arose in Judah itself, resulting in the siege and conquest of Jerusalem in 701.

The collapse of an overextended Assyria and the rise of Babylon revived some hope, but a new aggressive Babylonian dynasty conquered Syria, Palestine and Egypt as well, and the king of Judah was imprisoned by Nebuchadnezzar. A last revolt in 586 B.C. ended with the conquest and burning of Jerusalem. Judah was utterly wiped out, the Temple sacked of its golden treasure and destroyed—even pots and pans and spoons and other objects of brass were carried off—and 10,000 persons, now including even craftsmen and smiths so that only rural peasants remained, were deported into the Babylonian Captivity (II Kings 24:10–16, 25:9–12; Jeremiah 39:9–10). When still another eastern empire arose, Cyrus the Persian allowed some of these exiles to return after half a century of the Captivity, although; for economic reasons, many others elected to stay in the great Babylonian cities. In a sense, the Babylonian Exile was the second scattering of the Jews, long before the third and final Great Diaspora under the Romans. Repeatedly, a proud and clannish people, so jealous of one another they could not set up for long a single kingdom, were traumatized by foreign conquest and humiliated by alien rule.[37] These ruthless and recurrent geopolitical events forever set the stamp of spiritual suffering upon the Jews. The Jews were chosen for suffering—chosen perhaps to show for all time that, anthropologically, there are no chosen people.

The acculturational sophistication of Jews had begun already in half-legendary days during the Egyptian Captivity, but the nativistic reaction to this experience was largely a still more fierce and fanatic assertion of tribalism. The Yahwistic religion, though a crisis-cult borrowing in the Wilderness, was to be the later core of an intense nationalism. During the conquest of Canaan in the troubled times of the Judges and the Kings, a Samuel was needed to reassert the federal faith amidst the Canaanitish *baal-* and revived earlier Hebraic clan-cults. But in the destruction of the Temple and of all Jerusalem, the Israelites suffered the most severe cultural trauma of all. The Babylonian Captivity was the greatest ghost-dance crisis heretofore in their history.

Babylonian culture had much influence over the urbanized Jerusalemic folk, and many Biblical myths were borrowed from Babylonia, e.g. the

Creation, the Fall, the Tower of Babel, and the Deluge.[38] The compulsively rigorous observation of the Sabbath was also Babylonian in origin; even down to Jesus there was constant criticism of the too-strict Sabbatarianism that emerged after the Babylonian Captivity. When political power was annihilated, priestcraft and theocracy flourished. It was in this period that traditional Judaism appeared, the new Law was elaborated and imposed in all its force, and the priestly projection of Hebrew origins became rampant. Goethe wrote that "The last four books of Moses have been made quite unreadable by a most melancholy, most incomprehensible revision. The course of the history is everywhere interrupted by the insertion of innumerable laws, with regard to the greater part of which it is impossible to see any reason for their being inserted where they are." The renowned literary man was justified in this judgment on stylistic grounds alone, for he sensed the contrast, later teazed out by higher criticism, between the fresh and charmingly naïve Yahwistic narrative and the stiflingly jejune, artificial, pedantic, legalistic prose of the Priestly Code.

Changes in the secular situation of the Jews are nowhere better reflected than in the changes of their politico-religious functionaries. The judges were patriarchs and sheikhs of living tribes, experienced and responsible men, their authority founded on their fatherhood of lineages; the Jerusalemic kings, sheikh-patriarchs grown larger, were Davidic war leaders and wise Solomons who "judged Israel" quite as Jehovah continually judged his People. The Judges and the Kings were all fallible men, in need of the sa*tanas*[39] and the prophet to enlarge the issue, present alternative views, and sway their mighty judgments. Job[40] addressed Jehovah with the same confident logic a satanas would bring to confront a sheikh or tribal judge,[41] the same privilege with which a prophet would address a king. The new Judean priesthood, however, took from Babylonian theocrats their arrogant claims as well as new notions of worship; and after the final and complete political annihilation of the nation in later Roman times, Judaism became the *religious community* that it has remained even down to the modern Zionist state of Israel.

Scholarly rabbis, teachers of the Law, were the leaders and preservers of religious continuity in the often small and scattered groups that existed after the Diaspora while the Jews awaited a God-sent messiah king to rescue and reunite them.[42] But priests were the officiants of the compulsive state cult in post-exilic Jerusalem, litigious to a degree that matched their vatic certitude. Both rabbis and priests are guardians of a fixed dogmatic divine code. Their authority rests on revealed and received tradition. But Jerusalemic priests had a larger clientele than did most medieval village rabbis. Rabbinical acumen managed to adapt centuries-old laws to new conditions, not without the aid of important medieval Jewish mystics and, later, on occasion hereditary charismatic *tzaddikim*. Rabbis were scholars of the Law who could always find a reasonable precedent for a wise ad hoc interpretation. Biblical Hebrew religion from Palestine was transformed into Rabbinic Judaism of the Diaspora, shaping a Talmudism that enabled Jews to survive two millennia in alien environments at best unfriendly and often murderously hostile.

Shamans and prophets, however, in contrast to priests, are religious individualists, in direct contact with the divine powers in more archaic times. Moses had been just this, "the chief shaman, or *kahin*" in Meek's words,[43] during the tribal wanderings in the wilderness. It is not that Moses does not speak with authority; it is a question of the nature of the authority. Moses brooks no rebellion, and he speaks with the more asperity and rage precisely because his Yahweh had rivals in the wilderness—his brother Aaron was at times a rival shaman—as Yahweh had rivals even long afterward in the land of Canaan. Magic power, derived from Yahweh on direct instruction and contact, is Moses' strength, not a long written tradition of the Book. The relationship is made explicit when Moses complains that he is a man of poor speech, whereupon he is made a god to Aaron "and thou shalt speak unto him, and put words in his mouth: and I will be with thy mouth, and with his mouth, and will teach you what ye shall do. And he shall be thy spokesman unto the people: and he shall be, even he shall be to thee instead of a mouth, and thou shalt be to him instead of God (Exodus 4:15–16). The divine Patriarch and the human patriarch are here as one. But the god-man relation and the locus of omnipotence here define magic, not religion: for in religion the priest and his god are sharply distinguished. In times of later sore distress, Judaism more than once regressed from oedipal father-son distinctness to messianic fusion. Christianity is therefore, strictly speaking, a heresy of Judaism. And when the God-man was united with the Father, Christians again borrow from Jesus an expectation of the Coming—as if the blasphemy of human godhood were a mere aberrant episode in the worship of the eternal One.

In all the historic phases of Judaism, then, one must carefully attend to the oedipal and political paradigms of power in order to understand the religion. The ancient jinn-haunted Hebrews of the Negeb had no sense of orderly and predictable forces in a lawful consolidated universe, since this view requires for its secular paradigm a settled civic life under a unified and legal state. They inhabited instead a wild world of spirits, in temperament not unlike themselves, violent, willful, unpredictable and small-scale in their power. In a superb oedipal myth, a human Jacob personally overcame a jinn in hand-to-hand combat one night, "battler of *el*"! In the mysterious world of open deserts, mountains, springs, animals and storms, the Hebrew herdsman indeed knew of powers greater than himself on which he depended. But herdsmen are self-reliant, if dependent on patriarchs, hence the still human scale and nature of religious projections. Exceptional men in fact could incorporate enough mana to become great shamans, medicine-men and wonder-workers, just as powerful sheikhs could dominate lesser men. Such a wonder-worker was the sacred counterpart of a sheikh in the secular world, and indeed Jacob was both, and so were Abraham and Moses. The old Hebrew *kôhēn* (Arabic *kāhin*) was originally a shaman, medium and soothsayer, the intermediary between men and spirits, some of which were clearly totemic animal-familiars. For example, *nāhash,* "divination," is related to the word *nāhāsh,* "serpent," tribal deity of the Levites, and hence the power of divination came from the wise serpent as animal-familiar.

Early prophets like Samuel, called *rô'eh* or "seer" (from the root *rā'āh* "to see") were also oracles of the shamanistic type. Ecstatic possession is made quite clear in such phrases as "Yahweh put his spirit upon," "poured his spirit upon," or "the spirit of God (or Yahweh) was upon," "rested upon," "came upon," "fell upon," "entered into," "spoke by," or "the power [literally hand] of Yahweh was upon" such and such a man. Samuel "turned into another man" when he prophesied (I Samuel 10:6). Some prophets seemed to be, or were, insane: Elisha is a "mad fellow" (II Kings 9:11), and in later times "every man that is mad, and maketh himself a prophet" had to be put into prison and in stocks (Jeremiah 29:26). The ecstatic reaction is violent and contagious, so that even King Saul, in good shamanistic fashion, "even he stripped off his clothes also, and prophesied before Samuel in like manner, and lay down naked all that day and all that night" (I Samuel 19:24)—evidently so characteristic a behavior as to inspire the saying that Saul also was among the prophets. King David, too, took off his clothes and, wearing only a linen ephod, danced ecstatically before the Ark on its way to Jerusalem. When Michal, daughter of the former King Saul, mocked David "the glorious king of Israel" for such shamelessness, like the angered fertility daemon that he embodied, he appropriately cursed her with barrenness to the end of her days (II Samuel 6:14 and 20–23).

A synonym for *rô'eh* is *hozēh,* from *hāzah,* "to see or to see ecstatically."

The older term for prophet, *rô'eh,* was later almost entirely replaced by *nābî',* a root not found in Hebrew but cognate with the Akkadian *nabû,* "to call, to speak out." The Septuagint correctly translates this as προφήτης, "spokesman, speaker in behalf of." Moses was just this sort of prophet (Deuteronomy 18:15; Hosea 12:13) even to later men, and Deborah was quite clearly an ecstatic shamaness in the oldest portion of the Old Testament, the "Song of Deborah." It is significant that both Moses and Deborah came in times of stress, and were resorted to as oracles for advice and guidance (Exodus 15:15; Judges 4:5). The later prophets were in the same tradition as Samuel, and they too arose particularly in times of stress. They also evidenced standard shamanistic powers, for example Elijah had an inexhaustible cruze of oil, made a return from the land of the dead, a journey to heaven, etc.

Indeed, a case could be made that the prophets were always joined to troubled times. After the sundering of Israel and Judah came Elijah, who contemned the Baal-temple of Ahab's queen Jezebel; Elisha, who persuaded the captain Jehu to fulfill Elijah's prophecy of a bad end for Ahab and his dynasty; and Amos, the grim Judaean shepherd who interrupted the feast at Bethel with forebodings of Assyrian conquest and the destruction of Damascus and Israel. Hosea and Micah, the great moralists, came during the rise of Assyria, shortly before and after the fall of Samaria; and Zephaniah, after the sinful Manasseh's dictatorship. Isaiah, always close to the seats of power, saw the downfall of Samaria and threatened Judah with similar chastisements if Ahaz joined the Assyrians against Israel and Syria; Judah was subjected anyway, whereupon Isaiah fought to maintain the status quo and King Hezekiah's retaining of Jerusalem. A second Isaiah, or his editor, knew of the terrible Exile two hundred years later; the Messiah (the rising Persian?) would set political matters aright. Jeremiah aided in the reforms under Josiah, but he lived on after the king was killed in the battle of Megiddo; the Lamentations of Jeremiah followed the destruction of Jerusalem that he had so bitterly fought to prevent. The prophet Nahum knew the fall of Nineveh; Obadiah, of Babylon; Habakkuk, the battle of Carchemish; and Ezekiel, the first deportation. Joel and Zechariah may have been contemporaries of Alexander and his world-shaking conquests; "Jonah," of the Greco-Egyptian Ptolemies and their rule. The late Book of Daniel pretends that the prophet was taken captive to Babylon; but the book's author lived in the bloody and bootless Maccabean revolt of Israel against the Roman Empire, in 167–164 B.C. But the apocalyptic Daniel stayed in the same tradition of dire prediction, and from first to last the prophets witnessed catastrophe.

Prophets flourished from 1000 B.C. onward, especially in the afflicted southern kingdom of Judah. Not only social but also personal turmoil are clearly visible in their lives. Amos seems sound enough—though perhaps only great emotional pressure would force a humble shepherd to prophecy before the mighty of the land—but some of the ecstatics give evidence of distinct mental instability. Isaiah went naked for three years, suggesting a psychotic variance with a society so notable for physical modesty, an ecdysiasm surely beyond even the prophetic stereotype. Jeremiah denied himself any sexual life; and Ezekiel's schizophrenia can hardly be doubted.[44] A bewildered society is the more ready to listen to its neurotic and psychotic olonists; if a smugly comfortable establishment were as able to listen to its psychic dissidents it might expect usefully to be edified of its own pathogenic trends also, for to distance the "crazy" overmuch is to destroy their potentially therapeutic function and to project into scapegoats merely unacknowledged faults.

Possession by angry spirits was culturally expected of the Hebrew prophet or *nabi,* for *hitnabbē* means "to rage, to fume, to be crazy." More wisely than modern men, the ancient Hebrews used their prophets as social olonists rather more than we do. The early prophets Elijah and Elisha took direct part in the internecine struggles, and since the kings treated them with great severity, it is evident that they were criticizing authority. In this, the prophets before the kings somewhat resembled the old legal figure of the *satanas* or "adversary" to the judges, the sheikhs from whom the kingship emerged. Some dignity of the son-defendant in the court of the father-judge is not to be minimized in importance; for whereas other Semitic patriarchates to the east evolved into monstrous and absolute autocracies, Hebraic authority remained human in scale and modesty. However litigious and logic-splitting Talmudic Judaism later was to become, respect for reason in scrutinizing the Law remained basic. The anti-Pharisaical trend is visible even down to Christ, the antinomian tinge a logical ally of Christianity against the Roman empire; and without this element in early Christianity, the Reformation would have lost a weapon. By contrast, the only response to a Semitic Allah is a quietist kismet.

In any case, the Hebraic prophets typically defended the humble against the mighty, and widows, orphans, poor and other dispossessed against grasping and unfeeling rich men; and, though respected, these prophets were at the same time feared and sometimes despised outsiders. Nevertheless, the Hebrew *nabi* was not a simple creature of adolescent crisis. Only adult males had weight in influencing opinion. Prophecy emerged in men of mature years. The emotional and spiritual identification of prophets with Yahweh was complete; and it was this authority's demonic rage that they exemplified and to which they gave witness.

Furthermore, all the great prophets were not simply antinomian but preached a responsible moral reform, articulate even to details. Mere moral negativists and easy anarchists lack a sufficient sense of the mature necessity of culture. The prophets attacked formalism and hypocrisy as well as idolatry and oppression, and in this they often opposed both priest and king. The Eternal desires mercy, not sacrifice (Hosea 6:6); he rejects the oblations of the wicked (Amos 5:21–25); he adjures the worshiper first to put away the evil of his doings (Isaiah 1:16–17); and Jeremiah, in an extreme protest against cult practices, even seems to proscribe burnt offerings altogether (Jeremiah 7:21–23). Jeremiah was the first prophet of priestly lineage, though the prophet predominated in him. Furthermore, the prophets consistently attacked the compulsive priestly formalism that spread like a pall over Judaism in the last five centuries before Christ. And with good reason: formalism and fundamentalism, with all the answers in, easily becomes mechanical magic; only oedipal *persons* have the emotional and cognitive freedom for reform. Earnestly sought *moral imperative* is basic to Judaism.

In the light of Ghost Dance theory it is interesting to note that priestcraft and its offices first flourished after the dislocation of the Babylonian Captivity, in a kind of social regression of ego-autonomy. The priests emphasized many ritual formalities such as, significantly, in circumcision; and to Priestly revisions are due the confusions in the Pentateuch on this matter. Even down to Jesus and Paul, moralists reiterated that the real sin was to be "uncircumcised of heart." After the Babylonian Exile, as noted above, the priests also developed an obsessive Sabbatarianism.[45] The old Hebrew Sabbath was in essence a joyful time of rest and family communion with God, but now the Sabbath became a monstrous tangle of fearful Priestly taboos.[46] The Law was also proliferated, often into sheer sacerdotal nonsense,[47] and to such a degree that only a truly authoritarian personality could possibly live within it.[48]

The patriarchal strain in Judaism does make for an inordinately demanding superego, but ambivalent compulsiveness soon makes a mockery of meaning and intention. If one aspect of Judaism is "fossil," this was already fossilized after the Destruction of the Temple. Toynbee, however, is not only incomplete and unfair, but exactly wrong with respect to another aspect of traditional Judaism, its intrinsic moral and intellectual progressivism. To attend only to Zealots and Pharisees is to neglect the Sadducees and the Essenes. These latter strains not only survived in Judaism but also produced both Christianity and, in the last analysis,

Protestantism. The spirit of the Old Testament prophets has never really died. Indeed, progressivism and reform is the taproot of the American ethic, and it is no accident so often to find Judaism on the side of the American dream.

Nevertheless, the persistence of filial culture-dependency and its reciprocal, the compulsively priestly, may not be ignored. It is possible that hereditary shamanship remained in the line of Moses, perhaps in the oldest houses at Dan and Shiloh that claimed descent from him. But quite characteristic of some revitalization movements is retrospective falsification, with the result that anyone who reads the received Pentateuch with ethnographic attentiveness is often roughly jarred by the non-"period" elements in it. The Priestly Code systematically falsified the past and brazenly borrowed the traditional prestige of Moses in the interests of the later priestly hierarchy, but often with gross illogicality. For example, the twelve secular tribes had a synthetic occupational "tribe" of Levi added to them, the sons of Aaron, who alone were priests, plus "Levites" who were hieroduli, or lesser officiants. The Levites manifestly could not have been an authentic functioning tribe and also have officiated dispersed among many other tribes; in fact, the Levites were adjured to leave their various families and to serve only the cult. Thus they were not so much an authentic tribe as an artificial clerical group.

The Priestly Code made further falsifications of the ethnic past. The Tabernacle is a priestly fiction designed to give pre-existence to the Temple and national unity of worship. Actually, older and more contemporary sources in the Old Testament indicate that the Ark in David's time and before was sheltered in a tent; and there were many other similar fetishes then. Furthermore, obviously in retrospect, David was in Chronicles much idealized at priestly hands, the number and unity of his supporters greatly exaggerated, and even the slaying of Goliath by Elhanan son of Jair (II Samuel 21:19) was falsely attributed to David (I Samuel 17) as a hero to whom other heroic legends accrue. Chronicles itself is a tendentious Priestly rewriting of Kings and is of much later date, the purpose being to exalt the monarchy which fitted a priestly hierarchy centered in Jerusalem. The priestly cult, evidently for good reason, seemed to have an inordinate appetite for historical legitimacy, and it is admittedly a difficult accomplishment to discover continuity in the gods of Abraham, of Jacob, of Moses-Aaron-Joshua, of David, and of the post-Babylonian Priestly Code.

The Priestly Code also invented exorbitant tithes and inserted them into older documents, now including cattle and sheep in addition to the proper measure of corn and oil and wine—almost a blasphemy in terms of the older religion. The worthless sons of Eli even arrogantly demanded raw meat to roast before making burnt offering to Jehovah, instead of eating the boiled meat speared in more modest random lot out of the pot with the traditional shamanistic trident (I Samuel 2:13).[49] Again, the assignment of cities to priests, or the assignment of land and its products, was an outrage against the original view that the earth literally was the Lord's and the fullness thereof. As the older Owner or Master of Animals, deity *owned* the animals (whence the very rationale of ritual sacrifice). The pouring out of blood on tribal altars was merely rendering back the substance of life to God who had given it. The burning of fat, source of fertility and fire, was especially and naturally his proper portion on the altar, "table of the Lord." In fact, meat was less commonly used than milk, fruit and grain; and all slaughter properly speaking was sacrifice, combined with a meal by the natural society of gathered family and clan. As Wellhausen writes, "With the Hebrews, as with the whole ancient world, sacrifice constituted the main part of worship."[50] Indeed, the prophets Amos, Hosea, Isaiah, and Micah all later inveighed against this naïve older notion of the proper relationship of God and man, saying that men confounded ritual (sacrifice, which God now despised) with religion (a contrite heart, which alone was an acceptable sacrifice).

"One might as well try to hear the grass growing as attempt to derive from such a source [as Chronicles] a historical knowledge of the conditions of ancient Israel," wrote Wellhausen in scholarly exasperation.[51] The Priestly Code is one of the earliest of pious "modernist" ethnography-fakings, completely obtuse to the reality of culture and of history; Jonah and Daniel too, as well as a number of apocryphal writings such as Maccabees, show this tendency to cast reflections of the present back into the past. The change of economic conditions from pastoralism to agriculture is easy to see; the Priestly Code could not conceivably have applied in the Wilderness. The old ritual of worship was of course pastoral, viz. the sacrifice of animals—that is, of common-property domesticated animals cared for by the group, for these alone were subject to the severest food taboos and later most fantastic ritual observances—for to hunted animals these priestly rules of late date did not apply. By no stretch could the Priestly Code be carried back to paleolithic hunting times!

Furthermore, in Deuteronomic law, festivals rest on agriculture and the yearly cycle, and only the Passover can therefore belong to ancient pastoral rites.[52] But agriculture was learned by the Hebrews from the Canaanites among whom they settled. Land ownership was not a developed concept among early pastoralists, and many pastoral skirmishes were over grazing lands unowned in their wanderings; by contrast, the tribes had to ask Egypt to permit grazing their flocks in the Land of Goshen. But the same view of God's rights remainecd. In agriculture the land now becomes the basis of life and of religion. Jehovah is given as having promised the land and its products; in tithes he now receives back the best of the first-fruits, in thankfulness and in recognition of his seignorial rights. In the first contract between God and his chosen people he gave them the land in fee. But is this not already false archaizing? The Covenant as the rite of circumcision is authentic, either as an old puberty rite or mark of tribal identity, and in context it is conceivably even Stone Age in antiquity, since only flints might be used. But is not the contractual promise of land, and this view of land, not reading back *ex post facto* into the Covenant in the Wilderness the possession of Canaan, which happened historically only much later?[53] Again, as place daemon, fertility god, husband of the land, pastoral bull god and storm king, as shamanic lord of battle, fire, earthquake, volcano, lightning or whatever, Jehovah is authentically archaic. But as the revenue-producing capital property of priests he is post-Babylonian only, and even mercantile in concept.

Hence the post-exilic, deuteronomic elements in Judaism seem contrived, inauthentically traditional, and borrowed. Again, Jehovah demanded in the contract only that the Israelites should have no other god before him, in the tumultuous Mosaic days of many cults. A monotheistic god is the product of a later and different political milieu, the kingly state. The picture the Code would give us is that of a whole unified people driven hither and thither by the same inner and outer compulsions, with everything that happens depending on the seesaw of Jehovah's favor and wrath as interpreted by the priests, in a crazy alternation of absolute peace and utter affliction—a priestly artifact possible to imagination only after experience of a wealthy centralized and settled kingdom of Solomon, followed by the tribulation of the Exile. And surely idyllic Davidic lands untroubled by alien invaders need no despairing Ghose Dance, but only an easy traditional cult of quid pro quo.

The concept of a politico-military messiah who would reaffirm the state as it was in the golden days of King David appeared only after the revolt from the royal house of David. Early Old Testament allusions to the messiah as a supernatural culture hero are sporadic, ambiguous and obscure, and even these are not above suspicion of being later interpolations. This kind of messianic hope is later; certainly Isaiah put his faith in a purely secular messiah, King Hezekiah. Messianic hopes developed especially after the Fall of Jerusalem. Haggai and Zechariah show that messianism preoccupied Jews at the time of the captivity, and the influence of the Deuteronomy newly "discovered" in the Temple pervaded the whole century of the exile. Sometimes even foreign rulers were looked to as the messiah, e.g. the Persian Cyrus who would conquer Babylon and deliver the Jews. Sometimes foreign rulers shrewdly exploited this hope, which was at first more a popular than a priestly belief. Nebuchadnezzar, for instance, appointed Gedaliah of the house of David, but in a rebellion against the foreigners Gedaliah was murdered, a Babylonian official was appointed in his place, and many persons (including Jeremiah) fled to Egypt. The tree of the Davidic dynasty had been cut down, but the prophecy of a shoot growing from its roots began a new messianic conception (Zechariah 3:8 and 6:12). Messianism was not taken very seriously by either Philo or Josephus, but hatred of the rule of the Herods and the Romans made messianism especially strong in the first centuries B.C. and A.D. The New Testament evidence for belief in a spiritual Messiah is voluminous, and of course a similar belief became an integral part of Judaism at the Diaspora. The "teacher of righteousness" in the Essene writings, for example, is one prototype of the Christ.

Factionalism is characteristic of ghost-dance periods of crisis and unrest, and factionalism was not absent in Judaism of the last century before Christ. Pharisaism emerged especially in the Maccabean conflict with surrounding heathenisms, and was dominant in the three centuries from John Hyrcanus to A.D. 135. The Pharisees elaborated the old idea of Sheol (originally no more than a dim animistic Greek-like Hades where unhappy spirits survived after leaving the body and this world) into a doctrine of the immortality of souls—a recurrent and immemorial belief when the secular world is particularly unsatisfying, and here not inconceivably influenced by a neo-Platonic ideal hieratic state—puritans who transformed the Law into a way of life (*Halakha*); argued, perhaps under both Babylonian and Egyptian ideas of Fate, that all save human will is determined by God; and believed in immortality and the torture of the damned, that is, of those who did not accede to Pharisaism. In the present-day world there is a tendency to secularize more and more aspects of life, but the Pharisaic ideal was (and is) the exact opposite of such progressivism. Pharisees strove to bring all departments of human activity under the dominance of religious law, in a way quite paralleled by another Semitic religion, that of Islam. Pharisaism was the major force in shaping Jewish Orthodoxy and became permanent in the rabbinical system of later Judaism, surviving among that relatively small minority of Orthodox Jews who would make the modern State of Israel a strict theocracy under Mosaic-Rabbinic law.

Josephus portrays the opposite faction, the Sadducees, as representing the wealth and political engrossment of nobles. Perhaps a more secular and worldly view may be seen in the Sadducean beliefs that Fate has no influence, that God may not be blamed for the actions of men whose wills are free and responsible, and that there are neither angels nor spirits (Acts 23:8) and hence neither immortality of souls nor reward and punishment after death (Mark 12:18). One must not neglect to note, however, that the doctrinal differences of Sadducees from Pharisees were also based on politico-religious grounds. Sadducees rejected the doctrine of a Davidic messiah because they regarded prophetic teaching on this matter to be contrary to the Torah; resurrection was not taught in the Torah either, and hence Sadducees rejected this new development as well. In conservative Pharisaic circles the very name Sadducee came to be synonymous with infidel. Nevertheless, the rational and secularizing trend of the Sadducees survived too in Jewish intellectual tradition, and it is a strong component of Reformed Judaism.

Wellhausen emphasizes that mercantilism[54] among the Jews came only after they had learned trade from the Palestinean Phoenicians and had become used to settled life in cities. Mercantilism received another impetus after leaders had become used to urban life in the great trading cities in Babylonia and when they returned to Israel found themselves displaced from their agricultural lands. Kautsky[55] argues that, in trade, purchase and sale are removed from one another in space and time; and that, whereas handicraft stimulates a sense of the concrete, mercantilism stimulates abstract thought. It may be overstressing a point to say that unproductive trade in principle foments scientific study; but certainly scientific thought needs surplus wealth, and also leisure, urbanity, and disinterested investigation. Perhaps also, for the repeatedly displaced Jews, easily transportable money and jewels were more suited than livestock and agricultural land as a form of wealth. But wealth may be a problem in inviting dangerous envy. After Alexander the Great, the glory of the Phoenician trade cities declined; Palestine, as a troubled buffer state between Asia Minor and Egypt, had been a scene of many wars but presently became less a route of trade, which now went by sea.

In response to this, mercantile Jews accumulated in the great commercial cities elsewhere, since urban trade afforded the greatest opportunities for displaced leaders to gather wealth. Mommsen wrote that Alexandria was as much a city of Jews as of Greeks; and Alexandrian

Jews were soon peers to those of Jerusalem in numbers, wealth, cultivation, intelligence and organization, especially now that Jerusalem was somewhat a stranded Venice. In the first imperial census, there were a million Jews to eight million Egyptians, and Strabo says that Alexandrian Jews were actually given a sort of extraterritorial government, much as later mercantile Europeans were to have in the Far East. In any case, from having once been rural nomads Jews became and remained predominantly an urban people, as in Alexandria, Rome, London, the great Netherlands ports, and New York. Perhaps city life offers even greater stimulation to wits than money.

After the conquest by Alexander the Great, Judaea was ruled by the Ptolemies from 320 B.C. until the Seleucids of 189 B.C., both dynasties descended from Alexander's generals. Antiochus IV persecuted the Jews and provoked them to rebellion under the leadership of Judas Maccabaeus, son of the priest Mattathias. The Maccabees were a numerous and powerful family descended from the Asmonean pontiffs, so-called from Mattathias' great-grandfather. After initial striking successes, the rebellion dragged on inconclusively for a long time. One of the Maccabees, Simon, finally took the title Prince of the Jews in 142 B.C. and his successors—Hyrcanus, Aristobulus and Alexander Jannaeus—were simultaneously kings and high priests in the final triumph of Judaean theocracy.

But political and religious dominance was not all. It is interesting that, for good economic reasons, Aramaic linguistically conquered all western Asia.[56] As Babylonian had been in the second, so Aramaic became the language of commerce and diplomacy in the first millennium B.C. Only the post-Alexander rise of Greek as a universal language set a limit to the spread of Aramaic. This linguistic dominance is unquestionably a further index of wealth and influence. But the making of money can be easily displaced by the taking of it, as Jews have repeatedly learned to their sorrow.

Julius Caesar knew well the power in money. Suetonius wrote that Caesar early received money from Rome's allies when he was Proconsul in Spain, money he sometimes begged from them to pay his towering debts, due both to his extravagances and to the needs of his personal army. Pretending that they were hostile, Caesar sacked several cities in Lusitania, although they had complied with his orders and opened their gates to him. Later, in Gaul, with experienced rapacity, he destroyed temples and sanctuaries richly stored with gifts, and attacked cities more for their booty than their rebellion. Irish gold in the royal towns of south England beckoned him to invade even Britain, though his politico-religious pontificate also led him to extinguish rival Druidism transplanted from Gaul to Britain. In his western campaigns, in fact, Caesar collected so much gold that he offered and sold it in Italy for three thousand sesterces a pound, thus forcing the price of gold down twenty-five percent from its usual four thousand sesterces or $200 a pound.

Next Caesar conspired with two of the wealthiest financiers of Rome, Pompey and Crassus, to seize the power of the state. As First Consul he stole three thousand pounds or $450,000 worth of gold from the Capitol, replacing it with an equal weight of gilt copper. In his growing power he sold kingdoms and alliances for money, six thousand talents or $7,500,000 alone coming from the Ptolemy of Egypt to be divided with Pompey. Booty led him to a break with Pompey, who had to seek glory elsewhere, and at the end of the civil war between them Caesar gave each soldier 5000 Attic drachmas, over $1000, twice this amount to non-commissioned officers, and twice that or 20,000 drachmas to each officer. Now in total command of the army, Caesar's authority was never publicly disputed until his assassination at the hands of a group including Brutus, said by some to be his own son. His heirs Antony and Augustus destroyed all opposition, and the Roman Republic hard-won from the old Tarquinian kings was now dead. Democratic process ended, the whole Empire became the possession of the Emperor and his dominion over it his own private affair. Small wonder a new Owner soon became a god.

If political dominance was the life breath of imperial Rome and armies its muscle, money was its life blood, and the one can often secure the other. And if Rome could bear no rival in Carthage, the trans-Saharan port of the gold and riches of Africa, so also Rome could not bear a rival in the great mercantile city of Jerusalem, the largest in Judaea, and door to the wealth of Asia.[57] Jerusalem, now under the Asmonean ruler Hyrcanus II, was conquered by the luckless Pompey. Later, Herod of Idumaea, son of a minister of Hyrcanus, received a puppet's crown from another member of the triumvirate, Mark Antony. Later Roman procurators left little power to the three tetrarchies divided among Herod's children.

The insatiable Roman thirst for money provoked a general Judaean revolt against Rome in 66 A.D. A vigorous political life flourished longer in Jerusalem, center of the last stronghold of independence in the Roman Empire. A long and stubborn siege under Vespasian (emperor 69–79 A.D.) and his son Titus, later emperor himself, was required to capture Jerusalem, which was destroyed in 70 A.D. In 132, the false messiah Bar Kokhba led a final hopeless insurrection and the last fortress at Bethar fell into Roman hands. The defenders were massacred or sold as slaves. In 135 A.D., near the height of Roman expansion, Hadrian founded a Roman colony on the dead ruins of Jerusalem. But all national life of the Jews was utterly extinguished for nearly two millennia until after World War II. Those that had first lived by the swords of Saul and Jonathan (I Samuel 13:22) now perished by the sword.

Dispersed all over the world,[58] only the religion of Judaism now served to keep the sacred community alive, an event unique of its kind in history. Instead of melding anonymously into the many peoples among whom they sojourned, the Jews stubbornly retained their religious identity. Outcasts forbidden land ownership, political responsibilities, and honorable professional callings, imprisoned in squalid ghettos, the Jews of Dark Age and medieval Europe suffered unspeakable miseries. Hated always, often plundered, and in times of public tragedy or fear treated as scapegoats both by conniving rulers and ignorant blood-crazy mobs, the Jews in the Enlightenment of the eighteenth century seemed to find a hope of better days, and in the nineteenth a Jew rose to be Prime Minister of the chief empire on earth—only for the Jews to undergo in the twentieth the most ghastly and disastrous genocide in history, under a sick nativism and a psychotic messiah.

The continuity of the Judaic tradition, in the face of repeated calamities, is one of the most spectacular in all ethnology. There are perhaps three reasons for this phenomenal endurance: a literate tradition (Baron notes most medieval Jews were as educated as Christian clergy, amidst mass illiteracy), close adherance to and deep respect for teachers of that Law. The Law gave continuity to Judaism. The ancient Mosaic sheikh was a politico-religious leader and lawgiver or judge. The early Judges in Canaan gave way to charismatic kings like Saul and David. But even after the disappearance of the Jewish state, the medieval rabbi was still essentially part priest and part teacher of the Law and judge. Community leadership was founded primarily on knowledge and wisdom regarding the Law. The rabbi essentially governed the community, rendered decisions on civil disputes, and was consulted on every question whether an act was permitted or not permitted according to the traditional Talmudic interpretation of the Mosaic law.[59]

In modern times the rabbinical tradition of learning has developed into that of the Jewish scientist and intellectual—both in some ways a constant *satanas* to the tyranny of tradition, and in this context they were inescapably liberalist, humanist and progressive. Freud may be adduced as an example of this type. It is interesting that Freud abandoned the study of law for the interpretation of individual dreams and aspirations. He enjoyed collecting various primitive "idols" but often quite privately considered himself a new Moses, seeking liberation from internal tyrants in an entirely new way. Freud sought emancipation from the forgotten past both ethnic and individual, but coupled with an insistence on fresh assessment of current and past reality by the maturing ego.[60]

It is also interesting that Freud so valued individual, conscious autonomy that he abandoned the study of a pain-repressing drug that distorted consciousness, so that the credit for "discovering" cocaine went to another person. He also abandoned hypnotism, which facile mountebanks still use in the "cure" of hysterias, because this authoritarian magic did not have the participation of the patient's conscious ego. Freud indeed was a new Moses, who led us into a new and strange land of the unconscious mind. He deeply valued and respected the sources of spontaneity, genius and art. But he would have profoundly pitied the culture-alienated who seek escape from the oedipal problems of growing up, in a psychedelic drug-induced fantasy. To Freud this would have seemed an *ersatz* religionist illusion, a defensive cowardice, and the gravest possible impiety toward the Reality Principle. Besides, what is man without history, to serve as foil for intellectual growth?

The Jewish tradition is rich and complex; it is not to be encompassed within a *simpliste* formula of a group compulsion neurosis of a whole people. For there has existed also the constantly liberating tradition of Jewish mysticism (in which Bakan argues Freud was embedded) that in medieval days served something of the reformist function of biblical prophet and seer. In a daily irrational world of alien culture, Jews never stayed exclusively bound to a sunny realm of humanist Greek rationalism, for their variety of enclosed minority group living would always tap dark rich streams of humanist feeling as well. And in an irrational world it was a Jew who first taught us to fathom irrationality. Bakan[61] says Orthodox Jews believe study keeps temptation at a distance (i.e. is psychoanalytically repressive), and immersion in Talmudic lore protects from Satan and alien thoughts (i.e. serves as a compulsive-obsessive defense). Perhaps. And yet the earnest litigiousness of the Jewish Talmudic tradition seeking truth in the Law, it might be argued, is preadaptive to the careful search for and statement of scientific laws. Cultural alienation is itself emancipation from each cognitive Establishment. It might be argued also that suffering and a tragic sense of life are required to escape stolid fundamentalist self-imprisonment of mind.

In any case, suffering, alienation, and exile have been the nourishment that history has provided the Jew.

Judaism is therefore not so much the consequence of a single ghost dance of Moses and the Children of Israel in the Wilderness, nor of the Babylonian Captivity, not even of the Diaspora, as it is the rein-scribed palimpsest scroll recording a fantastic series of historic vicissitudes, each one of which has reinforced the same response to tribulation of an eternal minority people: the re-examination of conscience before the wrath of a punitive and patriarchal righteous God. The Greeks con-tinually modified their view of God-Nature; the Hebrews continually struggled to know the moral will of the eternal That Which Is. The Greeks sought to know *physis;* Hebrews the Law, the *nomos* of the Unknowable One.

Greek and Jew[62] historically meet in the Holy Bible—the Old Testa-ment a long history of successive crisis cults of the Jews, but mutilated as a document by the last ghost dance of post-exilic Judaism; the New Testament the intellectual ruins of post-Platonic Greece, adulterated with the detritus of numerous Near-Eastern cults; the whole administered by the political ghost of Rome. In a few centuries after the fall of Athens and the razing of Jerusalem, Christianity became a kind of dictatorship of the proletariat which in time complexly merged with the old religio-political dictatorship of the god-Caesars of Rome, late the Papacy that long ruled a still larger Christendom—the whole a long struggle of men to understand the moral burden of freedom and the proper uses of authority. It is useless to hate the past; a man can only struggle to recover from it, and to modify as we can what time has made of us. Will Jews ever have outlived the usefulness of taught anger and memorized anguish? Or are they chosen forever to be the lightning rod of other men's miseries?

A glance at another martyr people, the American Negro, may aid us in understanding the Jew. In each case we hate whom we hurt, for hurting gives good grounds for self-hate. But beyond this similarity there are differences. The racist, basically, attacks the Negro under the pretense of making a virtuous superego attack on the id: we identify the Negro with our own infantile and wicked impulses and then punish them by attacking him.[63] Much folklore exists to confirm the thesis that the racist attacks the Negro as the projective scapegoat of the racists' own sins. But attacking the Jew as "diabolic" is often really to attack not one's own impulses but an alien conscience—that is, both "racially" alien and (to the psychopath) ego-alien as despised and resisted con-science. And is, perhaps, an alternative oedipal stance (father-bound

Judaic religion) not the most anxiety-arousing, hateful, and unforgivable of differences?

Again, to the paranoid character that cannot abide difference, the Negro presents the target of visible race difference. But nothing so sets the teeth on edge of the anthropologically informed individual as the allegation that Jews are a "race."[64] The Habiru were not a single people even when they entered the Promised Land! And one glance around the streets of modern Jerusalem, millennia after the Diaspora, would support no claim for racial homogeneity. The existence of otherwise wholly Chinese "Jews" re-emphasizes the fact that Judaism is really only a *historic religious community.* It is thus anthropologically absurd to call the Jews a "race." Anti-Semitism on "racial" grounds is consequently as ridiculous as an attack on "dolichocephalic" Christianity, or the critique of a "phaenozygous" dictionary with high cheekbones. It is a certain sign that the speaker literally does not know what he is talking about. Worse, it misses the whole meaning of anti-Semitism.

Halevi cried, "Israel is the martyr-people; it is the 'heart of the nations,' feeling every pain and disorder of the great body of mankind."[65] But what makes Israel martyred? What is there about Jews that accounts for the persistent, hateful, and sometimes murderous response to them? This cannot be explained on superficial, ideological "Christian" grounds that (to rationalize the irrational) have falsified history concerning the Jews —because the same response occurs among anti-Christian nativistic Germans and Moslem Arabs as well. Is it simply that Jews are defiantly different—with historic pride and defensive combativeness, an unforgivably magnificent *panache,* mocking irony, self-discernment, and intense self-identity—and that these other persons are unwilling and unable to grant such culture-shocking difference a right to exist? Worse too, each Jew, as a member of a minority, has beside his defiant pride some touch of self-doubt—and can anything be more maddening, more totally infuriating to the authoritarian personality!

A significant clue to anti-Semitism may be that it appears especially during nativistic culture crises. As Wirth points out,[66] the segregation of Jews into medieval ghettos did not begin from any formal edict of church or state, and was not the arbitrary plan of authority to deal with an alien people, but rather a natural withdrawal of a minority group into a geographic enclave, in order to preserve ethnic custom and religious heritage, long before such segregation became compulsory. So long as a peculiarly urban group like the Jew is geographically segregated and thus identifiable in the ghetto (as the Negro is *always* and *everywhere* identifiable by his skin color), the group is easily available in pogroms as the scapegoat for every frightened crisis-nativism. But precisely because assimilated German Jewry was "racially" unidentifiable, there had to be visible badge-identification by the Star of David. Thus the paranoid could still react violently to the "race-proud" Jew, whose very ethnic existence is a red flag to ethnocentrism.

We have traced the long chronicle of what history has done to the Jews. What now can be said of the effect of Jews upon history? Surely our unique Europe would never have been Europe without the Jews, for their historic suffering has brought unprecedented gifts to all men. Jews are the martyr people of history, externally; internally, they converted each new suffering into moral sensitivity and self-criticism. If the consummately rational Greeks were the mind, the Jews have been the conscience of mankind—the visible, concrete, and punitively available protagonists of hateful conscience, yet born to infuriate every fundamentalism they meet up with. And, like the Greeks, the Jews are a people categorically indispensable to western history.

First of all, their tribalism ironically has rescued mankind from tribalism. Greek humanism, encountering acculturation, collapsed into nativistic platonism and Hellenistic despair; but Jews suffered eternally in every acculturative context by striving to reject acculturation. If the choice has seemed staggeringly masochistic, inviting every calamity, it has also been greatly edifying: only the continuous brave spectacle of an intransigent *alternative* culture can force men to discover and acknowledge the reality of culture as such. Epistemologically, science can rise above folklore only through the recognition that two competing culture-hypotheses have similar traditionalist claim to validity—and that every such authoritarian verification technique by mere tradition is wholly inadequate. Culture and neurosis are both largely fossil habit. Some other better grounds for belief than habitual *nomos* must be found, some supra-tribal touchstone for truth, and rational argument must be produced concerning why and how *physis,* re-encountered, compels credence in one contingent hypothesis over another.

The Jew gave cognitive heterosis to Europe. In Europe alone has acute and systematic epistemological sophistication arisen, and for this result were required both Greek and Jew. Each man possessing Greek integrity and humanistic self-respect inevitably seeks the masculine-disciplined world-view of science. But Greeks erroneously supposed that truth emerged from group manhood; Job knew at last that moral reasoning can legislate in no way the laws of nature. Science is a secularized piety toward That Which Is; hypotheses only its man-worded laws. Each man who thinks adaptation to That Which Is both morally and biologically significant, is in this belief a Jew.

Only a Greek could have written *Prometheus Bound,* and only a Jew the *Book of Job.* The one advances the claims of the power-seeking son, the other the power and majesty of the father. But in the dialogue of father and son, the omnipotence and narcissism of both must yield if moral maturity is to arise in either human estate. In another sense, Prometheus asserts the intrinsic and honorable need of the organism; but the Voice out of the whirlwind states the inexorability of the environment, physical and moral. Both the Pleasure Principle and the dignity of man, the Reality Principle and the way things are must be respected and attended to. Only a Greek tragedian could have written the cycle of Oedipus; and only a Moses, the Tables of the Law. The law of human Solons creates oedipal responsibilities; but only a theocratic Law direct from God can provoke fanatic loyalty. The Jew asserts the eternity of the Father, but vainly if he means nomos and not physis; the humanistic Greek vainly, too, if the eternity is that either of father or son. The death of his father is the most dire event in a man's life, for henceforth he must embody his own moral logos.

It is a mistake, however, to suppose that Jews historically were the passive automata of a traditional culture. From Job to modern scientist, the son has kept up a lively dialogue with That Which Is; and inevitably we see in this the deep influence of the legal concept of the *satanas,* the Adversary in the very court of the sheikh-father promulgating the law, and the prophet standing before priest and king. It is not, simply, that urbanized Jews have undergone "natural" selection for intelligence, or even that an urban environment may in fact stimulate psychic vivacity. It is, rather, that all their institutions—legal, mercantile, or rabbinical—have exalted competitive intelligence, which is ethnically another facet of the Jews' functional relationship to the rise of science. Again, in always being part of a dissident minority, and not historically accustomed to the reward for majority conformity, the Jew, in a sense, is "preadapted" to take the minority opinion that each new scientific viewpoint constitutes. That is, within his minority society, the Jewish intellectual is expected to seek, both rationally and argumentatively, the intent and meaning of the Law; what matter that all the Aristotles in history oppose him if the Eternal sustain him, if he have some lone converse with God, some new insight into a law of nature?

Here, to adopt the scientific posture is to become a Jew. Perhaps Jewish intellectualism has constantly an anti-establishment tone, for in compulsiveness of loyalty lies hidden ambivalence and surreptitious private revolt against one's own Jewish humanly impossible orthodoxy piled Pelion on Ossa throughout endless Talmudic maundering on the Torah. The forced habit of fresh assessment by oneself of each mooted issue perhaps also inevitably gives to the Jewish intellectual an anti-authoritarian bias. In learning to cope with the inbuilt fundamentalism of his culture, the Jew has taught others how to deal with fundamentalism in any other mind-imprisoning sphere; certainly complacent fundamentalist minds are invariably deeply disturbed by the inveterate intellectual combativeness of Jews. The enforced moral need of fresh self-assessment of one's integrity in lone battle may also encourage an anti-Pharisaical contempt for protective pretense. Bakan has brilliantly made the point that, for all his stubbornly rational integrity, the liberating spirit of Freud derived significantly from deep libertarian trends in medieval Jewish mysticism.

Again, as Reik has pointed out, "Jewish jokes started with heresies and allusions to timid aggression against the exaggerated demands made in the name of religion and will end with the abolishment of the illusions of religion,"[67] when men become able to take responsibility for their beliefs instead of projecting them outward. Jewish humor and its sources, then, is one part of Jewish leadership in the struggle for a rational and humanistic morality. The superb self-discernment in Jewish humor anticipates and renders feckless and naïve any anti-Semitic judgment. Pride in historic identity is the abrasive whetstone that hones each sharp redefinition of hypothetical new ways of being human. It is the very historicity of Jews that forearms them easily to cope with cognitively changing history; historicity is both the mold and the foil of their anguished and cherished identity. Perhaps only the field-anthropologist, professionally inured to the epistemic stolidity of other tribes, can fully relish this exquisite and endearing quality in the Jewish ethos. Against this, measure the fatuousness of Rome "forgiving" the Jews for millennia of punishment through tendentious anti-Semitic misinterpretation of the trial of Jesus!

Classic Greeks explored the mystique of political brotherhood in the open society of men—but then found humanistic rationalism inadequate. The Hebrews explored the religious mystique of fatherhood—and then had to fight their way out of the intellectual tyranny of authoritarian tribalism. The problem set by our humanity remains. How to accept and how to embody male *authority,* how to express and when to modulate aggressiveness against other men—how, in short, to be father and son, government and citizen—these still remain the towering problems of the oedipal animal. And make no mistake of it: our human nature is built upon volcanoes and the tensions of potential earthquakes, the clear rational mind lies uneasily above archaic Titans fettered beneath in darkness. The relation of fathers and sons is mysterious and terrifying. It has never been rational, nor will it ever be. It is not the only relationship that men must suffer. But father and son form the most critical and dangerous animal relationship on earth, and to suppose otherwise is to invite catastrophe. For it is by no means delivered to us that this species-paradigm will survive annihilation in blind self-slaughter through some displaced pathology of this relationship. No man ever grows beyond the reach of its influence. To maintain that he does is to mask anguish with the coward lie of self-deceiving denial and false indifference. And that anguish is the root of religion, the way we suffer that anguish the secret of who we are.

NOTES

(XVII The Immortal People)

1. J. A. Wilson, *op. cit.*, p. 81.

2. Sarton, *op. cit.*, I:105, 136; J. A. Wilson, *op. cit.*, p. 244.

3. W. F. Albright, *Archaeology and the Religion of Israel* (Baltimore: Johns Hopkins Press, 1941), and *From Stone Age to Christianity, Monotheism and the Historical Process* (Baltimore: Johns Hopkins Press, 1940). Many believe that biblical archeology simply confirms the truth of Holy Writ, as of course it will if that is the intent. The problem is, which rewriting of Holy Writ is thus confirmed? Sardonically citing the most formidably learned biblical prehistorians, the anthropologically trained Rabbi M. L. Zigmond ("Archaeology and the 'Patriarchal Age' of the Old Testament," in Goodenough, *op. cit.*, pp. 571–98) notes that the date of Abraham has been placed all the way from the Middle Bronze I Period of the twenty-first to nineteenth centuries B.C. (Glueck), nineteenth to eighteenth in the Aramaean migration (Noth), 1750 B.C. with the Hurrian migration (Meek) or the Amoritic invasion (Anderson), the eighteenth to seventeenth centuries or else 1650 B.C. (Rowley), seventeenth century (Böhl), c. 1400 B.C. in connection with Hittite and Hyksos movements (Gordon, Schmidtke), after 1350 B.C. (Kaufman), until "c. 1311 (1700?)" (Kraeling)—a range of 800 years! Abraham is also regarded as a shepherd and small cultivator (De Vaux), a merchant prince (Gordon), landowner and farmer (Helling), nomad (Saggs, Speiser), a donkey caravaneer (Albright), a military leader (De Vaux), and a considerable king (Gordon); the problem is complicated by Abraham's relationship to the camel (dromedary, donkey). "The trouble with the Habiru is that they seem to be doing something different on every occasion they are met with (John C. L. Gibson, "Observations on Some Important Ethnic Terms in the Pentateuch," *Journal of Near Eastern Studies*, 20 [1961] 217–38, p. 234). "Perhaps the only safe generalization possible is that the critical orthodoxy of a generation ago, with its apparent certainties and assured results, has gone, but that no new consensus has taken its place" (John Bright, "Modern Study of Old Testament Literature," in G. Ernest Wright [ed.], *The Bible and the Near East: Essays in Honor of William Foxwell Albright*, Garden City: Doubleday, 1961, 13–31, p. 14). Many of the apparent ambiguities would be obviated by the assumption that several Abrahams may be implicated, perhaps discernible in different manuscript cycles, but that the basic Abraham was a nomadic sheikh (patriarch, war leader, judge) and shaman (religious officiant), perhaps occasional bandit-raider of caravans from an oasis-seat (agriculture) and hence "trader" (of the loot). It is not inconsistent with the functions of the ancient shaman that he combine political, military, economic and magic power. We should ignore our differentiated and specialized categories of a later time, in order to perceive a perfectly expectable archaic shaman-sheikh of the Bronze Age.

4. On the Merneptah inscription, the Tel-el-Amarna letter of Abdi-Hiba, Andrew Peto, "The Development of Ethical Monotheism," in W. Muensterberger and S. Axelrad (eds.), *The Psychoanalytic Study of Society* (New York: International Universities Press, 1960, I:311–76, pp. 312–13).

5. Kathleen Kenyon, "Ancient Jerusalem," *Scientific American*, 213 #1 (July 1965) 84–91; and *Archaeology in the Holy Land* (New York: Praeger, 1960).

6. J. A. Wilson, *op. cit.*, pp. 100–1.

7. Diodorus Siculus, xx, 14, 6; cf. Minucius Felix and Tertullian.

8. Two inscriptions from the Tanit precinct at Carthage expressly mention child sacrifice (Harden, *op. cit.*, p. 104).

9. Jeremiah 19:5; I Kings 16:34; II Kings 3:27. See also Peto, *op. cit.*, pp. 335–36. Perhaps "going through the fire" is a ritual relic of this immolation (Leviticus 18:21; II Kings 16:3; and Ezekiel 20:26), on which see Julius Wellhausen, *Prolegomena to the History of Ancient Israel* (New York: Meridian Books, 1957, pp. 403 n 1, and 421). That God required of Abraham a crime, Kierkegaard triumphantly used to prove the distinction of religion and morality (Heller, *op. cit.*, citing Max Brod, *Das Schloss* [Frankfurt-am-Main: S. Fischer, 1964, p. 317], a dramatization of Franz Kafka, *The Castle*. It is, rather, one ethnographic period judging the religious impulses of another. On such grounds one could judge Job a ninny.

10. Theodor Reik, *Mystery on the Mountain;* Géza Róheim, "The Covenant of Abraham," *International Journal of Psycho-Analysis,* 20 (1939) 452–59; Arthur B. Brenner, "The Covenant with Abraham," *Psychoanalytic Review,* 39 (1952) 34–52; Erich Wellisch, *Isaac and Oedipus* (London: Routledge & Kegan Paul, 1954); and R. R. Money-Kyrle, *The Meaning of Sacrifice.* Freud, curiously, sees the oedipal *Akedah* in reverse: instead of the father's not killing the son, the sons do kill the father, whence the origin of guilt and of religion. But why guilt before parricide was a religious crime? And does not projection of current oedipal conflict into the mystic past really serve as a defense mechanism? A Jungian archetype of gene-remembered "original sin" disculpates us all individually, but makes God unjust in punishing us for Adam's sin. The etiological myth masks the biological facts in *each* family. No wonder we need myths about it.

11. Perhaps with Abraham in mind, Heinrich Heine observed that whenever the Jews think something, they declare that God told them so (Reik, *Mystery on the Mountain,* p. 149). However, for reasons elaborated in earlier chapters on human biology, psychodynamically this is not exclusively Jewish but rather a human propensity.

12. The ingenuity used to "explain" circumcision in terms conceptually comfortable to us is remarkable. J. W. M. Whiting ("Effects of Climate on Certain Cultural Practices," in Goodenough, *op. cit.*, pp. 511–44) has an intricate statistical theory that circumcision is related to patrilocal polygyny, rainy tropics and *kwashiorkor* protein-deficiency, the last two hard to apply to desert milk- and meat-eaters—a theory flawed in *being* etic-objectivist: to ignore native emics is the subtlest of ethnocentrisms. The Zipporah episode and perhaps Leviticus 21:6–9 indicate that circumcision was apotropaic, perhaps originally at puberty (Genesis 17:25) as it still is in Southern Arabia (R. Patai, *Society, Culture and Change in the Middle East* (Philadelphia: University of Pennsylvania Press, 1971, pp. 444–59. It is highly significant that the symbolisms of an ancient ethnozoology in which circumcision is rooted are almost obsessively profuse in both Testaments, and elsewhere in the ancient Mediterranean, including Greece (W. La Barre, *They Shall Take Up Serpents,* pp. 78–84, 107). That Christian baptism *specifically replaces* Judaic circumcision in the Pauline New Testament and that baptism symbolizes death and resurrection (Colossians 2:12 and Romans 6:4), the most distinctive features of primitive initiation, additionally confirm the apotropaic nature of these rituals against danger or death. That the symbols and beliefs are "scientifically mistaken" and "incorrect" in our terms means exactly nothing at all: since when have human motivations needed to be rational? Especially when pursuing impossible goals like immortality! It remains only to remark that, significantly, the moving forward from puberty of both circumcision and baptism to shortly after birth replaces the difficult ethical-oedipal mastery with the cremaster or dartos (Genesis 32:32; cf.

easy magical mastery of the problem. Similarly, Christianity replaces with easy pregenital symbolisms (the Eucharistic oral-incorporation of God, baptismal washing away of sin-dirt) the painful, but more relevant, genital mutilation. To be significantly oedipal and ethical, initiation rites should occur at puberty and be genital in symbolism. Cf. Freud, *Moses and Monotheism*, pp. 44–45, and Reik, *Mystery on the Mountain*, pp. 179–80.

13. Through Ishmael, of course, Father Abraham was additionally the father of other nations; although Abraham and Jacob-Israel were not themselves fertility daemons, certainly they were both aided by these spirit-familiars.

14. The rivalry between the herdsman Jacob and the hunter Esau (is Esau hairy because he metamorphizes into an animal familiar? for Jacob must wear skins to similate Esau) recalls the rivalry of the herdsman Abel and the agriculturalist Cain (Genesis 4:2). In this lineage, Tubal and Tubalcain, musician and smith, are even more clearly culture heroes (Genesis 4:21–22). In non-canonical myth Noah the animal-guardian invented the plow, scythe, hoe and other agricultural instruments, but lost the epithet "pious" when he began to cultivate the vine (Ginsberg, *op. cit.*, pp. 67, 79).

15. Wily and vengeful Jacob used *peeled rods* in fertility magic to influence pre-natally color in Laban's flocks (Ginsberg, *op. cit.*, p. 177; for Jewish legends concerning circumcision, pp. 109, 306, 323, 437).

16. Genesis 31:19, and 32:34. Like Jacob's peeled rods, the god-images of Rachel are magic fertility fetishes. The Hebraic "el" was the *numen* or *anima* (personalized spirit), the Canaanite *baal* an object's *genius* or *mana*, in the characterization of T. H. Gaster ("The Religion of the Canaanites," in V. Ferm [ed.], *Forgotten Religions*, New York: Philosophical Library, 1950, pp. 119–20). *Baal* as fertility daemon or "husband" of the land (Hosea, *passim*, and Isaiah 62:4) is an old shamanistic notion. As a divine title, Robertson Smith (*op. cit.*, pp. 101, 108) thinks "baal" entered Arabia with the introduced date palm—a dioecious tree with the sexes in separate trees, requiring fertilization by man's intervention or cherubim wind-spirits, and thus more assimilable to human sexuality and fit candidate for the Tree in Eden. The localized "god of the land" is related to the fertility daemon (e.g. the *el* of the majestic deep ravine at Jabbok)—both close to the fertility-shaman of the Stone Age cave, the Owner and dancing god (e.g., in another late form, Shiva).

17. The Priestly Code, in spite of great disparities, is at pains to have the god of all the patriarchs the same as the post-Babylonian traditional Ark-Tabernacle, Joseph-David bull God of Victory. But the repetition of blessings to Abraham and to Jacob (if genii-loci, geographically far-separated!) and the curious reduplication of the Covenant by Abraham and by Moses, would be less problem if one took the non-theological ethnographic view of separate shamanistic contracts, each with his contemporary power: Abraham with a totemic ram, Jacob and his shamanistic contest with a place-deity, one "Moses" with a serpent in Egypt and the Wilderness, another with a volcanic mountain in Sinai, the Golden Calf, etc. Albright (*Stone Age to Christianity*, pp. 188, 198) notes the marked specificity of references to pre-Yahwistic Hebrew deities as "god of Abraham," "kinsman of Jacob," "champion of Jacob," and observes that "Each Patriarch is represented by Hebrew tradition as choosing his god for himself." That is, *each one was the spirit-familiar of the individual*. Again, from Mosaic time ("Thou shalt not take the name of the Lord thy God in vain") to that of Jesus ("In my name shalt thou case out devils"), the magical power of the god-name is clearly shamanistic.

18. Whether the Jabbok daemon touched the hollow of Jacob's thigh to give him fertility, or Jacob grasped the daemon there to extort the blessing could be argued from the pronouns of Genesis 32:25; but the "sinew that shrank" is plainly

Genesis 24:2 and 9). In any case, the hollow of Jacob's thigh was out of joint, and Jacob got the blessing—from the daemon as he did from his father.

19. A. T. Sandison, "The Study of Mummified and Dried Human Tissues," in Brothwell and Higgs, *op. cit.*, pp. 413–25, p. 422.

20. On legendary motifs in Moses' life see O. Rank, *The Myth of the Birth of the Hero* (New Yodk: Robert Brunner, 1952, pp. 13–15); J. G. Frazer, *Folklore in the Old Testament* (New York: Macmillan, 3 vols., 1919, II:437–55; Red Sea passage and Waters at Meribah, pp. 456–64); Reinach, *Orpheus*, p. 190; Róheim, "The Passage of the Red Sea," *Man*, 23 (1923) 152–55; cf. Lord Raglan, "The Hero of Tradition," in Alan Dundes (ed.), *The Study of Folklore* (Englewood Cliffs: Prentice-Hall, 1965, pp. 142–57). On cherubim cf. R. Patai, *The Hebrew Goddess* (New York: 1967, pp. 101 ff.).

21. Robertson Smith sufficiently demonstrated Hebraic origins in totemism; in fact, the ancient sacrifice—of swine, dogs, mice (Isaiah 65:3 ff., and 66:3, 17; Ezekiel 8:10)—persisted or re-emerged intact in the crisis of the Babylonian Exile (*op. cit.*, pp. 357–59; cf. Porphyrius, *De Abstinentia ab animalibus necandis* (Cantabrigiae: G. Morden, 1655; more accessibly in *Porphyry, on Abstinence from Animal Food* [New York: Barnes & Noble, 1965] iv, 16). The term "totemism" has been bankrupt in any ethnographic sense referring to a specific social structure ever since the exhaustive discussions by Schmidt, Swanton, Wundt, Radcliffe-Brown, Trilles, Rivers, Reuterskiöld, Hocart, Thomas, Graebner, Goldenweiser, Ankermann, Hill-Tout and Boas in Wilhelm Schmidt (ed.), *Das Problem des Totemismus*, in the volumes 9–11 (1914–16) of *Anthropos*. Nevertheless, the *psychiatric* use of "totemism" is still valid to signify the *projection onto animals of social structures and attitudes appropriate only to human beings.* Totemism is the mystique of family and society projected onto animals and plants (W. La Barre, "Totemism," *Encyclopedia Britannica*, 1963, 22:317–20). The displacement to the phobic animal of a child's unmanageable attitudes toward his father is of course thoroughly documented by Freud's "little Hans" and Ferenczi's "little Arpad." A counsel of perfection, but perhaps henceforth no ethnographer should use the term unless he knows what he is talking about phychiatrically.

22. What is lost sight of by naïve theorists is that totemism is a subject *psychiatrically difficult* to think about. Really to understand the paranoia of totemism is to be denuded even of *alternative* institutionalized defense mechanisms: though eternally recurrent in symbol and rite, and heavily dramatized in psychoses and neuroses, the oral-symbolic introjection of the paternal is massively repressed in normal persons, who yet innocently avail themselves of it in their sacred group-neurotic culture.

23. "As Freud pointed out, by giving up animal sacrifices and making God invisible, the Jews transformed him from a material parental image to a spiritual collective superego that, according to Simmel, demanded greater mental sacrifice from the human race than it was ready for. Christianity, by introducing the primitive totem feast in the form of Holy Communion, again allowed some gratification" (John S. Peck, "Ernst Simmel," in F. Alexander, S. Eisenstein, and Martin Grotjahn [eds.], *Psychoanalytic Pioneers*, New York: Basic Books, 1966, 373–83, p. 381). On the significance of Hebraic aniconism and instinctual renunciation, Freud, *Moses and Monotheism*, p. 187; cf. Reik, *Mystery on the Mountain*, p. 163. The supposed aniconism of Islam finds no support in Mohammed's *Koran*, but only in the *Hadith* or traditional sayings of the Prophet. When saying that no angel will enter a house in which there are images, idols are clearly meant, not all realistic representations whatsoever; indeed, Indo-Iranian Moslem art is especially rich in naturalistic portrayal (Ernest J. Grube, *The World of Islam*, New York:

McGraw-Hill, 1966, pp. 11–12). L. B. Patton (*op. cit.*, p. 285) contrasts Indoeuropean naturism and the resultant pantheism with the *baal*-separability and transcendentalism of Yahweh, as a basic conceptual difference in Greek and Hebrew religion.

24. With reference to the Bible, Higher Criticism (the rigorous critique of internal documentary consistency) was first used by Johann Gottfried Eichhorn (J. R. Driver, *An Introduction to the Literature of the Old Testament*, New York: Charles Scribner's Sons, 10th ed. revised and enlarged, 1902, p. 3).

25. On the "Mosaic" theocracy, new conceptions of sacrifice, endowment with cities, and the supposed unity of Israel, Wellhausen, *op. cit.*, pp. 150–51, 157, 159, 234; on the absence of a hierarchy in Hebrew antiquity, p. 5; the possibility of hereditary shamanship in the house of Moses at Dan and Shiloh, p. 143.

26. The J manuscript (Jahvistic) belonged to the Southern Kingdom of Judah; the E (Elohistic) is northern or Ephraimite; the P (Priestly Code) belongs to the period of the Babylonian Captivity (Driver, *op. cit.*, pp. 122, 136; on the contrasting styles, pp. 8, 12). The J and E documents were consolidated about 722 B.C.; they are quasi-parallel and usefully redundant in part. In 621 the D document or core of Deuteronomy ("second law") was mysteriously "discovered" in the Temple at Jerusalem; about 400 B.C. the P or Priestly Code was promulgated in which all pre-existing documents were devised and re-edited (Brenner, *Covenant*, p. 35). The "God of Justice" like the cosmic principle $\delta i\kappa\eta$ of Anaximander seems influenced by the Egyptian *ma'at* and is hardly "Mosaic."

27. Raglan in Dundes, *op. cit.*, p. 153; cf. Wellhausen, *op. cit.*, pp. 287–88 on Elijah; R. Patai, "The Control of Rain in Ancient Palestine," *Hebrew University College Annual*, 14 (1934) 251–86.

28. My view of Moses owes greatly to Peto, *op. cit.*, pp. 317–25, and to Wellhausen, *op. cit.*, pp. 346–47, 354. Interestingly, in view of Moses as a shaman, Jewish legend has it that Yahweh imposed celibacy upon Moses (Ginsberg, *op. cit.*, pp. 399–400, 424; cf. 457, 459). On the "horns" of Moses, S. Freud, "The Moses of Michelangelo," in *Collected Papers*, 4:257–87; on his "shining," Ginsberg, *op. cit.*, pp. 406, 470. In Durkheimian terms, Freud's monotheistic Moses would fit only if an *Egyptian* Moses borrowed an Egyptian Ikhnaton's monotheism (which latter is exactly what Freud did argue); but classic Jerusalemic Priestly monotheism would hardly be expected of village Kenites. At the same time, the "rages" of Moses would seem to fit the stereotypes of the old Semitic visionary shaman or *nabi*.

29. The bitterness of the Hebrew-Philistine conflict was colored by a deep contrast in ethos: the father-centered Hebrew could not tolerate the blasphemy of an incestuous mother-son divine pair that did not know the oedipal father—even though the uniform fate of all these Levantine son-gods was dramatic ritual castration and death in refertilizing the Great Mother (Edith Weigert-Vowinckel, "The Cult and Mythology of the Magna Mater from the Standpoint of Psychoanalysis," *Psychiatry*, 1 [1938] 347–78). It is not only in a disenchantment with many messiahs that Judaism contrasts with Christianity; Jews have a profound ethical reluctance to admit of a son-god beside Yahweh. The West-Semitic son-god did return in the Deutero-Isaiah in the sixth century B.C. but, significantly, as the figure of the Suffering Servant. With characteristic irony, Heine wrote, "No Jew can become a true Christian, for no Jew can ever believe in the divinity of another Jew" (Reik, *Mystery on the Mountain*, pp. 172–74). In psychiatric parlance: no Jew can contemplate the murder of the Father and his replacement by the son. Derivatively: to murder tradition is to murder oneself, the identity and essence of one's Judaism. Even in Christianity, it is the Son who dies in atoning to the Father. Only in a modern era of existentialist anomie and alienation is God him-

self dead. These alternative oedipal paradigms are at the core of political and intellectual history, no less than of religion.

30. A. B. Brenner considers the Akedah a standard primitive initiation rite ("The Great Mother Goddess: Puberty Initiation Rites and the Covenant of Abraham," *Psychoanalytic Review*, 37 [1950] 320–40). Indeed, the shaman-led communal cult of a tutelary deity is only a more developed form of the shaman and his individual familiar (in Americanist terms, initiation into a "medicine society"). Initiation rites are the center of primitive education; in fact much of Judaic ritual is the teaching of tribal lore and traditional history to children, e.g., the question-and-answer catechism in the Passover or Seder ceremonies (Géza Róheim, "Passover and Initiation," *Man*, 23 [1923] 178, and *Covenant of Abraham*, pp. 452–59). In a sense, revelation is an initiation into divine secrets—which the shaman then shares. An individual crisis-revelation becomes a group puberty-rite: males become tribal or ritual brothers when they share the same mystic father-imago and learn the same mythic "facts of life." The magic "blood-brotherhood" sib then becomes the paradigm of the state. Under Moses and his simulacrum in the divine tutelary-spirit sheikh-patriarch, scattered Habiru tribelets become the whole ritual-contractual (Akedah) people of Israel, initiated into the secret society of Yahweh-worshipers.

31. In the 1930s the suggestion of the date 1475–1400 B.C. for the Exodus made by Garstang and Jack was generally accepted; but prevailing opinion now is that the oppression occurred under Rameses II (c. 1299–1232 B.C.), and the Exodus at the accession of his successor Merenptah when a famous stele records revolts in Gezer and Ashkelon (James, *Sky God*, p. 45). Psalm 104 strikingly resembles Ikhnaton's hymn to the Sun, in part word for word; as to any influence of Egyptian monotheism on Moses, it should be kept in mind that the dates of Ikhnaton IV are 1375–1358 B.C.

32. J. A. Wilson, *op. cit.*, p. 260.

33. Theologically, we cannot know which god of which tribe at which time is the true god, only ethnographically that a given tribe had a given god at a given time. As to changing views of god epistemologically, in folkloristic terms the past *explains* the present, not the reverse; to suppose past tradition *sustains* present folklore requires retrospective falsification of revelation. We believe what we believe about the Unknown partly for historical reasons, and partly for projective psychological, not cognitive reasons. Cognitive science is essentially anti-historical; it seeks ahistorical validities on grounds of *present* testing, not of traditional authority or of sacred *past* revelation. More than any other, this epistemological shibboleth of *ground for belief* critically distinguishes the adult mind from the infantile authoritarian personality.

34. Wellhausen, *op. cit.*, pp. 172–187; Peto, *op. cit.*, p. 332.

35. On the origin of the Davidic state in Bedouin-like Habiru brigandage, and final establishment athwart the ancient trade route, see Karl Kautsky, *Foundations of Christianity* (New York: International Publishers, 1925, pp. 213–15); on Jewish origins in general, pp. 188, 212, 214, 220, 229–30.

36. Peto, *op. cit.*, pp. 332–33.

37. As Kautsky notes (*op. cit.*, p. 237), "It is precisely during the time of the Exile, at the lowest point in their humiliation and despair, that this peculiar feeling of superiority over the rest of humanity first appears among the Jews."

38. The Tower of Babel legend is ultimately Sumerian—but while the Sumerians interestingly regarded man's fall as due to jealousy among the gods, the Hebrews characteristically saw in it Elohims' jealousy of man's wish to be like gods (S. N. Kramer, *op. cit.*, p. 223). A naturalistic explanation: the brickwork on the top

of the Birs-Nimrod (ancient Borsippa) *ziggurat,* known locally as the Tower of Babel, is vitrified into a porcelain-like mass and great blocks of it are blasted about, which may have been caused by lightning (Seton Lloyd, "Building Brick and Stone," in Singer, *op. cit.,* I:456–94, p. 468). Frazer, *Folklore in the Old Testament* discusses parallel stories of the Creation (I:3–5), the Fall (I:45–77), the Flood (I:104–46), and the Tower of Babel (I:362–77). Cf. R. Graves and R. Patai, *Hebrew Myths* (New York: Doubleday 1964, pp. 125 ff.).

39. The *satanas* or "adversary" was a legal functionary in the court of the traditional sheikh presiding as judge, a sort of "devil's advocate" or protagonist of the accused (Margaret B. Crook, *The Cruel God: Job's Search for the Meaning of Suffering,* Boston: Beacon Press, 1959, p. 11).

40. To understand Job is to take a long step toward understanding the Jew. The *satan,* not yet a defiant power in his own right, in the ancient story still functions within the heavenly court. The satan implies "Small wonder Job is pious, for look at the rewards for his piety!"—his family, wealth, servants, etc. In making his case the satan is here a tester of Job's integrity, through ordeals. But the suffering Job, proud in the conviction of his righteousness, would take God to task for injustice. Eliphaz counsels: You invite punishment; no man can bring a charge against God and win; humbly submit your case. Bildad: You presume too far; recognize the authority of the fathers and desist. Job, ironically, "Am I Leviathan?" (Why does He not pick on someone his own size?) Bildad, mis-understanding, thinks Job is talking blasphemously as God's equal. Zophar, bril-liantly, with the self-assurance of one steeped in knowledge, can point out to others, often derisively, the limits of their knowledge of God, but sometimes crosses these lines himself. Job: Does not God watch over man? Does not human suffering have a claim to His attention? There is no equity, no ruling hand directs the universe? Then there is no difference between God's persecuting me and the acts of wicked men! And God answers, mightily, out of the whirlwind.

41. Job's placing himself on an equal level with God in judging what is right, and what wicked, is his wrong relationship to That Which Is, and his sin (Meyer Fortes, *Oedipus and Job,* p. 17). Fortes applies these mythic figures to African materials as alternative paradigms in a typical social-anthropological exercise that exemplifies the same Frazerian irrelevance social anthropologists criticize. Mindful of the Greeks, I would rather see the Job-God colloquy as the dialogue between presumptuous cultural man and his physical environment: the organism ar-rogantly supposing it knows both ultimate nomos and physis, and calling upon reality to behave according to the organism's concepts and need. (But this is not the original meaning!)

42. Joseph Klausner, *The Messianic Idea in Israel, From its Beginning to the Completion of the Mishna* (New York: Macmillan, 1955).

43. T. J. Meek, *Hebrew Origins* (New York: Harper, rev. ed., 1960, p. 36).

44. On the psychological traits of the prophets, see Peto, *op. cit.,* pp. 344, 346, 355, 365–66; on their times, Reinach, *Orpheus,* pp. 193–96, and Wellhausen, *op. cit.,* pp. 397–402, 420–21.

45. Pharisaical fanatic Sabbatarianism was already criticized by as good a Jew as Jesus. The Stoic Seneca condemned the Sabbath because through observing it one lost a seventh part of a life of work (quoted by St. Augustine, *De civitate dei,* vi, 11); certainly the Protestant ethic turned Sunday into a dour stoic punish-ment and refrainment from all pleasure. But the Jewish Sabbath was a time of family congregation and holiday rejoicing. It might be argued that the day of rest, in later times, has been the starting point of emancipation of oppressed serfs from feudal to modern industrial times.

46. Strict Sabbatarianism brought difficulties already to the Maccabean armies:

having experienced the peril of not fighting on the Sabbath, they then discriminated between offensive and defensive warfare. But Pompey took mean advantage even of this; he raised an offensive earthwork but kept his Roman soldiers from fighting on the Sabbath, still to the Jews' disadvantage (Josephus, *Bellum Judaicum,* I, vii, 3). Nevertheless rigid Sabbatarianism proliferated in later history. Karaites said it was unlawful to light a candle on Friday night, for the *consequence* of this work, burning, would extend into the Sabbath; therefore his followers sat in darkness, for so they interpret Exodus 35:3 (*Hastings Encyclopedia* 7:663). Among Jerusalemic Jews of the last century, fingernails were to be cut early in the week, lest the supposedly excess work of *beginning to regrow* should occur on the Sabbath (*Folklore,* 15 [1904] 187).

47. Deuteronomy knows only two laws, the Decalogue and the statutes Moses received on Mount Horeb (Wellhausen, *op. cit.,* p. 370), but the Priestly recension interpolated in the Pentateuch an extraordinary number of new laws. Rabbinical commentaries, and commentaries on commentaries, elaborated one of these, "Thou shalt not seeth a kid in its mother's milk"—originally a simple injunction not to practice a certain heathen Canaanitish rite—into a fantastic set of taboos about milk and meat dishes. The ultra-orthodox have continued to compete with one another in invidious holiness. The N'tureî Kartá "Guardians of the City" group in modern Jerusalem even excludes other orthodox Jews and has retired into a new self-chosen ghetto, Mea Shearim, within this all-Jewish city. Their conviction of merit and prestige sometimes seems in neighborly eyes to derive from casuistrics. For example, the prohibition against "marring" the edges of the beard (Leviticus 19:27) is thought to be limited by a restatement (Leviticus 21:5) against "shaving" the edges of their beards, hence anything except a razor may be used to *trim* the beard, and *blunt* scissors are used as being farthest from a razor. They do not carry a handkerchief but wind it around the belt, since the prohibition against work on the Sabbath occurs in the *same chapter* (Exodus 35) which orders the building of the Tabernacle, said activities being discriminated by rabbinical commentaries into thirty-nine categories one of which was carrying objects—but the handkerchief must never be knotted, since tying knots on the *Sabbath* is one of the thirty-nine prohibitions. To be sure, the handkerchief is not actually mentioned in the Talmud and every day is not the Sabbath; but a sixteenth-century compilation, *Shulḥán Arúkh,* explains it should be worn "below the outer garment" which, being interpreted, therefore means not knotted but wound around the belt. Men do not shake hands with women, and a husband may not look his wife in the face; in intercourse, which cannot take place in any visible light unless both parties are dressed, a special method obviates this (Edmund Wilson, *Red, Black, Blond and Olive,* New York: Oxford University Press, 1956, pp. 436–39).

48. In the fine modern Hotel Deborah of Tel Aviv, elevator buttons may not be touched (=work) on the Sabbath, so elevators are pre-set before this day to stop and open and close, automatically, at each floor, all day, both going up and down. Since stoves can continue to operate if turned on before the Sabbath, all food is cooked before Friday night and left to simmer. *Halakha* forbids tearing toilet tissue on the Sabbath, so each Friday afternoon maids put white baskets with pre-separated sheets in each room. Lights are turned off and on by electric clocks (but would their action not be a Sabbath *consequence* of clock-making or pre-setting work done at another time?). Of course one may not check in or out or pay charges on the Sabbath. In these circumstances, only irony and humor can serve against turning life into dour puritanism! But, characteristically, this irony is found even in the Talmud (E. Wilson, *op. cit.,* pp. 449–50). Many American Jews, indeed, consider that turning modern Israel into an exclusive theocratic state constitutes "racism" in reverse.

49. Wellhausen, *op. cit.,* p. 153.

50. Wellhausen, *op. cit.,* pp. 52, 56, 63–64, 67, 78.

51. Wellhausen, *op.cit.,* p. 215; cf. p. 227.

52. Géza Róheim, *Passover and Initiation,* p. 178.

53. Wellhausen, *op. cit.,* pp. 91–93. For the notion that a god cannot be worshiped outside his own land, I Samuel 26:19; Hosea 9:4; cf. Ezekiel 8:12 (cited by Robertson Smith, *op. cit.,* p. 93)—a position consistent with the old placedaemon or "husband of the land "=paleolithic shaman>fertility daemon.

54. Wellhausen, *op. cit.,* p. 108.

55. Kautsky, *op. cit.,* pp. 205–7, 246–48.

56. The Jews could not maintain the use of Hebrew even in Palestine but took the language of the people around them, Aramaic, which was that of the common people like Jesus (who, incidentally, made the pun not on Greek *petros,* "rock," on which the Roman Church at least claims to be founded), but in Aramaic, in which the name of Petrus was Cephas, "rock" (John 1:42; Matthew 16:18). In the third century B.C. the Jews of Alexandria translated their sacred books into Greek, since few of them understood Hebrew; it was religion, and to a lesser degree commercial activity, not language, that was the strongest bond among Jews.

57. On Julius Caesar versus the Roman Republic and Jerusalem, Kautsky, *op. cit.,* pp. 111–13.

58. In the Roman Diaspora, Jews reached a fantastic scattering. For example, in the seventeenth century Ricci discovered an "orphan colony" of about a dozen families of Jews in remote China who recognized religious pictures and had a scroll of the Law about 500 years old, some of whom could read their several copies of the Torah in old Hebrew characters, who circumcised, and abstained from eating pork (A. M. Hyamson, "China (Jews in)," *Hastings Encyclopedia,* 3:556–60; James Finn, *The Jews in China* (London: B. Wertheim, 1843), and *The Orphan Colony of Jews in China* (London: Nisbet, 1872). Some authorities say they came in the reign of the Han emperor Ming Ti (56–78 A.D.), others say with Tamerlane, but Laufer thinks that about 70 families came between 960 and 1126 from Persia and India by sea. They reverenced Esther (*Issetha Mama*) and called theirs the *Tiao-chin Chiao* or "Pluck-Sinew Religion" that worshiped *Etunoi* (Adonai). The best and summarizing source is William Charles White, *Chinese Jews* (Toronto: University of Toronto Press, 3 vols., 1943, I. Historical; II. Inscriptional; and III. [with the collaboration of R. J. Williams] Genealogical). Again, Jewish merchants visited Japan at least 1000 years ago; and Jews were among the sixteenth-century traders when the port of Nagasaki was opened to them; in 1945, an atomic bomb destroyed a Jewish cemetery near the present granite pillar memorializing the holocaust, the last trace of a Jewish colony there (*New York Times,* 3 August 1964). An analytical survey of the total Diaspora as it exists today after progressive dispersal since Roman times, and a partial reversal since the establishment of Israel in 1948, can be found in R. Patai, *Tents of Jacobi: The Diaspora Yesterday and Today* (Englewood Cliffs: Prentice-Hall, 1971).

59. David Bakan, *Sigmund Freud and the Jewish Mystical Tradition* (New York: Schocken Books, 1965, p. 132).

60. A fresh assessment of Freud's *Beyond the Pleasure Principle* is by Herbert Marcuse, *Eros and Civilization* (Boston: Beacon Press, 1955).

61. Bakan, *op. cit.,* pp. 244–45.

62. Warner Muensterberger, "Remarks on the Function of Mythology," in Muensterberger and Axelrad, *op. cit.,* 3 (1964) 94–97; cf. Zimmern, *op. cit.,* p. 84 n 2.

63. Arthur B. Brenner, "Some Psychoanalytic Speculations on Anti-Semitism,"

Psychoanalytic Review, 35 (1948) 20–32. See also E. Simmel, "Anti-Semitism and Mass Psychopathology," in E. Simmel (ed.), *Anti-Semitism, A Social Disease* (New York: International Universities Press, 1946, ch. III, pp. 33–78); R. M. Loewenstein, "The Historical and Cultural Roots of Anti-Semitism," in Muensterberger and Axelrad, *op. cit.*, 1 (1947) 313–56; and Otto Fenichel, "Psychoanalysis of Antisemitism," *American Imago*, 1, #2 (1940) 24–39.

64. Carl C. Seltzer, "The Jew: His Racial Status," in Earl W. Count (ed.), *This Is Race* (New York: Henry Schuman, 1950, pp. 608–18).

65. Morris Joseph, quoting Halevi in "Halevi," *Hastings Encyclopedia*, 6:478–89, p. 479.

66. Louis Wirth, *The Ghetto* (Chicago: University of Chicago Press, 1956, p. 18).

67. Joseph M. Natterson, "Theodor Reik," in Alexander, Eisenstein and Grotjahn, *op. cit.*, 249–64, p. 262; see also Theodor Reik, *Jewish Wit* (New York: Gamut Press, 1962). In dynamic relation to the antinomian uses of wit, Jewish tradition (curiously like Freud) at times even roundly approves of transgression of the literal law, in the interest of common sense and independent judgment. In the Talmud, for example, Resh Lakish blessed Moses for courage in smashing the Tables of the Law, to keep the children of Israel from putting them to bad use (Ernst Simon, "Sigmund Freud, the Jew," *Leo Baeck Institute Yearbook*, 2 [1957] 207–305). There was also the story of the Hasidic rabbi who chopped wood on the Sabbath to help a poor widow; he died of course, but "by this sacrilegious action, they said, he ascended even higher" (Reik, pp. 106–7). The Old Testament calls the Jews a stiff-necked people. But even the rationalization is wryly traditional. "Since Jacob wrestled with God [says Reik], they continue to challenge their deity towards whom they remained unfailingly recalcitrant." The Hellenist Gilbert Murray well understood the Jew in describing him "at once the child of tradition and a rebel against it" (Reik, 209–10).

Old Testament studies have undergone many revolutions since the Higher Criticism. Meticulous archeological and historical studies have placed Babylonian, Canaanite, Egyptian and other foreign influences in better perspective. Tell el-Amarna produced datable documents for Old Testament comparison, as the Scrolls did especially for the New; and Ugaritic Ras Shamra tablets recovered since 1929 show Hebrew Psalm parallels closer than those of Babylonian or Egyptian texts. Throughout, Robertson Smith's concern with origins has indicated that ritual (e.g. sacrifice-communion) is exceedingly conservative, with more *continuity* (my own view) than is apparent from Wellhausen. Mowinckel's "situation in life" approach adds a certain ethnographic realism to mere textual criticism. And the Yahwist writer may have organized the "Priestly" rationale from the beginning; for monotheism, or at least henotheism, lies deep in Hebrew tradition.

I wish to thank Professors Raphael Patai and Mac Linscott Ricketts for criticisms I have sought to respond to in this chapter. An anthropologist without expertise in modern Semitology, I am aware of but do not control the mass of polemic reinterpretation. The ethnographer is here, if ever, an object lesson in the limitations of ethnography. What blood-brother rite can confer *cultural* membership? No outsider can ever become, above all, an honorary Jew. Interest, respect, study notwithstanding, to be densely ignorant of another tradition not lived through is to be expected. To make even gross errors in interpretation is easy. But one can never be in error in his admiration for Greek and Jew.

Epilogue

GREEK and Jew contrast sharply in Temple and Parthenon, in the Mosaic Tables of the Law and the trilogy of Sophocles. But both are rooted in the oedipal condition of man, the biological conflict of the generations. Greeks emphasized the organic Inside, the self, the humanistic, the mortal body, the Pleasure Principle; and Christ the Son is the endpoint of a Greek tradition beginning with the *koros* and the *ephebe* as the social cynosure. Jews asserted fervent loyalty to the Outside, the Not-Self, the divine environment, That Which Is, the Reality Principle; and from beginning to end they exalt God the Father and the parentalism of the orient. Hellenes, first to last, in a sense were shamanic: and from Zeus to Hermes Trismegistus the only divinity remained the human and manlike in earth and sky. Hebrews alone have taught the necessary separateness from man of That Which Is, the non-human environment, as Job learned. The eternal discreteness in total reality of environment and organism, fact and wish, is the epistemic inheritance of Europe, the ethos and morality of secular science. Humanism was born in Greece, but the ultimate error of Plato was to suppose subjective paradigm had objective existence.

Paul, another vatic with inchoate ego boundaries, achieved only a paranoid identification of the divine Hebraic Father with the divinized Hellenistic Son; it is his own paranoid pathology projected, and he aids us very little in understanding human fathers and sons. Another tender-minded platonist, Plotinus, would abolish the whole material world in his worship of the sacred subjective male principle. Like Paul, Plotinus is an endpoint of the Platonic sickness, which whines that the worst evil to the soul is its connection with the body. But though they both persist in an oedipal apperception of the world, neither Greek nor Jew can ignore the mother. Whatever their spiritual connection, the reality of father and son is material, their inescapable vexatious bond and battle-ground is Materia.

The significance of Hebraic monotheism is socially profound in moral effect. If there is but one God, our Father, then all men must be brothers. At the same time, if God is a single person, then man's relation to him can regain the intensity and immediacy of a child's relation to his father. In the concept of an incorporeal deity is a God who cannot be killed, who never dies[1] and, not represented by a tangible idol, who could not be broken or repudiated or destroyed or evaded. No female consort was associated with the Hebrew father-god, and oedipal conflict was thus muted. Since the father had never repressed adult sexuality in his sons, but on the contrary bade them be fruitful and multiply, Judaism does not suffer from ascetic anti-sexuality.[2] Identification is with a paternal fertility daemon who promised and gave the patriarchs Abraham and Jacob progeny.

The heresy-treason of the Pauline Son against the Hebraic Father, however, is massively guilt-ridden. To it is joined the asexuality of Christ and of his earthly vicar, monastic asceticism, and (from the fourth century onward) priestly celibacy. The pervasive Christian anti-sexuality developed, also, from the struggle against earlier fertility religions of the Mother, ancient in the eastern Mediterranean. In escaping the literal castration of the son-gods in the worship of the Magna Mater, Pauline Christianity also gave up the token sacrifice of circumcision to the Hebraic Yahweh, but was left with functional moral castration. But desexualization had also to accompany the new Mother. The great fertility goddess of the Levant was transfigured into the Virgin. Where once the mother was ruled out of the familial trinity in older Hebraism, in Christianity Joseph is the father denied the dignity of human fatherhood—and is replaced by the messenger bird, Aphrodite's dove, bringing Logos from the Father to the Virgin's ear. Christianity, then, has abolished sexuality in Jesus, Joseph, and Mary. All that is left is the Holy Ghost.

Closeness to the Father demanded obedience, but allowed identification and manhood; the good man Job had wealth and many children. Closeness to the Mother requires asexuality, and gives dependency at the price of eternal infantilization. In dubious battle, the familial Trinity is fragmented, one member or the other denied. But symbolic denial in myth is not to resolve the problem. In Melville's quarrel with God the oedipal logic is not shirked—for "if we obey God, we must disobey ourselves; and it is in this disobeying ourselves, wherein the hardness of obeying God consists."[3] And for Melville at last a mutilated promethean

Ahab is sunk with all his crew, except for the forsaken and alienated Ishmael; and Leviathan still swims the seas.

One's problem in reading modern theologians is that, beneath all the turgidity and self-ignorance, there are only disguised clinical autobiographies, and these certainly written with none of the subtlety and grace of literary artists. The same difficulty attends assessing the theologians' often violently different views on the meaning of the Dead Sea Scrolls. On these recently found documents, at no great distance in time from the origins of Christianity, many scholars have now voluminously expressed themselves.[4] But as they have so indulged their biases, I may be privileged to expose my own. It seems to me that certain of these scholars do not really welcome the documents, since in general effect the Scrolls tend to minimize the supernatural uniqueness of Jesus. Hence they seek strenuously to separate a character they must needs preserve charismatic, from his obvious secular origins. Others, like myself, take delight in the increased ethnographic relevance and historic plausibility of this important culture hero of early Europe.

We can discern men very much like ourselves at the dawn of Christianity, along with all the familiar types of reaction to acculturative stress and unease in the four crisis sects of Judaism: the Establishment tory, the detached cynic, the drop-out, and the True Believer. Quite characteristic of ghost dance periods is the development of sometimes violent sectarianism, as these types of men join with one another and do battle with the others. Josephus on the Jewish Wars reads like a modern newspaper. In his account, the Sadducees were a sophisticated and urbane group, representing nobility and wealth and power, engrossed in worldly political and practical affairs. Sadducees rejected belief in angels and spirits (Acts 28:8) as well as the Pharisaical doctrines of the Davidic Messiah and the resurrection of the body, as prophetic notions both, and plainly in conflict with the Torah. Though a relatively small group, the Sadducees were entrenched in the Temple until about 50–60 A.D., when the reactionary Pharisees wrenched power from them.[5] The rationalist Sadducees are an honorable and legitimate ancestor of Reformed Jewry.

The Zealots[6] were men of direct military action, in the secular messianic tradition of the Jews, in spirit the first Zionists so to speak—as opposed to the Essenes, a contemplative and scholarly monastic order that chose a Hellenistic retreat from the world to await the Teacher of Righteousness. The Jesus of the earlier gospels showed elements of Zealot and Essene alike, but was apart from both. Of lowly artisan origin, and not himself a priest, he was vigorously critical of the priestly Pharisaical group and their excessive post-Babylonian sabbatarianism.

In this, Jesus was in a sense the end of a long line of Jewish prophets preaching reform. This prophetic Jesus must be accounted capable of error, however, since the imminent supernatural Kingdom of God, if indeed he predicted it, has not yet arrived. Unfortunately for our assessment of him, the earliest gospels, Mark (written between 60 and 65 A.D.) and Matthew (67 A.D.) leave at best some thirty years between the death of Jesus and these first records of his life.

Albert Schweitzer's defense of this Jesus against critics of his sanity[7] would seem logically impregnable. These critics, not holding to the most authentic sources, Mark and Matthew, as proper scholarly method would dictate, would instead "bring together everything which is said in the four Gospels, collectively, and then sit in judgment on a personality which is in reality fictitious and consequently cannot be pronounced abnormal."[8] But in the psychiatric defense of Jesus through such higher criticism, both the infallibility of Scripture is impugned and the "historical" Jesus begins to recede. Significantly, it is from St. John's gospel that the main arguments for the mental unsoundness of Jesus are drawn. It is John, then, an innovative and ecstatic figure, whose gospel is the most difficult to bring into synoptic agreement; it is John on whom is based the projective figure of an unhistorical and psychiatrically dubious Jesus. Thus, so runs Schweitzer's argument, only this legendary Jesus can be paranoid.

Of course any argument based on the mythological and metaphysical Jesus of Paul too would be similarly invalid in attacking an "historical" Jesus. A very considerable difficulty is that Paul never knew Jesus, and either did not know or combatted the testimony of the Jerusalemic group that had known him, but instead made up through personal revelation his own version of the Christ. Paul's Christ is not historical. It remains only to note that of the fourteen supposedly "Pauline" epistles, computer analysis of style (by the Reverend A. Q. Morton of the Church of Scotland and Professor G. H. C. MacGregor of the University of Glasgow)[9] reveals that only five epistles were actually written by Paul, and the rest by at least five other authors.

Repeated historic traumata to the Jews meant that the tradition dominant at the destruction of the Temple in 70 A.D., under these blows gradually solidified into Orthodoxy. Whereas the European trend since the Renaissance has been more and more to secularize all departments of human life—education, scholarship, law and the state, with progress equivalent to emancipation from Rome and to imitation of Florence where modern man was born—by contrast, the Jewish Orthodox ideal has been to bring life more and more under the rule of religious observance.

This ideal was already consolidated in the medieval rabbinical period, during the desperate struggle of a minority to stay alive. A parallel to this theocratic trend may be found in Islam, a late prophet-inspired Semitism dating from the seventh century A.D.

It was the fourth sect of crisis Hebraism that chiefly survived in Judaism. Pharisaism emerged in the Maccabean conflict with surrounding heathenisms and was influential from the time of John Hyrcanus (135–105 B.C.) onward. Pharisaism was the major influence on the development of orthodox Judaism, which took its permanent character in the rabbinical system.[10] The compulsive-obsessive Priestly-Pharisaical system is shown in the mushroom-like proliferation of the Law. The authentic beginnings of the Law in Moses are modest, adequate, and limited: the Decalogue and the Mount Horeb statutes. Priestly Pharisaism essentially began with the post-exilic recension of the Pentateuch, and has continued with medieval rabbinical commentaries on the Talmud into modern times.

Christianity took its tradition separated from Judaism in the teachings of Paul.[11] Though his original name was that of the mighty first king of the Hebrews, the apostle Paul was a pathetically unprepossessing man, small, bowlegged, blind in one eye, and he apparently also suffered from a slight deformity of the trunk. He had a speech defect, was epileptic, and had violently murdered his brother while in an evidently epileptic-equivalent state, and on his own testimony had severe sexual problems (Romans 4:14). He was unmarried and had nothing sexually to do with women, whom he hated and feared, although he accepted money, food and shelter from them. In personality, Paul was doctrinaire and bigoted. In behavior, he was vindictive, bitter, jealous, masochistic, hypochondriacal, timorous and cravenly submissive to authority, irascible with colleagues, and in the Scriptural account quarrelsome even with a fatherly benefactor. Only the gentle and effeminate Timothy was able to tolerate Paul for any length of time. A number of psychiatrists have discussed Paul's passive homosexual trends.[12]

Paul had not been a disciple of Jesus,[13] had never even known him, and earlier had himself persecuted Christians. Although he was a Pharisee of the Pharisees at first, Paul had a conversion in connection with an epileptic seizure some time after the Crucifixion. But it was a conversion to his own self-created notion of Christianity. All sources agree that he was not taught or converted by any of the original community of disciples living in Jerusalem. Paul's dogma derived from hearsay and his own personal revelations, and it was Paul's doctrine that eventually replaced the teaching of the Jerusalemic group. They had known Jesus, but taught "another Jesus" than, according to Paul himself, did Paul; and Paul in time successfully subverted their sect with his differing direct revelation from God. Christianity is thus not historically continuous with Christ, or, more precisely with Jesus of Nazareth, in all the teachings of Paul.

Paul's preaching to the Gentiles, heretical and obnoxious to the main body of Jerusalemic Christians, might well have disappeared after his death in Rome (to which he had fled about 55 A.D.) except for one cataclysmic event—the total destruction of Jerusalem in 70 A.D., when the Essene-like Jewish Christians of Jerusalem disappeared from history. A Hellenized Jew, Paul repudiated the religion of his forefathers, renounced ritual circumcision, and completely transformed the traditional Jewish concept of the messiah. Paul was largely uninformed about or ignored the still-remembered tradition of Jesus' ministry in Palestine, but through industrious travel and writing he promulgated the teaching of his own personal sect.

In rejecting Judaic aspects of the Jewish Jesus and his group, especially the unpleasant but basic Jewish rite of circumcision, the opportunistic Paul made his Christ acceptable to the Gentiles. He did this by incorporating a mixed ideology compounded of non-Hebraic Semitic (Syrian), Egyptian Gnostic, neoplatonic and Greek Mystery elements— all already current and commonly known in the Hellenistic world of his time, but entirely alien to the Nazarene teaching in the Gospels. Paul was quite familiar with the platonic Noble Lie (Romans 3:7) and boldly proclaimed his own: that the Messiah had succeeded by failing, that he had died but not died, that he was actually God sacrificed to God, and that through faith in this new Mystery all mortals would share his immortal godhood. All these fantasies were thoroughly un-Jewish, indeed preposterous and blasphemous in Judaic terms. They were also preposterous and blasphemous in classic Greek terms.

The great Hellenic and Hebraic culture traditions, here both grossly distorted, melded in the turbid and sick mind of Paul. Paul placed no emphasis on the life and works of Jesus, for he knew little of either, but only on faith in the mystery of his sacrificial death, a faith invented and promulgated by Paul. Paul simply appropriated Jesus and made him the vehicle of his own personal revelation. In a curiously masochistic identification with his Messiah, Paul proclaimed that Christ was a human sacrifice that God commanded to mollify God's wrath (Romans 3:25). If Abraham had abolished human sacrifice of the Firstborn, and later Jews had abolished even animal sacrifice, Paul restored human sacrifice —but now with a jumble of symbolisms of the archaic scapegoat, Paschal lamb, the murdered son-god of the Great Mother, and the Orphic Dying God who was eaten to confer immortality! In this, Pauline Christianity lacks entirely the self-consistency inherent in the style of any authentic culture; it is a typical ghost-dance *mélange adultère de tout*. The difference, in this case, is that the documents, including his own, are voluminous enough for us to discern the sick man who made this curiously eclectic selection of the available folklore. No theologian since ever has or ever can make sense of the mixture as godly truth, most especially the relationship in time and in nature of God the Father and God the Son. The amalgam is simply Paul's personal neurosis, approachable not super-natural-historically but only clinically and ethnographically. It is of course quite impossible to "believe" it, unless one succeed in exactly replicating Paul's personal pathology.

Hesiod could never reconcile the two alien sets of gods in his *Theogony,* nor could Greek history finally abide peaceably with both. But at least Hesiod tried manfully to preserve all the folklore he could, contradictory or not. But the tamperings with the Old Testament in a clumsy attempt to erase old Hebraic history and to make of it one homogenized whole must be a vexation to the historic Jew. But, worse, the New Testament is explicitly a hopeless ghost-dance tangle of conflicting ethnologies and culture heroes over which Christians can argue endlessly. Its false "problems" can only be solved by new improvisation. It is not worth intellectual attention as a potential source of truth or belief. Rather than continuing to theologize upon its themes—that is, to improvise one's own liberal-Modernist fantasies *ad hoc* and *ad lib*—it seems to me more reasonable to approach Scripture as an objective ethnographic document, more useful to discriminate in its many time-strata the timeless struggle of humans with their humanity, and yet to discern the unbroken and unmysterious ethnographic continuity of the modern European with Stone Age man. I have tried also to understand the psychological reasons for the animistic projections, the displacements and disguises of vatic shamans however charisma-laden, and the pseudo-profundities of theologians, and yet to return faithfully to what they were originally talking about: the facts of life and death, fathers and sons.

Old Stone Age man had to imagine magic because he was so feeble and frightened a little animal to hunt behemoth beasts, as he had to do to stay precariously alive. And Neolithic man sorely needed religions with comforting and protective cosmic parents, because there gaped so terrifying a chasm between his needs and his knowledge of the world and of himself. But today, protected by the technical accomplishments of his many brave dead fathers, can not man now know and accept his nature and his limitations with equanimity, and receive with cool confidence and gladly the legacy of his manhood, without any antic self-cozening ghost dance? Can Atomic Age man afford any less?

NOTES
(Epilogue)

1. As a principle necessary to explain the existence of life, God the Father died on November 24, 1859. On that day was published Charles Darwin's book *On the Origin of Species by Means of Natural Selection; or, the Preservation of Favoured Races in the Struggle for Life* (London: J. Murray, 1859).

2. Reik, *Mystery on the Mountain*, p. 150; Brenner, *Covenant*, pp. 37–38.

3. Melville, *op. cit.*, p. 60.

4. J. M. Allegro, *The Dead Sea Scrolls* (Baltimore: Pelican Books, 1956); Millar Burrows, *The Dead Sea Scrolls* (New York: Viking Press, 1956); F. M. Cross, Jr., *The Ancient Library of Qumran* (Garden City: Doubleday Anchor Books, revised, 1961); A. Powell Davies, *The Meaning of the Dead Sea Scrolls* (New York: New American Library, 1956); A. Dupont-Sommer, *The Dead Sea Scrolls: A Preliminary Survey* (Oxford: B. Blackwell, 1952), *The Jewish Sect of Qumran and the Essenes: New Studies on the Old Dead Sea Scrolls* (New York: Macmillan, 1955), and *The Essene Writings from Qumran* (New York: Meridian Books, 1961); Theodor H. Gaster, *The Dead Sea Scriptures in English Translation* (Garden City: Doubleday Anchor Books, 1956); R. K. Harrison, *The Dead Sea Scrolls: An Introduction* (New York: Harper Torchbooks, 1961); G. Vermes, *The Dead Sea Scrolls in English* (Harmondsworth: Pelican Books, 1962); and, a layman for laymen, Edmund Wilson, *The Scrolls from the Dead Sea* (New York: Oxford University Press, 1956).

5. G. H. Box, "Sadducees," *Hastings Encyclopedia*, 11:43–46, pp. 44–45.

6. S. G. F. Brandon, *Jesus and the Zealots*, *The Trial of Jesus*, and *The Zealots*.

7. Georg de Loosten, Hirsch, Binet-Sanglé, and E. Rasmussen, *op. cit.*, in Schweitzer, *Psychiatric Study of Jesus*.

8. Albert Schweitzer, *Out of My Life and Thought* (New York: Henry Holt, 1933, p. 89). The elegant scholarship of the late Albert Schweitzer in his lengthy *Quest of the Historical Jesus* evokes only admiration, but even more admirable is his rockbound intellectual integrity. Despite earnest yearning he found Him not, had the clarity and integrity to know he had not, and the moral courage to state he had not. The subsequent masochism of flight to Lambaréné of this severely compulsive personality and adornment of European civilization was punishment enough for the discovery; but as an existentialist moral statement and social sublimation it is above criticism and can not be contemned.

9. "St. Paul and the Computer," *Scientific American*, 201, ⚹1 (January 1964) 56.

10. G. H. Box, "Pharisees," *Hastings Encyclopedia*, 9:831–36, p. 836.

11. My view of Paul has been influenced by S. G. F. Brandon, "Paul and His Opponents," *Horizon*, 10, ⚹1 (1968) 106–11; and Sidney Tarachow, "St. Paul and Early Christianity, A Psychoanalytic and Historical Study," in Muensterberger and Axelrad, *op. cit.*, 4 (1955) 223–81. On some of Paul's sources, see Edwin Hatch, *The Influence of Greek Ideas on Christianity* (New York: Harper Torchbooks, 1959).

12. Tarachow, *op. cit.*; H. Nunberg, *Problems of Bisexuality as Reflected in Circumcision* (London: Imago Publishing Co., 1949); O. Pfister, "Die Entwicklung des Apostle Paulus, Eine religionsgeschichtliche und psychologische Skizze," *Imago*, 6 (1920) 243–90; and Clara Thompson, "Identification with the Enemy and Loss of Sense of Self," *Psychoanalytic Quarterly*, 9 (1940) 37–50; on Paul's epilepsy, see

Cavendish Moxon, "Epileptic Traits in Paul of Tarsus," *Psychoanalytic Review,* **9** (1922) 60–66.

13. Besides Schweitzer's *Quest,* which after all deals with a special epistemological-theological question, the only sufficiently scholarly and unsentimental study is the modern work of the fair, cool, and acerb Marcello Craveri, *The Life of Jesus* (New York: Grove Press, 1967).

APPENDIX I
The False Messiahs

An ADEQUATE theory of crisis cults must take cognizance of the negative instance, that of the "failed messiah." What circumstances of defective charisma or cultural ambience account for the success of one culture hero and not another? Is some charisma *real* and some not? Can we recognize true messiahs only by historical hindsight? Is there a social "pathology" of the prophetic process so to speak? Are these vatic personages only a sociological type, or are they a psychological type also? Unfortunately, except for Handsome Lake, John Slocum of the Shakers, and a few others, the information we have from ethnographers is cursory or unsophisticated psychologically. Better documented are the histories of certain false messiahs in our western tradition. Here we find, however, no easy dichotomy into true and false messiahs but rather a continuous gamut, if authenticity be measured by success. Some messiahs failed in secular battle, and some made impossible reality-claims that were doomed to early disaster. But others, in spite of their ultimate defeat, have had a large if temporary impact on history, and several of them founded still-existing religious societies.

New revelation is a thorn in the flesh of an established church that is based on historic revelation. This is especially the case in a literate tradition with a religion of the book, because here ethnographic fact is set and available for later authoritative reference; the discrepancies with changed "common sense" are more conspicuous and vexing than in the case of an easily anonymous step-by-step culture drift in a preliterate society, where the currently tribal is the only manifest commonsense. Among preliterates even what the "ancestors" said can be modulated in the unconscious editing by each vatic repository of tradition. But were a historic church ever to deny the possibility of overt new revelation, it

would then bring into question the validity of the revelation on which
the church itself was established.

The compulsive maintenance of belief in one Messiah throughout
western history tends to make for easy rejection of the more grandiose of
the new messiahs. Enormous charisma is required of a new prophet for
retrospective falsification of history. However, here too ignorance of the
exact tradition among his followers is an ally of the folk leader in new
crisis cults. Only the literate custodians of ancient revelation are burdened
with the necessary logic-chopping and modernizing re-interpretation; hence
theologians write mainly for one another, and folk evangelists neither
know nor care about the enormous intervening culture change. But even
on the folk level a new leader's conviction must rise sometimes to paranoid heights to be heard. In crisis situations, since impotence in the
individual demands omnipotence in the savior, it is therefore to be expected that many charismatic leaders would be paranoid. It is really
astonishing how very massive clinical paranoia can be and yet go unrec-
ognized by the ordinary observer—or even the self-supposed "expert"
for that matter. Hence many retrospectively "false" messiahs achieve in
their time a cult of weighty cultural proportions. At times the paranoiac
disrupts history with the violence of a Caesar or a Hitler. More commonly
the crisis-cult messiah obtains credence only among the dispossessed and
the ignorant, those with insufficient knowledge and ability to manipulate
the Great Tradition which throughout remains in power. The petty protest of many a proletarian ghost dance is often unimportant; but their
very "escape" from achieving a larger historicity leaves them naïvely
fresh as psychological documents and undefiled by the defensive accretions
of later times in more successful cults.

The supposed supernatural uniqueness of Jesus assumes different secular proportions in its ethnographic context; indeed it is only the much
later historic magnitude of the crisis cult emergent from his secular
failure and crucifixion that retrospectively imposes on us a false sense of
his importance to his time. After the final disaster of the independent
Jewish State there were still many prophets of hope and self-appointed
leaders of a return to the ancestral lands in the dark days of the Diaspora.
Some early leaders were associated with military revolts and came almost
invariably at times and places of the sorest political persecution. But
there were also many "supernatural" local messiahs at the opening of the
Christian era. In 44 A.D. one Theudas told his followers he would divide
the Jordan that they might cross it dryshod; but before he could accomplish this promise the whole assemblage was massacred by the Roman
soldiery.[1] Again, a certain Egyptian gathered 30,000 on the Mount of

Olives to await the fall of the fortified walls of Jerusalem which would magically occur at his command; but the prompt arrival of the soldiers of Felix precluded this miracle.[2] A third messiah was about to lead his people into the wilderness when he was destroyed by the troops of the Procurator Festus.[3] All these prophets ran head-on into the overwhelming military power of the Roman Empire. Like the ghost dances and cargo cults of primitives, these nativistic movements did not succeed in taking the measure of military and other extratribal forces in their historical environment.

A more successful secular leader was Menahem, grandson of the Hezekiah who had led the Zealots. He seized the fort of Masada and its store of arms, and then set out to attack Jerusalem. When he beat back the soldiers of Agrippa II and captured the outpost village of Antonia, he was emboldened to claim leadership over all his co-conspirators. Jealous of this leadership, however, they assassinated him and the revolt failed. Menahem was the last Judean messiah before the destruction of the Temple. Contemporary with him were the Samaritan messiahs: Simon Magus, who sought to have the early Christians join him, but who ended in being converted together with his followers; and Dositheus who, failing to restore the Jewish State, founded a Samaritan sect that survived until the sixth century.[4]

For sixty years after the Temple was destroyed there was no new messiah. But when Hadrian succeeded the milder Trajan, his repressions aroused the Jews to rebellion. Bar Kokhba, "Son of the Star" (so named from a prophecy in Numbers 24:17) did not pretend to be the Messiah, though he was acclaimed as such by the Rabbi Akiba and others. Allegedly 400,000 to 580,000 males were gathered into a Jewish army, and the Romans hastily abandoned Judaea, Samaria, and Galilee. Julius Severus, the greatest Roman soldier of his time, was brought back from wars in Britain to cope with the insurrection. But even he was largely on the defensive for a time and attacked only small parties and supply trains. Some fifty battles were fought, and Bar Kokhba's following increased with each victory, being swelled by Jews arriving from far-off colonies. Bar Kokhba took Jerusalem, which he made his capital, was there proclaimed King and ruled for three years, meanwhile taking 50 walled towns and 985 villages. But after a desperate struggle the Romans recaptured Jerusalem and razed it to the ground. Bar Kokhba was driven to a last stand at Bethar, but dissensions in the garrison gradually weakened the revolt until the Romans stormed Bethar, killed Bar Kokhba, and bore his body away in triumph. The carnage was tremendous. More people were killed at Bethar than were said to have been in the Exodus from Egypt. Tens of thousands lay dead, and thousands of males were later slaughtered in the pacification, while many thousands of women and children were sold into slavery. All who could escape death by torture fled, many to Arabia, where a large Jewish population became established, though after two millennia almost all have returned to Israel. Rabbi Akiba, imprisoned at the outbreak of the revolt, died under Roman torture. This war led to the final break between the Jews and the Judaeo-Christians who had not joined them.

Not until the fifth century did another messiah arise. This time it was in accordance with a Talmudic computation. Moses of Crete promised to lead his followers dryshod from island to island. A crowd of them gathered at a peninsula and started out. Many were drowned, and the messiah himself disappeared.[5] At the end of the seventh century, Isaac ben Yakub of Ishfahan was miraculously cured of leprosy and as miraculously learned instantly to read. He was proclaimed the messiah, but his movement became a political revolt against the chaotic khalifate of the time. After his defeat in battle, the Isavite Sect arose, the earliest of the Jewish sects of the Diaspora and one which lasted several centuries. His disciple Yudghan of Hamadan, called al-Ra'i "the shepherd," had followers who insisted on his messiahship, and when Yudghan died, they said he was not dead but would come again. About 720 the Syrian Serenus, a politico-religious reformer, promised to take the Jews back to the Holy Land. His influence spread even to Spain; but, captured by the khalif Yazid II, he claimed he was only cozening his followers and amusing himself. The khalif therefore turned him over to the Jews for punishment.

David Alroy of Kurdistan came about 1160 to Baghdad, where there were great political disturbances incident to the Christian Crusades. Alroy claimed to be the Messiah, and he promised to overthrow the weak Sultan and lead the Jews back to Palestine. He was held to be a great magician, and legends tell of his miraculous escape from the Sultan's prison. Though he was killed in a futile attack on the fortress of Amadia, a sect remained worshiping him for many years. In 1172 a minor prophet rose in Yemen; the next year he was beheaded at his own request, to prove by his return that he was really the Messiah. In 1281 the kabbalist Abraham ben Samuel Abulafia went to Rome to convert the Pope to Judaism, but with little success. He was said miraculously to have escaped the Pope's dungeons; in any case he was in Sicily in 1285, when he proclaimed himself the Messiah and announced the Millennium for the year 1290. Although this did not arrive on schedule, Abraham of Avila announced the Millennium again for 1295. But when the Jews gathered in the synagogue, miraculous crosses appeared on their clothing and many were converted to Christianity. In 1502, Asher Lämmlein promised in Istria that the Messiah would come if fasting and prayer and almsgiving were made general. Both Christians and Jews accepted him, but he subsequently disappeared, it is said with the alms.

In the early sixteenth century a most remarkable imposter, David Reubeni, came to the west from a mysterious kingdom of Khaibar, as emissary from his brother the king, to obtain aid against the Sultan. He was in Venice in 1524, later saw Pope Clement II, and proceeded in 1525 to Portugal to persuade John III to ally himself with the King of Khaibar. He obtained the promise of eight ships and four thousand cannon. The Jews thought him superhuman, not the least of his miracles being his influence unmolested at the court of one of the cruellest persecutors of the Jews. But his conversion from Christianity of Solomon Molkho, a man of Jewish descent, shook Reubeni's position at court. Molkho himself fled to Turkey, where he developed a confused mysticism foretelling the Messiah in 1540. Meanwhile, however, Reubeni's ship was wrecked on the coast of Spain, and for a time he was in the hands of the Inquisition. He was released by Charles V and went to Avignon, then ruled by the Pope.

Next ensued a conflict of the two fantastics, Molkho and Reubeni. Molkho went to Rome and had visions foretelling earthquakes and floods which, in fact, did occur. He was protected by Pope Clement VII and certain cardinals who shrewdly thought he was harming Jewry, but actually his Jewish critics at this time were few and his influence increased. Molkho met Reubeni again in Venice, having once been his disciple but now become his equal. Reubeni was still engaged in obtaining allies for his brother, the alleged King of Khaibar. Molkho actually achieved an indefinite postponing of the introduction of the Inquisition into Portugal. But his Jewish enemies, rising especially in Venice, finally had him condemned to auto da fé as a renegade Christian. The victim was burned —but it was a substitute provided by the Pope! Smuggled out of the papal apartments, Molkho joined Reubeni at Ratisbon to plead the cause of the Jews of Khaibar. But when Molkho attempted to convert to Judaism the Holy Roman Emperor Charles V, he was sent to the Inquisition in Mantua where he was burned. Reubeni was sent to Spain, where he too seems to have died at the hands of the Holy Office of the Inquisition. Each of this pair was acclaimed as the Messiah by his followers. Scholars, highly skeptical of the Kingdom of Khaibar, claim that Reubeni's *Journal,* on internal evidence, must have been written by a German Jew. There are few more colorful psychopaths in history.

But the false messiahs were not exclusively Jewish. Even in Hellenistic times some Gnostics[6] had claimed original insight into the mind of God and indeed to participation in the Divinity. The Gnostics were subjective idealists whose *gnosis* or revelation maintained that the world was intrinsically evil. In this lowest realm, the earth, the soul was kept captive by planetary powers, to win freedom from which the soul had to ascend the spheres they ruled, subduing or deceiving the demons with numerological charms and passwords. The Gnostics were descended philosophically from the Pythagoreans and bore a relationship to the Kabbalists, whose mystic numerology was based on the customary use of letters for the cardinal numbers in Hebrew. The secret knowledge of the Gnostics was mainly directed toward the circumvention of the hostile planetary rulers.

Modern psychiatry is disposed to consider Gnosticism a paranoid system, with the usual persecutory delusions of reference and of magical omnipotence. Gnosticism was an individual magic-working against which early institutionalized Christianity was forced to take arms for its own survival as the one ordained supernatural system; traditional Judaism has had the same suspicion and distrust of Kabbalism, since it substitutes the practitioner's magical claims for the religious worship of the Most High. But some Christian scholars regard it as unfortunate that the Church set itself against Gnosticism, since in order to check its inroads into Christianity the Church had to forbid freedom of belief, make dogma rigid, and prohibit any new revelations; and from this cause, ecclesiastical government became rigidly official and repressive. But what else can true religion do, against its enemy magic?

The Christian heretics in general made no messianic claims but merely criticized the official interpretations of Scrupture by the Church. The inevitable new revelations of mystics were with large success incorporated into Catholicism, since the Church had the powerful weapon of passing on the authenticity of saints and their visions.[7] But the pressures built up by the increasingly rigid and enlarging body of dogma broke forth ultimately in the Protestant Reformation, not a petty protest but a massive social movement in the mainstream of western civilization. Once Protestants had won the victory of private (or in Lutheran and Calvinist sects their special but in any case non-Catholic) interpretation of the Bible, a number of non-Jewish messiahs began to appear.

A great many Gentile messiahs took their pattern from the extraordinary and widely famed Jewish messiah, Shabbathai Zevi (1626–76).[8] Shabbathai had been a beautiful and introspective child, the son of a Sephardic agent of an English mercantile firm. The father took an almost worshipful attitude toward his adored son. Shabbathai disliked the Talmud but ardently loved Kabbalistic studies, in which as a young man he had already attained fame, added to by his asceticism, his obvious belief in his magical powers, and his determined aversion to marriage—this last an attitude unprecedented in the society in which he lived. Through business contacts, his father learned of English millenarian sects whose favored date for impending supernatural events was 1666. According to his computations of the Zohar, Shabbathai selected 1648 as the proper date and announced to a small group of followers that he was the Messiah. In support of this claim he uttered the Tetragrammaton, permitted only to the high priest in the Temple on the Day of Atonement. The rabbis thereupon excommunicated him as well as his enlarging group of fervent followers.

Banished from Smyrna, Shabbathai went to Constantinople where the respected scholar Moses Pinheiro and the distinguished teacher Abraham Yachini supported his claims. Intoxicated with his role, Shabbathai wandered widely about the Near East. He was expelled from Salonika by the rabbis, but in Cairo about 1660 he got the support of the wealthy and powerful mystic, Raphael Joseph Chelebi of Aleppo, who had long impatiently awaited the Coming. In Jerusalem Shabbathai was accepted by the people and sent abroad to collect money. A romantic and eccentric Polish Jewess, orphaned at six and reputedly living an immoral life at Leghorn, next proclaimed she was to be the bride of the Messiah, although she put forth this announcement without consulting him. He sent for her, and the vehemently bachelor messiah, now almost forty, succumbed to her charms and in 1662 married her in Cairo. At Gaza Shabbathai met Nathan Benjamin Levi, who became his Elijah, the traditional forerunner of the Messiah. Levi announced the Messianic Age for 1666, a prophecy that spread even to the North Sea, where millenarians had for some time decided on the same date. Shabbathai made a triumphal entry into Smyrna where he was extravagantly welcomed, and formally announced his Messiahship to the local Jewish community which this time at once gave their local son absolute power over them.

Business in many parts of Europe came to a standstill. Merchants in North Sea ports worte their oriental agents for more information. Embassies visited the King of Kings from all over the world, and tribute poured in upon him. He was publicly acclaimed the Messiah in the synagogues of three continents. In Hamburg, Protestants for a time worried about the fate of Christianity itself. In Persia, farmers ceased work to await the Lord. After giving the various kingdoms of the earth to his chief followers, Shabbathai went to Constantinople early in 1666. But there the Sultan arrested him on landing and took him to the Moslem capital in chains, though this little affected the tribute that continued to pour in. Shabbathai's courage did not match his convictions however, and when examined by the authorities he said he was only a rabbi sent from Jerusalem to gather alms for charity. Nevertheless he continued to hold court in prison for both Jews and Moslems who believed in him. Two months later he was removed to the castle at Abydos, where his court increased in protocol and became the center of excited pilgrimages from Jewish communities all over the world.

Next, Nehemiah Ha-Kohen, who claimed to be a forerunner of the Messiah, was summoned by Shabbathai to his court. But neither prophet nor messiah was satisfied at the encounter. Fearing assassination, Nehemiah fled to Constantinople, turned Moslem, and denounced Shabbathai's plots. Taken to Adrianople, Shabbathai in turn became frightened and also turned Moslem, announcing God had commanded he become an Ishmaelite. World Jewry was shocked at the apostasy, and Turkish Jews were terrified at the consequent choice between apostasy or massacre. The Sultan, pleased at the conversion, made Shabbathai one of his doorkeepers. But Shabbathai never really gave up his claims and founded the Dönmeh, a Judaeo-Moslem sect that still survives in Salonika. After a time he fell into disgrace at the Turkish court and was banished to Dulcigno where he died, leaving long controversy behind him and a line of petty messiahs.

Jacob Querido, younger brother of Shabbathai's fourth wife who pretended he was her son by the Messiah, was succeeded in turn by his son Berehaih (1695–1740). Still other Shabbathaian messiahs tried to step into his place when Shabbathai died: Miguel Cardoso (1630–1706), a Marrano; Mordecai Mokiah (1650–1729) of Eisenstadt, who preached widely in Italy and Poland; Löbele Prossnitz (died about 1750), a clumsy conjurer who was successful both in Germany and Austria; Judah Hasid, founder of a group emphasising penitence and enthusiastic prayer, who took a large group of his followers to Jerusalem, where he died upon arrival. Jankiev Lejbovisz (1726–91) a distiller born in Podolia, was an undisguised charlatan and an apostate from several religions. An anti-rabbinical Kabbalist, he obtained the support of the Bishop of Kamenetz, but when the Bishop died and his situation was reversed Lejbovisz became an outward Christian, though still secretly a Jew. He was arrested for heresy in 1760 and imprisoned for thirteen years in Czentschow Castle, from which he promulgated his teachings. Liberated in the Russian invasion of 1722, he made a triumphal progress through Poland, Bohemia and Moravia. He lived in state in various continental capitals, latterly as the Baron of Offenbach, always with a vast retinue and an immense income from his infatuated communicants, He died in 1791, the last messiah with any influence on Judaism.

In 1651 Lodowicke Muggleton (1609–98), originally a Puritan but influenced by the mystic Boehm and the prophets Thomas Tany and John Robins, had a revelation.[9] The next year Muggleton's cousin, John Reeve (1608–58) had another revelation, which denounced both Robins and Tany, announced Reeve himself as the third and last messiah, and appointed Muggleton as his "mouth" in accordance with Revelation 11. In 1652 came Muggleton and Reeve's *Transcendent Spirituall Treatise;* in 1653 they were imprisoned for blasphemy, but issued two more pamphlets. In 1656 they published *The Divine Looking Glass, or the Third and Last Testament,* which contained an extraordinary theology and in 1672 obtained the distinction of being denounced by William Penn. Many Muggletonian scriptures were reprinted in 1756, after Swedenborg had announced a similar system, *The Looking Glass* being reprinted as late as 1846. Reeve became a Ranter, but the Muggletonians held their own services until 1870.

In the deeply disturbed days of mid-seventeenth-century England came the Ranters,[10] one of many sects whose adherents practiced convulsive ecstasy, hypnotism, prophecy and miracle working. In 1650 one Ranter prophet claimed he reincarnated Melchizedek and, later, God. Certain living persons, he said, were Cain, Judas, Jeremiah and the like, whom he had raised from the dead. He could also cause apparitions and floating lights in the dark. George Fox believed he had the gift of prophecy, clairvoyance, and healing by word of mouth. After an apocalyptic vision in the village of Lichfield he predicted the great London fire of 1666. Fox was the founder of the Society of Friends, called Quakers because of the violent tremblings coming from the Spirit in their early days. The "Fifth Monarchy Men"[11] proclaimed the coming of the fifth monarchy prophesied by Daniel, when Christ would come down from heaven and rule for a thousand years. In 1657 they plotted to kill Cromwell. One night in 1661 they broke out in an insurrection, parading the streets of London with the lion banner of "King Jesus." Troops were called out, but the Fifth Monarchy Men, believing themselves invulnerable and invincible through divine assistance, fought until nearly all were shot down. The surviving leaders were tried for treason and executed.

At the end of the seventeenth century, an ecstatic sect was driven out of France. In 1706 they reached England, where they were known as the "French Prophets."[12] They had convulsive trance performances, with visions and prophecies. Charles Wesley once stopped for a night with a gentleman, not knowing he was of this sect. When about to go to bed,

his new friend fell into a fit and began to gobble like a turkey. Frightened at this and other things, Wesley exorcized the Devil out of him.
Later, with some friends this time, Wesley visited a prophetess of this cult
who spoke as in the Person of God. The Jumpers[13] began in Wales in
1740; they too were subject to violent physical agitations. A contemporary
writer once saw ten thousand of them at a meeting, shouting and jump-
ing in the midst of the sermon. In 1750, the prophetess "Mother" Ann
Lee, an incarnation of Christ, founded the millenarian Shakers.[14] They
had the gift of tongues, of healing, and of prophecy and were in constant
contact with the spirit world through visions. Persecuted in England
for their violent shaking, dancing, visions and prophecies, they came to
New Lebanon in New York about 1780.

Joanna Southcott (1750–1814) was the woman chosen by God to
fulfill the Promise made to women at the Fall: her seed, Christ, should
bruise the serpent's head and put an end to evil.[15] Both men and
women would be brides of Christ. But she was to be his bride in a special
sense, thus fulfilling Revelation 12. She began her prophecies in 1792,
and when many of her predictions eventuated in fact, Foley, rector of Old
Swinford, gathered friends at Exeter in 1801 to examine her gifts systematically. They were convinced and were themselves hailed by followers
as the "Seven Stars." In August 1802 Joanna retired to have a seven-
day dispute with Satan which she later published. Those who read and
accepted at least two of her works were given a certification on which
was written: "The Sealed of the Lord—the Elect Precious Man's Redemp-
tion—To Inherit the Tree of Life—To be made Heirs of God and Joint-
Heirs with Jesus Christ. Joanna Southcott." About fourteen thousand
people were thus "sealed" within five years. In 1813 she wrote personal
letters to every member of the House of Commons, every bishop and
peer in the realm, and to all the important newspapers. The next spring
she announced she was pregnant with Shiloh, attracting much attention
by this, even in medical circles. Fourteen doctors were invited to examine
her. But she died two days after Christmas. Southcottians still exist in
Canada, the United States, and Australia.

When "Mother" Ann Lee died in 1784, she was succeeded by Joseph
Meacham and Lucy Wright. Like the Rappites, they believed that God
was a dual person, male and female, and that Adam likewise had had in
himself both sexes, being created in the image of God. Ann Lee had
believed that sexual lust was the evil of evils, and no soul could follow
Christ who indulged it, for Christ had never had sexual intercourse. The
Shakers therefore stressed celibacy, though they lived in communal fashion
in "families" of eighty to ninety persons, with open confession of sins.[16]

The Bimmelers originated in Würtemburg with Joseph Bäumler and became the Society of Separatists at Zoar, Ohio, in 1817. At first this sect prohibited marriage, though Bäumler himself married one of the colonists. About 1834, John Noyes, a graduate of Dartmouth College, founded the Perfectionist Community of Oneida. They were the reverse of the Bimmelers, however, and advocated that every man should be the husband of every woman, and every woman wife to every man. Requests for intercourse were made through a third person, man or woman, but no individual thus solicited was obliged to accede unwillingly. After weaning, children were placed in a common nursery, where their parents lost all rights to them and were supposed to show no special interest in them. The sect is extinct.

In 1827, Joseph Smith discovered the ancient Book of Mormon, allegedly written on plates of gold.[17] Smith deciphered these books, full of a strange theology and the muddled superstitions of a rural mind. References to contemporary agitations against Freemasonry, Deism and Catholicism, as well as references to Swedenborgianism, have led a majority of scholars to question the antiquity of the Book of Mormon, and the gold plates seem early to have disappeared again without adequate authentication by impartial witnesses. A current theory that the Indians were the Ten Lost Tribes of Israel also became a part of the belief of the Church of Jesus Christ of Latter-Day Saints. The Nephites were descended from Joseph and Judah and would go to a glorious Zion in America. Partly through repeated revelations, and partly by the armed compulsion of their successive neighbors, the Mormons were driven to Utah where for many years they practiced polygyny and a kind of communism. Mormonism remains the dominant religio-political power in the state of Utah, and from their Tabernacle in Salt Lake City they send proselytizing missionaries all over the world.

In 1828, Edward Irving[18] asserted the carnal sinfulness of Christ's humanity and for this pronouncement was excommunicated by the Presbyterian Church of Scotland. Known as "Irvingites," his communicants in the Catholic Apostolic Church spoke with tongues, healed the sick, and believed in the imminent Millennian Coming. William Caird took the cult to Germany where it became the New Apostolic Church, with H. Niehaus, the "Stammapostel," as its incarnation of Christ.

About 1831, a minister named William Miller[19] began to preach the end of the world and the Coming of Christ, basing his predictions on the Bible. He began his mission in New England and New York but traveled southward, giving it is said over three thousand sermons on the Advent. More than fifty thousand Adventists awaited the Trump of Doom, predicted for the summer of 1843. Many sold their property and arrayed themselves in white "ascension robes," which were put on sale by enterprising if sometimes unbelieving Yankee storekeepers. When the year 1843 passed without Apocalypse, Miller discovered an error in his mathematical calculations. Fifteen or twenty thousand Adventists remained at the beginning of the twentieth century, most of them in southern Michigan, but in this troubled century their numbers have since increased.

In 1843, a preacher named Henry James Prince[20] wrote a long letter in which he explained the steps through which the Holy Ghost had become identified with his own personality. Ordained in 1840, he joined Starky, rector of the parish assigned to him, and together they led a great revival in 1841, whence the group was called "Starkyites." The Bishop of Bath and Wells revoked the preaching license of Prince, and the Bishops of Salisbury and Ely likewise frustrated him, at which he began to preach outside the Church in barns. Starky and Prince were the Two Witnesses of Revelation 11 and declared the Biblical injunction of community of goods was still binding. Many people sold their lands and brought the proceeding money to Prince. About this time, by direct revelation, Prince announced himself as Elijah. In 1849, Prince and Starky set up Agapemone, "the Abode of Love," near Spaxton village. Money poured in, and a large and beautiful mansion was built which Prince lived in until his death in 1899. Prince had an especial influence over wealthy persons, a number of whom renounced the world and deposited their money in the Bank of England in the name of "Brother Prince," thereafter coming to live at Agapemone. Letters came addressed to "Our Holy Lord God at Spaxton." Prince stood at his throne in the auditorium defying all the powers of evil, until even the doubters quailed and trembled. He promised them that neither he nor his believers would ever die or suffer grief and sickness, since the Lord in his person[21] had come to redeem the flesh. He then set up in royal state, having bought the Queen Dowager's equipage and four cream-colored horses. He often drove rapidly around Bridgewater accompanied by bloodhounds, which lent an element of fear to the spectacle. When he took a party to see the Great Exhibition of 1851 he was accompanied by outriders, bareheaded because they were in the presence of the Lord. He took the title "Beloved" and signed his books and letters with a B. In the trial of a lawsuit over property brought by a cult backslider, it transpired that "free love" had been practiced at Agapemone. Prince's *Little Book Open* aroused such scandalous feeling that the order came from Agapemone to destroy all copies; but a copy survives in the British Museum, describing the erotic "Voices" that Prince heard. After the trial his income from collections dwindled, but a wealthy London merchant gave Prince all his property, humbly entered the brotherhood as a butler, and preserved Agapemone.

The Reverend J. H. Smyth-Pigott was the official successor to H. J. Prince. His "Children of the Resurrection," as they were now called, in 1892 built an elaborate "Ark of the Covenant" costing 16,000 pounds. In September 1902, shortly after Prince's death, Smyth-Pigott announced himself as Jesus Christ, at which revelation riotous excesses ensued for several weeks at Agapemone. Smyth-Pigott thereafter lived in retirement, worshiped as divine by a small group, and the Ark was closed.

Thomas Lake Harris founded the Mountain Cove Community of Spiritualists[22] in 1851 on the original site of the Garden of Eden in Virginia. However, for some reason he left Eden and in 1866 founded the Brotherhood of the New Life at Salem-on-Erie. His system was rigorously patriarchal, all communicants being guests or slaves of Harris and having to do exactly as they were told. Later Harris and others went to Santa Rosa, California, and began still a third community.

About this time Mrs. Martha MacWhirter founded the Women's Commonwealth[23] at Belton, Texas. They did not exclude men from their membership, but the only man who joined them withdrew after a few years. Though they were diligent, thrifty, pious, and a great material success, the Texans persecuted them. They therefore removed to Washington, D.C., where in 1906 they still numbered eighteen. This manless Commonwealth is now extinct.

About 1875, Mrs. Dora Beekman, wife of a Congregationalist minister in Rockford, Illinois, announced herself the spiritual Mother of Christ in the Second Coming, this person being a young Methodist minister, the Reverend Mr. George J. Schweinfurth. For about twenty years three or four hundred communicants formed the Church Triumphant, or the Church of the Redeemed. They are also known as "Beekmanites,"[24] though the Reverend Beekman did not believe in them and became psychotic while trying to persuade his wife of her folly. Dora Beekman claimed immortality, but when she died her messianic essence passed into Schweinfurth who became "the risen Christ, the Lord of heaven and the immortal maker and ruler of the earth." He is dead now.

About 1881, John Ballou Newbrough, dentist by trade but spiritualist by avocation, began to hear angels' revelations, which he wrote down on his typewriter for half an hour daily. After fifty weeks the "Book of Oahspe" emerged, being published in Boston in 1882, and reprinted in London in 1910. Its eight hundred pages concerning the hierarchy of

Lord, Lord God, God, Orion Chief, Nirvanian Chief, and Jehovih (sic); its mythical earth made up of Whaga, Jud, Thouri, Vohu, and Dis; its fantastic anthropology of the Asu'ans, Druks, I'hins, Yak, and Ong'wee; and its Triunes named Ennochissa, Kabalactes, and Loveamong—all these constitute the beliefs of the "Faithists."[25] About 1894 the Faithists founded a community called Shalam in New Mexico, in accordance with the Book of Jehovih's Kingdom on Earth.

In 1888, in Soddy, a small village in eastern Tennessee, a man named Patterson[26] began to preach that a strange and wonderful thing was soon to happen. After a time he said that Christ had come in the person of A. J. Brown, who had been his assistant. Shortly afterward Brown disappeared, having gone into the mountains for a fast of forty days and nights. On a Sunday morning in June, the people followed Patterson to the hills, where Brown suddenly appeared clothed in white and with uplifted hands. The people rushed shouting toward him and kissed his feet, and many who were ill were healed by his touch. Among the most fanatic was a young girl who cried she was ready to die for her faith, and some believers became so fearful of human sacrifice that they sent to Chattanooga for the sheriff. It took all the forces he could muster to persuade Patterson and Brown to leave the county.

In 1889 and 1890 a messianic craze[27] developed among the Negroes along the Savannah River in Georgia and South Carolina. One person after another declared himself the Christ, drawing excited worshipers from their work and greatly alarming the whites. The chief Christ was a mulatto named Bell who preached his divinity and exhorted the negroes to follow him from the cotton fields, the sawmills and the turpentine woods. These "Wilderness Worshipers" obeyed his every word and set up a "temple" of circular seats around an oak tree. The excitement so increased that he was arrested by the civil authorities. His followers would have resisted, but he said an angel would open his prison door at night. Since no legal charge could be brought against him he was shortly released, whereupon he preached to even greater crowds. He announced the end of the world for 16 August 1890, when all Negroes would turn white and all white men turn black. All who wished to ascend on the Last Day should purchase wings from him. He was at length adjudged insane. But in the following year King Solomon arose, and Nebuchadnezzar, who emphasized his claim by eating grass on all fours. When a woman was killed by the enthusiasts, King Solomon and Nebuchadnezzar were sent to join Bell in an asylum for the insane.

In 1888, after a somewhat dissolute life, Huntsman T. Muason had visions of both God and the Devil in a Methodist revival meeting in

New York City. After many privations he wandered to Park Ridge, New Jersey, where he received the power to heal by the laying on of hands. "His strange appearance, in which he sought to imitate the traditional portraits of Christ, and his wonderfully magnetic will power, aided by a musical voice, evident sincerity, and easy flow of speech, made a strong impression upon men and women alike." In 1890, at Hackensack, he founded his "Angel Dancers,"[28] so called because they believe the Devil is at times among them. The Angel Dancers hold everything in common, kill no living thing, are vegetarians, and believe in free love. Herman Storm's farm near Hackensack became known as "the Lord's Farm" because of his extreme hospitality to vagrants, a practice which alarmed the neighborhood. In May 1893, Muason and several followers were arrested and jailed for maintaining a disorderly house. But the demeanor of the Angel Dancers under sentence to a year of hard labor won them much public sympathy, and they afterward returned to Storm's farm, where they quietly continued to tend to their affairs.

One hot day in the summer of 1909, in Grasshopper Valley, Tennessee, George Went Hensley,[29] then in his early thirties, was pondering in his mind a text from Mark 16:17–18.

And these signs shall follow them that believe; In my name they shall cast out devils; they shall speak with new tongues;
They shall take up serpents; and if they drink any deadly thing, it shall not hurt them; they shall lay hands on the sick and they shall recover.

These words of Jesus after the Resurrection and before the Ascension were a command, Hensley felt, he was bound to test out and obey. So he climbed White Oak Mountain, east of Grasshopper Valley, and found a large rattlesnake in a rocky gap. A few days later he began his mission, citing the Bible texts and thrusting the rattlesnake at the people to take up in their hands and thus prove their faith. In this manner was founded "The Dolley Pond Church of God With Signs Following," an ascetic rural sect that prohibited cosmetics, tea, coffee, and even carbonated beverages. The Coca-Cola heresy came when a deacon said in meeting he had had a "Coke" one hot spell and saw no lessening of his snake-handling powers. The potential schism was defeated, however, when he was challenged to find a Bible text permitting Coca-Cola to the elect.

The snake-handling cult spread in later decades all over the rural Southeast, into Kentucky, Virginia, both Carolinas, Georgia, and Florida. The use of blow-torches was taken up in Virginia, and later, allegedly, poison drinking.[30] Faith healing was a central practice in the cult; ecstatic seizures and speaking with tongues were other common features.

Police from Chattanooga began the suppression of the cult in Tennessee, culminating in a state law prohibiting the public handling of snakes. Kentucky and Virginia later also passed similar state laws. In 1946, Benjamin R. Massey brought snake handling to Durham, North Carolina, where he joined with the Reverend Colonel Hartman Bunn of the Zion Tabernacle. In mid-October 1948, Bunn organized an interstate convention of the snake-handling cult which was held at Durham. Much nationwide publicity attended this event, but Bunn was sentenced to prison for violation of a Durham municipal ordinance against snake handling, after the State Supreme Court upheld the local ordinance.

Sixteen persons died between 1940 and 1955 from the effects of poisonous snakebites received in snake-handling meetings, including a woman cultist in Long Beach, California. But the culmination was reached when the founder of the religion, Hensley, was himself bitten on the wrist by a diamondback rattlesnake at a prayer meeting in Lester's Shed near Altha, Florida, on Sunday night the twenty-fourth of July 1955. The aged prophet of the cult, now over seventy, had been handling poisonous snakes for forty-six years before this retribution. He refused all medical treatment in order to prove his faith, and died it is said vomiting blood. At protracted funeral services held by the Reverend Obis Lassiter, cultists testified to Hensley's "doing the right thing in giving his life to God" and vowed their determination to maintain the snake-handling religion. The Reverend Hensley's widow said she would move from Georgia to the pinelands of northwest Florida to continue her late husband's work.[31]

Active snake-handling churches survive to this day in the Appalachian Mountains. On the eighteenth of August 1968, Oscar Franklin Pelfrey, a retired coal miner and lay minister in his late sixties, was bitten on the temple near his right eye while handling two timber rattlesnakes during services in the Holiness Church of God in Jesus Name, at Big Stone Gap in Virginia. Pelfrey refused medical aid and died in his home six hours later. The Reverend Kenneth Short of Harlan, Kentucky, and three other men were charged under the Code of Virginia (Section 18.1–72) with violating the state anti-snake-handling law, and were indicted for murder. The visiting minister was found innocent by the circuit court in a trial at the county seat in Wise, Virginia, but Roscoe Mullins, who handed the snake to Pelfrey a few minutes before it struck, was given a thirty-day sentence and fined $50. Released on $2,000 bond, Mullins (whose right hand had been amputated after a rattlesnake bite in 1953) said he would appeal all the way to the United States Supreme Court, on the ground that the Virginia law violated his constitutional right to freedom of religion.[32]

The disposition of Southern urban folk is freely to call these snake cultists "crazy." But however much we share the opinion that handling poisonous snakes is dangerous and unrealistic behavior, we must point out that this definition is not sufficiently refined. In all belief systems, as noted earlier, there is a quantitative spectrum. There is, first of all, the psychosis of an individual, that is, the personality or the "culture" of a single person; next, the folie à deux, a "psychosis" present in two persons that is no longer simple personality but already an incipient culture; next, the folie à N, or the minority cult, the sub-culture of a segment of the society; and finally the belief system of the majority in a society, the common content of belief in many personalities, that is, their culture.

The characteristic trait in all these cults is that they all fail of wider social credence and achieve at best a very limited historicity. But the *size* of the believing group is no adequate criterion of truth. It is merely our quantitative (and inaccurate) rule of thumb in discriminating among psychoses, cults, and cultures. The question that concerns us, however, is not the complex one of metaphysical truth but rather the simpler one of descriptive scientific fact, both ethnographic and psychiatric. For this purpose any cult has equal status with any culture and must be treated with the same respect. Indeed, in its greater proximity to the psychosis end of the belief-gamut, the cult has had technical advantages over the culture for the present study.

Modern psychiatric judgment would undoubtedly agree with the common-sense opinion that all these individual prophets were psychotic or psychopathic. As a matter of fact, the snake-handling beliefs were taken as bona fide evidence of psychosis in a patient at the psychiatric clinic of Duke Medical School until it was discovered that these beliefs had a bona fide cultural status as well. How, then, are we to assess them? At many points the tradition of our own Christian majority culture gives powerful support to some of these cultist fantasies and a necessary clinical judgment of the patient becomes still more embarrassed. Indeed, persons who are more impressed by the social mass of believers than by their own judgment—that is those who would depend more on tradition than on their own intelligence—would prefer for that reason to side-step judgment entirely. They would say evasively that each prophet was "a child of his time," that cultural beliefs must be given the courtesy of escaping scientific scrutiny and assessment especially insofar as they are religious, and that the prophet is to this degree not accountable for his fantasies. But judgment may not so easily be shirked; this merely shifts the onus of error to the whole society in question. Only to the degree that their contemporaries rejected the prophets would the society stand exonerated.

Once we accept the method of belief-testing we call science, we are forced to maintain that we know what we know. Anyone who holds today the opinions that these prophets did, cannot escape being judged clinically. And to the extent that a society shared these errors of belief, the society was in error as well. Events did not substantiate the prophets' claims, and their personalities were pathological. The cult-society was disoriented too, to the degree it shared the prophet's delusions. *Once we accept and only if we accept the possibility that the "culture" of a society may be as much in error as the "personality" of a psychotic do we have the wit and the need to invent the as-if method of a scientific hypothesis.* If . . . then makes sense only if we have learned to say "if."

These quasi-historical messiahs and their movements exhibit many of the familiar traits we have found already in the similar cults of primitives. Manahem and Bar Kokhba were primarily political and secular messiahs in the old Hebraic tradition, and they are to be equated functionally with such military leaders as Pontiac, Chief Joseph, and Sitting Bull. Others were primarily cultist miracle workers, that is *magicians:* Theudas, the Egyptian messiah, the prophet destroyed by Festus, Simon Magus, Dositheus, Moses of Crete, Isaac ben Yakub of Ishfahan, Yudghan of Hamadan, David Alroy of Kurdistan, the beheaded Yemenite prophet, Abraham ben Samuel, and Abraham of Avila—as were also a number of the later gentile miracle-working messiahs. These magicians were all evidently of a paranoid-omipotent trend. Gnosticism and Kabbalism, with their large claims to magic power, were especially attractive to paranoid personalities like the messiah Shabbathai Sebi. The clinical impression we get of others is of characteristic psychopathic personalities: the Syrian Serenus who "amused" himself at the expense of the Jews; Asher Lämmlein who absconded with the alms he gathered; Reubeni and Molkho, both gifted with *pseudologia phantastica;* the mountebank Prossnitz; and Lejbovisz, the "Baron of Offenbach." All these, whatever other symptoms they exhibited, were at least well oriented enough to be able to mulct their followers economically.

Several of the cults are most interesting in their beginning literally as the classic folie à deux. Among these one might place Shabbathai and Levi, and again Shabbathai and Kohen (though it was a less successful collaboration, as was also that of Molkho and Reubeni), Muggleton and his cousin Reeve, Prince and Starky, Southcott and Foley, Beekman and Schweinfurth, Patterson and Brown, and perhaps others. The megalomania of paranoiacs is manifest in the prophetess of the Fifth Monarchy Men who spoke in the Person of God; in Mother Ann Lee, the incarnation of Christ; the "Stämmapostel" Niehaus of the New Apostolic Church, another incarnation of Christ; "Brother" Prince who became "Our Holy Lord at Spaxton"; his successor Smyth-Pigott, the new Jesus Christ; Mrs. Beekman's Rev. Schweinfurth-Christ; Patterson's assistant, A. J. Brown; several of the Wilderness Worshipers who were God or Christ; and Muason of the Angel Dancers, who at least assiduously imitated the appearance of the Savior. Hysteroid "mothers of God" may be seen perhaps in the first and fourth wives of Shabbathai; in Mrs. Dora Beekman, "spiritual mother" of the Rev. Schweinfurth; and in Joanna Southcott, who was to bear the Messiah Shiloh (a *pseudocyesis hysterica?*).

Other anticipated features are variously present. George Fox predicted the Apocalypse, as also did the Fifth Monarchy Men, the Millerites or Adventists, the Wilderness Worshipers, and others. Melchizedek of the Ranters could raise the dead. The Fifth Monarchy Men believed themselves invulnerable. The English Shakers practiced public confession, quite as did the Indian Shakers. Sexual ascetics include the Shakers, the Bimmelers, and perhaps the members of the Women's Commonwealth. Sexual communism, by contrast, was advocated by the Oneida community and at Agapemone; and polygyny was long a practice in Mormonism. Economic communism was also present among the Mormons, the Shakers, at Agapemone, and among the Angel Dancers.

History is constantly shocking in its unbelievability. We ask, How could even sub-societies accept the delusions of these prophets? And yet the social fact is that they did. More useful are operational questions such as, Why did these minor prophets succeed as they did? Why do some prophets succeed and others fail? Certain of the cult features may explain success. For example, sexual revolutionaries emancipate their communicants from cultural repressions such as monogamy and cultural burdens such as individual enterprise. But at the same time, these fantasies were often closer to the prophet's id than to any useful social superego. Perhaps, in general, it is a question of the relative narcissism of the prophet. The more he expressed a real social need, the more he succeeded; but the more he expressed a mere narcissistic wish, the more he failed.

The closer to the solitary olonist "acting out" his anti-social conflicts, as in the frankly exploitative psychopathic prophets, the more limited was the prophet's success; only portions of his social ambient aided what success he had. On the other hand, the closer to the socialized shaman and culture hero of a society the prophet was, the greater his historical reality. Moses and Aaron handled snakes, and so did George Went Hensley. But Moses and Aaron also embodied larger social and ethical ends; the Southern snake handlers, absorbed in strictly personal sins, were a poor second in this feature. The *Book of Oaspe* and the *Book of*

Mormon are alike in their fantastic unreality and pseudo-history; but the second was connected with other economic and social features that gave it a larger life and institutional success. The larger social ambient in turn is also functionally a part of cult success. The Mormons removed themselves to an isolated state; but the communism of the Angel Dancers accorded ill with local American capitalism and free enterprise. Again, the Welsh Jumpers, the Quakers, and the Shakers together were part of a much wider contemporary group of like sects; but the Angel Dancers were an isolated cult. The Wilderness Worshipers and the Cargo Cultists were alike in their belief in the reversal of skin color; but both were submerged by more powerful nearby white cultures. Adaptation to the larger society is also evidently a differentiating feature. The seventeenth-century Quakers and Ranters were identical in their antinomianism and ecstatic trend toward individual autonomy. But the Quakers achieved a *Book of Discipline* and changed from an ecstatic cult to the most staid of modern sects in their behavior, whereas the violent Ranters disappeared or were absorbed into Quakerism, perhaps the most committed social-activist group of our day. At the same time, Quakerism gradually more and more abjured the more alarming politico-economic ideas of the Ranters and the Fifth Monarchy Men, adapted to the trend of the times, and under William Penn the Quakers went on to become some of the most successful and respected capitalists in America.

The small social distance of the visionary from his communicants, is highlighted by another feature: the greater social distance of the cult from the Great Culture, and of one culture from another in "nativistic" cult. Acculturation clashes are more visible in the invasion-from-a-distance—both geographically and psychologically—of one society by another, as when Indo-European Greeks poured down from northern Europe into Mediterranean Helladic Greece. Most discernible of all are crisis cults incident to the meeting of the most profoundly different and historically most separate traditions, as when the advanced Old World Iron Age societies of Europe invaded the New World societies of American Indians with their variously mesolithic, neolithic and Bronze Age cultures.

Here most transparently of all we can see the sad *irrationality* of the defenses of the weaker society, its technological culture hopelessly outclassed by that of another more powerful society—as when Indians had to meet firearms with bows and arrows, and confront powerful national states with their tribal bands and loose confederations. Their defenses were irrational of necessity; for if they had somehow managed under stress to achieve genuinely adaptive technical defenses of a superior type, then they would not have been defeated in the arena of history. Thus, since Indians were technologically weaker in material culture, their sacred culture had no prestige or little later diffusion among us.

This is all easy to accept, since our own society won easily in the struggle. But what of the origins of the "sacred culture" within our own tradition? Surely these upsetting insights are not relevant to our own Ghost Dance defenses! And yet our own sacred culture derives from *the same kind of unresolved problems*. Many of the old unresolved problems, perhaps unresolvable like individual death, are still with us. This remains the major content of our fantasies, and we still cherish religiously the false autistic "solutions" of the past. Faced in history with traumata they could not master, societies of men culturally ancestral to us have passed their fantasies intact on down to us—quite as the neurotic adult has inherited the buried conflicts of his inadequate and impotent child-mind. Our sects are sub-societies of men with the same fears and the same unresolved problems, all compulsively defending their sacred fundamentalist ignorance from new knowledge, for fear that old traumata be again uncovered. We have forgotten what the symbols meant, and have substituted the compulsive symbols for the lost realities. Often we have even forgotten what our sacred theses were, and what questions they were shaped to answer. "But faith, like a jackal, feeds among the tombs, and even from these dead doubts she gathers her most vital hope."[33]

The tragic, ironic fact is that secular culture in many instances has long since discovered answers to some problems that our sacred culture is still vexed about (for example, the genetic relationship of father and son). Our civilization differs from mere tribalism in two important ways: in the possession of science as a method of investigation, and in the possession of documentation of our long past. By contrast, our sacred culture preserves the ruins of tribalisms in which three Mediterranean cultures foundered in their ghost-dance paroxysms. Consequently, throughout western history, secular science has wrested more and more intellectual territory once occupied by the terrors of the sacred and the supernatural, though not without titanic struggles against the Olympian powers of the rational mind. The melancholy fact is that many men persist in cherishing old errors in preference to new knowledge. "What perversity," cried Cicero, "can make men feed on acorns after grain has been discovered?"[34]

That "perversity" is only frightened ignorance. It is the origins of group neuroses and the historic process of emancipation from them that we have here examined. And it is in our having a method to view the recoverable past of our literate civilization that the possibility of therapy lies, in a kind of phylo-analysis of past intellectual history. As in neurosis, protective narcissism is our worst enemy. With much pain the narcissistic pride of man has suffered blows at the hands of science, quite like the insults to omnipotence the child experiences in his growth. Man was displaced from the center of the solar system by Copernicus, by Darwin from his position as the unique animal at the center of creation, and now by Freud from the easy and complacent notion that he knows his past and that he is master of his own mind.

A number of recent anthropologists and psychologists have aided our understanding of the crisis cult.[35] As to the charismatic cult leader, Devereux points out a critical difference between the culture hero and the failed messiah. The public shaman and the private neurotic differ in that the conflicts of the shaman "are located in the unconscious segments of his ethnic personality, rather than in the idiosyncratic portion of his unconscious."[36] The shaman's conflicts may be more intense than those of most men, but they are closer to conventional conflicts than are the lone psychotic's, and the shaman skillfully manipulates the institutionalized and ritualized devices that his society has elaborated for such purposes. "In brief, [unlike the alienated psychotic] the shaman is ill for conventional reasons and in a conventional way." Successful shamanism, therefore, is a species of phatic communication, not disjunctive autism. Thus normal persons in the society "echo" so readily the shaman's intrapsychic conflicts, and find his "symptoms" (ritual acts) so reassuring; his appositeness is "uncanny" because his cult impinges squarely on what is already familiar in the unconscious wish.

The supernatural "other world" is that of dreams and visions, not of existential spirits. The bad dream must be told and socially shared; it is unfinished dream work. The culture-alien observer of this process cannot discriminate the culture-hero from the psychotic, if his ethnography is merely static-descriptive and wholly unpsychological. We must understand *what culture is for* in the ecology of the mind of this neotenous animal, as Róheim has urged. At the same time, without Devereux's distinction the ethnographer also cannot distinguish the personality of the shaman from the alien culture he studies. Hence the non-dynamic observer finds the shamanic personality "normal" to the culture, and he fails to see how a culture too can be "psychotic" in terms of reality-orientation. But an attractive folly can gull evidently an indefinite number of wishful thinkers.

In the antique clashes of culture and culture some gods may seem to have died. But this, in one sense, is an illusion. Being gods they remain immortal, all of them, in our sacred culture. The sacred culture of any society is the storehouse of its emotional and intellectual defeats in the forgotten past. Sacred culture is the autistic side of history. Each ghost dance is a failure in the secular adaptiveness of a society from which later men must somehow extricate themselves. History, cried young Stephen Dedalus, is a nightmare from which I am struggling to awaken!

We must face our phobias and examine them. The difficulties are great. Not only are our sacred institutions cumulatively deeper than in most societies and more compulsive in the defense of fossil folklore, but they also constantly resist the increasingly adequate discoveries of the secular realm, material, social, and ethical. "The sacred is that which is specifically unalterable," Max Weber wrote.[37] Those who "find no conflict" between contemporary sacred and secular culture lack not merely any sense of what happened in history but also any insight into the meaning, nature, and purpose of their beliefs, and the grounds on which they are held. For each dead society has bequeathed to us its historical sickness—the Greeks, Platonism as the Great Tradition in western philosophy; the Hebrews, the fallen temple of their ancient tribalism and their lost Davidic messiah; and the Romans, the ghost of Rome, the Church and western patterns of political and intellectual despotism. The Pythagorean brotherhood is still alive; the prehistoric, Orphic immortality-song of the Master of Animals still sweetly seduces us.

NOTES

(Appendix i: The False Messiahs)

1. Josephus, *Jewish Antiquities* (tr. H. St. J. Thackeray, 9 vols., New York: G. P. Putnam's Sons and Cambridge: Harvard University Press, 1926–65, vols. 4–9, 9:441–43, XX, v, 1). See also Acts 5:36.

2. Josephus, *op. cit.*, 9:473–81, XX, viii, 6. See also Acts 21:38.

3. Josephus, *op. cit.*, 9:489–91, XX, viii, 10.

4. Albert M. Hyamson, "Messiahs (Pseudo-Messiahs)," *Hastings Encyclopedia*, 8:581–88, is the major source for the Jewish pseudo-messiahs from Manahem and Bar Kokhba through Reubeni and Molkho discussed here.

5. Herbert Loewe, "Judaism," *Hastings Encyclopedia*, 7:581–609, p. 598.

6. E. F. Scott, "Gnosticism," *Hastings Encyclopedia*, 6:231–42. A good summary may be found in Friess and Schneider, *op. cit.*, pp. 310–11.

7. The line between mystic and heretic is admittedly difficult to draw. How would one classify the following? Wilhelmina of Bohemia said she was an incarnation of the Spirit made to save Jews, Saracens, and false Christians; after her death in 1281 her sect was exterminated. Conrad Schmidt, a Flagellant of Thuringia, an incarnation of Enoch, founded the "Brethren of the Cross" which the Inquisition quashed. Savonarola had mystic visions but refused to put his claims to the test of fire. The Alumbrados of Spain spoke with both the Lord and the Virgin. Nicolas Storch, a Silesian weaver of Zwickau, temporarily convinced the authorities at Wittenberg of the validity of his visions—until it transpired they were of Luther and Satan. Melchior Hoffman, a Swabian tailor who claimed to be Elijah, predicted the end of the world for 1533. Jan Matthys, or "Enoch" incarnated, said Münster would be the New Jerusalem and gathered 1400 people into his cult in eight days (W. T. Whitley, "Enthusiasts (Religious)," *Hastings Encyclopedia*, 5:317–20).

8. In addition to Hyamson, *op. cit.*, information on Shabbathai is from Loewe, *op. cit.*, p. 605; and William G. Schauffler, "Shabbathai Zevi and His Followers," *American Oriental Society*, 2 (1851) 3–26.

9. W. T. Whitley, "Muggletonians," *Hastings Encyclopedia*, 8:871.

10. Mooney, *op. cit.*, p. 938.

11. Mooney, *loc. cit.*

12. Mooney, *op. cit.*, pp. 938–39.

13. Mooney, *op. cit.*, p. 939.

14. Mooney, *op. cit.*, pp. 941–42.

15. W. T. Whitley, "Southcottians," *Hastings Encyclopedia*, 11:756.

16. Early Shakerism was close to an institutionalized compulsion neurosis. "Hervey Elkins, who had spent fifteen years as a Shaker, wrote: 'Not a single action of life, whether spiritual or temporal, from the initiative of confession, or cleansing the habitation of Christ, to that of dressing the right side first, stepping first with the right foot as you ascend a flight of stairs, folding the hands with the right thumb and fingers above those of the rest, kneeling and rising with the right knee first, and harnessing first the right-hand beast, but has a rule for its perfect and strict performance.'" (R. Bruce Taylor, "Communistic Societies of America," *Hastings Encyclopedia*, 3:782–83, p. 783).

17. I. Woodridge Riley, "Saints, Latter-Day," *Hastings Encyclopedia*, 11:82–90; Friess and Schneider, *op. cit.*, pp. 457, 551.

18. J. G. Simpson, "Irving and the Catholic Apostolic Church," *Hastings Encyclopedia,* 7:422–28.

19. Mooney, *op. cit.,* pp. 944–45.

20. Edwin J. Dukes, "Agapemone," *Hastings Encyclopedia,* 1:175–77.

21. Paranoiac identification with God is not uncommon. Gadadhar Chatterji (1834–1886) was an incarnation of Krishna (A. A. MacDowell, "Ramakrishna," *Hastings Encyclopedia,* 10:567–69). Siva Dayal Saheb, the *guru* Sant Satguru who founded the Radha Soamis, was identical with the Supreme Being (J. N. Farquhar, "Radha Soamis," *loc. cit.,* 10:558–59). Mīrzā Ghulam Ahmad (1839–1908) was the promised Messiah of the Jews, the Mahdi of the Moslems, an *avatar* of Vishnu, the new *guru* of the Parsis, and the Buddha (H. A. Walter, "Qādiāni," *loc. cit.,* 10:530–31). Abu 'l-Mughith Husain ibn Mansur al-Hallaj was barbarously executed in Baghdad on the 26th March 922 on the charge of pretending to be an incarnation of God (Reynold A. Nicholson, "Hallaj," *loc. cit.,* 6:480–82). In Russia, the Khlysti or Flagellants were founded in 1645 by a man who said he was God; in reaction to him the Skoptzi ("Castrators") were founded in 1770 by God incarnate; Mary Anne Girling announced herself as the final revelation of God and stated the dogma of her personal immortality, but her death in 1886 ruined her sect, the "Children of God" (W. T. Whitley, "Enthusiasts (Religious)," *loc. cit.,* 5:317–20, p. 319).

22. R. B. Taylor, *op. cit.,* p. 787.

23. R. B. Taylor, *loc. cit.*

24. Mooney, *op. cit.,* pp. 945–46; W. T. Whitley, "Sects (Christian)," *Hastings Encyclopedia,* 11:315–29, p. 326.

25. Louis H. Gray, "Oahspe," *Hastings Encyclopedia,* 9:428–30.

26. Mooney, *op. cit.,* p. 946.

27. Mooney, *op. cit.,* pp. 946–47.

28. F. D. van Arsdale, "Angel Dancers," *Hastings Encyclopedia,* 1:474–75.

29. W. La Barre, *They Shall Take Up Serpents,* pp. 11–33.

30. In late August 1947, a thirty-year-old farmer named Ernest Davis died of drinking a "salvation cocktail" made of strychnine, in a Summerville, Georgia, snake-handling meeting led by the Reverend Gordon Miller (according to *Time,* 8 September 1947).

31. In addition to the Big Stone Gap center of continuing snake handling, there is another in Fayette County, West Virginia (Nathan L. Gerrard, "Scrabble Creek Folk," two manuscript books, *circa* 1966).

32. Articles in the national press served by the Washington Post-Los Angeles Times News Service, 15 September 1968. The article in *Time,* 1 November 1958, p. 86, contains minor errors. I am grateful to Dr. Helen Lewis, my former graduate assistant, now of Wise, Virginia, for additional information.

33. Melville, *op. cit.,* p. 52.

34. Cicero, *Orator* (tr. H. M. Hubbell, Cambridge: Harvard University Press, 1939, ix, 31, p. 327).

35. In addition to articles cited in my *Current Anthropology* study, several works are apposite to the theme of the "false messiah," such as B. Bernardi, *The Mugwe, A Failing Prophet;* and Benson Saler, *op. cit.* A contrast of the prophetic (others-oriented, ethical-emotional conflict, unexpected vision, and demands by deity) with the mystical experience (self-oriented, serenity at achieved neutrality, induced and sensory-dependent experience, and "oceanic" fusion with deity) is made by I. Thorner, "Prophetic and Mystic Experience: Comparison and Consequences," *Journal for the Scientific Study of Religion,* 5 (1965) 82–96.

36. George Devereux, *Normal and Abnormal,* pp. 10–11.

37. Max Weber, *Wirtschaft und Gesellschaft,* p. 231.

Index of Names

Subject Index